MW01268698

David m
c592

THE N-TOWN PLAY
Cotton MS Vespasian D. 8
VOL. II

EARLY ENGLISH TEXT SOCIETY
S.S. 12
1991

he chargyht þ ʒe haft ʒolk for he is redy bent
lolk to iacobþs dot ʒo comyng

he byddyth ʒolk fortheymo⁷ in handys þ ʒo haue
& sayþ þhte to do oþey at of ʒolk ʒo bryng
may not i pay ʒolk

my lord do i say ʒolk   is ful redy dyght
now to iacobþs ʒolk

Jn lyght

2 Joseph

¶ Benedicite i can not vndyr stande
þat our prince of prestys doth mow
þ euery man þat come & bryng it hyt a whande
&byt to be mappod þ it not i so mote i throw
i haue be maydon dyz & dyz mo⁷ þolo ban
i chaungyd not ʒot of all my long lyf
& now to be mappod hu man þolo þow
it is astraunge thyng an old man to take a ʒonge wyf

¶ but vndyrz þ loffe no dout of the must forth to toluo
now neythei & bynyfmon loto no forþy go
i xal take a whand in my hand & cast of my þolfno
ʒef i fallo, yu i xallo, gronyn foi tho

he so take a way my ftaff i fay he beſ my fo
ʒo be mow þ may þolo pow go ʒo þe foi
i am old & also colde walkyng doth mo tho
yⁱ foi now þolo i so my ftaff holde i yⁱ þ mymy to þoſ

epis

¶ Þat ʒe xal vndyrz stande
þ yⁱ is þ cawſe of o⁷ comyng
& þis þ on of ʒolk bryng yt it whande
foi of god þe haue knowlyng⁷

hoi is to be mayyde a mayde ʒynge
at ʒo iodbye ʒo xal bryngo up to me
& on hoſo iodbo þ yⁱ holy goſt is syttynge
he xal þ hyſband of yⁱᵉ may be

þis portent vij doi

Joseph

Cotton MS Vespasian D. 8, f. 53ʳ

THE
N-TOWN PLAY
Cotton MS Vespasian D. 8

EDITED BY

STEPHEN SPECTOR

VOL. II
COMMENTARY, APPENDICES AND GLOSSARY

Published for
THE EARLY ENGLISH TEXT SOCIETY
by the
OXFORD UNIVERSITY PRESS
1991

Oxford University Press, Walton Street, Oxford OX2 6DP

Oxford New York Toronto
Delhi Bombay Calcutta Madras Karachi
Petaling Jaya Singapore Hong Kong Tokyo
Nairobi Dar es Salaam Cape Town
Melbourne Auckland

Associated companies in Beirut Berlin Ibadan Nicosia

Oxford is a trade mark of Oxford University Press

© *Early English Text Society, 1991*

All rights reserved. No part of this publication may be reproduced,
stored in a retrieval system, or transmitted, in any form or by any means,
electronic, mechanical, photocopying, recording, or otherwise, without
the prior permission of Oxford University Press

British Library Cataloguing in Publication Data
The N-town play: Cotton MS Vespasian D. 8.—(Early English
Text Society, S.S., 11–12).
1. English drama
I. Spector, Stephen   II. Early English Text Society
III. Series
822.0516
ISBN 0–19–722411–3 v. 1
ISBN 0–19–722412–1 v. 2

Set by Joshua Associates Ltd, Oxford
Printed in Great Britain
by Ipswich Book Company Ltd

CONTENTS

COMMENTARY

ABBREVIATIONS IN THE COMMENTARY

Anderson	M. D. Anderson, *Drama and Imagery in English Medieval Churches* (Cambridge, 1963).
Bevington	*Medieval Drama*, ed. David Bevington (Boston, 1975).
Block	*Ludus Coventriae*, ed. K. S. Block, EETS ES 120 (1922).
Castle	*The Castle of Perseverance*, in *The Macro Plays*, ed. Mark Eccles, EETS OS 262 (1969).
Chester	*The Chester Mystery Cycle*, eds. R. M. Lumiansky and David Mills, EETS SS 3 (1974).
Cornish plays:	
Creacion	*The Creacion of the World*, ed. and transl. Paula Neuss (New York and London, 1983).
Origo Mundi, *Passio Domini Nostri*, and *Resurrexio*	*The Ancient Cornish Drama*, ed. and transl. Edwin Norris, 2 vols. (New York and London, 1859, reissued 1968).
Coventry	*Two Coventry Corpus Christi Plays*, ed. Hardin Craig, EETS ES 87 (1902, reprinted 1967).
Cursor Mundi	*Cursor Mundi*, ed. Richard Morris, EETS OS 57, 59, 62, 66, 68, 99 (1874–78, 1892).
Davies	*The Corpus Christi Play of the English Middle Ages*, ed. R. T. Davies (Totowa, New Jersey, 1972).
De Nativitate	*De Nativitate Mariae*, in *Evangelia Apocrypha*, ed. C. von Tischendorf (1876).
Digby	*The Late Medieval Religious Plays of Bodleian MSS Digby 133 and E Museo 160*, eds. Donald C. Baker, John L. Murphy, and Louis B. Hall, Jr., EETS OS 283 (1982).
Dutka	JoAnna Dutka, *Music in the English Mystery Plays* (Kalamazoo, 1980).
EETS	Early English Text Society OS Original Series ES Extra Series SS Supplementary Series
Falke	Ernst Falke, *Die Quellen des sogenannten Ludus Coventriae* (Leipzig, 1908).
Fry	Timothy Fry, 'The Unity of the *Ludus Coventriae*', *Studies in Philology* 48 (1951), 527–70.

Gauvin   Claude Gauvin, *Un Cycle du Théâtre Religieux Anglais du Moyen Age* (Paris, 1973).

Greban   *Le Mystère de la Passion D'Arnoul Greban*, ed. Gaston Paris and Gaston Raynaud (Paris, 1878).

Greg   W. W. Greg, *Bibliographical and Textual Problems of the English Miracle Cycles* (London, 1914).

Halliwell   *Ludus Coventriae*, ed. James Orchard Halliwell (London, 1841).

Kretzmann   Paul Edward Kretzmann, *The Liturgical Element in the Earliest Forms of the Medieval Drama* (Minneapolis, 1916).

Legenda Aurea   *Legenda Aurea*, ed. Th. Graesse (Dresden, 1846).

Love's *Mirrour*   *The Mirrour of the Blessed Lyf of Jesu Christ*, ed. Lawrence F. Powell (Oxford, 1908).

Luke, Cornelius   'The Rôle of the Virgin Mary in the Coventry, York, Chester and Towneley Cycles', Catholic University Ph.D. thesis (1933).

Mankind   In *The Macro Plays*, cited above.

MED   *Middle English Dictionary*, eds. Kurath, Kuhn, and Lewis (Ann Arbor, 1954–).

OED   *Oxford English Dictionary* (Oxford, 1933).

PL   *Patrologia Latina*, ed. Migne (Paris, 1844–64).

Play of the Sacrament   In *Non-Cycle Plays and Fragments*, ed. Norman Davis, EETS ss 1 (1970).

Pseudo-Matthew   In *Evangelia Apocrypha*, cited above.

Swenson   Esther L. Swenson, *An Inquiry into the Composition and Structure of the Ludus Coventriae* (Minneapolis, 1914).

Towneley   *The Towneley Plays*, eds. George England and Alfred W. Pollard, EETS es 71 (1897).

Viel Testament   *Le Mistére du Viel Testament*, ed. James de Rothschild, vol. 1 (Paris, 1878).

Vriend   J. Vriend, *The Blessed Virgin Mary in the Medieval Drama of England* (Purmerend, 1928).

Whiting   Bartlett Jere Whiting and Helen Wescott Whiting, *Proverbs, Sentences, and Proverbial Phrases* (Cambridge, Mass., 1968).

Woolf   Rosemary Woolf, *The English Mystery Plays* (Berkeley and Los Angeles, 1972).

York   *The York Plays*, ed. Richard Beadle (London, 1982).

Young   Karl Young, *The Drama of the Medieval Church*, 2 vols. (Oxford, 1933, reprinted 1967).

PROCLAMATION

The N-town Proclamation, like the banns preceding the *Castle of Perseverance* and the *Play of the Sacrament*, is an advertisement, delivered by banner-bearers, for dramatic performances to be mounted within the following week: N-town will be presented 'A Sunday next' (525), the *Castle* 'þis day seuenenyt' (133), and the *Play of the Sacrament* at 'Croxston on Monday' (74). Unlike the *Play of the Sacrament*, the N-town and *Castle* manuscripts do not name the place of performance. The 'N' in 'N-town' (527) is generally taken to stand for *nomen*, with the name of each town in which the plays were put on supplied in place of the 'N'. The *Castle* leaves blank spaces for the name of the town, suggesting a similar arrangement.

The Proclamation describes forty pageants. The numbering of pageants 8–14 has been altered to take into account the addition of several Marian plays; but the revision is incomplete, with the result that pageant 16, according to the new numbering, is followed by pageant 15, as reckoned by the old system. Several Proclamation accounts display detailed thematic parallels to the plays they describe, sometimes even echoing the language of those plays. In other cases, however, the Proclamation contains significant discrepancies from correlative plays, and in several instances, notably the Marian plays, omits any mention of the plays.

The basal stanza of the Proclamation is the Proclamation thirteener, rhyming ababababcdddc. Long thirteeners appear in 40–52 describing the Fall, and in 386–437, describing the Passion, Burial, Harrowing of Hell, and Resurrection. Two quatrains also appear, in 183–90, describing the Trial of Joseph and Mary and the Nativity.

Pr 36 *blake*: 'yellow'; so rendered by E. V. Gordon in *Pearl*, 27: 'Blomeȝ blayke and blwe and rede' (*Pearl* (Oxford, 1953)). *MED* cites Pr 36 under *blak* adj. 6(b) in the sense 'white', but cf. 2/23 (a line that Pr 36 recalls): 'Red and qwyte, bothe blew and blake'. Rendering *blake* as 'white' in 2/23 would be redundant, since *qwyte* already appears in the line.

Pr 44 *delyte*: 'crime, sin'; cf. *MED*, *delīte* n. (3) and Latin *delictum*.

Pr 45 *Bothe to askuse hem*: 'that they both might exonerate themselves'.

Pr 153–4 Cf. 10/324, which is, however, spoken by Mary, in reaffirmation of her vow of chastity. Brother C. Philip Deasy observes that, according to St Thomas, Joseph too vowed to be chaste ('St. Joseph in the English Mystery Plays', Catholic University Ph.D. thesis (1937), p. 32). Cf. 10/291–2.

Pr 183–90 These two quatrains are each followed by sufficient blank space to allow them to be expanded into thirteeners. Greg (p. 131) says that this unfinished state of affairs indicates that the Trial play was added as the codex was being transcribed; the present version of the Nativity play may also have been added at that time. Revision of the Trial is further evidenced by Den's prologue (see the note to 14/1–33). Greg observes that Pr 191 places Jesus' birth at the beginning of the Shepherds play, indicating that the cycle at an earlier stage had no distinct Nativity play.

Pr 259–60 'In the best manner that we can devise, we shall make the Holy Ghost hover above him.'

Pr 350 *Thre thevys*: cf. 31/170 s.d.

Pr 399 *oure pleyn place*: cf. the *Castle*, 160 'þis propyr pleyn place', rendered by Eccles as 'this fine open space'.

Pr 432 'That it is a joy to her [i.e. Mary] to engage in their conversation'; Bevington renders *devyse* as 'discern'.

Pr 438 *Maryes thre*: see note to 36/1st s.d.

Pr 495 *þe cenacle*: the upper room in which the apostles met; cf. Acts 1: 13, Mark 14: 15, Luke 22: 12.

Pr 525–6 Performance at 6 a.m. on a Sunday precludes the possibility of presentation on Corpus Christi Day, which was celebrated on Thursdays. Cf. the *Castle*, 138, 'we schul be onward be vnderne of þe day', which Eccles takes to mean either 'We must be on with the play by mid-morning', or, more likely, 'We must be moving on by noon' or 'by afternoon'.

Pr 527 *N-town*: 'N' stands for *nomen* in the church marriage service; cf. *Wisdom* 834. The presence of this feature may indicate itinerance (see the headnote). But 'N' could also represent a single name, as for example in *The Book of Margery Kempe* (eds. Sanford Brown Meech and Hope Emily Allen, EETS os 212 (1940; reprint 1961), p. 9). See p. xvi n. 1 in the present edition.

PLAY 1

Omitting the biblical work of the first day, the creation of light and the separating and naming of day and night, N-town represents instead the creation of heaven, which in Gen. 1: 6–8 occurs on the second day. The play also includes on the first day the extra-biblical creation of the angels. Jubilees 2: 2 also allocates that event to the first day, and Augustine asserts in *De Civitate Dei* that the angels were themselves the light that was called 'day'. The Fall of the Angels derives from Patristic interpretation of Old and New Testament texts.

The play comprises six Proclamation thirteeners and the first four lines of another stanza in this form.

1/a Rev. 1: 8.

1/1–28 Cf. the Athanasian Creed, which declares that God is one God in three persons, uncreated, eternal, and omnipotent. See A. C. Cawley, 'Middle English Metrical Versions of the Decalogue with Reference to the English Corpus Christi Cycles', *Leeds Studies in English* 8 (1975), 132, 142 note 23.

1/5–6 Cf. Towneley 1/13.

1/12–13 Cf. the Athanasian Creed: 'Unum Deum in Trinitate, et Trinitatem in Unitate veneremur; neque confundentes personas: neque substantiam separantes.'

1/30–1 Cf. Baruch 3: 34, Job 38: 7.

1/35 *belde*: *MED* cites this line under *bēlden* v. 2(a) 'to protect (sb.), defend, give shelter to', but *belde* here is more probably a form of *bilden* 'to create', as in 4/93.

1/39 s.d. *Tibi omnes angeli*. . . : a section of the *Te Deum*; see Dutka, 42–3.

1/53 ff. Cf. Isaiah 14: 12 ff.

1/81 Cf. 2/273. Martial Rose points out that the sound of the 'fearful farting of a frustrated fiend' was made to carry through the use of gunpowder, as set out in the stage plan of the *Castle* ('The Staging of the Hegge Plays', *Medieval Drama*, Stratford-upon-Avon Studies, 16 (1973), p. 218).

PLAY 2

The portrayal of the second up to the fifth days of Creation is based on Gen. 1: 6–25, though here, as in the other cycle Creation plays, the biblical order of events has been changed. The creation of beasts, which occurs on the sixth day in Genesis, is moved to the fifth day, setting the creation of man off from all God's previous work. The two creations of man, in Gen. 1: 26 ff. and Gen. 2, are conflated and extremely compressed, with the act of creating Eve not represented in dialogue at all. The story of the Fall is ultimately based on Gen. 3. In portraying the serpent as a 'werm with an aungelys face' (220), the play joins the apocryphal idea that the tempter was an angel, with the discrete tradition, expressed in the *Historia Scholastica*, that the serpent had a maiden's face. The play contains thematic parallels to the *Mistére du Viel Testament*, and later portions of the play contain verbal reminiscences of the *Life of Adam and Eve*.

The play begins at the fifth line of a thirteener, the first four lines of which serve as the conclusion to Play 1. This sharing of a stanza suggests that these two plays had earlier been a continuous unit (see p. 549 n. 1). Greg (p. 122) says that the extreme compression in Play 2 resulted from revision, and this idea is confirmed by the fact that the events of the fourth to the sixth days are represented in a single abababab octave, a rare stanzaic form in the cycle that is associated with revision elsewhere in the codex.

The play principally consists of Proclamation thirteeners, except for the 9-line stanza and octave mentioned above, and the punishment scene in 195–282, which is in tail-rhyme. (126–38 form the unusual pattern abababababcaaac.) In addition, quatrains appear in 57–60 and immediately before the tail-rhyme, in 191–4. Greg (p. 123) notes that the Proclamation, which does not identify the serpent with the devil, accords with the thirteeners in the play, which use the speaker heading 'Serpens'; the tail-rhyme portion, by contrast, uses 'Diabolus'.

The Proclamation describes the Fall of Lucifer and the Fall of Man as two distinct pageants, corresponding to the present division of plays 1 and 2.

2/38 *þis tre þat is of cunnyng*: this formulation is rare in the English drama, though the A Text of the *Norwich Grocers' Play* refers to the 'tre of connyng' (ed. Norman Davis, EETS ss 1 (1970), II/26). Cf. 'frute of cunnyng' in Pr 38. Kathleen M. Ashley observes that cunning is a central concept in this and other plays in N-town, and that the promise that man can be as 'wys of connyng' as God is repeated so often as to have almost an incantatory effect on Eve. The limits of man's cunning are also a central concern in the Doctors play: cf. 21/28, 40, and 120 ('"Wyt" and "Wysdam" in the N-town Cycle', *PQ* 58 (1979), 121–35).

2/42–3 Cf. Gen. 2: 17.

2/49–56 Cf. Gen. 2: 2–3, in which God blesses, however, not his creatures but rather the seventh day. The prohibition against work on the sabbath first appears in Exodus: cf. Exod. 16: 22–30, 20: 8–11, 23: 12, 31: 12–17.

2/91–103 Cf. Gen. 3: 2–5, and see Carleton Brown, 'Sermons and Miracle Plays', *Modern Language Notes* 44 (1934), 395.

2/149 'You shall be established as God's equal'.

2/156 *A fayr aungell*: Woolf (p. 117) conjectures that Satan appears in this play as an angel, rather than a serpent, following a tradition that derives from the Book of Enoch and is employed in *Genesis B*. Cf. the Norwich Grocers' plays, A/74 and B/40, and the Cornish *Origo Mundi*, 215. M. D. Johnson traces this motif to the *Life of Adam and Eve* (*The Old Testament Pseudepigrapha*, ed. James H. Charlesworth (N.Y., 1985), 2: 256). Cf. 2 Cor. 11: 14, and Irenaeus: '[Eve] was led astray by the word of an angel' (*Ante-Nicene Fathers*, eds. Alexander Roberts and James Donaldson (Buffalo, 1866), I: 547). The speaker heading 'Serpens' in the present play suggests that Satan appears here not as an angel, but as 'A werm with an aungelys face', Eve's description of him in 220. In the Cornish *Creacion of the World*, the serpent has a face like a fair maiden, and Eve refers to it as an angel (499–501, 759–61); cf. Chester 2/193–6, and the English translation of Grosseteste's *Chasteau d'Amour* in *Minor Poems of the Vernon MS* (ed. C. Horstmann, EETS os 98 (1892), 409/53). The idea that the serpent had a woman's head appears in the *Historia Scholastica* (*PL* 198: 1072), is dramatized in the *Viel Testament*, and was common in art, e.g. the Holkham Bible Picture Book; see John K. Bonnell, 'The Serpent with a Human Head in Art and in Mystery Play', *American Journal of Archaeology* 21 (1917), 255–91, and J. B. Trapp, 'The Iconography of the Fall of Man', in *Approaches to Paradise Lost*, ed. C. A. Patrides (London, 1968), pp. 223–65.

2/167–90 Cf. Gen. 3: 7.

2/205–8 Cf. Gen. 3: 12.

2/235–42 Cf. Cassian: 'the occasion of the envy and seduction, which led him to deceive man, arose from the ground of his previous fall, in that he saw that man . . . was to be called to that glory, from which he remembered that he himself, while still one of the princes, had fallen' (*Coll.* viii. 9–10, in Evans, *Paradise Lost*, p. 83). Fry (p. 540) notes that Gregory the Great, Peter Lombard, Anselm, and Thomas also attribute the motive of envy to the devil; see Gayley, p. 245, and compare *The Book of Adam and Eve*, trans. S. C. Malan, in *The Forgotten Books of Eden* (N.Y., 1927; reprinted 1972), p. 31, and *Wisdom*, 325–8.

2/243–50 Cf. Gen. 3: 17–19.

2/251–8 Cf. Gen. 3: 16.

2/259–66 Cf. Gen. 3: 14–15; Hilda Graef, *Mary: A History of Doctrine and Devotion* (N.Y., 1963), p. 1; N-town 2/292–5 and the note, and 7/51–2. Falke (p. 15) observes that although 263–5 offer a common intepretation of 'ipsa conteret caput tuum' in Gen. 3: 15, among the French and English mystery plays, only the *Mystère d'Adam* and N-town explicitly include this motif. In Philippe de Mézières' play on the Presentation of Mary in the Temple, Mary pounds on the prostrate Lucifer with her feet (Young, 2: 238–9).

2/272 *to qweke*: 'to quake'; or 'to fart' (*MED, queken* v (b) cites this instance only; the word is derived from *quek(e)* interj. and MDu. *quacken*).

2/273 Cf. 1/81 and 23/195.

2/275–82 s.d. Cf. Gen. 3: 23–4.

2/292–5 Cf. Chester 2/399–400.

2/303–23 M. D. Johnson (2: 256) asserts that Eve's request that Adam slay her derives from the *Life of Adam and Eve*. The affinities to the play are apparent in this Middle English version of the *Life*: 'Thanne seyde Eue to Adam . . . "Wolde God þat I myȝte dye, or ellis þat I were slayen of þee, for-whi for me is God wrooþ wiþ þee". . . . Thanne seyde Adam: "Eue, speke no moore so, leste oure Lord God sende his malysoun upon us . . . how myȝte it be þat I schulde sle my fleisch? But aryse, go we and seke we where-wiþ to lyue. . .."' (*The Wheatley Manuscript*, ed. Mabel Day, EETS os 155 (1921), 81/1–16). Cf. 'Canticum de Creatione' and 'þe lyff of Adam and Eue' in *Sammlung altenglischer Legenden*, ed. C. Horstmann (Heilbronn, 1878), 128, 141, 223; York 6/155–60; and *Le Mystère d'Adam*, ed. Paul Aebischer (Geneva and Paris, 1964), 461–72, 559–90. Fry (p. 540 note 46) cites the dejection of Adam and Eve in Augustine, *De Genesi ad litteram* (*PL* 34: 432).

2/304 *fonde*: 'proceed, go'; alternatively, 'strive, endeavour (to go)'. Block suggests 'findest, provest', and Davies 'thou mayest find, experience (it to be so)'.

2/316 *Short lykyng xal be longe bought*: cf. Towneley 13/97–9, Whiting, M642.

2/322–34 Cf. Gen. 3: 17–19; *Origo Mundi*, 367–70; the Cornish *Creacion*, 1029–37; Falke, p. 16.

2/325 'Our bliss utterly reduced to suffering and sorrow'.

PLAY 3

Play 3 is an elaboration of Gen. 4: 1–16. Adam's speech on the duty of sacrifice recalls the *Historia Scholastica*, and was dramatized in English, Cornish, and Continental plays. It is also portrayed in the Holkham Bible Picture Book. The impropriety of Cain's sacrifice appears in Hebrew tradition and Latin commentary, and the presentation of the sacrifices in terms of tithing derives from Patristic exposition. Cain's using the jawbone of an ass as the instrument of fratricide appears to have been a native English tradition.

The play is prosodically irregular. It begins with a quatrain and three 9-line stanzas in which Abel and Cain go to their father, then has Adam deliver a thirteener rhyming ababbabacdddc, a very peculiar stanzaic form in this collection; another such thirteener occurs in 66–78. Lines 45–61 constitute a still more unusual 17-line stanza rhyming ababbababababacdddc (the absence of a capitulum at 49, and the rhyme scheme, suggest that these lines were intended as a single stanza). Another quatrain appears in 62–5. The remainder of the play, starting with line 79, is in Proclamation thirteeners, with the exception of an odd thirteener rhyming ababacacdeeed in 105–17 (the bad rhymes may indicate that this stanza consists of stanzaic fragments).

The Proclamation thirteeners in the play agree with the Proclamation description. Like that description, they emphasize the tithing, a motif virtually neglected in the other stanzaic forms in the play. The opening scene with Adam, comprising most of the irregular prosodic forms, is not mentioned in the Proclamation. Kenneth Cameron and Stanley J. Kahrl consider the scene an interpolation ('Staging the N-Town Cycle', *Theatre Notebook* 21 (1967), 153).

3/13 *knowe for oure levynge*: 'learn how to live'. *MED*, however, cites this line under *knouen* v. 10a (c) 'to worship'.

3/16 y^t for 'yet' is very unusual in the MS; cf. 4/250.

3/26 i.e. 'as sincerely as we may'.

3/32–44 Adam's advice on the duty of sacrifice appears in the *Historia Scholastica* (*PL* 198: 1077). Adam similarly tells his sons to offer sacrifice in Chester 2, the Cornish *Creacion*, and the *Origo Mundi*; cf. the *Book of Adam and Eve* (p. 55), Towneley 2, the *Viel Testament* (2231–44), and the Holkham Bible Picture Book (5^r).

3/36 *another portature*: 'a different appearance'. *MED* cites this line under *portraiture* n. (d) 'shaping, construction, method of construction', but cf. the

Book of Adam and Eve, in which Adam and Eve say, 'Our body is changed from the similitude in which it was at first, when we were created' (p. 16).

3/37 *herd seyd*: cf. *Franklin's Tale*, V 1547; Tauno F. Mustanoja, *A Middle English Syntax* (Helsinki, 1960), 1: 554; and N-town 9/39.

3/75–8 Woolf (pp. 124, 374 note 55) observes that this is the only English mystery play to make explicit the parallelism between Abel's lamb and Christ, though this assocation is usual in German plays. She says elsewhere that, outside of the Chester cycle, this is the only actual statement of an Old Testament type in the English mysteries ('The Effect of Typology on the English Mediaeval Plays of Abraham and Isaac', *Speculum*, 32 (1957), 809); but this is mistaken: N-town explicitly refers to Old Testament types in 7/42–4 and 69–72.

3/92ff. Cf. Matt. 5: 22. Gen. 4: 3–4 says only that Cain offered the fruit of the ground while Abel offered the firstlings of his flock and of their fat portions. The impropriety of Cain's offering, a motif deriving from Jewish tradition, is mentioned by Ambrose, Alcuin, and Peter Comestor. Various Fathers took the sacrifices to suggest tithing (Oliver F. Emerson, 'Legends of Cain, Especially in Old and Middle English', *PMLA* 21 (1906), 849–51).

3/111–12 'How would God be the better for it, you tell me, if I were to give him my best sheaf. . . .'

3/123 'For I find few people who share your doctrine'.

3/149 Cain also uses a jawbone as his weapon in the Cornish *Creacion* and a 'cheke bon' in Towneley 2/324. Emerson (pp. 851 ff.) suggests that the motif derived from confusion with the story of Samson. He notes that Hebrew and Patristic commentators do not refer to this weapon, though such references do appear in *Salomon and Saturn*, *Cursor Mundi*, the prose 'Life of Adam and Eve', and the English and Cornish drama. See also the *Middle English Metrical Paraphrase of the Old Testament*, 236, and John K. Bonnell, 'Cain's Jaw Bone', *PMLA* 39 (1924), 140–6. Meyer Schapiro notes the existence of this image in English art from the eleventh to the sixteenth century, and proposes that the Old English *cinbān* 'jawbone' may have derived from *Cain bana* 'Cain the bane' ('Cain's Jaw-Bone That Did the First Murder', *Art Bulletin* 24 (1942), 205–12). Cain uses a jawbone in the Holkham Bible Picture Book, and W. O. Hassall notes that this was a common English motif that spread to Northern Europe (*The Holkham Bible Picture Book* (London, 1954), p. 67).

3/153 *boy*: E. J. Dobson ('The Etymology and Meaning of Boy', *Medium Ævum* 9 (1940), 135) cites this instance of *boy*, as well as those in 18/86 and 41/37, as a vague term of contempt or abuse. Cf. 12/75 and the note to 4/152.

3/156 Cain also buries Abel in the *Book of Adam and Eve* (p. 58). This motif is illustrated in the Holkham Bible Picture Book and Queen Mary's Psalter (Hassall, p. 68).

3/159–65 Gen. 4: 9.

3/168–73 Cf. Gen. 4: 10–12.

3/176–80 Cf. Gen. 4: 14–15.

3/188 *strete and stage*: 'at street level and on the scaffold'. Cf. Rose, 'Staging', p. 204.

PLAY 4

The biblical account of the Flood in Gen. 6–8 is here compressed, altered in detail, and interrupted by the intrusion of Lamech's killing of Cain. The latter story developed as an attempt to explain the ancient song of Lamech's blood-revenge in Gen. 4: 23–4. It began as a Hebrew tradition, appears in the *Book of Adam and Eve*, and is a frequent subject in Patristic exegesis. Rabanus Maurus accepts the story, as does Peter Comestor, and it is cited in the *Glossa Ordinaria* (see Edmund Reiss, 'The Story of Lamech and Its Place in Medieval Drama', *Journal of Medieval and Renaissance Studies* 2 (1972), 39–41; see also Hardin Craig (*English Religious Drama* (Oxford, 1955), pp. 65, 258), who notes a reading on Lamech in the Cologne breviary). The episode appears in such works as the Caedmonian *Genesis*, the Middle English *Genesis*, *Cursor Mundi*, the *Polychronicon* (in an account based on Comestor), Wyntoun's *Original Chronicle*, and Lydgate's *Fall of Princes* (Emerson, pp. 874–7; Reiss, p. 43). It is a common motif in art (Hassall, p. 70; Anderson, p. 145; Woolf, p. 376 note 9; Reiss, pp. 41–2; also see Emile Mâle, *The Gothic Image*, translated by Dora Nussey (N.Y., 1958), p. 205). In the drama, this episode occurs in the Cornish *Creacion* and in Continental plays, including the *Viel Testament*, though among the English mysteries, the motif is unique to N-town. The *Historia Scholastica* may well have been the proximate source for the N-town play, as evidenced by verbal parallels.

In the present play, the Lamech episode has been interpolated into the midst of the Noah story, a chronological arrangement that has been found elsewhere only in the Egerton Genesis illuminations (see Ellin M. Kelly, '"Ludus Coventriae" Play 4 and the Egerton "Genesis"', *Notes and Queries* 217 (1972), 443–4). In this position in the cycle, the episode exemplifies the evil that the Flood is intended to punish, and allows Noah and his family to exit in order to fetch (or build) the ark.

The play is atypical of English drama in several other particulars as well, such as the portrayal of Uxɵr Noe as obedient rather than contentious. Woolf (p. 133) says that N-town follows the Continental drama in this regard. The Cornish *Creacion* and *Origo Mundi* also present the Uxor as basically agree-able, and the *Creacion*, like the *Viel Testament*, includes a Lamech episode.

Play 4 consists of Proclamation thirteeners until the speech of the angel at 118, with the exception of 53–65, an anomalous thirteener rhyming ababb abacdddc (perhaps a quatrain joined to a 9-line stanza, but cf. 3/32–44 and

3/66–78). From the angel's speech on, the play contains long-lined octaves, which Swenson (p. 7) says are written in tumbling metre. The Proclamation description makes no mention of the Lamech scene.

4/14–17 Although St Gregory proposed that there were five historical ages, Augustine and others declared that there were seven, the first of which was initiated by Adam, and the second by Noah. See O. B. Hardison, Jr., *Christian Rite and Christian Drama in the Middle Ages* (Baltimore, 1965; paperback, 1969), p. 88 note 6, and V. A. Kolve, *The Play Called Corpus Christi* (Stanford, 1966), pp. 88 ff.

4/34 *lyvys bylle*: 'the book of life'; cf. Psalm 68: 29 (Vulgate), Rev. 3: 5, 13: 8, 17: 8, *et passim*.

4/36 *sclepp*: perhaps 'slip', but the rhymes with *depp* 'deep' and *crepp* 'creep' suggest the rendering 'sleep', as does the form *sclep* for 'sleep' in 28/70. Cf. *synful sownde* 'sinful swoon' in 4/5, and the rhymes in 4/75–7.

4/96 ff. The play contradicts Gen. 6: 13 ff. by having an angel, rather than God himself, address Noah. The same arrangement occurs in the Newcastle Noah play and the *Viel Testament*. Joan Broadbent observes that God sends an angel to warn Noah of the Flood in the Book of Enoch ('An Edition of the Noah Pageant in the English Corpus Christi Cycles', Leeds MA thesis (1955), p. xxxviii), and F. Holthausen notes the angel's appearance in Alcimus Ecdicius Avitus' *De Diluvio Mundi* ('Die Quelle des Noahspiels von Newcastle upon Tyne', *Shakespeare Jahrbuch* 36 (1900), 277–9). See the note to 5/73–88.

4/98–9 'Bid him forthwith to undertake to build a ship for himself and his family....'

4/105–6 *Fecisse hominem nunc penitet me*: cf. Gen. 6: 6: Deus 'poenituit eum quod hominem fecisset in terra'; and Gen. 6: 7: 'poenitet enim me fecisse eos', translated in line 106. Cf. also 11/169. 'Poenitet me fecisse hominem' appears in Bernard's *In Festo Annuntiationis Beatae Mariae Virginis* (*PL* 183: 389), in the *Historia Scholastica* (*PL* 198: 1082), and, with slight revision, in Greban's *Passion*, 587.

4/118–19 Cf. Gen. 6: 14. Atypically, the dialogue here omits the dimensions of the ark, which were often taken as symbolic; see Woolf, p. 136.

4/120–5 Cf. Gen. 6: 17–19.

4/127 The play contradicts the biblical account in making Noah five hundred years old at this point. In Gen. 5: 32, Noah's sons are born *after* he is five hundred years old, but in the play, his sons are already married by this time. The contradiction may result from inconsistency within the play, since the sons and their wives speak in thirteeners, while the present line occurs in the octave portion of the play. Lines 206–7, also in an octave, have Noah say that he has worked on the ark for one hundred years; this brings the play into agreement with Gen. 7: 6, which makes Noah six hundred years old at the time of the Flood. Cf. York 8/91, 114–15.

4/141 s.d.–189 Cf. the *Historia Scholastica*: 'Lamech vero vir sagittarius diu vivendo caliginem oculorum incurrit, et habens adolescentem ducem; dum exerceret venationem, pro delectione tantum, et usu pellium, quia non erat usus carnium ante diluvium, casu interfecit Cain inter fructeta, aestimans feram, quem, quia ad indicium juvenis dirigens sagittam, interfecit. Et cum experiretur quod hominem, scilicet Cain, interfecisset, iratus illic cum arcu ad mortem verberavit eum' (*PL* 198: 1079). This episode individualizes some of the evil that God is about to punish, a feature that Woolf (p. 132) finds only in the *Viel Testament*. Broadbent (pp. lxxv–lxxvii) considers the Lamech story to serve as an exemplum within the larger homiletic structure of the play. See Alicia K. Nitecki, 'The N-Town Lamech and the Convention of Maximainus' [*sic*] First Elegy', *American Notes and Queries* 17 (1979), 122–4.

4/152 Dobson (pp. 140, 146) takes *boy* here to signify 'servant child' and states that any fifteenth-century text in which this sense, 'urchin', or 'male child' is certainly intended is likely to be from the Southeast Midlands. The speaker heading in the play, 'Adolescens', agrees with the *Historia Scholastica* and Gen. 4: 23, while the Cornish *Creacion* refers to the boy as a servant and the *Viel Testament* makes him Tubal Cain.

4/166 Cf. the *Historia Scholastica*, quoted above. Cain is also killed while in a bush in the Cornish *Creacion* and the *Viel Testament*; cf. the Holkham Bible Picture Book (6ᵛ). The boy's mistaking Cain for an animal also parallels the *Viel Testament*, as well as the Cornish *Creacion*, in which Cain has a horn on his forehead and is covered with hair. Emerson (p. 873) notes that Cain's bestial appearance is ultimately a Hebrew tradition, and Hassall (p. 71) says that Cain is generally represented as covered with hair like an animal. Paula Neuss points out Cain's resemblance to the wild man of the woods in folk plays (the Cornish *Creacion*, p. 228).

4/174–7 Cf. the Cornish *Creacion*:

>O, alas ['Owt, aylas' in the Cornish] I'm dead!
>I have no longer to live!
>I'm pierced through the ribs,
>and the arrow has gone right through me. (1568–71)

Compare the *Viel Testament*:

>Dyables! qui esse qui m'a frappè?
>C'est fait de moy; je vois mourir. (4763–4)

4/176 *to tundyr*: Block suggests 'to tinder'; Broadbent renders as 'turned to fire'.

4/178–85 Cf. the *Viel Testament*, 4771–83.

4/185 s.d. This stage direction echoes the *Historia Scholastica*: 'cum arcu ad mortem verberavit eum'. Falke (p. 21) notes the slightly different language used in the *Viel Testament*: 'Il le frappe de son arc' (4783 s.d.). The Cornish

Creacion, by contrast, has Lamech kill his servant with a staff. The *Poly-chronicon* omits this passage.

4/218–25, 235–37 Cf. Gen. 6: 2. The *Book of Adam and Eve* recognizes adultery as a chief cause of the Flood, and rabbinic commentary especially stressed the licentiousness of the generation of the Flood (Jack P. Lewis, *A Study of the Interpretation of Noah and the Flood in Jewish and Christian Literature* (Leiden, 1968, pp. 127–8). Charles Mills Gayley, *Plays of Our Forefathers* (New York, 1907), p. 243, says that lasciviousness was considered the *initium peccati* until Chrysostom and Augustine began to identify the Sons of God with Seth's descendants, and the daughters of men with Cain's. Cf. the *Historia Scholastica*, *PL* 198: 1081; also 'þe lyff of Adam and Eue': 'And Adam comaunded to Seth þat non of his kuynde schulde felauschupe wiþ Caymes kuynde ne wedde non wyues in Caymes kuynde—for þo þat coomen of Seþes kuynde ben cleped godes sones, and Caymes kuynde to men sones. And þenne at þe fiftene hondred winteres ende heo bigunnen to don heore lecherie priueliche, & afturward openliche. And þo afturward heo weddeden þe to kuynde in to þat oþur, and geeten geauns. And þenne god tok wreche & adreynte al þe world . . .' (Horstmann, *Sammlung*, p. 225). Lamech's presence itself reinforces the emphasis on lechery as the cause of the Flood, since he was known as the first adulterer (Reiss, pp. 35 ff.). See Daniel P. Poteet II, 'Symbolic Character and Form in the *Ludus Coventriae* "Play of Noah"', *American Benedictine Review* 26 (1975), 75–88.

4/223–4 'Very severely transgressed when they were sinfully driven (by desire) to the daughters of Cain'.

4/242–5 s.d. Cf. Gen. 8: 6–7.

4/246 The raven's eating carrion is non-biblical. It was a common rabbinic and Christian theme, found in commentary by Augustine, in Isidore's *Etymologiae*, and in verse by Prudentius and Avitus (Lewis, p. 146; Don Cameron Allen, *The Legend of Noah* (Urbana, 1963), pp. 72–3, 163). It is portrayed pictorially in the Holkham Bible Picture Book, Queen Mary's Psalter, a Norwich roof-boss, and elsewhere; cf. Hassall, p. 74; E. P. Evans, *Animal Symbolism in Ecclesiastical Architecture* (London, 1896), p. 76; and Arieh Sachs, 'The Raven and the Dove', in *Studies in the Drama*, ed. Arieh Sachs (Jerusalem, 1967), pp. 181–208. In the drama, the motif is alluded to in the Towneley and York cycles, the Cornish *Creacion* and *Origo Mundi*, and the *Viel Testament*.

4/247–51 Cf. Gen. 8: 10–11.

4/249 s.d. *viridi*: Meredith and Kahrl (p. xiii) alternatively propose *viridis*.

4/250 *frende* is perhaps an error for *refrende* 'restrained': 'We may now rejoice, who till now were restrained from mirth'. Or *frende* may be mean 'alienated' (cf. *MED*, *fremed* adj. a., with the form *frend* cited under the entry for the *Promptorium Parvulorum*). *yet* is written *y'*; cf. 3/16.

4/253 s.d. *Non nobis, Domine . . .*: cf. Psalms 113A. 3, 113B. 1 (Vulgate), the

liturgical piece cited by Dutka, pp. 34–5, and Marjorie D. Coogan Downing,
'The Influence of the Liturgy on the English Cycle Plays', Yale Ph.D. thesis
(1942), pp. 148–9.

PLAY 5

This play embellishes the story of the binding of Isaac in Gen. 22: 1–19,
supplying extended expression of affection and anguish where the biblical
narrative is silent, and emphasizing the typological element of the father's
sacrifice of the son.

The play consists of octaves rhyming ababbcbc. Like plays 4 and 6, but
atypically in the manuscript as a whole, it is preceded by *introitus*; and like
Play 6, it ends with *explicit*. The play generally corresponds to the Proclamation account (but see the note to 199–202).

5/72 Cf. Psalm 21: 21 (Vulgate), cited in Davies, p. 103 note 2.

5/73–88 Cf. Gen. 22: 1–2. Here, as in the Noah play, the text contradicts the
biblical source by having an angel, rather than God himself, speak to man.
The *Viel Testament* similarly has an angel speak in both instances, and the
York, Northampton, and Brome Abraham plays have an angel address
Abraham.

5/125–30 Cf. Gen. 22: 7–8.

5/140 *Alas, þat evyr þis bowe was bent*: see the note to 12/55–6.

5/158 *rod*: 'rod', referring to the wood Isaac carries; or 'rood', typologically,
and connoting 'suffering'. The MS reading, *reed*, rhymes badly with *God* in
160.

5/179 The extra-biblical motif of Abraham's covering Isaac's eyes is also
depicted in the York, Chester, and Brome plays, as well as the *Viel Testament*.
See Thomas Rendall, 'Visual Typology in the Abraham and Isaac Plays',
Modern Philology 3 (1984), 227–8, and Anderson, p. 109.

5/185–92 Cf. Gen. 22: 11–12.

5/199–202 Rendall (pp. 229–30) proposes that the 'shepe' sacrificed in the
present play is a lamb rather than the biblical ram. Howard R. Patch notes that
the play, in having Abraham conceive of the sacrifice, differs from the
Proclamation description, in which an angel bids him 'a shep to kyl' (Pr 90).
Observing that the Northampton Abraham play is consistent with the
Proclamation in this regard, and that it contains tail-rhyme and thirteeners,
Patch endorses the theory that the Northampton play was once part of the
N-town collection ('The *Ludus Coventriae* and the Digby *Massacre*', *PMLA* 35
(1920), 336). This conclusion is doubtful. The angel's suggesting the sacrifice
was a familiar dramatic motif, and its appearance in the Proclamation

indicates no special connection with the Northampton play. The prosodic affinities that Patch cites are also questionable.

5/205–28 Cf. Gen. 22: 14–18.

PLAY 6

The Moses play drastically compresses events in Exodus, conflating the episode of the burning bush with the giving of the Ten Commandments. The burning bush appears in Exod. 3: 1 ff., while the Decalogue is presented in Exod. 20: 1–17, and reiterated in somewhat different form in Deut. 5: 6–21. The extra-metrical Latin quotations from the Decalogue follow the formulations in Exodus, though sometimes inexactly; but in the ninth and tenth commandments, the play harmonizes the language of Exodus with the order of prohibitions in the Deuteronomic version.

Moses' teaching of the law essentially constitutes a versified sermon employing several conventional motifs that appear in homiletic literature and Latin commentary. Falke (p. 28) cites similar expositions of the Commandments in texts including the *Historia Scholastica* and the English translation of the *Chasteu d'Amour*; Block (p. li) cites affinities to the *Court of Sapience* and St John's College, Oxford, MS 94 (edited by James Finch Royster, 'A Middle English Treatise on the Ten Commandments', *Studies in Philology* 6 (1910), 3–35); G. R. Owst cites St Albans Cath. MS, f. 45 (*Literature and Pulpit in Medieval England* (Cambridge, 1933), p. 468 note 5); Cawley notes parallels in the *Lay Folks' Catechism*, and cites an early fifteenth-century reference to possible dramatizations of the Decalogue ('Metrical Versions', pp. 131, 136, 143–4). Compare 'X mandata' in BL MS Harl. 665, edited by Julius Zupitza in 'Zwei Umschreibungen der Zehn Gebote in mittelenglischen Versen', *Archiv* 85 (1890), 44–6; also *The Book of Vices and Virtues*, ed. W. Nelson Francis, EETS os 217 (1942), pp. 1–6.

As Greg (p. 124) observes, the Proclamation omits to mention the burning bush, but it does accord with the play in including Moses' teaching the Ten Commandments. Block (p. lv note 4) interprets Pr 101–2 ('þe Ten Comaundementys . . . 3e xal hem sene') to indicate that the play apparently included a procession of the Commandments. These lines could, however, simply refer to a written Decalogue; cf. Towneley 7/34–6.

The play is written in octaves rhyming ababbcbc, with a single couplet in 49–50. Like Play 5, this play begins with *introitus* and ends with *explicit*.

6/21 The burning bush as a type of Mary, which seems to have been current in Church commentary by the fourth century (Graef, p. 60), was a familiar image in English literature. See, for example, Chaucer's *ABC* and the prologue to the *Prioress' Tale*; Lydgate's 'To Mary, the Queen of Heaven',

'Ave, Jesse Virgula!' (*Minor Poems of John Lydgate*, ed. Henry Noble
MacCracken, EETS ES 107 (1911), I: 286/33, 299/6), and the *Life of Our Lady*
(ed. Joseph A. Lauritis, Pittsburgh, 1961, II: 799–802); and the *Myroure of oure
Ladye* (ed. John Henry Blunt, EETS ES 19 (1873), p. 296); also Towneley 12/
359–67 and Chester 19/80–7. See E. Harris, 'Mary in the Burning Bush',
Journal of the Warburg Institute 1 (1937–8), 281–6, and Anderson, pp. 24–5.

6/23–32 Cf. Exod. 3: 3–5.

6/37–40 Cf. Exod. 31: 18, 24: 12.

6/43–4 i.e. 'So that my laws are obeyed in every respect'.

6/48a Deut. 6: 17.

6/49–58 Cf. Deut. 6: 1–3.

6/61–4 Cf. the *Historia Scholastica*: 'Praeterea dicit Augustinus tria fuisse in
una tabula, et septem in alia. . . . Forte quia Augustinus voluit tria pertinere ad
dilectionem Dei, et septem ad dilectionem proximi . . .' (*PL* 198: 1164; cf. *PL*
34: 620) Isidore of Seville, Bede, and Hugh of St Victor were among those who
accepted this division of the Ten Commandments. See the *Lay Folks'
Catechism* (ed. T. F. Simmons and H. E. Nolloth, EETS OS 118 (1901), p. 30);
'How a man schal lyue parfytly' (*Vernon MS.*, 241/771–6); the *Book of Vices and
Virtues*, p. 6; and P. E. Dustoor, 'The Origin of the Play of "Moses and the
Tables of the Law"', *Modern Language Review* 19 (1924), 462.

6/66a–82 Cf. Exod. 20: 3, and compare the *Lay Folks' Catechism*: 'Couetyse ys
worschepyng of fals goddys' (p. 33), and 'Who brekys þe fyrste maundement?
. . . wordly men . . . for þey make worldly godys ['goods'] her god' (p. 35). See
'A Middle English Treatise on the Ten Commandments', p. 15; the *Book of
Vices and Virtues*, p. 1; and *Middle English Sermons*, ed. W. O. Ross, EETS OS 209
(1940), pp. 22, 107 (cited by Cawley, 'Metrical Versions', p. 143). Also see
D. W. Robertson, Jr., 'Certain Theological Conventions in Mannyng's Treatment of the Commandments', *Modern Language Notes*, 61 (1946), 506. Cawley
(p. 143) says that the omission of the prohibition against image-worship in this
commandment may indicate an anti-Lollard attitude to images. The reference
to 'vanyté' in line 74 may, however, connote idols, which are spoken of in the
Vulgate and in commentary as vanities and vain things.

6/82a–98 Exod. 20: 7; cf. Matt. 5: 33–5, Ecclus. 23: 7–20 (Vulgate); also the
Lay Folks' Catechism, p. 39, the *Book of Vices and Virtues*, p. 2, and *Middle English
Sermons*, pp. 23, 109.

6/98a–114 Cf. Exod. 20: 8, and compare the 'X mandata':

> Haue mynd to halow thyn holy day,
> Thow and all thyn with good entent:
> Leve servyle werkes and mych a-ray;
> Thys ys the tryd comaundement. (Zupitza, p. 45)

See also 'A Middle English Treatise on the Ten Commandments', pp. 21–2,
the *Lay Folks' Catechism*, p. 43, and N-town 26/65–87.

6/103-6 Cf. Hoccleve's *Regement of Princes* (*Hoccleve's Works*, ed. Frederick J. Furnivall, EETS es 72 (1897), p. 16).

6/114a Exod. 20: 12.

6/123-8 Cf. the exposition of the fourth commandment in 'A Middle English Treatise on the Ten Commandments': 'þou schalt worschup þi modur holy chirche & hir seruantes. for þai been oure gostly fadurus' (p. 24); also the *Lay Folks' Catechism*, pp. 42–5, and the *Book of Vices and Virtues*, p. 3.

6/130a-8 Exod. 20: 13. The exposition given here was conventional in medieval texts. Cf. Hugh of St Victor: 'Homicidium sit istis modis: manu, lingua, consensu' (*PL* 176: 122; also 176: 356). The *Lay Folks' Catechism* bids 'Sle noman with wykkyd wyl; In word ne dede . . .' (p. 47). See also 'A notabill Tretys off the ten Comandementys' (*Yorkshire Writers*, ed. C. Horstmann (London, 1895), I: 196), the 'Spore of Love' (*Vernon MS.*, 282/529), 'A Middle English Treatise on the Ten Commandments', pp. 25–7, and Towneley 18/ 153–4. Cf. Robertson, 'Certain Theological Conventions', pp. 509–10.

6/138a-46 Exod. 20: 14. Cf. the *Lay Folks' Catechism*, p. 48.

6/146a Exod. 20: 15.

6/152 *handys lymyd*: cf. 'To yow also, thevys of other men is godes. . . . Ye have handes, lymed euere ready to take . . .' in the *Middle English Pilgrimage of the Soul*, cited by *MED*, *līmen* v. (1) 3 (b).

6/154a Exod. 20: 16.

6/162a This commandment employs the language of Exod. 20: 17 in the Vulgate, but the order of Deut. 5: 21. This was considered the ninth commandment by Clement of Alexandria, Augustine, and other Fathers, and this manner of enumerating the commandments is now customary among Roman Catholics and Lutherans. Cf. Towneley 18/169–76 and York 20/187– 92.

6/170a Exod. 20: 17.

6/179-82 Cf. Augustine: 'in illis duobus praeceptis, non moechandi et non furandi, ipsa opera notata sunt; in his vero extremis [i.e. the ninth and tenth commandments] ipsa concupiscentia' (*in Exod.*, *PL* 34: 621, cited by Cawley, 'Metrical Versions', p. 143 note 39). Compare Hugh of St Victor: 'Hic opponitur de hoc quod Dominus in Evangelio, cum suppleret illud praeceptum, "Non moechaberis" dicit: "Ego autem dico vobis: Qui viderit mulierem ad concupiscendum eam am moechatus est eam." Sed hoc non fuit superaddere cum in lege idem prohibeatur, ut in hoc praecepto: "Non concupisces uxorem proximi tui." Hic enim concupiscentia prohiberi videtur sicut ibi. Ad quod potest dici quod vere hoc praeceptum bene intellectum et actum prohibet . . .' (*PL* 220: 420–1). Cf. the *Book of Vices and Virtues*, p. 5.

PLAY 7

This play merges the traditions of the dramatic *Prophetae* with the iconographic *Radix Jesse* to produce a 'Jesse Root' play that is unique in the extant English drama. Like a *Prophetae*, it has Old Testament prophets testify to New Testament salvific events. But like a Jesse Tree, the play also includes the ancestors of Christ, in this case thirteen of the kings listed in the genealogy of Jesus in Matthew 1.

The inclusion of thirteen prophets, and a matching number of kings, presumably derives from the pseudo-Augustinian *Contra Judaeos, Paganos, et Arianos Sermo de Symbolo*, which also contains thirteen prophets (Young 2: 143). The *Ordo Prophetarum* of Limoges presents the same number of prophets, and the Towneley *Prima Pastorum* refers to thirteen prophets, twelve of whom are the same as those listed in the *Sermo de Symbolo* (A. C. Cawley, *The Wakefield Pageants in the Towneley Cycle* (Manchester, 1958), p. 102). Only four of the N-town prophets and one king, David, are included in the *Sermo de Symbolo*, but all of the prophets in this play, save Baruch, appear in the Rouen prophets play.

John K. Bonnell ('The Source in Art of the So-Called *Prophets Play* in the Hegge Collection', *PMLA* 29 (1914), 327–40), followed by Anderson (p. 37), argues that this play was inspired by pictorial rather than textual models. Vriend, however, disputes this idea, stating that a diligent search revealed no iconographic Jesse Tree in which kings are supplied with prophecy scrolls (p. 16). Brother Cornelius Luke (pp. 8 ff.) argues that Bonnell's theory overlooks the prominence of the Marian element in the play, which, he says, overshadows the importance of the Jesse Tree. And Kretzmann (pp. 30–4) argues that the play originated in liturgy; see Thomas B. Campbell, 'The Prophets' Pageant in the English Mystery Cycles: Its Origin and Function', *Research Opportunities in Renaissance Drama* 17 (1974), 107–21.

This play develops specific themes, including Christ's royal and priestly lineage and the temple as a type of Mary. It also recapitulates, in the form of prophecy, principal episodes in salvation history. Rehoboam, Micah, and Daniel employ images of the Fall in prophesying salvation, all the while emphasizing Mary's central role. Subsequent speakers then offer a chronology of New Testament events that conforms to a credal pattern. Such figures as Jonah and Joel appear according to the chronology of the events that they prefigure and prophesy, rather than in order of the prophetic books in the Vulgate. Anderson's sugestion (p. 37) that the play may once have been longer seems unlikely: the allusions to Doomsday in the last stanzas bring the chronology of events to a conclusion, and the number of prophets in the play as we have it has important precedents, as noted above.

Marius Sepet notes the mixing of kings and prophets in French drama, and cites a reference to one such procession at Mayenne about 1655 (*Les Prophètes du Christ* (Paris, 1878), p. 168 n. 1). Chambers (2: 368) records a Jesse play at

Hereford, and Craig (p. 278) and others have proposed that entries in the Lincoln corporation minute book refer to the kings in a Jesse play.

The Proclamation, accurately describing the play as a Jesse Root, emphasizes that the prophecies therein will apply to Mary. Swenson (p. 17) observes that the play is consistent with this Marian interest, since it contains no fewer than fifteen direct references to the Virgin, as compared to only one in the Towneley Prophets play. Prophecies in N-town 7 also apply, of course, to Jesus, both independently and in conjunction with Mary (see Robert A. Brawer, 'The Form and Function of the Prophetic Procession in the Middle English Cycle Play', *Annuale Mediaevale* 13 (1972), 124). A focus on Mary was characteristic of many Jesse trees, and the words *virga* and *virgo* were commonly identified in this context. The Holkham Bible Picture Book (10ʳ), like many Jesse windows, places Mary atop the tree (see Anderson, p. 37).

The play is written in ababbcbc octaves.

7/4-5 Cf. Isaiah 7: 14. Isaiah's prophecy is cited in the *Sermo de Symbolo*, in early Christmas tropes and liturgical *Pastores*, and in each of the English cycles and both Coventry plays; see Arthur Watson, *The Early Iconography of the Tree of Jesse* (London, 1934), p. 155, and Cawley, *Wakefield Pageants*, p. 113.

7/6 *Zabulon*: *Le Mystère de la Passion*, 5461, includes Zabulon in a list of devils. Block (p. 382) says that in the *Gospel of Nicodemus* (cap. xiii. 9) Zabulon is associated with the 'regio umbrae mortis' and that Zabulus occurs with the meaning 'devil' in *De Nugis Curialium*.

7/9-10 Cf. Isaiah 7: 14.

7/13 Cf. 37–8, in which Jeremiah declares that Jesus descended from priests as well as kings. The genealogy in Matt. 1 illustrates the Davidic ancestry of Joseph; cf. Heb. 7: 14—24, Luke 3: 23—38, and Marshall D. Johnson, *The Purpose of the Biblical Genealogies* (Cambridge, 1969), pp. 139ff. The apocryphal *De Nativitate Mariae* and several later texts declare that Mary too was of the royal stock of David (see N-town 15/49–52 and the note). The *Legenda Aurea*, however, says that Mary's royal tribe had bonds of kinship with the priestly tribe, so that Mary was descended from both. Thus Jesus was 'rex et sacerdos' (Cap. cxxxi, p. 587). Kretzmann (pp. 31–2) cites a similar theme in liturgy, and Davies (p. 450 note 16) refers to a citation in Hone's *Apocryphal New Testament* that says Mary was of the tribe of Levi. In N-town 14/113, the bishop declares that Mary is his blood relative. And in Play 18, Baltazare speaks of Christ's kingship, Melchizar of his priesthood.

7/17-24 Cf. Isaiah 11: 1, widely cited in the drama. Bonnell (p. 332) observes that in a typical Jesse tree, Jesse sleeps at the foot of the tree, or the tree grows out of his body, with the kings appearing on the branches and the prophets forming a border.

7/25-32 Watson (pp. 152–3) traces David's speeches in the *Sermo de Symbolo* and in Continental Jesse plays to Psalms 21: 28, 71: 11, 84: 12–13, and 109: 1.

See Thomas Livius, *The Blessed Virgin in the Fathers of the First Six Centuries* (London, 1893), pp. 77–90.

7/33–40 Cf. Jer. 33: 14–18 and *Life of Our Lady*, III: 638–53, 941–68; also, Towneley 12/359, Chester 5/328a–44 (MS H), the Coventry Weavers' pageant, 68–74, and Davies, p. 450 note 17.

7/42–3 The temple was a common type of the Virgin, cited in Ambrose and Rabanus Maurus; see Graef, p. 88 and F. J. E. Raby, *A History of Christian-Latin Poetry* (Oxford, 1927; 2nd edition 1953), p. 366. Gail McMurray Gibson cites this motif in *Christ I* '"Porta Haec Clausa Erit": Comedy, Conception, and Ezekiel's Closed Door in the *Ludus Coventriae* Play of "Joseph's Return"', *Journal of Medieval and Renaissance Studies* 8 (1978), 143; cf. 'A Song to Mary' in Davies, *Medieval English Lyrics*, no. 34, l. 31.

7/45–8 Cf. Ezek. 44: 1–3. Ambrose, Aquinas, and others took Ezekiel's closed gate of the temple to be symbolic of Mary's virginity *in partu*, during the Nativity (Graef, p. 80 *et passim*, Livius, pp. 114–16, Raby, pp. 373–4. Gibson traces this motif in *Christ I*, Lydgate's *Life of Our Lady*, several lyrics, and Greban's passion play, as well as in the visual arts. She notes that in the *Speculum Humanae Salvationis*, the *porta clausa* is juxtaposed to the Jesse tree. See Watson, pp. 153–4, Anderson, pp. 159–60, and Ch. Cahier, *Caractéristiques des Saints dans L'Art Populaire* (Paris, 1867; reprint 1966), p. 713. In drama, this prophecy is evoked in the Rouen *Festum Asinorum* (Young 2: 162) and Chester 5/312a–28 (MS H).

7/51–2 Cf. Gen. 3: 15 and N-town 2/263–5.

7/53–6 The prophet Micah addresses Christ during the Harrowing of Hell in the *Gospel of Nicodemus*, citing Mic. 7: 18–20. In the Rouen *ordo*, Micah refers to Mic. 1: 3, and in Chester 5/392a–400 (MS H), he paraphrases Mic. 5: 2; cf. Chester 8/310a–14. For artistic treatments, see Watson, p. 158, and Davies, p. 450 note 17.

7/61–4 That Christ was the fruit of redemption for man, who had fallen by eating the forbidden fruit, was a familiar literary and iconographic motif. Patrick J. Collins observes that Adam of St Victor praised the Virgin for restoring the *pomum veritum* or *fructum vitae*, which had been lost by Adam and Eve. He notes that Deguilleville's *Pelerinage de l'Ame* recounts how man was damned until the Jesse tree brought forth a divine fruit, and adds that illuminated English psalters frequently incorporate the pictorial type of the Virgin with the fruit into their depictions of the Jesse Tree (*The N-town Plays and Medieval Picture Cycles*, Early Drama, Art, and Music Monograph Series, 2 (Kalamazoo, 1979), pp. 4–5). Martin Stevens adds that the maiden's fruit is the retributive signal that God has made the Tree of Life intact again (*Four Middle English Mystery Cycles* (Princeton, 1987), p. 241). Bonnell (pp. 334–5) says that Daniel's vision of 'maydenys frute' on a tree seems to be an incorrect allusion to Nebuchadnezzar's vision of a tree reaching heaven in Dan. 4: 10ff.; cf. the deuterocanonical story of Susanna, as well as Seth's vision of the new-born Christ-child at the top of the tree in Eden ('Canticum de Creatione', ed. Horstmann, p. 133; *Cursor Mundi*, 1337–59; *Northern Passion*, pp. 150–3; see J. H. Mozley, 'the "Vita Adae"', *Journal of Theological Studies* 30 (1929), 123–4).

7/63 Cf. Pr 115.

7/65–88 The events rehearsed in these lines approximate a credal pattern and specifically recall the Creed Page of the Arundel Psalter, in which prophets and apostles, holding inscribed scrolls, illustrate the Apostles' Creed. Ten of the twelve prophets on the Creed Page also appear in the play; see Anderson, pp. 39–40; also, Brawer, pp. 108–9, and Cahier, p. 719.

7/69–72 Cf. Jonah 1: 17, Matt. 12: 39–40, the Rouen *Ordo* (Young 2: 160), Chester 5/344a–60 (MS H), and N-town 38/115–18.

7/77–80 In the Rouen *ordo* and, in art, at St Michael's, Hildesheim, Obadiah cites Obad. verse 17 (Young, 2: 160; Watson, p. 159).

7/81–2 'I too, Joras, the seventh king of the Jesse root. . . .' Kretzmann (p. 32) cites the following from a liturgical exposition of the genealogy in Matt. 1: '*Joras*: Nemo ascendit in caelum nisi qui descendit de caelo: Filius hominis qui est in caelo'.

7/86–8 These lines recall the Apostles' Creed: 'He ascended into heaven, and sitteth on the right hand of God the Father Almighty: From thence He shall come to judge the quick and the dead'. In the *Gospel of Nicodemus* Habakkuk greets Christ by quoting from Hab. 3: 13. In the *Sermo de Symbolo* he recites Hab. 3: 2. Cf. the Rouen *ordo* (Young, 2: 158), Watson, p. 154, and the note to N-town 15/100.

7/93–6 Cf. Joel 2: 28. The Rouen Joel also alludes to this passage. Cf. York 12/85ff. and Chester 5/376a–84 (MS H).

7/101–4 Cf. Ezek. 34: 23 and Ezekiel's prophecy in *Life of Our Lady*, III: 1532–37. Haggai paraphrases Hag. 2: 8 (Vulgate) in the Rouen play and in Jesse trees in art (Young 2: 161, Watson, p. 154).

7/105–8 Cf. 2 Kings 16, Is. 7: 1–17.

7/125–8 Cf. the *Life of Our Lady*, p. 536, which has Baruch cite Jer. 23: 5:

> Baruk . . . sayde of Dauid a burioun and the spryng
> Shall be susteynede and Regne like a kyng.
> And he shall do, thourgh his worthynesse,
> Dome in erthe and also Rightwysnesse.

Falke (p. 32) cites Isa. 3: 13–14. Baruch is the only prophet in the play who does not appear in the Rouen *ordo*. He is also the only N-town prophet who is unaccounted for in the Jesse window from St Chad's, now at St Mary's church, Shrewsbury (Anderson, p. 37).

7/Notations Genealogical notes concerning St Anne and a list of the five Annes are written below the text on the final page of Play 7, and below Contemplacio's opening speech in Play 8. Meredith observes that the names listed here are very similar to those given in the genealogies in the Commonplace Book of Robert Reynes. This information was available in the *Legenda Aurea* and elsewhere, but interestingly, both N-town and the Commonplace Book erroneously refer to St 'Geruasius', rather than the 'Servatius' of the *Legenda* (*The Mary Play* (London and New York, 1987), p. 11). Greg (p. 143) and others infer from the genealogical tables here and on ff. 21–22ᵛ, and from the notes on the dimensions of the ark in the margin of f. 24, that the codex was used for private reading rather than acting. Several revisions and notations, however, notably those by Scribe C, suggest that at least portions of the codex were used as prompt-copy. See Spector, *Genesis of the N-town Cycle*, pp. 145–6; Peter Meredith and Stanley J. Kahrl, *The N-town Plays* (Leeds, 1977), p. xxiv; and pp. xxiii–xxiv and 543 n. 1 below.

PLAY 8

This play follows and often echoes the *Legenda Aurea*, which incorporates much of the *De Nativitate Mariae*. In some instances, the play draws details from the *Legenda* that do not appear in the earlier apocryphal source, including Episcopus' allusion to three annual feasts, the reference to Sarah's being ninety when she conceived Isaac, and the phrase *regal sacerdocium*. A few details, such as the bishop's name, Ysakar, recall the *De Nativitate* rather than the *Legenda*, but this information could have been transmitted by other accounts. The *Life of St. Anne*, for example, also names Isakar, and is generally similar to the Marian plays in N-town. But despite claims by Roscoe E. Parker (*The Middle English Stanzaic Versions of the Life of Saint Anne*, EETS os 174 (1928), pp. xxxiv ff.), it does not seem to have been a significant source of the cycle. Liturgical influence on the play is apparent in the singing of the sequence 'Benedicta sit beata Trinitas' and the hymn 'Exultet celum laudibus', and in the chanting of Latin formularies. Kretzmann (p. 157) notes that Anna's Barrenness is treated in the lectiones for the festival Anna Matris Mariae.

The expositor Contemplacio makes his first appearance in this play, introducing what appears to be an independent sequence of Marian plays that was interpolated into the cycle as the codex was being transcribed. (See Spector, 'The Composition and Development of an Eclectic Manuscript', *Leeds Studies in English* 9 (1977), 62–83, and *The Genesis of the N-town Cycle* (New York and London, 1988).) In diction, tone, and function, Contemplacio's speeches in these plays closely resemble those of his counterpart, Poeta, in the Digby St Paul and Candlemas plays (but see the headnote to Play 11). David Hobart Carnahan observes that most of Contemplacio's speeches, in their inclusion of sermon elements, discussion of preceding and following plays, apology for the manner of presentation, and pleas for silence, resemble the speeches of Continental expositors and doctors ('The Prologue in the Old French and

Provençal Mystery', Yale Ph.D. thesis, 1905). Woolf (p. 164) adds that when Contemplacio reappears in Passion Play 2 dressed as 'an exposytour in doctorys wede' (29/first s.d.), he is also identical in appearance to Continental expositors. She detects further Continental affinities in the fact that the early life of Mary was dramatized in the *Mystère de la Conception de la Vierge*, the *Passion de Valenciennes*, Jean Michel's *Mystère de la Passion*, and the *Egerer Fronleichnamsspiel.* In extant English drama, by contrast, the matter of this play and the next are unique to N-town.

The bulk of the play is in long-lined ababbcbc octaves. The third stanza of Contemplacio's speech (17–25) is a 9-line stanza which may well be revisional. Quatrains appear in 145–8 and 250–3. Lines 237–49 form either an octave and a 5-line stanza or a thirteener rhyming ababbcbcdeeed. This play is not mentioned in the Proclamation.

8/1–25 The five Marian episodes and the conclusion that Contemplacio promises are presented in plays 8–11 and 13. In Play 9, he adds the promise of a Parliament of Heaven, which appears in Play 11. Sister M. Patricia Forrest notes that Contemplacio's rhetorically embellished opening stanza in the present play recalls the *ante-theme* of medieval homily and that his first two lines may echo the liturgical formula of a collect. She adds that his concluding blessing in Play 13 and his promise of pardon for saying daily prayers were similarly standard features of sermons ('The Role of the Expositor Contemplacio in the St. Anne's Day Plays of the Hegge Cycle', *Medieval Studies* 28 (1966), 65–7, 74). See Carnahan, pp. 63–7, and Owst, *Preaching in Medieval England* (Cambridge, 1926), pp. 316–17; also see the note to N-town 13/156A–57A, however. Forrest (p. 64) says that Contemplacio's name seems to represent contemplation of scripture, while Woolf (p. 382 note 21) proposes that his name may have been suggested by the marginal notation 'Contemplacio' in Love's *Mirrour*. The doctor in the chapter house in the *Abbaye of the Holy Ghost*, a text associated with a major source of Play 11, is named Contemplacyon.

8/9 *Modyr of Mercy*: Meredith, observing that this is a common epithet for Mary (cf. 9/8), cites the phrase *mater misericordiae* in the antiphon *Salve Regina* (*Mary Play*, p. 86).

8/12–13 Contemplacio's statement that the portrayal of the Annunciation will be followed by the Visit to Elizabeth agrees with the order of events in Luke 1. He makes no reference to Joseph's Doubt, depicted in Play 12, which is based on Matthew. See the notes to 11/310 and 11/340 s.d.

8/26–7 Cf. Lev. 21: 6. Meredith notes the use of this text during the mass on Corpus Christi day (*Mary Play*, p. 87).

8/30 The high priest is named Isakar (or Issachar) in the *De Nativitate*, and in such English works as the *Life of St. Anne*, Bokenham's *Legendys*, and Mirk's *Festial.* Alan J. Fletcher notes that the Sarum Breviary also names the bishop

Ysachar ('The Design of the N-Town Play of Mary's Conception', *Modern Philology*, 79 (1981), 168).

8/34–37 Cf. the *Legenda Aurea*: 'Cujus rei gratia cum singulis annis in tribus festis praecipuis Jerusalem frequentarent, in festo encaeniorum Joachim cum contribulibus suis Hierusalem adscendit, et cum caeteris ad altare accedens oblationem suam offerre voluit' (Graesse, Cap. CXXXI, p. 587). Cf. John 10: 22. Meredith cites Isidore's rendering of *Encaenia* as 'nova templi dedicatio' and his comment, 'Graece enim καινὸν dicitur novum. Quando enim aliquid novum dedicatur, encaenia dicitur' (*Mary Play*, p. 87).

8/38 *dysspyse*: cf. *De Nativitate*: 'despexit eum' (Tishendorf, Cap. II); also, Bokenham's *Vita S. Annae* in *Bokenham's Legendys of Hooly Wummen*, ed. Mary S. Serjeantson, EETS os 206 (1938), 51/1852–3, and the *Life of St. Anne*, 3/86.

8/40 *regal sacerdocium*: cf. the *Legenda Aurea*: 'soli sacerdotes et reges et prophetae in lege veteri inungebantur, unde et nos a Christo christiani dicimur et genus electum et *regale sacerdotium* appellamur' (Cap. CXXXI, p. 587; italics mine). Meredith points out that in 1 Pet. 2: 9, and in the *Legenda*, this phrase refers to all Christians, while in the present context it emphasizes the grandeur of the temple and its officers (*Mary Play*, pp. 15–16).

8/41 The *Speculum Sacerdotale* lists 'prayingis, fastyngis, almes dede and wakyngis' as ways of purifying oneself of sin (*Mary Play*, p. 88).

8/47 Isidore renders Joachim as 'ubi est praeparatio' (*Mary Play*, p. 88).

8/50 *ryghtful*: Bokenham's Joachym is 'symple, rihtfulle & eke petous', and 'ryhtful to god' (45/1634, 1658).

8/51–53 These lines very closely agree with the *Legenda Aurea*: 'omnemque suam substantiam trifarie dividebant, unam partem templo et templi servitoribus impendebant, aliam peregrinis et pauperibus erogabant, tertiam sibi et familiae suae usibus reservabant' (Cap. CXXXI, p. 587). This passage adopts the *De Nativitate* almost exactly. Pseudo-Matthew includes this motif, but in slightly different language. Cf. Bokenham, 45/1651–7, and the *Life of St. Anne* 2/37–48.

8/53 '. . . the third part for those (who) dwell with me'.

8/58–65 Cf. the *Legenda Aurea*: 'Et ita per annos XX prolem ex conjugio non habentes voverunt domino, quod, si iis sobolem concederet, eam servitio domini manciparent' (Cap. CXXXI, p. 587). Cf. Bokenham, 45–6/1658–71; *Life of St. Anne*, 2/61–6.

8/68 Cf. Bokenham, 41/1498, and the *Life of St. Anne* (Trinity MS), 96/211. Fletcher cites a lection for St Anne's feast day: 'Anna dicitur, id est gratia, quia gratia plena est' ('Design', p. 168).

8/70 Cf. Isa. 7: 14.

8/81 Cf. Whiting, 5515.

8/91 '. . . may God bring you back again safe and sound'.

8/97 s.d. *Benedicta sit beata Trinitas*: cf. Dutka, pp. 22–3. Kretzmann (p. 159) says that this sequence is primarily for the festival of the Trinity, and that part of the Trinity service was used on the festival of Anna.

8/98–105 Cf. the *Legenda Aurea*: 'Quem videns sacerdos *cum indignatione nimia repulit*, et cur ad altare Dei accedere *praesumeret*, increpavit asserens non esse conveniens, maledicto legis obnoxium oblationem domino legis offerre, nec *inter foecundos infoecundum . . . adstare*' (Cap. CXXXI, p. 587; italics mine). *presume and abuse* (103): *presume* echoes *praesumeret* in the *Legenda*; *OED* (*abuse* v. 7b) cites this instance only of 'abuse' as an intransitive form meaning 'malign, revile', but *MED* (*abūsen* v. 3) offers the preferable rendering 'behave improperly'.

8/105 s.d. Meredith conjectures that *refudit* is a form of *refutit* or is *refundit* with a missing abbreviation mark (*Mary Play*, p. 89).

8/110–16 Fletcher notes that the antiphonal lines in 110–13 are commonly connected with Mass liturgy, normally occurring a little before the Kyries. He adds that Episcopus' concluding blessing in 114–15 corresponds to the feast of the Trinity, as does 'Benedicta sit beata Trinitas' ('Design', p. 168). Dutka (p. 72) observes that the precise words of this benediction do not occur in the Sarum or York manuals.

8/123–4 These lines generally follow the accounts in Pseudo-Matthew and the *Legenda Aurea*, and recall Bokenham, 47/1702–5; cf. the *Life of St. Anne*, 3/97–8.

8/130 Cf. the *Legenda Aurea*: 'Secedens igitur ad pastores suos, cum ibi aliquamdiu fuisset' (Cap. CXXXI, p. 587). See also *De Nativitate*, Cap. II, Bokenham, 47/1706–9, and the *Life of St. Anne*, 3/100–3. *shepherdys*: Meredith suggests that the manuscript reading, *sherherdys*, may be an otherwise un-recorded noun denoting sheep shearers (*Mary Play*, p. 90).

8/133–212 Roughly-drawn lines before and after this section mark it off, as does the notation 'pastores', written by another hand at the right of 133. Letters have been written in the left margins by another hand: 'a' before 135, 'b' before 139 and 141, 'c' before 143, and 'd' before 145. This lettering may have been connected to the cancellation at 139 of the speaker heading 'ijus Pastor' and the writing of 'Joachym' above it.

8/141 Cf. Luke 1: 52.

8/143 Cf. Whiting B325; compare 8/226.

8/155 Cf. Apoc. 3: 19.

8/168 *3e*: in suggesting the emendation from *he*, despite the shift in gram-matical person that results, Meredith cites a similar shift in 11/333.

8/172 s.d. *Exultet celum laudibus*: a hymn for Lauds at the feast of the Apostles

(Meredith, *Mary Play*, p. 91). Fletcher says that 'archangelorum' has been sub-
stituted for 'apostolorum' in this hymn, making it fit the context of the play
('Design', p. 169). But the text of the hymn reproduced by Dutka (p. 27), has
the word 'archangelorum'. *The Conversion of St. Paul* concludes with 'To whoys
lawd ye syng: "*Exultet celum laudibus!*"' (*The Late Medieval Religious Plays of Bod-
leian MSS Digby 133 and E Museo 160*, EETS os 283 (1982), eds. Donald C. Baker
et al.).

8/173–99 The angel's speech in large measure faithfully renders the *Legenda
Aurea*: 'quaedam dei ei soli angelus cum magna claritate apparuit et de ejus
visione turbatum, ne timeret, admonuit, dicens: ego sum angelus domini missus
ad te, ut annuntiem tibi preces tuas exauditas esse et elemosinas tuas in conspectu domini adscendisse; vidi enim pudorem tuum et audivi sterilitatis
opprobrium non recte tibi objectum. Peccati quippe, non naturae ultor est Deus
et ideo, cum alicujus uterum claudit, ad hoc facit, ut mirabilior denuo aperiat, et
non libidinis esse, quod nascitur, sed divini fore muneris cognoscatur. Prima
gentis vestrae mater Sara nonne usque ad nonagesimum annum sterilitatis
opprobrium pertulit et tamen Ysaac, qui repromissa erat omnium gentium
benedictio, generavit? Rachel etiam nonne diu sterilis fuit et tamen Josephum
genuit, qui totius Aegypti dominium habuit? Quis fortior Samsone vel sanctior
Samuele? Et tamen hi ambo matres steriles habuere. Rationi igitur et exemplis
crede, dilatos diu conceptus et steriles partus mirabiliores esse solere. Proinde
Anna uxor tua pariet tibi filiam et vacabis nomen ejus Mariam. Haec, ut vovistis,
erit ab infantia domino consecrata et adhuc ex utero matris suae spiritu sancto
plena, nec forinsecus inter populares, sed in templo domini semper morabitur,
ne quid sinistrum de ea aliquis suspicetur Et sicut ipsa ex sterili matre nascetur,
ita et mirabiliter ex ea altissimi filius generabitur, cujus nomen erit Jesus, et per
eum omnibus gentibus erit salus. Et tibi hoc signum: cum perveneris Hierosoli-
mis ad auream portam, Annam uxorem tuam obviam habebis, quae de tua tarda-
tione modo sollicita tunc in conspectu tuo gaudebit. His dictis angelus ab eo
recessit' (Cap. CXXXI, pp. 587–8).

8/191 *joys fyff*: The Five Joys of Mary usually include the Annunciation, the
Nativity, the Resurrection, the Ascension, and the Assumption.

8/198 *Gyldyn Gate*: this gate, specified in Pseudo-Matthew, the *De Nativitate*,
and the *Legenda Aurea*, has been identified as the Beautiful gate of Acts 3: 2.
Meredith, citing the *Wanderings of Felix Fabri*, says that the Golden Gate was
the eastern gate through which Jesus entered Jerusalem on Palm Sunday
(*Mary Play*, 92).

8/213–24 Cf. the *Legenda Aurea*: 'Anna autem, cum amare fleret et, quonam
vir suus ivisset, ignoraret, idem angelus eidem apparuit et sibi eadem, quae
viro annuntiaverat, patefecit addens, ut pro signo Hierusalem ad auream
portam pergeret et ibidem viro suo redeunti obviaret' (Cap. CXXXI, p. 588).

8/226 *Aftere grett sorwe evyr grett gladnes is had*: Cf. Whiting, T484, B52, B325,
E161, etc.

8/227 *myn inbassett*: Bokenham refers to the angel's mission as 'his ambacyat' (49/1791).

8/237–53 Cf. the *Legenda Aurea*: 'Igitur juxta angeli praeceptum ambo sibi invicem obviantes de mutua visione laetati et de prole promissa securi adorato domino domum redierunt divinum promissum hilariter exspectantes' (Cap. CXXXI, p. 588).

8/238 Anne's creeping to Joachim contradicts the accounts in the *Protevangelium* and Pseudo-Matthew, in which she runs to him. The *De Nativitate* and the *Legenda* are silent on this point. Meredith observes that the visual arts usually show Joachim and Anne standing as they meet (*Mary Play*, p. 92).

8/241 *kusse of clennesse*: Fry (p. 545 note 55) says that the kiss of cleanness was once used as proof of the doctrine of the Immaculate Conception. Vriend (pp. 36–7, 41), while noting the kiss, says that the play makes no mention of Mary's conception being immaculate in the theological sense. Brother Cornelius Luke (p. 31) prefers to believe that the playwright remained aloof from this controversy. Cf. lines 221–5.

PLAY 9

The apocryphal story of the Presentation of Mary in the temple is here augmented and segmented into motifs principally developed on numerical themes: the fifteen steps of the temple corresponding to the fifteen Gradual Psalms, the Ten Commandments reduced to two, Mary's five maidens, seven priests, and seven petitions, and the five letters in 'Maria'. In comprehending all of these motifs, the play or its source has conflated several earlier sources. A number of earlier texts, for example, refer to the fifteen steps. But Pseudo-Matthew, the *De Nativitate*, the *Legenda Aurea*, and the *Life of St. Anne* are among the few to associate the steps with the psalms, and none of these has Mary recite the psalms as she ascends, as she does in the play (this motif may derive from Bede). Nor do they include the seven petitions. This last motif and others in the play do appear in the *Meditationes Vitae Christi* and Love's *Mirrour*, which, however, omit the fifteen steps. And Lydgate's *Life of Our Lady* includes an embellished version of the seven petitions, and mentions the fifteen steps, but not the psalms. In presenting the seven petitions, the play differs from these analogues by excluding the commitment to righteous hatred, thereby gentling Mary's speeches. The play also places special emphasis on love.

The first dramatization of the Presentation of Mary was by Philippe de Mézières, perhaps as early as the 1360s. Young (2: 244–5) observes that Mézière's play appears to be unique in liturgical drama, and that one must look to the vernacular for wider acceptance of this theme in drama. The N-town version, however, is unique among extant English plays, and Woolf

(p. 162) says that Mary's recitation of the Gradual Psalms is found elsewhere in the drama only in the sixteenth-century *Passion de Valenciennes*.

One of the group presided over by Contemplacio, this play is not described in the Proclamation. The play is chiefly in long-lined ababbcbc octaves, though 210–17 rhyme ababbaba. The translation of the psalms is in quatrains, as are 218–21 and 294–301. The second stanza in Contemplacio's opening speech and his final stanza in the play are 9-line stanzas rhyming ababcdddc, both of which may be revisional (see the notes to 1–17 s.d. and 294–310).

9/1–17 s.d. Blank space left below 17 s.d. on f. 42ʳ indicates that the body of the play, beginning on f. 42ᵛ, was transcribed before Contemplacio's speech had been fully copied out.

9/17 s.d. Mézière's Presentation play specifies that Mary is to be played by a beautiful virgin three or four years old, dressed in a white tunic and a white mantle tied by a golden cord, with a gold frieze on the collar of the tunic and the opening of the mantle and a gold circlet on her head.

9/29 Brother Cornelius Luke (pp. 32–3), while noting that the angel makes no such prophecy in the preceding play, observes that queenship was a traditional appendage to the title 'Mother of God'.

9/30 '. . . (who) will be your husband'.

9/39–41 Cf. Mézière's *Livre du Sacrament de Mariage et du reconfort des dames mariées*: 'she prayed sweetly to God that she might see this virgin and serve her by washing her feet' (*Figurative Representation of the Presentation of the Virgin Mary in the Temple*, translated and edited by Robert S. Haller (Lincoln, Nebraska, 1971), p. 79).

9/39 *I have herd ȝow seyd*: Cf. 3/37 and note.

9/43 Cf. the Hereford Infancy Gospel: 'non iam infantula estimaretur esse sed magna et quasi iam xx esset annorum' (M. R. James, *Latin Infancy Gospels, A New Text, with a Parallel Version from Irish* (Cambridge, 1927), p. 23. Mézière's *Livre du sacrament de Mariage*, and Lydgate's *Life of Our Lady*, by contrast, follow Pseudo-Matthew in saying that Mary spoke as if she were thirty years old.

9/49 *wys husbond*: Meredith, arguing that this does not sound like Anne's normal speech, treats *wys* as an aphetic form of *iwys*. He adds that 'wise' is never spelled without a final *-e* in the Marian group of plays (*Mary Play*, pp. 93–4). However, Elizabeth's words, 'wys fadyr Joseph', in 13/143 corroborate the present reading (Meredith treats *wys* there too as an aphetic form). The spelling *wys* does appear in the 2/102, 113, 120, 150, and 41/296.

9/54 Cf. 8/100–8, and see the note to 8/30.

9/79 'May that Lord be loved (who) keeps you so'.

9/94–167 Mary climbs the fifteen steps of temple while reciting the opening verses of the fifteen Gradual Psalms (the Song of Ascents), Psalms 119–33 in the Vulgate. See the headnote for discussion of sources and analogues of this motif. Bede asserts that one of these psalms was recited while ascending each of the steps of the temple (*Psalmorum Librum exegesis*, *PL* 93/1084–92); Cassiodorus says that the psalms as a whole are steps to the perfect love of God (*Expositio Psalmorum*, *PL* 70/901–61; cited by Meredith, *Mary Play*, p. 94). In his Presentation play, Mézières does not specify the number of steps, but his note about the 1385 performance does, and his letter concerning the feast relates the steps to the Gradual Psalms; see M. Catherine Rupp's introduction to *Figurative Representation of the Presentation of the Virgin Mary in the Temple*, p. xxiii. In the present play, Mary's English renderings of these verses are in some instances awkwardly literal or otherwise problematic. In each case, they are preceded by 'gostly' interpretations that reflect Mary's own spiritual posture. Their relevance to Mary, and the absence of a single source, suggest to Meredith that these spiritual applications were made specifically for the play (*Mary Play*, pp. 16, 95).

9/112 'I am glad about these tidings (that) have been told me'.

9/115 *þe planetys sefne*: in order of their accepted distances from the earth according to Ptolemaic astronomy: the moon, Mercury, Venus, the sun, Mars, Jupiter, and Saturn.

9/119 'So that we may not be without God'.

9/121 This line translates not the first verse of Ps. 123, but much of verses 2–3.

9/129 (?) 'Then are we made like joyous merry ones', or 'like the joyous, merry'.

9/140–1 'Often youth is attacked by vexation of this kind'. The form *ȝough*, unattested in *OED*, is perhaps *ȝongh*, a form of *ȝonge*; cf. 5/41, 21/165. Line 141, possibly drawing on the interpretation of *Israel* as 'seeing God', seems to translate *dicat nunc Israel* as: 'Thou, seeing God, called Israel, say so'. Cf. Augustine's commentary on Ps. 120: 4 and Isidore's *Etymologiarum* (VII. vii. 6), cited by Meredith (*Mary Play*, p. 95).

9/149 *lokynge abowte*: in the place of 'elati sunt', this line suggests a self-restraint that complements Mary's humility.

9/158 The words 'on acorde' denote the harmony that Cassiodorus emphasizes in this psalm (957–61; cited by Meredith, *Mary Play*, p. 95).

9/170–87 Cf. Matt. 22: 37–9, Mark 12: 29–31, Luke 10: 27; also, the *Lay Folks' Catechism*, p. 61. Cf. the Three Laws in the *Meditationes* and Love, which also contain a parallel to 186: 'hate [the soul's] enemyes / that is to saie vices and synnes' (Love, p. 20). For 187, cf. Matt. 5: 44.

9/172–3 Meredith relates these lines to Luke 10: 25–8 (*Mary Play*, p. 96).

9/176–7 Meredith cites this common idea in the *Ancrene Riwle*, and in lyrics and drama (*Mary Play*, p. 96).

9/180 This is the first of several instances in the cycle in which Christ is specifically associated with wisdom. Ashley (p. 124) considers this association to be an essential element of the Christology of N-town. Wisdom is also an attribute of the second person of the trinity in the Parliament of Heaven in Play 11 (cf. 11/173, 174, and 179), as well as the Doctors play (21/90), and the play of the Assumption (41/94 and the speaker heading in 107). It is spoken of as a quality or gift of God in 9/223, 11/124, and 21/34.

9/190 Meredith's emendation of the line to read, 'For with prayʒer come grace and mercy', is consistent with the *Meditationes*: 'nulla gratia descendit in animam, nisi per orationem et corporis afflictionem' (*Mary Play*, p. 96).

9/194–205 Five maidens similarly appear in the Presentation of Mary scene of the Kinwarton alabaster (Anderson, p. 134 and plate 7b).

9/196 'This manner of living pleases me as much as my life itself'.

9/200 *Fruyssyon*: 'the joy of communion with God', which the Wycliffite *Lanterne of Liʒt* defines as the fourth spiritual endowment, 'vse of þe godhed & loue of God euerlasting' (ed. L. M. Swinburn, EETS os 151 (1917), 26/24, cited by *MED*, *fruicioun*, n.). Meredith, noting that the names of the maidens all represent qualities of Mary, observes that *fruyssyon* is the only one of these terms that was not commonplace. He relates the word to the *Legenda*, which says of Mary, 'et visione divina quotidie fruebatur' (p. 589; *Mary Play*, p. 97).

9/206–13 The seven alliterative qualities personified by the priests are devotional and intellectual, in keeping with their function as stated in 208–9. Divination (in 213) was often represented as a pagan practice, and was sometimes linked to necromancy (see the note to 21/17). In its present context, however, the word denotes prophecy or, as *MED* suggests, foresight or wisdom (*divinacioun*, n. 2 [b], citing this instance only). Meredith points out an approbative biblical use of *divinatio* in Prov. 16: 10, and, for the view that the seven priests are related to the seven gifts of the Holy Ghost, refers the reader to *NQ* 27 (1980), 295–7 (*Mary Play*, p. 97).

9/222–3 'May he through whose wisdom the entire world was created grant your soul solace'.

9/230–43 Mary's third petition is gentler than the corresponding request in the *Meditationes* and Love, to hate and eschew all things that God hates, and, in Lydgate, to hate the devil. The fifth petition in these analogues is here made the seventh. See 'Revelationes B. Elizabeth', ed. L. Oliger, *Antonianum*, 1 (1926), 54–6, and 'De Sancta Maria', in *Yorkshire Writers*, 1: 158–9). Cf. the seven petitions in Love's *Mirrour*:

First / I asked grace of all myʒty god / thoruʒ the whiche I myʒt fulfille the heste of loue / that is to say / forto loue hym with al my herte / &c.: the secounde / I asked that I myʒt loue myn neighebour after his wil and his likynge / and that he wolde make me to loue alle that he loueth: the thridde / that he wolde make me to hate and eschewe alle thing that he hateth: the ferthe / I asked mekenes / pacience / benignyte / and swettenesse / and alle othere vertues by the whiche I my3t be graciose and plesynge to goddes si3te: the fifte peticioun I made to god / that he wolde lete me se the tyme in the whiche that blessid mayden schulde be born that schulde conceiue and bere goddes sone; and that he wolde kepe myne ey3en that I my3t see hire / myne eris that I my3t here hir speke / my tunge that I my3t preise hir / myne hondes that I my3t serue hir with / my feete that I my3te goo to hir seruise and myne knees with the whiche I my3te honoure and worschippe goddes sone in hir barme. In the sixte peticioun I asked grace to be obesiaunt to the biddynges and the ordenaunces of the bisshop of the temple. And in the seuenthe I prayde god to kepe all the peple to his seruise (p. 21).

9/232 *as myself dere*: 'as dearly as I do myself'.

9/241 *wyttys fyve*: the five senses, as in *Cursor Mundi*, 17015–18, though often alluding to the inner wits, as in *Wisdom*, 163. See N-town 10/317.

9/242 '. . . and if it does not, it is pointless to contend to the contrary'.

9/245 cf. S. of S. 5: 2.

9/245 s.d. *confeccyons*: prepared dishes, especially ones containing fruit and spices. Exod. 16: 31 says that manna was like coriander seed, tasting like wafers made with honey. The sources of the play do not refer to manna, but they do have Mary accept food from angels (see the note to 246–51 below). Since manna was commonly referred to as angel's meat (as in 248 below; cf. Ps. 77: 25), it is represented here as the food given to Mary. Manna was considered to prefigure the bread of the Eucharist: cf. the Digby *Mary Magdalen* (2065–8), cited by Meredith, who adds that in the Paris *Resurrection*, manna is described as resembling large coins. He suggests that the angelic song in this stage direction may have been 'Jhesu corona virginum', as in 277 s.d. below (*Mary Play*, p. 98).

9/246–51, 278–93 Mary eats angel's food and distributes her earthly food among the poor in Pseudo-Matthew and several later texts, including the *Meditationes* and Love, the *Life of St. Anne* (Bodl. MS), and the *Life of Our Lady*.

9/250 The daily angelic appearance to serve Mary was a common element in the story, specified in Pseudo-Matthew, the *De Nativitate*, the *Legenda*, the *Meditationes*, and other accounts. The *Meditationes* and Love's *Mirrour* follow Pseudo-Matthew in noting that Mary often spoke with the angels.

9/256–7 Manna is 'in tast celestialle of savoure' in the Digby *Killing of the Children*, 12, and 'fode of most delycyte' in *Mary Magdalen*, 2038 (*Mary Play*, p. 98).

9/262–7 George C. Taylor notes the highly conventionalized nature of these lines ('The Relation of the English Corpus Christi Play to the Middle English Religious Lyric', *Modern Philology*, 5 (1907), 6) and Halliwell (p. 412) notes that Lydgate gives three similar acrostics in Harl. MS 2255. But Woolf (pp. 162–3) says that the angel's ornate acrostic of Mary's name in the present play appears to be an original embellishment.

9/266 For Mary's descent from Jesse and her position at the peak of Jesse trees, see the headnote to Play 7 and the note to 7/13.

9/267 *anceter*: the MS reading, *antecer*, is otherwise unattested. It may be an error for *antecesser*, but the emended form assumes a simple confusion of *c* and *t* (*Mary Play*, p. 99).

9/268–9 Cf. Phil. 2: 10.

✓ **9/277 s.d.** *Jesu Corona Virginum*: Sister M. Patricia Forrest notes that this hymn in the Sarum use is sung at Lauds on the feasts of the Virgins ('Apocryphal Sources of the St. Anne's Day Plays in the Hegge Cycle', *Medievalia et Humanistica*, 17 (1966), 47 note 71). See Dutka, pp. 32–3. Kretzman (pp. 159–60) discusses the liturgical associations of this play.

9/284 Meredith notes that Mary's sharing her food with her maidens is not in the sources (*Mary Play*, p. 99).

9/285 Cf. Whiting G228, G231.

9/288 *hertyly*: 'amply, to the satisfaction of appetite'. *MED* offers no gloss in this sense; the earliest citation with this meaning in *OED* is from about 1613 (*heartily*, adv. 3).

9/291 *þe dedys of mercy*: see the headnote to Play 42 and the note to 42/79–86.

9/294–310 The atypical prosody of Contemplacio's speech, and the fact that he did not mention the Parliament of Heaven in his opening list of plays (8/9–13), suggest that this speech is revisional. This is confirmed by the fact that it is written on a short page. The playnumber '10' written opposite 301–4 further evidences revision, since the same playnumber stands on f. 49ʳ, at the opening of the play proper.

9/296–7 Mary's allocation of her days in the temple to prayer, study, or work is specified in Pseudo-Matthew, the *Legenda Aurea* (but not the *De Nativitate*), and the *Meditationes* (which cites Jerome), as well as such English accounts as the *Life of St. Anne*, Love's *Mirrour*, and the *Life of Our Lady*; see Theresa Coletti, 'Devotional Iconography in the N-Town Marian Plays', in *The Drama of the Middle Ages*, ed. Clifford Davidson, C. J. Gianakaris, John H. Stroupe (New York, 1982), p. 251.

9/303 9/15, 10/30, and most analogues make Mary fourteen at the time of her betrothal, which occurs eleven years after her presentation in the temple.

PLAY 10

The Proclamation thirteeners in this play in several instances recall Pseudo-Matthew, with the names of Mary's handmaidens, for example, ultimately deriving from that source. The octaves and quatrains, by contrast, display thematic and verbal indebtedness to the *Legenda Aurea*, which substantially adopts the account of Mary's betrothal in the *De Nativitate*. The thirteeners contradict events in the preceding Marian plays, indicating their different origin, and in some particulars agree most closely with the analogues in the York and Towneley collections.

The play consists chiefly of Proclamation thirteeners, long-lined ababbcbc octaves, and quatrains. Lines 14–26 constitute an unusual thirteener rhyming ababacacdeeed (perhaps a quatrain joined to a 9-line stanza, but cf. 3/105–17). 237 is an ametrical line placed within an octave. The interpolated E Quire, containing two ababbcbc octaves and a quatrain, divides a Proclamation thirteener, which begins on f. 50^v and is completed on f. 53^r.

In the Proclamation, prior to its renumbering, the Marriage consistuted two distinct pageants, as described by three stanzas. This description closely accords with the Proclamation thirteeners in the play, in several instances echoing them.

10/first s.d. *Abysakar*: Halliwell prints as 'ab Ysakar', presumably to conform to 'Ysakar' in Play 8, but cf. 'Abizachar' in 14/105 s.d. In Pr 118, the bishop who summons the young women to marry is called Abyacar. Cf. Pseudo-Matthew, which names the high priest Abiathar. The *Life of St. Anne* refers to the bishop as Abaythar.

10/7 *for what þat ȝe owe*: 'as you should' ('for the sake of your obligation': cf. *MED*, *ouen*, v. 4c); or, more assertively, 'at all costs' ('for all that you own'; suggested by Meredith, *Mary Play*, p. 100).

10/14 ff. Mary's being at home in Play 10 after having been left in the temple in Play 9 reflects incongruity between textual strata (see Appendix 1). There may, however, be a parallel in art: the Croughton church frescoes show Mary being led from her parents' home between the scenes of the Presentation in the Temple and the Betrothal (M. R. James and E. W. Tristram, 'Wall-paintings in Croughton Church', *Archaeologia*, 76 (1927), 179ff.;, cited by Anderson, pp. 113–14, 229 note 13, and Woolf, p. 382 note 19). Cf. the *De Nativitate*, in which the virgins brought up in the temple are sent home to marry and Mary alone refuses to leave. Also see Graef, p. 188.

10/18 *rowse*: *MED* cites only this instance and 10/472 in the sense 'say, utter' (*rōsen*, v. 3). Halliwell read *rowse* as *kowse*, and *OED* consequently glosses it under *couse*, v., 'to say'.

10/36–78 Cf. Pseudo-Matthew, Cap. VIII, *De Nativitate*, Cap. VII, *Legenda Aurea*, Cap. CXXXI.

10/70–1 'My heart possesses purity and chastity (that) no earthly creature can ever banish'; *owth* 'possesses' is possibly 'owes', evoking Mary's vow of chastity; *showe*: cf. 3/129.

10/92–115 s.d. These three octaves on f. 48^v are intended for interpolation after line 91, as indicated by reference marks and the copying of key lines of text to mark the beginning and end of the interpolation. In addition, the letters 'A', 'B', 'C', and 'D' have been written in the left margins to mark the bishop's first four speeches on folios 49^r–50^r, and an 'E' is written before his speech in one of the interpolated stanzas on f. 48^v. 'F' and 'G' appear before his speeches on f. 50^v. The fact that the interpolated stanzas were written on f. 48^v, the last leaf of the quire preceding Play 10, shows that they were added after the play had been at least partially copied out. The interpolation follows the *Legenda Aurea*: 'Tunc anxiatus est pontifex eo, quod neque contra scripturam, quae dicit: vovete et reddite, votum infringendum putaret nec morem genti insuetum introducere auderet. Ad imminentem festivitatem Judaeorum senioribus convocatis omnium haec una fuit sententia, ut in re tam dubia consilium domini quaereretur' (Cap. CXXXI, p. 589). For fuller discussion of interpolation in this play, see Spector, 'Composition and Development of an Eclectic Manuscript', pp. 65–9, and *Genesis of the N-town Cycle*, pp. 39–50.

10/112 *fynyte*: apparently an error for *infynyte*, but cf. *MED*, *finial*, adj. (c) 'everlasting, eternal'.

10/115 s.d. *Veni Creator*: The hymn 'Veni Creator Spiritus' is also included in Mézières' Presentation play. See Dutka, pp. 43–4, 69. Meredith observes that this hymn is associated with requests for guidance in deliberations (*Mary Play*, p. 100).

10/120–32 Cf. the angel's words in the *Protevangelium*: 'go out and assemble the widowers of the people, and let them bring each his rod; and to whomsoever the Lord shall show a sign, his wife shall she be' (p. 363). In Pseudo-Matthew, the angel does not appear until later in the story. Cf. Num. 17: 1–11 (*Mary Play*, p. 101).

10/126 *kynsmen of Dauyd*: The candidates in the *De Nativitate* and the *Legenda* are the unmarried men of the house of David. The *Protevangelium* contradicts the play in having the bishop summon widowers: see the notes to 10/120–32 and 10/179–80. In Pseudo-Matthew, the lot falls on the tribe of Judah; cf. Towneley 10/242–4.

10/128 *whyte ʒardys*: cf. 'white wand' in the Towneley account of the Marriage, 10/245. For the use of the word *ʒerd(e)* in the thirteeners and *wand* in the octaves and quatrains, see Appendix 1, p. 539 n. 1.

10/131–2 See the note to 262 below.

10/138ff. Cf. Pseudo-Matthew: '. . . inventum est tale consilium ut mitteretur praeco per omnes tribus Israel, ut omnes die tertia in templum domini convenirent . . . et cecidit sors super tribum Iuda. Dixitque sacerdos: Insequenti die quicumque sine uxore est veniat et deferat virgam in manu sua' (Cap. VIII, pp. 66–7).

10/155–74 Folios 51–2, two leaves of a paperstock bearing the watermark of a one-armed pot surmounted by a cross, constitute the interpolated E Quire. The two octaves and a quatrain that make up these lines are written on f. 51^r, with the remainder of the quire blank. The lines are written by Scribe B. Reference marks at the left of line 155 and before line 175 indicate the intended position of the interpolation. The present edition reunites the Proclamation thirteener (142–54) that was split by the insertion of E quire.

10/175 The cancellation of the speaker heading 'Primus Generacionis Dauid' in favour of 'Joseph' may indicate a change in plans during transcription: 203 ff. may originally have been intended for inclusion here. See Appendix 1, p. 539 n. 2.

10/179–80 Joseph's virginity, asserted in this octave, is consistent with the *Legenda Aurea*, but contradicts Pseudo-Matthew and other accounts in which Joseph says that he is a widower, or has children.

10/186–90 The scribe employs pointing to indicate internal rhyme in these lines.

10/189 Cf. Joseph's declaration in Chester 6/134: 'I am both ould and could'.

10/190 *to wore*: 'were taken', i.e. 'completed'. Cf. *to schulde* 'had to go to' in *Sir Gawain and the Green Knight*, 1671, where *to* 'might be a verb "go"—either an error for *te* . . . or a form of *take*' (*Sir Gawain and the Green Knight*, eds. J. R. R. Tolkien and E. V. Gordon (Oxford, 1925; reprint 1955), p. 109).

10/220–8 Towneley offers a near analogue in having Joseph say 'ffor I was old I stode be syde' (10/249). In the *Legenda* he leaves no branch on the altar.

10/229–32 Meredith conjectures that this quatrain may once have completed an octave begun with 199–202, and that 298–301 may similarly have once formed an octave with 255–8 (*Mary Play*, p. 102–3).

10/231–2 The speaker heading 'Vox' recalls the *Legenda Aurea*, in which a voice instructs the high priest. The thirteeners in the play, by contrast, agree with Pseudo-Matthew in having an angel appear. The substance of these lines follows the *Legenda Aurea*, which has the Lord say, 'quod solus ille virgam suam non attulit, cui virgo desponsari deberet' (Cap. CXXXI, p. 589).

10/246 *sterrys seven*: the Pleiades or the seven planets; see the note to 9/115.

10/262 In this thirteener, as in Pr 150 and 10/131–2, Joseph's selection is indicated only by the flowering of his rod, with no reference to the appearance of a dove. This miraculous flowering seems to be a dramatic tradition, since it occurs in the York and Towneley plays. The dove is not mentioned in the present play until line 300, in a quatrain. This makes the play accord with the *Legenda Aurea*, which contains the miracles of both the flowering and the dove. Pseudo-Matthew mentions only the dove. See Deasy, pp. 6–7.

10/282–3 *clowte my cote*: 'beat me' (cited in this sense by *MED*, *clouten*, v. [2]); cf. 'pay thaym on the cote', Towneley 16/326. This rendering seems preferable to Meredith's 'patch my coat', i.e. 'make things worse'. *Blere myn ey*: 'hoodwink me' (Meredith suggests 'blear with weeping'). *pyke out a mote* extends the image of the eyes, alluding to the mote and beam in Matt. 7: 3–5 and Luke 6: 41–2; the implication is 'dwell on trifling faults in me to distract from her own sins'. Joseph's protest against a January–May marriage was a dramatic convention: cf. Towneley 10/263–8, York 13/1–50, the Coventry Shearmen and Taylors pageant, 133–5.

10/285–90 In Pseudo-Matthew, the high priest also warns Joseph to accept

God's will and marry Mary, and Joseph replies: 'Ego quidem non contemno voluntatem dei, sed custos eius ero' (Cap. VIII, p. 69).

10/291–2 See the note to Pr 153–4.

10/301 s.d. *Benedicta sit beata Trinitas*: see the notes to 8/97 s.d. and 10/334.

10/302 ff. The terms *desponsata* and *desponsatam* in Matt. 1: 18 and Luke 1: 27 respectively resulted in doctrinal controversy about whether Mary and Joseph were in fact married or merely betrothed at the time of Joseph's Doubt (Deasy, pp. 3–4). Deasy says that the apocrypha make it clear that they were only affianced at that point, and adds that Thomas Aquinas affirmed this belief. The *Legenda Aurea* too refers to espousals, with a wedding to follow. The *Life of St. Anne*, by contrast, refers to their *matremony* (16/587). The *Life of Our Lady*, as well as York 13 and Towneley 10, refers to their wedding; cf. Chester 6/114. Among English plays, N-town alone dramatizes the wedding ceremony.

10/302–3 These lines recall the marriage service in English, but Meredith questions how apparent this would have been to the audience, since service books normally gave only the vows of the man and the woman in English. He adds that these English vows do bear similarities to the present lines (*Mary Play*, pp. 103–4).

10/310–13 The first two lines paraphrase the marriage service in the Sarum Missal, as does 320.

10/317 *wyttys fyff*: see the note to 9/241.

10/324 See the note to Pr 153–4.

10/332 *þe hyʒ names of oure Lord we wole now syng hy*: cf. 334, containing the opening line of the sequence 'Alma chorus', which consists principally of names and titles of God (*Mary Play*, p. 104; cf. Dutka, p. 19).

10/334 The sequence 'Alma chorus' was used in the English marriage service, as was 'Benedicta sit beata Trinitas' in 301 s.d. (Dutka, pp. 6–7, 19–20, 138–9 note 23; Vriend, p. 58 note 1). Meredith observes that 'Alma chorus' was sung during the nuptual mass in all uses but York (*Mary Play*, p. 104).

10/350 *in stage*: 'on the scaffold'. Block suggests 'now, at this time, straightway'.

10/353–5 The names of the three damsels derive from Pseudo-Matthew, which lists five: Rebecca, Sephora, Susanna, Abigea, and Zahel.

10/421–56 Mary's reading and praising the psalms in the temple while Joseph rents a house is not in the sources.

10/436 Cf. *The Myroure of oure Ladye*: 'the propertye of these psalmes deuoutly songe is to dryue away fendes, & all euel spirites' (p. 36).

10/446 *Swetter to say than any ony*: cf. Ezek. 3: 3; compare the *Myroure of oure Ladye*: 'oure lorde god hathe made a drynke by his seruante Dauid whiche is swete to taste. . . . This drinke is these psalmes, that ar swetely harde when they ar songe' (p. 37); and *Yorkshire Writers*: 'Dona michi, queso, deus meus, vt per hec sacrosancta verba psalterii celesti melle anima mea saginetur' (I: 398, cited by Meredith, *Mary Play*, p. 105).

10/447 'You teach them to love the Lord. . . .'

10/455 Psalm 84: 2 (Vulgate). Verses 11–12 of this psalm provide the basis for the Debate of the Four Daughters of God in Play 11 (Fry, pp. 546–7); see the headnote to that play. Meredith observes that this verse interweaves the liturgy at the end of the period after Trinity Sunday with that of Advent, and so prepares for the Annunciation in the following play (*Mary Play*, p. 105).

10/465–9 Cf. Pseudo-Matthew: 'Ioseph in Capharnaum maritima erat in opere occupatus, erat enim faber ligni: ubi moratus est mensibus novem (Cap. X, p. 71). Cf. Towneley 10/275–81.

10/469 Joseph's nine-month absence is specified in Pseudo-Matthew, Ch. X.

PLAY 11

This play comprises appeals for divine mercy spoken by Contemplacio and the Virtues, the Debate of the Four Daughters of God, and the Salutation and Conception.

Contemplacio's speech differs markedly from his prosaic prologues, epilogues, and links elsewhere in the Marian group of plays. Here, by contrast, his lines are impassioned and integral to the play proper. He adopts in these speeches the voices of Isaiah and Jeremiah, who in fact speak many of the same biblical verses in the nearest analogue to this portion of the play, the *Charter of the Abbey of the Holy Ghost*. Woolf (pp. 164–6) notes the influence on Contemplacio's speech of the seven great O-antiphons and other liturgical sources, and considers it reasonably certain that a work like the *Passion de Valenciennes* provided the idea for Contemplacio's speech.

Angelic intercessions in man's behalf precede the Debate of the Four Daughters of God in the *Meditationes* and several later texts. N-town follows this tradition by having the Virtues, one of the angelic orders, pursue the appeal after Contemplacio has spoken.

The Debate of the Four Daughters of God is based ultimately on Psalm 84: 11 (Vulgate). This theme, expanded in midrash, was later adopted by Christian writers, including Bernard of Clairvaux, whose version the *Meditationes* adopted and modified. N-town comprehends elements that appear in the *Meditationes* and Love's *Mirrour*, as well as in three other English manuscripts: the *Charter of the Abbey of the Holy Ghost*, noted above; Trinity College, Dublin, MS 423; and Trinity College, Cambridge, MS B. 2. 18. The play contains several of the same biblical citations that appear in these last three texts, and shares with them as well the unusual reckoning that man lay in hell for 4,604 years. Like the Dublin and Cambridge manuscripts, but unlike the *Charter*, N-town places the Debate in its traditional context, prior to the Incarnation. And it includes the Virtues' search for the intercessor who will die for man, a motif that appears in Bernard, the *Meditationes*, and Love, but not in the *Charter* or the Dublin or Cambridge manuscripts. The argument for selecting the Son to carry out this task, presented in the play in lines 173–6, is given in Love, while God's paraphrase of Gen. 6–7 in the play (lines 169–70) appears in Bernard and the *Meditationes*, but not in Love.

The Debate is also presented in the *Castle of Perseverance* and in several other English and Continental texts. See Hope Traver, *The Four Daughters of God*, Bryn Mawr College Monographs, VI (1907), pp. 138–9, who posits a common ancestor for the Debate in N-town, the *Charter*, and the *Castle*. See also Peter Meredith and Lynette Muir, who compare this episode in the *Eerste Bliscap* and other Continental texts with N-town and other English versions ('The Trial in Heaven in the "Eerste Bliscap" and Other European Plays', *Dutch Crossing*, 22 (1984), 84–92).

The Annunciation scene is an elaboration of Luke 1: 26–38, with extensive borrowing from Love in lines 261–84.

The play as it stands is not the one described in the Proclamation, which omits any reference to the Debate, and mentions a detail not included in the dialogue of the play: the fact that Mary's maidens overhear her conversation with the angel. The bulk of the play is in ababbcbc octaves. Quatrains appear in 185–8, 213–20, and 293–6. Three octaves rhyming abababab appear in 261–84. Another such octave, in 321–8, is preceded by two quatrains and followed by a third.

11/1–32 Greg's conclusion (pp. 125–6 note 1) that Contemplacio was written into this play at a late stage may well be correct, but his speculation about the original speakers of these lines is most likely mistaken. Citing the marginal notations '1us' above line 1 and '2' at the left of line 17, and the Virtues' reference to 'Aungelys, archaungelys, we thre' (line 37), Greg concludes that 1–16 were originally spoken by Angels, and 17–32 by Archangels. This is improbable, however. As Forrest observes, Contemplacio seems instead to assume the voices of Isaiah and Jeremiah. These four stanzas are spoken from the perspective of earthdwellers, not angels (cf. lines 10 and 15), and later references in the play indicate that *prophets* have made supplication (cf. lines 35 and 53). In several analogues, prophets and angels utter laments prior to the Debate, and the same seems originally to have happened here. The notation '1us' in fact precedes citations from Isaiah, while '2' marks off the material from Jeremiah and Lamentations. In the *Charter*, Isaiah and Jeremiah actually speak several of these same lines in Latin and English. See Forrest, 'Role of the Expositor Contemplacio', pp. 69–73; also, Davies, p. 450 note 20; Peter Meredith and Stanley J. Kahrl, *The N-Town Plays* (Leeds, 1977), p. xvii; and Alan J. Fletcher, 'The "Contemplacio" Prologue to the N-Town Play of the Parliament of Heaven', *Notes and Queries*, new ser. 27 (1980), 111–12.

11/1–3 *Fowre thowsand sex vndryd foure*: Alfred W. Pollard observes that there were nearly two hundred computations of the number of years between Creation and the Nativity (*English Miracle Plays, Moralities, and Interludes*

(Oxford, 1909), p. 192), and Samuel B. Hemingway notes that of the 108 computations of the year of Creation recorded in *L'Art de Vérifier les Dates*, none can be made to agree with the figure 4,604 (*English Nativity Plays* (New York, 1909; reprint 1964), p. 242). The *Book of Adam and Eve* says there were 5,500 years from the Fall to the Redemption, and the *Gospel of Nicodemus* gives the same period from Creation to the Nativity. The *Legenda Aurea* gives several reckonings, and the *Meditationes* and Love's *Mirrour* say man spent 5,000 years in hell, a figure also given by Greban. The York and Towneley Harrowing of Hell plays, which have Adam say that man has been in hell for 4,600 years, are closer to the N-town play, and the *Charter* and the Trinity and Dublin manuscripts give precisely the same figure as N-town: 4,604 years; the 'Lyff of Adam and Eue' also gives this figure (Horstmann, *Sammlung*, p. 226). N-town does not truly agree with these last texts, however, since they, like the York and Towneley plays, reckon man's total term in hell, till the Harrowing, not till the Annunciation, as in the present play. The figure 4,604 was evidently arrived at by adding the 5,500 years between Creation and the Nativity (as in the *Gospel of Nicodemus*) to Jesus' lifespan ('ny3 þre and þritty 3ere and an half' says the *Polychronicon*, IV, 274–5), and subtracting the 930 years that Adam lived before going to hell (Hemingway, pp. 242–3).

11/7–8 Pollard (p. 192) suggests that these lines refer to Isa. 63: 15. But Isaiah may simply have identified himself in line 7 before this speech was given to Contemplacio.

11/9–10 Cf. Isa. 64: 1, quoted in the *Charter*, p. 347: 'Isaye . . . seyde þus: "*Vtinam dirumperes celos & descenderes*, wolde god, he seyd, þou woldest bresten heuene & come adoon . . ."' (*Yorkshire Writers*, I: 347). Kretzmann (p. 40) associates line 9 with the Advent 'Rorate coeli desuper'.

11/10 *erth*: a bad rhyme with 'fede'. Pollard (p. 192) suggests emending to 'this stede'.

11/13 *þi thrysté*: 'thy thirsty ones'. The MS reads *thryste*, which Block renders as 'thirst'. Pollard (p. 192) says that we should have expected 'their thirst'. Forrest takes 'thy thirst' to refer to Christ's words on the cross, 'I thirst', piously interpreted to indicate a spiritual thirst, which can be quenched only by the grace given through his suffering and death ('Role of the Expositor Contemplacio', p. 71).

11/17–18 Cf. Jer. 45: 3, spoken in Latin and English by Jeremiah in the *Charter*, p. 347.

11/25–7 Cf. Jer. 9: 1, also quoted in the *Charter*.

11/29 Woolf (p. 166) observes that this line derives from an antiphon sung on Holy Thursday. Compare Lam. 2: 13, which is cited by Jeremiah in the *Charter*. Cf. *Wisdom*, 996.

11/30 Lam. 5: 16, also spoken by Jeremiah in the *Charter*.

11/33–48 The Virtues constitute one of the nine orders of angels. In 37–8

they are said to be in the first angelic hierarchy, with the Angels and Archangels. This contradicts the system of angelic orders attributed to pseudo-
Dionysius, which places Virtues in the second hierarchy, with Angels and
Archangels in the third. Gayley (p. 234), however, notes that the *Book of Enoch*,
which contains what he asserts is the original arrangement of the nine angelic
orders, has Angels, Archangels, and Virtues make up the first ternary. Gregory
the Great cites them as the first three in his list of angels, as does the *Myroure of
oure Lady*, p. 184. Trevisa and other writers list Angels, Archangels, and
Virtues in the same hierarchy, but it is not the first; cf. Chester 1/52–9, *Viel
Testament* I: 53–6, and the Cornish *Creacion*, 59–65. Pollard (p. 193) suggests
that the angelic Virtues here are the same as the Virtues who are about to
debate. This would be analogous to Continental versions, in which Miseri-
corde issues an appeal prior to the Debate proper.

11/44 *he*: Lucifer.

11/47–8 Cf. Love's *Mirrour*: 'alle the blessid spirites of heuene desirynge the
restorynge of her companye / that was fallen doun with lucifer / hadden grete
compassioun of so longe meschief of man that was made to here restorynge /
and preiden often for his restorynge' (p. 13). The familiar idea that man should
fill the place vacated by the fallen angels was expressed in drama in Towneley
1/262–5 and 3/28–9, York 7/23–4, the *Castle*, 3496–3507, and *Wisdom*, 327–8;
cf. N-town 11/203–4.

11/48a Psalm 11: 6 (Vulgate) translated in 49–51. The psalm is appropriate to
the play: Augustine comments that God spoke this psalm as a promise to send
his son (*Expositions on the Book of Psalms by St. Augustine*, trans. J. Tweed *et al.*
(Oxford, 1847–57), I: 103; cited by Meredith in *Mary Play*, p. 108).

11/52 *Tyme is come*: the issue of the timing of the Redemption, emphasized at
the opening of the play, is here raised again. Cf. Gal. 4: 4–5, which influenced
Bernard and the *Meditationes* (*Mary Play*, p. 108).

11/53–4 Cf. the *Charter*: 'whan almiȝty god had hard þus þes prophetis, wiþ
many oþere men, ma[k]e mochel mone ... he had grete pyte of hem þat þei
ferden so, & þat mannus soule was þerfore in prisone of the pyne of helle'
(p. 348).

11/56 *MED* (*exorten*, v.) cites this instance only of *exorte* in the sense 'issue
forth'. Meredith suggests that it may have been suggested by 'Exortum est in
tenebris' (Ps. 111: 4), an antiphon for second vespers at the Nativity (*Mary
Play*, p. 108).

11/61–4 Cf. the *Charter*: 'þou seydest þat what-tyme þat man ete of þat appul,
þat he schulde dieye & gon to helle; þerfore ȝif þou delyuerest man þanne out
of þat prisoun, þou destroyest me' (p. 349; the Dublin and Cambridge manuscripts agree almost exactly).

11/65 Cf. Psalm 116: 2 (Vulgate), cited in the *Charter*, the Dublin and Cambridge manuscripts, the *Castle*, and the *Court of Sapience*. Cf. the *Charter*: '*Quia Veritas domini manet in eternum*, for whi goddys treuþe schulde dwellen eueremore wiþ-outen ende' (p. 349).

11/71 Cf. Psalm 50: 8 (Vulgate), spoken by Truth in the *Charter*, the Dublin and Cambridge manuscripts, and the *Castle*.

11/73–4 Cf. 2 Cor. 1: 3–4. Mercy quotes this passage in the *Charter*, the Dublin and Trinity manuscripts, and the *Castle*. Meredith observes that the play is closer to the biblical passage than to the translation in the *Charter* (*Mary Play*, p. 108).

11/80 *Ther prayers*: 'Their prayers . . .' or 'Where prayers . . . .'

11/81 'Truth says, then, that she has always existed'.

11/83 Cf. Psalm 88: 29 (Vulgate), 'In aeternum servabo illi misericordiam meam', cited by Mercy in the *Charter*, the Dublin and Cambridge manuscripts, and the *Castle*.

11/85 Psalm 88: 25 (Vulgate), not included in the analogues listed above.

11/91–6 Cf. Psalm 10: 8 (Vulgate) and Deut. 32: 18. N-town agrees very closely with the *Charter*, the Dublin and Cambridge manuscripts, and the *Castle*. Cf. the *Charter*: 'þanne seyde Riȝtfulnesse: "Nay, nay, scho seiþ, it may not ben so: *Quia iustus dominus & iusticias dilexit*, for whi, lord, scho seiþ, þou art riȝtful & þou louest riȝtfulnesse. . . . *Dominum qui se genuit dereliquit, & oblitus est dei creatoris sui*, he forsoke god þat haþ forþe-Ibrouȝt hym, & he, lord, for-ȝat þe þat maydest hym of nouȝt' (p. 350).

11/97 Cf. Gen. 3: 5.

11/100 Cf. Psalm 110: 3 (Vulgate), which Justice also quotes in the *Charter*, and the Dublin and Cambridge manuscripts; cf. the *Castle*, 3440.

11/101–2 Cf. Riȝtfulnesse's conclusion in the *Charter*: '& þerfore, leue lord, scho seiþ, lat mannus soule be stille as it is' (p. 350; the Dublin and Cambridge manuscripts agree almost exactly).

11/107 Cf. Psalm 144: 9 (Vulgate), which Mercy quotes to Justice in the *Charter*, the Dublin and Cambridge manuscripts, and the *Castle*; cf. also the *Court of Sapience*.

11/108 *he*: i.e. man.

11/112 Cf. Psalm 102: 17 (Vulgate), cited in the *Charter*, the Dublin and Cambridge manuscripts, the *Castle*, and the *Court of Sapience*.

11/113–14 Cf. the *Meditationes*: 'Peace now said, "Cease this debate. It is not virtuous so to contend"' (*Meditations on the Life of Christ*, eds. Isa Ragusa and Rosalie B. Green (Princeton, 1961), p. 8).

11/115–20 Cf. Phil. 4: 7. These lines closely accord with Peace's speech in the *Charter*: '*Pax domini exsuperat omnem sensum* . . . þouȝ it be so, sche seiyt, þat Truþe seiþ a grete skile why mannus soule schulde not be saued, & Riȝtfulnesse seiþ also, neuerþeles me þenkeþ þat Mercy seiþ alþerbest . . . þere

schulde also, ȝif man were stille in helle, ben a discord by-twene god & man
... so þat I, þat am pees, schulde a ben forsaken' (p. 351; nearly verbatim in
the Cambridge and Dublin manuscripts). Cf. Love's *Mirrour*, in which 'Pees'
says, 'I may not abide ne dwelle there as is stryf or disencioun' (p. 16).

11/137 ff. Meredith and Muir (p. 85) observe that the Son does not appear in
the Debate in French drama, except in the twenty-day Valenciennes play performed in 1549. They also note that N-town and the *Eerste Bliscap* are the only
plays to include the entire Trinity in the debate.

11/137 Cf. Jer. 29: 11, quoted by the Father in the *Charter* with this translation: 'I þenke, he seyde, þouȝtis of pees & not of wickednesse' (p. 351; nearly
verbatim in the Dublin and Cambridge manuscripts). Pater also quotes this
biblical passage in the *Castle*, 3560a. The extended affinities among the
Debate scenes in N-town, the *Charter*, and the Dublin and Cambridge texts
cease after this point.

11/138–68 Cf. the *Meditationes*: 'Then the King wrote His decision. . . . "The
one side says, 'I perish if Adam does not die', and the other, 'I perish if he does
not receive mercy'. . . . Let there be found someone prepared to die out of
charity, yet not guilty of death. Death will not be able to keep the innocent
man". . . . But where could such a one be found? . . . Truth searched the earth
but found no one pure of evil, not even a new-born child. And Mercy searched
in heaven and found no one with sufficient charity, for . . . we are worthless
servants (Luke xvii, 10). . . . Said Peace . . . "There is no one who will do good,
not a single one (Psalm xiii, 1). But let Him who gave the advice now lend His
help"' (pp. 8–9). Though Love contains fewer affinities to the present lines in
the play, compare lines 154–5 to the *Mirrour*, p. 18: 'there was none founden
clene of synne / no / not the child of one dayes birthe'.

11/149 'Go and see where such a one is'; *prevyde*: cf. *prevideo* 'go beforehand'
in R. E. Latham, *Revised Medieval Latin Word-List* (London, 1965). *MED* cites
this instance in the sense 'look, search' (*prēviden*, v. 1 [b]).

11/156 'Nor any (that) will be bound to that death'.

11/165 'There is only one person (who) can do that good deed'.

11/168 'For the resolution of all this depends on him'.

11/169–70 Cf. the *Meditationes*: 'I regret that I made man and now I must do
penance for the man I created' (p. 9). These words, based on Gen. 6: 7, recall
Bernard's version of the Debate (*In Festo Annuntiationis Beatae Mariae Virginis*,
PL, 183: 389). They are omitted by Love and the Dublin and Cambridge
manuscripts. *peyne I must suffre fore*: 'I must suffer pain for that (i.e. creating
man)'. See the note to 4/105–6.

11/171 Cf. the Dublin manuscript: 'Alle myghty god . . . ordeyned a counseyll
of the holy trinite' (quoted from Robert A. Klinefelter, 'The Four Daughters
of God: A New Version', *JEGP*, 52 (1953), 94; nearly verbatim in the Cambridge manuscript); compare the *Court of Sapience*, p. 155.

11/173-6 Cf. Love's *Mirrour*, p. 19, the *Court of Sapience*, p. 146, and N-town 21/115–32 and note, and 28/59–60.

11/177 Cf. the Dublin manuscript: 'And þere fore he þat shulde do þat dede, he most be boþe god and man' (p. 45; verbatim in the Cambridge manuscript). Meredith notes that this idea originated with Anselm's *Cur Deus homo* and is expressed in *Cursor Mundi*, 9799–9802 (*Mary Play*, p. 112).

11/181 Cf. the Athanasian Creed: 'Spiritus Sanctus a Patre et Filio: non factus, nec creatus, nec genitus: sed procedens' (*Mary Play*, p. 112).

11/183 *I, Love*: Woolf (p. 383 note 34) observes that St Thomas gives particular emphasis to the Holy Ghost's role in the Conception, in part because 'Spiritus enim Sanctus est amor Patris et Filii' (*Summa Theologica*, III, xxxii, I). Cf. the *Lay Folks' Catechism*, in the discussion of the Apostles' Creed: 'The iiij articule of þis parte seys þat crist was conseyuyd of þe holy gost . . . þe whyche ys lyf [love]' (16/274–7).

11/187-8 Psalm 84: 11 (Vulgate).

11/189-212 The father's speech closely follows Luke 1: 26–7, the Holy Ghost's paraphrases Luke 1: 34–7. The play does not draw substantially on God's words to Gabriel in the *Meditationes* and Love, and, moreover, divides the instructions, spoken by God the father in those texts, among the persons of the trinity. But compare the Son's words in 199–201 with the description of Gabriel's descent to Mary in the *Mirrour*: 'and ȝit also swiftly as he flewh his lord was come byfore / and there he fonde alle the holy trinite . . .' (p. 25).

11/189 *god*: Meredith, acknowledging the awkwardness of the reading, prints *God*. He argues that it renders the Latin *a Deo* and conforms to the spelling pattern in the Marian plays, which, he says, invariably spell 'good' as *gode* or *good*. The spelling *god* for 'good' is infrequent in the codex, but appears in 11/165; also, unequivocally, in 14/368 (though Play 14 is not part of the Marian group).

11/197 *withowte wo*: see the note to 11/219–20.

11/203-4 Cf. the third of three reasons given in the *Legenda Aurea* why an angel delivered the Annunciation: 'Tercio ratione lapsus angelici reparandi. Quia enim incarnatio non tantum faciebat ad reparationem humani lapsus, sed etiam ad reparationem ruinae angelicae . . .' (p. 216). Compare 11/47–8 and the note.

11/216a-18 Luke 1: 28; see the note to 13/151A–155A. *Maria* has been crossed through after *Ave* in 216a, bringing it into agreement with the translation in 217 and Contemplacio's commentary in 13/151A–155A. Meredith suggests that the main scribe may himself have cancelled *Maria* in this line in consideration of Contemplacio's words (*Mary Play*, pp. 113–14).

11/219-20 The parallelism between Eve and Mary was introduced by Justin Martyr in the second century (Graef, p. 37), and the transformation of 'Eva' into 'Ave' became a familiar medieval motif. It appears, for example, in the *Lay Folks' Catechism*, Lydgate's 'Ave Jesse Virgula', and the hymn 'Ave Maris

Stella'. Compare the present lines to the *Myroure of oure Ladye*: 'And so Eua is turned in to Aue. for our sorowe is turned in to ioy. by meane of our lady. For Eua ys as moche to saye as woo. & Aue is as moche to say as Ioye. or wythout woo' (p. 78). See Woolf, pp. 172, 384 note 44; Raby, *History of Christian-Latin Poetry*, p. 368; and Hemingway, p. 248.

11/220–8 Hemingway (pp. 248–9) says that these lines seem to have been inspired by Bonaventura's *Speculum B. Mariae Virginis.*

11/224 Cf. the *Myroure of oure Ladye*: 'neuer creature had the fulnesse of all graces. but our lady alone' (p. 79).

11/230–1 Cf. Luke 1: 29.

11/232–3 The *Ormulum* also says that Mary was concerned because Gabriel appeared to her in the form of a man ('aness weress hewe'; ed. Robert Meadows White (Oxford, 1852), l. 2182, cited in *Mary Play*, p. 114). Cf. Love's *Mirrour*: 'sche was not ... agaste of his presence / for sche was wont to aungels presence and the siȝt of hem' (p. 26). Compare the *Meditationes*, p. 17, the *De Nativitate*, Cap. IX, p. 119, and *Legenda Aurea*, Cap. LI, p. 218.

11/235–6 Cf. Love's *Mirrour*: 'shamefast and dredful / sche hild hir pes and answered not' (p. 27); cf. also the *Meditationes*, p. 17.

11/237–44 Cf. Luke 1: 30–3.

11/245–59 Cf. Luke 1: 34–7. 249–50 recall the *De Nativitate*: 'His angeli verbis virgo non incredula, sed modum scire volens respondit: Quomodo istud fieri potest' (Cap. IX, p. 120).

11/253–4 'Therefore that holy one (who) shall be born of you. . . .' Cf. Luke 1: 35: 'Ideoque et quod nascetur ex te sanctum, vocabitur Filius Dei'.

11/261–82 Here, as elsewhere in the cycle, the abababab octaves contain extended echoes of Love's *Mirrour*: 'Now take here good hede and haue in mynde how first all the holy trinyte is there abydynge a fynal answere and assent of his blessid douȝter marye .. and furthermore howe alle the blessid spirites of heuene / and alle the riȝtwis lyuynge men in erthe / and alle the chosen soules that weren that tyme in helle / as adam / abraham / dauid / and alle othere desireden hir assent; in the whiche stood the sauacioun of all man-kynde' (pp. 29–30). The corresponding passage in the *Meditationes* is far less similar to N-town. Love's version is reminiscent of one of Bernard's homilies on the *Missus est* (*PL* 183: 83), which Woolf (pp. 167–8) proposes as the source of these lines. The play is closer to Love's version, though it does render two of Bernard's passages that do not appear in Love: 'Da, Virgo, responsum festinanter' (cf. 11/261) and 'patres scilicet tui' (cf. 11/274); the first of these is also found in the *Legenda Aurea*, however.

11/272 *levers*: 'those who live', recalling Love's 'alle the riȝtwis lyuynge men in erthe', cited above: the word also denotes 'believers'.

11/287–8 Cf. Luke 1: 38.

11/292 s.d. The association of light with the Incarnation was widespread in Latin and vernacular texts as well as iconography; cf. N-town 21/97–100. Coletti (p. 256) discusses the influence of the *Revelations of St. Bridget* in this regard. Davies (p. 450 note 22) suggests that beams of wood would have been employed in this play, but Kahrl notes a mid-fifteenth-century instance in Barcelona in which an undertaking was made to present an Annunciation play employing rays of light or fire that did no damage (*Traditions of Medieval English Drama* (London, 1974), p. 51, citing N. D. Shergold, *History of the Spanish Stage* (London, 1967)). David Mills suggests that the 'bemys' may be trumpet blasts, and that Mary's 'bosom' here may refer either to her heart or womb or to her embrace ('Concerning a Stage Direction in the *Ludus Coventriae*', *ELN* 11 (1974), 162–4).

11/293–8 The Christ-child's having his complete form from the moment of conception is found in the *Legenda Aurea*, the *Pepysian Gospel Harmony*, the *Meditationes*, and Love's *Mirrour*. Downing (p. 100) cites a parallel in the Sarum Breviary.

11/300–2 Meredith observes that painlessness was a common feature of the birth of Christ, but was rarely associated with the conception, which was typically characterized as free of stain (*Mary Play*, p. 116). Cf. Epiphanius, in Migne, *PG* 43: 443 (cited by Miriam J. Benkovitz in 'Some Notes on the "Prologue of Demon" of *Ludus Coventriae*', *MLN*, 60 (1945), p. 82).

11/304 'Your son, now my son, deserves the distinction (—or privilege—of being born in this way)'.

11/310 This line suggests that the Visit to Elizabeth will follow immediately, in accordance with Luke 1, and as promised by Contemplacio; see the notes to 8/12–13 and 11/340 s.d.

11/322–4 Cf. Love (p. 14), who cites Bernard in saying that Gabriel received a special revelation concerning the Incarnation.

11/325–7 'I pray you to make it a customary practice to visit me often during my pregnancy', or 'through the intervening pregnancy'. Meredith renders *passage* as 'time', giving *mene passage* the sense 'the meantime' (*Mary Play*, p. 116).

11/330–1 'You noblest of ancestry and most exalted of kindred (of any of those) who reign on earth in any degree'.

11/335 Cf. 'Hayl! oure patron & lady of erthe, / Qwhene of heuen & emprys of helle', in Carleton Brown, *Religious Lyrics of the XVth Century* (Oxford, 1939; reprint 1967), no. 26, lines 1–2.

11/337 'Through your body (that) bears the babe (who) shall renew our bliss'. That the difficulty in this line was caused by the ellipsis of *that* after *body* was suggested by Kittredge and cited by John Matthews Manly in *Specimens of the Pre-Shaksperean Drama* (New York, 1897; reprinted 1967), I: 93.

11/338 *Modyr of Mercy*: see the note to 8/9.

11/340 '(That) gladdened heaven and earth. . . .' *Enjouyd*: alternatively, *Enjonyd* 'Joined', but cf. *enjoyd* and *injouyid* in 13/54 and 85. Meredith reads as 'heaven and earth united' (*Mary Play*, p. 117).

11/340 s.d. *Aue Maria, gratia plena, dominus tecum, uirgo serena*: cf. Dutka, p. 21. *And þan Mary seyth*: cancelled in red, these words may have led directly into Play 13, which opens with Mary's speech; see the notes to 8/12–13 and 11/310, and compare Block, p. xxi.

PLAY 12

The play of Joseph's Doubt is based on Matt. 1: 18–25, with embellishment from apocryphal and meditative texts, and affinities to dramatic analogues. Joseph's accusatory dialogue ultimately derives from the *Protevangelium*, and his indignation at the claim that Mary has been impregnated by an angel appears in Pseudo-Matthew. Joseph's distress and Mary's prayer are indebted to Love's *Mirrour*. And specific details in the play, including Joseph's lament about his January–May marriage, appear in the other English cycles and the Coventry Shearmen and Taylors' pageant.

The location of this episode, between the Annunciation and the Visit to Elizabeth, is unusual. The Gospels offer no chronological order for these events since Joseph's Doubt occurs in Matthew while the Annunciation and Visit are in Luke. The Proclamation, like Pseudo-Matthew, places Joseph's Doubt after the Annunciation, with no treatment at all of the Visit (the same arrangement obtains in the *De Nativitate*, the *Life of St. Anne*, and the Coventry Shearmen and Taylors' play). When these episodes were harmonized in N-town, Joseph's Doubt was not placed in its traditional position in art and literature, following the Visit to Elizabeth, but rather before the Visit, as in the Towneley cycle. This arrangement may in fact have been dictated by Play 13, which has Joseph already at home and ready to accompany Mary during the Visit.

The play is constituted mainly of Proclamation thirteeners and 10-line stanzas. The thirteeners are consistent with the Proclamation description and recall Pseudo-Matthew and other Joseph plays. The 10-line stanzas, by contrast, closely follow Love's *Mirrour*, sometimes echoing that source. In one instance the 10-line stanzas contradict material in other prosodic forms (see the note to 133–6). The 10-line stanzas in 88–117 appear to have split a thirteener into a quatrain (84–7) and a 9-line stanza (118–26). The play begins with an ababab octave and ends with another such octave and a quatrain. Quatrains also appear in 9–12 and, with longer lines, in 13–20. A couplet appears in 47–8, and a 9-line stanza (perhaps a fragment of a thirteener) in 62–70.

12/3 Susanna, like Sephor in 67–70, is named in Pseudo-Matthew; see the note to 10/353–5.

12/9–12 See the note to 10/465–9.

12/15–16 Gibson ('"Porta Haec"', p. 154) cites the *Glossa Ordinaria*, In Matthaeum, I, 25 (*PL* 114: 72): 'Dicitur quod Joseph Mariam facie ad faciem videre non poterat, quam Spiritus sanctus a conceptione impleverat penitus'. She relates this motif to the radiant tabernacle in the Gradual of the Advent Mass. Cf. Graef, 1: 260, and N-town 15/162–7.

12/38 Cf. Towneley 10/187, 195, and York 13/103, 159.

12/55–6 As in 5/140, the bending of the bow signifies setting actions in motion, though in this instance the context, the image, and the reference to the 'French manner' suggest lechery, as in 14/165. Deasy (p. 82) takes these lines to refer to Continental farce and light poetry on the subject of cuckoldry. See Joseph L. Baird and Lorrayne Y. Baird, 'Fabliau Form and the Hegge *Joseph's Return*', *Chaucer Review*, 8 (1973), 160; Davies, p. 451 note 25; *Early English Carols*, ed. R. L. Greene (Oxford, 1977):, no. 466 and p. 499; John Stevens, *Music and Poetry in the Early Tudor Court* (London, 1961), pp. 249–50, 400–1; and Whiting, pp. 55–6. Cf. *Handlyng Synne*: 'Frenshe men synne yn lecherye / And Englys men yn enuye' (ed. F. J. Furnivall, EETS os 119 (1901), 4151–2).

12/59ff. Joseph's proposed flight from Mary appears in Pseudo-Matthew. Deasy (pp. 72–3) observes that the other apocrypha accord with Matt. 1: 19 in having Joseph decide to put Mary away privately (though *dimittere* can be rendered 'leave'; cf. Matt. 19: 5). His decision to flee is found in the other English Joseph plays as well as such narrative accounts as the *Meditationes*, Love's *Mirrour*, the *Life of Our Lady*, and the *Life of St. Anne*.

12/67–70 Sephor's speech refers back to the maidens' overhearing Mary's conversation with Gabriel, an action mentioned in Pr 161–4 but not presented in the cycle as we have it (Greg, pp. 128–9).

12/71–7 Cf. Pseudo-Matthew: 'Ut quid me seducitis ut credam vobis quia angelus domini impraegnavit eam? Potest enim fieri ut quisquam se finxerit angelum domini et deceperit eam' (Cap. X, p. 72). Cf. also the *Life of Our Lady*, II: 1219–28, *Life of St. Anne*, 20/764–8, Towneley 10/293–8, and York 13/134–42.

12/82–3 Hemingway (p. 253) cites *Les Proverbes Communs*, Jean de la Veprie, Paris, 1498: 'Vous battez les buissons dont une autre a les oysissons'. Whiting, B604, cites this proverb first in the *Confessio Amantis*.

12/96–7 Cf. Lev. 20: 10, Deut. 22: 22, Ezek. 16: 40, John 8: 5. Neither the *Meditationes* nor Love mentions stoning Mary, but Albert S. Cook finds it in a pseudo-Augustinian dialogue between Joseph and Mary ('A Remote Analogue to the Miracle Play', *JEGP*, 4 (1903), 426, 447). Cf. 'La estorie del Euangelie' (*Minor Poems of the Vernon MS*); also N-town 24/105–8.

12/101–7 Cf. Love's *Mirrour*: For on the tone side he sawh hir lyf so holy and
no tokene of synne in hir / neither in contenaunce / neither in word in speche
/ nor in dede that he dorste not openly accuse hir of avoutrie; and on that
other side he knewe nouȝt how that sche myȝte conceyue bot by man' (p. 41).
Cf. also the *Life of Our Lady*, II: 1157–8, York 13/209–13, Towneley 10/203–8.

12/127–32 Cf. Love's *Mirrour*: 'But her with sche prayed god that he wolde
sende remedye in this caas / and that he wolde / as it were his wille / putte
away fro hir and fro hire housbonde this tribulacioun and this disese' (p. 42).

12/133–6 Greg (p. 129) suggested the emendation in 133 from the manuscript
form *respyte* to *despyte*, which agrees with the probable source of this passage,
Love's *Mirrour*: 'sche suffred and hilde hir pes mekely and kepte priue that
grete ȝifte of god / and chese rathere to be holde as wickid / vicious / and
vnworthy / than sche wolde make open that grete sacrament of god' (p. 42). In
this 10-line stanza, however, Mary's determination to keep silent until God
reveals the truth of the Incarnation conflicts with the fact that she has already
spoken at length about the Incarnation in a Proclamation thirteener (38–42)
and elsewhere.

12/147 ff. Unlike the accounts in Matthew, the apocrypha, and most
analogues, in which Joseph sleeps as the angel addresses him, N-town
presents Joseph as awake and crying aloud. Cf. pseudo-Chrysostom, *Homily on
the Annunciation* (*PG* 60: 755–9, cited by Cook, p. 433); the *South English Legen-
dary*, line 273; the Holkham Bible Picture Book (f. 12); and Towneley 10/
321 ff.

12/160 ff. Cf. Pseudo-Matthew: 'Exsurgens autem Ioseph a somno gratias
egit deo suo, et locutus est Mariae et virginibus' (Cap. XI, p. 72).

12/172–3 Cf. Matt. 1: 21–2.

12/182–4 Cf. Pseudo-Matthew: 'Et consolatus est super Maria, dicens:
Peccavi, quoniam suspicionem aliquam habui in te' (Cap. XI, p. 73).

12/211–20 Cf. Love's *Mirrour*: 'Than after this reuelacioun Joseph asked
oure lady of this wonderful conceyuynge; and sche gladly tolde hym the ordre
and the manere therof' (p. 42); cf. also the *Meditationes*, pp. 29–30.

12/224 '. . . that Lord (who) so provided for me'.

PLAY 13

Mary's Visit to Elizabeth is based on Luke 1: 39–79. Contemplacio's speech in
23–42, recounting the story of Zachary's dumbness, closely follows the *Legenda
Aurea*, at times echoing it; the story itself ultimately derives from Luke 1: 5–25.
Several elements in the play, such as Joseph's presence during the visit, as
well as Mary's reasons for urging that they walk in haste, appear in the *Meditationes*, Love's *Mirrour*, and related English accounts. The idea that Mary

served Elizabeth during the visit appears in the *Legenda* as well as the *Meditationes*, Love, and the related accounts; these texts also state explicitly that Mary was present at the time of John's birth, a detail in the play that is unclear in Luke. Revisional stanzas in Contemplacio's Conclusion, which describe Mary's stay until after John's birth, follow Love's *Mirrour* so faithfully as to essentially versify it.

This is the last play of the Marian group presided over by Contemplacio, who speaks while Mary and Joseph travel around the 'place' and later delivers his Conclusion, as he had promised in 8/13. Like most of the plays in this group, the present play is not mentioned in the Proclamation. And like them, it is basically constituted of long-lined ababbcbc octaves, though the Magnificat and its English translation are in quatrains.

The latter part of this play has been substantially revised. The main scribe has written several abababab octaves and associated quatrains in a compressed hand, two lines as one, in blank spaces left on ff. 73ᵛ and 74ʳ. These stanzas provide two alternate endings to the play (see the note to 147–185A).

In addition to the stanzas noted above, quatrains appear in 1–4 and 39–42; the latter has a curious three-stress pattern and was perhaps intended as an extension of Contemplacio's octave in 31–8. An incomplete octave preceding the Magnificat (75–81) may evidence textual grafting. 21–2 form a couplet, and 122 is ametrical.

13/1 'Bvtt' at the head of this line may imply the continuation of some preceding dialogue between Mary and Joseph, perhaps the stanzas at the end of Play 12. Alan J. Fletcher proposes that the opening of Play 13 may once have followed directly after 12/17–20, with 13/1–4 completing an ababbcbc octave ('Layers of Revision in the N-Town Marian Cycle', *Neophilologus*, 66 (1982), 471).

13/2 *cosyn Elyzabeth*: 'Elisabeth cognata tua' in Luke 1: 36. Genealogies of Mary, including those in the *Legenda* (p. 586) and in marginal notations in the N-town codex (f. 37), make Mary and Elizabeth cousins in the strict modern sense, as Meredith observes (*Mary Play*, p. 117): Elizabeth is said to be the daughter of Anne's sister Hismeria (Emeria in the N-town version).

13/7 *Montana*: cf. Luke 1: 39: 'Exsurgens autem Maria in diebus illis abiit *in montana* . . .' (italics mine).

13/8 *þe cety of Juda*: this formulation appears in Tatian's *Diatessaron*.

13/14–15 Cf. Love's *Mirrour*: 'Sche taried not and letted not for the longe and disesy way / but anone with haste sche wente; for sche wolde not longe be seyen in the open amonge folk' (p. 37). Mary's haste ultimately derives from her travelling 'cum festinatione' in Luke 1: 39; compare the *Legenda*, p. 885 (*Mary Play*, p. 117).

13/17 The *Middle English Translation of the Rosarium Theologiae* says that pilgrimages 'ow to be done wiþ gret hastyng & deuoute' (ed. Christina von

Nolcken, Middle English Texts 10 (Heidelberg, 1979), p. 80; cited by Meredith, *Mary Play*, p. 117).

13/19 *icast*: 'say'. *MED* (*icasten*, v.) cites this as the sole instance of this form. Alternatively, it can be read *I cast* 'I purpose', or 'I say'.

13/23-7 Cf. the *Legenda Aurea*: 'David enim rex, sicut habetur in hystoria scholastica, volens cultum Dei ampliare, XXIV summos sacerdotes instituit, quorum tamen unus major erat, qui princeps sacerdotum dicebatur' (Cap. LXXXXVI, p. 357). The manuscript reading in 25, *let*, is here emended to *lot* following the *Legenda*: 'et secundum sortes dedit unicuique hebdomadam vicis suae . . .' (p. 357). Cf. Luke 1: 9, 1 Chron. 24; also Bonaventura, *Expositio in Cap. I. S. Lucae* (*Opera*, vol. 6, cited by Hemingway, p. 254).

13/28-33 Cf. Luke 1: 5-13; also, the *Legenda Aurea*: 'Erant autem Zacharias et uxor ejus senes et absque liberis. Cum ergo Zacharias templum domini, ut incensum poneret, ingressus fuisset . . . apparuit ei Gabriel archangelus. . . . Annunciat igitur Gabriel Zachariae, se filium habiturum' (Cap. LXXXXVI, p. 357).

13/34-6 Cf. the *Legenda Aurea*: 'Zacharias autem considerans sui senectutem et uxoris sterilitatem dubitare coepit . . . angelus autem pro eo, quod verbis suis non credit, ipsum taciturnitatis plaga percussit . . . completa autem septimana officii sui abiit in domum suam et concepit Elizabeth' (Cap. LXXXVI, pp. 357-8). The emendation of the manuscript reading *Hese juge* in 34 to *He, seinge*, suggested by Peter Meredith, accords with this source (see 'A Reconsideration of Some Textual Problems in the N-town Manuscript (BL MS Cotton Vespasian D Viii)', *Leeds Studies in English* 9 (1977), 35-9). Cf. also Luke 1: 18-24.

13/36 *Thei wenten hom*: Meredith ('A Reconsideration', p. 39) notes that in the *Legenda Aurea*, Zacharias goes home alone (see the note above). He adds that in *Cursor Mundi*, by contrast, the crowd outside the temple leads him home, an influence of the sort that might account for the plural pronoun in the present line.

13/41 *God be oure begynnynge*: Meredith notes that this translates *Deus sit in principio*, commonly spoken to ask God's blessing at the beginning of an enterprise (*Mary Play*, p. 118).

13/51-5 Cf. Luke 1: 41. John's kneeling is not in Luke (which says 'exsultavit infans in utero eius') or the other principal sources, but is occasionally represented iconographically. See Gertrud Schiller, *Iconography of Christian Art*, trans. Janet Seligman (London, 1971), I, plates 16, 133 (cited in *Mary Play*, p. 118). Robert J. Leonard considers this image to be part of a larger pattern of kneeling in the cycle ('Patterns of Dramatic Unity in the N-town Cycle', SUNY, Stony Brook Ph.D. thesis, 1984, pp. 47-8). Cf. Theresa Coletti, 'Devotional Iconography in the N-Town Marian Plays', in *Drama of the Middle Ages*, pp. 249-71.

13/57–61 Cf. Luke 1: 42–3.

13/63–4 Cf. Luke 1: 45.

13/65–80 Mary and Elizabeth exchange tales of the conception of Jesus and John in the *Meditationes*, Love's *Mirrour*, and the Dublin and Cambridge manuscripts.

13/78 *hym thought nay*: i.e. 'Zacharias doubted'.

13/81 *For*: see the note to 9/190. Meredith suggests rendering *for* as 'therefore', but the sense is not fully satisfactory, and, as Meredith notes, *MED* does not give this meaning (*Mary Play*, p. 119). *þis holy psalme*: the Magnificat, like the Creed, the Pater Noster, and other sacred recitations, was often called a psalm; cf. 13/127, 19/146 s.d.

13/82–117 Cf. Luke 1: 46–55. The recitation and translation of the Magnificat, like the treatment of the Gradual Psalms in Play 9, is in quatrains. This translation, like that earlier one, is often awkward and sometimes textually problematic. Unlike the recital of the psalms in the earlier Marian play, the Magnificat here rhymes the Latin lines with the English. In consequence, several of the English lines conclude with phrases that depart from the Latin meaning for the sake of rhyme.

13/84–5 'Through the Holy Ghost God's son has joyously come into you because your spirit so rejoiced in God's salvation'. 84 is an adaptation rather than a translation of the Latin. For 85, compare the Dublin manuscript: 'my spyrit hath Ioyed in god whiche is my hele' (quoted from Peggy Ann McQuillan, 'A Critical Edition of *The Life of the Virgin Mary and the Christ*', Duquesne University MA thesis (1951), p. 54). Compare the *Myroure of oure Ladye*, p. 158.

13/88–9 *handmayde, ȝe*: written as one word, and printed by Block as a plural, 'handmaydeȝe', but the sense and the rhyme with 'sue' in 86 require the present form. *Lo, ferforthe*: 'Lo' renders the Latin *Ecce* in 87; the emendation from the manuscript form 'So' is easily justified graphically. 'Ferforthe', rendering *ex hoc* is not inconceivably an error for 'hensforthe', but the present form, in the sense of 'far into the future' (or, less likely, 'greatly'), is acceptable.

13/112 Cf. Wyclif's rendering of Luke 1: 54: 'He, hauyng mynde of his mercy, took vp Israel, his child' (cited by *OED* under *take*, v. 90, i). *Suscipe*, as a term in Roman law, meant to lift a new-born child from the ground, and so to adopt it (Graef, p. 84).

13/113 *for hese þat be*: 'for those that are his'.

13/116 *in clos*: 'privately, face to face'; or 'in secret', by types and prophecies (suggested by Meredith, *Mary Play*, p. 120).

13/118–26 Hemingway (p. 255) observes that the inclusion of the Gloria Patri shows the influence of the liturgical version of the Magnificat.

13/122 This line is ametrical, or linked to the subsequent stanza in an irregular prosodic pattern.

13/129-30 From an early date, the Magnificat has been the canticle of Vespers in the Western Church. Cf. the *Myroure of oure Ladye*: '*Magnificat*, Thys ys oure ladyes songe, and yt ys sayde euery daye at euensonge' (p. 157, cited with additional analogues in *Mary Play*, p. 120).

13/131-4 Cf. Luke 1: 56, and see the headnote to this play.

13/143 *wys*: see the note to 9/49.

13/147-185A These lines provide two alternative conclusions to the play. In the first of these, Mary and Joseph depart promptly, and Elizabeth beseeches Zacharias to go to the temple with her (147-74). In the alternate ending, these speeches are omitted, and Contemplacio instead tells the audience that Mary and Joseph remained with Elizabeth until after John's birth. The latter conclusion was accomplished by the interpolation of 147A-149A, which are written at the foot of f. 73^v, and preceded by 'Si placet'. A marginal notation shows that they are to be placed after 146, and the speaker heading 'Contemplacio' at the right of 149A indicates that Contemplacio's Conclusion is to follow directly after this line. Most of the stanzas involved in both conclusions appear to be revisional, written in insufficient space as the manuscript was being transcribed. The scribe copied out the text to 146 on f. 73^v in his normal hand with normal spacing; apparently leaving space for later additions, he transcribed the first stanza of Contemplacio's Conclusion (150A-157A) on f. 74^r, again in his normal hand. He then evidently received more text than anticipated to fill in the space he had left before Contemplacio's stanza, and consequently squeezed 147-74 into their present position, writing two lines as one in smaller script. These added stanzas, a quatrain and three abababab octaves, depict Mary and Joseph's departure. To present the alternative ending, the scribe compressed three quatrains, an abababab octave, and an ababbcbc octave into the limited space below Contemplacio's first stanza on f. 74^r, again writing two lines as one in a smaller hand. The abababab octave and the associated quatrains, like the octaves in this rhyme scheme in Play 11, are in large measure indebted to Love's *Mirrour*, at times essentially reducing that source to verse.

13/149-50 Cf. Prov. 3: 12.

13/151A-155A Cf. Luke 1: 28, 42. In the Hail Mary, 'Mary' and 'Jesus' are added to the scriptural salutations of Gabriel and Elizabeth respectively. Cf. the *Lay Folks' Catechism*, p. 12.

13/156A-157A *Oure Ladyes Sawtere*: the name given to the rosary because it contains the repetition of 150 Aves, the same number as there are psalms in the Psalter. *He hath pardon ten thowsand and eyte hundryd зer*: cf. *Festyuall*, 1515: 'pope Urban and pope Iohan [say] to all beynge in clene lyfe that . . . as ofte as thou sayst oure ladyes psalter / so ofte thou hast of pardon. xxxiiii. yere and xxx. wekes' (cited in the *Lay Folks' Catechism*, p. 108). By contrast, Text L of the *Lay Folks' Catechism* (pp. 13-14), attributed by the editors probably to Wyclif, cautions against believing that men will receive pardon too lightly, such as ten thousand years' pardon for saying Our Lady's Psalter daily for a year!

13/162A–165A Cf. Love's *Mirrour*, the apparent source of these lines: 'A lord god / what house was that / or what chambre / and what bedde in the whiche dwelleden to gidre and resteden so worthi moderes with so noble sones / that is to saie Marie and Eliȝabeth / Jesu and John! And also with hem dwellynge tho worschipful olde men / Ȝacharie and Joseph' (p. 39).

13/166A–167A In Luke 1: 56, Mary returns home, and John's birth is not noted until the following verse. The *Legenda Aurea*, the *Meditationes*, Love's *Mirrour*, and the Dublin and Cambridge manuscripts have her stay with Elizabeth until after John is born.

13/168A–171A Cf. Luke 1: 64, 67 ff.

13/172A–173A Cf. Love's *Mirrour*: 'And so in that hous ... *Magnificat* and *benedictus* / weren first spoken and made' (p. 40; similarly expressed in the *Meditationes* and the Dublin and Cambridge manuscripts).

13/174A–177A Cf. Love's *Mirrour*: 'And at the laste whan al this was done / sche toke hir leue at Eliȝabeth and ȝacharye / and blessid the child John' (p. 40). Compare the following passage in the *Meditationes*, which Love omits: 'Ipsa laetanter colludebatur eidem, et osculabatur jucunde' (cited by Hemingway, p. 257).

13/184A–185A With '*Aue*' *we begunne*: Davies (p. 451 note 31) says that Contemplacio's Conclusion begins with a discussion of the 'Ave Maria' and ends with 'Ave Regina Celorum'. But Fletcher ('Layers of Revision', p. 474) proposes that the 'Ave' mentioned in 184A may refer to 11/216a. *Ave Regina Celorum*: cf. Dutka, pp. 21–2, York 44/194 s.d. Meredith observes that this antiphon, used in processions at the Nativity of the Blessed Virgin Mary and at the entrance to the choir on other liturgical occasions, would be particularly appropriate for a processional ending to the play (*Mary Play*, p. 121).

PLAY 14

The Trial of Mary and Joseph is unique to N-town among the extant English mysteries, and Woolf (p. 174) notes that none of the Continental cycles includes it. The play derives from Pseudo-Matthew, but transforms the setting into a medieval ecclesiastical court, and consequently supplies such figures as the summoner and the scandalous detractors.

The summoner's prologue, which appears to have been written after the body of the play had been at least partially transcribed, comprises an initial quatrain and four tail-rhyme stanzas (see the note to 21–33). It is prosodically distinct from the rest of the play, which consists of ababbcbc octaves and a single quatrain (402–5). This play, like the Nativity, which follows it, is

described in the Proclamation by only a quatrain, with sufficient space left
blank to complete a 13-line description: see the note to Pr 183–90.

The summoner, probably addressing the audience in his prologue as 'Johan
Jurdon', 'Malkyn Mylkedoke', etc., may be taking a collection, or preparing
the audience for one later in the play.

14/1–33 Greg (p. 130) says that Den's prologue on f. 74^v was not originally
contemplated by the scribe, who began to copy the play on f. 75^r, the page on
which he wrote the playnumber 14. Greg conjectures that the scribe had left
f. 74^v blank in order to allow for possible expansion of Contemplacio's Conclusion in Play 13. Halliwell (p. 413) cites a similar list of names in *Cocke
Lorelles Bote*, including Pers Potter and Phyllyp Fletcher.

14/21–33 Halliwell and Block print 28 and 29 as a single line. In the manuscript, however, 29 stands below 28, and is looped in red. This arrangement,
the prosody, and the sense all indicate that 29 was intended as a separate line.
21–8 constitute a tail-rhyme stanza rhyming aaabcccb, and, 29–33, rhyming
abbba, may be a fragment of a tail-rhyme stanza.

14/25 This line, and Den's demand for 'mede' in 158, may indicate that a collection was taken during the play. Cf. William Hone, *Ancient Mysteries
Described* (London, 1823), p. 57; J. P. Collier, *The History of English Dramatic Poetry* (London, 1831), II: 178; Halliwell, p. 413; and Joseph Allen Bryant, Jr., who
compares this play to *Mankind*, 454 ff. ('The Function of *Ludus Coventriae* 14',
JEGP, 52 (1953), 340–45); but Woolf (p. 385 note 50) is sceptical.

14/62–3 Cf. Bacbytere in the *Castle*, 647–98.

14/105 s.d. ff. *Abizachar*: cf. 10/first s.d. and the note. In Pseudo-Matthew
and Lydgate's *Life of Our Lady* and 'Fifteen Joys and Sorrows of Mary', the
bishop is Abiathar. Woolf (p. 175) notes that the play transforms the apocryphal source so that the trial is set in an ecclesiastical court, with a bishop, two
learned clerics, a summoner, and, as in all cases of alleged adultery, two wit-
nesses. Lynn Squires discusses topical implications in the trial in 'Law and
Disorder in the *Ludus Coventriae*' (*The Drama of the Middle Ages*, pp. 277–8).

14/113 See the note to 7/13.

14/129 Halliwell (p. 414) compares this line to the ballad of *The Cokwoldes
Daunce*: 'cokwoldes schuld begynne the bord, / And sytt hyest in the halle'.

14/156 'If in my haste I enrol you (in the list of people to be summoned)'.

14/159 Bryant, p. 344, says that Den's 'gret rough toth' may recall tooth-
drawing in mummers plays, or perhaps refers to the staff a summoner was
entitled to carry.

14/165–66, 169 See the note to 12/55–6.

14/232 ff. Cf. Numbers 5. 11–31, to which Pseudo-Matthew adds the detail of
circumambulating the altar seven times, and the idea that guilt would be
revealed by a sign on one's face. Cf. also the *Life of St. Anne*, 22/829–31.

14/257 'Because of your mercy grant me now your protection'.

14/286–8 Cf. Pseudo-Matthew: 'Et vocantes Mariam dixerunt ei: Tu quam excusationem poteris habere? aut quod signum maius apparebit in te quam hoc quod prodit te conceptus ventris tui? . . . confitearis quis est qui te decepit' (Cap. XII, p. 74).

14/306–13 The story of the snow-child, deriving from Latin poems of the tenth to the twelfth century and later fabliaux, is found in F. J. E. Raby, *A History of Secular Latin Poetry in the Middle Ages* (Oxford, 1934), 1: 295–7, 2: 34; cf. Anatole de Montaiglon, *Recueil Général . . . des Fabliaux* (Paris, 1872), 1: 162–7, and Joseph Bédier, *Les Fabliaux*, sixth edition (Geneva and Paris, 1982), 460–1. See also Holthausen, 'Das Märchen vom Schneekind', *Anglia Bleiblatt*, 35, pp. 95–6, and Woolf, p. 176.

14/320 *þe trewth, devyse*: 'the truth, consider'. Block suggests *trewe devyse* 'true device, trick'; Davies proposes 'true intent'.

14/333 s.d. ff. Cf. Pseudo-Matthew: 'Et accessit ad altare domine confidenter et bibit aquam potationis et septies circuivit altare, et non est inventa in ea ulla macula' (Cap. XII, p. 74).

PLAY 15

The story of the bowing cherry tree recalls a similar scene in Pseudo-Matthew, which, however, involves a palm tree, and is set during the Flight into Egypt. Among English plays, this motif is dramatized only in N-town. The Nativity is found in Luke 2: 1–7, while the story of the Midwives is based on Pseudo-Matthew, which the play follows nearly verbatim in several instances. There is also minor indebtedness to the *Protevangelium of James*. *Obstetrices* have a long history in liturgical drama, having appeared in the *Officium Pastorum* from Padua and elsewhere (Young, 2: 5 ff.). The Chester cycle, like N-town, includes them in the Nativity.

The chief stanzaic forms of this play are ababbcbc octaves and quatrains. 1–9, 44–52, and 57–65 are 9-line stanzas (57–65 rhyme ababbcccb); 22–3 form a couplet. Swenson (p. 33) says that the Cherry Tree scene is the only portion of the play written in tumbling metre, and Block (p. xxvii) notes that in this play, the scribe made regular use of pointing only in this scene.

Like the preceding play of the Trial of Mary and Joseph, the present play is described in the Proclamation by only a quatrain, followed by enough blank space to add several more lines; see the note to Pr 183–90. The Proclamation description accords with the play in alluding to the episode of the Midwives.

15/3 *besought*: 'summoned'; Davies renders this word as 'strongly requested'.
15/24 ff. Cf. Pseudo-Matthew, Cap. XX; *Cursor Mundi*, 11,657 ff.; the Infancy of Christ poems in Horstmann, *Altenglische Legenden*, p. 5, and *Sammlung*,

p. 102; and the Holkham Bible Picture Book, f. 15. Fletcher Collins, Jr., describes the cherry-tree episode in a liturgical dramatization of the Annunciation (*The Production of Medieval Church Music-Drama* (Charlottesville, 1972), p. 262).

15/39 Cf. the Cherry-Tree Carol: 'O then bespoke Joseph, / with words most unkind: / "Let him pluck thee a cherry / that brought thee with child"' (*English and Scottish Popular Ballads*, eds. Helen Child Sargent and George Lyman Kittredge (Boston, New York, 1904; reprinted 1932, no. 54). Cook cites similar rebukes in Eastern dialogues.

15/49–52 Cf. the *De Nativitate*: 'virgo Maria de stirpe regia et familia David oriunda' (Cap. I, p. 113). Mary's royal ancestry is also referred to in several later texts, such as the *Legenda Aurea*, *Cursor Mundi*, the *Life of St. Anne*, *Bokenham's Legendys*, and the Coventry Shearmen and Taylors' pageant; also, in homily (Cook, pp. 431, 434, 447). Cf. Livius, pp. 128–9 *et passim*, and the note to N-town 7/13.

15/68–73 Cf. York 14/8–12.

15/84–5 Cf. Vriend, pp. 93–5, 110–12.

15/92 'Christ, (who) within me has taken bodily form'.

15/100 Habakkuk's famous prophecy that the Christ-child will be found between two beasts appears in the Old Latin rendering of Hab. 3: 2: 'In medio duorum animalium cognosceris' (*Bibliorum Sacrorum, Latinae Versiones Antiquae*, ed. Sabatier). The prophecy is repeated in Pseudo-Matthew and the *Sermo de Symbolo*, and Woolf (p. 385 note 62) cites it in liturgy.

15/162–77 Cf. Pseudo-Matthew: 'Ego tibi Zelomi et Salomen obstetrices adduxi, quae foris ante speluncam stant et prae splendore nimio huc introire non audent' (Cap. XIII, p. 77). Cf. the *Life of Our Lady*, III: 204–21, and Anderson's discussion of the Norwich Cathedral roof bosses, p. 94.

15/177 s.d.–187 Cf. Pseudo-Matthew: 'Audiens autem haec Maria subrisit. Cui Ioseph dixit: Noli subridere, sed cauta esto, ne forte indigeas medicina' (Cap. XIII, pp. 77–8).

15/192 '. . . the child (who) has created this world. . . .'

15/218–41 Cf. Pseudo-Matthew: 'Cumque ingressa esset Zelomi, ad Mariam dixit: Dimitte me ut tangam te. Cumque permisisset se Maria tangi, exclamavit voce magna obstetrix et dixit: Domine domine magna, miserere. Numquam hoc auditum est nec in suspicione habitum, ut mamillae plenae sint lacte et natus masculus matrem suam virginem ostendat. Nulla pollutio sanguinis facta est in nascente, nullus dolor in parturiente. Virgo concepit, virgo peperit, virgo permansit' (Cap. XIII, p. 78).

15/221 'If you have pain as other women do'.

15/246–9 Cf. the *Protevangelium*: 'Then said Salome: As the Lord my God liveth, unless I thrust in my finger, and search the parts, I will not believe that a virgin has brought forth' (*Ante-Nicene Fathers*, VIII: 365).

15/250ff. Cf. Pseudo-Matthew: 'Cumque permisisset Maria ut eam palparet, misit manum suam Salome. Et cum misisset et tangeret, statim aruit manus eius, et prae dolore coepit flere vehementissime et angustari' (Cap. XIII, p. 78). See Hassall, pp. 88–9.

15/254–7 Cf. the *Protevangelium*: 'Salome . . . cried out, and said: Woe is me for mine iniquity and mine unbelief . . . my hand is dropping off . . .' (p. 365).

15/266–309 Cf. Pseudo-Matthew: 'Domine, tu nosti quia semper te timui, et omnes pauperes sine retributione acceptionis curavi, de vidua et orphano nihil accepi, et inopem vacuum a me ire numquam dimisi. Et ecce misera facta sum propter incredulitatem meam, quia ausa fui temptare virginem tuam. Cumque haec diceret, apparuit iuxta illam iuvenis quidam valde splendidus dicens ei: Accede ad infantem et adora eum et continge de manu tua, et ipse salvabit te, quia ipse est salvator seculi et omnium sperantium in se. Quae confestim ad infantem accessit, et adorans eum tetigit fimbrias pannorum, in quibus infans erat involutus, et statim sanata est manus eius. Et exiens foras clamare coepit et dicere magnalia virtutem quae viderat et quae passa fuerat, et quemadmodum curata fuerat . . .' (Cap. XIII, pp. 78–9).

PLAY 16

The Shepherds play is based on Luke 2: 8–20, but contains much extra-biblical detail. Although there was little development of this episode in apocryphal and meditative literature, elaborations occurred from an early date in liturgical performances. The shepherds' association with prophecy, for instance, appears in an eleventh-century text from Limoges, and their glorifi-cation of the Christ-child at the manger is also found in early liturgical drama. These motifs became dramatic conventions, and inform much of the present play. The shepherds' comic imitation of the angelic song recalls the corre-sponding Chester play, and is represented in the Holkham Bible Picture Book. Woolf (p. 183) suggests that the unexpected learning of the N-town shepherds may reflect the influence of Virgil's eclogues and Patristic exposi-tions in which the *pastores* signify the clergy.

This play has been extensively revised. 'Gloria in excelsis Deo' in the initial stage direction, for example, has been crossed through, presumably because a later stage direction, amid tail-rhyme stanzas, also calls for this hymn. And the angel's joyous announcement in the subsequent thirteener (1–13) goes wholly unnoticed by the shepherds, who remark (in tail-rhyme) only upon the bright light they have seen. In addition, three quatrains written on f. 90ʳ (lines 62–73) are intended for interpolation on f. 89ᵛ. A speech seems to have been lost after 89 s.d. as a result of revision. Much of the remainder of the play is in tail-rhyme octaves, several of which have two- and three-stress lines. 90–102 make up a long thirteener, and the final stanza is an abab quatrain.

The play was further revised by Scribe C, who altered several lines on ff. 88ᵛ–89ᵛ.

The Proclamation says that in the Shepherds pageant 'Cryst xal be born' (191); see the note to Pr 183–90.

16/first s.d.–2 Cf. Luke 2: 14, Dutka, pp. 28–9, and the headnote above.

16/5 The seven sacraments: Baptism, Confirmation, the Eucharist, Penance, Extreme Unction, Ordination, and Matrimony.

16/10 *is gloryed*: 'is glorified'; perhaps 'rejoices', as in *MED*, *glōrīen*, v. (1) 2 (b), which cites only this line and *Mankind*, 773—but Eccles renders the instance in *Mankind* as 'puffed up greatly'.

16/14ff. The star appears in the Magi episode in Matt. 2, not in the story of the shepherds in Luke 2.

16/15 *with shene shyne*: 'with a brilliant radiance'; or perhaps 'shine with brightness', but *OED* does not cite *sheen* as a noun meaning 'brightness' until 1602, or *shine* in the sense 'radiance' until a. 1529.

16/23 'I have watched the same (object, i.e. the star) pass by'.

16/26–9 Cf. Num. 24: 17, commonly interpreted to refer to Jesus, and widely cited in medieval texts. See, for example, 18/159–62; compare Rev. 22: 16.

16/32–3 The cross may refer to the brazen serpent. Cf. Num. 21: 8–9, John 3: 14–15; also, Tertullian's 'An Answer to the Jews': 'Moses ... set forth a brazen serpent, placed on a "tree", in a hanging posture ... in this case he was exhibiting the Lord's *cross* on which the "serpent" the devil was "made a show of"' (*Ante-Nicene Fathers*, III: 166). E. P. Evans, however, points out that Patristic interpretations associate Moses with the cross in other ways as well (*Animal Symbolism in Ecclesiastical Architecture*, pp. 247ff.). See Watson, p. 53.

16/39–40 Cf. 26–9. *skye* 'star' is apparently a unique usage; compare 18/159–62.

16/46–9 Falke (p. 50) cites Amos 9: 11, Hemingway (p. 261) proposes Amos 9: 13, and Davies (p. 172) suggests Amos 8: 1–2.

16/54–7 Cf. Dan. 7: 13–14 and the note to N-town 7/61–4.

16/62–89 s.d. In the manuscript, the two tail-rhyme stanzas and the stage direction here numbered 74–89 s.d. follow immediately upon 61 s.d., but are marked 'B' in the left margin. The subsequent three quatrains are marked 'A', and so are here placed first, as 62–73. A 'C' stands at the left of 90. Block (p. 148 note 1) observes that the quatrains resemble the humorous imitation of the angelic song in the Chester Shepherds play, but Woolf (p. 386 note 5) says that there is no reason to connect these stanzas specifically with Chester, since the joke was widespread in England. Cf. the Holkham Bible Picture Book (f. 13ʳ), in which the phrase 'Glum glo' anticipates line 69 in the present play. The first and second shepherds speak in 74–89, but the third shepherd's speech seems to have been lost, presumably as a consequence of the revision of this portion of the play.

16/89 s.d. *Stella celi extirpauit*: cf. Dutka, pp. 37–8.

16/90ff. N-town curiously omits the shepherds' giving of gifts, a motif that Woolf (p. 183) says is common to all western European Shepherds plays.

16/119ff. Cf. Luke 2: 20. Kretzmann (p. 50) says that lines 119–22 recall the 'Dicite quidnam vidistis' of the liturgical plays.

PLAY 17

There is no Play 17. The playnumbering, however, running directly from 16 (the Shepherds play) to 18 (the Magi), indicates that some subject was contemplated for inclusion as Play 17. This may well have been the Purification of Mary, which in Luke 2 follows almost immediately after the Shepherds episode. In the cycle as we have it, the Purification stands as Play 19, preceding the Slaughter of the Innocents (Play 20). Block (p. xxviii) proposes that a rubricated 'I' erased before the playnumber '20' on f. 101ʳ may evidence an earlier plan to place the Purification after Play 16. For if the Purification had indeed been 17, the Slaughter would have been 19: hence the erased 'I'. Such an ordering would have agreed with Pseudo-Matthew, the Arabic Infancy Gospel, and the *Diatessaron*; a similar arrangement obtains in *Cursor Mundi* and the *Life of St. Anne*. The present order of plays, however, conforms to a far more common pattern in medieval narrative.

PLAY 18

The Magi story of Matt. 2: 1–12 is here compressed by the omission of Herod's inquiry into the place of Christ's birth, but also extended by the inclusion of Patristic and other amplification. The idea that the Magi were three in number, for example, derives from Church commentary, as do their identification with the kings of Psalm 71: 9–11 (Vulgate) and the association of the star with Balaam's prophecy in Numbers 24: 17. The role of Herod's messenger was suggested in the *Protevangelium*. And the *Herodes iratus*, adumbrated in Matt. 2 and reinforced by apocryphal and Patristic accounts, became a familiar figure in liturgical and cycle plays.

Herod opens the play in long-line quatrains. Later, after changing his costume, he delivers two densely alliterative 'Herod thirteeners' rhyming ababababbcccb (69–94). He also speaks a Proclamation thirteener in 217–29. The remainder of the play is in tail-rhyme, predominantly rhyming aaabcccb (or aaabaaab), but also with short-lined stanzas rhyming aaabcccb, aabccb, and aaaaaa (259–64). 273–90 comprise aabccb stanzas, and 230–34 form an incomplete stanza rhyming abaab.

Folios 95–6 are an interpolated bifolium bearing a Hand watermark that is not found elsewhere in the codex. The text on these leaves was written by Scribe C, who also altered lines elsewhere in the play.

The play generally agrees with the Proclamation description.

18/4–12 Laudation of Herod's beauty was a dramatic convention. See, for example, York 19/8, Chester 10/86–9, and especially the Coventry Shearmen and Taylors' pageant, 507–13. Robertson points out that Herod was interpreted to mean 'vainglorious' or 'glorying in clothing' (*A Preface to Chaucer* (Princeton, 1962), p. 385). And Penelope B. R. Doob says that the medieval emphasis on Herod's rich clothes and divinity seems to recall Herod Agrippa's behaviour in Acts 12 (*Nebuchadnezzar's Children: Conventions of Madness in Middle English Literature* (New Haven and London, 1974), p. 124 note 56).

18/17 Herod evidently enters on horseback, as do the Magi in 21–2.

18/19—20 Herod's use of *ȝe* indicates that *mynstrell* is plural. Cf. 20/153, and also 20/231–2, in which the plurality of *menstrell* appears to be confirmed by *buccinant* in 232 s.d. Dutka (p. 87) says that this verb denotes the playing of some type of trumpet.

18/25–68 The Magi's names correspond to the traditional names given in the *Collectanea et Flores*, the *Historia Scholastica*, and the *Legenda Aurea* (see Winifred Sturdevant, *The Misterio de los Reyes Magos* (Baltimore and Paris, 1927), pp. 21–7). The traditional form Melchior appears here as Melchizar; cf. Melcisar in the Irish 'Legends of the Childhood of Christ', in M. R. James' *Latin Infancy Gospels* (Cambridge, 1927), p. 112. The symbolism of the Magi's gifts ultimately derives from Irenaeus, though N-town (lines 45–52) recalls Augustine's interpretation that the incense suggests priesthood (Young, 2: 32; Sturdevant, pp. 11–12, 17). Saba and Tarys, the kingdoms of Baltazare and Melchizar respectively, are taken from Psalm 71: 10 (Vulgate), but Jasper's allusion to Ypotan and Archage is problematic. 'Archage' may be Arcadia (cf. 23/164 and Archade in the *Confessio amantis* 5. 1007, cited by *MED* under *Archade*). Block (p. 379) cites Artage, apparently for Arcadia in the *Parliament of the Three Ages*. 'Ypotan' may recall ἀπὸ ποταμοῦ from Psalm 71: 8 in the Septuagint. Gauvin (p. 155) renders it as 'Mesopotamia'.

18/82–94 This Herod thirteener is misplaced. In these lines, Herod is already informed about Jesus' birth, and he announces that he will dispatch soldiers to kill the male children—a declaration that should more properly appear in Play 20. At this point in the story, in fact, Herod has not yet met the Magi. And in the subsequent tail-rhyme stanzas, he seems unaware of any specific danger.

18/83 *cruel and curryd*: Davies proposes 'curly-haired and well-combed'; alternatively, perhaps 'fierce and excellent', though the weak ending of *curryd* would be suspect. Block suggests that *curryd* is an error for *cursyd*.

18/88 *pap-hawk*: 'suckling child'; *MED* cites only this instance and the plural form in 20/11. *preuyn*: 'put to the test'; alternatively, the word may be read *prenyn* 'pierce'. *MED* cites this line under *proinen*, v. (b), 'to trim the feathers of (a bird)'.

18/92 Mahound (from OF *Mahon*, a shortening of *Mahomet*) is a principal devil and Herod's false god in each of the English Magi plays. The Nuncius in Towneley 16/54 calls him Herod's 'cosyn'. Evil figures in the drama often refer to Mahound in terms parodic of references to God. Cf. Michael Paull, 'The Figure of Mahomet in the Towneley Cycle', *Comparative Drama*, 6 (1972), 187–204; Ward, I: 87; and Norman Daniel, *Heroes and Saracens* (Edinburgh, 1984), Ch. 7 *et passim*.

18/93–4 'Bitter death will deliver up the life of anyone (who) would threaten me in this way'.

18/123–6 '(that) he may put (in) us intelligence to find God's noble offspring. . . .' *pete* 'put' may, alternatively, be 'pity' (*MED* cites this instance under *pitien*, v.): 'He may pity us'. *be glete*: perhaps 'in the midst of sin' (see *MED*, *glet*, n. 1. c); or *glete* may be an eccentric form of the past participle of *glīden*: 'has passed into flesh'. *be-glete* could be a variant of the dialectal *be-clede* 'clothed': 'clothed in flesh'. Block renders *be glete* as 'by the gleam (of the star)'.

18/131 *Where kyng gynnyth wyde*: (?) 'Where the king goes'. See *OED*, *wade*, v. 1, 'go, advance'; perhaps also suggesting 'be or become mad' (*OED*, *wede*, v.).

18/159–62 Balaam's prophecy was associated with the Magi by Irenaeus (Sturdevant, pp. 11–12) and became a conventional element in the liturgical *Officium Stellae* as well as the cycle Magi plays. See the note to 16/26–9.

18/221–302 The interpolated ff. 95–6 blend thematically and prosodically with the surrounding text, which is incomplete without them, and may well record lost material from the play. The first nine lines on f. 95ʳ, in fact, complete a Proclamation thirteener begun on the preceding page, while the last four lines of the interpolation begin a tail-rhyme stanza that is completed on f. 97ʳ. Given Scribe C's extensive alteration of text elsewhere in the cycle, however, it is possible that he revised much of this portion of the play.

18/223–4 Cf. the Shearmen and Taylors' pageant, 682, 687.

18/229 'So that they shall come this way in darkness'.

PLAY 19

The Purification of Mary and the story of Simeon and Anna the Prophetess derive from Luke 2: 22–38. The presentation of Jesus in the temple and his redemption for 'fyff pens' accord with the commands concerning the firstborn, especially in Exodus 13: 2 and Numbers 18: 15–16. In dramatizing these ceremonies, N-town draws on elements of the Candlemas liturgy, including the prayer 'Suscepimus deus misericordiam tuam', the 'psalm' 'Nunc dimittis', and the procession with candles. The play also exhibits verbal reminiscences of Love's *Mirrour* and shares in such dramatic conventions as

Simeon's laments about old age. The inclusion of liturgical elements is also a feature of other English Candlemas plays, especially the Digby play; see Vriend, pp. 118–22, and Woolf, p. 197.

This play is not mentioned in the Proclamation, and it interrupts the otherwise continuous action of the Magi and Herod plays; see the headnote to Play 17 and the note to 20/first s.d.

The play consists of 10-line stanzas rhyming aabaabbcbc. One stanza, rhyming aabaab (91–6) is presumably fragmentary.

19/39–40 Cf. the York *Purification*, 97.

19/44 The three-stress pattern, unusual in this position in the stanza, suggests that a word has been omitted, probably *þu*.

19/64–5 'Prophetess Anne, if you knew why (I make mirth), you would also, I vow'.

19/81–3 'In the temple of God, if the truth were known, today shall be presented with gracious heart he who is king of all'.

19/86 'Without declaring [calling out] a reason'. Cf. Matt. 27: 23 and N-Town 38/33.

19/87–90 Cf. Luke 2: 35.

19/97–106 Cf. Lev. 12; Ex. 13: 2, 11–13, 22: 29, 34: 20; Num. 3: 13 etc.

19/107–14 Similar reasoning appears in the *Legenda Aurea* and several English narrative and dramatic texts.

19/115–16 Cf. Luke 2: 24, Lev. 12: 6–8. The *Legenda Aurea*, like Love's *Mirrour*, observes that doves were the offering of the poor, while the rich offered a lamb.

19/136a–144 Psalm 47: 10 (Vulgate), included in the Sarum Missal (Woolf, p. 390 note 44). Cf. Love's *Mirrour*: 'Lord god / we haue resceyued this day thy grete mercy in myddes of thy temple / and therfore after thy grete name / so be thy louynge and thy worschippe in to the ferthest ende of al the worlde' (p. 61).

19/146aff. *Nunc dimittis*: cf. Dutka, p. 35, Luke 2: 29–32; sung in Chester 11/166 s.d.

19/158 '(Who) for more than eighty-two years'; cf. Luke 2: 37.

19/177–80 Cf. Num. 18: 15–16; also represented in the *Legenda Aurea*, the *Meditationes*, and such English texts as Love's *Mirrour* and the *Life of Our Lady*.

19/190–203 Cf. Love's *Mirrour*: 'And after / sche toke the forseide briddes of Joseph / and knelynge adoun and liftynge vp her eyȝen deuoutely vnto heuene / holdynge hem in her hondes offred hem / seienge thus: Al miȝty and merciful fader of heuene / vnderfonge ȝe this litel ȝifte and offerynge / and the firste ȝifte that ȝoure litel child this day presenteth vnto ȝoure hiȝe maieste of his symple pouerte' (pp. 62–3). Compare the *Meditationes*, pp. 63–4, and the Dublin manuscript, p. 70.

PLAY 20

The Slaughter of the Innocents is based on Matt. 2: 16–18. The mothers' laments dramatize Rachel's weeping for her children, a motif already movingly depicted in liturgical drama. Herod's death, alluded to in Matt. 2: 19, is here presented almost immediately after the Slaughter, an arrangement employed as early as the Benediktbeuern Christmas Play, which, like N-town, has Herod's soul go directly to hell. Herod also dies in the Chester and Digby Innocents plays, though N-town is unique among the English mysteries in having personified Death slay him.

Lines 1–8 and 73–104 form tail-rhyme stanzas in the pattern aaabcccb, while 41–72 and 105–28 have the same rhyme scheme but short lines; 22–7 follow the pattern aabccb. Herod speaks two Herod thirteeners (9–21, 28–40), and there are seven long thirteeners (129–54, 168–232). 155–67 and the last four stanzas of the play are Proclamation thirteeners.

The Proclamation divides the story into two pageants, the first depicting the Slaughter and the Flight into Egypt, the second, Herod's death. The first pageant agrees with the play generally, the second more specifically, with several close verbal and thematic parallels.

20/first s.d. Senescallus also appears in Play 18. His reappearance here, along with the thematic continuity and prosodic similarity between these plays, indicates that the present play once followed directly upon the Magi play. This is confirmed by the absence in this play of a traditional threatening or laudatory opening speech; see Greg, p. 133.

20/6 *Galylé*: in Matt. 2: 3, Herod appears to be in Jerusalem at the time of the Magi's arrival. The reference here to his being in Galilee may conflate this Herod with Herod Antipas, tetrarch of Galilee. Cf. Chester 8/199, N-town 29/78–85, and S. S. Hussey, 'How Many Herods in the Middle English Drama?', *Neophilologus*, 48 (1964), 252.

20/11 *Popetys* is both an ironic term of endearment for children and an anticipation of the probable use of dolls in staging the Slaughter. *pap-hawkys*: see the note to 18/88.

20/12 *to-pend*: MED (*pinden*, v. f) cites this line and 32/187 in the sense 'pinch, press; thrust, stab'; the *Catholicon* glosses 'To Pynde' with *jncludere*, *trudere*. Modern East Anglian survivals of this form are cited by Robert Forby, *The Vocabulary of East Anglia* (London, 1830; reprinted, Devon, 1970), 2: 248, and Edward Moor, *Suffolk Words and Phrases* (London, 1823; reprinted, Devon, 1970), p. 272.

20/13 'The gold-crowned children will never thrive', or 'The children will not profit from (bribery with) gold crowns'. The reference is less probably to the Magi, the men with gold crowns, whom Herod tries to intercept and kill in Pseudo-Matthew. *gomys* has been altered, perhaps to *gollys*. If glossed 'gulls, unfledged birds' (i.e. the Innocents), this would be consistent with Herod's avian imagery in this stanza.

20/15 *Do howlott howtyn*: the owlets are evidently the mothers of the Innocents. *howtyn* means 'cry out', and also recalls the sound of owls, as well as the typical outcry of the anguished mothers in Innocents plays, 'Out!' Cf. line 112. Both *hoberd* and *heyn* denote 'knave, rascal', though they seem to be used here as personal names.

20/21 'Because of one (whom) I called wicked', i.e. Jesus; cf. Towneley 16/101.

20/30 *Shewyth*: 'display', or perhaps 'shove'; cf. 3/129, in which *showe* rhymes with *aboue*.

20/31 *schelchownys*: perhaps a variant of *schelchene*, rendered in *OED* as 'female servant', though very possibly a scribal error for *scheltrownys* 'formations of troops'.

20/32 *rakynge*: 'fast-moving'; *MED* (*rāken*, v. 2. b) cites this instance in the sense 'of spears: thrusting, piercing'. The *English Dialect Dictionary* cites *raft* as meaning 'thin stick' in Norwich use.

20/34 'Let no child remain behind unbeaten', or 'unbeaten on the back'.

20/36 *Mahound*: see the note to 18/92.

20/58 *therlys*: 'piercings'; see *OED*, *thirl*, sb. 1. Block glosses this word as 'thralls, serfs'. Cf. *OED*, *thrill*, sb.².

20/136 'I shall smite those rogues and rake them in a group'. *rappe*: 'smite' or 'seize'. *rake*: 'sweep away', i.e. 'destroy'; Halliwell conjectures 'rack'. *on rought*: 'in a group' or 'one at a time'.

20/143 'It seems to me high time that we were at dinner'. *dyner*, the first large meal of the day, here suggests 'feast'.

20/168–206, 246–84 Compare Death's speeches in the *Castle*, 2778–2842, *Everyman* (ed. A. C. Cawley, Manchester, 1961), 64 ff., and the Cornish *Creacion*, 984–1004, as well as the Prolocutor's description of Death's role in the *Pride of Life*. Woolf (p. 393 note 86) cites figures of death in the Valencia play of Adam and Eve and the *Alsfelder Passionspiel*, and Neuss (p. 223) notes Death's appearance in the Breton Creation play. Death's warnings in the present play comprise traditional motifs exemplified in various genres. Owst notes similar homiletic treatments (*Literature and Pulpit*, pp. 530–1; see also *Preaching in Medieval England* (Cambridge, 1926), pp. 341–4). Woolf (p. 393 note 87) cites thematic affinities to lyric poetry. Warren E. Tomlinson associates Death's appearance in N-town with the *Totentanz* (*Der Herodes-Charakter im englischen Drama*, Palaestra 195 (1934), p. 48), and Chambers observes that Death's incursion into this play marks the principal influence of the Dance of Death upon the English mystery plays (*English Literature at the Close of the Middle Ages* (Oxford, 1945), p. 53). Cf. Gail McMurray Gibson, 'East Anglian Drama and the Dance of Death', *Early Drama, Art, and Music Newsletter*

(Fall, 1982), 1–9. In Dance of Death poetry, Death often speaks to his victims in terms appropriate to their roles in society, and Death's warnings here are suited to Herod, specifically recalling his earlier boasts and threats, and echoing his language; see Doob, p. 124, and David Staines, 'To Out-Herod Herod: The Development of a Dramatic Character', in *The Drama of the Middle Ages*, p. 218.

20/168 *a page*: cf. the *Pride of Life*, 437–42.

20/177–8 Cf. the Cornish *Creacion*, 'I am Death, God's messenger, appointed by him here' (984–5); also, *Everyman*, 63.

20/182 Cf. Herod's boast in 18/11, also Whiting, D78, and N-town 25/357.

20/191–2 Cf. *Everyman*: 'I gyue the no respyte' (line 130).

20/195 *he wenyth to leve evyrmore*: cf. the *Pride of Life*, 175, 193, 211.

20/196 *ȝeve hym such an hete*: *OED* cites this line under *hit*, sb. 1, though *hete* may, alternatively, be 'heat', recalling Herod's fever in the account of his death in the *Legenda Aurea* (see the note to 232 s.d.); cf. *to give a heat* (*OED*, *heat*, sb. 8). *MED*'s gloss of this line in the sense 'rebuke, reprove' (*hete*, n. 2. c) is less satisfactory, since Death intends a physical assault.

20/200 *I xal hym owt swete*: 'I shall sweat out of him' (see *OED*, *sweat* v. 13, in a sense first cited from 1686). Moor and *EDD* cite *sweat* as a modern Suffolk word meaning 'to beat'.

20/205 *my spere*: in the *Castle*, Death carries a lance, in the Cornish *Creacion* and *Everyman* a dart. See Cawley, *Everyman*, p. 30 note 76, the *Pardoner's Tale*, (C) 675–7, and N-town 25/63.

20/220, 222 Dobson stresses the abusive quality of *boys* in 220, and the sense of 'low birth' in *boy* in 222 ('Etymology and Meaning of Boy', pp. 132, 138).

20/231–2 Cf. 18/19–20 and note.

20/232 s.d. Herod's death, referred to in Matt. 2: 19, is described in gruesome detail in Josephus' *Jewish Antiquities*, briefly in Bede's *Martyrology*, more extensively in the *Historia Scholastica*, and in the following passage from the *Legenda Aurea*: 'Ipse autem Herodes cum jam annos LXX haberet, in gravissimam aegritudinem cecidit, nam febre valida, prurigine corporis, continuis tormentis, pedum inflammatione, vermescentibus testiculis, intolerabili foetore, crebro anhelitu et interruptis suspiriis torquebatur' (Cap. X, pp. 65–6). N-town may allude to these symptoms (see the notes to 196 and 272–83), and the feast scene may recall Eusebius' citation of Josephus' account of Herod's death: 'there was also an excessive desire and craving after food' (*The Ecclesiastical History of Eusebius Pamphilus*, translated by C. F. Crusé (Philadelphia, 1833), p. 36); compare Holbein's Dance of Death, in which Death comes while the king is feasting. Woolf (p. 209) notes that dramatists beginning with the author of the Benediktbeuern Christmas Play often disregarded historical chronology in making Herod die almost immediately after the Slaughter; cf. Chester 10 and the Digby *Killing of the Children*. Tomlinson

(p. 49) compares this episode with Death's killing of the King of Life in the *Pride of Life*.

20/233–45 Cf. the Benediktbeuern Christmas Play and Chester 10/434–57. A Norwich roof-boss shows devils dragging Herod's soul from his body (Anderson, p. 97 and plate 11f).

20/237–8 Cf. the *Legenda Aurea*: 'mallem esse Herodis porcus quam filius' (Cap. X, p. 65).

20/250 *whan I come I cannot spare*: cf. the *Pride of Life*, 55–6, *Everyman*, 116, and the *Dance of Death* (ed. Florence Warren, EETS os 181 (1931)), lines 9, 48, 54.

20/261 *feynt felachep in me is fownde*: cf. 25/277.

20/265 *I come sodeynly within a stownde*: cf. *Everyman*, 170, and 'Death, the Soul's Friend' in *Religious Lyrics of the Fifteenth Century*, no. 163, line 31.

20/266 *Me withstande may no castel*: cf. Lydgate's 'Death's Warning' (*Minor Poems*, II: 655), and 'Against Death Is no Defense', *Religious Lyrics of the Fifteenth Century*, no. 156, lines 27–8.

20/272–83 Death's costume is apparently that of a decaying body covered by worms; cf. 42/44. Falke (p. 54) and Thomas Ramey Watson ('N Town Death of Herod', *Explicator* 40 (1981), 3–4) say that Herod's death is modelled on Acts 12: 23, in which Herod Agrippa is struck dead by an angel and eaten by worms. Compare the description of Herod's death in the *Legenda Aurea* (in the note to 232 s.d. above).

PLAY 21

The story of Christ and the Doctors is based on Luke 2: 41–51. The play transforms that episode, in which Jesus merely listens to, questions, and answers the teachers in the temple, into a disputation inspired by New Testament apocrypha. In Pseudo-Matthew, for example, Jesus rebukes his schoolmaster for thinking himself without equal in learning. And the Arabic Infancy Gospel introduces philosophers learned in astronomy and medicine, and has Jesus display his knowledge of these and other fields, as well as scripture. N-town similarly has the doctors boast of their mastery of astronomy, medicine, and other subjects. Jesus then chastises them for the pride they take in their knowledge, and expounds central mysteries of Christianity.

The play is distinct from the textually-interrelated versions of Coventry, Chester, Towneley, and York, all of which centre on Jesus' teaching of the Decalogue. Block (p. liii) considers this perhaps the clearest illustration of N-town's independence as a cycle. A treatment of this episode that parallels the present play in several details is the 'disputison bi twene chi[l]d Jhu. & Maistres of þe lawe of Jewus' (Horstmann, *Altenglische Legenden*, pp. 212–14). Cf. also the 'Kindheit Jesu' in Horstmann, *Sammlung*, pp. 104–5.

The play is written in ababbcbc octaves, with many comparatively long lines. It generally accords with the Proclamation description.

21/1-32 Included in the list of subjects that the doctors boast they have mastered are the seven liberal arts: grammar, logic, and rhetoric (the trivium), and arithmetic, music, geometry, and astronomy (the quadrivium). Also included are higher branches of learning: medicine, philosophy, and canon and civil law. The doctors claim to be recognized experts on scripture, but they do not specifically mention theology, and it is in theological mysteries that Jesus magisterially instructs them.

21/3 Cf. Peter Dronke, *Medieval Latin and the Rise of European Love-Lyric* (Oxford, 1968), I: 181–92.

21/17 Necromancy and *calculacyon* 'astrological computation' were some-times linked, as in this line and in Lydgate's *Siege of Thebes*: 'what stood hym stede his Nigromancye, Calculacioun or astronomye' (EETS es 108 (1911), ed. Axel Erdmann, 4051–2). Jeffrey Burton Russell notes that necromancy could be associated with high magic and divination, rather than diabolism or classi-cal witchcraft (*Witchcraft in the Middle Ages* (Ithaca and London, 1972), pp. 85–6). Lynn Thorndike's *History of Magic and Experimental Science* cites late medieval instances of necromancy, including a case in 1468 when the local parliament forbade a member of the medical faculty of the neighbouring Uni-versity of Toulouse to continue his necromantic practices (New York, 1934, IV: 124).

21/19 *jematrye*: 'geometry'. *OED* cites this line under *Geometry*, but *MED* doubtfully cites is under *gēmetrī(e)*, n. 2 (b), as 'an occult art related to geomancy'.

21/22 *Caton, Gryscysme, nor Doctrynal*: The *Disticha de Moribus*, attributed to Dionysius Cato, was a collection of versified maxims and proverbs used as an elementary reader. The *Graecismus* and the *Doctrinale* were epoch-making versified textbooks of speculative grammar; the latter, according to Louis John Paetow, was still in use at the University of Toulouse in 1489 ('The Arts Course at Medieval Universities with Special Reference to Grammar and Rhetoric' (University of Pennsylvania Ph.D. thesis, 1910), p. 51).

21/33 Cf. Ecclus. 1: 1, here altered to suit the context.

21/36 'Thank earnestly that Lord (that) has sent it to you'.

21/40 'Many men like you (in respect of) your knowledge'. Alternatively, *lech* may be a form of *lach* 'catch, ensnare'.

21/41-8 Cf. 155–6. In Luke 2 and the Arabic Infancy Gospel, Jesus is twelve years old during this episode. In Pseudo-Matthew, however, he is only five when he confronts the learned schoolmaster and the Pharisees.

21/63 'Come to the understanding of such profound knowledge', or 'Attain the capacity for such profound comprehension'.

21/66 *oo God in Trynité*: cf. the Athanasian Creed: 'Fides autem catholica haec est: ut unum Deum in Trinitate . . . veneremur'.

21/81–4 Block (p. liii note 2) observes that the comparison of the Trinity to *ignis, splendor, calor* goes back to Augustine and is found in Vincent of Beauvais. Falke (pp. 55–6) cites a similar sermon in Anton E. Schönbach, *Altdeutsche Predigten* (Graz, 1888), II, no. 44. Cf. *Cursor Mundi*, 287–94, and *Piers Plowman*, C. xx. 168–76, and compare the conceit of the taper in the Digby Candlemas Play, 486–92.

21/84 Cf. the Athanasian Creed: 'Et tamen non tres omnipotentes: sed unus omnipotens'.

21/89 *þe Fadyr of Myght*: cf. the Athanasian Creed: 'omnipotens Pater'.

21/92 Cf. the Athanasian Creed: 'Neque confundentes personas: neque substantiam separantes'. Compare N-town 1/12–13 *et passim*.

21/97–100 Cf. the *Life of Our Lady*, II: 521–7, St. Idelphonsus, *Sermo XIII* (*PL*, 96: 282), the 'disputison bi twene chi[l]d Jhu. & Maistres of þe lawe of Jewus', p. 213, and N-town 36/18. Halliwell (p. 415) cites Sloan MS 3160, f. 38.

21/106 Cf. Pseudo-Matthew: 'aut certe angelus dei loquitur in eo' (Cap. XXXI, p. 102).

21/109 'Which of the three persons (of the Trinity) assumed human form'.

21/115–32 Woolf (p. 215) notes that Jesus' response is a traditional argument found, for example, in the *Summa Theologica*. Cf. Love's *Mirrour*, p. 19, the *Court of Sapience* (cited below), and N-town 11/173–6 and 28/59–60.

21/121–5 Cf. the *Court of Sapience*: 'O lady Sapyence / . . . Vouchesauf to telle . . . / Why myght, wysedom, and godenes, as ye rede, / To thre persones, whiche are in one godhede / Appropred ben . . . the Fader ful of myght, / The Sone of wyt, the Spyryte of goodnesse' (ed. E. Ruth Harvey (Toronto, Buffalo, London, 1984), p. 21).

21/129–30 'The attribute of the second person (of the Trinity) alone was involved in the temptation'.

21/135–6 Cf. Pseudo-Matthew: 'Responderunt Pharisaei: Nos nunquam audivimus talia verba ab infante alio dicta in tali infantia' (Cap. XXX, p. 99).

21/137–40 Cf. Pseudo-Matthew: 'Cum enim me putarem habere discipulum, inveni magistrum meum, ignorans eum' (Cap. XXXI, pp. 101–2); the Arabic Infancy Gospel reads similarly.

21/151–2 Cf. York 20/107–8, Towneley 18/79–80, Pseudo-Matthew, Cap. XXX, pp. 98–9, and the Athanasian Creed: 'Jesus Christus Dei Filius . . . ante secula genitus'.

21/157–64 Cf. Isidore's *Etymologiarum*: 'bis genitus dicitur sive quia Pater eum genuit sine Matre in aeternitate sive quia Mater sine Patre in tempore' (vii, vol. 2, p. 265, Migne, cited by Block, p. liii note 2). See also the Athanasian Creed: 'Aeternus Pater: aeternus Filius: aeternus et Spiritus Sanctus. . . . Deus

est ex substantia Patris ... et homo ex substantia matris, in seculo natus. ...
Aequalis Patri secundum divinitatem: minor Patre secundum humanitatem'.

21/179–84 Cf. Isa. 7: 14 and the *Life of St. Anne*, 75/2905–13.

21/211–13 Cf. Luke 2: 46.

21/216–20 Cf. Luke 2: 44–5.

21/221–4 Vriend (pp. 124–5) detects in these lines an acquaintance with the infancy legends in the apocryphal Gospel of Thomas.

21/241–56 Fry (p. 536), citing Jerome and Thomas Aquinas, argues that the 'holy deceit' of having Joseph marry Mary in order to prevent the devil from suspecting Jesus' divine birth was 'an integral part of the abuse-of-power theory of the Redemption'. Block (p. liii note 2) says that two of the reasons given here for Mary's marriage appear in Bonaventura and Comestor, while Vincent of Beauvais gives four. See David L. Wee, 'The Temptation of Christ and the Motif of Divine Duplicity in the Corpus Christi Cycle Drama', *Modern Philology*, 72 (1974), 1–16. Cf. York 12/25–30, the *Life of St. Anne*, 123–25/365–416, and Mirk's *Festial*, p. 108.

21/257–64 Cf. Luke 2: 48–9. Lydgate includes Christ's being left behind in Jerusalem as one of Mary's fifteen sorrows in 'The Fifteen Joys and Sorrows of Mary' (*Minor Poems*, I: 276).

21/273–8 Cf. Luke 2: 51.

PLAY 22

The Baptism play, based on the accounts in Matt. 3, Mark 1: 1–11, Luke 3: 1–22, and John 1: 6–34, is informed in large part by John's preaching the baptism of repentance. John's opening the play with a sermon on penance is paralleled in Continental drama, for example in Greban's *Passion*. In the English mysteries, the Baptism is dramatized in York 21 and Towneley 19.

Until Jesus' exit, this play consists of Proclamation thirteeners, which exhibit several verbal affinities to the Proclamation description. The final four stanzas, in which John further declares the necessity of penance, are long thirteeners.

Folio 112 is an interpolated leaf in the hand of Scribe C. It is unwatermarked, but from a different paperstock than is the remainder of J Quire.

22/1–53 The interpolated f. 112, like the interpolated ff. 95–6 in Play 18, was transcribed by Scribe C. Like them, it is thematically and prosodically consistent with the rest of its play. It may, therefore, record original play material; see the note to 18/221–302. Folio 112 is unrubricated, and in this codex it is the only initial leaf of a play that lacks a playnumber.

22/1 Cf. Matt. 3: 3, Mark 1: 3, Luke 3: 4, John 1: 23.

22/14–15 Cf. Matt. 3: 2 and Greban's *Passion*, 10,044 ff., in which John's opening speech is punctuated by the exhortation 'Penitenciam agite'.

22/27–35 Cf. Luke 3: 16.

22/40 Cf. John 1: 29. Unlike 1 and 14, this Latin line is extra-metrical.

22/67–72 Cf. Matt. 3: 14–15. Cf. Love's *Mirrour*, p. 87. Sister Marian Davis notes Love's influence here and elsewhere in this play ('Nicholas Love and the N-Town Cycle', Auburn Univ. Ph.D. thesis, 1979).

22/74–7 Cf. Love's *Mirrour*: 'but now doo as I bidde and baptise me / for now is tyme of mekenesse' (p. 87).

22/83 *su..tere*: Halliwell prints *sutere*, and *OED* cites this line from his edition under *suitor*, sb. 2 'adherent, follower, disciple'.

22/92 s.d.–98 Cf. Matt. 3: 16–17; also Mark 1: 10–11, Luke 3: 22.

22/100–1 Cf. Love's *Mirrour*: 'This is my byloued sone / in whom it liketh me wele; *and therfore here ȝe hym*' (p. 88, italics mine).

22/121–31 Cf. Matt. 4: 1–2, Mark 1: 12–13, Luke 4: 1–2.

22/151 Contrition, confession, and satisfaction, followed by absolution, constitute the sacrament of penance.

22/158–9 Cf. Matt. 3: 10, Luke 3: 9.

22/171–4 Cf. Matt. 3: 12, Luke 3: 17.

PLAY 23

The Temptation play is based on Matt. 4: 1–11, though the episode is also presented in Luke 4: 1–13, and Mark 1: 12–13. The biblical basis of the play is enhanced by tradition and commentary. The Parliament of Hell at the opening of the play, for example, resembles Continental analogues (Woolf, p. 220). And the Temptation itself explicitly recalls Gregory the Great's interpretation that Jesus triumphed over precisely the same sins to which Adam had succumbed: gluttony, vainglory, and covetousness.

The basal stanza of this play is the Proclamation thirteener. The first three stanzas, opening the demonic dialogue, are long thirteeners, as is Satan's speech in 144–82. 40–52 form the pattern ababababaccca.

The Proclamation answers very closely to the play in describing the demonic council, a motif that is not included in the other extant English Temptation plays.

23/1–65 Demonic dialogues of the sort presented here appear in the *Gospel of Nicodemus* and the *Deuelis Perlament*. See Olin H. Moore, 'The Infernal Council', *Modern Philology*, 16 (1918), 169–93, and Mason Hammond, '*Concilia Deorum* from Homer through Milton', *Studies in Philology*, 30 (1933), 1–16.

23/50–2 'To tempt him in the three sins that always cause man's frail nature to fall most quickly'.

23/63 *Mahound*: see the note to 18/92.

23/66–73 Cf. Matt. 4: 1–2; also, Luke 4: 1–2.

23/79–99 Cf. Matt. 4: 3–4, Luke 4: 3–4.

23/107–43 Cf. Matt. 4: 5–7; also, Luke 4: 9–12, in which this is the third temptation.

23/144–7 In Gregory the Great's influential formulation, Jesus conquered in the Temptation the same three sins in which Adam had fallen: gluttony, vainglory, and covetousness. Cf. Chester 12/169–216, York, 22/47, 93, 131, the *Meditationes*, pp. 122–3, Love's *Mirrour*, pp. 94–5; and see Morton W. Bloomfield, *The Seven Deadly Sins* (Michigan State College Press, 1952), p. 111 *et passim*; Elizabeth Marie Pope, *Paradise Regained* (Baltimore, 1947), pp. 51–5; and Donald R. Howard, *The Three Temptations* (Princeton, 1966), p. 50 and note 16.

23/153–86 Cf. Matt. 4: 8–10; also presented in Luke 4: 5–8. Greban similarly has Satan list the lands he offers Jesus during this temptation, but Satan's catalogue in the present play resembles more closely the lists of places that fear Herod in Towneley 16 and obey Mundus in the *Castle*, 170–82. It also includes several of the places named by Arystory in the *Play of the Sacrament*, 86–148. The N-town Satan conspicuously omits to declare his ownership of England, though he does claim Ireland, Scotland, and Wales. He includes as well Zabulon, Nephthalim, and Galilaea, which are mentioned in Matt. 4: 15, a few verses below the story of the Temptation; this biblical passage is echoed in the *Gospel of Nicodemus*. Zebee and Salmana are kings of Midian in Judges, 8: 5; see also Psalm 82: 12 (Vulgate). 'Archage' may be Arcadia, and is one of the countries where Jasper is king in Play 18 (see the note to 18/25–68; Gauvin, p. 163, takes 'Archas' in 172 to be a form of 'Archage'). For 'Pownteys', see *The World and the Child* (*Six Anonymous Plays*, ed. John S. Farmer (London, 1905), p. 170); cf. *Hickscorner* (Farmer, p. 137) and *Reliquiae Antiquae*, eds. Thomas Wright and James Orchard Halliwell (London, 1841), I: 271–3.

23/195 Cf. 1/81, 2/273.

23/195 s.d. Cf. Matt. 4: 11, Mark 1: 13, and Dutka, pp. 72–3.

23/215–16 Cf. 1 Cor. 10: 13.

PLAY 24

The play of the Woman Taken in Adultery extends the spare account in John 8: 3–11 by dramatizing both traditional and other amplifications of this episode. It portrays, for example, Augustine's explanation that the Pharisees and scribes brought the adulteress before Jesus in order to force him to contradict either the Mosaic law of justice or his own teaching of mercy. It depicts the extra-biblical idea that the evil figures recognized their own sins in Jesus' writing. And, unlike the account in John, the play has the woman explicitly repent and beg forgiveness, another motif developed by Augustine (see Peter Meredith, '"Nolo Mortem" and the *Ludus Coventriae* Play of the *Woman Taken in Adultery*', *Medium Aevum* 38 (1969), 42). N-town also incorporates several coarsely realistic elements, including the role of the gleefully malicious Accusator, the breaking in of the woman's door, the partially-clothed adulterer's bold escape, and the crude vilification of the adulteress.

The play is written in ababbcbc octaves. The Proclamation description agrees with the play thematically, and, to a degree, verbally. This episode is treated briefly in the York and Chester cycles.

24/1–2 Cf. Ezek. 18: 23, 32, and 33: 11. Meredith ('"Nolo Mortem"', pp. 40–3) notes that 'Nolo mortem peccatoris' is part of the weekday antiphon for the psalms at Prime during the first four weeks of Lent. The phrase has a common liturgical background with the story of the adulteress, and Meredith argues that the body of the play constitutes a sermon for which 'Nolo mortem peccatoris' is the text. Woolf (p. 395 note 33) points out that the phrase and the story had already been brought together in Ludolf's *Vita Jesu Christi.* Line 1 seems to have been omitted initially. The main scribe then wrote it at the right of the title, wrote 'gyn at Nolo morte[m]' in the top margin, and preceded line 1 with a capitulum.

24/17–24 Cf. Rosemary Woolf, *The English Religious Lyric in the Middle Ages* (Oxford, 1968), pp. 214–18.

24/89–112 Cf. *Cursor Mundi*, 13, 715–25.

24/97–100 Cf. Chester 12/294–6.

24/106–8 See the note to 12/96–7.

24/132 *or he xal me*: 'before he kills me'.

24/147 *bych clowte*: 'rag of a whore', or perhaps 'cursed rag'.

24/152 *kepe þi kutte*: (euphemistically) 'defend your virtue'. *OED* cites this line (*cut*, sb². 34) in the innocent sense 'keep one's distance, be coy or reserved'. *MED* also cites this instance, with a similar rendering (*cut*, n. (2), 2 (b)). However, Helge Kökeritz refers to this line in his discussion of the obscene meanings of *cut*, which, he notes, escaped the searching eye of Eric Partridge (*Shakespeare's Pronunciation* (New York and London, 1953; reprint 1966), p. 133). Cf. Woolf, p. 395 note 31.

24/193–208 s.d. Cf. John 8: 3–6.

24/221–56 Cf. John 8: 7–9.

24/265–80 Cf. John 8: 10–11.

24/285 A reviser has cancelled the speaker heading 'Jesus' and replaced it with 'Doctor', indicating that at some point this closing speech was assigned to an expositor.

PLAY 25

The Lazarus play faithfully follows John 11: 1–44, principally embellishing that account by developing Martha and Mary's laments and the comforters' attempted condolence. Amplifications of this kind were dramatic traditions, appearing in Hilarius' twelfth-century *Svscitacio Lazari* and in the Fleury play-book. In the present play, expressions of grief and consolation are more extended than in any other Middle English Lazarus play, and become central and unifying motifs.

The play is written in ababbcbc octaves; 377–92 and 425–48 constitute comparatively long-lined stanzas. The Proclamation description agrees with the play in general terms. This episode also appears in the York, Towneley, and Chester collections, and in the Digby *Mary Magdalen*. Woolf (p. 227) says that N-town resembles Continental analogues in its use of invention at the beginning of the play.

25/9 *Mawdelyn*: Mary of Bethany is here identified as Mary Magdalene, following an association made by Gregory the Great, and generally adopted by the Latin Church.

25/61–80 Woolf (p. 228) notes that the *consolatores*, by attempting to dissuade Lazarus from accepting the inevitability of death, contradict the advice given in the *Visitatio infirmorum* about fostering patience in the sick; see *Yorkshire Writers*, II: 449–53.

25/89–90 Cf. John 11: 3.

25/102 Cf. *Cursor Mundi*, 14,142, and Greban's *Passion*, 14,702–3.

25/115 *For who*: 'On account of woe'.

25/130 *deth is dew to every man*: cf. lines 275–6; also *Wisdom*, 876, and Whiting, D97–D101.

25/131-2 Cf. Whiting, D96.

25/134 *þe blood of kynde nature*: 'blood relatives, by their inherent nature'.

25/201-4 Cf. John 11: 4.

25/213-44 Cf. John 11: 7–16. In 241–4, as in *Cursor Mundi*, 14,218–29, Thomas expresses the wish to die with Lazarus. In York 24/144–5, by contrast, the apostle indicates his willingness to die with Jesus. Cf. John 11: 16, also Towneley 31/37–8.

25/213–16 Cf. John 11: 6, in which Jesus waits two days before going to Judea.

25/277 *Deth to no wyht can be a frende*: cf. 20/261 and Whiting, D85.

25/281-4 Cf. John 11: 20.

25/289–316 Cf. John 11: 17–27.

25/314 *þiself is sone*: 'You are his son'.

25/315 *these wordlys*: 'this world's'.

25/337-40 Cf. John 11: 28.

25/343 Cf. John 11: 29.

25/345-56 Cf. John 11: 31-2.

25/357 Cf. 'Against Death Is no Defence', *Religious Lyrics of the Fifteenth Century*, no. 156, and Whiting, D78.

25/360 Cf. John 11: 5.

25/369-84 Cf. John 11: 33-7.

25/391-400 Cf. John 11: 39-40.

25/412 s.d.-422 Cf. John 11: 41-3.

25/428 s.d.-430 Cf. John 11: 44.

PLAY 26

This play opens the first of two Passion sequences to which I refer as Passion Plays 1 and 2 (adapting titles used by Block). Passion Play 1 includes plays 26–8 and the 'Procession of Saints', and may, in an earlier state, have existed independently of the cycle. Like Passion Play 2, it differs from the bulk of the collection prosodically and in its use of sources, notably the *Northern Passion*. The Passion Plays are unique in the collection in their elaborate English stage directions, which include detailed description of costume, settings, and movement in a polyscenic theatre employing scaffolds and a playing place. The main scribe very probably copied out the Passion sequences at a different time from the rest of the codex: except for minor interpolations, his hand is more untidy and irregular in these sequences, and his orthographic and graphemic patterns are distinct from his habits in surrounding plays (see pp. xxii–xxiii and xxxiv). In addition, except for the interpolations, he recorded Passion Plays 1 and 2 on different paper stocks than he used in the remainder of the codex (see pp. xviii-xxi, 541 n. 1). The Passion Plays were evidently mounted in successive years, as indicated by Contemplacio in Play 29. Each of the Passion sequences seems intended for continuous performance, but the rubricator added play numbers to segment them into rough correspondence with the Proclamation. The agreement is inexact, however, and Passion Play 2 disagrees substantially with the Proclamation accounts. See Spector, *Genesis of the N-town Cycle*, pp. 109–13.

Play 26 comprises prologues by Satan and John the Baptist, and portrayals of the Council of the Jews, the disciples' fetching of the ass and foal, and the Entry into Jerusalem.

In his prologue, Satan recounts events that have preceded the Passion, especially those in which he has played a central part, and promises to instigate conspiracies against Christ. Woolf (p. 239) says that in this speech, and in his later actions in the Passion, the N-town Satan takes on a role so crucial as to suggest Continental influence. His sartorial display recalls homiletic denunciations of such clothing as expressions of pride. In the religious drama, costume of this sort is typically associated with devils and other sinful figures, and in the present instance, it draws attention to the thematic implications of clothing in the Passion plays.

Citing his own earlier bidding to prepare the way of the Lord and make his paths straight, John the Baptist delivers a prologue that is appropriate to the play, in which the citizens and children literally prepare the path as Jesus enters. John's sermon here is an exposition of the path to salvation, and a specific counterbalance to Satan's speech.

The depiction of the Conspiracy and the Entry conflates the accounts in the Synoptic Gospels and John. The Conspiracy appears in John 11: 47–53, as well as Matt. 26: 1–5, Mark 14: 1–2, and Luke 22: 1–2. The Entry is in John 12: 12ff., and Matt. 21: 8ff., Mark 11: 8ff., and Luke 19: 36ff. In presenting the Conspiracy before the Entry, the play follows the order in John, contradicting that of the Synoptics. The dialogue includes elements from all four Gospels, however, and the Entry is enhanced by a liturgical addition, the 'Gloria laus'. Two scenes in the play, the fetching of the beasts and the healing of the blind men, are themselves conflations of the Synoptic Gospels, and the latter scene has been moved from its proper biblical position.

Satan's prologue consists of long-lined quatrains and long-lined ababbcbc octaves, many of which are concatenated by rhyme between the final line of one stanza and the initial line of the next. Shifts between these stanzaic forms roughly correspond to thematic changes in the speech. John the Baptist's prologue is made up of five octaves, with lines somewhat less hypermetric than Satan's. The Conspiracy and Entry, with the exception of the interpolated f. 143, are constituted of quatrains and ababbcbc octaves, several of which are long-lined or hybrid forms; here too there is some concatenation by rhyme. The unrhymed lines 341–2 at the foot of f. 142ᵛ are a stanzaic fragment that no doubt resulted from the inclusion of f. 143. That interpolated leaf contains three Proclamation thirteeners, a quatrain, and the first six lines of an octave, which is completed (though with imperfect rhyme) on f. 144ʳ.

The brief Proclamation description, only four lines, mentions neither the Conspiracy nor the fetching of the animals.

The Towneley collection does not represent the Entry, and the York and Chester cycles, unlike N-town, depict the Entry before the Conspiracy.

26/1–40 Satan's account in several instances contradicts earlier plays in the cycle, especially the Temptation play (Play 23). His assertion that the third temptation was a test of vainglory, for instance, disagrees with Play 23 (see the notes to 23/144–7 and 26/32). He uses the names Lucifer and Satan in this play, though these are distinct devils in the Temptation play. He also says in line 40 that Christ has already forgiven Mary Magdalene's sins, but her exorcism is not portrayed until Play 27, where it is interpolated into the Last supper.

26/4 'Who appears among you to speak about a matter'.

26/17–20 Cf. Rev. 12: 4.

26/22 'And consider what cunning outrages I caused to be performed in heaven'.

26/23 Cf. Tutivillus' boast in the Towneley Judgment play:
> I haue brought to youre hande / of saules, dar I say,
> Mo than ten thowsand / in an howre of a day. (30/215–16)

26/28 'After he fasted forty days, in defiance of his strong physical needs (or 'physical strength') and reason'.

26/32 Howard (pp. 49–50) notes that Rabanus Maurus took the temptation on the mount to evidence vanity, while the word 'gloriam' in Matt. 4: 8 suggested vainglory, as in the present line. Gregory the Great associated this temptation with avarice; see the note to 23/144–7.

26/37 *provaylys*: cf. *provayl(e)* in 193 and 251. *MED* (*prēvailen*, v.) cites two instances of this form in a Paston letter of 1465.

26/47 'According to this ancient text, remembered in support of my meaning', or 'Let this ancient text be remembered in support of my meaning'.

26/48 *Quia in inferno nulla est redempcio*: from the Office of the Dead, attributed to Job in the York and Towneley Harrowing of Hell plays (York 37/285–8, Towneley 25/299–302) and other texts. See the *Castle*, 3096–7, and Eccles' note, which cites Job 7: 9: 'qui descenderit ad inferos, non ascendet'.

26/49–60 Fry (pp. 558–9) cites assertions by Leo the Great and Chrysostom that Satan incited the Pharisees, the scribes, and Judas. Cf. Satan's claim in the *Gospel of Nicodemus*: 'There is one of the race of the Jews, Jesus by name, who calls himself the Son of God. But he is (only) a man, and at our instigation the Jews crucified him' (*New Testament Apocrypha*, eds. Edgar Hennecke and Wilhelm Schneemelcher (Philadelphia, 1959; reprint 1963), 1: 472). The *Meditationes* and Love's *Mirrour* similarly implicate the devil. See Miriam J. Benkovitz, 'Some Notes on the "Prologue of Demon" of *Ludus Coventriae*', *Modern Language Notes*, 60 (1945), 79–80.

26/58 *in trost is treson*: cf. *Mankind*, 750, and Eccles' note; also Whiting, T492.

26/64 'Poverty shall not befall you because of (your) great prosperity'.

26/65–108 Satan's costume is similar to the sinful Galaunt's in *Mary Magdalen*, 496–505, and Pryde's in *Nature* (*The Plays of Henry Medwall*, ed. Alan H. Nelson (Cambridge and Totowa, N.J., 1980), 110/739 ff.). It also recalls Lucifer's disguise as 'a goodly galont' in *Wisdom*, 380 s.d. Cf. Superbia's advice on dress in the *Castle*, 1058–60, and Tutiuillus' description of contemporary fashions in the Towneley Judgment play (30/233 ff.); also see Tony Davenport, 'Lusty fresche galaunts', in *Aspects of Early English Drama*, ed. Paula Neuss (Cambridge, 1983), pp. 111–28. The N-town Satan's apparel also resembles that of the devils in the *Vision of Edmund Leversedge*: 'the sayd aray the going of ✓

the sayd deuyllys . . . was in shorte gownes and dowblettes, closse hosyn, longe
heere, vpon here browes, pykes on ther shon of a foot in lengh and more, hygh
bonettes. . . . j charge the put away thi dublettes stuffid with woll and bolsters,
and neuer were ne use suche stuffid dublettes fro this tyme forth. . . . kutt thi
here short and shewe thy face . . . were no high bonettes. . . . neuer vse mo
close hoose' (*Somerset & Dorset Notes & Queries*, 9 (1905), 25, 29).

Satan's dress seems to fit with a date between the mid-1460s and about the
1480s, and can tentatively be placed toward the end of that period. Long piked
shoes, having gone in and out of favour earlier, were especially fashionable
from about 1460 until about 1485. At about the same time that these shoes were
going out of style, stomachers were becoming popular for men. Thus Leversedge's *Vision*, of May 1465, includes long-piked shoes, but makes no mention
of a stomacher. Similarly, a satirical list of proud garments, dated not later
than 1467, includes 'long peked shone', but says nothing of stomachers
(Harley MS 372, in *Satirical Songs and Poems on Costume*, ed. Frederick W. Fair-
holt (London, 1849), pp. 55–7). By contrast, the sinful costumes in *Nature* and
Mary Magdalen, both of which have been dated to the 1490s, include
stomachers, but not long-piked shoes. Since N-town refers to both garments,
this speech may date from the 1470s or 1480s, when both were fashionable. See
Francis Kelly and Randolph Schwabe, *A Short History of Costume & Armour*
(New York, 1931; reprint 1968), p. 41; Dorothy Hartley, *Mediaeval Costume and
Life* (London, 1931), p. 127; Iris Brooke, *English Costume of the Later Middle Ages*
(London, 1935), p. 78; Nancy Bradfield, *Historical Costumes of England* (London,
Toronto, Wellington, Sydney, 1938; reprint 1970), pp. 59, 63; C. Willett Cun-
nington and Phillis Cunnington, *Handbook of English Mediaeval Costume*
(Boston, 1969), p. 139; and Marion Sichel, *Costume Reference 1: Roman Britain
and the Middle Ages* (Boston, 1977), p. 60. 'Huff! A Galaunt', in a manuscript of
the second half of the fifteenth century, also refers to both a stomacher and
'pykyd schone' (Rossell Hope Robbins, *Historical Poems of the XIVth and XVth
Centuries* (New York, 1959), no. 52). Robbins (p. 323) cites a papal bull of 1468
denouncing 'pykys passynge ij yenchys of lengthe'. *OED* first cites *stomacher*
as a man's garment in 1466 and 1478 (along with the present line). Slips to be
used in the *MED* entry show appearances of this word about 1474 (in the
Paston letters), in 1480, and about 1500 (Robert E. Lewis, private correspondence); Lydgate uses *stomachers* to denote a female garment in the *Fall of
Princes*. Compare Gauvin, p. 235.

26/65 'Behold the diversity of my newfangled and showy variety (in dress)'.
The sin of 'varietas vestium' was declared a sign of English decadence in a
sermon cited by Owst (*Literature and Pulpit*, pp. 406–7).

26/66–7 'Each article placed in its due and proper position, and each part
harmoniously suited in its appearance'.

26/70, 72 A fifteenth-century English nobleman would have worn long hose
laced to the lining of his doublet or surcoat by leather strings (*points*) with

ornamental metal tabs (*aglottys* or *aiglets*) through as many as a dozen pairs of eyelet holes. See Austin Lane Poole, *Medieval England* (Oxford, 1958), I: 308, and Cunnington and Cunnington, p. 108.

26/71 Criticism of wearing expensive clothes in imitation of one's betters was a common homiletic motif: see Owst, *Literature and Pulpit*, 369–70, 406, and 410, and compare the *Regement of Princes* (*Hoccleve's Works*, ed. Frederick J. Furnivall, EETS ES 72 (1897)), 435–48, 505–11.

26/73 *care not for þe payment*: cf. the *Regement of Princes*, 487–90.

26/75 Cf. Towneley 30/237 and the *Regement of Princes*, 428–31.

26/77–8 Cf. Harl. MS 372: 'your short stuffede dowblettys and your pleytid gownys', and Towneley 30/288. See Poole, I: 309, and Sichel, pp. 49 and 59. Joel Scott Branham cites sumptuary laws of 1463 and 1483 forbidding the 'stuffing of wool, cotton or caddis' in doublets by yeomen or men of lower degree ('The Hegge Cycle in Relation to the Medieval Church' (Columbia University MA thesis, 1947), pp. 81–2).

26/81 *A gowne of thre ʒerdys*: cf. *Fulgens and Lucres*:

B   And yet he puttyth in a gown communely–
     How many brode yardis, as ye gesse?
A   Mary, two or thre.
B   Nay, seven and no lesse!
     (*Plays of Henry Medwall*, 50/740–2).

26/81–2 '. . . see to it that you present yourself every day as equal to people of all social ranks surpassing yours'. Cf. the *Castle*, 1068, and *Fulgens and Lucres*, 50/754–7.

26/83 *a daggere*: cf. *Nature*, 772.

26/85–6 *syde lokkys*: cf. *Nature*: 'I love yt well to have syde here / Halfe a fote byneth myne ere' (755–6); also Towneley 30/243.

26/87 *An hey smal bonet*: cf. Harl. MS 372, 'your hygh cappis witlesse'; Leversedge's *Vision*; and *Nature*, 747–8.

26/95 Oaths were often by Christ's body and were said to dismember him. Cf. the *Parson's Tale*, 590, and the *Pardoner's Tale*, 472–5.

26/100 *hem*: i.e. 'men'.

26/109–15 *newe names*: Satan supplies euphemisms for six of the seven Deadly Sins, omitting sloth. Cf. Bernard Spivack, *Shakespeare and the Allegory of Evil* (New York and London, 1958), pp. 155–61, and Glynne Wickham, *Early English Stages* (London, Henley, New York, 1981), 3: 100–9.

26/111 *kalle pride onesté*: the devil's daughter Pride 'is callyd "Honestye"' and 'A prowde man is callyd an honest man' in a sermon cited by Owst (*Literature and Pulpit*, pp. 96, 314). In *Mary Magdalene*, 550, Pride is called Curiosity.

26/113 *Wreth, 'manhod'*: cf. Lewis Wager's *Marie Magdalene*: 'Wrathe putteth on the coate of manlynesse' (ed. Frederic Ives Carpenter (Chicago, 1902), p. 7).

Cf. *Hickscorner*, p. 145, and 'The Bel-man of London' (*Non-Dramatic Works of Thomas Dekker*, ed. Alexander B. Grosart (London, 1885), III: 116).

26/115 *let abstynawnce beyn absent*: cf. the *Parson's Tale*, 831: 'Agayns Glotenye is the remedie abstinence, as seith Galien'.

26/123 Cf. John 14: 18. Like much of Satan's speech, this line parodies pleas and assurances traditionally attributed to Jesus.

26/125–64 Prosser (pp. 122–3) argues that John's sermon directly responds to Satan's prologue, and is illustrated by actions in subsequent plays. John's references to 'enherytawns' of heaven, trust, avoidance of sensual sin, etc., specifically recall and rebut Satan's speech.

26/126–8 Cf. Mark 1: 7, Luke 3: 16; also N-town 22/31–2.

26/130 *þe mortall dedys sevyn*: pride, envy, wrath, covetousness, gluttony, sloth, and lechery.

26/131 Cf. Matt. 3: 2.

26/133–5 Cf. Matt. 3: 3, Mark 1: 3, Luke 3: 4; also John 1: 23.

26/164 s.d. *Annas*: cf. Luke 3: 2, John 18: 13ff., Acts 4: 6. Anderson (p. 162) notes that medieval stained glass shows high priests vested as bishops, and that the windows at Malvern have a high priest wearing the archaic form of closed mitre. The Holkham Bible Picture Book (f. 30) also shows the leaders of the Jews wearing mitres. Iris Brooke finds dress like that in the present stage direction illustrated in the Valenciennes MS (*Medieval Theatre Costume* (London, 1967), pp. 79–80). Lynn Squires observes that the two doctors with Annas wear the traditional dress of fifteenth-century lay and ecclesiastical judges, and that the striped robes of Rewfyn and Leyon identify them as sergeants-at-law ('Law and Disorder', p. 279).

26/183–4 Cf. John 11: 48.

26/191 'If any proven failing is reported about you. . . .'

26/194 *Rewfyn and Leyon*: L. W. Cushman notes that these names appear in lists of German dramatic devils, and asserts, without warrant, that these figures are devils in the present play (*The Devil and the Vice* (London, 1900; reprint New York, 1970), pp. 18, 26). See Gauvin, p. 171 note 3.

26/196 *ȝoure cosyn Cayphas*: Annas is Caiaphas's father-in-law in John 18: 13. Cf. Matt. 26: 3 and John 11: 49.

26/295 *and sythe present*: 'and then claims'.

26/311 *Bothe in word and in werke*: Prosser (p. 126) observes that these words ironically echo the act of contrition.

26/333–4 Cf. Matt. 26: 5 and Mark 14: 2.

26/343–91 The interpolated f. 143 appears to have been written at a different time from the rest of Passion Play 1. Though unwatermarked, it resembles the YHS in a Sun paper that precedes and follows the Passion Play sequences. And the main scribe's hand here is tidier and more regular than it is in the bulk of Passion Play 1. Block (p. xiii) observes that this interpolation resulted in duplication of the passage beginning 'Frendys, beholde' on f. 143ʳ as well as f. 145ᵛ, and in Peter and John's both remaining and also advancing toward Jerusalem.

26/343–6 Cf. John 12: 31.

26/347–85 This presentation of the fetching of the beasts conflates the accounts in Matt. 21: 1–7, Mark 11: 1–7, and Luke 19: 29–35. Cf. John 12: 14.

26/362–3 The *Meditationes* and Love's *Mirrour* include the extra-biblical idea that the ass and colt were designated to serve the poor. Cf. York 25/57.

26/386–417 Woolf (p. 396 note 50) cites a similar allegorical exposition of healing the man born blind in the *Vita Jesu Christi*.

26/401 'And therefore I should call you spiritually deaf'.

26/426–8 Cf. Zech. 9: 9.

26/439 'I wouldn't have us be late for anything' (Bevington, p. 495).

26/443 *hefly*: MED cites this form under *hevenlī*, adj., as a possible error, but accepts *heveliche*. OED lists *hefly* under *heavenly*, a. The form occurs again in 32/215.

26/447 'To do that which would reverence him'.

26/448–9 s.d. Cf. Matt. 21: 8, Mark 11: 8; also Luke 19: 36.

26/450–1 Cf. Matt. 21: 9, Mark 11: 10 (Vulgate), Luke 19: 38, John 12: 13.

26/453 s.d. *Gloria laus*: Dutka (pp. 68–9) observes that by including this Palm Sunday hymn, the play attempts to reproduce the Palm Sunday procession. She notes that this hymn also appears in the Passion Play in the Carmina Burana manuscript. *Cursor Mundi*, 15,033 ff., also includes the hymn in the Entry into Jerusalem.

26/458–61 These lines repeat 343–6 with only minor change, and stand here as the first four lines of an octave; see Prosser, p. 127.

26/470–85 This scene conflates and relocates in time and space the accounts in Matt. 20: 29–34, Mark 10: 46–52, and Luke 18: 35–43. In each of these Gospel accounts, this story is set near Jericho prior to Jesus' entry into Jerusalem. Cf. York 25/321 ff. Daniel P. Poteet II argues that such alterations of chronology in Passion Play 1 emphasize the contrastive relationship between existing time and theoretical eternity, which he considers the subject of this sequence of plays ('Time, Eternity, and Dramatic Form in *Ludus Coventriae* "Passion Play I"', in *The Drama of the Middle Ages*, p. 235.

26/470, 474 Cf. Matt. 20: 31.

26/478 Cf. Mark 10: 52, Luke 18: 42.

PLAY 27

This play harmonizes and telescopes events, conflates characters, and imports Old Testament Passover laws and Christian commentary to produce the most elaborately detailed and reconstituted portrayal of the Last Supper in the Middle English drama. In a drastic and unusual conflation, the Passover supper is identified with the earlier meal with Simon the leper in Bethany. Mary of Bethany, who anoints Jesus at that meal, appears here as Mary Magdalene, and events are further compressed when Jesus exorcises seven devils from her. Judas' betrayal of Jesus, which in Matthew and Mark occurs after the anointing at Bethany, is also depicted in the Last Supper play. Chester 14 similarly portrays the exorcism in the same scene with Magdalene's anointing of Jesus' feet, though Chester places the anointing in its traditional position, prior to the Passover.

The plan to set the Last Supper in the house of Simon the leper is apparent early in the play (36 s.d.), but Magdalene's appearance was an addition, in the interpolated O quire. Jesus' prediction that he will be betrayed, and the disciples' responses (205 ff.), were also interpolated in O quire. As a result, the play includes two versions of this episode, which are to a large extent complementary. Woolf (p. 397 note 55) observes that such a double prediction of Judas' treason commonly resulted from harmonization of the Gospels, and was often dramatized on the Continent. It appears in *Cursor Mundi* and the *Pepysian Gospel Harmony*, but its occurrence in N-town is unique in the English drama.

The Last Supper is described in Matt. 26: 17–29, Mark 14: 12–25, Luke 22: 7–23, 31–4, and John 13: 1–38, though the meal itself is celebrated in the play in accordance with the Passover laws in Exodus 12. Paraphrasing and echoing commentary on those laws, Jesus expounds their significance in terms of the new law. Much of the play contains close verbal resemblances to the *Northern Passion*.

The bulk of the play is written in short-lined ababbcbc octaves and quatrains. The interpolated f. 149 contains four Proclamation thirteeners, a tail-rhyme stanza, and a quatrain. Folios 150–1, also interpolated, consist of long-lined octaves. Folios 154–5 are mainly constituted of long-lined quatrains, though lines 365–80 are octaves and lines 449–52 and 462–5 form couplets; 490–1 also make up a couplet.

The Proclamation description is brief, but its declaration that the Supper shall be played 'with wordys fewe' (315) does not apply to the play as we have it.

27/1–16 Cf. Matt. 23: 37–9, 24: 15–22; Luke 13: 34–5, 19: 43–4, 21: 20–4; and Chester 14/209–24.

27/13 'The time is coming when Jerusalem shall suffer woe'. *hes woo*: 'its woe' or 'the woe of God'.

27/17–24 Cf. Matt. 26: 17, Mark 14: 12, Luke 22: 7–9.

27/25–32 Cf. Matt. 26: 18, Mark 14: 13–15, Luke 22: 10–12, and compare the *Northern Passion*:

> Go he seyde. 3e schul mete
> A man wyth watyr in þe strete. . . .
> þe lorde of þe house. 3e xul fynde
> A symple man. of symple kynde. (Camb. Ii. 4. 9/181–2, 185–6)

Syon: cf. the *Meditationes*: 'at the command of the Lord Jesus, Peter and John went to the house of a very dear friend on Mount Sion, where there was a large dining room arranged and set for the Pasch' (p. 310; Love's *Mirrour* is similar).

27/36 s.d. *Symon leprows*: in Matt. 26: 6–13 and Mark 14: 3–9, the woman anoints Jesus' head at the house of Simon the leper in Bethany; cf. John 12: 1–8. In Mark and John, this occurs at a meal, but all these accounts place this event prior to Passover. Foster notes that Simon the leper also hosts the Last Supper in Robert de Boron's *Roman du Saint-Graal* (*Northern Passion*, II: 180–1); cf. Achille Jubinal, *Mystère Inedits* (Paris, 1837), II: 167 ff.

27/37–8, 41 Cf. the *Northern Passion*:

> To hym 3e schul speke And seye
> þat I com sone in the weye
> I wyll me restyn in hys halle
> I And my dyscyples alle. (Camb. Ii. 4. 9/187–90)

27/53 *þis path is calsydon*: Block, citing Bede's *On the Apocalypse* and the *Court of Sapience*, refers to the hardness of chalcedony, and to the association of this stone with those who show forth the light within them when called upon to give public display of their faith. Other extraordinary qualities were also attributed to chalcedony: see *English Mediaeval Lapidaries*, ed. Joan Evans and Mary S. Serjeantson, EETS os 190 (1933), pp. 29–30, 49, 75; Joan Evans, *Magical Jewels of the Middle Ages and the Renaissance* (Oxford, 1922), pp. 24, 35; also Paul Studer and Joan Evans, *Anglo-Norman Lapidaries* (Paris, 1924). Meredith's proposed emendation of *calcydon* to *cald Syon* ('A Reconsideration', p. 41) is very plausible.

27/81–7 Cf. John 11: 48.

27/86 'Lead the people according to their own wishes'.

27/90–2 Cf. John 11: 50.

27/101 Gamalyel, who has not previously been referred to by name, is presumably one of the priests mentioned in 76 s.d. A Gamaliel is listed in the *Gospel of Nicodemus* among the delegation of Jews who come to Pilate to accuse Jesus.

27/141–268 O quire (ff. 149–51) is an interpolation. It consists of different paper from that of the surrounding quires, and its scribal characteristics suggest that it was written at a different time from the bulk of the Passion sequence, though still by the main scribe. The play seems to have originally had Judas appear after line 140, deliver his speech (now 269ff.), and go directly to make his bargain with Annas, Cayphas, *et al.* Folios 150–1, containing Jesus' accusation and the disciples' responses, were then interpolated. The stage direction and speaker heading on f. 148ᵛ, calling for Judas' speech, were cancelled, and the appropriate speaker heading and catchword added. Folio 149, depicting the scene with Magdalene, was then included, requiring the further alteration of the speaker heading and catchword to their present form (see Swenson, pp. 54–5, and Greg, p. 115). Folio 151ʳ is a short page and f. 151ᵛ is blank, suggesting that these leaves are not physical survivals of a complete play, but rather were copied out for purposes of interpolation here. The fact that the stage direction on f. 151ʳ refers to Judas' speech on f. 152ʳ, the first leaf of P quire, confirms this. The stage direction at the foot of f. 149ᵛ may have been written with ff. 150–1 in mind, suggesting that f. 149 too may have been transcribed at the time of its inclusion in the play. Three distinctive stains in the shape of elongated triangles appear on f. 151ᵛ. There is no matching stain on the facing page (though a similar stain does appear on the flyleaf of Passion Play 2), indicating that the leaves constituting O quire were once stored separately.

27/141–92 The woman who anoints Jesus' head in Matt. 26: 6–7 and Mark 14: 3 is unnamed. In John 11: 1–2 and 12: 1–3, she is Mary of Bethany, who was commonly identified with Magdalene (see the note to 25/9). The play follows the account in John by having Mary anoint Jesus' feet, and conflates this episode with the exorcism of Magdalene, which is alluded to in Luke 8: 2 and Mark 16: 9.

27/167–83 Cf. Chester 14/133–6.

27/182–3 Prosser (p. 133) notes that these lines echo the act of contrition.

27/193–200 John 12: 4–5 has Judas complain about the anointing. Judas' speech in the play most closely agrees with Mark 14: 4–5 (which does not name Judas as the speaker); cf. Matt. 26: 8–9, and compare lines 193–4 with the *Northern Passion*:

>   Me thynke he sayse þou duse full ill
>   þat lattys þis oygnement þus spyll. (Camb. Gg. 5. 31/127–8).

27/201–4 Cf. Matt. 26: 10–12, Mark 14: 6–8, John 12: 7–8, and compare line 202 with the *Northern Passion*: 'agaynes this womane ȝe hafe wrange' (Add./ 140).

27/204 s.d. The last three words, 'gohth here outh', have been crossed through in black and red ink. Prosser (p. 134) concludes that Magdalene remains on stage throughout the Last Supper and accompanies Jesus to Gethsemane, inferences that Woolf (p. 396 note 53) rejects. See the note to 28/148 s.d.–192.

27/213-20 Cf. John 13: 23-5.

27/235 'He who intends to carry out this deed against him (i.e. Jesus). . . .'

27/253-6 Thaddaeus, the eleventh apostle in Matt. 10: 3 and Mark 3: 18, corresponds to Jude in the lists in Luke 6: 16 and Acts 1: 13. The N-town Procession of Saints, line 30, gives the name Judas (i.e. Jude).

27/257 'He (who) will perform this betrayal is eating in my dish'. Cf. Matt. 26: 23, Mark 14: 20.

27/258-60 Cf. Matt. 26: 24, Mark 14: 21; also Luke 22: 22.

27/264-5 Cf. Matt. 26: 25

27/269ff. Prosser (p. 136) says that the *Northern Passion*, which has Judas slip
X out of the dinner at Bethany to make his bargain and then sneak back in, probably provided the model for Judãs' movements in N-town.

27/270-2 Cf. the *Northern Passion*:
> To þe iewes I xal þe sellyn
> Al thy maystrye for to fellyn. (Camb. Ii. 4. 9/149-50).

27/304 *mony makyth schapman*: cf. Whiting, M629.

27/305 Cf. Matt. 26: 15.

27/317-23 Cf. the *Northern Passion*:
> the iewes spake hem by twen
> To the traytoure Iudas so kene
> where by schul we thy lorde knowe
> Summe of vs hym neuyr sawe. (Camb. Ii. 4. 9/519-22)

Compare Towneley 20/588-90, Chester 14/409-10, the Cornish *Passio Domini Nostri*, 965-70, and York 26/253-4.

27/326-8 Cf. the *Northern Passion*:
> Iudas seyde 3e thar noughte mysse
> Takyth hym that I schal kysse. (Camb. Ii. 4. 9/523-4)

27/342-4 Cf. John 18: 3. *Cressetys* 'oil lamps': Robert R. Edwards notes that oil lamps are employed in the arrest of Jesus as early as the twelfth-century
X Montecassino Passion, and proposes that their inclusion may reflect the influence of the visual arts ('Iconography and the Montecassino Passion', *Comparative Drama* 6 (1972), 282).

27/349ff. The foods and accoutrements of the Last Supper are taken from the commands regarding the first Passover feast, in Exod. 12. Jesus follows the order of Exod. 12: 8-11 when he says in 353-60 that the lamb is eaten ✓ with unleavened bread and bitter herbs, the head with the feet, and that the participants have their loins girded and are wearing shoes, carrying staves, and eating in haste. The idea that the participants stand while eating is not biblical, but does appear in the *Meditationes*, which provides a model for the introduction of the Passover laws into the play. Love's *Mirrour* also alludes to standing and carrying staves at the Last Supper, as does the *Meditations on* *the Supper of Our Lord.* Jesus' 'gostly interpretacyon' of the Passover laws in 393ff. agrees very closely with Rabanus Maurus' exegesis in *Commentariorum in Exodum, Lib. I* (*P.L.* 108: 48–52). Woolf (p. 234) notes that this scene must have resembled the somewhat unusual iconograpy of Fra Angelico's fresco of the Last Supper in the Convent of San Marco, which represents a liturgical act of communion rather than a historical Last Supper. See Theresa Coletti, 'Sacra- ⌐ ment and Sacrifice in the N-Town Passion', *Mediaevalia* 7 (1984), 239–64.

27/365-8 Cf. Luke 22: 15–16.

27/369-465 s.d. This second scene of accusation and denial may be an inter- polation. The gathering in which it is depicted, Q quire, contains only two leaves, typically a sign of textual alteration in this codex. In addition, this quire lacks a catchword, and the material it contains is metrically distinct from the remainder of the play. For further discussion of this point, see my 'Symmetry in Watermark Sequences', *Studies in Bibliography* 31 (1978), 174.

27/369 'And just as the paschal lamb (that) we have eaten. . . .'

27/375-6 Cf. the Athanasian Creed: 'Aequalis Patri secundum diuinitatem: minor Patri secundum humanitatem'.

27/389-92 Cf. John 1: 29, Exod. 12: 5.

27/396 *replye*: *OED* and *MED* offer no appropriate gloss. Block renders the word here and in 41/173 as 'apply'.

27/397-400 Cf. Rabanus: '*Et azymos panes cum lactucis agrestibus.* Panes quippe sine fermento comedit, qui recta opera sine corruptione vanae gloriae exercet; qui mandata misericordiae sine admixtione peccati exhibit' (*PL* 108: 50). The *byttyr bred* in 397, representing bitterness, hatred, and envy, stands in the place of 'leavened bread', and is contrasted with the *suete* or 'unleavened' bread of love and charity. Cf. the *Speculum Christiani*, which contrasts the 'soure' or leavened dough of sin to the 'swete brede' of good deeds (ed. Gustaf Holm- stedt, EETS os 182 (1933), 182/6–10), and see Matt. 16: 6, 12, Mark 8: 15, and Luke 12: 1.

27/405-8 Cf. Rabanus: 'Caput ergo agni vorare, est divinitatem illius fide percipere. Pedes vero agni vorare, est vestigia humanitatis ejus amando et imitando perquirere' (108/51). Compare Bede: 'In capite, divinitatis signum; in pedibus, humanitatis' (*In Pentateuchum Commentarii-Exodus*, *PL* 91: 306).

27/417-20 Cf. Rabanus, *PL* 108: 51–2.

27/421-4 Cf. Rabanus: *Calceamenta habebitis in pedibus.* Quid sunt etenim pedes nostri nisi opera? Quid vero calceamenta nisi pelles mortuorum animalium? Calceamenta autem pedes muniunt. Quae vero sunt mortua animalia ex quorum pellibus nostri muniantur pedes, nisi antiqui Patres qui nos ad aeternam patriam praecesserunt, quorum dum exempla conspicimus, nostri operis pedes munimus? Calceamenta ergo in pedibus habere est mortu- orum vitam conspicere, et nostra vestigia a peccati vulnere custodire (108: 52).

27/429–36 Cf. Rabanus: '*Et comedetis festinantes.* Notandum vero quod dicitur *festinantes*, nos admonere quo mandata Dei, mysteria Redemptoris, coelestis Patris gaudia cum festinatione cognoscamus, et praecepta vitae cum festinatione implere curemus. Quia enim adhuc hodie licet bene agere scimus, utrum cras liceat, ignoramus (108: 52).

27/448 s.d.–449 Cf. Matt. 26: 26, Mark 14: 22, Luke 22: 19.

27/457–8 Cf. Luke 22: 21.

27/459–60 Cf. Matt. 26: 24, Mark 14: 21.

27/460 s.d.–461 The disciples' denials are extra-biblical. Cf. the *Northern Passion*, which says of the disciples,

> ffyrst they lokyd Amonges hem Alle
> Of whom the treson myghte be falle
> Alle they settyn vp A crye
> And seyde lorde was it oughte I. (Camb. Ii. 4. 9/254–8)

27/462–3 Cf. Matt. 26: 25.

27/465 Cf. John 13: 27.

27/465 s.d.–477 Cf. John 13: 27, 30. Patrick J. Collins notes the iconographic ✓ tradition of associating Judas with Satan (*The N-town Plays and Medieval Picture Cycles* (Kalamazoo, 1979), p. 13), and Anderson (p. 214) points out that the Drayton Alabaster shows a demon in the foreground of the Betrayal scene.

27/478–9 Cf. John 13: 31.

27/482–9 Cf. 1 Cor. 11: 25, Matt. 26: 27–8, Mark 14: 23–4, Luke 22: 20; also the *Northern Passion*, 225–36.

27/497 Cf. John 21: 15–17.

27/511 s.d. Cf. John 13: 1–5.

27/516–27 Cf. John 13: 6–9 and the *Northern Passion*:

> 'It fals noght maister vnto me
> Slike seruise forto tak of þe.'
> þan said ihesus: 'bot I do þis,
> þou gettes no part with me in blis.'
> þan said peter and oþer ma:
> 'þat blis, lord, lat vs noght forga,
> Wasche heuid and hend lord pray we þe. . . .' (Harl./339–45)

27/528 *þis wasshyng xal now prevayll*: the washing of feet was an act of charity and humility (cf. 1 Tim. 5: 10), and was performed as a rite on Holy Thursday (the Mandatum).

27/529–39 Cf. John 13: 13–14; also the *Northern Passion*:

> So schul ʒe don echon to othere
> As eche of ʒou were otherys brothere
> Gode exsample I haue ʒou ʒeuyn
> To be mylde of herte whyle ʒe leuyn

I xal ȝou qwyte welle ȝowre mede
In heuene. . . . (Camb. Ii. 4. 9/363–8)
Compare *Cursor Mundi*, 15,329–33.

27/540–2 Cf. the *Northern Passion*:
the tyme is comen þat I xal fulfylle
þe prophecye for alle mannys sake
Spekyth of deth þat I xal take
And ȝe schul ben to day for drede. . . . (Camb. Ii. 4. 9/374–7)

27/548–55 Cf. Matt. 26: 31–2; also Mark 14: 27–8. Compare the *Northern Passion*:
þare of sall ȝhe be all adrede
When I sall fore ȝow be ledde
ffull fast sall ȝhe fro me flee
And some of ȝhow forsake mee. . . .
for I sall dy and breke þe lay
And ryse apon þe thyrd day
þan sall ȝhe me seke and see
In þe land of galyle. (Camb. Gg. 5. 31/377–80, 389–92)

27/556–9 Cf. Matt. 26: 33, Mark 14: 29, Luke 22: 33, John 13: 37.

27/560–1 'Take care not to say more than you know with respect to that promise'.

27/562–3 Cf. Mark 14: 30.

27/564–8 Cf. the *Northern Passion*:
Ryse ȝe vp And folowe me
ffor here wyl I no lengere be
To A toun they toke the weye
þat men clepyn bethayne. (Camb. Ii. 4. 9/423–6)

PLAY 28

The Betrayal play harmonizes and embellishes the accounts in Matt. 26: 36–55, Mark 14: 32–49, Luke 22: 39–53, and John 18: 1–12. It contains several echoes of the *Northern Passion*, and Mary's lament at the conclusion of the play is influenced by the *Meditationes*. Woolf (p. 253) says that in giving names to the usually anonymous figures who arrest Jesus, N-town agrees with the practice in Continental drama.

The play is written in short-lined octaves and quatrains until Magdalene's speech and Mary's lament, which consist of long-lined octaves and quatrains.

The Proclamation mentions the disciples' flight in the same pageant as the arrest of Jesus. Their fleeing is not referred to in the play, though it may well have been depicted.

28/8 *Mannys sowle, my spovse*: the bride of the Song of Songs was interpreted by Gregory of Nyssa, Bernard of Clairvaux, and others to be the soul. Cf. *Medieval English Lyrics* (ed. Davies), no. 45/95–8, and the *Meditations on the Life and Passion of Christ* (ed. Charlotte D'Evelyn, EETS os 158 (1921)), p. 44.

28/9 *þe oyle of mercy*: in the pseudepigraphic *Life of Adam and Eve*, Seth journeys to Paradise in quest of the oil of mercy, and the archangel Michael tells him that the oil will be made available to man only in the last days. In the *Gospel of Nicodemus*, Seth says that Michael told him that the Son of God will anoint with the oil of mercy all those who believe in him. Cf. the 'Life of Adam and Eve' (*Wheatley Manuscript*), pp. 92–5; the 'Canticum de Creatione' (Horstmann, *Sammlung*), pp. 132–3; *Legends of the Holy Rood*, ed. Richard Morris, EETS os 46 (1871), pp. 66–8; *Cursor Mundi*, 1237ff.; the *Northern Passion*, p. 146; *Wisdom*, 321.

28/16 s.d.–24 Cf. Mark 14: 32–4; also Matt. 26: 36–8. Compare the *Northern Passion*:

> Here ȝe schuln me A byde
> þe qwylys I go here be syde
> þere I haue sum dele to seyne
> whan I haue don I com A geyne. . . .
> My flessche it is al in quakynge. (Camb. Ii. 4. 9/429–32, 442)

28/24 s.d. Cf. Luke 22: 41.

28/25–32 Cf. Matt. 26: 39, Mark 14: 36, Luke 22: 42, and compare Towneley 20/520–1:

> Dere fader, thou here my wyll!
> this passyon thou put fro me away.

28/29–31 Cf. the *Northern Passion*:

> But if it byhoueth Al wey so
> I Am redy al thy wylle to do. (Camb. Ii. 4. 9/451–2)

28/32 s.d.–36 Cf. Matt. 26: 40, Mark 14: 37; also Luke 22: 45–6.

28/36 s.d.–38 Cf. the *Northern Passion*:

> On knees he fel doun wepynge
> for hys tyme was ny comynge
> he bade hys fader in trynite
> þat he myghte the peyne flee (Camb. Ii. 4. 9/479–82)

28/41–2, 52 Cf. Luke 22: 44; also John 19: 34 and York 28/50.

28/44 s.d. Cf. Matt. 26: 43; also Mark 14: 40.

28/45–6 Cf. the *Northern Passion*:

> þe thredde tyme Aȝen he ȝede
> hys Arende fully for to spede. (Camb. Ii. 4. 9/487–8)

28/52 s.d.–64 s.d. Cf. Luke 22: 43; also the *Meditationes*, p. 323, Love's *Mirrour*, 222–3, and York 28/113–22. Woolf (pp. 236, 397 note 62) says that

the angel's appearing with a chalice and the Host accords with late iconographic representations of this scene, and cites Marie Bartmuss, *Die Entwick-
lung der Gethsemane-Darstellung bis um 1400* (Halle, 1935).

28/57–8 Cf. Play 11 and Contemplacio's reference to the 'Parlement of
Hefne' in 9/307.

28/59–60 For the reasons underlying the Son's special redemptive role, see
11/173–6 and the note, and 21/115–32 and the note.

28/62 '(That) for man's sin. . . .'

28/65–8 Cf. Matt. 26: 39, Mark 14: 36, Luke 22: 42.

28/68 s.d.–76 Cf. Matt. 26: 45–6, Mark 14: 41–2.

28/71–2 Downing (p. 176) notes that Judas is not mentioned by name at this
point in the Gospels, but is named in a responsory sung on the Wednesday of
Holy Week or on Holy Thursday. Jesus also mentions Judas' name in this
context in the *Northern Passion*, Love's *Mirrour*, and Towneley 20/652–5.

28/73–6 Cf. the *Northern Passion*:
> Ryse vppe all for my sake
> I se þaime come þat wyll me take. (Camb. Gg. 5. 31/501–2)

28/77–80 Cf. the *Northern Passion*:
> whane þou seest that I am take
> And A monge Alle my frendys for sake
> Counforth þou thyn breþeren Alle. (Camb. Ii. 4. 9/325–7)

Compare *Cursor Mundi*, 15,527–8.

28/80 s.d. Cf. Matt. 26: 47, Mark 14: 43, John 18: 3; also Luke 22: 47. Compare the *Northern Passion*:
> Iudas come þane with gret rowte
> To by sett Ihesu al abowte
> with swerdis glayues maces gude. . . .
> In lanterns þay broghtene lyghte. (Add./513–15, 517)

28/82 Cf. the *Northern Passion*: 'for here wyl I 30u nought flee' (Camb. Ii. 4.
9/542).

28/84–100 Cf. John 18: 4–8.

28/86 'A traitor (who) is. . . .'

28/93 Cf. the *Northern Passion*: 'whom seke 3e fast haue 3e gone' (Camb. Ii. 4.
9/537).

28/101–4 s.d. Cf. Matt. 26: 49, Mark 14: 45–6. Compare the *Northern Passion*:
> Welcom Maystyr Iudas gan calle
> þe iewes comen Abovte hym alle
> þey leyden hondes vp on hys clothys
> And sworen hys deth wyth gret othes. (Camb. Ii. 4. 9/547–50)

28/104 s.d. Kolve (p. 197) observes that N-town is unlike the other cycles in that it contains relatively little new dialogue for the *tortores*, and also in its comparing the tormentors to madmen here and in 28/143.

28/105–6 s.d. Cf. Luke 22: 50–1, Matt. 26: 51, Mark 14: 47, John 18: 10. Compare the *Northern Passion*:

> Ihesu . . . tok þe ere þat was of schorn
> and sette it on aȝen al bledande
> & blissid it wiþ his holy hande. (Camb. Dd. 1. 1/583–6)

Edward Wilson, citing *'tys* in 106 s.d., proposes that this form may have arisen in Norfolk, and in Middle English may be regarded as characteristic of Norfolk dialect ('The Earliest 'Tis = "It Is"', *Notes and Queries* (April, 1974), 127–8).

28/107–8 Cf. Matt. 26: 52, and compare Towneley 20/698–9 and the *Southern Passion* (ed. Beatrice Daw Brown, EETS os 169 (1927), 42/1162).

28/111–12 Cf. 27/260 and the note, and compare the *Northern Passion*:

> Body and saule alle was for lorne
> allas þat euir was he borne. (Add./863–4)

28/116 Cf. John 18: 12.

28/117–20 Cf. the *Meditations on the Supper of Our Lord*:

> Thou seyst þat þou art goddes sone,
> Helpe þy self ȝyf þou kone. (437–8)

28/121–2 Cf. Matt. 26: 57, Mark 14: 53, Luke 22: 54.

28/133–42 Cf. Matt. 26: 55, Mark 14: 48–9, Luke 22: 52–3, and Towneley 20/702–5, and compare the *Northern Passion*:

> Ihesu sayde ȝe bynde me here
> Righte als I were a thefes fere
> with me ȝe done alle vnryghte
> thus to fare with me one nyghte. (Add./591–4)

28/148 s.d.–192 George C. Taylor says that in no other English verse *planctus* is Mary introduced speaking at this point in the narrative ('The English "Planctus Mariae"', *Modern Philology* 4 (1907), 624). Brother Cornelius Luke (p. 102) proposes that her lament is misplaced here, but Woolf (p. 263) notes that the French cycles also locate Mary's sorrow early in the Passion. Woolf (p. 403 note 56) adds that, in the tradition of the *Meditationes*, it is normally St John, not Magdalene, who brings the Virgin the news of Jesus' capture. Vriend (pp. 126–7) points out that this is St John's role in the *Acta Pilati*, Lydgate's 'Fifteen Joys and Sorrows of Mary', Love's *Mirrour*, and the York and Towneley plays. Graef (I: 261) observes, however, that in the *Vita Beatae Virginis et Salvatoris Rhythmica*, Magdalene tells Mary that Jesus has been scourged. And Hermann Thien cites Magdalene's similar role in the 'Prosacompassio' and the 'Devozione del Giovedi e' del Venerdi santo' ('Über die englischen Marienklagen' (Kiel. Ph.D. thesis, 1906), p. 54).

28/161–4 Cf. Towneley 23/399.

28/174 'þe swerd of sorwe' refers back to Simeon's prophecy in Luke 2: 35 (see N-town 19/87–90 and York 36/159).

28/177–8 Cf. Towneley 23/435–40. Thien (p. 54) cites the 'Prosacompassio': 'A, holy fader, where be þi trewe behestis? why woldist thou ordeyn me to be a moder. . . .'

28/179 Cf. 15/100 and the note.

28/181–6 Cf. the *Meditationes*: 'Eternal Father, is my Son Jesus to die? He has done no evil. But, just Father, if you wish the redemption of mankind, I implore you to effect it in another way' (p. 327). Love's *Mirrour* and the *Meditations on the Supper of Our Lord* read similarly.

THE PROCESSION OF SAINTS

This procession presents eleven apostles, in agreement with the list in Acts 1: 13. It appropriately omits Matthias, who has not yet been selected to complement the Twelve, but includes John the Baptist and Paul, resulting in thirteen figures.

The procession is transcribed on f. 163, the last leaf of the final quire in Passion Play 1. In this regard it recalls the Corpus Christi tableaux, which 'all to a greater or lesser extent have a concluding section made up of apostles, saints, doctors of the church' (Woolf, p. 75). Bevington (p. 520) conjectures that the procession may be incomplete, but the fact that the number of saints, thirteen, is the same as the number of prophets and kings in Play 7, suggests a symmetry that may argue against this conclusion.

The procession comprises ten quatrains.

PS 15–16 Cf. John 1: 35–42, Matt. 4: 18–20, Mark 1: 16–18.

PS 21–2 Philip the deacon, also known as Philip the evangelist, preached in Samaria. On the road from Jerusalem to Gaza, he converted the eunuch of the Ethiopian queen, Candace (Acts 6: 5; 8: 5–13, 26–39; 21: 8). This Philip is evidently conflated here with Philip the apostle.

PS 23–4 James the son of Alpheus, one of the twelve apostles, was traditionally identified with James the son of Mary, who is called James the lesser in Mark 15: 40. A very early Church tradition identifies him with James the 'brother' of Jesus, who was head of the early Church at Jerusalem.

PS 25–7 The *Legenda Aurea* stresses Matthew's avarice as a keeper of the customs.

PS 35–6 Cf. John 20: 24–9.

PS 40 Cf. the note to 22/1.

PLAY 29

This is the first play in Passion Play 2. Like Passion Play 1, this sequence differs prosodically and orthographically from other plays in the collection, and is distinct in its dependence on the *Northern Passion*. The extensive English stage directions, found only in the two Passion sequences, specify production involving a playing place and scaffolds (see pp. 544–9). The main scribe recorded the Passion Plays in a comparatively untidy hand, using different paper from that in the rest of the manuscript (see the headnote to Play 26 and pp. xviii–xxi and 541 n. 1). This second Passion sequence dramatizes events from Jesus' trial before Caiaphas and Annas until the Crucifixion, and includes at least part of the Burial play. In his prologue to the sequence (29/1–20), Contemplacio is vague about its constituents. Though several scholars have concluded that Passion Play 2 dovetails into other cycle material, they disagree about where this occurs. One can say, however, that the stanzaic forms and other features characteristic of the Passion sequences appear in plays 29–31, and in plays 32 and 34 up to the points of transition to the tail-rhyme material (on ff. 184–5 and 190 respectively). With those transitions, the prosody, elaborate stage directions, and use of literary sources typical of the Passion Plays cease, the paper stock changes, and close approximation to the Proclamation is restored (see p. 541 and Spector, 'Composition and Development of an Eclectic Manuscript', 72–6, and *Genesis of the N-town Cycle*, pp. 113–18).

Play 29 opens with the prologue by Contemplacio, whose list of subjects dramatized the 'last 3ere' corresponds to, and in some instances echoes, Passion Play 1. Contemplacio is also the name of the expositor of the Marian plays, but the present speech is prosodically and stylistically distinct from those of that earlier figure. A brief list of episodes presented the previous year also appears in Poeta's prologue to the Digby Candlemas Play.

The bulk of the play proper harmonizes, revises, and amplifies the questioning and beating of Jesus, and Peter's denials, in Matt. 26: 57–75, Mark 14: 53–72, Luke 22: 54–71, and John 18: 12–27. Like several of its dramatic analogues, the play develops the element of game in the buffeting, which it presents as a variant of blind man's buff.

Contemplacio's speech comprises five long-lined quatrains. Herod and his soldiers speak in long- and short-lined octaves and quatrains, with 37–49 constituting a quatrain followed by a 9-line stanza. After the messenger's entrance, the play is in long- and short-lined quatrains, except for the Judei's speeches and Peter's denials (177–208), which are largely in couplets. A line is apparently wanting after 166, and 187 and 192 are ametric.

The Proclamation description agrees with the play generally, but differs in details.

29/first s.d. *þat processyon* may refer to the Procession of Saints.

29/20 s.d.–89 Woolf (p. 250) says that the depiction of Herod as a persecutor of Christians seems to derive from hagiography. His threats and dispatching of spies recall the behaviour of Herod the Great in Play 18, who may similarly denounce Christians (see the partially-lost lines 73–6 in that play).

29/29 *his feyth*: i.e. belief in Mahound.

29/35–6 'To drive them into dungeons, for dragons to gnaw and to tear apart their flesh and bones for their food'.

29/97 'And one whom I was near to received a blow'.

29/98–101 Cf. 28/105–8 and the notes to those lines.

29/102–11 Cf. John 18: 4–8 and N-town 28/84–100.

29/124–5 Cf. Matt. 26: 15 and N-town 27/305.

29/126 *now art oure*: 'now you are ours'.

29/130–45 Cf. John 18: 19–23.

29/150–3 The doctor here cites Jesus' words in John 2: 19 in the context of Matt. 26: 60–1 and Mark 14: 57–8.

29/162–6 Cf. Matt. 26: 62–3, Mark 14: 60–1.

29/167–8 Cf. Matt. 26: 63; also Mark 14: 61, Luke 22: 70.

29/169–72 Jesus' response in Matt. 26: 64, Mark 14: 62, and Luke 22: 67–9 is here conflated with declarations that the Son of Man will come in glory to judge men (cf. Matt. 16: 27 and parallels, and 25: 31 ff.). Compare the *Northern Passion*, 663–7, and the Cornish *Passio Domini Nostri*, 1325–34, 1481–8, 1665–70.

29/173–8 Cf. Matt. 26: 65–6, Mark 14: 63–4, Luke 22: 71.

29/180 s.d.–192 Cf. Luke 22: 63–5, Matt. 26: 67–8, and Mark 14: 65. Owst cites homilies that identify the medieval game *Qui fery?*, or Hot Cockles, with this episode in the Gospels (*Literature and Pulpit*, p. 510). Woolf (p. 254) lists variations on the game in Continental treatments of the Passion. Kolve (pp. 185–6) notes that this scene and the throwing of dice for Christ's robe are the only parts of the Passion that are commonly described in medieval narrative as games.

29/192 s.d.–224 The portrayal of Peter's denial conflates the Synoptics and John. The cock's crowing twice, for example, is from Mark 14: 72 (cf. 27/562–3), Jesus' casting a look on Peter is from Luke 22: 61, and Malchus' kinsman identifies Peter in John 18: 26.

PLAY 30

Judas' suicide follows the version in Matt. 27: 3–5. The trial before Pilate harmonizes the accounts in Matt. 27: 11–14, Mark 15: 2–5, Luke 23: 2–5, and

John 18: 28–38, and includes many echoes of the *Northern Passion*. The sub-sequent trial before Herod is based on Luke 23: 6–12, though several of Herod's speeches are modelled on Pilate's words and actions in the Gospels and the *Northern Passion*.

In having Pilate try Jesus both before and after Herod does, N-town agrees with the arrangement in Tatian's *Diatessaron* and the *Pepysian Gospel Harmony*. The York and Chester cycles follow the same pattern; cf. Towneley 22/98–9.

This play is principally in quatrains, with couplets (of two-, three-, and four-stress lines) appearing in 1–2, 23–4, and 89–112. Caiaphas' opening dis-cussion with the messenger includes four long-lined quatrains and one quatrain with three- and four-stress lines. 113–88 mix quatrains and octaves, and, after 144, several discrete stanzas are concatenated by rhyme. 245–9 form a 5-line stanza rhyming abbba.

The play does not agree with the Proclamation description, which makes no reference to a trial before Herod, describes Judas' suicide as a separate pageant, and has thieves tried with Christ (a scene not dramatized until Play 31). The Proclamation description of Pilate's wife's going to rest prior to Judas' suicide is not portrayed here (see Swenson, p. 57).

30/24 s.d.–32 s.d. Cf. Matt. 27: 3–5. Woolf (pp. 243, 399 note 15) suggests that a brief dumb show depicted Judas' suicide, and notes that dumb shows occur in no mystery cycle except N-town, where they are fairly frequent in the Passion plays; see, for example, 31/57 s.d.

30/31 Cf. 29/125.

30/33–40 s.d. Cf. Matt. 27: 1–2, Mark 15: 1, Luke 23: 1, John 18: 28.

30/45–6 Cf. Luke 23: 5.

30/48 '(Which he) shows to the people . . .' (Bevington, p. 529).

30/49–52 Cf. Luke 23: 2 and compare the *Northern Passion*:
And ȝit þare es anoþer thing,
He sais þat he es iews king,
And þat es ogains þe honoure
Of sir Sesar oure emperoure. (Harl./911–14)

30/57–61 Cf. the *Northern Passion*:
Ihesu he sayde by thynk now the
alle this folke haldes one the
ffor thou takes newe lawes
that were noghte vsede in oure dawes. (Add./1141–4)
Ihesu seyde in hys þoughte
Of here wordes me recche ryth noughte. (Camb. Ii. 4. 9/1145–6)

30/64 Cf. the *Northern Passion*: 'My fadrys wylle schal forth go' (Camb. Ii. 4. 9/1156).

30/65 Cf. John 18: 37.

30/70–2 Cf. the *Northern Pasion*:
> And in thys worlde I was born
> I cam to sekyn that was for lorn. (Camb. Ii. 4. 9/1161–2)

30/73–6 Cf. John 18: 37 and compare the *Northern Passion*, 1165–6b.

30/78–80 'Don't you all think, considering the matter rationally, that things may well be just as he says, and that they should be so, according to this reasoning'.

30/81–2 Cf. Luke 23: 4, John 18: 38. Compare the *Northern Passion*:
> I ne fynd in hym no gilt
> Whar fore þat he suld be spylt. (Camb. Gg. 5. 31/927–8)

30/81 *obecyon*: 'ground for reproach or accusation'. Cf. Godefroy's quotations under *obicier*, and Lewis and Short, *obicio*, II. B.

30/89–98 Cf. John 18: 29–31.

30/103–4 Cf. Matt. 27: 11, Mark 15: 2, Luke 23: 3; also John 18: 33, 37.

30/107–10 Cf. John 18: 36.

30/111–20 Cf. Luke 23: 4–5; also John 18: 38 and the *Northern Passion*, 933–8.

30/121–52 s.d. Cf. Luke 23: 6–7.

30/122 *outborn*: 'born out of the region'. H. Kökeritz feasibly conjectures that *outborn* is in fact *out born* 'in any respect (aught) born' ('Out Born in *Ludus Coventriae*', *Modern Language Notes* 44 (1949), 89–90). *MED*, in evident agreement with this reading, does not include the sense I propose here (see *outbēren*, v.). However, the seven variant forms of *ought* 'aught' in N-town do not include *out*. And *OED* (*outborn*, a.) gives two illustrations of the sense 'born out of the country' (1532 and *c.* 1550) in addition to the present instance.

30/162 *shewyd present*: 'shown here and now'.

30/167–8 Cf. Luke 23: 12.

30/170, 193 ff. Cf. Luke 23: 8–9.

30/173 ff. Cf. Luke 23: 10.

30/197–204 Cf. the *Northern Passion*:
> I hafe herd speke of þi ganyng
> þou has done many selcouth thyng
> þe blynd men þou makys to se
> þe dume to speke þe deefe to here þe
> Crowkid men þou has done gone
> And wode men made hale onone
> Do now for þe luf of me
> Some myracle þat I may se. (Camb. Gg. 5. 31/981–90)

Compare York 30/441–9, Towneley 22/161–78.

30/209 ff. Herod's extra-biblical sentiment recalls Pilate's words in John 19: 10. Cf. Cayphas' speech in 29/162–5. Theo Stemmler cites similar transfers from Pilate to Herod Antipas in Greban's *Passion* and the Passion Play from Alsfeld ('Typological Transfer in Liturgical Offices and Religious Plays of the Middle Ages', *Studies in the Literary Imagination* 8 (1975), 142 note 74).

30/221 Cf. York 32/188: 'þou onhanged harlott, harke what I saie'.

30/231–44 s.d. Cf. the *Northern Passion*:
> heroudes be gan Ihesu fast to threte
> And dyde hym spoylen And to bete. (Camb. Ii. 4. 9/995–6)

This scene in N-town resembles the stripping and whipping of Jesus during the *second* trial before Pilate in the *Northern Passion*, 1189ff.

30/247 Herod's words recall Pilate's in the *Northern Passion*: 'þow ert full strong to suffyr schame' (Camb. Gg. 5. 31/1224).

30/252–5 Cf. Luke 23: 11–12.

PLAY 31

Satan's belligerent opening stanzas in this play reiterate his personal involvement in bringing about Jesus' death, asserted earlier, in his prologue to Play 26. Pilate's wife's dream derives from Matt. 27: 19, as amplified by the *Gospel of Nicodemus* and by Comestor's *Historia Scholastica*, which attributes the dream to the devil. The Middle English *Gospel of Nicodemus* follows Comestor in this, and, like the present play, has Pilate's wife tell him of the dream in person. N-town imports dialogue from an entirely distinct episode, the Harrowing of Hell in the *Gospel of Nicodemus*, to establish Satan's motive in trying to prevent the crucifixion; cf. *Cursor Mundi*, 17,977ff. Pilate's wife's warning and several subsequent speeches in the play follow and often echo the *Northern Passion*. The freeing of Barabbas and the condemnation of Jesus are ultimately based on Matt. 27: 15–31, Mark 15: 6–20, Luke 23: 14–25, and John 18: 38–19: 17.

The trial before Pilate was a common dramatic subject, and Pilate's wife's dream appears in the York cycle, the Cornish *Passio Domini Nostri*, and in Continental plays, including Greban's *Passion* (see Woolf, pp. 244, 399 note 18).

The play is written principally in quatrains and couplets until 152, and in couplets thereafter, except for two quatrains (189–96). A few of the quatrains are concatenated by rhyme. There is no capitulum before 5, and 1–8 are therefore treated as an octave. 94–103 and 126–30 are 5-line stanzas rhyming abbba; 33–41 also seem to be in this form (see the note to these lines).

The play contradicts the corresponding Proclamation description, which follows Matthew in having Pilate's wife send her message to him.

31/first s.d. Cf. Luke 23: 11.

31/7 *bras*: molten copper, used for torture. Brass and brimstone were associated with hell, as in the *Castle*, 3590–93.

31/17–29 Cf. the *Gospel of Nicodemus*, in which Satan says to Hades, 'I have tempted him . . . and I have prepared wood to crucify him, and nails to pierce him, and his death is near at hand, that I may bring him to thee' (*Ante-Nicene Fathers*, VIII: 449). For the sins associated with the Temptation, see the note to 23/144–7.

31/33–41 I treat 33–41 as two 5-line stanzas, with 38–41 wanting an initial line. 38 is not preceded by a capitulum, however, and an unusually careless rhyme-bracket connects 37 to 41.

31/33–4 Cf. the *Gospel of Nicodemus*: 'Satan, the prince and leader of death, said to Hades: Make thyself ready to receive Jesus, who boasts himself to be the Son of God' (VIII: 449).

31/35 *none*: three p.m. Cf. Matt. 27: 45–50, Mark 15: 34–7, and Luke 23: 44–6.

31/38–41 Cf. the *Gospel of Nicodemus*: 'And when Hades heard this, he said to him: I adjure thee by thy powers and mine, do not bring him to me. . . . But if thou bring Him to me, all who are here shut up . . . He will let loose' (VIII: 449–50).

31/43 'Unless some stratagem helps me, I shall suffer a vile turn of affairs'.

31/57 s.d. Cf. the *Northern Passion*:
> Vp sche roos and styrte fro slepe
> for drede sche be gan to wepe
> A non sche went to syr pylate (Camb. Ii. 4. 9/1088a–1089)
> thare he in the Mote haulle satte. (Add./1090)

31/58–9 Cf. the *Northern Passion*, 1093–4.

31/60–5 Cf. the *Northern Passion*:
> Byd þi lord with gude rede
> þat he do noght ihesu to ded
> ffor þai þat procurd ihesu to fall
> þai sall be condempnyd all. (Camb. Gg. 5. 31/1079–82)
> As I lay And slepte I þe telle
> A beest I wene þer cam fro helle
> lothlech he malasyd me. . . .
> I was neuyr so for drede
> Sythen I was of my modyr fedde. (Camb. Ii. 4. 9/1097–1099, 1105–6)

31/79–81 Cf. the *Northern Passion*:
> Sone þai tald hym tythyng glad
> þat herode was his frende made
> Of ihesu he bad þe do þi wyll
> Whethir þow will hym safe or spyll. (Camb. Gg. 5. 31/1009–12)

31/86–93 Cf. Luke 23: 14–15; also John 18: 38. Compare the *Northern Passion*:
> And said: 'for soth, ʒe er to blame,
> þat ʒe do ihesu all þis schame,
> ffor no cause can I in him find
> Wharfore men suld him bete & bind. (Harl./1015–18)

31/94-9 Cf. Matt. 27: 15, Mark 15: 6, and John 18: 39, and compare the *Northern Passion*:

> It is þe custome in thys londe
> Of thys paske þat is nowe in honde [Add. MS: 'nere hande']
> If þat ony man be nowe in preson
> for man slaughte or for treson
> he of preson delyuyred schulde be
> wyth owten dom he schulde go free. (Camb. Ii. 4. 9/1021-6)

31/98-9 Block prints 99 before 98, but the rhyme-scheme and the position of these lines in the manuscript require the present order.

31/100-4 Cf. Mark 15: 9-10, Matt. 27: 17-18, and John 18: 39, and compare Pilate's advice in the *Northern Passion*:

> I rede þat we Ihesu take
> and late hym alle qwytte skape. (Add./1027-8).

31/105-7 Cf. Luke 23: 18-19; also Matt. 27: 21, Mark 15: 11, John 18: 40.

31/108-13 Cf. Matt. 27: 22-3, Mark 15: 12-14; also Luke 23: 20-3.

31/120-3 Cf. the *Northern Passion*

> Pilate sayd vnto ihesu
> þai luf þe noght and what says þou
> In pese þou myght be for me (Camb. Gg. 5. 31/1119-21)
> Bot for þe mene of thi countree
> the Byschope of þe lawes with Envie
> thoghte to done the grete folye. (Add./1122-24)

31/127-32 Cf. John 19: 10-11.

31/135-6 Cf. John 19: 11.

31/140 s.d. S. W. Reid suggests that *into* is an error for *vnto* ('Two Emendations in "Passion Play II" of the *Ludus Coventriae*', *English Language Notes* 11 (1973), 86-7); *into* can, however, mean 'to, unto' (see *MED*, *in-to*, prep. 9. a).

31/141-4 Cf. John 19: 12, and compare the *Northern Passion*:

> alswa sone he sayde the Iewes vn to
> what will 3e with Ihesu doo
> Synne it es to spylle his blode
> ffor I ne fynd in hym bot gude
> and gude it es we latyne hym gaa. (Add. 1173-7)

31/149-52 Cf. John 19: 12.

31/153-60 Cf. Matt. 27: 24-5.

31/161-2 Cf. John 19: 4.

31/163-6 Cf. John 19: 15.

31/167 ff. The freeing of Barabbas derives from Matt. 27: 26, Mark 15: 15, and Luke 23: 25: cf. John 18: 40. This scene in the play recalls the charge to a jury and the rendering of a verdict in a medieval criminal proceeding.

31/179 *Dysmas and Jesmas*: the non-biblical names Dysmas and Gestas are given the thieves in the *Gospel of Nicodemus*. The speaker heading in N-town 32/117 gives the name 'Jestes'. Cf. 'Gesmas' in *Cursor Mundi*, 16,739.

31/189–92 Block (p. li note 2) observes that in the *Dialogus Beatae Mariae et Anselmi de Passione Domini*, the *populus* are sympathetic after the Crucifixion while the *Iudaei* continue to persecute Jesus' friends.

31/193–6 Cf. Matt. 27: 26, Mark 15: 15, John 19: 1. Gauvin (p. 184) discusses the non-biblical tradition that Jesus was bound to a pillar, a type of the Cross which became the object of a liturgical office.

31/210 s.d.–212 s.d. Cf. Matt. 27: 27–31, Mark 15: 16–20; John 19: 2–3, 17.

31/212 s.d. Davies (p. 455 note 67) observes that forks are also used to force the crown down in an alabaster representation and in the Holkham Bible Picture Book (f. 29ᵛ). Cf. Owst, *Literature and Pulpit*, p. 508.

PLAY 32

This play harmonizes the accounts of the Crucifixion in the Synoptic Gospels and John, and embellishes them with motifs from apocryphal, meditative, and dramatic traditions. The result is a series of brief scenes achieving rapid shifts in emotional extremes. Matt. 27: 32–50, Mark 15: 21–37, Luke 23: 26–46, and John 19: 17–30 provide the biblical basis of the play. The Veronica story is apocryphal. The coercion of Simon is influenced by the *Northern Passion*, as is the gruesome stretching of Jesus' limbs to fit the Cross, a scene suggested by the *Meditationes* and depicted in each of the extant English cycles and the Cornish *Passio Domini Nostri.* Woolf (p. 260) takes the inclusion of the Veronica episode and other apocryphal elements, along with the dramatization of the final Seven Words, to indicate Continental influence.

Mary's suffering under the Cross was traditionally considered the fulfilment of Simeon's prophecy that a sword would pierce her soul (Luke 2: 35), which Origen had interpreted to signify that she would doubt during the Crucifixion (Graef, p. 45). The play depicts Mary's momentary incomprehension, as well as her yearning for death. This was an ancient motif that had become familiar by the medieval period and is portrayed in each of the English cycles and the Digby *Christ's Burial.*

The play is written principally in short-lined quatrains till 176, though longer lines appear in the 'Daughters of Jerusalem' speech (9–20), Mary's lament in 93–100, and Jesus' words to Mary and John in 145–56. 177–84 are couplets. The remainder of the play is in tail-rhyme stanzas rhyming aaabcccb; the initial three lines of the first tail-rhyme stanza (185–9) appear to be wanting, however. The matter of this play agrees with the description of Pageant 30, written in a long thirteener in the Proclamation.

32/1–20 Cf. Luke 23: 27–30.

32/20 s.d.–40 s.d. Cf. Matt. 27: 32, Mark 15: 21, Luke 23: 26.

32/22–4 Cf. the *Northern Passion*:

> he beris hym selfe þat Ilke tree
> whare one þat he schalle hangede be. (Add./1565–6)

32/25–8 Cf. the *Northern Passion*, 1569–72.

32/29–30 Cf. the *Northern Passion*:

> HE answerid & seyde nay
> I may not be þis day
> for I haue greet nedis to do. (Camb. Dd. 1. 1/1573–4a)

32/33–4 Cf. the *Northern Passion*:

> Off this harlotte it es grete skorne
> ffor sakes thou the rode tree
> To bere it whene we bydde [Camb. Dd. 1. 1: 'preyd'] thee.
> (Add./1576–8)

32/41–8 Veronica appears in the *Mors Pilati* and the *Legenda Aurea*. Woolf (p. 403 note 60) observes that her story occurs in the three great French Passions, and notes that Mâle credits the drama with bringing about the sudden appearance of Veronica in late medieval iconographic representations of the road to Calvary. Cf. York 34/183–9.

32/57–64 Cf. York 35/106, and compare the *Northern Passion*:

> vn to þe boris þei leyde his handis swete
> to lokin if þat þei were mete
> and as þei gan him make so
> his armis myghte not come þer to
> be a large fote wiþ outen lesing. (Camb. Dd. 1. 1/1605–9)

32/62 *to þe sore*: perhaps an error for 'to þe bore'; cf. the *Northern Passion*, 1618, and Towneley, 23/121.

32/65–76 Cf. the *Northern Passion*, 1614–34. W. L. Hildburgh cites the stretching of Jesus' limbs in an alabaster table ('English Alabaster Carvings as Records of the Medieval Religious Drama', *Archaeologia*, 93 (1949), 83–4, cited by Hassall, p. 132). See the Holkham Bible Picture Book, f. 31ᵛ.

32/76 s.d. Woolf (p. 258) notes that in some German plays the Jews similarly dance around the Cross.

32/81 Cf. Towneley 23/209–10.

32/85–7 Cf. the *Northern Passion*:

> lyghte now downe of þat harde tre
> kyng of Iewes ʒif þat þou be. (Add./1649–50)

32/87–8 Cf. Matt. 27: 42, Mark 15: 32.

32/92 s.d. Cf. Matt. 27: 35, 38, 55–6; Mark 15: 24, 27, 40; Luke 23: 33–4; John 19: 18, 24–6. Compare the *Meditationes*: 'our reverend Lady Mary, as well as

John, the Magdalen, and the sisters of the mother of the Lord, remained, sitting to one side of the cross' (p. 338). Anderson (pp. 160, 215) cites alabaster Crucifixion panels showing John seated and the soldiers brawling at the foot of the Cross. The Virgin's swooning in this scene was a familiar motif; Woolf (p. 265) notes the frequency with which this image appears in fifteenth-century art.

32/93-6 Cf. York 36/139-43.

32/97-100 s.d. Mary's yearning for death was a traditional motif made explicit in the *Meditationes* and its English derivatives and dramatized in Chester 16A, York 36, Towneley 23, and the Digby *Christ's Burial*. See Livius, p. 187, and Margaret Alexiou, *The Ritual Lament in Greek Tradition* (Cambridge, 1974), pp. 64-5.

32/100 s.d. *swonge*: cf. *synge* 'sign' in 41/455.

32/101-4 Cf. Luke 23: 34.

32/105-16 Cf. Matt. 27: 40, Mark 15: 29-30; also Luke 23: 37. *Vath*: the Vulgate gives the form *Vah*.

32/117-32 Cf. Luke 23: 39-43.

32/133-44 Cf. the Digby *Christ's Burial*, 172-5. Thien (p. 55) cites a correspondence between Mary's speech here and a passage in the 'Devozione del Giovedi e' del Venerdi santo'.

32/134 *defendyd*: 'offended'. Cf. *MED*, *dēfens(e)*, n. 5 (c).

32/145-8 Cf. John 19: 26-7.

32/149-56 Cf. York 36/144-7.

32/156 s.d.-64 Cf. the *Meditations on the Supper of our Lord*:
> To þe cros foote hastly she ran,
> And clypped þe cros faste yn here arme,
> And seyd, 'my sone here wyl y dey. . . .' (835-7)

32/168 s.d.-176 Cf. Matt. 27: 41-3; also Mark 15: 31-2, Luke 23: 35.

32/176 s.d.-182 Cf. John 19: 19-22; also Matt. 27: 37, Mark 15: 26, Luke 23: 38.

32/182 s.d. Reid ('Two Emendations', p. 87) proposes emending to *þer skaffaldys*.

32/183-5 Cf. Matt. 27: 46, Mark 15: 34.

32/190-3 Cf. Matt. 27: 47, 49, Mark 15: 35-6.

32/194-9 Cf. John 19: 28-9; also Matt. 27: 48, Mark 15: 36, Luke 23: 36.

32/200 *a mowe ʒe make*: cf. York 35/285-6, 36/78.

32/214-16 Cf. Luke 23: 46.

32/221 Cf. John 19: 30.

32/244-5 Cf. the *Meditationes*: 'from the sole of His foot to the crown of His head there is no health in Him' (p. 338).

32/258ff. Cf. John 19: 27.

32/267 Thien (p. 56) cites the 'Complaint of Mary Maudeleine': 'Thus arayde was neuer man before' (ed. Skeat (Zurich Ph.D. thesis, 1897)).

32/288 Cf. Psalm 41: 4 (Vulgate).

32/269 s.d. *semi-mortua*: cf. the *Meditationes*: 'either she was so absorbed by the multitude of her sorrows as to be insensible or was half-dead' (p. 337).

32/292 *handmay*: not listed in *OED* or *MED*.

PLAY 33

Christ's descent into hell was mentioned by most of the Church Fathers, included in creeds, and depicted at length in the *Gospel of Nicodemus*. Kretzmann (pp. 116–33) concludes that the N-town version is based on the *Gospel of Nicodemus* and vernacular treatments of the Harrowing, with no liturgical influence (see, however, Young, 1: 150). The Harrowing was a common subject in religious drama, but Fry (p. 562) observes that no other extant English mystery places it immediately after Christ's death, as N-town does. The action in the present play is interrupted by the Burial and Guarding of the Sepulchre in Play 34, and completed in Play 35.

This play comprises six tail-rhyme stanzas rhyming aaabcccb. The Proclamation describes the Harrowing as part of the same pageant as the Longinus episode.

33/24 s.d. Ps. 23: 7. For the marginal reference to Anima Latronis, see the note to 35/40; cf. the *Gospel of Nicodemus*, X: 452.

33/25 *sorwatorie*: apparently a form of *surquidry* 'pride'. Cf. the *w/qw* variation in *where/qwere*, *what/qwat* in this codex, and compare York 37/182: 'Vndo youre ȝatis, ȝe princis of pryde'.

33/33–40 *Belyall*: the *Gospel of Bartholomew* has Beliar discuss with Hades the identity of Christ as he approaches hell.

PLAY 34

The biblical basis for the Centurion's speech, the Deposition, the Burial, and the Guarding of the Sepulchre is found in Matt. 27: 54–66, Mark 15: 39–47, Luke 23: 47–56, and John 19: 31–42. Much of the play, including speeches by Pilate and the soldiers, recalls the *Northern Passion*.

Until nearly the end of f. 189ᵛ the play consists chiefly of quatrains, several of which are concatenated by rhyme, mixed with some ababbcbc octaves. The initial two octaves (1–16) contain rather long lines, and the subsequent stanza is in tail-rhyme. Line 113 is ametric. From 222 the play is in tail-rhyme, most often rhyming aaabcccb, with two-stress lines in 262–301. The final four speeches are written in short-lined stanzas rhyming aabccb (302–25).

The correlative Proclamation description, written in a long thirteener, disagrees with the play as we have it by making Nicodemus accompany Joseph of Arimathea to petition Pilate for Jesus' body, and by describing the guards' fear of the risen Christ. In the play, by contrast, the guards fall asleep before the Resurrection (but compare 35/193 ff.).

Certain elements of the play, for example the 'pieta' scene at the Cross, are not included in the other English cycles, though this motif is depicted in the Digby Burial play and occurs in the *Meditationes* and its English derivatives.

34/1–12 Cf. Matt. 27: 45, 51, 54; Mark 15: 33, 39; Luke 23: 44, 47; compare York 36/314, 38/91, and Towneley 26/116.

34/25–6 Cf. Matt. 27: 54, Mark 15: 39.

34/39–44 Cf. 138–9, 142–3, and the notes to those lines.

34/41–52 Cf. Matt. 27: 57–8, Mark 15: 42–3, Luke 23: 50–2, John 19: 31, 38.

34/57–9 Cf. Matt. 27: 58, Mark 15: 45, John 19: 38. Compare the *Northern Passion*:

> Pilate seyde I graunte it the
> But first I wile witen if he ded be. (Camb. Dd. 1. 1/1853–4)

34/67 Cf. the *Northern Passion*, 1860.

34/71 'Once we leave you. . . .'

34/80 s.d.–84 Cf. John 19: 33, and compare the *Northern Passion*:

> Sythen they stode in the place
> And lokyd Ihesu in þe face
> wele they wyst Ihesu was dede
> To brekyn hys lendys was it not nede. (Camb. Dd. 1. 1/1865–8)

34/85–113 Longinus was the name traditionally given to the soldier in John 19: 34 who pierces Jesus' side with a spear. In the *Gospel of Nicodemus*, Longinus is the centurion who affirms that Christ was the son of God. Foster (*Northern Passion*, II: 96) notes that N-town, like the *Northern Passion*, presents the Longinus episode after Joseph of Arimathea is given permission to bury Jesus' body, rather than before, as in John and the N-town Proclamation.

34/108 s.d.–113 Cf. the *Northern Passion*:

> wol sore he him gan to drede
> of him forto han his mede
> on his knes he be gan to falle
> of ihesu merci he dide þan calle. (Camb. Dd. 1. 1/1885–8).

Cf. also the *Southern Passion*, 1638–9, York 36/309–12, Chester 16A/392–9.

34/113 s.d.–121 s.d. Cf. John 19: 39 and compare 118–20 with the *Northern Passion*:

> thay layde his body in a graue
> Off hym thay wiste thaire mede to haue. (Add./1907–8)

34/121 s.d. Davies (p. 455 note 73), citing Joan Evans, says that the 'pieta' motif seems to have come to England from France in the early fifteenth century. He adds that this motif occurs in no other English cycle. It does appear in the *Meditationes* and Love's *Mirrour*, however, and was dramatized in the Digby Burial play. See Joan Evans, *English Art: 1307–1461* (Oxford, 1949), p. 88.

34/127 Cf. Love's *Mirrour*: 'Than sche wipeth his face and kisseth it' (p. 252; the *Meditationes* is similar).

34/138–9 Cf. Matt. 27: 59, Mark 15: 46, Luke 23: 53, and John 19: 40.

34/140–1 Cf. John 19: 39–40, the *Northern Passion*, 1899–1902, and York 36/400–3.

34/142–3 Cf. Matt. 27: 60.

34/146–7 Cf. Matt. 27: 60, Mark 15: 46.

34/154–7 s.d. Matthew and Mark put only Magdalane and another Mary at the Burial. Luke says that the women who had come with Jesus from Galilee were there. The *Gospel of Nicodemus* (Greek form), the *Meditationes*, and Love's *Mirrour*, however, have the Virgin Mary present at the Burial, as in N-town. Cf. the Cornish *Resurrexione* (ed. Norris), 439, and the Holkham Bible Picture Book (f. 33ᵛ).

34/157 s.d.ff. Cf. Matt. 27: 62–6.

34/182–205 The biblical Guarding of the Sepulchre was embellished in several Latin plays (see Young, I: 408ff.) and in each of the extant English cycles. The selection of four guards occurs in the *Northern Passion* and was a dramatic and iconographic convention (Gauvin, p. 193). Falke (pp. 84–5) points out that the treatment of the soldiers in N-town is related to that in a poem in MS Ashmole 61 published by Horstmann ('Nachträge zu den Legenden', *Archiv* 79 (1887), 441–7), which names the knights Amorant, Arfax, Gemorante, and Cosdram. Woolf (p. 407 note 22) cautions that the direction of the influence between the poem and the play is unclear. Dorothee Metlitzki cites the Saracen giant Sir Amoraunt who opposes Guy of Warwick (*The Matter of Araby in Medieval England* (New Haven and London, 1977), pp. 196–7). Woolf (p. 276) says that the portrayal of the soldiers in a manner recalling the Plautine *miles gloriosus* or the *soldat fanfaron* of French farce is typically Continental rather than English; but compare Chester 18.

34/194–7 Cf. the *Northern Passion*:

> O payn of lif þat 3e noght let,
> And all 3owre gudes to be forfet (Harl./1945–6)
> and appone catelle & appone wyfe. (Add./1946)

34/200–5 Cf. the *Northern Passion*:

> And if þai bring with þam in fere
> A hundreth men whils we er here,
> Hastily sall þai heuided be
> Omang vs foure, bot if þai fle. (Harl./1963–6)

34/214–94 The speaker headings for the four knights were numbered to reflect the order in which Pilate summons them in 182–4: Amorawnt, then Arphaxat, Cosdram, and Affraunt. The numbering has been revised, however, to indicate the order in which the knights actually speak in 214–29. Similar changes were made in 286 and 294.

34/214–25 Cf. the *Northern Passion*, 1955–60.

34/226 ff. Folio 190, beginning with line 226, is the first leaf of V quire. Consisting of a different paper stock from the preceding gatherings of Passion Play 2, this quire is prosodically and orthographically distinct from the Passion Play 2 material. In the present play, the joining of these discrete strata, one principally in quatrains and octaves, the other in tail-rhyme, resulted in contradictions and redundancy.

34/230–57 Cf. Matt. 27: 66.

34/262–5 'As fierce as wind, knights, now go (to the one) wrapped in a shroud, and guard him well'.

34/302–25 Cf. Matt. 28: 4. The *Northern Passion*, like N-town, contradicts the biblical account by having the guards fall asleep. The guards also sleep in the Chester version, and in the Cornish *Resurrexione*, but Woolf (p. 407 note 20) observes that only in N-town (as in many later French plays) do the soldiers become drowsy and lie down to rest one by one.

34/324 Block renders *taske* as 'tax, levy, i.e. seize, take'.

PLAY 35

The portrayal of the Harrowing of Hell, begun in Play 33, is completed in this play. The risen Christ's first speech (73–81) echoes the Middle English *Harrowing of Hell*. Christ's appearance to the Virgin Mary is not biblical, but Ambrose asserts that Mary was the first to see her son's Resurrection (Livius, p. 191; cf. Graef, p. 126), and the *Legenda Aurea* refers to the belief in this event. The *Meditationes* and Love's *Mirrour* portray this interview, including the words 'Salue, sancta parens', which appear in the play. Vriend (pp. 128–31) observes that this episode was seldom recognized in the liturgical prayers of the West, and points out that of the English mysteries, only N-town includes it. The appearance to Mary is also depicted in the Cornish *Resurrexione*, and Woolf (p. 279) notes that it was commonly dramatized in Germany, though in

France Greban alone depicted it. The soldiers' meeting with Pilate is a revision and elaboration of the account in Matt. 28: 11–15. Their decision to tell Pilate the truth about the Resurrection, and Pilate's denunciation of them, are non-biblical, but occur in the *Northern Passion* as well as each of the English cycles and the Cornish *Resurrexione.*

The play is written in tail-rhyme, principally in the form aaabcccb, mixed with stanzas of two-stress lines in the same rhyme-scheme.

The corresponding Proclamation description, a long thirteener, agrees with the play in mentioning the conclusion of the Harrowing of Hell, as well as the appearance to Mary. But it omits to mention the guards' meeting with Pilate.

35/1–4 Cf. the *Gospel of Nicodemus*: 'the King of glory stretched out His right hand, and took hold of our forefather Adam, and raised him. Then turning also to the rest, He said: Come all with me' (VIII: 437). Compare York 37/ 385–6.

35/9–10 Cf. the *Gospel of Nicodemus*: 'our forefather Adam seemed to be filled with joy, and said: I thank Thy majesty, O Lord, that Thou has brought me up out of the lowest Hades' (VIII: 437).

35/25–7 Cf. the *Gospel of Nicodemus*: 'I am John the Baptist. . . . I baptized Him in the river Jordan' (VIII: 456).

35/33–4 In the *City of God*, Augustine says that after the flood, Abraham initiated the third historical age; see the note to 4/14–17.

35/40 Marginal notations by Scribe C indicate that this play was expanded after the main scribe had copied it out. The marginal notes opposite 40 refer to Anima Caym, who is not included in the play as we have it. The note in the left margin concludes with 'as folow fayere frendys', thus returning to the opening words of Anima Christi's speech in 41. Notations by C in the margins of the next page (f. 192, starting opposite line 64) indicate that a speech by Cain was to be interpolated at that point. The marginal 'nota þe devyll' seems to indicate an added role for the devil as well, and C interlined between 64 and 65 what appear to be the opening words of a speech that was to be spoken by the devil: 'Thowght many be gon I am glad . . .' ('Though [?] many are gone, I am glad . . .'). He wrote the first two of these words again in the right margin, and beneath them 'hens I wyll þe bere', apparently the closing words of the devil's speech. C did not record the remainder of the speech. But what we have suggests that the devil was to express satisfaction here that, despite the loss of the patriarchs' souls, he expected to bear new souls to hell. Scribe C wrote 'þan crist' in the right margin to indicate that lines by Christ were to follow. In the left margin, and a bit lower on the page, C wrote 'And þan cayme xall sey his spech', again referring to lines that are not recorded in the manuscript. Below that, the note 'And þan crist xall sey, now ys your foo et cetera' returns the dialogue to Anima Christi's speech at 65, which begins with those words. The erased words in the margin after 56 evidence the decision to include the additions in their present position rather than one stanza above. In Play 33, a similar marginal notation, perhaps by C, introduces Anima Latronis into the first section of the Harrowing (opposite 33/24 s.d.); see the Introduction, p. xxiii–xxiv above.

35/43–56 Cf. the *Gospel of Nicodemus*: 'And, behold, the Lord Jesus Christ . . . bound Satan by the neck; and again tying his hands behind him, dashed him on his back into Tartarus, and placed His holy foot on his throat, saying: Through all ages thou hast done many evils. . . . To-day I deliver thee to ever-lasting fire' (VIII: 457).

35/73–81 Cf. the Middle English *Harrowing of Hell*:

> Hard gates haue y gon
> & suffred pines mani on;
> þritti winter & þridde half ȝere
> haue y wond in lond here. . . .
> þai bete me tyl y ran on blode. . . .
> alle for adams sinne ywis,
> þan haue I þoled þis.

(William Henry Hulme, ed., EETS ES 100 (1907), Auchinleck/43–6, 55, 57–8). In the poem Christ speaks these lines upon his arrival in hell. Woolf (p. 275) cites a less pronounced similarity to a four-line verse in John of Grimestone's preaching book.

35/89 *Salue, sancta parens*: cf. Love's *Mirrour*: 'sodeynly oure lord Jesu came and aperede to hir . . . gretynge hir on side half in thise wordes: *Salue / sancta parens /* that is to say Haile / holy moder' (pp. 263–4). Cf. the *Meditationes*, p. 359, and the Cornish *Resurrexione*, 455, and see the note to N-town 38/353–92. Audrey Davidson points out that *Salve sancte parens* is the Introit for the Lady-Mass ('*Alma Redemptoris Mater*: The Little Clergeon's Song', in *Studies in Medieval Culture*, ed. John R. Sommerfeldt, Larry Syndergaard, E. Rozanne Elder, Western Michigan University, IV (1974), 462).

35/138–44 Cf. Matt. 28: 2–4.

35/151–2 Cf. the *Northern Passion*: 'what maye we saye to sir pilate' (Add./2028).

35/153–68 Cf. Matt. 28: 11, York 38/329 ff., Towneley 26/472 ff., Chester 18/226 ff., the Cornish *Resurrexione*, 575 ff., and the *Northern Passion*, 2039 ff.

35/156–7 Cf. the *Northern Passion*: 'we will saye als we hafe sene' (Add./2047).

35/168 *gast*: this form is not listed in *OED*, *give*, 2 sg. indic. past.

35/169–208 Cf. York 38/363 ff., Towneley 26/506 ff., Chester 18/250 ff., the Cornish *Resurrexione*, 607 ff., and the *Northern Passion*, I: 244–5. The knights' account of their fear in 193–200 agrees with Matt. 28: 4 and N-town Pr 424, but compare 34/302–25.

35/222–4 'Those whom Christ's laws guide will never cease till the ones who brought him to death are themselves dead'.

35/233-304 Cf. Matt. 28: 12-15.

35/261-2 *mede doth most in every qwest*: cf. Whiting, M490, G296.

35/264 *With mede men may bynde berys*: cf. Whiting, B105.

PLAY 36

The depiction of the Visit to the Sepulchre was inspired by Matt. 28: 1-8 and Mark 16: 1-8 (compare Luke 24: 1-10, John 20: 1-2, and the Gospel of Peter 12: 50-13. 57). N-town conflates and embellishes its biblical sources, and, like the Chester and Cornish Resurrection plays, contradicts the order of events in Matthew's narrative by presenting this episode after Pilate's bribing of the soldiers. The disciples' running to the tomb and discovering Jesus' shroud closely follows John 20: 3-10.

Marshall (pp. 322-3) says that the order of events in the present play resembles that of several liturgical *Visitationes*, though the same sequence of episodes also appears in the *Historia Scholastica*. Woolf (p. 278) observes that N-town includes nearly all the separable segments of the Latin plays on this subject, and that Chester presents an even broader range of episodes, while York (like Towneley) omits the episode of Peter and John.

The play is in tail-rhyme up to line 94, chiefly rhyming aaabcccb; 1-8 rhyme aaabaaab, and 33-8 are two-stress lines rhyming aabccb. From 95, in the scene involving Peter and John, the play consists of octaves rhyming ababbcbc. The Proclamation description accords with the general action of the play.

36/first s.d. ff. In Mark 16: 1, the women who go to the tomb are Magdalene, Mary the mother of James, and Salome, whom the play names Mary Salome. As in the marginal genealogy on f. 37ʳ, the latter two Marys are here identified as sisters of the Virgin Mary, a reference to the trinubium, or threefold marriage of Anna, which resulted in the births of three Marys, each to a different father (Vriend, p. 42). Cf. *Mirk's Festial*, p. 215; also, Towneley 26/333 ff., Chester 18/309 ff., and the Cornish *Resurrexione*, 679 ff., and compare Matt. 28: 1, Luke 23: 55-24: 10, and John 20: 1.

36/9-13 See the notes to 27/141-92 and 167-83.

36/18 *as sunne in glas*: see 21/97-100 and the note.

36/29 *feyn*: Block conjectures a rendering of 'make faint', and Davies proposes emending to *freyn* 'bruise', but cf. *OED, fay*, v.¹ 1. 'to fix or fasten in position'.

36/63-78 Cf. Mark 16: 5-7, Matt. 28: 5-7.

36/79-86 Cf. Matt. 28: 8.

36/81 'He (who) lives now. . . .'

36/99 Scribe C altered text in this stanza and added lines in the margins of this and the next page in order to make the Marys refer to the risen Christ's appearance to them. That episode is not depicted in the cycle, and evidently represents a late expansion of the play. Cf. the note to 35/40, and see the Introduction, pp. xxiii–xxiv.

36/121–46 Cf. John 20: 3–10.

PLAY 37

This play closely follows and embellishes the story of Christ's appearance to Magdalene in John 20: 11–18 (compare Mark 16: 9–11). The play disagrees with John in having one angel, rather than two, address Magdalene at the sepulchre, and it appends Peter's extra-biblical final speech.

The play is principally written in ababbcbc octaves; 25–32 rhyme ababcbcb, an odd form in the cycle, and perhaps comprise two quatrains. 74–7 form a quatrain; line 37 is ametrical. The Proclamation description agrees with the play.

37/first s.d. Cf. John 20: 11.

37/9–16 Cf. John 20: 12–13.

37/21–4 Cf. John 20: 15.

37/33–8 Cf. John 20: 15–16.

37/38–41 Cf. Towneley 26/588–91 and the Cornish *Resurrexione*, 871–4.

37/42–9 Cf. John 20: 17.

37/56 'Yet, despite all this, lo, I shall ordain. . . .'

37/66–71 Magdalene's account of her sorrow follows John 20: 2, 11, but contradicts her declarations of mirth and joy in the empty tomb in 36/79–82; cf. Matt. 28: 8.

37/76–7 See the notes to 27/141–92 and 167–83.

37/80–93 Cf. John 20: 18; also Mark 16: 10.

PLAY 38

The *Peregrini* episode follows and expands upon the account in Luke 24: 13–35 (compare Mark 16: 12), while the Appearance to Thomas is based on John 20: 24–9.

This play elaborates extensively on the statement in Luke that Christ expounded the scriptures concerning himself. Woolf (p. 280) observes that while Greban presents this exposition as a long sermon, and Chester, by contrast, treats it briefly and perfunctorily, N-town presents it as a well designed debate. The play emphasizes the pilgrims' use of force in constraining Christ to remain with them, and it adds the non-biblical miracle of Christ's slicing the bread without a knife.

The Emmaus scene is constituted principally of ababbcbc octaves, with 209–16 forming quatrains. The Appearance to Thomas, from line 297, comprises long-lined octaves.

The Proclamation describes the Emmaus and Thomas episodes as separate pageants, the second of which is described in only four lines. The descriptions follow the Gospel accounts, and so agree with the play in general terms.

38/1–67 Cf. Luke 24: 13–20.

38/3 Alan H. Nelson says that although *castellum* in the Vulgate implies a village, the 'castel' of Emmaus was typically portrayed in art as a castle ('Some Configurations of Staging in Medieval English Drama', in *Medieval English Drama*, eds. Jerome Taylor and Alan H. Nelson (Chicago and London, 1972), p. 141).

38/5 Cleophas' companion, unnamed in the Gospel narrative, was traditionally identified as Luke; cf. Young, I: 688.

38/41–2 Cf. Pr 468–9.

38/45–8 Cf. Luke 24: 17 and the antiphon 'Qui sunt hi sermones' (Downing, p. 189).

38/49–50 Cf. Luke 24: 18 and the antiphon 'Tu solus peregrinus es' (Downing, p. 189).

38/73–8 Cf. Luke 24: 21–2.

38/81–94 Cf. Luke 24: 22–6. Cleophas' reference in 83 to a single angel who appeared to the Marys agrees with Play 36, which follows Matthew and Mark but contradicts Luke. Peter and John (in 85) are not named in Luke 24: 24.

38/89 *A, 3e fonnys and slought of herte*: cf. 'O stulti, et tardi corde' in Luke 24: 25, also in an antiphon cited by Downing (p. 189).

38/97–192 Cf. Luke 24: 27–9.

38/113 *Trewth dyd nevyr his maystyr shame*: cf. Whiting, T510.

38/115–20 Cf. Matt. 12: 40; also N-town 7/69–72 and the note to those lines.

38/129–36 Cf. Num. 17: 8. Woolf (p. 281) observes that Aaron's rod is less commonly a type of the Resurrection than of the Virgin Birth.

38/155–65 Cf. Luke 24: 29 and the versicle 'Mane nobiscum' (Downing, p. 189).

38/177–90 The disciples' use of force is based on Luke 24: 29. Woolf (p. 281) considers it likely that the N-town dramatist had an authoritative source associating this event with Jacob's wrestling with the angel.

38/213–20 Cf. Luke 24: 30–2; also the Cornish *Resurrexione*, 1321–6.

38/218 Cf. 'Nonne cor nostrum' in Luke 24: 32 and the versicle cited by Downing (p. 189).

38/226–8 Cf. Luke 24: 32.

38/233–40, 269–88 Cf. Luke 24: 33, 35.

38/269 Cleophas and Luke here meet Peter and Thomas, and perhaps other disciples.

38/273–6 In Luke 24: 13, Emmaus is sixty stadia from Jerusalem.

38/285–6 Cf. Towneley 28/265 and *Cleanness*, 1105–8 (ed. J. J. Anderson (New York, 1977)). Marshall (p. 327) proposes that Christ's miraculous slicing of the bread is also intended in the *Shrewsbury Fragments*, 75: 'He cutt oure bred withouten knyfe'.

38/301–4 Cf. Towneley 28/184, York 41/135–8.

38/305–8 Cf. Towneley 28/236–9, 260–3.

38/321–8 Cf. John 20: 25.

38/333–4 Cf. John 20: 26–7 and the antiphon 'Pax vobiscum, ego sum' (Downing, p. 189).

38/339 Cf. John 20: 27.

38/343–5 Cf. John 20: 27–8.

38/349–51 Cf. John 20: 29 and the antiphon 'Quia vidisti' (Downing, p. 190).

38/353–92 Falke (p. 91) notes a similarity between the refrains in these stanzas and in two lyrics edited by Furnivall in *Political, Religious, and Love Poems* (EETS os 15 (1866), pp. 233–42). The second of these lyrics, 'The Virgin's Complaint and Comfort', contains the refrain 'resurrexit! non mortuus est!' and includes the risen Christ's apparition to the Virgin with the salutation 'Salue, sancta parens'. Cf. N-town 35/89 and the note.

PLAY 39

This play faithfully follows scriptural sources with only slight elaboration. The depiction of the Ascension harmonizes the account in Acts 1: 4–11 with passages in Luke and Mark, and the Selection of Matthias derives from Acts 1: 15–26.

Block (p. xxxii) detects in this play signs of haste and incompleteness in compilation. She notes that only one of the two angels mentioned in the first stage direction speaks, for example, that a gap was left after the angel's speech, and that the subsequent speech lacks a speaker heading. Fry (p. 564 note 106) responds that the depiction of the Ascension, though brief, is complete.

The chief prosodic form of this play is a thirteener rhyming ababbcbc deeed. 1–4 and 44–7 are quatrains, and 48–56 is a 9-line stanza rhyming ababcdddc.

The Proclamation description, which comprises nine lines that complete a thirteener, does not mention the Selection of Matthias.

39/1 Cf. Luke 24: 36 (Vulgate).

39/4 *prynspal his he*: 'it is of the highest importance'.

39/5–8 Cf. Mark 16: 14.

39/10–13 The *Legenda Aurea* and the *Stanzaic Life of Christ* list eight scriptural apparitions by the risen Christ prior to this episode: to Magdalene, to the women, to Simon, to the pilgrims on the way to Emmaus, and to the disciples gathered at the cenacle; then, eight days after the Resurrection, to the disciples, including Thomas, to the disciples fishing in the lake of Galilee, and then on Mount Thabor. These texts also refer to three non-scriptural appearances, including the one to the Virgin Mary, presented in N-town Play 35. Counting that appearance among the eight referred to in line 10, however, would throw off the correspondence with the eight in the *Legenda*.

39/14–17 Cf. Luke 24: 41–3.

39/20–8 Cf. Acts 1: 4–5, also Luke 24: 44, 49, Matt. 3: 11, Mark 1: 8, Luke 3: 16, John 1: 26, 33, Acts 11: 16.

39/29–30 In Luke 24: 50, Christ leads the disciples to Bethany; the *Meditationes* and several English texts specify that they go to Olivet.

39/31–43 Cf. Acts 1: 6–8.

39/47 s.d.–54 Cf. Acts 1: 9–11 and Towneley 29/286–9, and compare Love's *Mirrour*: '. . . that he schulde come in that self forme bodily to deme alle quikke and dede, but that they schuld turne aȝen in to the citee' (p. 291). The stage direction refers to an unspecified song; Woolf (p. 284) points out that the other English cycles have the antiphon 'Ascendo ad patrem meum' sung during the Ascension.

39/57–62, 70–91 s.d. Cf. Acts 1: 15–26. N-town replaces the account of Judas' death in this chapter of Acts with the story of his suicide in Matt. 27: 5; cf. N-town 30/32 s.d. Line 57 lacks a speaker heading, but, as Falke (p. 91) observes, Peter is certainly the speaker, as in Acts 1: 15–20.

39/59–62 Acts 1: 20 refers to Psalms 68: 25 and 108: 8 (Vulgate). Davies (p. 361) also cites Ps. 40: 10.

39/90 *þe lott of Judas plas*: 'the position allotted to Judas'.

PLAY 40

The Pentecost play, like the preceding play of the Ascension, is extremely brief, closely follows its biblical source in Acts, and is written in the form ababbcbcdeeed, a stanzaic pattern found in the cycle only in these two plays (but see the headnote to Play 8). Block (p. xxxii) contends that this play, like Play 39, is incomplete, but Fry (p. 564 note 106) argues that the play presents the essential facts of the Pentecost and comprises a dramatic unit.

The Proclamation description broadly agrees with the action of the play, though it provides detail about which the play is silent.

40/1–4 Gauvin (pp. 204–5) proposes that each apostle receives from the Holy Ghost the virtue that he names in these lines.

40/14–15, 18 Cf. Acts 2: 13.

40/27–38 Cf. Acts 2: 14–36. Gauvin (p. 204) suggests emending *seyn* to *sleyn* in line 36, in keeping with Acts 2: 23–4, but lines 35–8 can be satisfactorily rendered without alteration: 'In which he speaks in plain language indeed about that (which) you have seen'.

PLAY 41

The Assumption of Mary play very closely follows its principal source, the *Legenda Aurea*, which substantially incorporates the *Transitus Mariae*. The play revises and reorders the *Legenda*, however, and often goes beyond it, dramatizing, for example, portions of the *Transitus Mariae* that have not come down to us in the *Legenda*. The play contains many liturgical pieces, including several from the feast of the Assumption. Most of these appear in the *Legenda*, though N-town sometimes follows the formulations of scripture or the liturgy rather than the *Legenda*.

Woolf (pp. 287–8) notes the importance of spectacle in this play, and cites the effective use of choral and instrumental music to signify sublime mysteries and accompany marvellous events; cf. Dutka, p. 72.

The chief stanzaic forms in this play are long-lined thirteeners rhyming ababababbcccb and long-lined abababab octaves. These thirteeners have the same rhyme-scheme as the 'Herod thirteeners' of plays 18 and 20, but have longer lines and less dense alliteration. 384–96 were presumably of this stanzaic type before the rhyme-words in 388 and 390 were obliterated; 410–22 are short lined. Six quatrains appear in the play (five of them with long lines), along with three long-lined thirteeners rhyming abababababcdddc (371–83, 397–409, 464–76), a long-lined thirteener rhyming ababababbaccca (153–65), and a long-lined octave rhyming ababbaba (356–63). Uniquely in this cycle, the Assumption play employs many intercalated couplets and single lines, linked by rhyme to contiguous stanzas. 92–3 and 242–3 comprise couplets that are not linked to surrounding stanzas in this way.

This play is an interpolation. It is not mentioned in the Proclamation, is written by a different hand on different paper from that found elsewhere in the codex, and is prosodically, stylistically, and orthographically distinct from the other plays.

41/1-13 Greg takes the rhyme-scheme in the tail of this stanza to be -cdddc (*The Assumption of the Virgin* (Oxford, 1915), p. 34).

41/2-4 Greg (*Assumption*, p. 65) renders *a book clepid apocriphum* as 'a book said to be apocryphal' (cf. *OED*, *apocrypha*, A. *adj*; also *MED*, *apocrif*, *-a*, *-um*). Compare the *Legenda Aurea*: 'Assumptio beatae Mariae uirginis qualiter facta sit ex quodam libello apocrypho, qui Iohanni euangelistae ascribitur, edocetur' (Cap. CXIIII). I quote from the 1482 Strassburg edition, reproduced by Greg (pp. 40–3), who notes that this text is superior to the Graesse edition in spelling, punctuation, and accuracy. Block (pp. xix, lvii) refutes Gayley's contention that the play was based on Caxton's Englished *Golden Legend*.

41/5-12 Cf. the *Legenda Aurea*: 'Et secundum quod ait Epiphanius uiginte quatuor annis post ascensionem filii sui superuixit. Refert ergo quod beata uirgo quando Christum concepit erat annorum quatuordecim et in quinto decimo ipsum peperit et uixit cum eo annis triginta tribus, et post mortem Christi superuixit uiginti quatuor annis. Et secundum hoc quando obiit erat annorum septuaginta duorum. Probabilius tamen uidetur quod alibi legitur, ut duodecim annis filio superuixerit, et sic sexagenaria sit assumpta, cum apostoli totidem annis predicauerint in Iudaea et circa partes illas, sicut ecclesiastica tradit historia.'

41/11 Cf. 'Assumpt aboue / the heuenly Ierarchie / Cristes Modre', lines Carleton Brown attributes to Lydgate in 'Lydgate's Verses on Queen Margaret's Entry into London', *Modern Language Review* 7 (1912), 230.

41/13 Falke (p. 92): 'Unter der Legenda Sanctorum ist die Legenda aurea . . . zu verstehen'.

41/14-21 Cf. the *Legenda Aurea*: 'Apostolis namque ob praedicationis gratiam diuersas mundi subeuntibus regiones uirgo beata in domo iuxta montem Sion posita dicitur remansisse. Omniaque loca filii sui, scilicet locum baptismi, ieiunii, orationis, passionis, sepulturae, resurrectionis et ascensionis, quoad uixit deuotione sedula uisitauit.'

41/17 Greg says that *went* is 'almost a technical term. You *go* to a pilgrimage' (*Assumption*, p. 65). But *MED*, *gōn*, v. 3 (a) cites more general applications of this usage; cf. N-town 13/14.

41/27 The speaker heading is cropped, *Mi* remaining. Greg says that this is 'no doubt *Miles*' (*Assumption*, p. 66).

41/31 *attayne*: Greg suggests emending to *attame* 'undertake, endeavour', in order to improve the sense and the rhyme (*Assumption*, p. 66). *MED* cites this line under *atteinen*, v. 1 (a) 'attain or achieve (a purpose, a desired end); obtain'. But 'find out' seems a more appropriate rendering (*OED*, *attain*, v. 9).

41/33 *pillid* is a term of abuse, but may best be rendered here as 'tonsured' (Greg, *Assumption*, p. 66; cf. *MED*, *pīlen*, v. (1), 6 (b)).

41/48-9 'We must not hesitate to deal severely with such rogues'. *won* in 48 is

COMMENTARY

perhaps a shortened form of *wonde* (OE *wandian*; compare *won* as a pp. of *wind*; *bon*, as a pp. of *bind*).

41/58 *Whoso clyme ouyrhie, he hath a foule fall*: cf. Whiting, C296; also *Wisdom*, 444, and Eccles' note.

41/63 *relefe*: Block and *MED* (*relēfen* v. b) render this as 'remain'. Cf. *relevys* 'remainder' in 9/290. Greg's 'relieve, rise again' is less likely here. Gower uses *relieve* reflexively in the sense 'essay, presume' (cited by *OED*, *relieve*, v. 6d.).

41/83 'But once that sister, Mary, that fart, is dead. . . .'

41/98–102 Cf. the *Legenda Aurea*: 'Die igitur quadam dum in filii desiderium cor uirginis uehementer accenditur aestuans animus commouetur et in exteriorem lacrimarum abundantiam excitatur, cumque ad tempus subtracti filii aequanimiter non ferret subtracta solacia. . . .'

41/116 s.d. Dutka (pp. 88, 92) says that these citharas are the only plucked instruments that are certainly played in any of the English cycles, and notes that the citharas and the organ referred to later (see 313 s.d. and the note) seem to have been used as principal instruments rather than as accompaniment for the angelic choir.

41/117–20 Cf. the *Legenda Aurea*: 'ecce angelus cum multo lumine eidem astitit et reuerenter utpote sui domini matrem salutauit. "Aue", inquit, "benedicta Maria suscipiens benedictionem illius qui mandauit salutem Iacob"'.

41/121 *seuer*: apparently a variant of (*as*)*sure*; cf. line 439.

41/123–4 Cf. the *Legenda Aurea*: 'Si inueni gratiam in oculis tuis obsecro ut nomen tuum mihi reuelare digneris'. Meredith ('A Reconsideration', p. 45) observes that *is* has been erased and reinserted at the end of line 124.

41/125, 127 Cf. the *Legenda Aurea*: 'Cui angelus, "Cur scire desideras, domina, nomen meum quod admirabile est et magnum?"'

41/128–30, 133–5 Cf. the *Legenda Aurea*: 'Ecce autem ramum palmae de paradiso ad te dominam attuli quem ante feretrum portare iubeas cum die tertia de corpore assumeris, nam filius tuus te matrem reuerendam expectat'.

41/132 Cf. York 44/26.

41/142–4 Cf. the *Legenda Aurea*: 'Sed hoc peto instantius ut filii et fratres mei apostoli ad me pariter congregentur, ut eos antequam moriar corporalibus oculis uideam'.

41/147–50 Cf. the *Legenda Aurea*: 'Nam qui olim prophetam de Iudaea in Babylonem in crine attulit subito, ipse procul dubio ad te apostolos adducere poterit in momento'. See Bel and the Dragon, Dan. 14: 30–42 (Vulgate).

41/148 *the lake of lyonys*: cf. 'in lacum leonum' in Dan. 14: 30.

41/153–4 Cf. the *Legenda Aurea*: 'Hoc iterum peto et obsecro ut anima mea de corpore exiens nullum spiritum teterrimum uideat, nullaque mihi Sathanae potestas occurrat'.

41/157–8 Cf. the *Legenda Aurea*: 'Malignum autem spiritum uidere cur metuis cum caput eius omnino contriueris et spoliaueris ipsum suae potestatis imperio?'

41/161 'He shall not attempt that'; or 'So that he shall not attempt (to act)'.

41/165 s.d. Cf. the *Legenda Aurea*: 'His dictis angelus cum multo lumine caelos ascendit'.

41/172-4 Cf. the *Transitus Mariae*: 'And she asked all her relations to [guard] her, and give her comfort. And she had along with her three virgins' (*Ante-Nicene Fathers*, VIII: 592). *replyeth*: *MED*, *replīen*, v. (1) 2 (b) cites this instance in the sense 'answer'. Block renders the word as 'apply'.

41/183 The missing word rhymes with 'Savyoure'. Greg suggests 'honoure' (*Assumption*, p. 68).

41/187 s.d.-191 Cf. the *Legenda Aurea*: 'Factum est autem, dum Iohannes in Epheso predicaret, caelum repente intonuit et nubes candida ipsum sustulit ac raptum ante Mariae ianuam collacauit'. *Sanctus Johannes Euangelista*: ancient tradition, going back to Clement of Alexandria, Tertullian, and the Muratorian Canon, identified John the Apostle as the author of the fourth gospel.

41/188-95 The erased rhyme-words *now* (?) in 188, 190, and 192, and *is* in 193 (?), 194, and 195, produced the atypical pattern ababacb. 194 was perhaps intended to conclude '. . . is moste brith now'. The present arrangement permits the abababab form characteristic of this play. 193-5 were incomplete without the erased words. Yet the rhyme-lines pass through the erasures, suggesting that the rhyming words were written and erased before the rhyme-brackets were drawn. The word 'is' was later interlined in 193-5.

41/195 s.d.-202 Cf. the *Legenda Aurea*: 'Percutiensque ostium interius introiuit et reuerenter uirgo uirginem salutauit. Quem felix Maria conspiciens uehementer obstupuit et prae gaudio lacrimas continere nequiuit. Dixitque, "Fili Iohannes, memor esto uerborum magistri tui quibus me tibi in matrem et te mihi in filium commendauit"'.

41/195 s.d. Greg: '*Sⁱ* is the usual contraction for *sibi*, which is perhaps not an impossible reading, though one would rather expect *sic* (*sᶜ*)' (*Assumption*, p. 68).

41/202 *And you me moder*: 'And (bade) you (call) me mother'.

41/212-18 John's lament recalls *Cursor Mundi*, 20,317-21 and 20,351-5; cf. York 44/48-52.

41/215 *þu*: Greg, observing that Scribe D usually preferred *th-* spellings to the use of the thorn, infers that the exemplar had a *y*-shaped thorn which occasionally led D to write *y* in error for *th* (*Assumption*, p. 68).

41/220-3 Cf. the *Legenda Aurea*: 'Tu igitur hanc palmam deferri facies ante feretrum cum corpus meum duxeritis ad sepulcrum'.

41/224-8 Cf. the *Legenda Aurea*: 'Audiui enim Iudaeos iniisse consilium, dicentes, "Expectemus, uiri fratres, quoadusque illa quae Iesum portauit subeat mortem et corpus eius continuo rapiemus ac iniectum ignibus comburemus"'.

41/233–5 Cf. the *Legenda Aurea*: 'Dixitque Iohannes, "O utinam hic essent omnes apostoli fratres mei. . . . Haec illo dicente omnes apostoli de locis in quibus praedicabant a nubibus rapiuntur et ante Mariae ostium collocantur. Qui uidentes se ibidem insimul congregatos mirabantur, dicentes, 'Quaenam causa est propter quam nos hic dominus insimul congragauit?'"' Compare York 44/57.

41/236–42 Cf. the *Transitus Mariae*: 'Peter was urging Paul to pray first, Paul answered and said: That is thy duty, to begin first, especially seeing that thou hast been chosen by God a pillar (Gal. ii. 9) of the Church, and thou hast precedence of all in the apostleship; but it is by no means mine, for I am the least of you all, and Christ was seen by me as one born out of due time (I Cor. xv. 8); nor do I presume to make myself equal to you: nevertheless by the grace of God I am what I am (I Cor. xv. 10). Then all the apostles, rejoicing [at the humility of Paul] with one mind, finished their prayer' (VIII: 596). 240–1 follow 1 Cor. 15: 9 rather than the *Transitus Mariae*; 242 is a corruption of 1 Cor. 15: 10.

41/249 *cherubyn halle*: 'the abode of the cherubim', or 'all cherubim' (Greg, *Assumption*, p. 69).

41/253–6, 263–70 Cf. the *Legenda Aurea*: 'Iohannes igitur ad eos exiit et dominam de corpore recessuram praedixit. Et addidit dicens, "Vidite, fratres, ne cum obierit aliquis eam defleat, ne hoc uidens populus conturbetur et dicat, 'Ecce quomodo isti timent mortem qui tamen aliis predicant resurrectionem!'"'

41/267 'For we say that all those (who) believe. . . .'

41/281–5 Cf. the *Transitus Mariae*: 'And she said to them: Peace be with you, most beloved brethren! How have you come hither? And they recounted to her how they had come, each one raised on a cloud by the Spirit of God, and set down in the same place' (VIII: 596). Compare *Cursor Mundi*, 20,441–4. Greg says that either *was* in 284 was attracted to the singular by the intervening object, or that *Diueris clowdys* was felt in a partitive sense (*Assumption*, p. 70).

41/297–9 Cf. the *Transitus Mariae*: 'Now therefore I implore you, that without intermission you all with one mind watch, even till that hour in which the Lord will come, and I shall depart from the body' (VIII: 596). Compare *Cursor Mundi*, 20,455–7.

41/303–9 Cf. Matt. 25: 1–13.

41/311 s.d.–313 s.d. Cf. the *Legenda Aurea*: 'Circa uero horam noctis tertiam Iesus aduenit cum angelorum ordinibus, patriarcharum coetibus, martyrum agminibus, confessorum acie, uirginumque choris, et ante torum uirginis acies ordinantur et dulcia cantica frequentantur'. Craig (p. 270) argues that the reference to an organ indicates that the play was or had been put on in a church, but Martial Rose ('The Staging of the Hegge Plays', in *Medieval*

Drama (Stratford-upon-Avon Studies, 16, 1973), p. 218) and Dutka (p. 88) observe that portative organs could have been used. Woolf (p. 411 note 67) says that *organa* in 313 s.d. could refer to a consort of musical instruments.

41/318–29 s.d. Cf. the *Legenda Aurea*: 'Nam prior ipse Iesus incohauit et dixit, "Veni, electa mea, et ponam in te thronum meum, quia concupiui speciem tuam." Et illa, "Paratum cor meum, domine, paratum cor meum." Tunc omnes qui cum Iesu uenerant dulciter intonauerunt, dicentes, "Haec est quae nesciuit torum in delictis, habebit fructum in refectione animarum sanctarum." Ipsa autem de semetipsa cecinit dicens, "Beatam me dicent omnes generationes quia fecit mihi magna qui potens est et sanctum nomen eius." Tunc cantor cantorum omnibus intonauit excellentius, "Veni de Libano, sponsa, veni, coronaberis." Et illa, "Ecce uenio quia in capite libri scriptum est de me ut facerem uoluntatem tuam, deus, quia exultauit spiritus meus in te salutari meo." Sicque Mariae anima de corpore egreditur et in ulnas filii aduolauit'. 'Veni electa mea' and 'Beatam me' appear in the liturgy for the feast of the Assumption (Dutka, p. 139). Dutka cites the respond 'Paratum cor meum' and the antiphon 'Hec est que nesciuit' in the Sarum Breviary (pp. 31, 35). For 'Veni de Libano' and 'Ecce venio', see Dutka, pp. 44–7 and 25. 'Veni electa mea' and 'Veni de Libano' are sung in the York Assumption play: see John Stevens' discussion in the Beadle edition.

41/318 *Veni tu, electa mea*: Dutka (pp. 47, 71) notes that N-town adds *tu* to the 'Veni electa mea' of the liturgy and the *Legenda*. She adds that both the N-town and the York versions have 'quia concupiuit rex speciem tuam', while the *Legenda* gives 'concupiui' and omits 'rex'.

41/320–1 These lines follow the text of the liturgical respond 'Paratum cor meum', and so diverge from the *Legenda* (Dutka, pp. 35, 71).

41/322–3 *Hec est que nesciuit*: compare the Sarum Breviary: 'Hec est que nesciuit thorum in delicto habebit fructum in refectione animarum sanctarum' (Dutka, p. 31). Dutka (p. 71) notes that the substitution of 'requiem' for 'fructum' and 'respectu' for 'refectione' make the dirge more appropriate to the context.

41/325 *Quia fecit michi magna*: N-town agrees with the *Legenda* and Luke 1: 49 rather than with the respond cited by Dutka (p. 22).

41/326 *Veni de Libano, sponsa mea*: N-town agrees with S. of S. 4: 8. The *Legenda* and the York cycle, by contrast, omit 'mea', as does the liturgical piece cited by Dutka (pp. 44, 71).

41/329 N-town agrees with Luke 1: 47 rather than with the *Legenda*.

41/332–7 Cf. the *Legenda Aurea*: 'Dixitque apostolis dominus, "Corpus uirginis matris in vallem Iosaphat deferte et in monumento nouo quod ibidem inuenietis illud recondite, et me ibidem triduo donec ad uos redeam exspectate"'.

41/336 *severe*: 'certainly, surely'; or 'secure'. Cf. lines 121 and 439.

41/342 Cf. the *Legenda Aurea*: 'Post eam apostoli clamitant dicentes. . . . "Esto nostri memor, o domina"'.

41/343–7 Cf. the *Legenda Aurea*: 'Tunc ad concentum ascendentium coetus qui remanserant admirati concite obuiam processerunt. Videntesque regem suum feminae animam in ulnis propriis baiulantem, illamque super illum innixam, obstupefacti clamare coeperunt, dicentes, "Quae est ista quae ascendit de deserto deliciis affluens innixa super dilectum suum?" Quibus concomitantes dixerunt, "Ista est speciosa inter filias Hierusalem sicut uidistis eam plenam caritate et dilectione." Sicque in caelum gaudens suscipitur et a dextris filii in throno gloriae collocatur'. The liturgical dialogue 'Que est ista que assendit de deserto' is from the feast of the Assumption (Woolf, p. 411 note 69). Cf. S. of S. 8: 5.

41/356–68 Cf. the *Legenda Aurea*: 'Dixitque Iohannes Petro, "Hanc palmam ante feretrum, Petre, portabis, quia dominus nobis te praetulit et suarum ouium pastorem et principem ordinauit." Cui Petrus, "Hanc potius portare te conuenit, quia uirgo a domino es electus et dignum est ut palmam uirginis uirgo ferat. Tu super pectus domini recumbere meruisti et exinde sapientiae ac gratiae plus ceteris fluenta potasti, et iustum uidetur ut qui a filio recepisti plus muneris impendas uirgini plus honoris. Tu igitur portare debes hanc palmam luminis. . . . Ergo autem portabo cum feretro sanctum corpus". . . . Paulus autem dixit ei, "Et ego qui minimus omnium uestrum sum portabo tecum"'.

41/360 Cf. John 13: 23. *seyng all celestly*: *seyng* is probably 'seeing' (rather than 'saying'): the *Northern Passion*, 271 ff., says that while John slept on Jesus' breast, an angel took his spirit to heaven, where he saw God (Block, p. l). Greg suggests 'everything heavenly' for *all celestly* (*Assumption*, p. 71).

41/368 s.d.–370 s.d. Cf. the *Legenda Aurea*: 'Eleuantes itaque Petrus et Paulus feretrum, Petrus incipit cantare ac dicere, "Exiit Israel de Aegypto, alleluia." Ceteri autem apostoli cantum dulciter prosequuntur. . . . Affuerunt et angeli cum ipsis concinentes et totam terram sonitu mirae suauitatis replentes'. N-town follows 'Exiit Israel', a psalm in the burial service, rather than the *Legenda* (Dutka, pp. 27, 68).

41/371–452 s.d. Cf. the *Legenda Aurea*: 'Excitati omnes ad tam dulcem sonum et melodiam de ciuitate uelocius exeunt, et quidnam hoc sit diligenter sciscitantur. Tunc exstitit qui diceret, "Mariam illam discipuli Iesu efferunt mortuam, circa illam hanc quam auditis concinunt melodiam." Tunc ad arma omnes concurrerunt, et se mutuo hortabantur, dicentes, "Venite omnes discipulos occidamus ac corpus illud quod seductorem illum portauit ignibus comburamus." Princeps autem sacerdotum hoc uidens obstupit et ira repletus ait, "Ecce tabernaculum illius qui nos et genus nostrum conturbauit, qualem gloriam nunc accipit." Et hoc dicens manus ad feretrum misit uolens illud euertere ac ad terram deducere. Tunc manus eius subito ambae aruerunt et lectulo adhaeserunt, ita ut ad lectulum manibus penderet et nimio cruciatu uexatus lamentabiliter eiularet. . . . Princeps autum sacerdotum clamabat, dicens, "Sancte Petre, in hac tribultione me non despicias sed pro me obsecro ad dominum preces fundas. Memor enim debes esse qualiter aliquando tibi astiti et qualiter te accusante ancilla ostiaria excusaui." Cui Petrus, "In obsequiis dominae nostrae impediti sumus et curationi tuae intendere non ualemus. Verum tamen si in dominum nostrum Iesum et in hanc quae ipsum genuit et portauit credideris spero quod continuo sanitatis beneficio potieris." Qui respondit, "Credo dominum Iesum Christum uerum esse filium dei et hanc sacratissimam matrem eius". . . . Dixitque ei Petrus, "Accipe hanc palmam de manu fratris nostri Iohannis et pones eam super populum excaecatum, et quicumque credere uoluerit recipiet uisum, qui autem credere noluerit uidere non poterit in aeternum." Mariam autem portantes apostoli in monumento posuerunt et iuxta illud ut dominus iusserat consederunt.'

41/408 Greg takes *stent* to be an error for *stene* 'stone' (*Assumption*, p. 71), but *OED* (*stint*, v. 9) cites this instance in the sense 'cause . . . to cease moving, bring to a stand'.

41/410–11 Cf. the *Legenda Aurea*: 'Dominus autem feretrum et apostolos nube protexit, ita quod ipsi non uidebantur sed tamen eorum uox audiebatur'.

41/415 'May the devil reward him (who) brought me here'.

41/417 *wyndand wod*: 'raving mad', perhaps 'wandering mad'; cf. 'welland wode' in Towneley 8/344.

41/453–4 The antiphon 'De terra' is from the ceremony of the inhumation of the dead (Dutka, p. 68). It does not appear in the *Legenda Aurea* account.

41/463 s.d.–475 Cf. the *Transitus Mariae*: 'when they heard the words of the chief who had been cured speaking, they believed in the Lord Jesus Christ; and when he put the palm over their eyes, they recovered sight. Five of them remaining in hardness of heart died' (VIII: 598).

41/467 '(Which) shall alleviate your sickness. . . .'

41/471 *belthe*: 'misfortune, evil' (OE *bealo*); *MED* cites this instance only, but cf. Greg, *Assumption*, p. 73.

41/477 *herne*: *MED* (*hirn(e)*, n. 1. d) cites this instance in the sense 'pit of hell', but 'corner' (sense 1. a) is also feasible. In view of the rhyme with *brenne*, *renne*, and *denne*, *herne* may be a metathesized form of *iren* 'iron chains', recalling Christ's binding of Satan during the Harrowing of Hell (*MED* lists *herne* as a variant of *iren*). Cf. Towneley 30/94–5: 'I was bonde . . . In yrens'.

41/478 *Vs fettyn*: 'Let us fetch', or 'We go to fetch' (see F. Th. Visser, *An Historical Syntax of the English Language* (Leiden, 1970), I: 245).

41/480 'Make ready for (the time that) we return to this (place), demon'.

41/495 s.d.–521 s.d. Cf. the *Legenda Aurea*: 'Tertia autem die ueniens Iesus cum multitudine angelorum ipsos salutauit, dicens, "Pax uobis." Qui responderunt, "Gloria tibi, deus, qui facis mirabilia magna solus." Et dixit apostolis dominus, "Quid gratiae et honoris uobis uidetur ut meae nunc conferam genetrici?" Et illi, "Iustum uidetur, domine, seruis tuis ut sicut tu deuicta morte regnas in saecula, sic tuae resuscites matris corpusculum et a dextris tuis colloces in aeternum." Quo annuente Michael angelus continuo affuit et Mariae animam coram domino praesentauit. Tunc saluator locutus est, dicens "Surge, proxima mea, columba mea, tabernaculum gloriae, uasculum uitae, templum caeleste, ut sicut per coitum labem non sensisti criminis, sic in sepulcro solutionem corporis minime patiaris." Statimque anima ad Mariae accessit corpusculum et de tumulo prodiit gloriosum. Sicque ad aetherium assumitur thalamum comitante secum multitudine angelorum.'

41/510–11 Cf. S. of S. 2: 10 and the antiphon 'Tota pulchra es' (Dutka, p. 72).

41/513 *clene... of alle synnys greyn*: 'free ... of the stain of any sin' (compare the *Legenda* above).

41/522 'Assumpta est Maria' is both an antiphon and an alleluia verse for the feast of the Assumption (Dutka, p. 68; Downing, p. 209). It does not appear in the *Legenda Aurea* account.

41/523–6 Cf. *Cursor Mundi*, 20,679–81), and York 46 and 46A.

PLAY 42

The Judgement Day play is ultimately based on Matt. 25: 31–46. In the play, Deus denounces the damned for their failure to perform the seven corporal works of mercy, and the devils then link each instance of this failure to one of the Seven Deadly Sins.

The Play is incomplete, and the text as we have it is spare in comparison to the other English Judgement plays. It is written in Proclamation thirteeners, and broadly agrees with the Proclamation, which describes the Judgement in general terms.

42/7–9 Sister Mary Margaret Walsh points out that these lines recall the *Dies Irae* sequence:

> Quid sum miser tunc dicturus?
> Quem patronum rogaturus,
> Cum vix justus sit securus?

('The Judgment Plays of the English Cycles', *American Benedictine Review* 20 (1969), 388). Cf. Owst, *Literature and Pulpit*, p. 275.

42/39 Cf. York 47/125–6.

42/40–2 *Venite, benedicti*: cf. Matt. 25: 34, Dutka, p. 51, Chester 24/453, and the Chester late banns (*Records of Early English Drama: Chester*, ed. Lawrence M. Clopper (Toronto and Buffalo, 1979), 246/34). Clifford Davidson notes that this invitation to the blessed is common in the visual arts ('Gesture in Medieval Drama with Special Reference to the Doomsday Plays in the

Middle English Cycles', *EDAM Newsletter* 6 (1983), 11). *Come hedyr to me* was a common line: cf. *Canterbury Tales*, A 672, *Pearl*, 763, and Chester 24/453.

42/44 See the note to 20/272–83.

42/53–6 Hildburgh cites alabasters showing similar scenes of welcome by Peter; see Davidson, 'Gesture', p. 13.

42/68 *rubbe*: perhaps 'run about' (cf. *OED*, *rub*, v.[1] 16, and compare N-town 41/416. Or the word may indicate an act of self-injury denoting despair (Davidson, 'Gesture', pp. 13–14).

42/79–86 Cf. Matt. 25: 42–3. The other English Judgement plays cite only the six corporal works of mercy given in Matt. 25. For the seventh, burial of the dead, see Tobit 1: 20 (Vulgate), Ecclus. 38: 16; and 2 Macc. 12: 39. Compare *Cursor Mundi*, 23,081–92.

42/92–5 Cf. York 47/337–9, Towneley 30/494–6.

42/118 *þu ssalte sewe*: 'you lecherous sow'. Davies suggests 'you shall follow (into hell)', but *salt* for 'shall' is unexampled in this manuscript.

APPENDIX 1
THE COMPOSITION AND DEVELOPMENT OF THE N-TOWN CYCLE

The cycle is manifestly eclectic. It contains over two dozen prosodic forms written by four scribes on at least seven kinds of paper. The Proclamation describes forty pageants, several of which do not correspond to the forty-one plays that have come down to us. There are many expositors and homilists in the cycle, three of whom preside over plays that are omitted by or largely incongruous with the Proclamation. And many of the plays in the collection are inconsistent, either internally or with respect to other plays. Given the intricate disharmonies of the text, one may understand why W. W. Greg called the cycle 'one of the chief puzzles of our early dramatic literature'.[1]

The textual complexity of the collection resulted from extensive compilation and revision that continued even after the main scribe had recorded the plays. Greg and Esther L. Swenson argued that the principal constituents of the text can be sorted out, however, by comparing the Proclamation descriptions with correlative plays. They further concluded that the textual layers of the collection are associated with specific verse forms. Subsequent studies, including my own, have attempted to extend and correct their findings by applying a wide variety of bibliographic and literary tests. Among these are an analysis of incongruity and redundancy within and between plays, as well as examination of expositors' speeches, the use of sources, linguistic patterns, and other manuscript and scribal evidence.[2]

My investigation of the plays confirms that the major strata of the

---

[1] W. W. Greg, *Bibliographical and Textual Problems of the English Miracle Cycles* (London, 1914), p. 108.

[2] See Greg, pp. 108–43; Swenson, *An Inquiry into the Composition and Structure of Ludus Coventriae* (Minneapolis, 1914); my 'Composition and Development of an Eclectic Manuscript: Cotton Vespasian D. Viii', *Leeds Studies in English* 9 (1977), 62–83 (which cites earlier studies of the composition of the cycle); and my 'Genesis of the N-Town Cycle' (Yale Ph.D. thesis, 1973), published in revised form as *The Genesis of the N-town Cycle* (New York and London, 1988). Prosodic evidence is less crucial to investigations of the strata of the cycle by K. S. Block (*Ludus Coventriae*, EETS ES 120 (1922), xiiff.) and Kenneth Cameron and Stanley J. Kahrl ('Staging the N-Town Cycle', *Theatre Notebook* 21 (1967), 124–8). See Appendix 3 for discussion of a recent challenge to the value of applying stanzaic tests to reconstruct the development of the cycle.

cycle tend to be written in characteristic stanza forms. Proclamation thirteeners in the cycle, for example, appear to constitute a discrete layer of text.[1] These thirteeners exhibit very close thematic and verbal affinities to the Proclamation. Most of the Proclamation descriptions are themselves written in proclamation thirteeners, and they show detailed and extensive correspondences only to plays and portions of plays that are written in the same stanzaic form. By contrast, the Proclamation often does not mention plays written in other verse forms, or describes different plays from the ones that have come down to us in those forms.[2] The Proclamation echoes several of the proclamation thirteeners in the 'Marriage of Mary and Joseph' (Play 10), for instance, but says nothing of the two preceding Marian plays, which are written chiefly in long-lined octaves and quatrains.[3]

In addition to their common prosody and consonance with the Proclamation, proclamation thirteeners exhibit thematic links across plays. And they are sometimes incongruous with events depicted in other stanzaic forms. In the thirteeners of the 'Marriage', for example, Joachim and Anna bring Mary to the temple, contradicting the fact that they have already left her there in the long-lined octaves of the preceding play, the 'Presentation of Mary'. Another thirteener in the 'Marriage' then has the bishop assign Mary three handmaidens, despite the fact that she has already been assigned five by the bishop in the octaves of the 'Presentation'.[4] Proclamation thirteeners also share a common indebtedness to Pseudo-Matthew, while showing little or no influence of the sources that inform the Marian and Passion Plays. And unlike the Marian plays, which contain mixed Latin and English stage directions, or the Passion Plays, with their elaborate English stage directions, the comparatively few stage directions accompanying these thirteeners are in Latin.[5]

[1] For the names and characteristics of the stanzaic forms, see pp. xli–xliii; also my *Genesis of the N-town Cycle*, pp. 6–17.

[2] Plays in short-lined octaves constitute the chief exception to this pattern. The Proclamation is generally consistent with such plays, but lacks the extensive verbal affinities that it bears to plays in proclamation thirteeners. For a list of the plays in which proclamation thirteeners appear, see p. xlii note 3.

[3] For verbal parallels between the Proclamation and the thirteeners in the 'Marriage' compare Pr 121–2 and 10/6–7, Pr 139–43 and 10/126–32, Pr 145–7 and 10/138–40, Pr 150 and 10/262, and Pr 153–4 and 10/324. The Proclamation does not mention the subjects of plays 8, 9, or 13, or the Parliament of Heaven in Play 11.

[4] Proclamation thirteeners also contradict 10-line stanzas in 'Joseph's Doubt': see the note to 12/133–6.

[5] The 'Purification of Mary' (Play 19) also contains Latin and English stage directions. Several brief Latin stage directions appear in Passion Play 2. Play 34 has English

The expositor Contemplacio presides over a series of Mary plays written chiefly in long-lined octaves and quatrains. These plays include 'Joachim and Anna', the 'Presentation', and the 'Visit to Elizabeth' (plays 8, 9, and 13); also very probably portions of Play 10, and perhaps of Play 11.[1] His speeches, though revised, describe a self-contained sequence, and may be survivals of a time when these plays existed independently of the cycle. Unlike the plays in thirteeners, the Marian plays are indebted to the *Legenda Aurea*, the *Meditationes Vitae Christi*, and Nicholas Love's *Mirrour of the Blessed Lyf of Jesu Christ*. The Proclamation's omission of the Marian plays suggests that they were incorporated into the cycle at a comparatively late date, and this is confirmed by the fact that the numbering of the Proclamation descriptions was altered to take the addition of the Mary plays into account (see the headnote to the Proclamation). Scribal and manuscript evidence shows, in fact, that Marian material in long-lined octaves was being added to the cycle as the codex was transcribed.[2] Indeed, the practice of dotting the loops of capitula preceding octaves and quatrains in the Marian plays and the 'Marriage' appears to have been a way of keeping track of these stanzas, and of distinguishing them from the thirteeners (see p. xxix).

stage directions until the beginning of tail-rhyme, in which stage directions are in both Latin and English. One English stage direction appears amid the tail-rhyme in Play 33, and one at the head of Play 37.

[1] Octaves and quatrains in Play 10 are linked to the surrounding Marian plays, and distinct from the thirteeners, prosodically and linguistically: the word *wand* for 'rod' appears exclusively in the octaves and quatrains, while *ȝerd(e)* occurs in the thirteeners of the Proclamation description and the play (see J. Vriend, *The Blessed Virgin Mary in the Medieval Drama of England* (Purmerend, 1928), p. 54 n. 2). The octaves and quatrains are also distinguished in the play by scribal notation (see the discussion below of the dotting of the loops of capitula), in their use of sources, and by their depiction of Minister, a figure who appears in the 'Presentation' but not in the thirteeners of the 'Marriage'. The Annunciation scene in Play 11 may also be a survival of the Contemplacio group. See Spector, 'Composition and Development of an Eclectic Manuscript', 65–72.

[2] The long-lined octaves on f. 48ᵛ were recorded for interpolation into the 'Marriage' only after that play had been at least partially transcribed (see the note to 10/92–115 s.d.). Three other octaves and a quatrain (ll. 175–202) may also have been added to the play at that time: before 10/175 the scribe wrote, then crossed through, the speaker heading 'Primus Generacionis Dauid', which now precedes the proclamation thirteener at line 203. This may evidence a change in plans during transcription, whereby the octaves and quatrain, preceded by dotted capitula, were interpolated into text that otherwise consists of thirteeners (see Spector, 'Genesis of the N-Town Cycle', p. 49, and Peter Meredith, *The Mary Play* (London and New York, 1987), p. 101). The renumbering of the Proclamation and the dotting of the capitula (discussed below) also suggest that the Marian plays had been incorporated into the collection only recently. The same may be true of the red notations surrounding Contemplacio's speech in Play 11 (see xxviii), and of the cancellation of the stage direction at the close of the Annunciation scene in the same play (see the note to 11/340 s.d.).

Octaves rhyming abababab are most often associated with the
Marian plays. In the 'Visit to Elizabeth' (Play 13) they are clearly revisional and seem to have been added as the manuscript was transcribed: squeezed into insufficient space that had been left for them,
these octaves provide two alternative endings for the play. Several of
the abababab octaves follow Love's *Mirrour* very closely.

The 10-line stanzas that make up some of 'Joseph's Doubt' (Play 12)
and nearly all of the 'Purification of Mary' (Play 19) are also indebted
to Love. The 'Purification' appears to be a late addition to the cycle: it
is not mentioned in the Proclamation, and is inserted between the
'Magi' and 'Innocents', plays apparently intended for continuous
presentation. The intrusion of this play in its present position may
account for the discontinuous numbering of plays in that part of the
cycle (see the headnote to Play 17). The 10-line stanzas in the Joseph
play also appear to be interpolated: they contradict the proclamation
thirteeners in the play and in one instance appear to have split a thirteener into two stanzas.[1]

The sequences that I refer to as Passion Plays 1 and 2 are characterized by their mixing long- and short-lined octaves, quatrains, and
couplets, as well as occasional 5-line stanzas and other forms. Passion
Play 1 comprises plays 26–8 and the 'Procession of Saints'. Passion
Play 2 includes plays 29–32 (except for the interpolated ff. 184–5, into
which Play 32 dovetails) and most of Play 34. Similar dovetailing
occurs at the foot of f. 189ᵛ, the last page of T quire (see p. 541 note 1
below and the headnote to Play 29). The Passion Play sequences are in
many ways distinct from the bulk of the manuscript, and may, in an
earlier state, have been independent of the N-town collection.
Prosodically unlike the rest of the cycle, and following sources (especially the *Northern Passion*) that had little influence on other plays in
the collection, these sequences alone are characterized by extensive
English stage directions that elaborately specify costume and movement on a polyscenic stage involving scaffolds and a playing place.
The Passion Plays also differ orthographically and graphemically
from surrounding plays (see pp. xxii–xxiii). They were copied out on

---

[1] See the headnote to Play 12. Below 12/12 the main scribe wrote, then cancelled,
'how hast', the opening words of the first proclamation thirteener in the play (lines 21–
33). This change of plans may indicate that lines 13–20 were interpolated during transcription, an idea corroborated by the dotted capitulum before line 17 (see p. xxix n. 1).
Cf. Spector, 'Genesis of the N-Town Cycle', pp. 52–3, and Peter Meredith, 'Scribes,
Texts and Performance', in *Aspects of Early English Drama*, ed. Paula Neuss (Cambridge,
1983), pp. 28–9. Compare the similar pattern in Play 10, cited on p. 539 n. 2 above.

paper that was not used elsewhere in the codex, and variations in the main scribe's hand show that he transcribed them at a different time from the rest of the manuscript.[1] Though each of the Passion Plays seems intended for continuous playing, the rubricator added play-numbers that roughly correspond to the Proclamation divisions. The Passion Plays, especially Passion Play 2, often disagree with the Proclamation accounts, however, suggesting that they displaced the plays that the Proclamation was written to describe. The tail-rhyme plays into which they merge, by contrast, agree closely with the long thirteeners that describe them in the Proclamation.[2]

The 'Assumption of Mary' (Play 41) is also not mentioned in the Proclamation, indicating that it too was probably incorporated at a comparatively late date. This play is, in fact, an interpolation written by Scribe D, though possibly rubricated and corrected by the main scribe. It faithfully follows the *Legenda Aurea*, though it often goes beyond that source to include, for example, elements of the *Transitus Mariae*.

CONCLUSIONS: THE HISTORY OF THE CYCLE

The patterns noted above suggest the following hypothetical recon-struction of the main stages in the compilation of the cycle:

Close verbal and thematic correspondences demonstrate that many

[1] See pp. xviii–xxi, xxii–xxiii, and xxxiv. Block was mistaken in her claim that the Passion Plays were already copied when incorporated into the collection (*Ludus Coven-triae*, p. xxxi). As he copied out Passion Play 2, the main scribe clearly had before him existing constituents of the cycle written in other metres on different paper stock. On f. 183ᵛ, for example, he wrote a transition to the interpolated ff. 184–5, which are linked in several ways to the plays surrounding the Passion sequences, and which agree with the Proclamation (these leaves include the first of two tail-rhyme plays on the Harrow-ing of Hell; see note 2). Writing tail-rhyme stanzas in a small hand on f. 183ᵛ, the scribe copied two lines as one in insufficient space, in order to reach the point of transition to the interpolated leaves. The scribe similarly wrote tail-rhyme at the foot of f. 189ᵛ, the last page of the Two Crossed Keys paper, as a transition to the tail-rhyme on the YHS in a Sun Paper of V quire.

[2] Five long thirteeners appear in the Proclamation, and all accurately describe plays containing tail-rhyme. Pr 40–52 include the punishment in Eden, which is portrayed in the tail-rhyme section of the Fall of Man play. Pr 386–437 describe the Crucifixion, the Burial, the Harrowing of Hell in two parts, and the risen Christ's Appearance to Mary, all of which are dramatized in tail-rhyme (starting at 32/185). The division of the Har-rowing, and the Appearance to Mary, are unique subjects in English drama, certainly indicating that the poet of the long thirteeners attempted to harmonize the Proclama-tion with tail-rhyme plays. The long thirteener accounts fail to describe accurately only those actions that are dramatized in stanzas other than tail-rhyme.

Proclamation accounts were written to describe plays written in proclamation thirteeners.[1] Other plays, principally the Marian sequence, are not mentioned by the Proclamation, though its numbering of pageants was adjusted in order to take the Marian plays into account.[2] This, along with evidence within the plays proper, indicates that the Marian plays were additions to the cycle, and were perhaps incorporated as the manuscript was transcribed. Revisional ababab octaves were also added at that time, providing alternative endings for the 'Visit to Elizabeth'. The 'Assumption of Mary', also omitted by the Proclamation, is an interpolation written by Scribe D on paper not used elsewhere in the codex. Several plays described by the Proclamation have not come down to us, but in their place stand other plays, notably Passion Plays 1 and 2.

Several marginal notations, minor corrections, and a few interpolated leaves written by other scribes were added after the codex had been copied out and rubricated. One such interpolation is E quire, in the hand of Scribe B. Others are ff. 95–6 and 112, written by Scribe C, who also made many minor alterations as well as notations. In the 'Harrowing of Hell' and the Three Marys play (36), C's marginal notations refer to extensions of the text that are not recorded in the codex. Other marginal notes suggest the existence of an expanded version of Play 26, the 'Entry into Jerusalem' (see pp. xxiv–xxv). These notations show that the process of accretion and revision continued even after the main scribe had completed his work.

The addition of the Passion Plays, the 'Assumption', and the minor interpolations created a bewildering distribution of paper varieties. The manuscript may previously have consisted of only two kinds of paper: Bunch of Grapes and YHS in a Sun (see pp. xviii–xxi).

Though the learned marginal genealogies and notes in the codex suggested to Greg (p. 143) that the manuscript was written for private reading rather than performance, several marginal notes indicate that

[1] As noted above, Proclamation accounts are broadly consistent with plays in short-lined octaves. I do not conjecture when those plays were included in the collection, but at least two of them, the 'Trial of Mary and Joseph' (Play 14) and the 'Nativity' (Play 15), may have been added at a later date. The Proclamation descriptions of these plays appear to be revisional (see the note to Pr 183–90), as do the accounts in long thirteeners (see p. 541 n. 2 above).

[2] Swenson (p. 7) identifies the last part of 'Noah' as an addition to the cycle, both because the Proclamation does not mention the Lamech episode depicted in these lines, and also because the prosody shifts at that point to long-lined octaves written in tumbling metre.

the text was used in play production.[1] The marginal entry on f. 196, 'finem 1ª die Nota', possibly written by C, appears to divide the production of this portion of the cycle into smaller units. This extends a pattern of segmentation already apparent in the reference to Passion plays that were presented 'last 3ere' (29/9), and in Contemplatio's description of a sequence of Marian plays (8/9–16).

The eclecticism of the text does not preclude the possibility of thematic and artistic unity. The earlier constituents may in fact have set a model for selection or further composition. As Rosemary Woolf concludes, the subjective impression of N-town as a cycle of striking imaginative unity does not clash irresolvably with the objective evidence of discrepancies within the text.[2] See Appendix 3 for further discussion of this issue.

---

[1] See the marginal notes cited on pp. xxiii–xxiv. Kenneth Cameron and Stanley J. Kahrl list 'Angelus' (ff. 97ᵛ, 101ᵛ), 'go hom wardys' (f. 102), 'here goth he his way' (f. 129), as well as 'finem 1ª die Nota' (f. 196) as notations used by a prompter or stage manager ('The N-Town Plays at Lincoln', *Theatre Notebook* 20 (1965–6), 64).

[2] Rosemary Woolf, *The English Mystery Plays* (Berkeley and Los Angeles, 1972), p. 310.

APPENDIX 2
STAGING

Indications about the methods of staging the N-town plays vary with the constituents of the collection. The Proclamation describes discrete pageants that will be begun on 'Sunday next . . . At vj of þe belle'. Plays that agree thematically with Proclamation accounts also tend to be discrete, and several are demarked by incipits and explicits.[1] By contrast, many plays that are omitted by or incongruous with the Proclamation bear signs of continuous performance. These principally include the Marian plays, presided over by the expositor Contemplacio, and the Passion sequences, which contain elaborate English stage directions alluding to the use of scaffolds in polyscenic production.

Several scholars have inferred that the cycle thus records processional methods of presentation for some plays, and continuous, polyscenic prodution for others. Greg (p. 142) concluded that it was only the revisers of the cycle who contemplated continuous performance on a polyscenic stage. More boldly, Swenson (p. 71) proposed that the plays were acted on movable vehicles up to the Marian plays, which were mounted on a fixed stage; the cycle then resumed processing through the streets until the performance of the Passion sequences, which were presented on another fixed stage; the players then proceeded to a church to give the 'Assumption of Mary' and possibly the Judgement play. She considered it more plausible, however, that pageants were rolled before a stationary audience, as suggested by Noah's entrance with the ark in Play 4, and by the stage direction 'Hic intrabit page[n]tum de Purgacione Marie et Joseph' in Play 14. In any case, Swenson suggested that N-town represents the transition from acting on movable pageants to more elaborate production on a fixed stage.

Kenneth Cameron and Stanley J. Kahrl extend the notion that N-town employed alternative methods of presentation. They argue that older plays in the cycle have only one or two locations each, suggesting processional 'pageant' staging, while the newer plays have the

---

[1] The Proclamation agrees principally with plays in proclamation thirteeners and short octaves, often echoing the former (see p. 538). The appearance of incipits and explicits is reported on p. xxvi.

multiple locations and simultaneous action characteristic of the in-the-round staging described by Richard Southern in *The Medieval Theatre in the Round.*[1] They suggest that Adam's reappearance in Play 3 and the Lamech episode in Play 4 are interpolations that may represent a late attempt to adapt processional plays to a fixed playing area. And they contend that the Mary plays have been reconstructed for central staging, as indicated by the common use of several fixed *loca* in succeeding plays. Cameron and Kahrl propose that the Ministry plays have processional characteristics, and that the central staging of the Passion Plays may have given way to sequential staging at the point marked by the marginal 'finem 1ª die Nota' (see p. 543 above). Thus two very different systems of presentation were, according to this reconstruction, put before the same audience on successive days.

Other scholars argue, however, that the entire cycle was presented continuously on a fixed stage. E. K. Chambers contended in a brief discussion in 1903 that the whole cycle was intended for such performance, as shown, for example, by the appearance of characters in more than one play, and by the absence of well marked breaks between pageants.[2] Block (p. xxix) concluded that Proclamation pageants 15–17, 27 and 29, and 31 and 33 form groups that could be presented simultaneously, indicating a standing and not a processional play. And Izola Curley Harrison suggested in 1929 that the staging of the entire cycle recalls French *mise en scène* production, with a raised platform containing definite stations and surrounded on three sides by the audience.[3]

More recently, Anne Cooper Gay has argued that the cycle bears the marks of continuous playing in a place-and-scaffold theatre of the kind described by Southern.[4] She identifies six stations in the Passion sequences: Passion Play 1 requires a heaven, a 'scaffold', a 'stage' (which Gay takes to be another scaffold), a council house, Simon's house, and Mount Olivet. At least the first three of these are elevated. In Passion Play 2, the two scaffolds are occupied by Herod and Pilate's wife, and both of these structures, Gay notes, are evidently equipped

---

[1] 'Staging the N-Town Cycle', 122–38, 152–65. Cameron and Kahrl note that the older plays contain Latin or Latin and English stage directions while the newer plays, *i.e.* the Passion sequences, have profuse English stage directions.

[2] *The Mediaeval Stage* (London, 1903), 2: 421.

[3] 'The Staging of the Ludus Coventriae', Univ. of Chicago MA thesis (1929).

[4] 'A Study of the Staging of the N. Towne Cycle', Univ. of Missouri M.A. thesis (1961), and 'The "Stage" and the Staging of the N-Town Plays', *Research Opportunities in Renaissance Drama* 10 (1967), 135–40.

with curtains, as are the council house and Simon's house. Gay observes that players must go into the undifferentiated playing area called the 'place' in order to move from one station to another, and that players who make their initial appearances on scaffolds must enter them from the 'place' before the action begins. She proposes that the other plays in the collection were also presented continuously: 1–4 constitute such a series, she believes, and 8–20 also form a·sequence, which could, like the Passion Plays, be produced with six stations.[1] She considers the reference 'Et sic transient circa placeam' (13/22 s.d.) to indicate the use of a 'place' in the 'Visit to Elizabeth', and suggests the same of the 'locum interludii' of the Noah play (4/141 s.d.). Gay adds that plays 22 and 23, as well as 36 and 37, are connected by stage directions. And she notes that the 'Assumption' (Play 41) has staging requirements similar to those of the Marian and Passion sequences, and employs spectacular devices like those in the Ascension and Pentecost plays (39 and 40). She concludes that nothing in the manuscript suggests that perambulatory staging was ever used, and that, in light of the work of Glynne Wickham, the use of wagons could in any case be consistent with stationary staging.[2]

Alan Nelson, arguing that N-town was always given stationary production, identifies clusters of *loca* employed in various plays.[3] One of these is the 'heaven complex'. Postulating that a single elevated heaven served as a stage area during each step of the cycle's develop-

[1] Other reconstructions of the *loca* of the Marian and Passion plays are offered by Cameron and Kahrl, and Martial Rose (cited below). David Bevington's proposed stage designs for the Passion sequences show a round with seven scaffolds surrounding the place. In the first Passion sequence, the council house and Gethsemane are located within the playing area; in the second, the moot hall/council house, as well as the sepulchre and Golgotha, are required (*Medieval Drama* (Atlanta, Dallas, etc., 1975), p. 480). Martin Stevens suggests a similar plan for Passion Play 1, but, unlike Bevington, does not note the use of a hell scaffold (*Four Middle English Mystery Cycles* (Princeton, 1987), p. 189). Peter Meredith argues that if one thinks in terms of place and scaffold staging, the Marian group would require an open space surrounded by five scaffolds or by three with doubling-up of locations (*The Mary Play*, pp. 20–1).

[2] Over fifty years earlier, Victor E. Albright had suggested that the scaffolds of the Passion Plays could have been pageant wagons (*The Shaksperian Stage* (New York, 1909; reprinted New York, 1965), p. 22). Claude Gauvin, after a detailed review of the staging requirements of the cycle, rejects Gay's argument, and concludes: 'Du point de vue de la mise en scène aussi le cycle est composite' (*Un Cycle du théâtre religieux anglais du moyen âge* (Paris, 1973), p. 278).

[3] 'Some Configurations of Staging in Medieval English Drama', in *Medieval English Drama: Essays Critical and Contextual*, eds. Jerome Taylor and Alan H. Nelson (Chicago and London, 1972), pp. 131–47. Nelson argues that the single starting time of 6:00 and the gratuitous redundancy of *loca* are not characteristic of true-processional production.

ment, Nelson observes that the N-town heaven was large enough to accommodate God and his throne, as well as a messenger angel, an angelic choir, and an organ; this heaven also had gates. Near heaven may have been paradise, a hill (which may have served in 'Abraham and Isaac' and the 'Temptation', also as Olivet), and the temple with an altar. The temple stood above the fifteen steps of the 'Presentation of Mary' and adjacent to the Golden Gate of 'Joachim and Anna'. Nelson suggests that the house of Joseph and Mary was also part of the heaven complex, and compares this scenic cluster to Continental models, rather than to the theatre-in-the-round discussed by Southern.[1] He adds that another cluster included a stable on a scaffold, and a hill with a tree and a star. And he identifies distinct *loca* that could have served in several plays, including a sepulchre and a castle. He agrees with Gay that the Passion Plays use the same major scaffolds in different ways. He notes, for example, that in Passion Play 1 Annas and Caiaphas have separate scaffolds, while in Passion Play 2 they share one and Pilate takes the other. He suggests too that Simon the leper's large scaffold in the first Passion sequence may become Herod's in the second.

Martial Rose also concludes that stationary staging was employed in presenting the entire collection.[2] He notes the frequent requirement for the use of 'the place', and develops Cameron and Kahrl's observation that a mansion often serves as a focal point in midst of the playing area. In the Passion Plays the focus is on the oratory, which doubles as the council house, and also, says Rose, perhaps as the sepulchre in 'Lazarus', the 'Assumption', and 'Judgement Day'. He refutes the possibility of processional performance of the Old Testament plays, stating that the patriarchs often walk out of the acting area, rather than being wheeled out on pageant-carts. And he agrees with other scholars that the repeated use of the same acting areas in the Marian and subsequent plays indicates performance on multiple stages.

[1] Nelson (p. 137) compares the N-town arrangement to the plan of the Lucerne Easter play and the Valenciennes 'theatre'. Eleanor Prosser (*Drama and Religion in the English Mystery Plays: A Re-Evaluation* (Stanford, 1961), p. 51) and Glynne Wickham (*Early English Stages* (London and New York, 1963), 1: 305) reach similar conclusions.
[2] 'The Staging of the Hegge Plays', in *Medieval Drama*, Stratford-upon-Avon Studies, 16 (1973), pp. 196–221. See Rose's *The Wakefield Mystery Plays* (New York, 1961), pp. 40–3.

CONCLUSIONS

These studies draw thoughtful and often persuasive inferences about the staging of plays and sequences in the collection. Discussion of the production of the entire cycle, however, is necessarily conjectural, and in some instances presupposes a unity of purpose that has not been demonstrated in so composite a text. The cycle as we have it is in any case not designed for presentation as an undivided whole. Rather, many plays constitute sequences with staging characteristics unlike those of the plays that precede and follow them. In addition, some individual plays reveal aspects of production that do not appear elsewhere in the codex. 'The Trial of Mary and Joseph', for example, is unique in the cycle not only in its initial stage direction, 'Hic intrabit page[n]tum de Purgacione Marie et Joseph', but also in its inclusion of Den's demand for money, perhaps an attempt to take a collection (see the note to 14/25). The 'Trial' and other constituents of the text may retain features of an earlier existence, and the degree to which they were integrated into the actual production of the cycle remains speculative.[1]

Although the Proclamation describes a collection of sequentially organized, independent pageants, it gives no explicit indication of processional staging. The word *pagent* here denotes 'play', and does not necessarily suggest pageant wagons. And the name 'N-town', even if it does imply itinerance, does not prove perambulatory production at designated stations.[2] Nor does the Proclamation offer definite signs of continuous production on a stationary stage. The reference to 'oure pleyn place' (Pr 399) most likely indicates no more than an unobstructed area. It may signify a specific site for mounting successive plays, but need not. Block's assertion that some Proclamation pageants are connected as groups, and so suggest a standing play, is misleading, for it is based upon the plays that have come down to us, not the Proclamation descriptions.[3]

[1] Swenson and Hardin Craig took the reference to an organ in the 'Assumption of Mary' to suggest that that play, unlike most others in the cycle, was put on in a church. The organ may, however, have been portable: see the note to 41/311 s.d.–313 s.d.

[2] See the note to Pr 527. The plays may have toured at an early point in their development, if at all. The staging requirements of the additions to the collection would have been formidable for a travelling troupe. Rose ('Staging', p. 219) estimates that over fifty actors are needed for production of the Passion Plays, and nearly as many for the 'Assumption'. Woolf (p. 308) considers it beyond belief that even a troupe capable of mounting the *Castle of Perseverence* could have put on the N-town cycle as we have it. Meredith ingeniously suggests that the manuscript rather than the cycle was itinerant ('Scribes, Texts and Performance', pp. 19–20).

[3] Cf. Hardin Craig, *English Religious Drama* (Oxford, 1955), pp. 244–5.

As a rule, plays that accord with the Proclamation thematically also agree with it structurally, in that they are suitable for independent performance.[1] These plays could have been mounted in an elaborate scaffold-and-place theatre, but their brief and infrequent stage directions, and their use of typically only a few *loca*, indicate more modest presentation. Indeed, positive evidence of continuous production on a fixed stage of any kind is limited in these plays. Adam's remaining onstage for 'Cain and Abel' has been cited as a revision that allows such performance, but his roles in plays 2 and 3 may have been played by different actors, representing him in youth and in age.

Other plays do form sequences designed for continuous acting, as noted above. But whether this quality was always preserved in the cycle is uncertain. The 'Magi' and 'Innocents', for example, are, as Block perceived, suited to uninterrupted presentation. Yet these plays have in fact been interrupted in the manuscript, by the intrusion of the 'Purification'.[2] This seems to suggest a tendency toward the isolation of plays rather than continuous acting, or indifference to such issues during compilation. On the other hand, the action of the 'Magi' and 'Innocents' may have continued silently during the intervening play, or merely been suspended.[3] The actual methods and circumstances of production in such instances remain open to conjecture.

[1] Occasional exceptions indicate some fluidity in the structuring of these plays. The two Creation plays are described as two pageants in the Proclamation, and so divided by the playnumber '2', but are written as a single unit sharing a stanza (see the headnote to Play 2). In addition, plays 10 and 20 correspond to two Proclamation pageants each. In these three instances, early plays are organized into larger units than are the Proclamation accounts, despite the fact that the descriptions (especially in the case of the Marriage play) were clearly written for these plays. This may suggest that much or all of the collection was intended at some early point for continuous performance and segmented into distinct plays only later. This is particularly likely in the case of plays 1 and 2 (see Spector, *Genesis of the N-town Cycle*, pp. 35–6). Stevens' theory (p. 186) that the play divisions represent no more than an attempt to match the numbering of the Proclamation may explain the awkward segmentation of the Creation and Fall plays, and probably of the Passion sequences as well. But it is incomplete and does not account for the discrepancies between the Proclamation divisions and plays 10 and 20.

[2] For discussion of the position of the 'Purification', see the headnote to Play 17 and p. xx. The 'Magi' and 'Innocents' are linked by their tail-rhyme metre, Latin stage directions, shared characters in a continuous action, and linguistic affinity (both use the word *pap-hawk(ys)*, a word not cited elsewhere in the English language). The reference to Herod as 'kynge in kage ful hye' (18/151) may suggest that these plays were intended to be mounted on scaffolds; cf. 18/54, 20/128.

[3] A similar arrangement may have obtained in presenting the Harrowing of Hell, which is divided into two parts surrounding the 'Burial'.

APPENDIX 3
THE PLAY

The N-town Cycle is impressive in its aesthetic and formal variety. Cycle drama is characteristically various, largely because of its impulse toward comprehensiveness and synthesis. Much of the particular diversity of N-town, however, derives from the eclecticism of the text (see Appendices 1 and 2). Several scholars have none the less observed thematic and tonal uniformity in the cycle, and some have identified in it a unique character, despite its compositiveness. Hardin Craig (p. 260) says that the special quality of N-town is 'its learning expressed with great theological correctness and dignity', and Arnold Williams concurs, calling it 'the most learned of all the cycles'.[1] Rosemary Woolf notes N-town's theological sophistication and dramatic sumptuousness. Like Eleanor Prosser, she praises its dramatic power.[2] And although she acknowledges the rough joins between different parts of the collection, Woolf remarks on its 'striking imaginative unity'.[3]

In an attempt to define the unity in N-town, Timothy Fry argues that the cycle is thematically organized to illustrate the Patristic abuse-of-power theory.[4] Satan, according to this theory, was deceived by Jesus' humanity, and so lost his right to take men's souls by attempting to claim Christ's. Though rebutted by Anselm, this theory of the Redemption no doubt remained well known, and is certainly present in the cycle. But the degree to which it unifies the collection has been questioned.

[1] Arnold Williams, *The Drama of Medieval England* (East Lansing, 1963), p. 122.
[2] See Eleanor Prosser, *Drama and Religion in the English Mystery Plays* (Stanford, 1961), p. 197.
[3] See Woolf, pp. 307–10. Cameron and Kahrl had spoken earlier of the cycle as the compilation of a 'single guiding intelligence' ('N-Town Plays at Lincoln', p. 64). Other critics have commented on the unity of segments of the collection, particularly Passion Play 1. Prosser (p. 121), for instance, speaks of this sequence as a unified sermon on repentance. Daniel P. Poteet II discusses the artistic and intellectual character of the sequence in 'Time, Eternity, and Dramatic Form in *Ludus Coventriae* "Passion Play I"', in *The Drama of the Middle Ages*, pp. 232–48. See also Miriam J. Benkovitz, 'Some Notes on the "Prologue of Demon" of *Ludus Coventriae*', *MLN* 60 (1945), 78–85.
[4] Timothy Fry, 'The Unity of the *Ludus Coventriae*, *SP* 48 (1951), 527–70. Gauvin argues that this theory provides 'une unité théologique et dramatique qui pourrait bien être la marque du dernier auteur-réviseur du cycle' (p. 216).

Patrick J. Collins has identified sets of imagistic and thematic patterns that appear periodically in the cycle.[1] He cites, for example, the frequent use of fruit imagery. In accordance with literary and iconographic tradition, the cycle often refers to fruit as the instrument of man's fall, but also of his redemption. Thus Christ in Play 7 is the redemptive fruit atop the Jesse Tree, which itself extends the agricultural imagery in the collection (as does the cherry tree in Play 15).[2] Unfruitfulness is a token of the loss of bliss in the cycle, and a torment for Anna and Joachim in play 8. In the next play, Mary has been born, and Joachim refers to her as fruit, just as Mary calls Jesus 'my frute' in the Doctors play (21/227). Collins observes that this and other motifs provide continuity and a 'principle of connection' in N-town.

Kathleen M. Ashley argues that a concern about the source and limits of wit and wisdom is a dominant theme in much of the cycle.[3] Ashley challenges the idea that N-town is unusually learned. It is not more theologically subtle or sophisticated than its counterparts, she asserts, but it does exhibit a recurring interest in learning itself. She observes that Christ is associated with wisdom several times in the collection, and that the words 'witt', 'wisdom', and 'cunnynge' appear repeatedly as the plays clarify the origin and proper applications of man's reason.[4]

Martin Stevens finds the N-town Cycle to be an artistically integrated dramatic whole. He argues that the peculiar genius of the cycle lies in its formal organization.[5] He divides the plays into seven 'acts' in order to reveal its dramatic structure.[6] He also develops the

---

[1] Patrick J. Collins, *The N-town Plays and Medieval Picture Cycles*, Early Drama, Art, and Music Monograph Series, 2 (1979).

[2] See the note to 7/61-4.

[3] Kathleen M. Ashley, '"Wyt" and "Wysdam" in the N-town Cycle', *PQ* 58 (1979), 121-35.

[4] See the headnote to Play 21 and the note to 21/1-32.

[5] Stevens, pp. 181-257. Stevens notes that several unpublished dissertations address the issue of unity in the cycle. Cf. Daniel Powell Poteet II, 'The *Hegge Plays*: An Approach to the Aesthetics of Medieval Drama', Univ. of Illinois Ph.D. thesis (1969); Richard Jacob Daniels, 'A Study of the Formal and Literary Unity of the N-town Mystery Cycle', Ohio State Univ. Ph.D. thesis (1972); Mary Lampland Tobin, 'A Study of the Formation and Auspices of the *Ludus Coventriae*', Rice Univ. Ph.D. thesis (1973); Sidney Jerry Vance, 'Unifying Patterns of Reconciliation in the *Ludus Coventriae*', Vanderbilt Univ. Ph.D. thesis (1975); Sandra Robertson Nelson, '"Goddys Worde": Revelation and Its Transmission in the N-Town Cycle', Duke Univ. Ph.D. thesis (1976); and Robert Joseph Leonard, 'Patterns of Dramatic Unity in the N-town Cycle', SUNY, Stony Brook, Ph.D. thesis (1984).

[6] Stevens suggests that an edition of N-town should be organized in such acts, and that the playnumbers should be de-emphasized and the Proclamation relegated to an

earlier arguments by Collins and Ashley, and offers an extended analysis of the typological transfers that create detailed parallels between the Marian plays and the plays that portray the life of Christ. The Marian 'Under-plot', he says, made N-town the first double-plot play on the English stage. Stevens concludes from these thematic and organizational patterns that the N-town collection is not an un-assimilated product of multiple authorship. He concedes that the cycle is a compilation. But, like Woolf, he suggests that the final editor and the author may have been one and the same.

CONCLUSIONS

The emphasis in N-town on learning and instruction does provide one kind of thematic continuity through much of the collection. In informative speeches, 'gostly' interpretation, depiction of exemplary behaviour, and even marginal notes, the cycle is persistently instruc-tive. It addresses such fundamental elements of the faith as the Atha-nasian and Apostles' creeds, the Ten Commandments, the sacraments of baptism and the eucharist, the seven corporal works of mercy, and the Seven Deadly Sins. Similar doctrinal concerns inform other cycle drama as well.[1] But N-town is unique in the English drama in much of its spiritual instruction about the Decalogue, the Gradual Psalms, the Last Supper, and other topics. An interest in learning is also apparent in the cycle in other ways, for example in its demonstration of Mary's intellectual precocity and devotion to study, and in the debate about the limits of man's knowledge in the Doctors play, discussed by Ashley.

Thematic congruence in the collection also results from cyclic pat-terns within the larger representation of the cycle of divine history. This is often achieved through figural correspondence and transfer. Mary's early life and the Assumption are presented, as Stevens shows,

appendix. His divisions, however, are admittedly arbitrary, and other scholars have seg-mented the collection with different results. Moreover, the play divisions may well carry information about both the staging and the development of the cycle (see appendices 1 and 2, especially p. 549 n. 1 above). In the present edition, I retain the play divisions of the manuscript in order to reflect the intentions of the main scribe and rubricator.

[1] A. C. Cawley cites these concerns in the Towneley plays as evidence that 'the doc-trinal content of the Corpus Christi plays was influenced by the official movement for the instruction of the laity in the elements of the faith' ('Middle English Metrical Versions of the Decalogue with Reference to the English Corpus Christi Cycles', *Leeds SE* 8 (1975), 132).

so as to anticipate and recall much of Christ's experience. Through another transfer, Herod's lines in Play 30 paraphrase the scriptural words of Pilate (see the note to 30/209ff.). The continuity created by typological transferral illustrates a broad tendency in the cycle toward symmetry and iteration. The Parliament in Heaven in Play 11 offsets the Parliament in Hell in Play 23, for example (anticipating the arrangement in *Paradise Lost*). Similar balance is apparent in Play 20, where Death's boasts and threats parodically echo his victim's, and in Play 26, where John the Baptist's prologue answers Demon's in specific detail.[1]

Characteristic artistic and intellectual habits also reappear at various points in the collection. A radical telescoping and dislocating of events, for example, obtains in both Old Testament and Passion plays. It occurs in the juxtaposition of the episodes of the Burning Bush and the giving of the Decalogue in Play 6, for instance, and in the conflation of the Last Supper, the anointing of Jesus' feet in Bethany, and the exorcism of seven devils from Magdalene in Play 27.[2]

The fact that these symmetries and repetitions often cut across the textual layers of the collection supports Woolf's suggestion that one poet composed a cycle and discrete sequences, then integrated them, sometimes carelessly. The conclusion that N-town comprises the work of different writers is at least as compelling, however. A variety of evidence indicates that the plays were recorded and edited over time. Extreme differences in dramatic focus and in indications of staging suggest composition under varying circumstances.[3] And the stark disparities in style and literary indebtedness, the use of some two dozen stanzaic forms, the unexplained prosodic shifts within plays, and the contradictions and redundancies between strata, all suggest composition by more than one poet. In either case, the intelligence and aesthetic sensibility in the compilation and editing of N-town are apparent. And the patterns in the cycle reveal some of the principles of selection and incorporation that were applied.[4] In

[1] Structural and artistic parallels also connect pairs of plays, such as the Trial and Nativity plays (14 and 15) and the plays of the adulteress and Lazarus (24 and 25): see Spector, *Genesis of the N-town Cycle*, pp. 71–4, and Stevens, p. 194.

[2] These arrangements are unique in the English religious drama and are not in the major sources. Poteet considers such features to illustrate the 'time suppressing' character of N-town (see the notes to 26/470–85, 27/36 s.d. and 27/141–92).

[3] In 'Staging the N-Town Cycle', Cameron and Kahrl discuss the different focal systems inherent in the staging of distinct parts of the collection. See pp. 544–5 above, but compare the other opinions cited in Appendix 2.

[4] The more general principles of selection in the cycles have been debated: see V. A.

fact, many bibliographic 'footprints' illustrate this editorial process at work creating and enhancing the patterns that are characteristic of the text. There are several indications that the Marian sequence and the Assumption play were added to the collection at a late stage, for example. And much of the drastic conflation in the Last Supper play was effected by an editor who introduced Magdalene into the play by interpolating a leaf (see the note to 27/141–268).

Many of the thematic emphases and figural parallels in the cycle were already present in the sources. And the imagistic and linguistic clusters that have been noted in the collection are in large part intensifications of theological, iconographic, and literary commonplaces. Much of the special character of N-town emerged from the selection, assimilation, and development of these features.

Kolve, *The Play Called Corpus Christi* (Stanford, 1966), ch. 4; Woolf, ch. 4; Alan H. Nelson, *The Medieval English Stage* (Chicago and London, 1974), ch. 1; and Patrick J. Collins, 'Narrative Bible Cycles in Medieval Art and Drama', in *Drama of the Middle Ages*, pp. 118–39.

GLOSSARY

The glossary is intended to explain words and senses now unfamiliar. The great orthographic variety of the text has made it desirable, however, to include current words that may be obscured by medieval spellings.

þ is treated as *th*; consonantal *y* is in its usual place, but vocalic *y* is treated as *i*; *u* and *v* are distinguished according to function. In the arrangement, ʒ is placed after *g*. The mark ~ signifies the headword in any of its forms.

Variants within entries are listed with the most common form first, then in order of declining frequency in the text. References are selective. Numbers refer to the play and the line, with 'Pr' denoting the Proclamation, 'PS' the Procession of Saints, and 's.d.' the stage direction following the line number given; 'n.' indicates that a form is discussed in the notes. Line numbers from the alternate conclusion to Play 13 are followed by 'A'. Emended forms are marked by asterisks.

a *pron.* he 32/77.

a *prep.* on (a specific date) Pr 525.

a, an, han *indef. art.* a, an Pr 25, 40, 41, 49, 70, 71, 34/202; ~ *x personys* ten people 28/80 s.d.

a see **haue, o** (*prep.*).

abak(ke) *adv.* back, away; *go(n)* ~ withdraw 23/183, 191.

abasche *imp. pl. refl.* be distressed 41/151.

abey *v.* obey 27/525.

abhomynable, abhomynabyl *adj.* abominable 11/98, 24/211, 258, 26/429.

abyde, abydyn *v.* **1** remain, stay Pr 13, 3/191, 4/217, 27/566, 29/12, 34/250; **abydyn** *pl.* 26/385 s.d.; **abod** *pa.t.* 13/159A, 166A; **abedyn** *pp.* 39/64; **abyde** *imp. sg.* 8/100, 210; **abyde, abydyth** *imp. pl.* 10/415, 35/234, 38/174; **2** dwell, live, sojourn *Pr 26, 113, 266; **abyde** *pl.* 8/53; **abydyng** *pr.p.* 28/150; **3** await 10/423, 15/95, 117; **abydyth, abidyth** *pr. 3 sg.* 11/264, 41/128; **abydynge** *pr.p.* 39/50; **abyde** *imp. sg.* 5/46; **abydyth** *imp. pl.* 39/21; **4** endure, suffer 12/133, 32/99; **5** continue, persist 13/126; **6** wait, be patient 26/334; **abydyth** *pr. 3 sg.* 30/35; **7** stand firm 27/340; **8** permit *41/82.

abydyng(e) *vbl. n.* dwelling 9/194; remaining 38/191.

abyl, able, habyl *adj.* able 10/178, 21/9; worthy, deserving 20/25, 26/409; sufficient 24/95; liable (as I am) 24/254.

abyl *pr. subj.* enable 9/41.

above, aboue *adv.* above 3/127, 11/251, 23/104, 35/128.

above, aboue, abovyn, abouen *prep.* above 1/57, 2/239, 9/115, 32/176 s.d., 41/249, 518; to a greater degree than 11/107, 26/406; superior to (in rank or authority) 18/180, 20/212.

abowt(e), abowth, about(e), abought, abowtyn, abouth *adv.* about, all around 2/50, 4/147, 6/41, 9/149, 14/5, 259, 20/108, 134, 25/417, 26/462, 27/348 s.d.; *rownd(e)* ~ Pr 254, 4/25, 14/279; ~ *was brought* 13/65; ~ *to be brought* to be done 21/55; *browth* ~ 34/211, 35/248; *prep.* about, around 8/174, 14/239, 254, 26/244 s.d., 337, 449 s.d., 27/511 s.d., 41/463.

absens, absence *n.* absence 8/160, 25/359, 41/178.

absent(e) *adj.* absent 21/270, 26/115, *41/214; *vs* ~ absent from us 41/261.

abstynawnce *n.* abstinence 26/115.

abundauns, habundawns *n.* prosperity, wealth 26/64; abundance 26/403.

abuse *v.* behave abusively or improperly 8/103n.

accende *pr. subj.* kindle 24/31.

accept *ppl. adj.* acceptable, pleasing Pr 58.

acceptyn *v.* accept, receive with favour 3/54.

accusatyff *adj.* self-accusing 9/142.

acorde *n.* sentiment, opinion: *of* (*with, be*) *on* ~ in agreement, in harmony 5/251, 9/158, 26/162; agreement 11/285; peace, harmony PS 32.

acorde *pr. 1 sg.* accord, agree 7/34; **acordyth** *pr. 3 sg.* (with *to*) is in agreement

acorde (*cont.*)
with 26/341; **ac(c)orde** *pl.* 27/298, 39/95; **acordynge** *pr.p.* 7/134; with (*to*) being harmoniously suited 26/67n.; **acordyd** *pp.* 27/138; **acorde** *pr. subj.* 11/121.

acorde *pr. subj.* 11/121.

acounte *impl. pl.* compute 41/9.

acquyte *v. refl.* free oneself, escape 24/244.

acursyd *ppl. adj.* accursed 3/175, 14/108.

ac(c)use *v.* accuse, charge Pr 337, 14/303, 24/265; **acuse** *pl.* 29/166; **acusid** *pa.t.* (with *of*) brought an accusation (concerning) 41/428; **acusyd** *pp.* 30/58.

acusyng *vbl. n.* act of accusing 30/61; charge, accusation 30/90.

adde *pr. 1 sg.* add 11/233; **addyd** *pa. t.* 13/155A; **haddyd** *pp.* 11/18.

adewe *interj.* adieu 24/143, 143.

adon *adv.* down 41/482.

adrad, adrede *ppl. adj.* afraid 8/173, 18/274.

advercyté, aduersyté, aduercyté *n.* adversity 13/148, 27/7, 28/166, 41/337.

aduocat *n.* advocate, intercessor 9/267.

advowterere *n.* adulterer 24/107; **advowtererys** *pl.* 24/168.

advowtrye, adultrye, advowtery *n.* adultery Pr 283, 24/85, 126, 159, 196.

affeccyon *n.* love, goodwill 12/210, 27/365; *myn* ~ the love due to me 26/61; desire, wish 28/156.

affendyn see **offende**.

af(f)erd(e) *ppl. adj.* afraid, fearful (that) 21/221, 23/77, 24/234.

affermynge *pr. p.* affirming, declaring, 7/36.

affyaunce *n.* faith 41/352.

affye *v.* have faith or trust 41/103.

afflyght *pp.* afraid 24/247.

affray *n.* attack, fray 24/141.

affray *v.* frighten 15/167.

af(f)rayd(e) *ppl. adj.* afraid Pr 115, 137, 2/99.

af(f)tyr, af(f)ter(e) *adv.* afterwards, after that Pr 501, 4/38, 9/277 s.d., 309, 13/38, 19/85; *prep.* after, following Pr 77, 4/16, 5/208; according to, in conformity with 1/9, 2/141, 155; in order to find or get 4/249, 26/194, 34/312; in the likeness of 26/164 s.d.

afore *adv.* beforehand 32/176 s.d.

aforn, afore *prep.* in front of 21/42, 32/92 s.d., 41/222.

aftyr, after *conj.* after 7/78; ~*þat* 27/456 s.d., 31/57 s.d.

aftyrwarde, afterewarde *adv.* afterwards, later 16/71, 19/190.

agast *ppl. adj.* aghast, frightened Pr 505, 13/16, 28/35.

age *n.* *þe Secunde* ~ the Second Era 4/14n.; *grett* ~ old age 4/127, 11/209; *of iij (thre, ij) 3ere* ~ three (two) years old 9/9, 17 s.d., 164, 20/46; *in* (*hyre*) ~ in (her) old age 10/281, 11/256; *a man of* ~ an old man 10/293; *of grett* ~ of mature years 27/268.

ageyn(e), a3en, agayn *adv.* again, once more Pr 428, 5/151, 7/78, 8/93, 234, 10/230, 24/207, 25/74, 298; back, back again Pr 180, 182, 365; in return 9/176, 24/20, 41/429.

ageyn, a3en *prep.* contrary to, in defiance of Pr 288, 10/24, 10/101, 14/299, 20/227, 21/183; against 7/6, 7, 127; with regard to 14/256; ~ . . . *sey wrech* should call for the punishment of 24/91; upon 23/127, 25/223; opposite, facing, in front of 23/159, 26/347; from 25/81; in view of, in comparison with 25/432; toward 26/278, 29/103; in the opposite direction from 32/66; in preparation for (the time that) 41/480.

a3encomynge *vbl. n.* return 10/423.

a3ens, ageyns *prep.* contrary to, in defiance of Pr 42, 291, 2/68, 7/31, 26/28, 229; *forfete* ~ disobey 2/81; against 4/141, 10/272, 15/263; over against, in comparison with 26/19; in preparation for 26/164.

agyd *ppl. adj.* aged 10/226.

aglottys *n.* metal tags or points (at ends of laces) 26/72.

agreve *v.* distress, grieve 4/69; **agrevyth** *pr. 3 sg.* 4/32, 5/134.

agryse *v.* offend 4/56; **agresyth** *pr. 3 sg.* frightens 34/7.

ay *adj.* eternal 9/153; *adv.* eternally 8/229, 23/99, 25/269; *for . . .* ~ forever 2/133, 12/61, 37/28.

ake *v.* ache 25/282.

alderers see **al(l)e(e)**.

algatys *adv.* in any case, no matter what 31/114, 167.

alyaunce, alyawns *n.*: *of* ~ of common

parentage (with us) 25/37; *lovys* ~ the
bond of love 26/62.

alye *n.* family 15/16; kinship 41/104.

alyve *adj.* alive 25/424.

al(l) *adv.* entirely, completely Pr 43, 110,
134.

al(l)as *interj.* alas Pr 362, 2/165, 165.

al(l)(e), hall *adj.* all Pr 1, 3, 37; ~ *us* us all
6/131; ~ *and som* every bit 30/27; ~ *þei*
all of them 31/104 s.d.; every, each Pr
62, 499, 2/32; *of* ~ of each (of the) 4/114;
any 7/76; perfect, complete 11/295; *as
noun* Pr 101, 122, 278, 30/145; *at* ~ in
every way Pr 189; ~ *is for* it is all
because of 4/202; *we prey* ~ we all pray
32/25; **al(l)ther(e), altheris, alderers**
gen. pl. oure ~ of us all Pr 392, 25/232,
35/135; *3oure* ~ of all of you 22/104.

al(l)myght *adj.* almighty 9/247, 36/10.

**al(l)myghty, almythy, al(l)mythty,
almyhtty** *adj.* almighty Pr 46, 3/62,
142, 4/27, 5/3, 28/63, 29/5, 32/101, 34/
152, 41/249; **Allmyhty** *as noun* 41/122.

allmyghtyfful *adj.* almighty 19/197.

al(l)ther(e) see **al(l)(e)**.

al(l)thyng(e), allþing(e) *n.* everything,
all things 1/11, 2/39, 40, 44, 3/63, 21/
150.

al(l)wey, al(l)way *adv.* in every way; forever 2/131; always, continually, all the
while 3/25, 4/36, 5/31, 6/94, 118, 13/79.

almaundys *n.* almonds 38/132.

almes, helmes *n.* alms-giving, charitable act(s) 8/41, 176, 40/21; alms,
charitable gifts 15/269.

alofte *adv.* aloft, upright 28/148 s.d.

alon(e) *adj.* and *adv.* alone Pr 331, 2/24,
8/90; single and unique 1/17, 21/76;
solely 25/203.

along *adv.* lengthwise, at full length 32/
48 s.d.

alow *v.* reward 27/332; **alowyht** *pr. 3 sg.*
accepts, is pleased with 3/143; **alowe**
pr. subj. permits 6/142.

altheris see **al(l)(e)**.

altitude *n.* acme PS 1.

alwyse *adv. in* ~ in any event 31/154.

amat *adj.* overwhelmed, confounded 29/
115.

amend(e) *v.* **1** relieve 4/249, 8/148, 11/28;
amende *imp. sg.* 37/45; **2** change for the
better, set right 8/168, 9/100, 12/206;
amend(e) *imp.* 12/41, 63, 86; **3** make
amends for 27/170; **amende** *imp. pl.*

34/36; **amende** *pr. subj.* 24/3; **4** care for
(wounds) 36/49; **5** reform or improve
(oneself) *in* **amend** *imp. sg. refl.* 6/79.

amendyng(e) *vbl. n.* correction, moral
improvement 4/210; repentance 22/
166.

amendys *n.* amends 20/192, 22/25, 27/
547.

amys *adj.* and *adv.* amiss 5/155, 6/73, 162.

among(e) *adv.* all together Pr 500; *with*
. . . ~ in company with 10/351; always,
continually 12/125, 34/34; *evyr* ~ 4/45.

among(e), amongys *prep.* among, from
among, amid Pr 332, 3/84, 92, 5/15,
8/103, 106.

an *conj.* and 12/91, 42/6.

an see **haue**.

anameryd *pp.* (with *upon*) enamoured
(of) 14/83.

anceter *n.* ancestor *9/267n.

and *conj.* if 8/76, 127, 168; as if 9/43.

anguysch *n.* anguish, suffering 9/264.

any, ony *n.* any 11/128, 15/16, 20/226, 21/
113, 34/190.

any, ony *adj.* any Pr 416, 2/82, 3/17, 176,
4/54, 10/446.

anythyng(e) *pron.* anything 18/99, 34/75.

anoynt(e) *v.* anoint 27/164, 34/141.

anon(e), anoon *adv.* at once Pr 337, 449,
1/70, 5/78, 79, 6/26; ~-*ryght* (*ryth*), ~
forthryght (*forthryth*), ~ *ful ryght* immediately Pr 149, 397, 3/158, 5/166, 10/22,
23/152, 25/381, 34/239; ~ *present* here
and now 2/146, 30/146.

anon *conj.*: ~ *as* as soon as 13/151.

another, anothyr, anodyr *pron.* another
one or thing 2/111, 8/53, 11/297, 27/
361, 30/49, 31/202.

another, anothyr *adj.* another 3/36, 11/
42, 12/83, 14/100, 124.

anothyr *adv.* secondly 19/111.

anow(e), inow *n.* an abundance 15/43;
seyn þerof ~ say plenty about it 34/54;
enough 19/181, 26/107, 27/115.

anow *adj.* abundant 2/62, 26/12; ~ *plenté*
in great abundance 3/19; enough 29/
219.

anow, inow *adv.* enough, very 27/330,
30/40, 34/98, 199, 41/66; enough, suffi-
ciently 32/74; completely 34/81.

ansuere, answere *n.* answer, response
Pr 510, 9/32, 10/92, 11/264, 279, 30/18
s.d., 42/7; **answerys** pl. 26/31.

answere *v.* answer 31/151; 190; reply 11/
235, (with *a3ens*) refute 30/133; **answer-**
yst *pr. 2 sg.* (with ellipsis of 'thou') 29/
162; **answere** *pl.* 9/43; **answerd,**
answeryd *pa. t.* Pr 246, 278; **answere**

apace, apase *adv.* quickly, promptly 18/
269, 24/185; *þu were there* ~ so that you
may get there quickly 11/199.

apayed *ppl. adj.* satisfied, pleased 7/61.

aper(e),   **aperyd,**   **aperyth**   see
ap(p)er(e).

apocriphum *adj.* apocryphal 41/4.

apostel, apostyll, apostle *n.* apostle PS
25, 39/71, 41/240; **apostelys, ap(p)os-**
telis, apostel, appostolis, postelis
pl. Pr 313, 483, 493, PS 13, 41/143, 150,
332, 358, 496.

apparaled *pp.* prepared 41/139.

apparens *n.* sight, perception 27/382.

appendyth *pr. 3 sg.* pertains: ~ *onto the* is
your responsibility 28/60.

ap(p)er(e) *v.* appear Pr 436, 452, 478;
aperyth *pr. 3 sg.* Pr 374, 26/4; **apperyth**
pl. 29/41; **ap(p)eryd** *pa. t. and pp.* Pr
496, 13/32, 77; **apere** *pr. subj.* 14/45.

appetyde *n.* physical need 29/88.

appyl, appel *n.* apple, fruit Pr 40, 2/37,
89.

applye *v. refl.* apply or devote oneself to
3/48; **applyande** *pr. p. be* ~ apply yourselves 26/134; **applyed** *pp.* expressed,
understood 9/102; obeyed, put into
practice 26/397.

appose, apposyn *v.* interrogate Pr 44,
42/10; engage in disputation Pr 245;
investigate, examine 14/187, 23/56.

aprevyn *v.* prove, demonstrate 38/371;
aprevyn *pl.* 34/3.

aproche *v.* befall, approach 26/64.

aproperyd *pp. to* . . . ~ is an attribute of,
is proper to **21/122.

aqwyte, aqwhyte *v.* requite, pay 5/192,
16/153, 34/120; **aqwhyte** *pp.* repaid 26/
417.

ar see **ar(e).**

aray *v.* prepare 26/133, 163; **aray(e)d** *pp.*
clothed 18/69, 26/208 s.d. 208 s.d.; in a
state or condition: *þus* . . . in this condition 14/214; **fowle** ~ unclean 15/238;
prepared, armed 41/90; **aray** *imp. pl.*
refl. apply yourselves 41/390.

aray see **ar(r)ay** *n.*

archaungelys *n.* archangels 11/37.

archere *n.* archer 4/150, 151, 14/169.

archerye *n.* archery 4/157.

arde see **hard(e).**

are *n.* hare 4/148.

ar(e), arne *pr. pl.* are 2/214, 3/32, 6/56,
8/99, 101, 166.

arere *v.* stir up, arouse 14/46; rouse, start
(a wild animal) 24/80; set going, devise
26/50.

areste *n.* place of residence 10/31.

argemente *n.* reasoning, argumentation
21/15.

aryght *adv.* properly 4/161.

aryse, arysyn *v.* arise, rise up 8/62, 25/
300, 35/71, 94; **aryseth** *pr. 3 sg.* Pr 423;
aresyn *pp.* Pr 440, 35/91, 145; **arys(e)**
imp. pl. 20/43, 43, 25/173.

arm(e) *n.* arm 13/100, 15/201, 32/54;
armys *pl.* 32/92 s.d.

armyd *pp.* armed 34/276.

arneys *n.* battle gear, armour 28/80 s.d.

ar(r)ay *n.* order, manner Pr 519; conduct:
what ~ *is þis?* what goes on here? 3/131;
clothing 6/102, 18/20, 27/26; state, condition 6/119, 16/150, 32/108; grandeur
18/2; *robys of* ~ magnificent clothing
18/70; appearance 20/272; *in gret* ~
with great ceremony 41/386.

arryn *v.* harass 31/210 s.d.

ars *n.* arse 14/157.

art(e), erte *pr. 2 sg.* are 2/192, 211, 3/79,
22/107; (with ellipsis of 'thou') 2/232,
29/126.

arwe *n.* arrow 4/171, 175, 177.

as *adv.* (introducing a request or command) 3/14, 12/197, 15/143; (as
emphatic) 9/127: ~ *tyght* immediately
3/160; ~ *þus* thus 13/170A; (in expressions of reference): ~ *in*, ~ *for*, ~ *to*
with respect to 7/59, 115, 12/199, 21/
269, 26/45, 27/561; ~ *be* by 14/196, 19/
95; ~ *for* for 19/182; ~ *in* in 19/192; ~
for as 23/186; ~ *for-than* therefore 37/
90; (introducing exemplification) 11/
277, 13/164A; also 28/80 s.d.

as *conj.* in the same way as, like 2/209,
3/117, 132; ~ *for* like Pr 353; in what
manner, to what degree: ~ *þat we kan*
(*may*) as we are able Pr 10, 312; as if
8/174, 25/282, 27/334; (preceding
parenthetic comment): ~ *þat* 24/114;
more . . . ~ more . . . than 29/54–5; **also**
as: ~ *sone as þat* as quickly as 26/358n.

asay, asayd(e), asayn see **as(s)ay.**
asayl see **as(s)ayle.**
ascende, ascendist, ascendyth see **assende.**
aschamyd, ashamyd *ppl. adj.* ashamed 10/202, 14/203, 24/233.
aschis *n.* ashes 41/84.
asclepe *adv.* asleep 28/44 s.d.; *browth ~* 40/20.
aseyth *n.* atonement through deeds, satisfaction 11/103.
asencyon *n.*: *to þe hyest ~* to the very top (of one's body) 26/68.
asent see **as(s)ent.**
asyde *adv.* aside 25/272; apart from others 32/92 s.d.
asygne *pr. pl.* assign, entrust 13/181A; **assygned** *pa. t.* prescribed (as punishment) Pr 47; **assygnyd** *pp.* assigned 10/286; ordained, assigned (the time for) 42/4.
askape *v.* recover from 25/254; escape from 29/77.
aske, haske, askyn *v.* 1 ask for, beg for Pr 346, 24/6, 40, 32/176 s.d., 34/42; **aske, haske** *pr. 1 sg.* 12/169, 15/194, 24/20, 27/448; **askyth** *pr. 3 sg.* 24/36; **aske** *pl.* 42/71, 128; **haskyng** *pr. p.* 32/140; **askyd** *pp.* 32/130; **haske, aske** *imp. sg.* 24/24, 157; **aske** *imp. pl.* 24/10; **aske, haske** *pr. subj.* 24/16, 38, 288; 2 ask, inquire 24/87; **aske** *pr. 1 sg.* 11/250, 21/93, 41/41; **askyst** *pr. 2 sg.* 27/266; **haskyd** *pa. t.* 29/104; **aske** *imp. sg.* 29/136, 137; **aske** *pr. subj.* 11/205, 26/352; 3 ask, request *in* **haske, aske** *pr. 1 sg.* 9/238, 34/323; **aske, askyght** *pl.* Pr 413, 15/270; **askyd** *pa. t.* 41/211, 42/79, 126; 4 cries out for *in* **askyht** *pr. 3 sg.* 3/169; 5 demand *in* **aske** *pl.* Pr 383.
askuse see **excuse.**
aslake *v.* keep away 25/448.
aslepe *adv.* asleep 31/51.
asmatryk *n.* art or science of measuring and calculating, arithmetic 21/18.
asoyle *imp. sg.* answer 3/158.
asondyr *adj.* separated 19/176; **asundyr, asondyr, asoundyr, asondre** *adv.* to pieces, asunder 21/208, 28/44, 176, 32/196, 38/259; apart 28/44, 38/291, 42/27; *losyth hem ~* untie them 25/430.
aspy(e), aspey *v.* 1 detect, discover, see 10/229, 24/237, 26/173, 28/98; **aspye** *pl.*

26/298; **aspyed** *pp.* 26/400; **aspye** *imp. sg.* look for 4/162; *~ afftere* 4/249; **aspye** *pr. subj.* 29/71; 2 consider; investigate 27/133, 32/191.
as(s)ay, asayn *v.* 1 try, attempt 2/119, 123, 10/.173, 15/36; **asayd(e)** *pa.t.* (with *of*) had experience of 14/213, 228; **as(s)ay** *imp.* 15/161, 23/43, 48; 2 taste 14/233, 30/240; **asay** *imp. pl.* 2/129; 3 tempt, put to the test 21/126; **assayde, hasayd** *pa. t.* 15/277, 31/19; 4 find out by testing 23/151, 32/49; 5 had intercourse with *in* **asayd** *pp.* 14/85; 6 tested 29/183; 7 examine *in* **asay** *imp. pl.* 15/251; **assay** *pr. subj.* 15/247.
as(s)ayl(e) *v.* 1 tempt 23/150, 204; 2 assail, attack 26/192; **asaylys** *pr. 3 sg.* 26/39.
asse *n.* ass 6/175, 20/84, 26/350.
assedually *adv.* assiduously 41/174.
Assencion *n.* Ascension 41/15.
assende, ascende *v.* 1 ascend 9/97, 37/49, 41/107, 130, 293; **assende, ascende** *pr. 1 sg.* 11/340, 41/165, 338; **ascendist** *pr. 2 sg.* 41/216; **ascendyth** *pr. 3 sg.* 28/64 s.d.; **ascende** *pp.* 37/43; **ascende, assende** *pr. subj.* 37/98; (forming *imp.*) 41/518; 2 ascended to, rose above *in* **assendid** *pa. t.* 41/21.
as(s)ent *n.* assent, agreement: *by (be) on ~, with on ~* with one mind, in unison 24/82, PS 16, 35/227; opinion 12/51.
assygnacyon *n.* order, directive; *3eve ~ (to)* issue an order regarding 10/107.
as(s)yse *n.* session of court 38/109; *þe last ~, þis grett ~* the Last Judgement 6/58, 42/5.
assystent *adj.* helpful, present to help 26/30.
Assumpcion, assumpcyon *n.* Assumption 41/2, 528.
assumpte *pa. t.* ascended 41/11; **assumpte** *pp.* taken to heaven 41/25.
ast see **haue.**
astat(e) *n.* rank, status 6/104, 26/82; *in (one's) ~* in a manner or position appropriate to one's rank Pr 349, 27/76 s.d., 30/152 s.d.; *staff of ~* staff of state 26/164 s.d.; condition, state 26/90; office, authority 27/85; exalted position 35/166.
astronomye *n.* astronomy, astrology 21/16.

asundyr see **asondyr.**
aswage *v.* alleviate, relieve 41/467; **aswage** *pr. subj.* 14/369.
atast *v.* taste, experience 2/278.
ateynt see **attayne.**
atent *n.* intent Pr 83.
athreste *adj.* thirsty 21/46.
atonys *adv.* together, at once 26/449 s.d., 456, 28/104 s.d.; immediately 41/406.
atoo *adv.* in two, to pieces 35/140.
atreyd *pp.* distressed, frightened 35/194.
at(t) *prep.* at: ~ *all* in every way Pr 189; with Pr 228, 12/170, 27/514; according to, in conformity with 1/7; on 7/132, 18/289, 35/75; to 9/226, 10/340, 27/265; of 10/406, 13/176A; from 11/238.
attayne, atteyn *v.* succeed in discerning 41/31n.; bring to judgement 41/73; **ateynt** *p.p.* infected, overcome 25/24.
attencyon *n.* attention 39/19.
attendauns, attendaunce *n. to his* ~ attending him 26/33; duty 41/348.
at(t)ende *v.* apply one's energies to, muster: *with all þe obedyens we kan* ~ as obediently as possible 27/22; pay attention 27/172; **attende** *imp. sg.* attend to 24/28; **attende, attendyth** *imp. pl.* pay attention 27/89, 39/57.
attrybute *n.* attribute 21/129.
atwynne *adv.* apart: *part* ~ part company 23/112.
audyens, audyence, audience *n.* audience, group of listeners 7/36, PS 4; opportunity to be heard 29/21, 41/26.
augrym *n.* computing or numbering with Arabic numerals 21/18.
aungel(l)(e), aungyl, angel(l) *n.* angel Pr 20, 49, 70, 168, 440, 1/8, 41/109, 121, 132; **aungel(l)ys, aungel, angelys** *gen. sg.* 2/220, 11/230, 12/77, 13/128, 36/88; **aungel(l)ys, angel(l)ys, aungell, angell, aungyl** *pl.* Pr 17, 18, 192, 486, 1/32, 36, 7/15, 9/250, *259, 10/435, 22/13, 26/14, 41/490; **aungell, aungelys, awngellys** *gen. pl.* 2/1, 9/248;. ~ *mete* sacramental bread 27/439; ~ *-songe* 39/46.
autentyk *adj.* trustworthy, authoritative 9/267.
autere see **awter(e).**
autorysyth *pr. 3 sg.* confirms 41/13.
avayl *v.* avail 13/158, 23/144; **avaylith** *pr. 3 sg.* 5/95.

auantorysly *adv.* by chance 34/100 s.d.
Aue, Ave *n.* and *interj.* hail, Ave 11/219, 339, 12/215.
avengere *n.* avenger 8/178.
auerter *n.* one who averts *9/264.
avexit *pr. 3 sg.* vexes, distresses 38/358, 366, 374; harasses 38/390.
avyse, avise *n.* plan, arrangement: *at þe best* ~ in the best way 5/128; advice 10/99, 104, 11/166; thought 38/111.
avysement *n.* consideration; consultation: *have* ~ take thought, confer 27/137.
avysyd *pp.* decided 27/451; **avyse, awyse** *imp. sg. refl.* resolve, determine 4/59; take thought, consider 14/315, 27/267, 30/29; **avyse** *imp. pl. refl.* take thought, consider 14/123, 21/197, 29/114.
avoyd *imp. pl.* make room, stand aside 14/1; *refl.* go away 15/115.
avow *n.* vow 8/163, 170, 9/20.
avow *pr. 1 sg.* vow 8/63; **avowyd** *pa. t.* Pr 132.
avowe *v.* affirm, declare 41/6.
awe *n.* power to inspire fear, overawing influence: *vndyr þer* ~ in their power Pr 293; *out of oure* ~ from our power 24/111; *onto hem set* ~ overawe them 41/44.
awey(e), away *adv.* away Pr 51, 222, 279, 324, 331, 437; absent 2/210; (as an order) move away! 14/150.
awntys *n.* aunts 36/28.
awter(e), autere *n.* altar 8/97 s.d., 9/229, 14/232, 239, 19/176 s.d.

bad(de) *adj.* bad 2/80, 3/139, 18/86.
baftys *adv.* behind 20/34.
baye *n.* stall 20/35.
baylé *n.* control, jurisdiction 29/83.
bayn *adj.* ready, willing 19/36, 190.
bakbyte *v.* backbite 42/101.
bak(e) *n.* back 22/52, 26/376, 32/240; **bakkys** *pl.* 9/108.
bake *v.* prepare, bring on 5/157.
bakere *n.* baker 14/24.
bakward *adv.* backward 28/148 s.d., 29/107.
balauns *n.* a set of scales: *in trewe* ~ when truly weighed 24/7.
bale *n.* suffering, trouble 2/249, 325, 5/93; **balys** *pl.* 11/21, 27/165.
balys *n. pl.* bales 23/171.

balke *n.* ridge, mound 34/299.

bane *n.* murderer 34/224.

banke *n.* hill, bank 18/277; **bankys** *pl.* 18/42, 105, 228.

baptym(e) *n.* baptism 22/23, 27, 29.

baptyze *n.* baptism 35/28.

baptyze, baptyse *v.* baptize Pr 257, 22/33, 68, 73; **baptyze** *pr. 1 sg.* 22/91; **baptysynge** *pr. p.* 39/25; **baptyzid** *pa. t.* and *pp.* 22/136, 35/27, 39/28; **baptyze** *imp. sg.* 22/65.

bare *adj.* sterile 8/101; absolute, sheer, manifest 20/248; bereft, devoid 21/260, 27/143, 35/183.

bareyn see **bar(r)eyn.**

bar(e)fo(o)t *adj.* barefoot 2/247, 6/33, 26/449 s.d.

barelegged, bareleggyd *adj.* and *adv.* barelegged 26/449 s.d., 31/170 s.d.

bargany *n.* bargain 27/310, 313.

barynes *n.* childlessness 8/168.

barn(e), baron *n.* child 16/34, 135, 18/86, 168, 219, 20/90; **barnys, barnis** *pl.* 20/16, 69, 115.

barre *n.* railing before a judge's seat 31/170 s.d.; *to pe ~* before the court 31/169, 170 s.d.

bar(r)eyn, barrany *adj.* barren, childless 8/101, 106, 179, 181, 195; (of a tree) without fruit 22/158.

basyn *n.* basin 27/511 s.d., 515 s.d.

bat *n.* contention, discord Pr 351.

batayle *n.* battle 21/110.

batte *n.* blow 29/183.

bawmys *n. gen. sg.* of balm 7/20, 16/47.

be, by(e) *prep.* by means of, with, through, by Pr 27, 96, 427, 489, 1/11, 2/144; *~ name* by name Pr 455, 2/15, 9/278; *~ name* in the name 30/245; (of manner) in: *~ opyn syth* in plain view Pr 29; *~ no way (wey)* not at all Pr 521, 28/14; *~ rowe* in order 5/220; *~ proces* in due time 8/223; in accordance with Pr 493, 6/95, 12/51; (in oaths, affirmations) 4/62, 67, 5/221; in, according to (writings, the Bible) 8/185; during 11/327; *~ nyth ne day (nyght nor day), ~ nyght and eke ~ day, ~ nyth (nyght)* 3/182, 4/19, 5/85, 18/229, 28/135, 35/276, 36/162; *~ pis day* today 14/37; *~ derk* by darkness 18/229; *~ and ~* at once 23/10, 27/527 s.d.; from 23/197, 24/168; near, beside, in the presence of 2/260, 15/84, 18/40, 279.

be, ben(e), byn, beyn *v.* be Pr 30, 34, 64, 67, 103, 106, 25/255, 26/115; **be(n), byn, beth, been, bene** *pl.* Pr 55, 122, 350, 418, 2/182, 4/241, 5/217, 6/61, 8/17, 26/313, 42/19; **beynge** *pr. p.* 9/17 s.d., 13/71: **be(n), ben(e)** *pp.* Pr 513, 4/156, 8/48; **beth, be** *imp. pl.* Pr 116, 5/149, 6/138, 8/228, 9/45.

becawse, because, bycause, bycawse *conj.* because Pr 69, 4/222, 10/49, 14/200, 355, 358, 24/267, 26/305; *~ pat* 8/60; in order that 30/226.

bed(de), bede, beed *n.* bed 10/295, 14/102, 16/76, 18/251, 35/102.

bede *pa. t. 2 sg.* offered 3/139.

bede see **byde.**

bedellys *n.* messengers 26/34.

bedene *adv.* indeed Pr 28, 183, 230; together Pr 101, 516; at once 18/15, 23/9.

bedyght *pp.* furnished: *in pe ~* with which you are endowed 9/184.

beed see **bed(de).**

beetys *n.* beets 2/25.

beffalle *v.* come to pass, occur 19/87; **befallyth** *pl.* 29/68; **befelle** *pa. t.* 14/68; **befalle** *pp.* 26/291; **befalle** *pr. subj.* 8/214, 18/121, 27/43.

beforn(e), bef(f)ore *adv.* in advance, beforehand 2/264, 5/215, 8/236, 10/188, 410, 16/25; in front, at the front 2/168, 20/94, 26/164 s.d.; previously 4/234, 7/71, 10/336; forward, ahead 13/22, 22/42; openly 41/141.

bef(f)orn, bef(f)or(e), byf(f)ore *prep.* in (into) the presence of Pr 195, 231, 325, 511, 7/36, 8/162, 11/271, 13/171A; in front of Pr 215, 9/229, 10/341; prior to, before Pr 296, 3/34, 7/75.

befornseyd *ppl. adj.* aforesaid 7/130, 27/76 s.d.

begat(t) *pa. t. ~ 30w with childe* (who) made you pregnant 15/39; begot 32/15.

begchis see **bych.**

beggere *n.* rascal, knave 20/35, 24/48; **beggerys** *gen. sg.* 26/101; **beggerys** *pl.* 26/87.

begyle *v.* 1 outwit, get the better of 24/120, 31/72; 2 beguile, delude 26/243; **begylyd, begylde** *pp.* 14/98, 23/25.

begynne *v.* 1 begin 1/29, 8/97, 10/281; **begynne** *pr. 1 sg.* 13/81, 19/12, 23/69; **begynnyth** *pr. 3 sg.* 4/15; **began, begunne** *pa. t.* Pr 11, 9/264, 11/179, 13/

begynne (*cont.*)
184A; **begonne** *pp.* 27/465, 474, 31/22;
begynne *imp. pl.* 16/89; **begynne** *pr.
subj.* 25/28; **2** do, undertake 9/188, 27/
257; *prophesye . . . dede* ~ prophesied 27/
391; **begynnyth** *pr. 3 sg.* (with infin.)
4/243, 32/219; **begownne** *pp.* performed, done: ~ *a synfull gyse* acted sinfully 12/31.

begynnyng(e) *vbl. n.* beginning Pr 2,
1/27, 9/7; *at þe* ~ first 27/49.

behest *pa. t.* vowed 10/58.

behestys *n.* promises 28/177.'

behete *pr. 1 sg.* promise 39/26.

behynde, behyndyn, byhynde *adv.*
behind, in back 2/168, 10/200, 222, 233,
32/240; ~ *and beforn* everywhere 20/94;
tardy, overdue 19/9.

behold(e) *v.* behold 9/46, 48, 15/32;
beholdyth, beheldyth *pr. 3 sg.* 11/260
s.d., 12/18, 29/194; **beholdyn** *pp.* 16/
23; **beholde, beheld** *imp. sg.* 11/215,
15/235, 18/97, 32/145; **behold(e),
byholde, beheldyth** *imp. pl.* 15/28, 22/
41, 25/373, 26/65, 32/169; **beholde** *pr.
subj.* observe, consider 26/311.

behovyth *impers.* is due to, is proper to
15/2; befits 21/45, 22/67; is necessary
39/59; **behove** *pr. subj. impers.* be necessary 28/29.

bey see **by(e), boy.**

beynge *vbl. n.* existence 1/5; a living
being, person 11/302.

belave see **beleve** (*v.*²).

belde see **bylde.**

beleve, belef *n.* belief 15/255, 274, 297;
bryng . . . in ~ convince 31/55.

beleve, belevyn, beleue *v.*¹ believe 15/
243, 21/95, 26/471, 485, 27/87, 411, 32/
111, 38/327; **beleve, beleue** *pr. 1 sg.*
7/65, 76, 9/68, 41/436; **beleve, beleue,
belevyn** *pl.* 24/53, 25/418, 26/452;
belevyd *pa. t.* 13/34, 63; **beleve,
beleue** *imp. sg.* 38/319, 342, 41/434;
belevyth *imp. pl.* 41/465.

beleve, belave *v.*² **1** remain 20/34, 41/
459; **2** lives, dwells *in* **belevyth** *pr. 3 sg.*
36/15; **3** is left over *in* **belevyth** *pr. 3 sg.*
27/413; **beleve** *pr. subj.* 9/289.

belyve, blyff, belyff *adv.* at once, quickly
Pr 379, 20/74, 22/149, 37/81; suddenly
35/147.

belle *n.* bell: *of þe* ~ o'clock Pr 526; *seyth
þe* ~ is spread abroad 14/120; *bere . . .*

þe ~ take the prize, am (are) the best
18/5, 21/2.

belthe *n.* (?) misfortune, evil 41/471n.

beltys *n.* belts 41/46.

bemys *n.* beams 11/292 s.d., 292 s.d., 292
s.d.n.

bench(e) *n.* bench 14/129n.; council,
assembly: *vpon this pleyn* ~ in this full
council 41/72.

bende *n.* captivity, bondage 18/48.

bende *v.* (of a bow) draw back the string
4/162; submit, yield 10/362; *my body* ~
strenuously apply myself 15/13; **bende**
pl. bend 9/268; **bent** *pa. t.* brought
about 38/31; **bent** *pp.* drawn Pr 85;
resolved (to do) Pr 55, 336, 451; (of a
bow) drawn back the string 4/155, 12/
55, 14/165; *þis bowe was* ~ this matter
was begun 5/140; stretched, fastened,
i.e. crucified 18/65; bound 18/141, 20/
78, 21/207; **bend** *imp. sg.* submit, yield
2/254.

benedicité *interj.* bless me (us) 10/175,
12/160.

benethe *prep.* beneath 16/3.

benygnely *adv.* humbly 39/86.

benyngne, benyng *adj.* obedient 10/3;
benign 28/183.

benyngnyté, benygnyté *n.* benignity
11/286, 41/98.

benyson *n.* blessing 9/216.

benyvolens, benevolens *n.* benevo-
lence, kindness 7/37, 14/382.

bent *ppl. adj.* resolved, determined 6/117.

berall *n.* beryl; crystal 42/46.

berde *n.* woman 27/143, 41/194; man 41/
121.

bere *n.* bier 25/64, 291, 41/135; tomb 38/
247.

bere, berun *v.* **1** give birth to 7/5, 108,
112; **bar(e)** *pa. t.* 28/179, 41/187, 351;
born(e), bore, iborn *pp.* born Pr 191,
2/263, 292, 8/195, 196, 204, 16/29; **bere**
imp. sg. 2/256; **2** bear (witness) 7/118,
39/80; **bere** *pr. 1 sg.* 7/109, 22/132, 36/
105; **bere** *pr. 3 sg.* ~ *it record* records,
bears witness *18/238n.; **bere** *pr. subj.*
6/156; **3** carry, bring 8/233, 9/284, 15/4;
~ *oure book* compare with us in scholar-
ship 21/9; **beryn't** carry it 31/212 s.d.,
32/35; **bere** *pr. 1 sg.* 2/118, 20/110, 36/
56; ~ *. . . þe belle* take the prize, am the
best 18/5; **beryth, beryght** *pr. 3 sg.* 11/
337, 15/47, 32/40 s.d.; ~ *hevy of* (who) is

heavily burdened by 32/23; **bere, beryn** *pl.* 18/139, 41/386, 435; carry (in one's womb) 13/56; ~ *þe belle* 21/2; ~ *þe prysse* surpass all others 21/7; ~ *þe maystrye* are pre-eminent 21/28; **beryng** *pr. p.* 27/27, 36 s.d.; **bar** *pa. t.* 8/218, 29/98; **bore** *pp.* 41/135, 222; **bere** *imp. sg.* 5/114, 32/27; **4** bear (flowers, fruit, nuts) 10/131, 22/158, 38/137; **beryth** *pr. 3 sg.* 10/262; **bare** *pa. t.* 38/132, 135; **5 beryth** *pl. all þat ~ lyff* all living things 10/426.

berere *n.* bearer 26/16.

bery(e), burry *v.* bury 25/155, 292, 34/43, 49; **burry** *pl.* 25/161; **beryed** *pa. t.* 25/388; **beryed, buryed, beryde** *pp.* Pr 305, 7/72, 25/140, 258, 260; **beryeth** *imp. pl.* 41/335; **bery** *pr. subj.* 34/79.

beryelys *n.* tombs Pr 508.

beryenge, burryenge *vbl. n.* burial 36/16; ~ *grownd* 34/306.

berys *n.* bears 35/264.

berst see **brest(e)** *n.*

beschrewe *v.* curse 14/192.

beseche *v.* **1** beseech, pray 32/115; **besech(e), beseke** *pr. 1 sg.* 8/76, 9/76, 168, 13/167, 41/123, 126; **besech(e), beseke** *pl.* 9/305, 29/7, 41/273; ~ *3ow of* ask of you 9/298, 13/179A; **besekyng(e), besechyng** *pr. p.* 3/43, 13/182A, 29/20, 41/173; **2** summoned *in* **besought** *pp.* 15/3n.

beseyn, beseen *pp.* arrayed 26/164 s.d., 28/80 s.d.; furnished 26/288 s.d.

besett *pp.* filled 15/68.

besy *adj.* busy, intent Pr 379, 9/297, 23/199; *3e be to ~ of 3oure langage* you talk too much 14/130.

besyde *adv.* to the side: *go ~* pass by 6/109; nearby, alongside 19/17; *prep.* beside 28/19.

besyly, besily, bisyli *adv.* diligently 9/212, 29/123, 32/147, 41/299, 305.

besynes *n.* occupation, affairs 9/201.

bestad *pp.* (of a difficulty) stopped, settled 8/211; lodged 16/118; placed, *or* afflicted 33/3.

best(e) *n.* beast 3/94, 117, 4/120, 163; ~ . . . *and foule* Pr 31; *foull and ~* 2/45; *byrd and* . . . ~ 2/136, 4/132; **bestys** *gen. sg.* 16/117, 26/376; **bestys** *pl.* 2/13, 22, 4/114; **bestys** *gen. pl.* Pr 74, 4/208, 18/28.

best(e) *adj. sup.* best 2/90, 3/83, 112; ~ *is* it is best 41/78; *as noun* 3/80, 81, 89; *of*

þe ~ of the best quality Pr 357, 20/149; *adv.* Pr 259, 3/130, 194.

bestryde *v.* bestride 18/10.

betake *pr. 1 sg.* entrust, commend 8/80; **betok** *pa. t.* entrusted to 41/203; **betake** *pp.* entrusted to 41/244.

bete *n.* bite, mouthful 2/138.

bete *v.* beat, whip 12/82, 29/180 s.d., 31/87; **bete** *pr. 1 sg.* 2/286; **betyn, bete** *pl.* *28/160; ~ *out* Pr 386; **bete** *pa. t.* Pr 51, 31/68; **betyn** *pp.* 30/244 s.d., 248, 31/197; ~ *owt(h)* 22/53, 34/23, 36/92; **bete, betyth** *imp. pl.* 29/179, 30/231, 243, 34/192.

beteche *pr. 1 sg.* ~ *3ow* entrust (you) to 8/19; **betaught** *pp.* entrusted 14/332.

bethynke *imp. sg. refl.* remember 29/222; **bethynke** *imp. pl. refl.* consider, keep in mind 25/274; **bethought, bethowth** *pp. I am ~ (of)* has come into my mind 21/233, 34/86.

betyde, betydyn *v.* **1** happen, come to pass 4/218; **betyd(de)** *pa. t.* 12/79, 24/249; **betydde** *pp. be ~* have come to pass 4/136; **betyde** *pr. subj.* 34/279; **2** befall, afflict 27/258.

betynge *vbl. n.* beating, scourging 18/67.

betrayd *pa. t.* betrayed 39/72; **betrayd** *pp.* 12/27, 27/457, 29/13; led astray 14/220.

bett *adv. comp.* better 4/160.

bet(t)yr *adj. comp.* better 4/236, 23/98, 25/365; *þe ~* better off 3/111; *hym were ~* it would be better for him 3/181; ~ *is* it is better 41/77; *he were ~* he would be better off 42/24; *as noun* 3/86, 12/116; *adv. comp.* 3/86, 5/57, 6/105; *þe ~* 10/376.

betwen(e), betwyn, bethwen, betweyn *prep.* between Pr 388, 9/17 s.d., 27, 10/312, 15/97, 26/144; among 25/151, 35/259.

betwyx *prep.* between 12/192, 26/159, 467; ~ *us tweyn* in private 31/117; among 27/320.

beware *v.* beware, be wary: ~ *be* take warning by 27/132; **bewar(e), bewhare** *imp. sg.* 6/87, 98, 136, 27/321; **bewar(e), bewhare** *imp. pl.* 14/310, 20/246, 260, 26/327; *refl.* 41/263.

bewray *imp. pl.* expose, accuse publicly 24/155.

bewté *n.* beauty 2/84, 14/84, 94.

Bybyl *n.* Bible Pr 52.

bych *n.* (opprobrious) bitch, whore: ~ *clowte* rag of a whore 24/147n.; **begchis** *pl.* curs, bitches 41/28.

bychyd, bygyd *ppl. adv.* vile, accursed 41/396, 404.

byd(de) *v.* command, bid Pr 224, 4/134, 207; **bydde** *pr. 1 sg.* 1/67, 4/109, 5/188; **byddyst** *pr. 2 sg.* 2/118; **byddyth, byddith, byddyt, biddith** *pr. 3 sg.* Pr 123, 126, 292, 6/139, 28/16 s.d., 41/135; **bydde** *pl.* 5/112, 256, 12/213; **bad** *pa. t.* Pr 90, 152, 2/73; **bad** *pp.* 9/280; **byd, bid** *imp. sg.* 4/99, 10/140, 12/140, 41/441; **byddyth** *imp. pl.* 11/87n.

byddyng(e) *vbl. n.* commandment, bidding 1/75, 2/34, 106.

byde *v.* reside, live 12/220; live to see 19/16, 53; **byde** *pr. 1 sg.* delay 11/216; **byde, byden** *pl.* dwell Pr 241; await 11/276; remain 42/38; **bede** *pp.* lived (in expectation of an event) 19/159; **bydyth** *imp. pl.* await 41/336; **byde** *pr. subj.* (forming *imp.*) stay, remain 41/461.

bydyng *vbl. n.* dwelling 2/17.

by(e), bey *v.* redeem, save 7/39, 16/40, 18/27; ~ *us to his blys(se)* purchase our salvation, bring us to heaven 7/12, 32/255; buy 26/106, 107, 27/196, 309; **bowth, bought, bowht** *pp.* bought, paid for Pr 368, 2/316, 4/194, 6/175, 14/328, 26/74, 27/199; acquired 26/99; redeemed 35/24.

bye see **be** *prep.*

bygyd see **bychyd.**

byholde see **behold(e).**

bylde, belde *pr. 1 sg.* create 1/32, 35n.; **byldyd** *pa. t.* 4/93.

bylle *n.* document: *lyttys* ~ the book of life 4/34n.

byn see **be** *v.*

bynd(e), byndyn *v.* bind 4/145, 24/203, 28/134, 31/210 s.d.; *do hym* ~ have him bound 26/231; oblige 12/176; tame, restrain 35/264; **bynde** *pr. 1 sg.* bind 35/50; **bownd** *pa. t.* bound 31/68; **bownd(e), bowndyn, bounde, boundyn, bounden** *pp.* bound, fettered, wrapped 2/224, 15/130, 16/116, 22/52, 25/32, 28/116, 34/271, 35/65, 198; ~ *vp* strung or tied up 41/46; obliged, committed 4/241, 6/28, 8/155; ~ *in brere* crowned with thorns 36/40; **bynde** *imp. pl.* bind 31/195.

bynne *n.* stall, stable 16/117, 18/40.

byrd *n.* bird: ~ *and best(e)* 2/136, 4/132; **byrdys** *pl.* 2/13, 20/183.

byrth(*e*) *n.* birth Pr 194, 202, 7/16; *of o day* ~ one day old 11/155; descent, parentage 21/157, 246.

bysmare *n.* wretch, contemptible creature 14/298, 24/146.

byte, byth *v.* bite Pr 40, 2/110; (with *of*) 2/100, 125, 148; **boot** *pa. t.* 2/243; **byte** *imp. pl.* 2/129.

byttyr, bytter *adj.* grievous, severe, cruel 1/73, 5/93, 18/59; bitter 18/62, 255, 25/323; see note to 27/397–400.

byttyrnesse *n.* bitterness 27/398.

blaberyn *pr.* talk foolishly 18/86.

blaberyng *vbl. n.* babbling 41/27.

blad see **blede.**

blak(e) *adj.* black Pr 25, 2/23, 299; yellow Pr 36n.; dirty 32/46.

blame *n.* offence, sin, fault Pr 45, 2/17, 14/144; flaw 6/20; disgrace, shame 8/122; *puttyn in* ~ accuse, disgrace 12/73, 24/58; *in* ~ culpable 14/185; reproof, rebuke 14/280; *pult me in* ~ rebuked me 7/107; *pult me in no* ~ 38/386.

blamyd *pp.* blamed, rebuked 15/31.

blasfemyng *vbl. n.* blaspheming 29/180.

blasfemyth *pr. 3 sg.* blasphemes 29/174.

blast *n.* (of a wind instrument) blast 18/19; **blastys** *pl.* gusts, blasts of wind 18/59.

blawe see **blowyn.**

ble *n.* colour, complexion 1/37; appearance 20/20, 41/331.

blede *v.* **1** bleed 4/153, 11/13, 16/42; **blede** *pr. pl.* 20/16; **bled(de)** *pa. t.* 35/80, 36/40, 38/127; **blede** *pr. subj.* 20/35; **2** cause to bleed 27/227; **blad** *pp.* 20/115; **3** bled out *in* **bledde** *pp.* 18/68.

blere *v.* blear: ~ *myn ey* deceive me 10/283.

blew *adj.* blue Pr 36, 2/23, 26/164 s.d.

blyff see **belyve.**

blyn *v.* cease 34/177.

blynd(e) *adj.* blind Pr 403, 4/143, 25/378; *as noun* 26/37, 392, 38/35.

blynde *v.* blind 26/228; ~ *... of ... knowlache* prevent from knowing 21/245.

blynd(e)nes(se) *n.* blindness 4/144, 32/12.

blys(s)(e), blyse, blis *n.* bliss Pr 203, 461, 1/35, 22/18, 22, 41/128, 283.

blys(se), blisse *v.* bless 5/212, 8/109, 230, 41/516; **blys(se)** *pr. 1 sg.* 18/329, 38/213, 41/166; **blyssyth** *pr. 3 sg.* 26/481 s.d., 27/527 s.d., 28/106 s.d.; **blysse** *pl.* (with future sense) 13/89; **blysse** *imp. pl.* 5/28, 9/69, 84; **blys(se)** *pr. subj.* 10/342, 15/312, 25/261.

blys(se)ful, blisful *adj.* blessed, full of bliss Pr 131, 194, 262, 12/178.

blyssyd, blissid, blessid, blys(s)id, blyssed, blessyd *ppl. adj.* blessed Pr 128, 160, 247, 5/228, 41/24, 163, 277, 297, 351, 366, 509, 527.

blyssydnes *n.* blessed state, blessedness 13/65.

blyssyng(e), blessyng *vbl. n.* blessing 2/47, 51, 5/30, 41/120.

blyth(e) *adj.* blithe, happy 2/74, 4/130, 10/264.

blod(e) see **blo(o)d(e).**

blody *adj.* bloody Pr 419, 16/93, 20/20; *adv.* with blood 33/13.

blome *n.* flower 16/92.

blome *v.* bloom, flower 7/22, 10/131; **blomyght** *pr. 3 sg.* 15/29; **blomyd** *pp.* grown, 'brought to flower' 18/164.

bloo *adj.* black-and-blue, bruised 34/123.

blo(o)d(e) *n.* blood Pr 386, 405, 3/168; kindred, offspring 4/195, 224, 5/172; *of* ~ by blood relationship 14/41, 113; lineage, stock 11/330, 15/7; person 30/26.

blosme *n.* offspring, blossom (i.e. Jesus) 18/39, 41/160.

blowyn, blowe *v.* (of wind) blow 18/59; boast loudly, bluster 20/135; **blawe** *pl.* deposit eggs (on), infect 41/46; **blowe** *pp. bost is* ~ is loudly boasted 18/87; **blow(e)** *imp. pl.* (of a wind instrument) blow, play: ~ *up* 18/19, 20/153, 232; make (a fire) burn harder 41/479.

bobbyd *pp.* struck 34/23.

bochere *n.* butcher, *or* botcher, patcher 14/16.

body(e), bodé *n.* body Pr 413, 414, 417, 12/217; person, living being 8/204, 9/38; trunk (of a man) 26/79; **bodyes** *gen. sg.* body's 33/16, 36/92; **bodyes** *pl.* 2/327, 41/87, 391; people 16/116.

bodyly, bodely, bodyli, bodily *adj.* physical, corporeal 2/332, 6/81, 124, 9/187, 192, 193, 41/289.

bodyly *adv.* bodily, physical 39/23.

boy, bey *n.* wicked fellow, rascal 3/153n., 12/75, 41/37; servant 4/152n., 162, 178;

commoner 26/71; **boys, boyes** *pl.* wicked fellows 18/86; boys, *or* rascals 20/220; servants 41/407.

boyle *v.* boil 41/483.

boyst *n.* container 36/56.

bold(e) *adj.* excellent, fair Pr 70, 5/12; bold, confident Pr 443, 4/130, 9/45; shameless, impudent 14/243, 298, 18/219.

boldnes *n.* boldness 18/5, 26/99.

bolt *n.* arrow 14/166.

bon *n.* bone 2/18, 18, 3/149; **bonys** *pl.* 29/36, 30/237, 32/86.

bond(e) *n.* rule, injunction 2/72; *harde* ~ distress 15/174; *in* ~ imprisoned 31/97; bond, fetter, shackle 35/38; **bondys** *pl.* bonds 25/430, 433.

bone, boun *n.* commandment 2/196; request, prayer 4/70, 87, 6/5, 15/40.

bone *adj.* good, gracious 2/270.

bonet *n.* cap 26/87.

book *n.* document, book Pr 97, 4/35, 10/431.

bo(o)rde *n.* table 27/458; (?) feast: *hurry-enge* ~ 36/16.

boot see **byte, bote.**

borys *n.* borings, holes 32/60.

borwe *n.* witness 8/169; surety, sponsor 35/135.

borwe *v.* rescue, redeem 11/104; **borwe** *imp. sg.* 11/21; **borwe** *pr. subj.* preserve, protect 4/81; rescue, redeem 27/160.

bost *n.* boast, bragging 18/87, 20/135, 248; *make no* ~ keep quiet (about it) 3/97; pride, *or* boasts, threats 35/209; **bostynge** *pr. p.* boasting 18/86.

bote, boot *n.* salvation Pr 107, 7/27, 18/47; remedy, relief 2/249, 27/165.

botel *n.* bottle 14/234, 294, 330.

both(e), bothyn *pron.* both Pr 45, 2/74, 231, 8/187, 21/240, 26/144; ~ *3oure* of both of you 11/123; **bothers, botherys** *gen.* of both: *3oure* – for you both 2/21; *here* –both of them 9/2.

both(e) *adj.* (pleonastically) ~ *to(o)* both 3/51, 53, 11/84.

both(e), bothyn, boþe *conj.* both Pr 7, 12, 36, 2/105, 10/135, 19/128; also 8/180, 9/75, 10/32.

boun see **bone** *n.*

bountevous *adj.* bounteous 26/9.

boure, bowre *n.* chamber, dwelling place 2/299, 10/64, 397, 11/316, 12/46, 27/177; town 16/79; stall 18/28.

bourgh *n.* town, village 15/5.
bow *n.* branch, bough 2/64, 10/300; *bete þe ~* beat the bush 12/82.
bowe *n.* bow 4/155, 162, 170; *þis ~ was bent* this matter was begun 5/140; *þi ~ is bent Newly now* your affairs now lie differently (also, with graphic eroticism, as in next instance) 12/55n.; *A cockoldeis ~ is... bent* 14/165.
bowyth *pr. 3 sg.* bows 15/42; **bowynge** *pr. p.* 11/286.
bowne *ppl. adj.*[1] ready, prepared 18/187.
bowne *ppl. adj.*[2] bound, compelled, certain 27/161.
box *n.* jar (of ointment) 27/197.
brace *n.* embrace 27/184.
bragge *v.* brag, boast 20/135; **bragge** *pr. subj.* should make noise 41/37.
brayde *n.* short time 25/255.
brayn *n.* brain 4/187, 25/454; mind 14/273, 25/77; brains 24/204, 40/18.
brake *n.* ferns, bracken 2/25.
bras *n.* molten copper 31/7.
braunch, braunce *n.* 1 line of genealogical descent 7/19, 21; 2 branch 41/134; **brawnchis** *pl.* 26/448.
brech(e) *n.* breeches 2/273, 24/139.
bred(e), breed *n.*[1] bread Pr 474, 3/155, 20/215, 38/286, 42/94; **bredys** *pl.* 27/353.
brede *n.*[2] breadth 4/156, 30/142.
brede, bredyn *v.* engender, bring forth 23/29, 41/70; **bredde, breed** *pp.* 5/11, 35/103; **brede** *pr. subj.* 4/60.
breff *adj.* brief 26/117.
breffly *adv.* concisely, in abridged form 8/11.
breffnes *n.* shortness (of time) 9/4.
breganderys *n.* body armour 28/80 s.d.
breke *v.* 1 (intr.) break, break up Pr 507, 32/143, 37/1; 2 violate 2/72, 196, 252; **brekyng** *pr. p.* 4/232; **brokyn** *pp.* 2/180, 231; 3 break open 11/9, 33/28; **brokyn** *pp.* 38/119; **breke** *imp. sg. ~ up* break open 24/121; 4 (trans.) break 30/237, 34/82, 38/259; **broke, brokyn** *pp.* 4/187, 35/38; **brekyth, breke** *imp. pl.* 29/151, 42/28; 5 escape, break out 36/158; 6 tear *in* **breke** *pr. 1 sg.* 2/273, 38/214; **brak** *pa. t.* tore 38/285.
brekyng(e) *vbl. n.* breaking Pr 474, 38/291.
brenne *v.* shine 16/21; (intr.) burn 27/

160, 41/479, 483; (trans.) burn 41/84, 228; **brennyth** *pr. 3 sg.* burns 3/132; **brennyng(e), brynnyng** *pr. p.* 22/9, 27/252, 28/148 s.d., PS 18; **brent** *pp.* Pr 57, 81, 5/141.
brennyng *vbl. n.* burning 1/73.
brennyng(e) *ppl. adj.* flaming, burning Pr 50, 497, 2/280.
brent *ppl. adj.* burnt 3/42.
brere *n.* (crown of) thorns 36/40.
brest(e), bryst, berst *n.* chest Pr 402, 443, 497, 21/42, 104, 32/240; breast (as seat of emotions, mind) 21/35, 38/84; *bolde ~* brave heart 21/103; bosom (of God) 18/51; **brestys** *pl.* 15/235, 29/92.
brest(e) *v.* 1 (intr.) burst Pr 507, 25/282, 28/164; **brest** *pr. 2 sg.* 32/97; 2 'break', put an end to 8/172; 3 (trans.) burst, break 24/204; **brest** *pr. subj.* 32/68; 4 overcome, conquer 31/41.
breth *n.* odour, scent 7/20, 16/47; voice 13/53; breath, breathing 25/105.
brethellys *n.* wretches 31/7.
brewe *v.* bring about, 'brew' 4/108.
brybe *n.* bribe 24/67.
brybory *n.* theft, swindling 26/90.
brybour *n.* scoundrel 20/135, 34/256.
brydde *n.* bird 12/83.
bryght(e), bryth, brith, bryht *adj.* bright, shining, resplendent Pr 17, 1/32, 37, 78, 3/132, 5/141, 6/19, 41/194, 353; fair 14/94, 15/262, 19/123, 41/353; *as noun* fair one 16/76; **bryghtere** *adj. comp.* 16/18, 18/316, 317.
bryghtnes *n.* brightness 15/163; radiance, splendour 40/4.
brymmys *n.* shores, banks 18/42.
bryng(e), bryngyn *v.* 1 bring Pr 74, 121, 123, 7/67, 27/421, 31/24; *~ aȝen* bring back Pr 365; *~ this to declaracyon* explain this 21/190; *~ the to... game* have sport with you 24/167; *~ in distemperaunce* deeply disturb 25/39; *~ o (a) dawe* kill 29/38, 129; *~... in belef* convince 31/55; **brynge(e)** *pr. 1 sg.* 10/208, 18/61, 255; **bryngyst** *pr. 2 sg.* (with *up*) produce 30/59; **bryngyth** *pr. 3 sg.* Pr 207, 9/245 s.d., 10/193; **bryng(e)** *pl.* Pr 128, 29/117 s.d., 30/99; **bryngyng** *pr. p.* 31/148; **brought, brouth, browth, brough** *pa. t.* Pr 78, 2/206, 9/219, 10/231, 21/117, 27/190, 30/92, 41/415; **brought, browth, brouth, browght, brout,**

browt *pp.* Pr 335, 350, 354, 10/12, 38/36; *in* ~ brought into 4/8; *my dethe is me* ~ I am killed 4/188; ~ *of dawe* put to death 29/149; **bryng(e), brenge** *imp. sg.* 10/221, 18/101, 27/465; *refl.* 28/120; **brynge** *imp. pl.* 20/149, 26/351, 355; **bryng(e)** *pr. subj.* Pr 203, 10/340, 38/391; *they hem* ~ let them bring them 34/253; (forming *imp.*) 41/493; **2** bring about 7/116.

brynke *n.* rim, edge (of the sepulchre) 34/322n.

brynnyng see **brenne.**

bryst see **brest(e)** *n.*

brith, bryth see **bryght(e).**

bryth *adv.* clearly, distinctly 34/102.

brithest *adj. sup. as noun* ~ *of ble* fairest one 41/331.

bronde *n.* torch 5/117; sword 20/137.

bronston *n.* brimstone 31/7.

bro(o)d *adj.* (of an arrow or spear) having a broad head 4/171, 175, 177.

brothel *n.* harlot, degenerate 24/146.

brother(e), brothyr, brothir(e), broþer *n.* brother Pr 54, 60, 3/3, 14/56, 18/279, 25/21, 33, 33, 37, 42; **brothers, brotherys** *gen. sg.* 3/161, 168, 25/178, 26/418; **bretheryn, brether(e), brederyn** *pl.* 9/157, 10/110, 11/27, 27/349, 41/143, 186, 213.

brotherles *adj.* brotherless 25/114.

brothyrly *adj.* brotherly, fraternal 9/154.

brougth, brout, brouth, browght see **bryng(e).**

brown(e) *adj.* of dark complexion 6/167; brown, dark 18/42, 105.

browstere *n.* brewer 14/30.

browt, browth see **bryng(e).**

buffett *n.* buffet, blow 24/190.

burgeys *n.* citizen 26/359 s.d.

burnyschith *pr. 3 sg.* burnishes 42/46.

burry see **bery(e).**

burryenge see **beryenge.**

busch(e) *n.* bush 4/166, 172, 6/18; branch 4/251; **busshys** *pl.* 2/299.

buske *pr. subj.* (forming *imp.*, *refl.*) go, hasten 16/79.

busshop(p), buschop(p), busschop, bushop, byschop *n.* bishop (i.e. high priest) Pr 118, 133, 155, 9/277 s.d., 10/3, 15, 115 s.d., 170, 14/187, 41/397; **beschoppys** *gen. sg.* 10/163; **buschop(p)ys, busshoppys** *pl.* 26/210, 288 s.d., 27/76 s.d., 31/122, 210 s.d.

but *adv.* no more than, only 3/16, 70, 121; **but, bvtt** *conj.* but Pr 20, 25, 129, 13/1; but rather Pr 99, 139, 352; unless 1/42, 9/120, 15/246; ~ *þat* except for the fact that 4/108; ~ *yf þat he deyd* without its dying 4/149; ~ *yf (if)* unless 9/132, 12/100, 14/216; but that, except that 15/149, 21/39; just, even 30/79.

buxum, buxom, buxhum, buxvm *adj.* obedient 5/110, 247, 10/3; gentle, humble, submissive 10/275, 393, 22/97.

cacche *v.* capture, arrest, catch 24/141; **kachyd** *pa. t.* received (a blow) 29/97; **cawth, cawght** *pp.* overcame, seized: *hevynese haue vs* ~ we are so drowsy 18/285; captured, arrested 24/96; ~ *away with* snatched away by 35/275.

cace see **cas(e).**

cadace *n.* cotton wool or other material for padding 26/77.

cadens *n.* rhythm of prose or poetry, rhetorical periods 21/8.

caysere see **kayser.**

caytyvys see **kaytyff.**

Calabere *n.* a kind of fur (apparently of squirrel) 26/105.

calculacyon *n.* computation, reckoning (mathematical or astrological) 21/7.

call *n.* *be* ~ for the asking, *or* by right 21/24.

call(e), kalle *v.* **1** summon, call 9/65, 14/116, 146; *gan vs* ~ *(from)* directed us away from 18/320; **call(e)** *pr. 1 sg.* 9/94, 10/97, 27/550; **calle** *imp. sg.* 25/319; **2** call, name, 41/201; *withowtyn cawse to* ~ with no justification that could be named 19/86; **callyth** *pr. 3 sg.* Pr 456; **call(e)** *pl.* 7/110, 14/36, 31/14; **calde, callyd** *pp.* Pr 385, 7/1, 53, 57, 117, 14/75; **3** speak of as, consider 26/111, 294, 27/116; **calle, kalle** *pr. 1 sg.* 1/22, 5/245; **kallyst** *pr. 2 sg.* 28/117; **callyth** *pr. 3 sg.* 29/66; **calle** *pl* 20/51; **4** call out 32/17; **calle, kall** *pr. 1 sg.* 5/5, 10/118, 34/313; **kall** *imp. sg.* 5/235.

callyng *vbl. n.* summons 5/108.

cammaka *n.* a rich fabric 18/82.

can, cannot(t), cannat see **kan.**

can *auxil. of pa. t.* did 14/128; cf. **gan** under **gynne.**

candele *n.* candle 41/303; **candelys** *pl.* 19/163.

canon, canoun *n.* canon law 21/25, 26/94.

cap(pe) *n.* headdress, cap 26/164 s.d.; **cappys** *pl.* 26/208 s.d.

captiuité, captyvyté *n.* captivity 9/128, 11/22.

care *n.* sorrow, distress Pr 430, 437, 2/286; concern 15/76, 20/149; **carys** *pl.* 24/151.

care *v.* be troubled, lament 8/157, 41/258.

car(e)ful(l) *adj.* sorrowful, full of care 2/287, 329, 5/144; *as noun* unfortunate or sorrowful person 8/145.

carefulnes *n.* sadness 25/116.

careyn *n.* carrion, corpse 4/246, 25/396.

carnalyté *n.* physical nature 11/295.

carnal(l) *adj.* bodily 9/138, PS 28; human 21/163.

carpynge *vbl. n.* talk 16/32, 18/177.

cas(e), cace *n.* case, instance 7/59, 115, 21/195; matter, affair, problem 10/97, 26/182, 221; reason, cause 10/159, 26/307; situation, state of affairs 10/370, 12/85, 14/332; way, manner 28/43; accusation, *or* fact 28/113.

cast *n.* intention, purpose 13/170.

cast(e), castyn *v.* **1** cast, throw, put 10/185, 18/227, 20/206, 29/180 s.d.; **cast** *pr. 1 sg.* ~ *hem in care* bring them to sorrow 20/270; **castyth** *pr. 3 sg.* 30/32 s.d.; **kest** *pa. t.* 29/221; **cast** *pp.* 2/241, 25/72, 26/15; ~ *in . . . care* 4/225, 20/252, 21/214; **cast** *imp. sg.* ~ *out* throw away 2/146; **cast, castyth** *imp. pl.* 20/29, 24/231, 32/51; **2** devised *in* **kast** *pp.* 31/46; **3** purpose, dispose (yourselves) *in* **cast** *imp. pl. refl.* 26/133, 27/420.

castel(l) *n.* **1** village Pr 465, 473, 26/347; **2** castle 18/129, 20/266; **castellys** *pl.* 23/176.

catel(le) *n.* property, chattel 20/233, 21/264, 23/37.

cause, cawse *v.* cause 14/93, 25/68, 26/100, 32/283; ~ *. . . þat þei xal se* cause to see 26/392; **causyth, cawsyth** *pr. 3 sg.* causes, brings about 4/33, 5/92, 13/74, 27/247.

caue, cave *n.* grave, cave 25/144, 165, 384, 409, 41/452.

cawdel *n.* warm drink, broth 14/272.

cawse, cause *n.* **1** reason, cause 4/142, 230, 10/43, 75, 26/431, 41/207; **cawsys** *pl.* 21/255, 26/147; **2** (legal) case 14/26, 332.

celestyal(l) *adj.* celestial 3/6, 21/161, 26/409.

celestly *adj.* and *adv.* heavenly 10/448; celestially 41/360n.

celle *n.* confined dwelling place, the pit of hell 20/234.

certayn, certeyn, serteyn *n. in* (*full*) ~ certainly, truly 2/115, 4/94, 178, 19/33, 191, 25/221, 37/27, 41/169; a certain number 26/453 s.d.

certayn, certan, certeyn see **serteyn** *adj.*, **serteyn(e)** *adv.*

certeynly see **serteynly.**

certefye, certyfyenge see **sertyfie.**

ces see **ses(e).**

cessacyon *n.* cessation 11/55.

ceté, cety(e) see **cyté.**

ceteceyn *n.* citizen 15/58; **ceteseynys** *pl.* 26/441 s.d., 449 s.d.

cetyward, cetéward *adv. onto* (*to*) *þe* ~ toward the city 26/423, 440.

cevyle, sevyle *adj.* civil (law) 21/25; *as noun* 26/94.

chaffare *v.* trade 27/239.

chalange *pr. 1 sg.* lay claim to 20/278.

chalys *n.* chalice 27/486, 28/52 s.d., 61.

chapmen see **schapman.**

chare *v.* and *imp. sg.* ~ *awey* drive away 32/213, 35/208.

chargyth, chargight *pr. 3 sg.* commands Pr 124, 10/146, 30/156, 159; **charged, chargyd** *pa. t.* Pr 96, 32/234.

chargyng *vbl. n.* commanding 10/210.

charyté *n.* charity, love, beneficence, *caritas* 9/205, 10/442, 11/158; *for* ~ for the sake of charity 8/25, 10/375, 21/108.

charle *n.* churl, villain 14/269; **scharlys** *pl.* 20/57.

chase *pr. subj.* urge on 2/59.

chast *adj.* chaste, virtuous 9/36, 14/79.

chast *adv.* in chastity 10/41.

chastement *n.* chastisement 26/113.

chastyse *v.* chastise, punish, subject to suffering 11/141, 13/149, 24/52.

chastyté *n.* chastity Pr 131, 154, 10/38.

chateryn *pr. pl.* chatter 40/19.

chauncel *n.* chancel 8/55.

chaunge, chawnge *v.* change 3/124, 25/49, 32/282, 35/266; **chaunge** *pr. 1 sg.* 18/20; **chaungyth** *pr. 3 sg.* 25/208; **chaungyd** *pa. t.* changed (one's course in life) 10/180; **chaungyd** *pp.* changed

(one's way of thinking) 14/204; altered
14/356; **chaunge, chawnge** *imp. sg.*
change 6/79, 12/154; **chaunge** *imp. pl.*
32/230, 38/103, 269; **chawnge** *pr. subj.*
38/329.

chavyl *n.* jaw: ~ *bon* jawbone 3/149.

chawmer(e), chaumbyr *n.* cabin, compartment 4/119; dwelling-place 11/316;
15/94, 112; chamber, room 18/20, 24/
72, 25/14.

chef *adj.* foremost, most prominent,
supreme 26/114, 215; ~ *of þis ordenawns*
foremost in this scheme 26/57; *þow
poverté be* ~ though poverty overcome
you 26/75.

cheke *n.* cheek 29/140, 141 s.d.

cheke *v.* place in check, arrest 30/230.

chene *n.* chain PS 19; **cheynes, chenys**
pl. 29/31, 32.

Cherch(e) see holy.

cher(e) *n.* good cheer, joy Pr 431, 14/102,
28/79; *do more* ~ bring more pleasure
14/102; *make . . .* ~ cheer 27/570; mood,
disposition, manner Pr 435, 5/134, 10/
133; *with gladsom (gladsum)* ~ cheerfully
Pr 458, 22/90; *what* ~ how are you? 10/
159, 13/49, 25/101; comfort 12/126;
facial expression 34/128.

chere *v.* console, comfort, cheer Pr 396,
15/169, 38/251; **chere** *imp. sg.* 12/153,
159; **chere** *imp. pl.* 25/53; *refl.* 25/80.

chery *n.* cherry 15/26; **cheryes, cheries**
pl. 15/33, 37, 39, 41.

cherysch *v.* cherish, favour, foster 11/
144; **cheryse** *imp. pl.* treat with loving
care 25/99.

cherubyn *n.* cherubim: ~ *halle* abode of
the cherubim, *or* all cherubim 41/249.

chese, chesyn *v.* choose 31/81, 39/89; *I
may not* ~ I have no choice 5/169; **ches**
pa. t. 11/95, 36/14; **chosyn, chose** *pp.*
10/419, 14/206, 338, 18/49; **chese** *imp.
sg. refl.* 10/34.

cheselys *n.* pebbles 5/222.

chete see shete.

cheteryn *pr. pl.* twitter 40/19.

cheve *v.* fare 16/145; **cheuyth** *pr. 3 sg.* ~
us sore grieves us 32/158.

cheverelle *n.* kid leather 26/72.

chevesauns *n.* stratagem 26/103.

chyde *v.* rebuke 34/282; (with *from*) drive
off with a rebuke 42/95; **chyde** *pr. subj.*
10/282.

child(e), chyld(e) *n.* child Pr 86, 128, 159,
190, 222, 5/24; **childys, chyldys** *gen. sg.*
Pr 91, 5/98, 197, 7/16, 12/36, 18/27;
**chylderyn, childeryn, chyldere,
chyldyr, childyr** *pl.* Pr 220, 226, 231,
310, 2/256, 4/11, 40, 49, 9/89, 31/160,
32/10, 34/196.

childely, chyldly *adj.* of a child 9/134,
11/295.

childhod *n.* state of being a child 11/298.

childyd *pa. t.* gave birth 41/6.

chille *v.* be chilled 41/483.

Chirch *n.* the Church 13/155A.

chyse *adj.* choice, excellent 20/42.

choyse *n.* someone chosen 6/170.

chosyn *ppl. adj.* chosen 11/275; *as noun*
41/525.

cyrcumstawns *n.* aspect: *with al þe* ~ in
every respect 26/210.

cyté, ceté, cety(e) *n.* town, city, village
(*civitas* in Vulgate) 8/43, 11/191, 13/8,
15/5, 12, 15, 68, 20/7, 23/155.

clad(de), clade *pp.* clad, covered 12/65,
15/300, 16/59, 18/235; ~ *in oure kende*
(one who is) incarnate 16/109; *vndyr
erth* ~ covered by earth 25/240.

clay(e), cley *n.* earth, clay Pr 305, 5/164,
11/94, 25/140, 142, 35/94; *from vndyr* ~
from the grave Pr 448.

clappyd *pp.* wrapped: ~ *in cloth* (the one)
wrapped in a shroud, i.e. Jesus 34/264.

clarefye *v.* make spiritually bright and
clear 19/48; **claryfieth** *pr. 3 sg.* purifies
10/442; **claryfyed** *pp.* glorified 27/478,
479.

clenche *pr. pl.* insist, affirm 41/68.

clene *adj.* spiritually pure, chaste 3/7,
6/111, 7/4; (with *to*) faithful to 6/145–6,
169–70; clean 15/237, 239, 243; pure,
free from admixture 22/171, 42/47.

clene, cleen *adv.* handsomely, splendidly 12/76; entirely 15/250, 24/232, 25/
419, 27/15; to a state of purity 26/155.

clenly *adv.* splendidly 26/288 s.d.

clennere *adj. comp.* spiritually purer,
more chaste 24/230.

clennes(se) *n.* purity, sinlessness 6/186,
8/241, 10/70; (as personif.) 9/199.

clennest *adj. sup.* (*as noun*) spiritually
purest one 41/514.

clensyth *pr. 3 sg.* cleans, purifies 42/47;
clensyd *pp.* purged 27/191.

clepe *pr. 1 sg.* **1** call 26/401; **clepe** *pl.* 8/34; **clepid** *pa. t. refl.* 41/53; **clepyd, clepid** *pp.* 8/50, 10/171, 431, 41/4, 18; **2** invited, summoned *in* **clepyd** *pp.* PS 26; **clepe** *pr. subj.* 13/46.

cler(e) *adj.* shining, bright Pr 16, 482, 1/37; pure, lovely, excellent Pr 434, 10/ 32, 366; innocent, *also* bright, clear 35/ 80; distinct Pr 456; (of vision) clear, keen 4/159, 25/227; (of water, tears, etc.) clear 8/177, 22/91, 34/10; certain 19/129; (of daylight) bright, clear 25/ 222; pure, sheer 26/74, 39/38; clearly visible 35/91, 41/498; innocent, un-defiled 41/5.

clere *adv.* brightly 15/165, 19/153; mani-festly 15/204; entirely 31/71; fully 34/ 276; to a state of purity, completely 42/47.

clergye *n.* knowledge 21/145.

clergyse *n.* learning, knowledge 21/2.

clerk(e) *n.* learned cleric, scholar 21/4, 9, 142; **clerkys** *pl.* Pr 248, 15/52, 21/7.

cleve, cleue *v.*[1] (intr.) break, split 5/164, 28/172, 32/197; hew asunder 18/149; (trans.) split, cut open 25/328, 38/326, 378; **clovyn, clevyd** *pp.* broken, split 4/177, 35/141; **cleue** *imp. pl.* 42/27.

cleue *v.*[2] remain: *In ... conscience ...* ~ truly accept 15/248.

clymbyn *v.* climb above 20/39; **clyme** *pr. subj.* should aspire, climb 41/58.

clyne *pr. 1 sg.* bow, submit 11/285.

clynge *v.* harden, *or* shrivel up 5/164.

clos *n. in* ~ privately, face to face 13/116n.

closyd *pp.* enclosed 1/6, 27/141, 185.

cloth(e) *n.* cloth garments 2/327; table-cloth 20/145; cloth 26/70, 375, 29/180 s.d.; shroud 34/264; **clothis** *pl.* bed-clothes Pr 357; clothes 6/104, 20/83, 26/ 449 s.d.; swaddling clothes 15/280, 292.

clothyd *pp.* dressed 12/76.

clothyng(e) *vbl. n.* clothing 18/296, 27/ 323; *oure* ~ i.e. human form 22/135.

clowde *n.* cloud 39/53, 41/191; **clowdys** *pl.* clouds 34/11, 41/284; clods 42/27.

clowte *n.*[1] a blow 14/261, 24/187, 29/97.

clowte *n.*[2] rag 24/147.

clowte *v.* strike, beat 10/282.

cognysion *n.* knowledge, comprehen-sion 21/63.

cok, kok *n.* cock Pr 342, 27/562, 29/221.

cok(e)wold(e), cokolde, kokewolde,

cockewold *n.* cuckold 12/55, 117, 14/ 98, 105, 129, 186, 225; **cockoldeis** *gen. sg.* 14/165.

cold(e) see **co(o)ld(e)**.

colere *n.* collar 26/85, 105.

colowre, colore, colour *n.* color 6/19; complexion 25/49, 208, 28/180, 35/184.

comawnde *v.* **1** command 26/167, 32/40; **comawnd(e)** *pr. 1 sg.* 30/245, 34/161; **comawndyth, comaundyth** *pr. 3 sg.* Pr 120, 26/397, 31/180; **comawnde** *pl.* 30/261; **comawndyd, comandyd** *pp.* 10/163, 27/351, 385; **2** commend *in* **comawnde** *pr. 1 sg. refl.* 30/147; **comawndyth** *pr. 3 sg. refl.* 30/20; **comawnde** *pl. refl.* 30/4; **comawndyd** *pa. t. refl.* 30/13; **comawnde** *imp. sg.* 30/ 15.

comaund(e)ment(e), comawndement, commaundement *n.* bidding, com-mandment 1/70, 2/75, 5/89, 6/49, 15/8, 26/93, 41/141; **comaundementys** *pl.* Pr 101, 9/170, 26/400.

comberaunce *n.* misfortune, distress 25/ 36.

combryd see **comeryd**.

combros *adj.* difficult, troublesome 35/ 247.

com(e), comyn, cum *v.* **1** come Pr 140, 195, 236, 488, 8/36, 9/109, 277 s.d., 13/ 112, 18/229; ~ *man* become human, be born 9/308; ~ *to* attain 21/63; ~ *hym bye* get at him 27/135; **com(e), cum** *pr. 1 sg.* 10/239, 14/39, 18/237; (with fut. sense) 5/48; **comyst** *pr. 2 sg.* 15/70, 22/ 117, 28/23; (with ellips. of 'thou') 10/ 223; **comyth** *pr. 3 sg.* Pr 171, 2/274, 9/123; ~ *of* derives from 7/60; **come, comyn, cum, comyth, cvm** *pl.* Pr 147, 204, 447, 18/136, 22/34, 27/327; ~ *at* arrive at 13/10; (with fut. sense) 18/215; **comyng(e)** *pr. p.* Pr 495, 9/277 s.d., 13/ 171; **cam, com(e), kam** *pa. t. 1, 3 sg.* 12/ 45, 214, 13/69, 24/19, 26/20, 396, 41/134; ~ *to* attained Pr 250; **camst** *pa. t. 2 sg.* (with ellips. of 'thou') 21/156; **come, comyn** *pa. t. pl.* 10/47, 38/82, 87; **com(e), cum, comyn** *pp.* 8/83, 95, 175; ~ *of, off ...* ~ descended from 7/102, 10/207, 18/162; **com(e), cum, coom** *imp. sg.* 2/31, 330, 3/157, 15/234; ~ *of* come on 11/261; **com(e), comyth, cum** *imp. pl.* 2/291, 9/57, 57; **com(e),**

cum *pr. subj.* 8/198, 10/145, 14/262; **com** *pa. subj.* 42/97; **2** go 35/64; **comyst** *pr. 2 sg.* 12/148; **come, cam** *pa. t.* 15/153, 25/215, 35/185.

comely *adj.* noble, holy; handsome 16/113; **comelyeste** *sup.* 18/9.

comendable *adj.* commendable 29/54.

comendacyon *n.* praise, commendation 9/270.

comende *pr. 1 sg. refl.* commend 9/218, 11/333; entrust, commit 32/216; **comendyd** *pp.* praised 11/234.

comeryd, combryd *pp.* (with *in*, *with*) encumbered (in), burdened (by) 11/31, 27/192.

comfortabyl *adj.* gratifying, comforting 11/321; **comfortablest** *sup.* 13/149A.

comfortacyon *n.* comfort, consolation 11/284, 328.

comfort(e), comforth *n.* comfort, consolation Pr 156, 431, 5/151, 208; *be of good ~* be of good cheer 25/65, 129; remedy, relief 2/328, 11/54, 167.

comfort(e), comfortyn *v.* 1 comfort Pr 487, 8/86, 13/4, 36/24; **comfortyth** *pr. 3 sg.* Pr 410, 13/161; **comforte** *pl.* 15/158; **comfort(e)** *imp.* 12/85, 32/167, 292; **2** relieve 25/116, 28/187, 41/337; **comfortyth** *pr. 3 sg.* Pr 430; **comfortyd** *pp.* 35/114; **comforte** *imp. sg.* 25/6; **comforte** *pr. subj.* 25/95.

comfortour *n.* one who gives spiritual strength of solace 19/117.

comyng(e) *vbl. n.* arrival, coming 10/147, 192, 13/74.

comly *adv.* fittingly 5/109.

comoun *adj.* of low rank, common 31/24.

comownys, comonys *n.* the common people 26/324, 32/88 s.d., 41/81.

company(e), compayné, compané *n.* fellowship, company 12/113, 15/315, 19/130, 186, 21/231, 29/211; intimate association 12/106.

comparycyon, comparison *n.* *make ~ (to, vnto)* claim equality (with) 26/71, 81.

compassyon *n.* compassion 11/16, 76, 24/270; (as personif.) 9/199.

compellyd *pp.* attracted, driven 4/224.

compiled *pp.* presented 8/11.

compleyn *imp. pl.* complain, make accusation 26/170.

compleynt *n.* complaint 4/141; **compleyntys** *pl.* charges 30/57.

comprehendyd *pp.* subsumed 9/171.

con see **kan**.

conceyte *n.* conception 8/8; **conseytis** *pl.* thoughts, minds 41/226.

conceyve see **conseyve**.

concente *pr. subj.* yield, surrender 23/205.

concepcyon *n.* conception 8/10, 188, 12/212.

concyens, conscience, consyens *n.* mind, heart 15/248; conscience, sense of justice 24/199, 205, 26/130; *thyrknes of ~* moral darkness PS 27.

conclaue *n.* private chamber 10/483; *dede ~* tomb Pr 419.

concludyd *pp.* confuted 29/128.

conclusyon *n.* concluding statement, end 7/129, 8/13, 13/150A; *I had ~* I was overcome, frustrated 26/29; decision, resolution, outcome 11/101, 152, 168; *in no ~* in no case 30/83.

concorde *n.* concord 9/154.

condempnyd *pp.* condemned 24/274, 277.

cone see **kan**.

confeccyons *n.* prepared dishes or delicacies 9/245 s.d.n. ✓

conferme *v.* 1 confirm 26/421; **conferme** *pr. 1 sg.* 7/58, 125; **2** institute, establish *in* 22/64; **confermyd** *pp.* 22/78; **3** strengthen *in* **conferme** *imp. sg.* 40/11

confermyng *vbl. n.* confirming 28/24.

confesse *imp. sg. refl.* make confession 26/155; **confesse** *pr. subj. refl.* 26/412.

confessyon *n.* confession 9/118, 142.

confidens, confydens *n.* belief, confidence 9/122, 26/419.

confusyon *n.* destruction, damnation; confusion 26/5, 51, 469.

congregacyon *n.* congregated people 8/1, PS 6, *41/239; act of congregating 41/235.

conyng see **kunnyng**.

conjowre, conjure *pr. 1 sg.* charge, adjure 27/176, 29/167; **conjure** *pl.* implore 31/38.

conjunccyon *n.* *copelyd be ~* joined together 26/158.

conjunct *pp.* (with *to*) joined (to), united (with) *41/100.

connyng(e), cunnyng(e), kunnyng *vbl. n.* knowledge, understanding Pr 38, 2/38, 102, 114, 150, 162, 21/28, 40, 120.

conqweryd *pp.* conquered 26/430.

conscience see **concyens.**

conseytis see **conceyte.**

conseyve, conceyve *v.* 1 conceive (a
child) 8/223, 11/239, 13/33, 78, 21/182;
conseyvenge *pr. p. was* ~ conceived
13/36; **conceyved, conceyvyd, conseyvyd, conseyved** *pa. t.* 11/301, 13/
70, 76, 41/5; **conseyvid, conseyved**
pp. 9/3, 11/256, 311, 41/15; 2 conceived
of, devised *in* **conseyvyd** *pa. t.* Pr 286.

conseyvyng(e) *vbl. n.* conception 13/73,
PS 38.

consent *v.* connive, consent 14/128; **con-
sente** *pr. 1 sg.* consent 11/129.

consentynge *vbl. n.* consent, agreement
13/70.

conserve *v.* protect, preserve 13/183A;
conserve *pr. subj.* 8/1.

consyder *v.* take into consideration 11/
110; **consydyr** *pl.* consider, take note
of 21/81; **consyderynge** *pr. p.* taking
into consideration 9/4; **consydyr** *imp.
sg.* ~ *to me* pity me 19/25.

consyens see **concyens.**

consolacyon *n.* pleasure, comfort Pr 302,
9/195, 28/154; relief, spiritual aid and
support, consolation 14/336, 405, 21/
285.

consorcyté *n.* company, fellowship 41/
116.

constreyn(e) *v.* compel, induce 25/369,
*27/121; govern 28/21.

consummacyon *n.* completion, conclusion, *or* performance 21/287.

contenawns *n.* appearance, countenance
28/1st s.d.; gestures 27/348 s.d., 28/80
s.d.

content(e) *adj.* content 8/8, 9/258, 11/
131.

contenue *v.* continue, carry on 26/227;
contewnyng *pr. p.* 27/57.

contynent *adj.* continent 27/419.

contynualy *adv.* continually PS 18.

contraryes *n.* antithetical qualities 11/
64.

contraryous *adj.* rebellious 11/43.

contraversy *n.* controversy, dispute 11/
138.

contrycyon, contryssyon, contryscyon
n. contrition 11/29, 22/151, 26/412, 27/
404, 448; (as personif.) 9/199.

contryte, contrite *n.* contrite 11/54, 22/
149, 24/289.

contryve *v.* discover, come to understand 21/54, 38/307; plan, devise 27/
125.

conuey, convey *v.* lead 27/54, 86; con-
vey *pr. 1 sg.* control, direct, *or* express
26/213; **conveyng** *pr. p.* leading 28/80
s.d.

convenyens *n.* appropriateness: *as* ~
wold seme as would seem appropriate
41/204.

conuenyent *adj.* proper, fitting 15/134.

conversacyon, conuersacyon *n.* manner of living 13/29, PS 26.

conuersaunt *pp. be* ~ (*in*) accompanied,
been associated with 39/77.

conuerte *v.* convert 38/377; **conuertyth**
pr. 3 sg. ~ *oure captiuité* brings us back
from (spiritual) captivity 9/128; **con-
uertyd** *pa. t.* PS 21, 22.

convycte, convicte *v.* 1 convict Pr 285; 2
defeat 21/102; **convycte** *pp.* 41/158.

convocacyon *n.* convocation, synod,
assembly 27/176 s.d.

co(o)ld(e), koid *adj.* cold Pr 72, 439, 10/
189; cold in death, dead 18/223; chill-
ing, distressing 24/151; ~ *stodye* state of
intense abstraction 24/225; *adv.* ~ *clade*
without warm clothing 18/235.

co(o)rs *n.* corpse 25/151, 161, 34/281.

coorte see **court(e).**

copelyd *pp.* linked, coupled 26/158.

copyl(l), cowpyl *n.* couple, pair of the
opposite sex 4/120, 208, 14/195.

corage *n.* spirit, courage 14/269.

corde *n.* accord: *perfyth of* ~ fulfilment of
the accord 26/467.

cordewan *n.* Cordovan leather 26/69.

cordys *n.* cords, ropes 28/116, 134, 159.

coryous *n.* skilfully made, elaborate,
costly 20/145.

corn(e) *n.* corn, grain 22/171, 32/212, 35/
207; **cornys** *pl.* corn, crops 3/98.

corner(e) *n.* corner 34/242, 254, 274;
cornerys *pl.* 34/247.

correcte *v.* punish, rebuke 26/242; **correcte** *imp. pl.* 29/82.

correxion *n.* punishment, rebuke 26/236.

cors see **co(o)rs.**

corteyn *n.* curtain 31/57 s.d.

cosyn *n.* kinswoman 11/208, 255, 310;
kinsman 26/196; **cosynys** *gen. sg.* kins-

man's 29/204; **cosynes, cosynys** *pl.*
kinspeople 13/159, 21/220.
cost *n.* outlying land: *crofte and* ~ 3/99;
land, region 20/131, 35/203.
coste *n.* expenditure, cost 20/149.
coste *v.* cost 20/148.
costyous *adj.* costly 26/70.
cote *n.*¹ cottage 10/201.
cote *n.*² coat, tunic: *clowte my* ~ strike me
10/282n.
countyrfe *v.* contrive, plot 26/55.
countré, contré, cowntré *n.* land,
region Pr 171, 175, 210, 29/70, 30/124,
41/68, 190; *all* ~ every land 6/154;
countrés, contreys *pl.* 18/58, 41/283.
course *v.* curse 27/6; **cursyd** *pp.* Pr 62,
3/170, 186.
court(e), coorte *n.* court 14/2, 4, 8, 140.
coveryd, couerid *pp.* covered Pr 357, 20/
145.
coverte *n.* covering 14/307.
covetyse *n.* covetousness, greed 23/147,
150; 26/112.
counawnt *n.* covenant 30/30.
coward *adj.* cowardly 41/393.
cowardis *n.* cowards 41/419.
cowde see **kan.**
cowncel(l)(e), counsel(l)(e), coun-
cel(l)(e), cownsel, counsayl, cown-
sayl *n.* counsel, advice Pr 380, 2/207,
3/50, 10/108, 13/154, 23/2, 26/123, 181,
186, 193, 197; *be my(n)* ~ I advise you
15/292, 20/260; council 11/171, 35/235;
~ *hous* building where a council meets
26/288 s.d., 27/76 s.d., 31/117 s.d.; a
secret: *kepe* ~ keep (a matter) secret 14/
118, 24/68, 35/301.
cownsell *v.* counsel *10/97; **councel(l),**
cowncell, cownselle, counseyll,
counsel *pr. 1 sg.* 2/88, 3/39, 10/107, 22/
23, 24/51, 26/129, 35/253, 38/107; **coun-**
sell *pr. 3 sg.* 11/74.
cownterfete *v.* 1 imitate, pretend to be
26/102; 2 contrived, devised *in* **cown-**
tyrfetyd *pp.* 27/267, 28/109; **cowntyr-**
fete *imp. pl.* 27/98.
cowpe *n.* vessel 9/245 s.d.
cowpyl see **copyl(l).**
cowthe *adj. makyth* ~ acquaints one with
10/442.
craft(e) *n.* 1 deceitful tricks, craft 30/177,
31/57; **craftys** *pl.* 30/47; 2 skills,
powers *in* **craftys** *pl.* 20/28.

craggyd *adj.* pointed, jagged 41/38.
crake *v.* crack 32/196; **crake** *pr. 1 sg. a fart
I* ~ I break wind 1/81; crack, break 34/
291.
crakke *n.* fart 23/195.
craue *v.* ask for, crave Pr 417, 18/143, 24/
286; **craue** *imp. sg.* 24/22.
creatour(e) *n.* creator 11/70, 19/118.
creature *n.* person, created being 8/8,
235, 9/87; **creaturys, creatures,**
creaturis *pl.* 2/50, 9/155, 10/93, 450,
41/103; **creaturys** *gen. pl.* 11/284.
credens *n.* credence 27/122, 384.
credyble *adj.* credible 11/212.
credyl, cradyl *n.* cradle 14/198, 21/47,
156; ~ *bende* swaddling clothes 20/16.
crenseyn *n.* crimson 26/70.
crepp(e), crepe *v.* 1 go, steal away 4/38;
2 creep 8/238, 40/18; **krepe** *pr. 1 sg.*
2/268, 10/479; **crepe** *pr.* 42/57; **crepte**
pa. t. 14/308; **crepe** *pr. subj.* (with *in*)
enter (into) 4/77.
cresset(t)ys *n.* vessels used as lamps 27/
342, 28/80 s.d.
cry *n.* outcry 4/179, 14/112.
crye, cryen *v.* 1 cry out Pr 362, 382, 24/
172, 31/104 s.d., 32/182 s.d.; **cry(e)** *pr. 1*
sg. 5/237, 10/118, 11/31; **cryeth** *pr. 3 sg.*
28/106 s.d.; **cry(e)** *pl.* 12/3, 31/11, 41/
376; **cryeng(e), criyng** *pr. p.* 11/22, 26/
457, PS 40, 29/89 s.d.; **cryed** *pp.* 9/104,
144; **crye** *imp. pl.* 41/488; 2 give forth a
call Pr 342; 3 beg, ask for 32/202; **cry(e)**
pr. 1 sg. 9/276, 41/310; **crye** *pl.* 10/257,
11/40, 54; 4 proclaimed *in* **cryed** *pp.*
15/5.
crystall *n.* crystal 42/47.
crystenyd *pa. t.* baptized 29/37; **cris-**
tenyd *pp.* 41/18.
Crystyn *n.* Christian 29/29; **Crystyn** *pl.*
29/33, 41.
Crystyn, Crysten *adj.* Christian 9/172,
29/47, 52.
crofte *n.* small enclosed field adjoining a
house: ~ *and cost* 3/99.
croyse *n.* cross 16/32.
crokyd *adj.* crippled 26/394, 402; *as noun*
26/37, 30/198.
crook *n.* crooked claw, hook, 'clutches'
23/135.
croppe *n.* belly, *or* throat 24/131.
cros(se) *n.* 25/456, 31/25, 110; **crosses,**
crossys *pl.* 32/89, 92 s.d.

crowch *n.* the cross 36/36.

crowe *n.* raven Pr 76, 4/244, 246.

crowe, crowyn *v.* crow Pr 342, 29/221; **crowe** *pp.* 27/562.

crowne, kroune *n.* crown 11/30, 18/41, 83, 31/212 s.d.; top (of head or hat) 26/87, 164 s.d.; mitre, *or* tonsure of a cleric 42/14; **crownys** *pl.* tops (of heads) 20/13n., 34/291.

crowne *pr. 1 sg.* crown 41/524; **crownyd** *pp.* 27/468; **crowne** *imp. pl.* 31/197.

crownyd *ppl. adj.* crowned 5/245.

cruel(l) *adj.* cruel, fierce Pr 219, 18/83n., 218.

cruelté *n.* cruelty 35/54.

cum see **com(e)**.

cunnyng(e) see **connyng(e)**.

curat *n.* curate, priest 8/54.

cure *n.* care, keeping 8/32; *takyth* ~ take charge of, care for 41/332; effort, diligence: *do* . . . ~ take pains 21/101, 27/435.

cure *v.* take care of 15/272.

curyng *vbl. n.* covering 26/87.

curyng see **kure**.

curryd *pp.* ? well combed; *or* excellent, choice 18/83n.

curs(e) *n.* curse 14/27, 24/133, 144.

cursyd *ppl. adj.* wicked, evil 3/166, 14/367, 372.

cursydnes *n.* wickedness, evil 4/26, 23/135.

curteys *adj.* courtly, courteous 18/13, 20/142.

curtesy *n.* courtesy 14/152, 20/262; *for þi* ~ if you please 18/172.

cus see **kys(se)**.

cusshonys *n.* cushions 26/288 s.d.

custom *n.* ~ *ocupacyon* customary activity 11/326.

custommably *adv.* habitually, often 10/441.

daggare, daggere *n.* dagger 24/131, 26/83.

day see **dey(e)**.

day(e), dawe *n.* day Pr 16, 148, 216; *all* ~ all day long, always 6/82; *be þis* ~ today 14/37, 30/9; *be* ~ *(as tag)* in the daytime 18/72; *brynge(e)* . . . *o (a)* ~ kill 29/38, 129; *browt of* ~ killed 29/149; ~ *dawe* dawn 30/14, 21; appointed time 20/278; period of time 39/37; *xij ȝere* ~ twelve

years 2/272; **days, day, dayes** *pl.* Pr 29, 75, 252, 22/130, 38/116, 41/174, 336.

dayly *adj.* daily 3/120, 28/154; *adv.* 9/189, 11/232, 13/156A.

daylyght, daylyth *n.* daylight 25/224, 38/78.

dale *n.* pit 2/321; **dalys** *pl.* dales 18/228.

dalyaunce, dalyawnce, dalyauns *n.* talk, words 14/135, 24/101, 38/171, 176.

dame *n.* 1 lady 2/87, 8/138, 12/1; **damys** *pl.* 15/158; 2 mother 41/60.

damesel, damysel *n.* damsel 10/10, 14/94, 268; **damysel(l)ys** *pl.* 10/6, 350.

dampnacyon *n.* damnation 5/157, 7/79, 26/433.

dampne *v.* damn, condemn Pr 287, 6/90, 22/36; **dampnyd, dempt** *pp.* 23/138, 27/243, 31/61, 69, 169.

dar(e), darst see **dur**.

dart *n.* spear 25/63.

datys *n.* dates 2/63.

daunger(e), dawngere *n.* danger, risk 2/257, 4/77, 19/145, 28/120; power 26/244.

dawe see **day(e)**.

dawns, dawncyn *v.* (euphemistically) dance 14/268; dance 32/76 s.d.

debat(e) *n.* dispute, strife 14/72, 15/73, 26/84.

debate *v.* quarrel, fight 15/74.

declaracyon *n.* story, representation Pr 298; elucidation, explanation 21/133; (as personif.) 9/213; *brynge this to* ~ explain this 21/190; *made* ~ explained *26/163.

declare *v.* show Pr 315, 9/14; tell 41/254; **declaryth** *pr. 3 sg.* declares, proclaims 40/38.

declinande, declynyng *pr. p.* deviating 26/146; *be not* ~ don't deviate 26/136.

ded(d)ly, deedly *adj.* deadly, mortal 11/159, 24/128, 25/24; destructive of the soul 42/23, 30.

ded(e), deed *n.* deed, act, conduct Pr 134, 2/143, 165, 208; *in werd and* ~ 5/231; *evyn in* ~ right in the act 20/271; **dedys** *pl.* 9/151, 291, 10/252, 18/72; *Mortal* ~, ~ *Mortal* Deadly Sins 26/130, 411.

ded(e), deed *adj.* dead Pr 150, 231, 305, 5/201, 25/38, 44; *be* ~ die 2/144, 153, 3/146.

dede see **deth(e)**.

dedly *adv. synnyst* ~ (with ellips. of 'thou') (you) commit a mortal sin 26/154.

dedmen *n.* dead men 29/111.
def *adj.* deaf 26/401; *as noun* 26/393.
defamacyon *n.* defamation 14/375.
defame *n.* disgrace, dishonour 14/141, 24/176.
defawth, defawte *n.* offence, sin 26/191, 30/84, 112, 31/91; **defawtys** pl. 30/249.
defende *v.* 1 protect, save, defend 9/220, 27/489, 506; **defende** *imp. sg.* 41/339; **defende, dyffende** *pr. subj.* 9/98, 18/261, 29/4; 2 offended *in* **defendyd** 32/134n.
defens *n. without* ~ without opposition or denial 13/153.
defens *v.* defend 7/7.
defye *v.* defy, repudiate 31/20.
defylyde *pp.* defiled Pr 129.
degré *n.* way, manner: *in al(l)* ~ in every way Pr 62, 2/103, 4/42; *in fele* ~ in many ways Pr 274; *in eche (iche)* ~ in every way 3/80, 10/123, 28/31; *in no* ~, *in no maner* ~ not in any way, not at all 4/61, 5/187, 21/210, 28/168; *in good* ~ properly 10/2; *in every* ~ 26/306; estate, position in the scale of dignity or rank 7/89, 11/331, 18/179; *in (at) (one's* ~ as befits (one's) rank or position 6/72, 20/156, 27/348 s.d.; *to ʒoure hey* ~ to your lordship 26/253; step (in a flight of stairs) 9/102; *in þis* ~ of such importance 10/102; condition, state 15/99; honour, prestige, standing 19/141, 21/24; *þe fyrst in* ~ the first 19/199; relative extent: *be more lengere in þer* ~ have lasted longer 21/271; **degrees** *pl. all* ~ persons of all ranks 26/82.
dey(e), dye, day, deyn, dyen *v.* die Pr 392, 2/93, 98, 214, 3/78, 11/62, 145, 19/85, 26/316, 34/193; *refl.* 25/245; **deye, dye** *pr. 1 sg.* 4/176, 186, 41/475; **deyst** *pr. 2 sg.* 34/37; (shall) die 2/43; **deyth** *pr. 3 sg.* 25/303; **deyd, dyed** *pa. t.* 4/149, 19/7, 24/293, 25/387; **deyd** *pp.* 11/139, 25/126, 32/247; **deye** *pr. subj.* 41/93.
deying *vbl. n.* dying 41/257.
deyté, deité *n.* Deity, God 9/274, 27/377; divinity, godliness 10/112, 41/94; divine state or condition 41/293, 493.
delacyon *n.* delay 26/260, 267; *make* ~ delay 27/101.
delay *v.* delay (to carry out) 26/357; **delayd** *pp.* withheld 26/43.
delayde *pp.* assuaged 15/278.

del(e) *n.* part, bit 25/97; *every* ~ entirely 27/471; *nevyr a* ~ none at all 27/509.
delectacyon *n.* delight PS 12.
deliberacyon, deliberacion, delyberacyon *n.* judiciousness, thoughtful consideration *13/181A, 21/58; (as personif.) 9/211.
delycyous *adj.* delicious, choice 27/445.
delyre *v.* go astray 22/163.
delyte *n.*¹ offence, crime Pr 44.
delyte, delyght *n.*² delight 14/93, 16/98, 26/89, 29/62, 38/154; pleasure *or* offence 14/301.
delyuerauns, delyverauns *n.* childbirth: *had* ~ gave birth Pr 190; deliverance 22/182.
delyveré *n.* release 31/172.
delyver(e), delyuere, delyvyr *v.* 1 save 16/36, 32/152, 175, 33/31; **delyuere** *imp. sg.* 28/47; 2 deliver (into someone's power) 29/14, 30/260; **delyveryd** *pp.* 30/110; **delyuere, dylyvere** *imp. pl.* 31/163, 163; 3 released *in* **delyveryd** *pp.* 26/479; **delyvere** *imp. pl.* 31/106.
delvyng *vbl. n.* digging 2/324.
demaunde *pr. 1 sg.* demand 41/41.
demawnde *n.* demand *30/259.
dem(e) *v.* 1 judge 7/88, 29/172, 30/211; 2 decide 11/124; 3 suppose, think, believe 26/304; **deme** *pl.* 25/236; **demyd** *pa. t.* 15/284; 4 declare (a decision) *in* **deme** *pr. 1 sg.* 11/138; 5 sentence, condemn *in* **deme** *pr. 1 sg.* 31/207; **demyd** *pp.* 2/214; **deme** *imp. sg.* 31/59; **demyth** *imp. pl.* 30/96; 6 suspect, assume *in* **demyst** *pr. 2 sg.* 14/358; 7 regarded as *in* **demyd** *pp.* 18/72.
demynge *vbl. n.* thinking, believing 15/297.
dene *n.* din 31/57 s.d.
deny(e), deney *v.* withhold, refuse 27/453; *she may it not* ~ she can't say no 26/108; prevent, forbid, repudiate 26/301; refuse (to do or suffer) 27/36, 28/7; deny, disavow 26/53, 168, 340; **denyid** *pp.* denied 26/398.
den(n)e *n.* den, pit 1/82, 41/483.
dent, dynt *n.* attack, blows 18/63; stroke, blow 20/186, 31/2; injury, wounds 36/57; **dentys, dentis, dyntys, dent** *pl.* strokes, blows 18/71, 256, 20/198, 34/225, 41/77.

departe *v.* cause to depart 25/35, 60;
departyth *pr. 3 sg.* departs 32/269;
departe *pl.* part company 8/81, 24/130;
departyd *pa. t.* Pr 501.

departyng *vbl. n.* departure 32/167.

depe, depp *adj.* deep 4/37, 25/422, 27/
256.

depe *adv.* deeply, deep 8/243, 9/81, 244.

depnes *n.* the depths 9/144.

deprave *v.* disparage 22/38.

dere *adj.*[1] grievous, severe Pr 480.

dere *adj.*[2] dear, excellent 2/181, 4/53, 96;
me ... ~ dear to me 27/564, 32/163;
derere *comp.* 5/131.

dere *adv.* at a high price 14/328, 18/27;
(love) dearly 9/232.

dere *v.* harm 6/98, 29/145; **dere** *imp. sg.*
6/158.

derysyon *n.* derision *21/61.

derk *n.* darkness 18/229.

derke, dyrk *adj.* dark 1/77, 18/226, 22/
105, 34/8.

derlyng(e) *n.* darling 5/132, 171, 15/77.

derth, dyrthe *n.* dearth 15/108, 20/214.

derwurthy *adj.* excellent, noble 23/1.

desert(e) *n.* desert, wilderness Pr 266,
22/128, PS 40.

desertnes *n.* barren desolation, desert
conditions 22/123.

desesyd, dyssesyd *pp.* distressed 12/
130; afflicted (by disease) 25/198.

desesse see **dys(s)ese**.

deseverid *pp.* separated, scattered 41/
145.

desideracyon *n.* desire, yearning 41/99.

desyre *n.* lust 6/185; desire, wish 9/103,
15/36, 22/58; **desyrys** *pl.* what one
desires 26/63.

desyre *v.* desire, wish 10/448, 41/106;
desyre *pr. 1 sg.* 29/64; **desyryth** *pr. 3 sg.*
19/131, 29/69, 41/257; **desyre** *pl.* 11/
279, 21/44, 41/162; **desyrynge, desy-
rand** *pr. p.* 19/3; *ben* ~ to wish (to
know) 41/125; **desyred, desyrid** *pa. t.*
30/170, 41/289; **desyryd** *pp.* 27/366, 30/
195; **desyre** *imp. sg.* covet, desire 6/165,
172, 174; **desyre** *pr. subj.* 26/80.

desolat *ppl. adj.* in ruinous condition 15/
102.

despyte see **dyspyte**.

deté *n.* song 10/437.

detent *pp.* withheld, removed 41/218.

determyn *v.* ordain, decide upon 9/274.

determynacyon *n.* (as personif.) doctrine, dogma 9/213.

deth(e), dede *n.* death Pr 306, 324, 466,
35/81; (as personif.) Pr 240, 20/177, 181;
~-*dredynge* fear of death 2/257; cause of
death 5/98, 139; **dethis** *gen. sg.* death's
2/224, 229, 35/22; **dethis** *pl.* deaths 11/
144.

detraccyon *n.* reproach, slander PS 8.

dette *n.* debt, obligation: *as is* ~ as is
(one's) obligation 9/114.

deve *v.* stupefy 18/148; **devid** *pp.* deaf-
ened 35/143.

devyde see **dyvyde**.

devyl, deuyl, devyll(e), devil *n.* devil Pr
242, 277, 374, 16/113, 18/226, 22/151,
23/198, 204, 27/506, 30/230; *in oaths: þe*
~ *hym sped* 32/63; **devel(l)ys, develis,
devyllys, devylis, devyl, dewelys**
gen. sg. 7/31, 16/43, 18/328, 22/12, 41/
27, 407, 474; *in þe* ~ *way, a* ~ *name* 32/
51, 41/403, 484; **develys, deuelys,
develis, devel** *pl.* Pr 269, 10/436, 20/
258, 22/105, 23/1, 62, 27/174, 31/3;
devyl *gen. pl. a xx*[ti] ~ *way* i.e. the devil
take you 24/143.

devyr *n.* duty 12/109.

devys(e) *n.* device Pr 259n.; intent 35/
251.

devyse, devise *v.* say Pr 432n., 21/51;
give 8/64; think of, conceive 21/5, 40/
26, 41/85; **devyse** *imp. sg.* consider 14/
320; **devyse** *pr. subj.* (forming *imp.*)
decide, plan 41/72.

devocyon, devoscyon *n.* devotion
9/244, 13/24, 19/204; (as personif.)
9/211; devoted service 26/83; **devocy-
onys** *n.* devotions, prayers 13/19.

devoyde *pr. 1 sg. refl.* leave, go away 26/
124; **devoydyng** *pr. p.* expelling, avoid-
ing 26/429.

devouth *adj.* devout 41/368; **devowtest**
sup. as noun 28/150.

devowtly, devouthly *adv.* devoutly 8/97,
10/334, 41/17, 223.

dew(e), du *adj.* prescribed by law or custom Pr 121, 8/41, 10/127, 204, 41/97;
inevitable, predestined 25/130; due,
proper 26/66, 424, 27/442.

dewly *adv.* according to desert 41/362.

dewté *n.* duty, obligation 36/53; **dewtys**
pl. 19/196.

dyaletyk *n.* dialectics, logic, formal reasoning 21/13.

dyce *n.* dice 32/92 s.d.

dych *n.* ditch 18/71, 20/116.

dye, dyed, dyen see **dey(e)**.

dyetis *n.* diets 21/20.

dyffende see **defende**.

diffynicyon *n.* limit 11/100.

dyffuse *adj.* difficult, uncertain 10/103.

dyggyng *vbl. n.* digging 2/324.

dyght, dyth *v.* offer 3/138; bring about 4/164, 27/210, 42/26; put (to death) 29/61; *refl.* prepare (oneself) Pr 510; go 16/83; direct (one's course) 25/451; **dyght(e), dith, dyth, dyht** *pp.* prepared, ready 1/82, 10/154, 213, 20/151, 41/300; ~ *þe to* prepared for you 26/379; given, dedicated 3/64, 10/249; brought about 3/150; appointed 3/164; saved 18/327; set, placed 26/384; treated 32/267; assigned 41/124; adorned 41/179; **dyth** *imp. sg. refl.* go 27/346.

dygne, dyngne *adj.* noble, worshipful 18/92, 41/94; *for ~ of* because of the worthiness of 20/132.

dygnyté, dygnité *n.* position of honour 7/91, 22/117, 39/71; official function, responsibility 8/38; worthiness, nobility, excellence 9/175, 40/3; high rank and office 20/132.

dyht see **dyght**.

dylexcyon *n.* (as personif.) spiritual love 9/211.

dylygens, dyligens, diligens, dilygens *n.* diligent attention or efforts 15/189, 20/208, 26/277, 424, 29/75; endeavour Pr 209; *do(n)* (*one's*) ~ endeavour, do (one's) utmost 3/10, 30/157, 205; dutifulness 21/279; *do (not)* (*one's*) ~ (don't) obey dutifully 29/52, 34/69.

dyligent *adj.* diligent 6/57.

dymysse *pr. 1 sg.* release 31/177.

dyne *v.* dine 3/52.

dyner *n.* first big meal of the day, dinner; feast 20/143, 21/45.

dyng(e) *v.* beat, drive (out, down) 2/281, 20/139; *byttyr dentys on þe þei xall* ~ they will strike you with bitter blows 18/256; **dynge** *pr. 1 sg.* 18/7.

dyngne see **dygne**.

dynt(ys) see **dent**.

dirige *n.* dirge 41/223, 317.

dyrk see **derke**.

dyrknes *n.* darkness 19/47, 25/226.

dyrthe see **derth**.

dysceyvyth *pr. 3 sg.* deceives 30/219; **dysceyved** *pp.* deceived, overcome by deceit 11/24.

dyscencyon *n.* dissension 11/114.

discendit(h) see **dyssende**.

dyscerne *v.* decide 10/96.

dysche *n.* dish 27/257.

dyscyple, dyscypil, dyscypyl *n.* disciple Pr 340, 27/322, 460 s.d., 29/100, 124; **dyscipulys, dyscyplis, disciplis, dysciplys, dyscyplys, dyscypulys, dyscipulis, discipulis, dyscyples, discyplis, dysypulys, dyscypulis, discipulys, dyscipelys** *pl.* Pr 327, 330, 442, 462, 7/92, 26/33, 53, 57, 348, 27/1st s.d., 41, 52 s.d., 60 s.d., 76 s.d., 204 s.d., 348 s.d., 448 s.d., 489 s.d., 28/16 s.d., 32 s.d., 44 s.d., 64, 80 s.d., 29/130, 194, 34/166, 190, 35/276, 41/86; **dyscipulys** *gen. pl.* 27/527 s.d.

dyscomforte *n.* cause of sorrow of dismay 19/10.

dyscres *v.* fall away Pr 327; diminish 25/31.

dyscressyon, dyscrecyon *n.* (as personif.) moral discernment, discretion 9/211; judgement, perception 26/60.

dyscrye *v.* describe 40/8.

dyscus *v.* decide about, settle on 9/274.

dysese see **dys(s)ese**.

dysgeysyd, dysgysed *pp.* disguised 26/102; costumed 28/80 s.d.

dysgysyd *ppl. adj.* fashioned to be modish and showy 26/65n.

dysmayd(e), dismayde *ppl. adj.* dismayed, perturbed Pr 116, 133, 10/329, 12/23.

dyspeyre *n.* despair 4/116.

dyspeyre *v.* drive to despair 13/101; despair 26/154; **dyspeyryng** *pr. p.* 26/386.

dysperacyon *n.* despair 26/143, 161.

dyspyte, dyspite, despyte, dyspyth, dispith *n.* disobedience Pr 46; contempt, disparagement, humiliation *12/133, 27/108, 28/147; *haue hem in* ~ despise them 26/88; *don . . .* ~ treat with contempt 41/85; injury, insult 31/102, 32/8, 266.

displesauns *n.* unhappiness 26/56.

displesaunte *adj.* displeasing 5/68.

dysplese *v.* displease 4/52, 32/154; **dys-plesyd, displesid** *pp.* 12/128, 41/99; **dysplese** *imp. sg.* 2/42; **dysplese, displese** *imp. pl. refl.* be displeased 10/458, 15/190, 32/37; **displese** *pr. subj.* 41/259.

dyspoyle *v.* despoil 31/87; **dyspoylyd, dyspoyled** *pp.* 32/2, 34/131.

dispose *v. refl.* prepare (oneself); ~ *me... redy* (with *to*) ready myself (for) 41/185; **dysspose** *imp. sg.* dispose, make fit 10/429; **dispose** *imp. pl. refl.* prepare (yourself) 41/140.

dysposyd *ppl. adj.* disposed, inclined 14/385.

dysposycyon, dysposysyon *n.* place, position 26/66; inclination 27/402.

dysprave, dyspravyn *v.* speak against, condemn 28/141, 35/204.

dysprevyd *pp.* refuted 31/187.

dysscryve *v.* describe, tell about 21/56.

dyssende *v.* descend 41/109; **dissende** *pr. 1 sg.* 41/115; **descendith, discendit, descendyth** *pr. 3 sg.* 11/292 s.d., 28/52 s.d.; ~ *þe hefne* comes down from heaven 8/172 s.d.; **dyssend** *pp.* 41/313; **dyscende** *imp. sg.* 12/137; **discendith** *imp. pl.* 41/491.

dys(s)ese, dissese, desesse *n.* ailment, disease, suffering 13/147, 25/6, 15, 83.

dyssesyd see **desesyd.**

dysseuerawns *n.* separation 26/159.

dys(s)pyse, dysspice, dyspyce *v.* despise, reject, treat as unworthy 8/38, 61, 10/52, 12/54; **dyspysyd** *pa. t.* 11/69.

dissponsacyon *n.* betrothal 9/302.

disteyne *v.* fade, *or* be sullied 24/59; **dysteyn** *imp. sg.* sully, desecrate 6/86.

distemperaunce *n.* derangement of the 'humours': *brynge in* ~ deeply disturb 25/39.

dystyllyth *pr. pl.* fall in drops 28/42.

dystresse *v.* distress, harass 24/119.

dystroy(e), distroye, dystrye, dysstroye *v.* destroy, overthrow 4/102, 7/23, 26/212, 300, 27/387, 29/55; **dystroyt** *pr. 3 sg.* 26/180; **dystroyd, dystroy** *pp.* 26/188, 27/3, 29/40, 30/176; **dystroye** *pr. subj.* 29/147.

dystruccyon *n.* destruction 27/100, 386.

dyswary *n.* doubt 41/4.

dyth see **dyght.**

dyvercyté, diuercyté *n.* diversity 26/65; adversity 41/114.

dyvers(e), dyverce, dyueris, diueris *adj.* diverse, various 9/277 s.d., 18/310, 26/35, 41/283, 284.

dyvyde, devyde *v.* **1** separate, divide 11/128; **devyde** *pr. 1 sg.* 8/51; **dyvide** *pp.* 26/468; **2** dismember 41/87.

dyvyne *adj.* divine 3/47.

dyvvynacyon *n.* (as personif.) prophecy, foresight 9/213n.

dyvinyté *n.* the divinity 11/265.

dyvvysyon, dyvicyon *n.* estrangement, division 11/119, 26/118.

do, don(e), doo *v.* **1** do, perform, commit 2/30, 208, 270, 4/68; ~ *oure dyligens* endeavour 3/10; ~ *resystens* resist, oppose 7/5; *is to* ~ is to be done 30/139; **dost** *pr. 2 sg.* 22/57, 26/452, 30/197; **do, don, doth** *pl.* 1/42, 14/161, 15/230, 26/234, 28/133; **doyng** *pr. p.* 27/228; **dede, dyd, dude** *pa. t.* Pr 381, 2/223, 12/87, 21/176, 26/331, 27/206, 28/40; **dedyst** *pa. 2 sg.* 12/123; **don(e), do** *pp.* Pr 42, 2/216, 275; **do, don(e)** *pr. subj.* 2/17, 4/91, 9/98; **2** act. behave, do 2/155, 3/1; **dost** *pr. 2 sg.* 3/105, 6/162, 12/151; **doth** *pr. 3 sg.* ~ *after* accords with 10/88; **don** *pl.* 25/263; **dede** *pa. t.* 28/182; **dedyst** *pa. 2 sg.* 12/58; **doth** *imp. pl.* 31/211; **dede** *pa. subj.* Pr 288; **3** cause, bring about 3/110, 5/20, 14/102; **dost** *pr. 2 sg.* 35/173; **doth** *pr. 3 sg.* 10/189, 14/143, 25/34; **don** *pl.* 32/102; **dede** *pa. t.* 2/236; **4** enforce 14/2; **5** cause (sth. to happen), cause to (with infin.) 14/157, 20/62, 21/248; *gan þer* ~ *play* caused to be performed there 26/22; ~ *hym bynde* have him bound 26/231; ~ *hym dey* have him killed 27/115; **doth** *pr. 3 sg.* 5/164, 27/179, 41/47; **doth** *pl.* 23/52; **dede** *pa. t.* 34/112; **do** *pp. han þe besyly* ~ *sowth* had you diligently searched for 29/123; *haue* ~ *made redy* have had prepared 31/25; **do** *imp. sg.* ~ *calle here* have her summoned 14/116; **do, doth** *imp. pl.* 20/15, 32, 26/239; ~ *hym day* kill him 34/193; ~ *gete* have brought 39/15; **6** show, exhibit 14/381, 21/276, 26/445; **done** *pp.* 5/230; **do** *imp. sg.* 6/127; **do** *imp. pl.* 14/154; **7** put, place 31/1st s.d., 128, 165; ~ *way* stop Pr 459; **don, do** *pp.* 31/110, 164; **do** *imp. sg.* ~ *wey* Stop! Enough of this! 32/121; **do** *imp. pl.* ~ *way* 12/74; **8** take: *of* ~

remove 31/193; **do(n)** *pp.* 36/44, 46; **do**
imp. pl. ~ *of* 14/153; **9** *aux.* (forming
with infin. the periphr. tense) **dost,
doyst** *pr. 2 sg.* 3/125, 5/190, 6/32, 27/
560; **doth(e), do** *pr. 3 sg.* Pr 98, 107, 142,
150; **do, doth, don** *pl.* Pr 228, 327, 329;
dede, dyd(e), dude *pa. 1, 3 sg., pl.* Pr 15,
69, 224; **dedyst, dudyst** *pa. 2 sg.* 3/138,
5/225, 12/58, 14/224; **dede** *pa. subj.* Pr
290; **10** fares *in* **doth** *pr. 3 sg.* 8/138; **do,
doth** *pl.* 8/140, 13/139, 139; **11** carries
out *in* **doth** *pr. 3 sg.* 4/213; **12** obeyed *in*
don *pp.* 5/89; **13** (for another verb)
5/128, 20/284, 30/135; **14** presented
9/300; **15** finished 10/115 s.d., 14/273,
18/192; **ha ~, haue ~** make an end,
hurry up 3/160, 16/89, 24/221; *here frute
was* ~ they were unfruitful 10/46; **16 do**
imp. pl. ~ *sewe* go 31/76; **17** grant, give
in **do** *pr. subj.* 8/96, 9/282.

dobbelet *n.* doublet 26/78.

dobyl *adj.* double 21/157, 157.

doctour *n.* learned authority, teacher PS
33; **doctorys** *gen. sg.* learned clergy-
man's 29/1st s.d.; **doctorys, doctoris**
pl. learned clergymen, authorities Pr
246, 26/164 s.d., 208 s.d.

doctryne, doctrine *n.* instruction, doctrine 3/45, 21/105, 29/131.

dodemvsyd *ppl. adj.* stupid and bemused
41/390.

dogge *n.* dog: ~ *whelpe* puppy 24/112;
doggys *pl.* 29/47, 52, 41/388.

doyl *n.* ~ *it is* it is distressing 4/215.

dolfol, dolful see **do(o)lful.**

dolfoly *adv.* painfully, in agony 3/78.

dolour(e), dolowre *n.* grief, suffering Pr
367, 10/399, 15/64, 32/259, 41/178.

dolve *pp.* buried 35/92.

dom(e) *n.* **1** command 10/209; **2** dominion, power 18/328; **3** judgement 24/194,
35/168; *Day of* ~ 42/4; **domys** *pl.* 8/49;
~ *þat longyth to phesyk* medical decisions
21/20.

dome see **dowm.**

domynacyon, dominacyon *n.* lordship,
control, authority 13/27, 26/45; *þin hyȝ*
~ 11/33; realm 41/102.

Domysday *n.* Judgement Day Pr 504,
4/78, 7/128.

dompnesse *n.* inability to speak, dumbness 13/35.

dongeon, donjoon, donjeon *n.* dun-

geon 1/82, 25/6, 27/256, 31/24; **doon-
genys, doungenys** 29/35, 31/6.

do(o)lful, dulfull, dolfol *adj.* sorrowful,
distressed 4/198, 25/155, 32/158, 259.

doolfulnes *n.* sorrow 25/117.

dore *n.* door 12/1, 5, 8.

doseyn *num.* dozen 26/72.

dowcet *adj.* sweet, delicious 2/77.

dowe, dove *n.* dove Pr 77, 4/248, 251, 41/
510; **dowys** *pl.* 19/116.

dowm, dome, dum *adj.* incapable of
speech, dumb 13/79, 169A, 26/410;
silent 22/162; *as noun* 26/37, 393.

down(e), doun *adv.* down Pr 408, 445,
1/65.

downryght *adv.* outright, utterly 4/102.

dowse *adj.* sweet, dear 10/20.

dowt(e), dowth, doute, dowhte *n.*
doubt, perplexity Pr 138, 253, 4/149, 10/
91, 119, 14/179, 15/250, 255, 20/230, 29/
132; *no ~ (of)* without doubt 9/167,
10/183; uncertainty, anxiety Pr 271,
23/4, 9; fear Pr 329, 5/152, 6/87; *for ~ of
drede* out of fear of danger 15/176; *for ~
of me* out of fear for my welfare 21/250;
in ~ fearful 25/205; *dyntys of ~* frightening blows 34/225; danger 18/102, 21/
188, 27/236; **dowtys** *pl.* doubtful
points, questions 21/195, 199; dangers,
fears 4/116.

dowte, dowth *v.* **1** fear 24/39, 27/436;
dowte *pr. 1 sg.* 41/156, 383; **dowth,
dowte** *imp. pl.* 27/330; *refl.* 41/397; **2**
doubt *in* **dowte** *pr. 1 sg.* 11/249; **dowte**
imp. sg. refl. 38/305.

dowtef(f)ul *adj.* uncertain, undecided
10/119, 38/343, 355.

dowteles *adv.* doubtlessly, surely 10/103,
26/167, 39/51.

dowtere, dowtyr, doughter *n.* daughter
9/22, 27, 29, 80, 10/16, 20, 172; **dow-
terys, douterys** *pl.* Pr 121, 32/9, 36/27.

dowty *adj.* worthy 10/174, 18/15; bold,
brave 16/44, 18/72, 31/2.

dowtynes *n.* strength, power 18/7.

dragonys *n.* dragons 29/35, 31/6.

draught, drawght *n.* drink 14/330, 362,
18/286.

drawe, drawyn *v.* **1** draw (a bow, sword,
arrow) 4/170; **drawe** *pr. 1 sg.* 28/105;
drawe *imp. sg.* 4/169; **2** bring, lead 16/
49; **drawyng** *pr. p.* 28/148 s.d.; **drowe**
pa. t. I ~ *in my tayle* I took along with me

drawe (*cont.*)

26/17; **drawyn** *pp.* brought forward 9/24; **drawe** *pr. subj.* 10/6; **3** pull to pieces 29/32; **drawe** *pp.* pulled to pieces, *or* dragged 27/111; **4** pull 31/212 s.d., 32/66; **drawe** *imp. sg.* 32/74; **5** come, go *in* **drawe** *pr. 1 sg. I* ~ *fast to an ende* I swiftly approach my death 19/26; **drawyth** *pr. 3 sg.* 26/440, 27/79, 565; **drawyth, drawe** *pl. aȝens þe* ~ turn against you 31/124; **drawe** *pr. subj.* (with *ageyn*) contradicts 24/109; **6** attracts *in* **drawyth** *pr. 3 sg.* 26/326; **7** disemboweled *in* **drawe** *pp.* 26/319, 27/292; **8** drawn 31/57 s.d.

dred(e), dreed *n.* dread, awe Pr 138, 333, 2/139, 36/74; danger 15/176; dreaded behaviour or qualities 16/43; doubt 24/79; *withowtyn* ~ certainly 19/111, 22/98, 25/293.

dred *ppl. adj.* feared, dreadful 31/2.

drede *v.* dread, stand in awe of 2/169, 3/40, 4/112; **drede** *pr. 1 sg.* 8/49, 58, 25/396; *refl.* 12/27, 15/145; **drede** *pl.* 9/136, 13/97; **drede** *imp. pl.* 4/50, 22/12; **drede** *pr. subj.* 20/274.

dredf(f)ul *adj.* dreadful, frightening 2/189, 4/78, 199.

dreye *v.* dry up 25/207.

drey see **drye** *adj.*

dreynt(e) *pp.* inundated 4/123, 139; drowned 4/200.

drem *n.* dream, vision experienced in sleep 18/316.

drepe *v.* droop, lie down 18/301.

dres(se) *v.* **1** bring about 7/120; **2** cause 21/124; **3** prepare 24/117; *refl.* prepare (oneself), turn (one's) attention to 10/90; **dresse** *imp. pl. refl.* prepare yourselves 26/424; **4** go 25/10; *refl.* 37/80; **dressyd** *pp.* 32/226; **dresse** *imp. sg. refl.* 14/249.

dreve, drevyn see **dryve.**

drewe *n.* morsel, bit 42/124; *but lytyl* ~ scarcely any food 3/121.

drye *n.* dry or clear weather 5/35.

drye, drey *adj.* dry 4/249, 18/228; dried out 15/256.

drynchyng *vbl. n.* drowning 4/100.

drynes *n.* dryness 32/197.

drynk(e), drynge *n.* drink 14/233, 235, 248, 250; the act of drinking 14/347.

drynk(e) *v.* drink 3/114, 14/295, 22/131;

~ *with yow a drawght* do as you do (i.e. sleep) 18/286; **drynke** *pr. 1 sg.* 14/333; **drynkyth** *pr. 3 sg.* 27/504; **drynk** *pr. subj.* 14/237, 508.

drynkerys *n.* drinkers 14/363.

dryve, dryvyn *v.* **1** chase away 22/151; **droff** *pa. t.* drove (off) 36/13; **2** drive by force 29/35; **dryve** *pr. 1 sg.* 18/71; **drevyn** *pp.* 7/79; **dryve** *imp. sg.* 9/244; **3** drive (a nail) 32/76; **dreve** *pp.* 32/72; **dryve** *imp. sg.* 32/69; **4** (of blows) struck, delivered *in* **drevyn** *pp.* 35/22.

dronkeshepp *n.* heavy drinking, drunkenness 42/115.

dronkyn, drunke *ppl. adj.* drunk 40/15, 30.

du see **dew(e).**

dubytacyon *n.* doubt 7/76.

duelle, duellyn see **dwell(e).**

duke *n.* lord, ruler 16/44, 18/92, 26/2; **dukys** *pl.* 18/15, 71.

dulfull see **do(o)lful.**

dullyth *pr. 3 sg.* grows dazed 34/302.

dum see **dowm.**

dur *v.* dare 27/550; **dar(e)** *pr. 1 sg.* 2/139, 155, 3/184; **durste, darst** *pr. 2 sg.* 8/103, 35/172; **dar** *pr. 3 sg.* 41/159; **durst** *pa. t.* 35/199; **durst** *pa. subj.* 29/157.

dure *adj.* hard 38/95.

dure *v.* still live 41/304.

duste *n.* ground, dust 38/147; *in* ~ in (one's) grave 25/72.

dwell(e), dwellyn, duelle, duellyn *v.* **1** dwell, live Pr 176, 1/69, 2/94, 7/12, 23/104, 26/120, 35/11; **dwellys, dwellyst** *pr. 2 sg.* 9/117, 19/46; **dwellyth, duellyth** *pr. 3 sg.* 9/125, 41/192; **dwelle** *pl.* Pr 161, 410, 13/7; **dwellyng(e)** *pr. p.* 20/259, 35/128, 39/23; **dwellyd, duellyd** *pa. t.* 2/240, 41/16; **dwelle** *imp. pl.* 38/174; **duelle** *pr. subj.* 5/216; **2** stay, remain Pr 58, 104, 275; **3** persist 11/44.

dwellyng(e) *vbl. n.* dwelling place 18/117, 297, 32/16.

dwere *n.* amazement, awe Pr 484; fear 2/112, 22/79; doubt: *withowtyn* (*withoutyn, without*) ~ certainly 2/54, 12/11, 20/179.

ebbe *v.* ebb 5/221.

Ebrew *n.* Hebrew Pr 500; *chylderyn of* ~ Hebrew children Pr 310.

ech(e), iche *adj.* each, every 3/80, 8/6,

9/258, 10/123, 14/397, 15/309; *as noun*
10/193, 26/282, 27/348 s.d.

echon(e), eche on, ichon *pron.* each one
2/22, 9/155, 235, 301, 15/4.

edyfy *v.* be exalted 26/345, 460; **edyfied**
pp. built 9/133.

eer see **or** *conj.* ²

eerly see **erth(e)ly**.

effectuously *adv.* truly, in fact 39/89.

efne see **hevyn**.

egal *adv.* equally 27/534.

ey *interj.* (expressing wonder or joy) 16/
62, 62.

eyd see **hed(e)** *n.* ²

ey(e) *n.* eye(s) 9/108, 19/283, 481; *sen at ~*
seen plainly 12/170; *~ syght* 4/145;
eyn(e), eynes *pl.* Pr 405, 2/182, 9/116,
11/25; *haue ~ (on)* lay eyes on, see 36/
31.

eylight see **heylyght**.

eylsum *adj.* beneficial, wholesome 10/
108.

eyr, eyer *n.* air 34/10, 41/372.

eyre *n.* heir 26/156.

eyte *card num. as adj.* eight 13/157A.

eyted *ord. num. as noun* eighth 9/130.

eyther *adj.* each 31/206.

eyther *conj.* either Pr 506.

eyzil *n.* vinegar 32/199, 38/30.

eke *adv.* also 4/19, 75, 25/9.

eld(e) see **old(e)**.

eleccyon *n.* God's choice, election PS 34.

elefnte *ord. num. as noun* eleventh 9/142.

ellys, ellis *adv.* else, 3/102, 9/173, 15/31;
otherwise 3/121, 9/242, 11/200, 41/444.

eloquens *n.* eloquence, *or* sophistry 41/
43.

empere *n.* dominion, empire 34/13, 41/
502.

emperour, empere *n.* emperor 15/3, 62,
19/121, 22/85; **emperorys, emper-
ourys** *gen. sg.* 15/8, 30/52, 55.

empres *n.* empress 11/335, 41/157.

enbawmyd *pp.* endued, impregnated
40/7.

enbrase, enbrace *v.* afflict 10/161, 24/
250.

encheson see **incheson**.

enclosyd *pp.* covered 26/70.

encrese *n.* increase, growth 10/11.

encres(e) *v.* increase (in number) 2/28,
5/218, 224; become more severe 25/26;
incressyd *pp.* 32/227.

ende, hende *n.* end 1/4, 2/246, 258, 20/
220, 32/81; *withowtyn ~* unceasingly,
eternally 9/185, 265, 11/65; *withowtyn ~*
eternal 11/112; *make myn ~* end my life
25/106; *on ~* incessantly 25/351; objective, purpose 22/60: resolution (of a
problem) 27/60; agreement, settle-
ment 28/12.

ende *pr. 1 sg.* conclude 11/339; **hendyth**
pr. 3 sg. 32/217; **endyd** *pp.* 19/146 s.d.

ende see **hende** *adj.*

end(e)les, hend(e)les *adj.* eternal 1/28,
80, 2/56, 21/159, 25/302, 307.

endyng(e), hendyng(e) *vbl. n.* end 8/7,
10/342, 16/154, 18/257, 21/56;*schortyn
his ~* hasten his death 41/57.

endyte see **indyte**.

endytynge *vbl. n.* writing, composing 21/
23.

endles *adv.* forever, ever 9/125.

endles(s)ly *adv.* forever, ever 11/4, 83,
227.

endure, indure *v.* continue, last 3/25,
21/57; remain 8/7, 11/72, 41/444.

eneryth, inheryte *v.* inherit 26/118, 413.

enforme *v.* instruct, teach 4/131, 6/54,
21/88; **informyng** *pr. p.* 22/138;
enforme *imp. sg.* 4/45, 6/14; *~ þu me*
resolve for me 10/119; **enforme** *pr. subj.*
imbue 38/331.

engendrure *n.* procreation 3/33.

engynes *n.* schemes, snares 26/50.

enherytawns see **inerytawns**.

enjoyd, enjouyd see **injoye**.

enmy(e) *n.* enemy 9/187, 27/387;
en(e)myes *pl.* 5/226, 9/121, 15/320.

ensawmple *n.* example to be imitated:
take ~ . . . by follow the example of 22/
76.

ensens, encence *n.* incense 8/26, 18/45,
52, 244.

ensensyth *pr. 3 sg.* fumigate with incense
8/97 s.d.; **insence** *imp. pl.* burn incense
41/452.

enspyre see **inspyre**.

ensure *pr. 1 sg.* assure 10/104, 26/413;
(without personal object) 12/108; **en-
suryd** *pp.* granted 26/40.

entent(e), ententis see **intent**.

enterly *adv.* sincerely, wholeheartedly
27/366.

entre *v.* enter 15/162, 38/94; **enteryth** *pr.
3 sg.* 27/76 s.d., 30/24 s.d., 31/1st s.d.;

entre *(cont.)*
  entre *pl.* enter, penetrate 11/292 s.d.;
  enteryd, entryd *pp.* 21/99, 29/1st s.d.,
  81.
envy(e) *n.* envy 2/237, 260, 26/113.
envyous *adj.* envious 35/54.
equyté *n.* fairness, righteousness 11/132.
eqwall *adj.* equal 27/375.
erand, errandys see her(r)and(e).
erbe *n.* plants *coll.*, vegetation 2/7, 20/
  185; erbys *pl.* 2/25, 248.
erde see herd *n.*, here *v.*
erdon see her(r)and(e).
er(e) *adv.* previously 21/136, 29/101, 197;
  previously, *or* here 31/44.
er(e) see here *n.*², he, or *conj.*¹, *conj.*².
erys see here *n.*².
eresye *n.* heresy 28/114.
eretyk *n.* heretic 26/170, 309; eretykys
  pl. 38/388.
ermyn *n.* ermine fur 26/105.
erraunt *adj.* wandering 22/152.
erre *v.* transgress 29/30; erre *pl.* 29/55.
errour *n.* false belief 29/60, 30/82; er-
  rouris *pl.* 26/212.
erste *adv.* (with *not*) then, and not earlier
  11/14.
erte see art(e).
erth(e), herth(e) *n.* earth, ground Pr 296,
  507, 2/5, 13/137, 18/8, 41/491; ~
  grownde the earth 16/2; ~ *qwave*, ~
  quake earthquake 34/11, 35/214.
erth(e)ly, erthelech, eerly *adj.* earthly,
  terrestrial 2/16, 277, 10/71, 11/273, 26/
  444.
ese *n.* pleasure, enjoyment 2/41; relief
  25/81, 32/45; benefit, good 30/171.
ese *v.* comfort, relieve 15/120; esyd *pp.*
  12/131.
est *n.* east 18/167, 25/285; *west and* ~ all
  directions Pr 495; ~ *and west* everywhere 2/51, 18/108, 35/262.
ete, etyn *v.* eat 2/88, 91, 119, 15/43, 20/
  283, 38/284; etyth, ete, etyht *pr. 3 sg.*
  27/76 s.d., 204 s.d., 257, 504; ete *pa. t.*
  27/360; etyn, ete *pp.* 27/350, 353, 369,
  397, 401, 458; ete *imp. sg.* 2/42, 89, 115;
  ete, etyth *imp. pl.* 20/157, 38/206; ete
  pr. subj. 2/96, 152, 222.
eternalyté *n.* eternalness PS 5.
eternal(l) *adj.* eternal 8/45, 9/96, 26/118.
eternyté *n.* eternal existence 3/66, 41/
  110.

ethe *adj.* easy 15/21.
Evangelyst, Euangelist *n.* Evangelist
  PS 25, 41/3.
evene see evyn *adv.*
every, euery, everych, everich, heuery
  adj. every, each Pr 65, 74, 352, 424, 2/21,
  70, 78, 198, 10/149, 26/404; *of* ~ *bestys* of
  each kind of animal Pr 74.
everychon(e), euerychon(e), euyry-
  chone *pron.* every one Pr 330, 22/34,
  23/129, 24/144, 268, 26/21, 41/271.
evesong *n.* evensong, vespers 13/130.
evy see hevy *adj.*
evydens *n. in* ~ as proof 1/55.
evyl, euyl *adj.* evil, wicked 8/194, 10/348,
  472, 12/25; difficult 35/248.
evyl, euyl(l) *adv.* badly 14/98, 30/229,
  234; ~*-gett good* ill-gotten goods 6/150;
  ~ *payd* displeased 12/197; with difficulty 10/238.
evyl-doere *n.* evil-doer 30/93.
evyn *n.* evening: ~ *and morn*, ~ *and*
  morwyn at all times 5/212, 27/8, 32/211.
euyn, evyn *adj.* straight, accurately
  alined 4/163, 168; ~*-Crystyn* fellow
  Christian, fellow man 9/174, 185, 232.
evyn, euyn, evene, ȝevene, ȝevyn,
  hevyn *adv.* indeed, in fact, even Pr 228,
  489, 6/78, 14/51; exactly, fully 2/101,
  5/105, 116, 35/291, 36/140; ~ *onto* all the
  way to 19/144; directly, right 5/83, 14/
  28, 16/20, 19/90; ~ *þer*, ~ *here* right
  there, right here Pr 395, 479, 3/87; ~
  pleyn, ryght ~ directly 23/157, 24/72;
  steadily 38/276; into equal portions,
  evenly 38/285, 291.
evyr, euyr, ever, hevyr, euere *adv.*
  always, continually, forever Pr 362,
  1/54, 72, 74, 3/24, 4/236, 8/143, 24/89,
  25/308; ever Pr 295, 363, 1/5.
evyrlestyng, evyrlastynge *ppl. adj.* eternal 18/4, 26/120.
evyrmo, euyrmo *adv.* always 11/71, 41/
  243.
evyrmor(e), euyrmore, evermore,
  heuyrmore, evyrmoor, euyrmare
  adv. always, continually 3/119, 4/82,
  237, 5/4, 6/117, 18/5, 24/29, 38/143, 41/
  260; forever Pr 198, 1/31, 36, 35/47.
evysum *adj.* sad, burdened 38/47.
examyne *v.* examine 31/117.
exawmple, exaunple, exawnpyl,
  exawmpyl *n.* instructive story, pre-

cedent *Pr 65, 38/122; example to be
imitated 26/428, 27/422, 512; *take ~ (of,
by)* 22/80, 23/196; **exawmplys** ex-
amples *pl.* 27/426.
excede *v.* 1 surpass, exceed 9/273, 21/
134, 26/60; **excedyth** *pr. 3 sg.* 27/442; 2
transgress 26/178; **excede** *pl.* 29/60;
excede *pr. subj.* 26/169.
**excellence, excellens, excyllence,
excillens** *n.* distinction, superiority,
excellence 21/13, 141, 25/444, PS 2, 29/
50, 40/3.
excellent, excyllent *adj.* excellent 29/27,
30/153, 181, 41/117, 179.
excepcyon *n.* objection, *or* exception 11/
79.
excitacyon *n.* urging, prompting 41/101.
excuse, askuse *v. refl.* exonerate (oneself) Pr 45, 14/305, 24/267; **excusyth**
pr. 3 sg. refl. 14/182.
exempt *pp. out of . . .* ~ not subject to 23/
134.
excercyse *pr. pl.* observe (a holy day)
8/35.
exilyd, exyled *pp.* exiled 8/126, 11/143.
exys *n.* axes 27/344.
exorte *v.*[1] exhort 8/83, 26/116; **exorte** *pl.*
(with *to*) implore 26/456.
exorte *v.*[2] issue forth 11/56.
expedyent *adj.* expedient, advantageous
27/90.
expelle *v.* expel 2/92, 37/62.
experyence *n.* proof, confirmation 26/
463.
expirand *pr. p.* dying 41/129.
exposytour *n.* expositor 29/1st s.d.
expowne, expownd *v.* explain, expound
Pr 470; ~ *þis oute* resolve this dilemma
10/87.
expres *v.* express 37/78; **expresse** *imp.
sg.* telle 27/216.
expres(se) *adj.* specially dispatched 11/
318; evident, manifest 21/164; clear,
explicit 36/118; *adv.* manifestly, particularly 9/151; expressly, explicitly,
specifically 10/89, 21/125, 39/80; without delay 25/231.
extende *pr. 1 sg.* (with *on*) bestow, grant
41/111; **extende** *imp. sg.* raise 5/187.

fabyll *n.* 1 fiction, myth, falsehood 6/85;
fablys, fablis *pl.* Pr 521; 2 lies, decep-
tions 2/228.

fac(c)yon *n.* fashion (of dress) 26/80; face
41/442.
face *n.* person: *bef(f)or(e) (byffore) (one's)*
~ in the presence of (someone) Pr 511,
11/271, 14/154; *in his* ~ openly, to his
face 4/31; *offende Goddys* ~ sin against
God 4/64; *fayre fare þi* ~ may you prosper 5/21; *beforn þe* ~ *of* in the sight of
19/150–1; appearance, expression 27/
334.
fade *imp. sg. from feyth . . .* ~ let (one's)
faith fade 38/373; **fade** *pr. subj.* (let)
vanish 42/48.
fad(e) see **fede.**
faderyn *v.* act as father of 14/100.
fadyr, fader(e) *n.* father Pr 263, 323, 1/18,
41/445; **faderys, fadyr, fadyres** *gen. sg.*
Pr 261, 3/11, 11/308, 14/354, 39/21;
faderys *pl.* 32/15.
fadyrles *adj.* fatherless 21/175.
fadyrly *adj.* fatherly 5/27.
fay(e), feye *n.* faith 32/119, 34/35; *in
(good)* ~ truly Pr 472, 4/17, 6/116;
Church, religion 41/358.
fayl(e) *n. withowt(e) (withowtyn)* ~ truly,
without doubt 13/152, 21/112, 27/530.
fayl(e), fayll, faylen *v.* fail (to do sth.)
4/173, 26/249; (with *of*) fail to attain 10/
443, 26/46, 27/324; fail to happen, mis-
carry 15/203; lack, want 19/12, 27/11;
come to an end 26/190; **faylid** *pp.*
missed 4/158; **fayle** *imp. pl.* fail 14/32;
fayl(e) *pr. subj.* fail (to do sth.) Pr 125,
14/7.
fayn(e), fawe *adj.* happy, willing, eager
Pr 181, 2/117, 5/149, 29/93; *adv.* gladly,
willingly 2/114, 172, 3/1.
fayr(e), fayere *adj.* shining 2/4; good,
dear, beautiful 2/84, 87, 128; clean, pure
15/222, 25/146; free from disease or
blemish 30/200; bright 27/198; *as noun*
ritually clean creatures 4/15; **fayrest**
sup. most beautiful, best 16/102; *as noun*
16/90, 26/16; *adv.* well 2/76, 5/21;
graciously, eloquently 12/215; directly,
or safely 18/166; civilly, carefully 28/
107; **fayrest** *sup.* 10/299.
fall(e) *n.* fall 2/272, 41/58; lapse 6/12.
fal(l)(e) *v.* 1 fall, descend, drop Pr 215,
279, 1/67; ~ *on* attack 28/135; (with *on,
vpon*) befall, descend on 24/32, 25/131,
27/8; (with *to*) join with, side with 26/
297; **fall(e)** *pr. 1 sg.* 2/267, 271, 3/28;

fal(l)(e) (*cont.*)

    fallyth *pr. 3 sg.* Pr 25, 457, 27/511 s.d.; **fall(e)** *pl.* 1/48, 65, 14/370; ~ ... *in age* grow old 13/140; **falle** *pp.* 11/30; fallen away 30/180; **falle** *imp.* 10/114, 32/19; **falle** *pr. subj.* 10/186; **2** fall (into sin) 3/8, 5/7; **3** decline, vanish 6/15; **4** belong to *in* **fallyth** *pr. pl.* 3/30; **5** alighted *in* **fall** *pp.* 4/246; **falle** *imp. sg.* 23/119; **6** let fall *in* **falle** *imp. pl.* 35/292; **falle** *pr. subj.* 42/44.

falsage *n.* wickedness, falseness 3/186.

fals(e) *adj.* deceitful, disloyal, wicked, etc. Pr 317, 361, 2/165; untrue 14/124; ~ *wyt(t)nes* 6/156, 158, 161.

false *v.* prove to be false 26/52.

falshed(e), falsed *n.* falsehood, treachery, deceitfulness Pr 284, 14/358, 24/61, 41/19.

falsly *adv.* wrongly, wickedly 7/106; deceitfully, treacherously 41/45.

falsnes(s)e *n.* treachery, deceitfulness, dishonesty 18/226, 30/174.

fame *n.* renown, honour 6/21, 25/195, 38/66; *speke gret* ~ speak of your renown 14/61; report, rumour 8/127, 194; reputation, good name 10/349, 14/278, 15/151.

fame *v.* defame 14/275.

famyt *ppl. adj.* famished 11/12.

fare *n.* behaviour, conduct 20/269; appearance, demeanour 21/261.

farewel(l), fareweyl(l), farwell *interj.* farewell 5/45, 53, 6/193, 8/205, 10/366, 396, 402, 25/108.

faryth *pr. 3 sg.* fares 25/42; **faryn** *pl.* fare, do, live 9/292; **ferd(e), faryn** *pp.* fared 12/10, 21; travelled 18/56.

fast(e) *adj.* strong, firm 29/112; *adv.* eagerly, stridently Pr 382; quickly Pr 510, 8/108, 10/239; firmly, securely 2/290, 27/306, 313; near: *evyn* ~ *þerby* near to it 23/160; severely, greatly 27/571; soundly 28/33, 31/51, 63.

faste *v.* fast Pr 268; **fast, fastyd** *pa. t.* 26/28, 41/19; **fastyd** *pp.* 23/67.

fastyng *vbl. n.* fasting 8/41.

favorabyl *adj.* disposed to be lenient 31/138.

fawe see **fayn(e)** *adj.*

fawte *n.* fault 8/67, 9/237, 24/23; default, want 27/498.

fe *n.* goods, money 20/124.

febyl(l) *adj.* feeble, deficient 3/109, 116; poor, wretched: ~ *of array* poorly clothed 42/123.

febyly *adv.* poorly 15/99.

febylnesse *n.* weakness, infirmity 10/157, 161.

feble *v.* grow weak or infirm 41/302.

fech(e), fecch *v.* fetch 21/103, 23/37, 33/22, 34/191; **fecch** *pl.* 26/359 s.d.

fede *v.* **1** eat 9/191; *refl.* 9/255, 280, 15/27; **fede** *imp. pl. refl.* 9/251, 288; **2** feed, nurture 11/12, 21/43, 239; **fed(de), fad(e)** *pp.* 2/76, 14/77, 101, 18/236, 27/493; **fede** *imp. pl.* 27/497.

feetly *adv.* craftily, neatly 14/128.

feye see **fay(e).**

feyn see **fyn(e).**

feyn *v.* [1] fix in position 36/29n.

feyn(e) *v.* [2] invent 24/57; hesitate, hold back 26/175; **feyne** *pl.* ~ *falsly* misrepresent 41/45.

feynnesse *adj.* feebleness, infirmity 4/129.

feynt *adj.* feeble, slight, unreliable: ~ *felachep in me is fownde* I am a poor friend 20/261; dispirited 25/22.

feyr see **fyre.**

feyth *n.* faith 9/150, 220, 11/108; *in* ~ truly 3/109, 8/208, 13/43.

feythf(f)ul(l) *adj.* faithful 25/398, 38/341, 347; *in me þat* ~ *is* who has faith in me 25/305.

feythffully *adv.* faithfully 7/76, 22/55, 38/319.

fekyll *adj.* false, treacherous 36/43.

felaw(e), fela *n.* equal 2/114, 131; friend, associate 16/14, 32/77; (ironic) 29/203; contemptible person 29/138; **felawys, felas, felawus** *pl.* fellows (as term of address) 8/133, 14/106, 29/181, 35/217; associates, colleagues 24/237, 243, 26/97.

felachep(p) *n.* company, companionship 8/126, 9/202, 22/152; *in* ~, *amongys* ~ in company Pr 469, 6/88, 38/42; intimate companionship 10/37; comradeship, friendship 20/261.

felde *n.* field, open country: *in* ~ *and town, be fryth and* ~, *in* ~, *in town* everywhere 3/188, 6/154, 15/88, 35/203; *in* ~ *nor town* (not) anywhere 5/260; *be* ~ *and fenne* 18/206; battlefield: *in þe (opyn)* ~

in battle 7/8, 21/102; **feldys** *pl.* fields 3/99.

fele *adj.*[1] many Pr 274, 38/272; *many and ~* very numerous 5/217.

fele *adj.*[2] excellent 2/64, 76.

fele *adv.* much 26/137, 146.

fele *v.* **1** discover by physical investigation 15/218; **fele** *pr. 1 sg.* 15/228; **2** feel 25/46; *refl.* 25/58; **fele** *pr. 1 sg.* 11/293, 306, 15/97; **felyd** *pa. t.* 38/378; **3** know, realize *in* **fele** *pr. 1 sg.* 9/202, 15/93; **4** smelled, tasted *in* **felt** *pa. t.* 9/257.

felle *n.* skin: *flesch and ~* the whole body 20/283, 35/67, 37/61.

fel(l)(e) *adj.* treacherous, fierce, cruel, wicked Pr 60, 273, 409; stern, *or* heavy Pr 174; grievous 1/73, 26/8; potent 9/139.

felle *v.* fell, vanquish 7/8, 12/218, 26/224; **fellyth** *pr. 3 sg.* casts down, fells 13/109, 29/65.

fellere *n.* one who fells (an adversary) 16/108.

felthe see **fylth.**

fenaunce *n.* ending 25/2.

fend(e), fynd(e) *n.* devil, fiend Pr 25, 273, 279, 409, 26/469; **fendys, fyndys, fendes** *gen. sg.* 12/218, 21/188, 27/184, 28/6, 36/13; **fendys, fyndys** *pl.* Pr 115, 7/63, 16/132, 27/244, 36/11.

fende *v.* defend 27/174.

fende see **fynd(e).**

fenne *n.* marshland, fen 18/166, 27/158.

fer see **fer(re)** *adj.*, **fyre.**

ferd *ppl. adj.* frightened 41/66, 266, 414.

ferd(e) see **faryth.**

ferdere see **ferther(e).**

fer(e) *n.*[1] fear 1/81, 2/147, 6/159; danger, frightening situation 41/430.

fer(e) *n.*[2] husband 4/44; friend, companion 10/34, 11/315, 22/134; equal 11/233; accomplice 28/136.

fere *n.*[3] company 32/96; *in ~* in company, together 5/104, 10/367, 11/277; *in ~* at the same time 15/202.

fere *v.* **1** frighten 41/155; **feryth** *pr. 3 sg.* inspires awe or fear (in) 10/440; **feryd** *pp.* 38/390; **2** fear: *refl.* be afraid 41/157; **fere** *pr. 1 sg.* 15/18, 27/472, 41/422; *refl.* 8/61, 171; **fere** *pl. refl.* 41/270; **feryng** *pr. p.*: *is ~* consists in my fearing (that) 8/158; **fere** *imp. pl. refl.* 41/232; **fere** *pr. subj.* 41/114.

fer(e) see **fer(r)e, fyre.**

ferforthe *adv.* (of time) 'far forth', into the future; *or* greatly 13/89n.

ferful *adj.* fearful 28/43.

ferly *adj.* miraculous, wonderful Pr 485.

ferne *n.* place overgrown by ferns 18/206.

fer(re) *adj.* distant, far Pr 171, 10/467, 12/10.

fer(r)e *adv.* far Pr 211, 10/135, 466; *haue ~ hom* have a long trip home 13/152; *~ as* as far as 41/42, by far 40/8.

fers *adj.* dangerous, fierce 9/139, 35/246, 38/23.

ferste see **fyrst** *adj.* and *adv.*

ferthe see **fourte.**

ferther(e), ferdere *adv.* further 13/158A, 21/12, 26/43, 183, 27/56on., 35/272.

ferthermore *adv.* furthermore 10/148, 11/269, 12/216.

fervent, veruent *adj.* burning, fervent 25/46, 207, 27/365.

fesyk see **phesyk.**

fest *n.* fast, *or* hardship 32/217.

fest *v.* join 41/506; **fest** *pp.* fettered, confined PS 27; fastened, fixed 31/199; **fest** *imp. sg.* fasten, tie 32/65, 73.

fest(e) *n.* **1** holy day Pr 491, 8/33, 35; **festys** *pl.* 6/110; **2** feast 35/267.

fett *v.* take away 25/171; **fettyn** *pl. vs ~* we go to get, *or* let us fetch 41/478; **fett** *pp.* (with *with*) taken away stealthily (by) 35/277.

fewe *adj.* few Pr 315, 8/14, 27/514; *as noun* 3/123, 42/122.

fewté *n.* fealty 36/52.

fy *interj.* fie! 12/71, 18/217, 217; *~ vpon (upon)* 35/171, 201, 41/419.

fyer(e) see **fyre.**

fyff, fyve *card. num. as adj.* five 8/191, 9/194, 241, 262, 10/317, 19/178.

fyfte *ord. num. as adj.* fifth Pr 79, 6/131; *as noun* 9/118, 235.

fyftene *card. num. as adj.* fifteen 9/97, 101.

fyftene, fiftene *ord. num. as adj.* fifteenth 41/6; *as noun* 9/158.

fyfty *card. num. as adj.* fifty 13/9.

fygge *n.* *~ levys* fig leaves 2/172.

fygure *n.* prefiguration, emblem 7/43, 62, 27/361.

fyguryth *pr. 3 sg.* prefigures 6/21; **fyguryd** *pp.* 7/71.

fylle *n.* *(one's) ~* one's fill 12/149, 15/27, 43.

fylth, felthe *n.* corruption, wickedness 35/40, 41/469; filth 42/48.

fynd(e), fyndys see **fend(e).**

fynd(e), fyndyn *v.* **1** find Pr 221, 2/172, 323, 26/349, 35/31; **fynd(e), fende** *pr. 1 sg.* 2/63, 166, 3/123; find (in prophesy) 19/91; **fyndyst** *pr. 2 sg.* (with future sense) 35/87; **fyndyth** *pr. 3 sg.* 28/32 s.d., 44 s.d., 68 s.d.; **fynde** *pl.* 24/201, 25/435, 26/226; **fownd(e), founde, fowndyn, ifownde, fownden, fownnde** *pp.* 3/98, 176, 4/3, 7, 8/29, 16/8, 90, 103, 20/24, 38/325, 42/23; **fynde, fyndyn** *pr. subj.* 18/185, 211, 24/93, 98; **2** receive Pr 514, 6/8; **3** recover, regain 16/126; **4** proved to be *in* **fowndyn, fownd, fownden** *pp.* 14/124, 136, 185, 18/50.

fyn(e), feyn *adj.* fine, pleasing 20/235; of select quality, costly 26/69, 73; pure 26/27; sheer, utter; ~ *fors* brute strength 34/285.

fynger, fyngyr *n.* finger 6/39, 38/323.

fynyaly, fynialy *adv.* permanently 11/143; finally, conclusively 11/185.

fynyte *adj.* 10/112 (see note).

fyre, fer(e), fyer(e), feyr *n.* fire Pr 57, 81, 497, 1/73, 81, 3/132, 136, 8/174, 15/103, 22/9, 28/80 s.d.; torch 5/114.

fyrst, ferste *ord. num. as adj.* first Pr 14, 16, 2/2, 41/106; *as noun* 6/61, 9/198, 10/353.

fyrst, ferste *adv.* first Pr 11, 1/30, 9/66, 41/18; first and foremost 3/39, 9/175, 228; formerly, beforehand 27/192, 34/10, 35/123.

fysch(e) *n.* fish, sea creatures 2/12, 20, 33.

fise *n.* (as term of abuse) fart, stink 41/83.

fistis *n.* hands, *perh.* power 41/229.

fyth, fytyn, fyght *v.* fight 26/91, 27/340, 32/92 s.d., 35/187; **fowth** *pp.* ~ *with* fought against 9/140.

fytt *n.* tune 20/232.

flamys *n.* flames 31/4, 41/479.

flammyng *ppl. adj.* flaming 2/285.

flanke *n.* flank *18/276.

flaterynge *vbl. n.* flattering 14/221.

fle *v.* flee, escape Pr 69, 175, 2/202; turn aside 11/133; **fleth** *imp. pl.* flee, fly 27/175, 177.

flecchere *n.* maker or seller of arrows 14/20.

flem *v.* drive away 28/6.

flesch(e), fles(s)he, flech, flessch *n.* flesh 2/18, 18, 311, 7/14, 18/125, 252;, 41/230, 302; *coll.* animals 2/33.

fleschly, flesly, flescly *adj.* earthly, corporeal, carnal 2/166, 182, 9/139, 14/212, 228.

flescly *adv.* physically 2/311.

flyes *n.* flies 41/46.

flynt *n.* flint 31/4; **flyntys** *pl.* hard stones 23/81.

flyth *n.* flight Pr 31, 11/216; **flithtis** *pl.* 41/355.

flytt, flitt(e) *v.* deliver, save 20/228; escape 34/244; flee 38/101; go 42/63; **flytt** *pp.* expelled, *or* fled 27/181; **flytt** *pr. subj.* go 35/272.

flok *n.* flock 3/84, 7/104; company: *þe ~ of gostly conuersacyon* i.e. the followers of Christ PS 26.

flokkys *n.* wool scraps 26/77.

flood, flod(e) *n.* flood Pr 75, 4/13, 123, 137, 199; **flodys** *gen. sg.* 4/112; **flodys** *pl.* waters 4/201, 234.

florens *n.* florins 18/181.

floreschyth *pr. 3 sg.* bears flowers 10/299; **floryschyd** *pa. t.* bloomed 38/131.

floure, flowre *v.* bloom, flower Pr 142, 150; flourish 27/178.

flowe *n.* surging 4/112; flood 35/34.

flowe *v.* move inshore 5/221; flow 21/152; **flowe** *pp.* risen Pr 75.

flowre, floure *n.* flower 7/22, 10/401, 16/8, 90, 99, 103; *erbe and* ~ 2/7; *seed and* ~ 10/63; **flourys, flowrys** *pl.* Pr 36, 310, 2/84, 26/448, 453 s.d., 38/131.

fo see **fo(o).**

fode see **food.**

fode *v.* nourish, feed: ~ *and fede* nourish and sustain 32/288.

foyson *n.* abundance (of grace) 7/29; abundance 9/285.

fol see **ful(l).**

folde *n.* many a ~ much 14/245; *be (in) many* ~ many times over 24/8, 26/127.

-folde *suffix vij-* ~ sevenfold 3/180, 4/192.

folde *v.* give way, buckle 4/129, 10/227, 14/267.

fole *n.* colt 26/350, 359 s.d.

fole see **fool, ful** *adj.*

folys see **fool.**

foly, folé *n.* folly, foolish act, sin 2/216, 8/29, 11/2, 30/161; **folyes** *pl.* 24/180.

folk(e) *n.* folk, people 9/292, 11/12, 15/4; **folkys** *pl.* 16/36.

folwe, folwyn *v.* **1** follow Pr 338, 10/360, 361; **folwe** *pr. 1 sg.* 25/343; **folwyth** *pr. 3* sg. Pr 490; ~ ... *sute* does the same as 22/160; **folwyn** *pl.* 29/130; **folwyng** *pr. p.* 8/12, 28/1st s.d.; **folwyd** *pp.* 18/25; **folwe** *imp. sg.* 10/461, 28/125; **folwyth, folwe, folwyht** *imp. pl.* 18/15, 127, 26/279, 39/29; **2** strive for 4/47; **3** obey, follow 5/255; **folwyth** *imp. pl.* 22/103; **4** be associated with 10/37; **5** keep, observe (doctrine, law) 26/11, 27/290; **6** act in accordance with 27/287; **7** follow spiritually 35/86; **folwygh** *pr. 3 sg.* 24/55; **folwyd** *pa. t.* PS 16.

folwerys *n.* followers 27/103, 136.

folwyng *ppl. adj.* following 27/465 s.d.

fomen *n.* foes 5/220, 7/127, 24/265.

fon see **fo(o)**.

fonde *v.* **1** try, undertake 2/326, 14/296, 24/284; **fond** *imp. sg.* 2/110; **fonde** *pr. subj.* 2/130; **2** proceed, go *in* **fonde** *imp. sg.* 2/304.

fonge *pr. subj.* endeavour, undertake 4/47, 26/131.

fonnyng *n.* foolishness, error 30/185.

fonnys *n.* fools 38/89.

fonnyst *pr. 2 sg.* act foolishly 3/117.

fo(o) *n.* foe 2/166, 5/144, 10/187; **fon(e)** *pl.* Pr 332, 21/221, 29/4.

food, fode *n.* food, nourishment 2/323, 3/120, 6/81, 9/255, 11/12, 23/98; young woman 15/145; young child, son 21/227.

fool, fole *n.* fool, rascal 20/48, 29/156, 32/121; **folys** *pl.* 3/92, 20/51.

foot(te), fote *n.* foot 12/208, 18/288, 23/128, 26/68, 27/1st s.d., 164; *upon* ~ on one's feet 29/109; foot (as unit of measurement) 32/64; power to stand, footing 34/320; **fete, feet, feyt** *pl.* Pr 458, 460, 1/65, 6/30, 14/260, 16/137, 32/264.

footmayd *n.* maidservant 8/73.

fop *n.* fool 29/164.

for, fore *prep.* because of, on account of Pr 46, 125, 321, 26/439; ~ *to* to, in order to Pr 71, 274, 294; for 10/412, 11/170n., 29/119; as, as being Pr 340, 1/59, 60; ~ *trewe*, ~ *trowth* 7/58, 119, 130; *as* ~ as if, like Pr 353; as regards: ~ *godys* as regards possessions 3/30; ~ *me* as far as I am concerned, for my part 14/226, 24/277, 27/95; ~ *hire* as far as she is concerned 14/227; out of regard for, for the sake of 4/44, 8/163, 164; (in asseverations, exclamations) 4/214, 5/100, 12/71; despite 14/347, 20/248, 23/200; ~ *any* whatever the 34/309, 315; through, by means of 28/64; *conj.* ~ *þat* because 5/211.

forbede *v.* forbid 6/182; **forbede** *pr. subj.* 4/53, 10/268, 12/98.

forevyr *adv.* forever 12/112, 13/125.

forfaderys *n.* forefathers 13/116.

forfare *v.* perish, go to ruin 4/226, 27/145.

forfete *n.* misdeed, offence 4/51, 12/40.

forfete, forfetyn, forffett *v.* transgress 2/81, 4/223, 237, 27/182; **forfett** *imp. sg.* 6/141.

forgete *v.* forget 8/201; **forgete** *imp. sg.* 32/127.

forgyf *pr. 1 sg.* forgive 30/167; **forgove, forʒovyn, forgevyn** *pp.* 32/138, 35/10, *21; **forgyf(f), forgeve, forʒeve, forʒeue** *imp. sg.* 14/373, 15/197, 32/102, 103, 103, 34/38, 109; **forʒeve** *imp. pl.* 9/77; **forʒeve** *pr. subj.* 14/374, 375.

forgyfnes *n.* forgiveness 12/169.

forhe(e)d *n.* forehead 42/92; *on here* ~ 42/76.

forkys *n.* forks (the tools) 31/212 s.d.n.

forlorn(e), forlore *pp.* lost, doomed Pr 197, 411, 2/294; destroyed, ruined 15/296.

formacyon *n. that were oure ferste* ~ who created us 41/106.

forme *n.* burrow 24/80; form 27/364, 394; manner: *in dewe* ~ properly, with proper devotion 27/442.

formere *n.* creator 16/107.

formest *adv.* first, in front 28/80 s.d.

form-faderys *n.* forefathers 27/423.

formyd *pp.* formed, created 1/45.

fors *n.* importance, value 3/104; force 34/285.

forsake, forsakyn *v.* **1** reject, repudiate, forsake Pr 38, 4/43, 46; **forsake** *pl.* (with ellipsis of 'you') 41/472; **forsakynge** *pr. p.* 38/365; **forsook, forsoke** *pa. t.* 11/94, 108, 108; **forsak(e)** *pr. subj.* 22/4, 10; **2** decline, refuse 14/160, 27/517; **forsake** *pr. subj.* 27/520; **3** refute, contradict *in* **forsake** *pr. 1 sg.* 21/75; **4** abandoned *in* **forsoke** *pa. t.* 29/206; **forsak** *pp.* 28/77; **5** denied *in* **forsoke** *pa. t.* 29/223; **forsake** *pp.* 29/214, 217.

forseyd *ppl. adj.* previously spoken 26/418; aforesaid 39/51.

forsoth(e) *adv.* in truth, truly Pr 106, 160, 1/53.

fortefye, fortyfye *v.* ensure 26/55; confirm, corroborate 26/58, 421; enforce, uphold 26/166, 314, 29/26; *aȝens . . . to ~* to fail to uphold, act contrary to 31/146; **fortefyet** *pr. 3 sg.* fortifies 27/400.

fortene *card. num. as adj.* fourteen 9/15.

for-than *adv.* and *conj.* for that reason, therefore 37/90; *natt ~* nevertheless 6/167.

forth(e) *adv.* forward, into view Pr 128, 149, 2/31; forth, ahead Pr 145, 466, 469; *must ~* must go forth 15/4; away, off 18/308, 20/242.

forthe see **fourte**.

forthy *conj. what ~* what of that? 12/104.

forthryght, forthryth *adv.* at once Pr 397, 5/166, 9/168, 20/152; precisely, fully 35/291.

fote see **foot(te)**.

foule, foull *n.* bird: *~ offlyth* flying birds Pr 31; *~ and best* 2/45; *fysch and ~* 2/105, 135; **fowlys, foulys** *pl.* 2/20, 4/114, 19/193, 196 s.d.

foulyng *n.* foul or filthy person 30/229.

fourte, ferthe, forthe, fowrte *ord. num. as adj.* fourth Pr 67, 2/11; *as noun* 2/9, 9/114, 234, 10/216, 19/165.

fourten(e) *card. num. as adj.* fourteen 41/5; *ord. num. as noun* fourteenth 9/154.

fourty *card. num. as adj.* forty 19/98, 20/101, 22/125.

fowle, foul(e) *adj.* foul, wicked, loathsome, ugly 2/216, 260, 271, 7/6, 52, 24/100; disgraceful 8/127; *as noun* ritually unclean creature 4/115.

fowle, foule *adv.* miserably 2/267; in an unclean manner 15/238, 303; (of smell) foully, badly 25/393, 38/148.

fowlyd *pp.* defiled 15/253, 27/158.

fowre, foure *card. num. as adj.* 11/1, 1, 13/24, 26/38; *as noun* 11/126, 144, 185.

fray *v.* attack 21/112; **frayth** *pr. 3 sg.* frightens Pr 424; **frayd** *pp.* frightened 35/211.

frankynsens *n.* frankincense Pr 205.

fraternyté *n. by ~* as a brother (to men) 11/267.

fraught *n.* burden, 'freight' 14/196.

fre(e) *adj.* excellent, noble Pr 80, 158, 5/103; unconstrained, unreserved Pr 208, 442, 5/61; free of sin 7/32, 15/180, 27/155; free, at liberty 31/98, 176, 178.

freke *n.* demon 2/271, 32/218.

frelnes *n.* frailty, weakness 11/110.

frelté *n.* frailty 23/51, 24/28, 32/186.

frenchep, frenshipp *n.* friendship Pr 514, 6/42, 16/8, 30/255.

frend(e) *n.* friend 2/166, 3/177, 16/107; *be (one's) ~* be favourable 6/91, 14/180, 15/56; kinsman 21/219, 22/54, 25/111; **frendys, fryndys** *pl.* Pr 426, 6/187, 193, 35/2; kinsmen 24/174.

frende 4/250. See note.

frendles *adj.* friendless, orphaned 15/271.

Frensche *adj.* French 12/56.

fresch(e) *adj.* fresh, unchanged by time 2/315; verdant 6/20; new, first (in a line of kings) 7/26; lusty, bold 14/87; (of appearance) blooming, youthful 14/91, 99, 16/80; unfaded, unwithered 15/304.

freschly *adv.* vigorously, eagerly 14/264.

frewte see **frute**.

fryndys see **frend(e)**.

fryth, fryght *n.* woodland, meadow 16/103; *be ~ and felde, be ~ and fenne* everywhere 15/88, 27/158; *~ and fe* landed and movable property 20/124; **fryhthis** *pl.* 18/181.

from(e) *prep.* from Pr 26, 51, 211; removed from 2/213, 6/16.

fro(o) *prep.* from Pr 69, 171, 253; of, belonging to 6/178; removed from 19/39; (of time) since 19/94; because of 26/64; of, concerning 26/401.

fruyssyon *n.* (as personif.) spiritual joy 9/200n.

frute, frewte, fruth *n.* fruit, crops Pr 38, 2/22, 33, 125; offspring, child 2/28, 5/62, 7/64, 12/194, 41/158, 456; *fyrst ~* 3/33, 42; *nothyr ~ nere chylde* no offspring 10/49; **frutys** *pl.* Pr 37, 2/64, 76.

fruteful *adj.* fruitful 8/102, 239; *as noun* 8/103, 9/56.

ful, fole *adj.* full, abounding in 2/221, 237, 259, 32/4; whole 19/79.

ful(l)fyll(e), fulffyl(le), fulffille *v.* **1** comply with, carry out 2/75, 10/35, 359, 15/36, 62, 26/270; **fulfyll** *pl.* 22/72; **fulfyllyd, fulfyllid** *pp.* 28/65, 39/59, 40/33, 41/262; **fulfylle** *pr. subj.* 34/65; **2** do, perform 24/180, 27/226, 235; **fulfylle** *pr. 1 sg.* 5/173; **fulfyllyd** *pp.* performed, brought about 15/101; **3** bring about 27/220; **4** accomplish 27/275; **5** fills,

fills up *in* **fulfyllyth** *pr. 3 sg.* 13/108; **fulfylt, fulfyllyd** *pp.* 11/211, 13/57.

ful(l), fol *adv.* very, completely Pr 6, 17, 25, 34/115; fully 10/30, 27/313, 39/64; ~ *every* on every, in every 2/64, 15/69.

fully, fullich, fullych, fulleche *adv.* fully 7/34, 13/160A, 19/175, 25/386, 28/46.

fullyth *pr. 3 sg.* grows full 34/303.

furlonge *n. pl.* furlongs 38/275.

furryd *pp.* trimmed or lined with fur 26/105, 164 s.d., 164 s.d.

furrys *n.* garments trimmed or lined with fur 18/198.

gaderyn, gadere *v.* **1** gather, pick 2/71, 15/43; **2** *refl.* assemble 26/92; **gadere** *pl.* Pr 270; **gaderyd, gaderid** *pp.* Pr 494, 41/29.

gay *adj.* bright, shining Pr 20, 49, 310; of bright colour Pr 310; elegant 6/105; beautiful 14/127, 24/70; pleasing, skilful, eloquent 24/54, 41/43.

gay *adv.* splendidly Pr 510, 12/76.

galaunt *n.* ladies' man, rake 14/87.

galle *n.* bitterness, sorrow 20/53; gall 25/323; *eyzil and* ~ 32/199, 38/30.

game *n.* play, dramatic production Pr 47, 519, 520; pleasure, joy 2/71, 10/264, 271; amorous play 12/75, 79; amusement, game 20/222, 29/188, 30/246; *brynge the to suche a* ~ have such sport with you 24/167; scheme, undertaking 31/44, 45.

gan see **gynne, go(o)**.

gardeyn *n.* garden 2/83.

gardener(e) *n.* gardener Pr 454, 2/69, 37/33.

garmentys *n.* garments 6/105, 28/80 s.d.

gast see **ʒeve**.

gate, ʒate, yate *n.*[1] gate, entrance 2/242, 7/47, 8/198, 236, 41/285; **ʒatys, gatys** *pl.* 2/302, 31/48, 33/24 s.d., 25, 28, 42/49.

gate, gatt *n.*[2] way: *þi* ~ *þu goo* go your way 5/86; *go(n)(one's)* ~ depart 35/282, 41/395; **gatys** *pl.* 35/73.

geawnt *n.* giant Pr 416.

gebettys see **jebet**.

gef see **ʒeve**.

geyn *n.* help, remedy *20/13.

geyne *v.* prevail against, oppose 41/399.

geynseyn *pr. pl.* gainsay 41/50.

gendyr *v.* engender 6/97.

geneologye, genealogye *n.* genealogy 7/114, 133.

generacyon *n.* stock, ancestral line 7/121; **generacyonys** *pl.* generations 13/89.

gent *adj.* attractive 14/126.

gentyl, gentyllest see **jentyl(l)**.

gentyllys *n.* nobles, gentry Pr 8.

gerle *n.* boy 20/110; **gerlys** *pl.* children: *knaue* ~ boys 20/59; boys, *or* young women (i.e. the mothers) 20/63.

gerth *n.* enclosed yard: *on grownd nere on* ~ (not) anywhere 20/212.

gesyn *n.* childbed 15/172.

gesse, gysse *pr. 1 sg.* suppose, think 3/117, 24/114, 25/13, 41/170.

gest(e) *n.* stranger, dangerous man, *or* tale 18/109; guest 18/306, 31/33.

get(e), gett *v.* **1** obtain, get Pr 515, 24/11, 25/54, 26/23, 104; *þe maystry...doth* ~ is victorious 21/139; **getyst** *pr. 2 sg.* (with fut. sense) 14/261; **gete** *pl.* (with fut. sense) 20/13; **2** earn 12/11.

gett *n.* manner: *on þe newe* ~ in the new fashion 32/208.

geve, gevyst, gevyth see **ʒeve**.

gyde *n.* guide Pr 265, 19/19, 22/122.

gyde *v.* guide, bring 32/272.

gyf(f), gyve see **ʒeve**.

Gylden, Golden *adj.* Golden 8/198, 221.

gyle *n.* guile, treachery 14/354.

gylt(e) *n.* sin, guilt 30/82, 42/23.

gylty *adj.* guilty 14/185, 240, 242.

gyltles *adj.* guiltless 14/251, 256, 31/158.

gynne *n.* instrument (of destruction) 4/124; scheme, trick, cunning 14/221; *þe devyllys* ~ the devil's wiles 22/12; spiritual trap or snare 23/108, 206.

gynne *v.* **1** begin 4/235; **gynnyst** *pr. 2 sg.* 38/301; **gynnyth** *pr. 3 sg.* Pr 175, 13/40; **gynne** *pl.* 28/143; (with fut. sense) Pr 526; **gunne** *pp.* 35/43; **2** *auxil.* do *in* **gynne** *pr. 1 sg.* 2/272, 20/167; **gynnyst** *pr. 2 sg.* ~ ...*gon* are 12/35; **gynnyth** *pr. 3 sg.* Pr 23, 394, 1/19; **gyn(ne)** *pl.* 4/129, 10/227, 14/184; **gan, gun(ne), gonne** *pa. t.* Pr 44, 311, 401, 2/226, 16/53, 35/45, 36/29.

gynnyng(e) *n.* beginning 1/4, 8/7, 187.

gyrdyl *n.* belt 27/417, 418.

gyrdyn *pa. t.* girt 27/358; **gyrt** *pp.* 27/511 s.d.

gyse *n.* behaviour, conduct Pr 350, 2/289, 12/31; manner, fashion 12/56, 26/208 s.d.; *þe newe* ~ the new state of affairs 29/113.

gysse see **gesse**.

glabereris *n.* loud or deceitful talkers 41/399.

glade *adj.* bright, shining 18/237; **glad-dere** *comp.* gladder 14/57.

glade *v.* gladden, encourage, comfort 38/372, 41/52.

gladnes *n.* gladness 8/222, 226, 9/110.

gladsom, gladsum *adj.* cheerful, glad Pr 458, 22/90.

glas *n.* glass 21/97, 98, 36/18.

glathe *v.* welcome 18/306; gladden 25/389.

gle(e) *n.* joy, rejoicing Pr 200, 2/71, 10/264.

gleyvys, gleyvis *n.* lances, spears 27/344, 28/80 s.d., 29/15.

glemynge *vbl. n.* gleaming 18/26.

glent *pa. t.* gleamed 41/209.

glete *n.* (see note) 18/125.

gleterynge *ppl. adj.* glittering 18/9.

glyde *v.* slither 2/261; go, travel 18/110, 118; pass (into joy) 20/167; charge: *amonge hem* ~ fall upon them 34/284; **glyde** *pl.* crawl 42/57.

glory(e), glorie *n.* glory Pr 2, 16/65, 70, 25/202.

gloryed *pp.* glorified 16/10n.

gloryfye *v.* glorify 25/204.

gloryous, glorious *adj.* glorious 4/2, 11/41, 15/56, 41/152.

glose *n.* deceit: *withowte (withowtyn)* ~ truly Pr 247, 14/190; deceitful explanation, misrepresentation 42/11.

gloteny(e), glotony(e) *n.* gluttony 6/112, 23/75, 106, 144, 42/114.

gnaggyd *pp.* pinned, hanged 41/47.

God(d)ys, God(d)is *n. gen. sg.* God's Pr 23, 27, 63, 41/54, 227, 278; **goddys** *pl.* 18/225.

god(e) see **go(o)d** *n.*, **good(e)** *adj.*

godys see **go(o)d** *n.*

Godhed(e), Godhyd *n.* Godhead, God 9/227, 11/198, 292 s.d., 332; **godhed** divinity 21/167, 27/406.

godly *adj.* of God, divine 9/159; *Fadyr* ~ holy Father 11/292 s.d.

godnesse see **go(o)dnes(se)**.

goyng *vbl. n.* going about 31/23.

gold(e) *n.* gold Pr 205, 6/120, 9/245 s.d.

gomys *n.* [1] male children 20/13.

gomys *n.* [2] gums, insides of mouth or throat 41/47.

gonge *n.* privy 35/58.

go(o), gon(e), gan, goon *v.* **1** go, move about Pr 465, 1/19, 56, 2/83, 4/37, 96, 5/254, 34/41; ~ *down* be weakened, defeated 20/56; ~ *abakke* withdraw 23/191; **go(o)** *pr. 1 sg.* 6/194, 11/215, 12/60; **gost** *pr. 2 sg.* 28/116; **goth** *pr. 3 sg.* Pr 157, 182, 356; **go(o), gon** *pl.* 2/12, 20, 5/121; ~ *in* follow 9/137; **goyng(e)** *pr. p.* 9/277 s.d., 26/449 s.d., 34/70; **gon(e), go** *pp.* Pr 448, 476, 2/306; **go(o)** *imp. sg.* 2/57, 245, 247; ~ *abak* withdraw 23/183; ~ *doun* kneel, prostrate yourself 41/437; **go(o), go(o)th, gon, goht** *imp. pl.* 8/142, 228, 9/64, 214, 10/335, 421, 20/25; **go(o), gon** *pr. subj.* 8/250, 10/386, 14/383; (forming *imp.*) 2/330, 8/242, 9/49; **2** proceed (to) 10/265; **3** be 12/35; **gon** *pl.* are, live 3/92; ~ *in travalynge* are giving birth 15/135; **4** (be able to) walk 26/394, 402; **5** ended, passed *in* go(o), gon *pp.* 20/98, 23/32, 34/173; *þi days be* ~ your life is over 3/150; **6** completed: *wolde be* ~ should be done 13/17; **7** travelled 21/259, 35/73; **8** ago: *iiij days* ~ 25/291, 394; **9** go to *in* **goht** *imp. pl.* 34/263.

go(o)d *n.* good, welfare, benefit Pr 392, 27/511; *a word of* ~ a good word 32/22; good or useful knowledge 15/143; good deed 11/165; **good, go(o)dys, gode** *pl.* goods, possessions, wealth 3/19, 30, 41, 5/182, 8/46, 51; good things, blessings 13/108, 29/1.

good(e), gode *adj.* good Pr 78, 83, 88, 5/123, 6/193, 9/94; *in* ~ *tyme* at a good time 18/301; ~ *tyme* it is high time 20/143.

goodly *adv.* in goodly fashion 35/179, 38/241.

go(o)dnes(se), goodnese *n.* goodness Pr 1, 352, 4/1, 22/37.

go(o)st *n.* soul 16/10, 35/210; devil 35/43; **Go(o)st** Holy Ghost 1/25, 21/122; *Holy* ~ Pr 166, 260, 265; **Gostis, Gostys** *gen. sg.* Holy Ghost's 1/20, 21/119, 41/355.

go(o)stly *adj.* spiritual, divine 3/57, 6/82, 126; *þe body* ~ 26/405; *adv.* in a spiritual manner 2/60, 9/102, 10/440.

gouernayl *n.* tutelage 41/203.

governawns, governauns *n.* control, custody 26/215; *in what* ~ in whose keeping 21/235; *I have in* ~ I have in my keeping 29/43; conduct 14/137.

governe *v.* **1** keep 8/20; **2** conduct (yourself) *in* **gouerne** *imp. sg. refl.* 2/60; **governe** *imp. pl. refl.* 8/205; **3** governed *in* **gouernyd** *pp.* 411/32.

gowne *n.* cloak 10/185; gown 26/164 s.d.; gown *or* cloak 26/81; **gownys** *pl.* gowns, cloaks 26/449 s.d.

grace, gras *n.* favour, goodwill Pr 281; divine grace 1/20, 26, 3/47, 310, 10/376, 16/24; mercy, pardon, reprieve Pr 515, 2/329, 4/211; divinizing gifts or power 2/221; fortune, fate: *evyl* ~ misfortune 14/65; (as imprecation) 14/153; **gracys** *pl.* divine gifts or favours 9/243.

gracyous, gracyows *adj.* merciful, benignant Pr 1, 3/90, 4/76, 41/126, 205; filled with grace 8/239, 9/8, 158; lovely 9/57.

gracyously *adv.* by God's grace 12/13.

graffe see **grave.**

grame *n.* sorrow 8/125, anger 15/184; *grevyd al with* ~ deeply vexed Pr 43; harm 15/156.

grame *v.* **1** anger, vex 2/177; **grame** *pr. subj.* 4/85; **2** enrage 24/63; **3** punished *in* **gramyd** *pp.* 14/321.

gramer *n.* (Latin) grammar 21/8.

gramercy, gromercy *interj.* (sometimes with *of*) thank you 3/45, 5/241, 242, 26/482, 41/131, 438.

gramly *adv.* grievously 41/399.

gratulacyon *n.* expression of thanks 41/97.

graunt, grawnt *v.* **1** grant, give, permit Pr 198, 414, 7/136, 10/57, 27/75; **graunt, grawnt** *pr. 1 sg.* 2/17, 47, 32/130; **grauntyst** *pr. 2 sg.* 5/248; **grawntyd, grauntyd, graunt** *pp.* granted 7/80, 8/235, 18/312, 19/52, 24/282, 28/9; **grawnt, graunt(e)** *imp.* 3/73, 4/70, 5/71, 6/11; **graunt, grawnt** *pr. subj.* 3/53, 4/86, 5/30; **2** ordain: *þe* ~ *present* ordain for you here and now 27/75; **grauntyd** *pp.* 12/135; **3** agree, assent *in* **grawnt, graunt** *pr. 1 sg.* 10/23, 11/82, 21/73; **graunte** *pl.* 34/234; **4** agree to *in* **graunt** *pr. 1 sg.* 32/71.

grave, graue, graffe *n.* grave Pr 415, 423, 427, 24/104, 25/148, 163, 34/231: **gravys** *pl.* Pr 508.

graue, gravyd *pp.* buried 25/142, 411, 36/21.

grecys *n.* steps, stairs 9/165. Cf. **grees.**

grede *v.* lament 37/31; **grede** *pr. subj.* cry out 20/63.

gredy *adj.* greedy 16/95.

grees *n.* steps, stairs 9/97.

gref *v.* harm 41/399.

gref(fe), greve *n.* hardship, distress, grief 3/110, 13/147, 15/128, 245, 16/144.

greyn *n.* stain 41/513n.

Grek *n.* Greek Pr 500.

grene *adj.* green, i.e. live 6/18, 20.

gres(se) *n.* plants, grass 2/25, 248, 3/156.

grete *v.* **1** greet 34/47; **grete** *pr. 1 sg.* greet, worship, honour 16/94; **gret** *pa. t.* greeted 12/215; **gret(e)** *imp. pl.* 26/256, 30/254; **2** (ironically) worship, salute *in* **grete** *pl.* 32/208, 210.

gretyng(e) *vbl. n.* greeting 11/231, 13/51, 30/155.

gret(t), grete, greet *adj.* great Pr 2, 22, 44, 46, 118, 11/5, 32/75; ~ *of myth* powerful 1/10; ~ *age* old age 4/126, 11/209, 21/242; eminent, noble Pr 118, 2/217; loud Pr 162, 31/210 s.d.; swollen 25/56; (of storms, etc.) severe 34/8, 11; *as noun* people of high rank: ~ *and small* everyone 42/6; **gretter(e), grettyr** *comp.* 1/51, 35/131, 37/25, 70; **grettest** *sup.* Pr 295, 16/94, 26/431.

gret(t)ly, gretlye *adv.* greatly, very much 4/241, 6/102, 162, 27/400.

grevauns, grevaunce, grevans *n.* offence, sin 4/85, 6/16, 24/5, 35/43; distress 4/205, 25/34, 26/54, 27/3; grievance, cause for complaint 26/59.

greve, grevyn *v.* **1** anger, trouble, grieve Pr 506, 14/89, 119, 134; **grevyd** *pp.* Pr 43, 4/122, 138; **greve** *pr. subj.* 25/78; **2** distresses *in* **grevyth, grevyht** *pr. 3 sg.* 4/94, 103, 107, 5/183, 11/77, 31/13; **3** (intr.) grieves 27/207; **4** harmed *in* **grevyd** *pp.* 38/11.

greve *n.* see **gref(fe).**

grevynge *vbl. n.* injury, physical distress 15/223.

grevous *adj.* grievous, severe Pr 47, 321, 2/186.

grylle *adj.* cruel, fierce 25/217.

grym *adj.* stern 7/128; fierce, cruel 25/217.

gryse *n.* boar 16/95.

grysly *adv.* terribly, horribly 16/95.

gryth *n.* peace Pr 200.

gromercy see **gramercy**.

grone, gronyn *v.* groan, moan 10/186, 20/107, 41/47; groan in childbirth 15/131; grunt, make animal sounds 16/95.

gronynge *vbl. n.* groaning, suffering 2/256; suffering in pregnancy 20/101.

grote *n.* groat 10/199.

groundyd, grownde *pp.* 1 (with *of*) established in, consisting of Pr 1; 2 established, confirmed, fixed 15/127; **grounde** *imp. sg.* 6/16.

growe *v.* 1 grow, increase 5/218, 14/71, 309; **growyth** *pr. 3 sg.* 23/171; **grow, growyn** *pl.* 13/50, 15/33; **growe** *pp.* 2/188; 2 comes *in* **growyht** *pr. 3 sg.* 8/143.

growyng *ppl. adj.* growing 2/6.

grown(n)d(e), ground(e) *n.* ground, earth Pr 457, 4/176, 5/250, 6/31, 14/370, 16/2; *on* (*þe*) ~ on earth 3/92, 170, 4/176; basis: *of grace* ~ the foundation of grace 4/1; field 20/212; place of burial 25/147; *beryenge* ~ 34/306.

grugge *v.* complain 25/175.

Grw *n.* Greek 20/22.

gutt *n.* belly, underside 2/261.

ȝa, ya *adv.* yea 4/94, 8/145, 246, 41/59, 384, 495.

ȝarde see **ȝerd(e)**.

ȝate, ȝatys see **gate** *n.* [1].

ȝe, ye *pron. 2 pl.* you Pr 13, 47, 58, 2/278, 10/160, 22/18; **ȝow** *nom.* 6/120, 11/89, 42/20; **ȝow, you, ȝou, yow, ye** *acc.* and *dat.* Pr 10, 33, 66, 100, 10/168, 169, 13/178A, 179A, 18/261, 286, 293, 41/26, 516; **ȝow** yourself 5/151; **ȝow, yow, you, ȝou** *refl.* 2/284, 8/205, 9/251; **ȝoure, your(e), ȝowre, yowr(e)** *poss.* your Pr 512, 528, 1/60, 2/28, 107, 5/157, 10/168, 18/263, 297, 302, 41/106, 137, 467; yours 12/44, 48, 37/47; **ȝoureself, ȝouresylf** yourself 9/188, 15/225, 25/70, 360; yourselves 32/10; *refl.* yourself 25/80, 333; *refl.* yourselves 22/150.

ȝede *pa. t.* went, lived 21/136.

ȝef see **if(f)**.

ȝelde *v.* requite 15/86; **ȝeld** *pr. 1 sg.* render 27/374; **ȝeld(e)** *pr. subj.* (forming *imp.*) render 10/301; requite 13/158.

ȝemanry *n.* yeomen Pr 8.

ȝenge see **ȝonge** *adj.*

ȝerd(e), ȝarde *n.* [1] rod Pr 142, 148, 10/131, 205, 208, 210; **ȝardys, ȝerdys** *pl.* Pr 141, 10/128, 130, 141; *of thre* ~ three yards long 26/81.

ȝerd *n.* [2] garden 29/205.

ȝer(e), yer *n.* year 8/35, 13/156A, 15/27, 41/6; ~ *and woke* continually Pr 99; **ȝer(e), ȝerys, yer(e), yeris** *pl.* Pr 244, 4/127, 206, 9/22, 10/17, 11/3, 41/7, 8, 9, 12; (*all*) *þis hundryd* (*thowsand*) ~ for the last hundred (thousand) years 4/206, 211, 14/48; *ninty* ~ *bareyn* childless for ninety years 8/181; ~ *age* years of age 9/9, 17 s.d., 164; *sefne* ~ *sorwynge* seven years of mourning 20/102; *xij* ~ *day* twelve years 21/272; years of age Pr 122, 9/15, 10/7.

ȝeve, gyf(f), ȝevyn, gyve, ȝeue, gef, geve *v.* give 3/55, 112, 6/82, 8/55, 9/216, 11/25, 14/266, 16/154, 23/182, 24/194, 25/378, 26/176, 27/295, 32/13; **gyf(f), ȝeve, ȝyf(f)** *pr. 1 sg.* 18/241, 22/27, 24/135; *I* ~ *not* ... *an hawe, I* ~ *no fors* I don't care in the least 3/22, 104, 29/33; ~ *hym such a trepett* so trip him up (in wrestling, that) 20/188; **gevyst** *pr. 2 sg.* (with ellips. of 'thou') 30/199; **gevyth, ȝevyth, ȝyvyth** *pr. 3 sg.* Pr 380, 9/179, 180, 811, 27/448 s.d.; **ȝeve** *pl.* 21/143; ~ ... *an aungel name* call an angel 12/77; **ȝevyng** *pr. p.* 29/11; **ȝaff, gyf, ȝove, gaf, gast, yaf** *pa. t.* 8/182, 11/167, 13/33, 15/269, 26/56, 31/21, 35/168, 41/120; ~ *dome* passed sentence on 35/168; **ȝovyn** *pa. t. pl.* 38/30; **ȝovyn, ȝove** *pp.* 2/65, 9/55, 170, 23/215; **ȝeve, gyf(f), geve, gef** *imp. sg.* 2/24, 26, 11/283, 28/80, 32/57; **gyf(f), ȝevyth, ȝyf, gevyth, gef, ȝeve** *imp. pl.* 19/174, 20/27, 26/61, 27/500, 29/21, 30/121, 32/57, 35/57, 39/19.

ȝevene, ȝevyn see **evyn** *adv.*

ȝewys see **Jewys**.

ȝiff, ȝyf(f) see **if(f)**.

ȝyft(e) *n.* offering 3/70; gift 12/20.

ȝynge(e) see **ȝonge** *n.* and *adj.*

ȝis, ȝys see **yis**.

ȝit(t), ȝet(t), ȝyt, yet, yit *adv.* yet, nevertheless Pr 303, 420, 3/16, 36; hitherto, up till now 4/148, 234, 250, 8/102; hereafter 7/51, 42/64; still 12/47, 14/172; as yet 14/230, 24/139, 30/63; *as*

~ 37/42; even now 15/69, 22/145, 27/
273; also, in addition 19/183, 21/93, 107,
30/49; ~ *onys* once again 23/153; furthermore 24/108; *conj.* and yet 2/232,
3/118, 122, 26/107, 41/59.

ʒon *pron.* that one 15/25; **ʒon(e), yon(e)**
adj. yon, that 2/67, 4/166, 169, 18/231,
41/270, 388.

ʒondyr *adv.* vonder 15/84, 34/87, 40/15.

ʒonge, ʒyng *n.* youth 5/41, 9/5.

ʒonge, ʒyng(e), yong, ʒoung, ʒenge
adj. young Pr 213, 7/43, 9/164, 10/182,
195, 279, 345, 15/137, 18/221, 282;
recent, new 21/149; *as noun* 7/96, 8/96,
30/182; **ʒonger** *comp.* 9/24; **ʒongest**
sup. 21/154.

ʒough, ʒoughʒ *n.* youth 9/140, 21/165.

ha see **haue.**

habyl see **abyl** *adj.*

habytacyon, habitacyon *n.* dwelling
place Pr 300, 26/409, 41/172; *haue (han)*
~ dwell 9/120, 27/5.

habundawns see **abundauns.**

habundaunt, habundawnt *adj.* abundant 14/395, 24/287, 41/111.

haddyd see **adde.**

hay *n.* net for catching wild animals *18/
81.

haht see **haue.**

hald(e), halt see **holde** *v.*

haly see **hoiv.**

hall see **al(l)(e)** *adj.*

hall(e) *n.* hall, dwelling place 2/269, 4/50,
5/244; *ʒoure (oure)* ~ 18/309, 321; **hal-
lys** *pl.* 18/18.

hals *n.* neck 34/277.

halse *v.* embrace 32/156 s.d.

halwe *v.* hallow, observe 6/100; **halwyd**
pp. hallowed 22/92.

halwyd *ppl. adj.* hallowed 10/449.

han see **a** *indef. art.,* **haue.**

hand(e), hond(e) *n.* 1 hand Pr 480, 2/46,
109, 128, 137, 139; *on ~ to* tan to undertake 4/98; *in* ~ in (one's) hand 4/155; 2
power, control: *hast in* ~ possess,
control 5/261; *had in* ~ possessed sexually 12/28; 3 protection 14/257; 4 person: *buxum to (one's)* ~, *obeyth to (one's)*
~ be (are) obedient to (sb.) 20/141, 33/
38; 5 side, direction 26/137, 31/208, 209;
~ *mayden*, ~ *mayd(e)*, ~ *may* hand-

maiden 11/287, 299, 13/88, 14/371, 387,
32/292; ~ *werk(e)* handiwork, creation
4/107, 5/264, 25/3; *per (here, etc.)* ~ 10/
128, 27/359, 30/241; **handys** *gen. sg.* 15/
260; **handys, hondys, handis** *pl.* Pr
141, 2/191, 3/151, 19/31, 22/68, 31/180,
41/250; *takyn in* ~ made captive 27/102.

handele *v.* touch, hold, handle 19/32.

hang(e), hangyn, honge *v.* 1 (trans.)
hang 24/179, 29/31, 32/88 s.d., 92 s.d.,
41/78; **hangyth** *pr. 3 sg. refl.* Pr 370, 30/
32 s.d.; **hyng** *pl.* hang, crucify Pr 389;
henge, hynge *pa. t.* 38/24, 26; *refl.* 39/
73; **hangyn, hangyd, hongyn** *pp.* 26/
319, 27/129, 292, 28/127, 31/209, 32/24;
hang(e) *imp. pl.* 32/90, 162; 2 (intr.) 31/
205, 32/92, 224, 34/53; **hangyst** *pr. 2 sg.*
32/86; (with ellips. of 'thou') 32/94;
hangyth *pr. 3 sg.* 32/170, 33/12, 34/105;
hangyng *pr. p.* Pr 390, 26/85; **hynge,
henge** *pa. t.* 35/69, 38/346, 41/200.

hangere *v.* anger 42/102.

hap(p) *n.* lot, fortune 2/313, 38/217, 225;
mishap, misfortune 12/181; *in* ~ perhaps 15/184, 24/32; **happys** *pl.* misfor-
tunes 20/104.

happend *pa. subj.* happened 34/176.

haras *n. hous of* ~ stable 15/84.

hardaunt *adj.* hardy Pr 418.

hard(e), arde *adj.* severe, harsh, bitter
2/313, 15/174, 20/104; troublesome,
difficult 10/100, 12/85, 35/73; hard 23/
82; stubborn: ~ *of truste* slow to trust 38/
145; ~ *of herte* 39/7; *adv.* firmly,
securely 35/44.

hardely *adv.* certainly, indeed 34/213.

hardy *adj.* foolhardy 29/23, 29.

hardnesse *n.* hardness 2/308.

harlot, harlat *n.* rogue 24/125, 30/221,
32/33, 35/171; **harlotis, harlotys** *pl.*
41/49, 395, 401, 406, 472, 481.

harlotry *n.* sexual immorality 24/148.

harme *v.* harm 4/113.

harpe *n.* harp 20/66.

harry *v.* drag 31/12.

harrow, herrow, harro, harraw *interj.* a
cry of distress 23/187, 33/33, 35/57, 41/
389, 475, 42/32.

Harwere *n.* Harrower 16/129.

hasayd see **as(s)ay.**

haske, haskyd, haskyng see **aske.**

hast(e) *n.* haste Pr 445, 509, 2/284; eager-
ness 11/201.

hast(e) *pr. 1 sg. refl.* go or come in haste 18/18, 19/71; **haste** *imp. sg. refl.* 11/261; **hast** *pr. subj. refl.* 10/146.

hastyly, hastely *adv.* rashly, hastily 2/196; quickly 13/3, 19/38, 27/360.

hat(e) *n.* hate Pr 353, 2/238, 14/70.

hatyst *pr. 2 sg.* hate 9/233; **hatyht, hatyth** *pr. 3 sg.* 3/145, 11/87.

hattyht see **hyght** *v.*

haue, han, have, hauyn, an *v.* 1 have Pr 294, 413, 446, 26/100, 107, 449 s.d., 27/139; ~ *in thought* keep in mind 22/176; ~ ... *delyverauns* (*of*) be saved (from) 22/182; ~ *lawe* receive judgement 24/182; have (as spouse) 10/311, 314; ~ *þe newe faccyon* be fashionable 26/80; **haue, have** *pr. 1 sg.* 1/67, 3/177, 4/142; ~ *a slepe* sleep 18/281; ~ *I grett merth* I am delighted 19/70; ~ *grett repentaunce* am most repentant 24/212; (with fut. sense) 31/43; **hast** *pr. 2 sg.* 5/261, 6/92, 122; **hath, has** *pr. 3 sg.* Pr 406, 435, 1/4, 24/291; **haue, han, have, hawe** *pl.* Pr 223, 271, 484, 14/179; ~ *þe hy3 excellence* are the most excellent 21/13; ~ *habytacyon* dwell 27/5; **havyng(e)** *pr. p.* 11/295, 13/27; **had(de)** *pa. t.* Pr 2, 156, 4/146; ~ *a towche* received a blow 29/99; **haddyst** *pa. 2 sg.* 12/80, 44/14; **haddyn** *pa. pl.* 15/271; **had** *pp. with 30w be* ~ should accompany you 8/209; **haue, ha, a, have** *imp. sg.* 2/112, 4/149, 5/31; ~ *don* make an end, hurry up 3/160; ~ *hem in dyspyte* despise them 26/88; **haue, ha, have** *imp. pl.* 5/152, 8/163, 11/6; ~ *do(n)* 16/89, 24/221; **haue** *pr. subj.* Pr 461, 3/19, 4/141; ~ *I blys* may I have bliss 14/54; **haddyst** *pa. subj. 2 sg.* 28/111, 30/248, 35/181; ~ *þu* (even) if you had 32/35; **2** *auxil.* **haue, have** *pr. 1 sg.* 2/44, 181, 203; **hast, ast** *pr. 2 sg.* 2/192, 195, 212, 5/230, 12/33, 27/464; **hath, haue, has, haht** *pr. 3 sg.* Pr 222, 232, 428, 18/285, 21/99, 35/21; has (done) 24/275; **haue, han, an, have** *pl.* Pr 59, 451, 516, 2/184, 4/157, 7/58, 8/150, 9/133, 10/327; (with ellipsis of subj.) 26/203; **a:** *xuld* ~ 4/158; *woldyst* (*wolde*) ~ 5/211, 11/97; *had* ... ~ 20/226–7, 26/252; **had(de)** *pa. subj.* had, would have Pr 190, 3/52, 121: *bettyr it* ~ *hym* it would have been better for him 27/459; **3** experience 3/154; **had** *pp.* 8/226,

33/2; **4** have in (one's) power 20/25, 27/307, 29/105; **haue** *pr. 1 sg.* 28/126; **han** *pl.* 26/98; **5** understand *in* **haue** *pr. 1 sg.* 16/64; **6** know *in* **haue** *pl.* 18/144; **7** accept, take *in* **haue** *imp.* 8/241, 19/132, 195; ~ *hym forth* take him away 28/147.

hawe *n.* fruit of the hawthorn, i.e. thing of little value 3/22, 21/27, 29/3.

he *pron. 3 sg.* it 4/149, 6/98, 12/16; **hym** *nom.* he 27/219; **hym, hem** *acc., dat.* him Pr 77, 89, 93, 18/234, 271, 22/37; himself 4/99, 8/57; *refl.* 20/251; **hem** *acc., dat. pl.* Pr 47, 51, 123; *refl.* Pr 45, 186, 329; **his(e), hes(e), is** *poss.* Pr 15, 24, 54, 60, 80, 117, 25/314; *mankynde* ~ mankind's 25/453; its 6/19, 21/98; *absol.* 4/99, 8/57, 13/113; **her(e), ere** *poss. pl.* Pr 55, 121, 140, 27/348 s.d.; **hymself, hymsylf, himself** *pron.* himself Pr 471, 2/95, 5/210; he himself 3/56, 4/110, 21/131; *refl.* Pr 24, 370, 25/76, 26/164 s.d., 208 s.d., 38/139; **hemself** *pl.* 24/267; *to hymward* towards him 8/238.

hed(e), heed *n.*[1] head 2/265, 4/197, 5/168, 11/30, 14/360, 365; ~ *ache* headache 25/8; *oure* ~ 41/387; **hedys** *pl.* 18/149, 26/164 s.d., 208 s.d.

hed(e), heed, heyd, eyd *n.*[2] heed, notice, attention 5/44, 209, 6/51, 10/2, 102, 131, 14/122, 22/102, 32/212.

hede see **hyde** *v.*

hedyr, heder *adv.* hither, here 5/101, 207, 8/135, 41/207.

hedyrcomynge *vbl. n.* coming to this place 13/75, 183A.

hefly, hefnely see **hevynly.**

hefne, heffne see **hevyn.**

heyd see **hed(e)** *n.*[2]

heyde see **hyde** *v.*

hey(e) ('haste') see **hye** *n.*

hey(e), hey3 see **hy3(e)** *adj.*

heyl(e) *adj.* healthy 38/256; ~ *be 3e*, ~ *be þu* may you be well 18/21, 151, 235.

heyl(e), heyll *interj.* hail! 2/87, 11/217, 15/57, 18/236, 237; *al(l)* ~ 15/170, 214, 19/61.

heylyght, heylith, eylight *pr. 3 sg.* ails, afflicts 14/263, 364, 25/55.

heylyng *pr. p.* greeting with 'hail!' 29/89 s.d.

heyn *n.* rascal: *as a name* 20/15.

heyned *pp.* exalted, raised 9/148.

heyth *n.* height: *vpon* ~ in a high position 13/105.

heldyn *pr. pl.* look 34/80 s.d.

hele *n.* health, well-being 25/61, 64, 74.

helyd *pp.* healed 15/296; **hele** *imp. sg.* PS 6.

hell(e) *n.* hell Pr 26, 269, 373; ~ *donjoon*, ~ *donjeon* 1/82, 27/256; ~ *logge* the prison of hell 2/233, 320, 33/43; ~ *sty* 2/241; ~ *pyt(t)* 2/269, 6/90, 20/253; ~ *qwelp*, ~ *hownde*, ~ *houndis* the hellhound(s) 5/72, 11/87, 41/488; ~ *cost* the land of hell 20/131; ~ *gatys* 31/48, 33/24 s.d., 30; ~ *gonge* the dungheap of hell 35/58.

helme *n.* helmets 34/269.

helmes see **almes**.

help(e) *n.* help Pr 136, 4/65, 188.

help(e) *v.* 1 help Pr 189, 5/70, 10/435; **helpyth** *pr. 3 sg.* 28/132, 32/79; **helpyht** *impers.* it avails us 25/446; **halpe** *pa. t.* helped 32/170, 41/429; **help(e)** *imp.* 12/131, 14/255, 274; **help** *pr. subj.* ~ *now* let him now help 32/172; **2** deliver, save 15/156; **help** *imp. sg.* 4/8, 14/277; **3** help (so that) 24/162; **helpe** *imp. pl.* 14/344, 25/140, 41/231; **4** relieve 25/119, 179, 264.

helpyngys *n.* missions to help (sb.) 13/17.

helth(e) *n.* health, well-being 6/82, 10/476, 20/264; *sowle-~* spiritual well-being 10/475; health, salvation 13/85, 41/465.

hem, hemself see **he.**

hende, ende *adj.* gracious, virtuous, kind Pr 143, 9/224, 10/360, 19/77; obedient 10/5, 38/237; **hendyr** *comp.* nearer 9/285.

hende see **ende** *n.*, **hynde** *adv.*

hend(e)les see **end(e)les.**

hendyng(e) see **endyng(e).**

hendyth see **ende** *pr. 1 sg.*

henge see **hang(e).**

hens *adv.* (away) from here 2/330, 3/12, 4/140; ~ *froo*, *from* ~ 14/385, 30/120; (with ellips. of vb. of motion) 41/403; from this time 41/129; *from* ~ 29/224.

hens-partyng *vbl. n.* death 3/60.

hent *pa. t.* (with *up*) picked up 25/387; **hent** *pp.* caught, taken Pr 340; **hent** *pr. subj.* take 10/148.

hepe *n.* pile: *on* ~ into a pile 20/83.

her see **or** *conj.*²

herborwe *n.* lodgings 15/59.

herborwe *v.* provide lodgings for 26/86; **herboryd** *pp.* lodged 15/85.

herde *n.* shepherd 16/31; **herdys** *pl.* 16/119.

herd, erde *n.* earth 28/59, 92 s.d.

herdmen *n.* shepherds 16/151.

her(e) *n.*¹ hair 25/109, 26/85, 41/149.

here, ere *n.*² ear 28/106 s.d., 106 s.d., 106 s.d., 29/99, 101, 204; **erys** *pl.* 18/107, 22/101, 35/143.

her(e) *adv.* here 1/15, 2/19, 35; ~-*levyng* life on earth 3/58.

here, heryn *v.* 1 hear Pr 391, 8/139, 212, 41/489; **here** *pr. 1 sg.* 2/194, 14/142, 22/109; **heryst** *pr. 2 sg.* (with ellips. of 'thou') 29/163, 166; **heryth** *pr. 3 sg.* 29/174; **here, heryn** *pl.* Pr 126, 30/73; **herd(e)** *pa. t.* 10/18, 62, 13/51; **herd(e), erde** *pp.* Pr 261, 263, 3/37, 30/77; ~ *seyde* 27/303; **here** *imp. sg.* 4/87, 9/145, 31/78; **here, heryth, heryght** *imp. pl.* 26/177, 34/185, 36/2, 39/18; **here, heryn** *pr. subj.* 8/127, 10/472, 28/152; **2** heard of *in* **herd** *pp.* 15/227.

her(e) see **he, she.**

hereabowth *adv.* near here 18/154.

hereafter(e) *adv.* after this 3/155, 9/272, 34/161.

herebeforn, herebefore *adv.* before now 8/246, *14/342, 19/58, 20/164.

herefore *adv.* for this 8/154; concerning this 11/175.

herein(ne) *adv.* into this place 2/291; in this place 29/189, 35/2, 37/4; in this circumstance 31/70.

heryght see **here** *v.*

heryng(e) *vbl. n.* speech 11/229; hearing 26/401.

herytage *n.* spiritual inheritance 7/40.

herytaunce *n.* inheritance 24/4.

herke *v.* 1 listen, take heed; *zoure erys to* ~ to give ear 22/101; **herk(e)** *imp.* 3/131, 4/178, 5/74; **2** listen to *in* **herk(e)** *imp.* 6/65, 23/3, 35/217.

herkenyth, herkyn *imp. pl.* listen, take heed 10/5, 41/36; listen to 41/39.

herne *n.* pit (of hell), *or* corner 41/477n.

herof *adv.* concerning this 41/263.

her(r)and(e), erdon, erand *n.* 1 intention, business 12/4; **2** errand, mission 21/206, 30/149, 32/32; **errandys** *pl.* 32/30; **3** petition, prayer 28/46.

hert *n.* hart 4/148.

hert(e) *n.* **1** heart, feelings Pr 174, 181, 208; *with* ~ sincerely, devoutly 14/282; **hertys** *gen. sg.* 27/365; **hertys** *pl.* 10/5, 54, 338; **hertys** *gen. pl.* 25/94; **2** heart, chest Pr 401, 404, 4/174; ~ *blood* life-blood 38/127, 340, 363; **3** courage, spirits 25/22, 33, 79; **4** mind 25/66; *thyn* ~ what you are thinking 5/124; **hertys** *pl.* 21/80.

herth(e) see **erth(e)**.

herty *adj.* heartfelt, fervent Pr 384, 4/89, 170.

hertyly, hert(e)ly *adj.* heartfelt 4/28, 10/69, 13/161A, 32/287, 37/1.

hertyly, hert(e)ly, hertylé *adv.* willingly, devoutly 3/83, 4/252, 5/111; earnestly, with feeling 5/22, 146, 236, 13/150, 41/294, 356; with good appetite 9/288.

hes(e) see **he**.

hesely *adv.* comfortably, easily 10/460.

hest *n.* command, behest Pr 493, 10/27.

hest *v.* wager 4/165; **hestyd** *pa. t.* vowed 10/68.

hete *n.*[1] injury, hit, *or* heat of a fever 20/196n.

hete *n.*[2] heat 21/82; heat of a fever 25/46, 207.

heve *imp. sg.* heave 34/99.

hevenynge *adv.* during the evening 4/72.

heuery see **every**.

hevy, evy *adj.* sorrowful Pr 173, 5/97, 134, 10/54, 14/134, 21/261; heavy Pr 421, 18/273, 276; *adv.* heavily: *beryth* ~ *of* (who) is heavily burdened by 32/33.

hevy, hevyin *v.* burden, make heavy 10/338; grieve 41/260.

hevyly *adv.* sorrowfully 8/137.

hevyn, hef(f)ne, hevene, efne *n.* heaven Pr 16, 26, 113, 434, 482, 1/67, 19/42, 27/539, 41/244; *þe* ~ 8/172 s.d., 9/245 s.d.; ~ *blys(s)e* the bliss of heaven Pr 461, 22/11, 18; ~ *tron(e)* the throne of heaven Pr 498, 1/21, 5/3; ~ *hille* the summit of heaven 2/158, 3/90; ~ *gate* (*ȝatys*) 2/242, 42/49; ~ *hall(e)* 2/269, *4/50, 10/120; ~ *kyng(e)* 3/9, 142; ~ *toure* (*towre*) the stronghold of heaven 5/39, 37/49; ~ *se* God's seat 16/153; ~ *holde* the kingdom of heaven 18/34; ~ *place* heaven hall 32/252; **hevenys, hefnys** the heavens 41/21, 518.

evyn see **evyn** *adv.*

hevynes(s)(e) *n.* sorrow, distress 8/123, 14/143, 25/95; drowsiness 18/285.

hevynly, hefnely, hefly *adj.* heavenly 9/99, 11/157, 21/133, 26/443, 32/215, 41/116, 317, 511.

hevyr see **evyr**.

heuyrmore see **evyrmor(e)**.

hewe *v.* hew 22/159, 23/33; **hewe** *imp. pl.* 20/26.

hyde *n.* skin 32/245.

hyde, hede, heyde, hide *v.* hide, conceal 2/171, 173, 4/197, 8/132, 20/251, 41/84; *refl.* Pr 329, 2/175, 3/195; blot out 22/26; keep secret 35/254; **hyd(de), hede** *pp.* hidden 15/179, 24/245, 32/20; wrapped 18/38; covered, clothed 18/252; **hyde** *imp. pl.* hide 32/18; **hyde** *pr. subj.* 6/157, 22/120.

hye, hey(e) *n.* haste: *on* (*in*) ~ quickly 16/86, 28/129, 30/215.

hy(e), hyȝe *v.* hasten, hurry 26/206, 37/44; *refl.* Pr 186, 8/236, 26/268; **hyȝ(e)** *imp. sg. refl.* 11/199; **hyȝ, hye** *imp. pl.* 37/44; *refl.* 2/284, 41/406.

hyghly see **hyȝly**.

hyght *n.* *on* ~ aloud, given openly 11/290; *in* ~ on high 19/102.

hyght, hyth, hygth *v.* **1** be named Pr 168, 504, 8/190, 224; *do* . . . ~ are called 21/87; **hyght, hattyht, hytht** *pr. 3 sg.* is called 16/31, 21/178, 41/501; **hyth, hyght** *pa. t.* 13/30, 38/65; **hyght** *pp.* called, named 12/214; **2** promised *in* **hyth, hyght** *pa. t.* 2/221, 40/6; **hyght** *pp.* 19/15, 35/290.

hyȝ(e), hy(e), hey(e), heyȝ, hygh, hie, high, hieȝ *adj.* exalted, holy, noble 3/6, 5/18, 239, 7/37, 89, 102, 135, 9/166, 175, 10/1, 11/39, 213, 319, 14/283, 401, 18/18, 41/123, 137; chief Pr 348; high 5/83, 14/129, 15/38; profound 21/63; full, complete 41/448; **hyest, hyȝest, heyest** *sup.* 8/33, 151, 11/8, 29/50; *hym* ~ he who is the highest 11/252; *as noun* 11/330; highest 23/110, 26/68; *adv.* high 10/255, 29/31; loudly 12/332.

hyȝht, hyght *n.* haste Pr 225, 10/150.

hyȝly, hyghly *adv.* highly 11/234; earnestly, devoutly 14/402, 21/36, 24/281.

hyȝnes(s) *n.* nobility, majesty, power 14/344, 25/93, 200.

hyll(e), hill(e), hyl *n.* hill Pr 87, 2/158, 5/83, 87, 107, 15/25, 23/154; **hyllys, hillis** *pl.* 32/17, 35/138, 41/191.

hylle *v.* cover 3/156, 26/376; **hylte** *pp.* buried 42/24.

hylle see **ill** *adj.*

hympne *n.* hymn 9/277 s.d.

hyn *pron.* him 32/84 s.d.

hynde *n.* hind 4/148.

hynde, hende *adv.* diligently 6/190; near 12/146; near at hand 41/155.

hynderawnce *n.* detriment 14/377.

hyndyr *v.* harm 3/110.

hyndrynge *vbl. n.* harm 25/333.

hyng(e) see **hang(e).**

hire, hyre see **she.**

hyryd *pp.* rented 10/459.

his(e) see **he, is.**

hyth, hytht see **hyght** *v.*

hitt *v.* hit 4/165; **hytte** *pl.* ~ *þe pynne* hit the mark, guess correctly 14/222; **hitte** *pp.* 4/157.

ho see **who(o).**

ho *v.* stop, cease 11/87.

Hoberd *n.* term of abuse used as name 20/15, 32/198, 206.

hod *n.* hood 29/157; **hodys** *pl.* 14/153, 26/164 s.d., 244 s.d.

hol see **ho(o)l.**

holde *n.* kingdom 18/34; *in* ~imprisoned 28/160, 31/174.

holde, holdyn, hald *v.* have, possess 10/311, 21/32; (with *with*) agree with 7/101; imprison 11/147; *in repreff . . .* ~ hold in contempt 12/115; (with *with*) obey 15/8, 34/267; engage in, carry on 21/110, 131; afflict 25/206; remain 26/138; depend 26/149; hold 27/425, 31/180; (with *a3ens*) resist, oppose 33/41–2; **hold(e), hald** *pr. 1 sg.* consider, regard as 3/16, 8/209, 10/26; (with *with*) agree with 7/85, 14/223; believe, suppose 3/93, 23/49, 27/242; hold 10/190, 34/289; **halt** *pr. 3 sg.* holds 31/172 s.d.; **holdyn, halt, halde** *pl.* ~ *on þi syde* side with you 1/68; ~ *hire wythall* support her 41/61; **considere** 41/88; **helde** *pa. t.* ~ *a3ens* challenged, disputed 15/263; **holde** *pp.* engaged in 24/148; **hold(e)** *imp. sg.* hold, keep 4/167, 4/248, 330; **holde** *imp. pl.* ~ *3oure pes* 25/137; **holde** *pr. subj.* ~ *stylle* should persist in 24/101.

holde see **old(e).**

holy, haly *adj.* holy 2/61, 6/31, 100, 108, 111, 7/102; ~ *G(o)st* Pr 166, 260, 265;

~ *Writ,* ~ *book* the Bible, Christian writings Pr 520, 23/131; ~ *Cherch(e),* ~ *Kyrke* 6/128, 19/196, 41/241; *as noun* holy one 11/253; **holyere** *comp. as noun* 8/186; **holyest** *sup.* 8/31, 10/298, 331.

holyly *adv.* holily 8/249.

holynese *n.* holiness 22/6.

Holond *n.* linen cloth made in Holland 26/73.

hom(e) *n.* home 5/46, 8/138, 9/226; *as adv.* homeward Pr 171, 180, 2/268; *I xal* ~ I shall go home 8/203.

homward(e) *adv.* homeward 8/118, 250, 13/156.

hond(e) see **hand(e).**

honesté *n.* propriety: *of 3oure* ~ out of decency 15/114; chastity, virtue 24/279.

honour(e), honowre, honure *v.* 1 worship, honour 6/114, 16/87, 18/190, 248, 26/425, 41/180; **honowre, honoure** *pr. 1 sg.* 5/4, 194, 10/217, 11/314; **honowre** *pl.* 1/50; **honouryng** *pr. p.* 41/17; **honouryd, onowryd** *pp.* 14/394, 37/95; **honure** *imp. sg.* 41/437; **honowre** *imp. pl.* 1/60; **honoure** *pr. subj.* 5/34; **2** honour, respect 10/303.

honowre, honour, honor, honure *n.* act of worship 1/64; honour, glory 5/259, 26/445, 27/374, 40/1, 41/180; *body of* ~ exalted body 41/433.

hont *v.* pursue, drive: ~ *hem vndyr hay* chase them into a net 18/81.

hoo see **who(o).**

ho(o)l *adj.* whole, entire Pr 517, 3/128, 9/301; healthy, sound, cured 28/106 s.d., 29/101, 30/200; safe, unharmed 28/119; intact 29/153.

hoold see **old(e).**

ho(o)so, whoso *pron.* whoever Pr 513, 6/42, 8/157, 10/187, 21/11, 24/38.

hoot see **hote.**

hope *n.* certitude, expectation 9/126, 26/160.

hope *pr. 1 sg.* think, believe, expect 14/149, 210, 291; (with *in*) trust in 25/311.

hore *n.* whore, adulteress 24/147.

horible, horryble see **orryble.**

hors *n.* horse 29/125, 30/31; **hors** *pl.* 27/111, 29/32.

hosyn *n.* hose, leggings 26/70.

hoso see **ho(o)so.**

hosoever *pron.* whoever 26/7.

hote, hoot adj. ardent 18/38; hot 27/252.

hougely adv. loudly 41/376.

hour(e) see **oure** n., **we**.

hous(e), howse n. house 6/113, 172, 8/222, 10/471, 18/247; ~ of haras stable 15/84; family 11/194, 244.

housholde n. household 10/468, 25/23.

how, whow, whov adv. how Pr 12, 15, 31, 8/103, 11/263, 270; ~ þat Pr 11, 81, 250; howsoever 18/121; why 19/64; as rel. pron. what 3/1, 30/77, 32/205.

how interj. ho! 5/73, 102, 6/25.

howe, howyth see **owe**.

howevyr adv. however 14/80.

howlott n. owlets, owls 20/15.

hownde n. dog 8/152, 11/87; **houndis** pl. 41/488.

howre, howrys see **oure** n.

howth see **ought**.

howtyn, howte v. cry out, hoot 20/15, 112.

humanyté, humanité n. human nature 27/407, 41/96.

humylyté, humylité n. humility 11/291, 15/116, 26/428.

hundryd, vndryd, honderyd, hunderyd card. num. as adj. 4/206, 211, 11/1, 13/157A, 34/204; as noun 34/200, 202.

hungyr n. hunger 23/68, 70, 71.

hurle v. ~ wyth hurl (oneself) against, assail 41/401.

hurt(e) n. hurt 15/128, 156, 23/117.

hurte v. hurt 25/396; **hurte** pl. 25/228; **hurte** pp. damaged: nott ~ of virgynité with virginity intact 15/233; not ~ of his nature undamaged, unaltered 21/98.

husbond(e), hosbonde, hosbund n. husband 2/111, 117, 122, 8/234, 12/63.

huswyff n. wife, housewife 14/189.

icast v. say 3/19.

iche see **ech(e)**.

idyl adj. futile, false 25/66.

ydolatrye n. idols 7/106.

ierarchie, ierarchye n. a division of angels 11/38; above the ~ higher than the angels 41/11.

if(f), yf(f), yif, 3yf(f), 3iff, 3ef conj. if Pr 58, 275, 287, 290, 2/141, 152, 8/64, 11/142, 14/124, 24/127, 26/173, 299, 29/29, 41/44, 56, 63; ~ þat Pr 13, 104, 525.

ignorans n. ignorance 34/112.

ilke adj. ~ a each, every 20/48.

ill, hylle adj. of poor quality 2/77; evil, harmful 26/218, 27/173.

ylle, ill adv. wrongly 3/105, 12/151, 27/193; bitterly, severely 4/32, 25/78; with displeasure: it lyke þe ... ~ it may displease you 24/181; harshly 34/55.

illusyon n. deception 7/31.

ymagynacyon n. act of imagination 14/350.

imcomparabyl, incomparabil adj. incomparable 8/201, 41/278.

immaculat, inmaculate adj. immaculate 27/409, 28/149.

immortalyté n. immortality 9/126.

impossyble, inpossible adj. impossible 11/210, 259, 41/146.

in, inne adv. in, inside Pr 74, 4/208, 24/21; ~ ondyr subordinate to 18/84.

in, inne, yn prep. in, into Pr 5, 14, 21, 3/56, 19/46, 20/210, 27/560, 41/231, 309; on Pr 94, 226, 296; (of time) at, during Pr 398, 5/180, 8/97 s.d.; as 8/198.

inasmyche adv. inasmuch 41/508.

inbassett n. message 8/227; mission 11/213.

incarnacyon n. incarnation 11/280, 324, 15/92.

incensynge vbl. n. offering of incense 13/77.

incheson, encheson n. causation 11/332; occasion, opportunity 27/271; reason: be þis ~ according to this reasoning 30/80.

inclyne v. refl. (with onto) accede (to) 3/50; **inclyne** pl. bow, kneel 14/388; **inclyne** imp. sg. direct, bestow 6/7.

includyd pp. included 6/123, 125.

incomperhensibele n. infinite being PS 2.

inconuenyens n. improper act or utterance 13/180A.

incressyd see **encres(e)** v.

indede adv. indeed Pr 48, 298, 4/15.

indew v. endue Pr 431.

indygnacyon n. indignation 8/105.

indyte, indite, endyte v. indict 24/51, 124; accuse, slander 42/103.

indure see **endure**.

indute ppl. adj. clothed, endued 22/164.

inerytawns, enherytawns n. inheritance 26/100, 157.

infaunte n. child 5/69.

inf(f)ormacyon *n.* information 21/192; *haue (more)* ~ be told (more) 9/197, 21/282; *of such* ~ so knowledgeable 21/135; *had* ~ been told 39/22; instruction: *brought to* ~ taught 21/65; *зeve* ~ instruct you 27/393, PS 10.

infynyth *adj.* infinite 41/95.

infyrmyté *n.* infirmity 41/464.

influens *n.* inspiration, influence 7/2; inherent nature 9/266; influx 21/192.

informyng see **enforme.**

inhabith *pp. was* ~ resided 41/4.

inheryte see **eneryth.**

iniquité, iniquyté *n.* iniquity 9/142, 11/24, 146.

injoye *v.* rejoice 41/520; **injoyeth** *pr. 3 sg.* rejoices 41/116; **enjouyd, enjoyd, injouyid** *pa. t.* gladdened 11/340; rejoiced 13/54; enjoyed, rejoiced in 13/85.

inke‾*n.* ink 32/176 s.d.

innovmberabyl *adj.* innumerable 26/54.

inow see **anow(e).**

inportable *adj.* unbearable 29/53.

inquysissyon *n.* inquiry 9/106.

inqwere *imp. sg.* investigate, inquire 26/336.

in-same *adv.* together 2/11, 20/185, 38/41.

inspyracyon *n.* divine communication 11/322.

inspyre *v.* inspire, fill 22/165; **inspyrynge** *pr. p.* 13/53; **inspyred** *pp.* 8/192; **enspyre** *pr. subj.* 4/28.

instawns, instawnce *n.* request 26/272, 27/63; urging, persuasion 26/27; *at his* ~ at his command 27/136.

intellygens, intelligence *n.* knowledge, news 26/273, 434; *зaff hym* ~ informed him 13/33; understanding 27/442.

intencyon *n.* meaning, significance 26/31; intention 26/47, 237; will, wish 26/63.

intende *pr. 1 sg.* intend 37/46; **intendyn** *pl.* 29/6.

intent, entent(e) *n.* **1** intention, will, desire Pr 147, 338, 457, 3/43, 26/32, 46; *to Goddys* ~ as God wished 9/12; *at (one's)* ~ at (one's) will 21/39, 26/205, 27/139; **ententis** *pl.* 41/75; **2** attention: *take good* ~ give heed 6/52; **3** mind 11/262; **4** opinion 14/168.

interpretacyon *n.* interpretation 27/395.

into *prep.* until 2/246, 258, 27/388.

invm *pp.* understood 16/67.

inwardly *adv.* ~ *in hert* sincerely, within the heart 3/26.

ypocryte, ypocrite *n.* hypocrite 24/42, 49, 58.

irke *v.* be weary 19/194.

yron *n.* iron chains 27/105.

is, ys, his *pr. 3 sg.* is Pr 18, 19, 21, 10/159, 171, 171, 11/149, 39/4; *pl.* are (by attraction to sg. noun) 21/263; (with two subjects) 2/210, 6/31, 9/75; *pl. aux.* 6/39.

is *poss. pron.* see **he.**

it, yt, itt *pron. 3 sg.* it Pr 19, 39, 135, 10/167, 25/138, 27/195, 414; he (i.e. his body) 34/135.

iwys, iwus *adv.* indeed, certainly Pr 199, 388, 462, 13/168A.

jape *v.* have sexual intercourse 12/44; **japyn** *pl.* ~ *with* mock, make sport of 31/10; **jape** *pr. subj.* speak foolishly or jokingly 14/314.

jebet *n.* gallows, i.e. the Cross 27/129; **gebettys** *pl.* 29/31.

jematrye *n.* geometry 21/19n.

jentyl(l), gentyl *adj.* noble, distinguished Pr 105, 7/49, 20/142, 34/89; excellent 2/37, 40/24; kind, gracious, good 10/14, 327, 470; **gentyllest** *sup. as noun* 11/330.

jentylman *n.* man of noble birth 26/71, 31/192.

jentylnesse *n.* generosity, kindness 34/73.

jentylwoman *n.* woman of noble birth 26/102.

Jesse *n.* genealogical tree of Christ 7/49; ~ *rote* Pr 105, 7/25, 74; (as personif.) 7/22.

jewge, juge *n.* judge 7/87, 26/166, 175, 211; **jewgys** *pl.* 26/195, 223, 238.

jewge *v.* **1** sentence, condemn 27/108; **jewge** *pr. subj.* 31/60; **2** govern 30/142.

jewgement see **jugement.**

Jewys, Juwys, Jewus, Зewys *n.* Jews Pr 320, 336, 382, 30/24, 32/180, 34/21.

joy(e) *n.* joy Pr 192, 432, 1/31; **joys, joyis** *pl.* 8/191, 234, 18/233, 27/73.

joye *v.* ~ *of* rejoice in 16/140; enjoy 35/104; **joyth** *pr. 3 sg.* gladdens 7/100.

joyful(l) *adj.* joyful 8/231, 9/47, 48; *as noun* 9/129n.

joyntys *n.* joints 28/44.

jolyere *adj. comp.* jollier 18/77.

juge see **jewge** *n.*

jugement, jewgement, jwgement *n.*
decree 2/144; punishment 9/173, 24/8,
87, 27/110, 29/49, 51, 31/85; verdict,
decision, judgement 24/260, 26/330,
30/128; *gyf* ~ pass judgement 26/292,
318, 335.

Juré, Jewry *n.* the Jews, Jewry 26/257, 30/
12, 103.

**jurnay, jurney, jorné, jorney, jurny,
jornay, jurné** *n.* journey 5/52, 10/157,
166, 190, 13/14, 20, 15/23, 311, 18/192,
26/385, 444, 41/185; business, task 20/
267, 23/64, 29/74.

**jurresdyccyon, jurediccyon, jurysdyc-
cyon** *n.* authority, power 29/71, 30/123,
143.

just(e) *adj.* just 24/95, 194.

justyce, justyse *n.* judge Pr 348, 14/317,
34/46, 35/249.

kachyd see **cacche**.

kage *n.* elevated stage or seat 18/54, 151.

kayser, caysere *n.* emperor, ruler 20/
134, 138, 22/85, 42/15.

kaytyff *n.* scoundrel 20/194; **caytyvys** *pl.*
2/170.

kall(e), kallyst see **call(e)**.

kan *n.* jar, can 27/36 s.d.

kan, can *pr. 1 sg.* 1 can, am able to 3/20,
67, 84, 8/63, 11/161, 25/122; **canst,
kanst, can, kone** *pr. 2 sg.* 6/169, 14/66,
21/48, 28/79, 30/216, 31/130, 32/147;
kan, can *pr. 3 sg.* 3/26, 11/154, 16/126,
20/240. 21/56, 25/132; **kan, can, con,
kone** *pl.* Pr 10, 8/144, 9/45, 14/167,
21/5, 53, 29/137, 31/185, 41/374;
cowde, kowde *pa. t.* 14/305, 24/267,
*31/19, 91; **kan, con** *pr. subj.* 19/30, 32/
109, 110; **cowde** *pa. subj.* 24/57, 63; 2
know 20/262; **kan** *pr. 3 sg.* 20/189; **kan**
pl. þat ~ *3oure good* who know what to
do 15/143; 3 offer, express (thanks) 30/
194; **cone** *pl.* 29/120; 4 is able (to be) *in*
can *pr. 3 sg.* 26/102; **cannot(t), kannot,
cannat, kannat** *pr. 2 sg.* (neg.) cannot
3/163, 6/22, 8/93, 10/175, 11/160, 235,
14/350, 37/7; **kannot** *pr. 3 sg.* 30/228;
kannot *pl.* 14/37, 30/53.

kary *v.* transport 15/18.

karpe *v.* cry out, wail 20/67.

kast see **cast(e)**.

keye *n.* key 2/302, 25/428; **keyes** *pl.* 41/
244.

ken see **kyn(ne)**.

ken *v.* acknowledge, proclaim, know 13/
122; recognize 29/200; **ken** *pr. 1 sg.*
know 13/56; **kenne** *pl.* know 40/9;
kende *pp.* called 11/191.

kend(e), kynde *n.* kindred 9/266; generation 13/96, 96; human form 16/59, 109;
class of creatures (i.e. humans) 19/95,
41/516; nature 26/10, 35/49; *in* ~ by
nature 2/262, 41/152; *of* ~ by nature, by
birth 11/242; *ageyn(s)* ~ contrary to
natural law 21/183, 26/229; *naterell* ~
human nature, instinct 26/111; way 28/
186; body, person 41/159; **kyndys,
kynnys** *gen. sg. euery* ~ every kind of
4/120; *in no* ~ *wyse* in no way 12/50.

kend(e), kynde *adj.* benevolent, gracious, noble 18/212, 259, 30/166, 32/83,
137, 38/13; *as noun* 16/104; brave, faithful 20/207; innate 25/134.

kendely, kyndely *adj.* natural 3/33;
beneficent, kindly, noble 19/117.

kendnessys *n.* kind deeds 28/184.

kene *adj.* brave, warlike 18/13, 20/28, 42/
15.

kep(e) *n.* care, attention 20/82, 25/27, 27/
499.

kepe, keppe, kepyn *v.* 1 keep, guard,
preserve Pr 419, 5/52, 8/92, 18/300, 34/
227; *refl.* 4/63; **kepyst** *pr. 2 sg.* 6/111;
kepe, kepyn *pl.* 22/171, 30/74; **kept(e)**
pp. 4/124, 11/83, 248; **kepe, kepp(e)**
imp. sg. 4/76, 8/164, 10/292, 470, 34/307;
refl. 6/101, 145, 169; **kepe, kepyth** *imp.
pl.* 8/241, 27/487, 27/510, 34/265; **kepe**
pr. subj. 4/71, 82, 5/158; 2 abide by, obey
2/73, 6/106, 187; **kept(e)** *pp.* 6/44, 21/
244, 26/408; ~ *of* observed by 9/172;
kepe *pr. subj.* 6/49; 3 reserve (for oneself) 3/95, 113, 8/57; **kepe** *pl.* 21/30; 4
look after, take care of 3/164, 10/315,
11/227; 5 keep imprisoned 11/88; 6
celebrate, conduct 27/17, 44, 366; 7
hold (by force) 38/178, 186; **kepe** *pl.* 38/
189; **keptyn** *pa. pl.* 38/283; 8 maintains,
preserves *in* **kepyth** *pr. 3 sg.* 1/24;
retains 6/19; **kepyng** *pr. p.* keeping,
continuing 26/136.

kepere *n.* keeper, protector 3/161, 10/
290, 30/12; **kepers** *pl.* Pr 417.

kepyng *vbl. n.* confinement, imprisonment 28/159; keeping 10/408, 11/225.

kerchere *n.* kerchief 5/179.

kerchy *n.* kerchief, the sudarium 32/44 s.d., 48.

kest see cast(e).

kyd(de) *pp.* known 5/9, 14/63, 18/37.

kyl(l)(e) *v.* kill Pr 90, 241, 382; kylle *pr. 1 sg.* 3/152, 41/38; kylle *pl.* 2/152; kylde, kyllyd *pa. t.* 38/67, 389; kyllyd *pp.* Pr 60, 4/180; kylle *imp. sg.* ~ ... *and scloo* put to death 5/88; kyllyth, kylle *imp. pl.* 20/29, 24/175; kylle *pr. subj.* 6/132.

kyllyng *vbl. n.* slaying Pr 233.

kyndam *n.* kingdom 41/524.

kynde see kend(e).

kyndely see kendely.

kyng(e) *n.* king Pr 194, 206, 209; kyngys *gen. sg.* 15/47; kyng(g)ys *pl.* Pr 109, 204, 208; kynggys *gen. pl.* 18/227.

kyngham, kyngdom, kyngdham, kingham, kyngdam *n.* kingdom 23/161, 26/132, 39/33; dominion, kingship 30/106, 107, 109.

kyn(ne), ken *n.* kin, family 10/216, 14/319, 18/162; *syb of þi* ~ your blood relative 14/114; *mannys* ~ mankind 16/12, 27/156, 33/31; people 27/200.

kynred(e), kynreed *n.* descendants, stock Pr 139, 146, 7/51; *of(f)* ~ *(to)* related (to), descended (from) 10/143, 164, 267; kindred, kinsfolk 8/83, 10/410, 11/274, 14/355, 25/112; kinship 15/51; kynredys *pl.* tribes 8/36.

kynsmen, kynnysmen *n.* kinsmen 10/126, 139, 184.

kyrke *n,* Church: see holy.

kyrtyl *n.* man's tunic or cloak 18/82; woman's gown 31/57 s.d.

kys(se) *v.* kiss Pr 326, 458, 9/76; kys(se), cus *pr. 1 sg.* 5/25, 174, 8/79, 9/276; kyssyth *pr. 3 sg.* 28/104 s.d.; kyssyng *pr. p.* 41/451; kyssyd *pa. t.* 13/177A; kysse *imp. sg.* 5/24, 10/389, 34/125; kys *pr. subj.* Pr 460.

kyth *n.* country 16/104.

kythe *imp. pl.* show 10/28.

kytt *v.* cut 25/143, 38/286.

knag *n.* pointed rock *41/38.

knave, knaue *n.* commoner 15/196, 35/212; rogue, knave 41/38; ~ *chylderyn (childeryn)*, ~ *gerlys* boys 18/91, 20/18,

29, 59; knavys *pl.* commoners, knaves 32/89.

knawe *v.* gnaw 29/35; knawe *pl.* 20/273.

knawe see know(e).

kne *n.* knee Pr 84, 3/28, 10/117; *on* ~ ... *fall, falle down on* ~ kneel Pr 215, 5/233, 10/114; *beforn my cruel* ~ before me in my cruelty 18/218; *oure* ~ our knees 5/250; knes, kneys *pl.* 1/48, 8/238, 9/229, 268.

knele, knelyn *v.* kneel 23/179, 32/83; knele *pr. 1 sg.* 9/204, 18/243, 251; knelyth *pr. 3 sg.* 19/20 s.d., 30/10 s.d.; knelyng(e), knelende, kneland *pr. p.* 5/250, 8/146, 10/117, 15/287, 41/39; knelyd *pa. t.* Pr 84, 135; knele *imp. sg.* 5/87; knelyth *imp. pl.* 9/216.

knyf(f) *n.* knife 2/319, 5/94, 200.

knyt, knyth, knett *pp.* united 1/13, 21/92, 26/162; fastened, knit 27/306, 35/279.

knok *n.* blow 29/141.

knyth, knyght *n.* knight Pr 403, 424, 16/13, 20/225, 31/192, 35/212; kepyng-~ keeper 3/162; knyghtys, knyt(t)ys, knyhtys, knythtys, knygtys, knyhtis *pl.* Pr 219, 228, 230, 241, 418, 18/13, 90, 20/28, 34/80 s.d., 35/266, 270, 273, 41/90.

knop *n.* tassel, tuft 26/164 s.d.

know(e), knawe *v.* 1 know 2/187, 11/145, 12/132, 21/150; know(e) *pr. 1 sg.* 3/165, 7/93, 12/167; knowyst, knowist *pr. 2 sg.* 12/128, 15/266, 18/153, 30/101; (with ellips. of 'thou') 31/128; knowyth *pr. 3 sg.* 8/140, 9/292, 30/228; know(e), knew, knowyth, knove, knawe *pl.* Pr 474, 10/370, 11/90, 25/237, 26/195, 28/144, 41/42; knowyng *pr. p.* 30/114; knownyn, knowe, iknowe, knawe *pp.* 1/1, 4/10, 7/50, 97, 113, 14/63, 310, 30/174; knowe *imp. pl.* 26/307; knowe *pr. subj.* 10/409; know of 18/184; 2 learn, find out 3/1, 15, 29; ~ *for oure levynge* learn how to live 3/13n.; knowyth, knowe *imp. pl.* 10/170, 26/186; 3 know by experience, practice 9/234; knew *pa. t.* ~ *of mannys maculacyon* sinned with man 14/334; 4 acknowledge, honour 10/3, 25/441; know *pr. 1 sg.* 18/242; knowyn *pp.* 14/404; 5 have consideration for, know 16/112; 6 know to be *in knowe pr. 1 sg.* 2/200; 7 recognize 33/46.

knowyng(e) *vbl. n.* knowledge: **haue** ~ know 9/107, 10/194, 13/2; *we haue* ~ we have been told 10/194; ~ *of* sexual intercourse with 11/247.

knowlech(e), knowlage, knowlege, knowlache *n.* knowledge Pr 250, 10/106, 113, 15/308, 21/245.

knowlych, knowlage, knowlege *pr. 1 sg.* acknowledge, declare 7/82, 12/203, 15/284; **knowlych** *imp. sg.* 14/225.

kok see **cok.**

kokewolde see **cok(e)wold(e).**

kold see **co(o)ld(e).**

kow *n.* cow 30/31.

krepe see **creppe(e).**

kroune see **crowne.**

kunnyng, conyng *ppl. adj.* wise, possessing knowledge 2/158; clever, learned 31/11.

kunnyng see **connyng(e)** *vbl. n.*

kure *pr. 1 sg.* cover 5/179; **curyng** *pr. p.* 41/284.

kusse *n.* kiss 8/241.

kutte *n.* private parts: *kepe þi* ~ defend your virtue 24/152n.

laboryn, labore *v.* work 10/467, 15/35; **laboryd** *pp.* 9/133, 12/12.

laboryng *vbl. n.* working 2/53.

labour, labore *n.* labour 2/277, 323, 10/155; task, exercise 9/192, 10/456; a difficult journey 15/13, 38/205; efforts, pains taken 23/149, 27/332.

lacche *v.* take 2/234.

Ladyes, Ladys *n. gen. sg.* Lady's Pr 172, 9/295, 13/156A, 34/121 s.d.

lay *n.*[1] practice, manner of life 6/140, 14/40, 42/119; law 18/4, 76; law, *or* way of life 20/40.

lay *n.*[2] tale 14/231.

lak *n. withowtyn* ~ without fail, truly 4/191.

lake *n.* pit 31/32, 41/148; grave 35/213, 37/8, 20.

lakke *pr. subj.* is lacking 26/103.

lame *v.* injure, wound 18/76.

lamentacyon *n.* lamentation 11/50.

langage *n.* words, talk Pr 248, 6/136, 14/130; *withoutyn* ~ putting it briefly (or plainly) 4/16; *hast þi* ~ speak, converse 6/92; *euyl (evyl)* ~ evil rumours 10/348, 472; language: *all maner* ~ every variety of language Pr 499.

langoris, langowrys *n.* afflictions, sufferings 26/390, 28/173.

langour *pr. pl.* languish 41/464.

lanterne *n.* lantern 11/292, 19/125, 29/98; **lanternys** *pl.* 27/342, 28/80 s.d.

lappe *n.* lap Pr 226, 21/41, 34/121 s.d.; *so nere oure* ~ so close to us 38/219.

lappyd *pa. t.* sealed 13/35.

large *adj.* full 32/64.

las *n.* snare 2/224.

lasse *conj.* unless 2/17.

las(se) see **lesse** *adj.*

lat(e) see **lete** *v.*

late, latt *adv.* lately, a short time ago 14/67, 21/156, 35/167; not for a long time 41/394.

Latyn *n.* Latin Pr 500.

laumpys *n.* lamps 41/299.

laue see **loff.**

lawe, lave *n.* law Pr 126, 291, 6/142, 41/40; ~ *of lyff* law about living 6/163; *haue* ~ receive judgement 24/182; teaching 3/18; practice, way of life 14/104; **lawys, lawes, lawis** *pl.* Pr 95, 97, 100, 4/232, 6/40, 43, 41/33; ~ *of lyff* 6/56.

lawful(l) *adj.* lawful 24/88, 31/148.

lawh₃, lawghe *v.* laugh, smile 14/69, 15/182; **lawghe** *pr. 1 sg.* 15/191; **lowh** *pr. 3 sg.* (with *on*) smiles (at) 2/66.

lec(c)herous *adj.* lecherous 6/140, 27/420, 42/119.

lech see **lyke.**

lech(e) *n.* healer, protector 18/184, 204, 230; **lechis** *pl.* physicians 20/197.

leche *v.* heal 22/144; tend (wounds) 36/3.

lechory, lycherye *n.* lechery 4/218, 235, 6/179, 26/89.

led see **leed(e)** *n.*

led(d)yr, leddere *n.* ladder 32/176 s.d., 34/121 s.d., 121 s.d.; **lederys** *pl.* 34/113 s.d.

lede, ledyn *v.* **1** lead, conduct (life) Pr 132, 154, 2/320, 334, 6/112, 10/324; **lede** *pr. 1 sg.* 10/155, 32/286; **ledyth** *pr. 3 sg.* 25/306; **lad** *pp. of goodly lyff* ~ of a well conducted life Pr 8; **2** lead, guide, take 11/183, 13/165, 24/74, 31/1st s.d.; **ledyth** *pr. 3 sg.* Pr 398, 31/117 s.d.; **lede, ledyn** *pl.* 28/148 s.d., 30/40 s.d., 152 s.d.; **ledyng** *pr. p.* 28/148 s.d.; **led(de), lede** *pa. t.* Pr 212, 16/75, 18/315; **led(de)** *pp.* Pr 222, 10/21, 18/166; **lede** *imp. sg.* 18/119; **lede** *imp. pl.* 30/144,

146, 253; **lede** *pr. subj.* 10/398, 28/146; **3** endure, suffer 27/224; **lede** *pr. 1 sg.* 28/51; **leed** *pa. t.* 35/101; **4** engaged in in **ledde** *pp.* 14/104; **lede** *imp. sg.* 6/183; **lede** *pr. subj.* 6/140; **5** guide, *or* teach in **leed** *pl.* 35/222n.

ledys *n.* landholdings, *or* peoples: *londys and* ~ lands and peoples, *or* landed property 20/123.

leed(e), led *n.* lead Pr 421, 18/273, 34/314.

leff *n.* leaf 2/174, 175; **levys** *pl.* 2/172.

lef(f) see **leve** *adj.* and *adv.*, **leve** *v.*[1]

lefful *adj.* permitted by law 10/93, 30/97.

left(e), lyfte, lefft *adj.* left (side or direction) 26/137, 143, 31/202, 209, 34/274.

leggys, legges *n.* legs 4/129, 10/227, 14/88, 26/79.

leyn, ley *v.* **1** bet, stake (as wager) 4/164, 29/157, 34/244, 35/221; **ley, lay** *pr. 1 sg.* 10/199, 14/60; **2** put, place, lay 9/41, 28/129, 31/212 s.d., 32/48 s.d., 41/450; **ley** *pr. 1 sg.* 20/83; *refl.* lie down 18/277; **leyth** *pr. 3 sg.* 19/176 s.d., 34/121 s.d.; **ley** *pl.* 28/104 s.d.; **leyd** *pa. t.* 29/112; *refl.* 35/195; **leyd(e), layde** *pp.* 15/280, 22/169, 25/16, 27/301; *his leggys to here hath* ~ i.e. has had sexual intercourse with her 14/88; *togedyr* ~ considered together 30/191; **ley** *imp.* 2/174; ~ *on hem* bind them with 27/105; **3** set aside 35/209; **ley** *imp. pl.* ~ . . . *downe* discontinue, put aside 18/176.

leyke *pr. subj.* (forming *imp.*) (let us) move quickly 16/75.

leysere *n.* opportune time 21/198; *be* ~ in the course of time, with deliberation *32/92 s.d.

leke see **lyke.**

lely-whyte, lely-wyte *adj.* lily-white 10/243, 15/305.

lemys see **lyme.**

lenage see **lynage.**

lende *imp. pl.*[1] go 18/263; **lent** *pp.* lived 24/85.

lende *v.*[2] lend 27/295; **lent** *pp.* given, granted 21/34.

lenyall *adj.* lineal 7/74.

lenth *n.* length 30/142.

lere *v.* learn 2/161, 3/18, 21/62; *be to* ~ need instruction 14/152; teach 28/139, 30/236, 35/242; **lere** *pr. 1 sg.* declare, *or* read 41/3; **lere, lare** *imp. sg.* learn 22/84; tell 41/252; teach 41/431.

lern(e) *v.* **1** learn Pr 95, 6/57, 190; **lerne** *imp. sg.* 5/41; **lerne** *imp. pl.* 11/111; **2** teach Pr 97, 9/209, 252; **lernyst** *pr. 2 sg.* 10/447; **lernyth** *pr. 3 sg.* 10/439; **lernyd** *pp.* 13/151A, 27/437.

lernyd *ppl. adj.* learned PS 9, 11; as *noun* 8/15.

lernynge *vbl. n.* knowledge, learning 21/35, 149.

lees, les see **les(se)** *n.*

lese, lesyn *v.* **1** ruin, destroy 23/19, **lese** *pl.* 10/276; **lorn(e), lore** *pp.* 4/231, 6/153, 11/58, 14/344, 20/254, 38/253; **2** kill 5/171; **lorn** *pp.* 5/213; **3** get no return from, waste 23/208; **lorn** *pp.* 23/149; **4** lose, be deprived of (with fut. sense) *in* **lese** *pl.* 34/197; **lorn** *pp.* 13/169A, 15/260, 19/175; **5** doomed *in* **lorn, lore** *pp.* 15/281, 24/23, 27/242; **6** missing, gone 25/325, 37/15, 38/163; **7** damn *in* **lese** *imp. sg.* 6/80.

lesyng *vbl. n.* lying: *without* ~ truly Pr 119.

les(se), lees *n.* falsehood, deceit Pr 321, 21/167, 25/75, 36/13; *without (withow-tyn)* ~ truly Pr 94, 6/27.

lesse, las(se) *adj. comp.* less, lesser 27/376; *þe* ~ *lay* the inferior law, i.e. Christianity 18/76; *þe* ~ 32/285, 36/22; as *noun* Pr 7, 39/81; *both(e) more and* ~ everything Pr 470, 14/376; *adv.* 21/127, 22/125.

lesse *conj.* ~ *þan* (than) unless 4/20, 6/142, 20/140.

lesse *v.* abate 25/15.

lest(e) *adj. sup.* least, smallest 24/12, 26/477; as *noun* 41/239.

lest(e), last(e) *v.* last, continue, endure 2/47, 10/349, 11/65, 13/174, 21/51, 25/280; **leste** *pr. 1 sg.* go on living 8/170; **lestyth, lestyght** *pr. 3 sg.* lasts 10/312, 23/99, 33/24, 39/34.

lest(e) see **lyst(e)** *n.*, **lyste** *v.*

lestyng *ppl. adj.* lasting: *evyrmore* ~ eternal Pr 198.

lete *v.* **1** let, allow 10/337, 24/207, 26/227; **let(e)** *pl.* Pr 332, 26/235; **latyng** *pr. p.* 28/44 s.d.; **lete, lett, late** *imp. sg.* 4/7, 5/7, 8, 24/39, 37/100; **let(e), lat(e), lett** *imp. pl.* 5/27, 11/101, 124; ~ *be(ne)* cease, desist 5/133, 10/280, 12/74; ~ *be* leave alone 12/186; **let(e), late, lett, latt** *pr. subj.* 26/183, 31/143, 149;

lete (*cont.*)
(forming *imp.*) 2/322, 3/3, 10; **2** lose (life) 2/98; **3** let pass 25/265; **lete** *pr. 1 sg.* ~ *a crakke* break wind 23/195; **4** cease 34/294; **5** leave: *doun* ~ forsake 24/283; **letyth** *pr. 3 sg.* 31/140 s.d.; **6** cause to, make *in* **let(e), lett, lat(e)** *imp. sg.* Pr 140, 11/47, 167; ~ *se(n)* let's see 5/79, 6/30, 45; **let(e)** *imp. pl.* 26/237, 240, 319; ~ *se(n)* 9/32, 45, 11/126.

lett *v.* **1** diminish, impair 20/40; **2** linger 32/207; **3** hinder, prevent 25/169, 26/354; **lett** *imp.* 12/150, 14/235, 19/73.

lettyng, latyng *vbl. n.* hindrance, obstacle Pr 125; delay 3/4; *withowte* ~ without hindrance or delay 27/20.

lettyr *n.* reading and writing 21/62; **letterys, letteris** *pl.* letters 9/262, 42/77.

leve, leue *n.* permission 13/155, 26/360, 29/5; *take (one's)* ~ (*of, at*) 9/66, 10/406, 14/389; *toke...* ~ *at* 13/175A.

leve, lef *adj.* dear 2/304, 310; pleasing (to sb.) 41/401; **levyr** *adj. comp.* had (*haue, haddyst*) ~ would rather 3/52, 12/11, 133; **leff** *adv.* gladly 27/261.

leve, lef *v.*[1] leave Pr 331, 9/63, 34/157 s.d.; disregard, leave (it) 3/102; leave alone: *þus hym* ~ let him persist in this way 27/82; **levyn't** omit it 27/465 s.d.; ~ *of* leave off, desist 32/76 s.d.; **lefte** *pa. t.* left 26/19; left undone 29/6; **left(e)** *pp.* left 8/90, 9/275, 24/266; **leff** *imp. sg.* desist from 19/41; **leve** *imp. pl.* stop 32/165.

leve, levyn, lyve, lyff *v.*[2] live 2/277, 239, 3/38, 5/8, 8/131, 248, 9/40, 19/53, 20/175; **leve** *pr. 1 sg.* 8/170, 32/222; **levyth, levith, lyvyth** *pr. 3 sg.* 5/119, 8/151, 25/303, 36/141, 38/293, 296; **leve** *pl.* 27/433; **levyng(e), lyvyng** *pr. p.* 9/261, 20/146, 38/371, 41/7; **levyd** *pa. t.* 9/12; **levyd, lyued, lyved** *pp.* 8/246, 14/335, 41/56, 380; *had* ~ would have lived 25/290; **levyth** *imp. pl.* 39/45; **leve** *pr. subj.* 24/279, 25/51.

leve *v.*[3] believe 26/230.

levers *n.* those who live, *or* believers 11/272n.

levyn *n.* light (of the sun, the star, or lightning) 16/3.

levyng(e) *vbl. n.* manner of living, conduct 3/13, 4/30, 82; *of* ~ in (one's) conduct 4/18, 22/7; *good men of* ~ men who live virtuously 22/173; sustenance 12/11; manner of living, *or* belief 19/40; life 30/199.

levynge, lyvenge *ppl. adj.* living 25/298, 35/180, 36/102, 38/221.

levyr *n.* liver 20/71.

lewd(e) *adj.* lewd, lascivious 24/283; *as noun* uneducated people 8/15.

lewdnes *n.* ignorance, foolishness, wickedness 15/265.

lyberary *n.* body (of laws) 9/252.

lyberté *n.* liberty; *at hese* ~ freely 11/148.

lycens, lysens *n.* permission 13/155, 31/178, 34/121.

lych(e) see **lyke.**

lycherye see **lechory.**

lycorys *n.* liquorice plant 2/35.

lycour *n.* spice 18/62.

ly(e), lyne *v.* **1** lie 18/279, 20/188, 25/64, 144, 384, 28/44 s.d.; **ly3** *pr. 1 sg.* 35/61; **lyggyst** *pr. 2 sg.* 16/111; **lyth(e)** *pr. 3 sg.* 20/99, 249, 25/110; **ly(e), lyth, lyne** *pl.* 10/160, 11/20, 20/116, 26/473, 30/212; ~ *in* depend on 30/208; **lyeng** *pr. p.* 29/108; **loyn** *pa. t.* 29/111; **loyn** *pp.* Pr 428; **ly** *pr. subj.* 25/32; **2** be, reside 11/4; **lyth, lyse** *pr. 3 sg.* Pr 430, 26/171, 31/82; ~ *not to me* doesn't fall to me 30/140; (with *in*) depends on 11/168; **ly** *pl.* 15/69; **loyn** *pp.* 11/3; **ly** *pr. subj.* 11/102; **3** lies, is located *in* **lyth, lyght** *pr. 3 sg.* Pr 213, 450, 10/156, 15/160; **4** appears, is found *in* **lyce** *pr. 3 sg.* 10/85; **5** leads, goes 18/16, 26/157; **6** was, occurred *in* **lay** *pa. t.* 35/219.

lyist, lyest *pr. 2 sg.* tell lies 12/43, 35/174; **lyede** *pa. t.* 20/174.

lyf(f)(e), lyve, lyue *n.* **1** life Pr 8, 91, 132, 306, 7/78, 9/196, 25/355; *on* ~ alive 3/182, 4/209, 217; **lyvys** *gen. sg.* 2/246, 258, 4/34; **lyvys** *pl.* 4/121, 34/194; **2** manner of living, conduct 2/213, 5/7, 6/56; *be maydonys o* ~ live as virgins 21/240; **3** lineage 7/29; **4** living person 20/227.

lyff see **leve** *v.*[2]

lyfte see **left(e)** *adj.*

lyfte *v.* lift, raise 10/255, 25/403; **lyftyth** *pr. 3 sg.* ~ *up* elevates, exalts 8/141; **lyfte** *pp.* 9/108; **lyfte** *imp.* 14/260, 25/22, 33.

lyght, lyth, lith *n.* spiritual light 1/25, 37, 9/181, 11/292, 16/100, 19/153, 41/245;

light 15/167, 177, 16/15; *sterrys of* ~
bright stars 1/30; **lithtis, lytys, lythis**
pl. lamps, lights 28/148 s.d., 41/299,
307; spiritual radiances, glories 41/177.
lyght, lyth *adj.*[1] bright 8/174, 19/48;
righteous, pure 9/252.
lyght, lyth *adj.*[2] light in weight, *or of*
small value 10/247; unchaste 14/96;
eager 18/324; easy to bear 32/261; swift
35/298; joyful 41/503; **lyghtere** *comp.*
more eager 19/57.
lyght see **lythtyn.**
lyghtly see **lythly.**
lyghtnes(se) *n.* brightness 15/165, PS 3.
lyke *n.* like, equal 22/30.
lyke, lych(e), lech, leke, like *adj.* similar, like 8/189; ~ *to* (*onto*) 9/245 s.d., 20/
276, 21/4; likely (to do or be) 13/10,
14/166; equal 18/3, 20/133; ~ *onto* equal
to 2/103; appropriate 39/71; appropriate for 41/362; *adv.* like 18/75, 29/111,
31/57 s.d.; ~ *as* just as, like 7/55, 14/
173, 293; ~ *as I was* the same as (when) I
was 14/173; ~ *to* 26/208 s.d., 28/16 s.d.;
alike 27/323; *prep.* equal to 21/21, 40n.,
223; similar to, like 27/322.
lykyng(e) *vbl. n.* pleasure 2/316; *at his* ~
as he likes Pr 235; *at my* ~ according to
my pleasure 1/17; *at þi* ~ as you please
2/36.
lykyst *pr. 2 sg.* wish, want 39/89; **likyth,
lyketh, lykyth** *impers.* pleases 9/196,
41/168, 225, 523; **lyke, liketh, like,
likyth** *pr. subj. impers.* pleases 41/98; *it*
~ *þe . . . ill* it may displease you 24/181;
yif it ~ if it please you 41/252; be
pleased: ~ (*it*) *yow* may (it) please you
41/1, 506.
lykkenyd *pp.* (is) symbolized 26/143.
lyknes *n.* form, likeness 3/75, 9/177, 11/
233.
lyme *n.* limb 18/276; **lemys** *pl.* 19/35, 36/
29.
lymyd *pp.* smeared with birdlime: *handis*
~ i.e. prepared for theft 6/152.
lympe *n.* lump 18/273.
lynage, lenage *n.* lineage 7/13, 21/157;
take ~ be descended 7/38.
lyne see **ly(e).**
lynyacyon *n.* use of lines (in geometry)
21/19.
lyonys *n.* lions 41/148.
lyppys, lippis *n.* lips 13/35, 29/24, 32/196.

lyst *conj.* lest: ~ *þat* 26/293.
lyst *pr. 3 sg.* wishes 30/218; **lyst** *impers.*
hym ~ pleases him 25/280; **lyst** *pl.*
wish, want to 8/142; **lyst** *pa. impers.*
pleased 41/96; **lyst** *pr. subj.* 8/168, 11/
111.
lyst(e), lest, liste *n.* desire, wish 18/305,
34/74, 77; joy 41/227.
lyste, lest *v.* **1** listen, pay heed 18/107,
21/44; **lyst, leste** *imp. sg.* 5/74, 10/33,
34/158; **lyst(e)** *imp. pl.* 24/269, 37/88; **2**
listen *to in* **lyst(e), lest** *imp. pl.* 14/120,
120, 40/32.
lysten *v.* **1** pay heed to, listen to 22/100;
lystenyth *imp.* Pr 7, 10/465; **2** pay
heed, listen *in* **lystenyth** *pl.* Pr 4;
lystenyth, listenyth *imp. pl.* 2/127,
10/1, 13/150A.
lytenyth *pr. 3 sg.* illuminates 10/436; **lyth**
pp. lighted, set burning 3/136; **lith** *imp.*
pl. light 41/304.
lyth *ppl. adj.* lighted 27/342, 28/80 s.d.
lith, lithtis, lyth, lythis, lytys see **lyght**
n.
lythly, lyghtly *adv.* in haste 9/299, 15/31;
easily 3/8; *wol not be* ~ won't easily be
(done) 15/38.
lythtyn, lyght, lyth *v.* descend, alight
18/161, 22/108, 26/449 s.d.; **lyght** *pa. t.*
35/77; **lyth** *pp.* Pr 166, 41/120.
lytel *n.* small amount 23/72.
lytyl(l), lytel, lytil *adj.* little 3/121, 6/89,
8/133, 10/459, 20/148, 25/284, 26/288
s.d., 35/238; *adv.* 11/309, 24/152, 27/204
s.d.
lyue, lyve, lyvys see **lyf(f)(e).**
lyvyng see **leve** *v.*[2]
lyvenge see **levynge** *ppl. adj.*
lo see **lo(o).**
loff, laue, loof *n.* loaf of bread 10/275,
23/72, 38/206, 285.
lofflyere *adj. comp.* more lovable, more
admirable, handsomer 18/4.
lofsummere *adj. comp.* more lovable,
more admirable, handsomer 18/4.
lofte *n. heyned on* ~ exalted 9/148; *on* ~ up
high 32/206.
logge *n.* prison, place of confinement
2/233, 320, 20/239; small building 15/
94, 160, 162.
logge *v.* lodge 15/79; **log(g)yd** *pp.* given
accommodations Pr 301, 15/99.

loggynge *n.* place of residence, lodgings 39/48.

logyk *n.* logic 21/14.

loyn see **ly(e).**

lok(e), look *n.* sight: *obeye to Goddys* ~ be obedient in the eyes of God 23/133; look, glance 29/221, 41/400; appearance, aspect 41/155.

lok see **lok(ke).**

lok(e), lokyn, look *v.* 1 observe *or* consult (laws) Pr 95; 2 look 3/100, 8/149, 24/70, 29/212 s.d., 32/168 s.d.; ~ *on book* read a book 21/48; **lokygh** *pr. 3 sg.* ~ *me lyche* resembles me 18/75; **look, lokyn** *pl.* 10/447, 32/48; **lokyng(e)** *pr. p.* 9/149, 27/372 s.d.; **loke** *imp. sg.* 23/157, 30/230; **loke** *pr. subj.* ~ *abowte* take heed 31/31; 3 find out 3/194, 4/197, 36/122; 4 see 4/159; 5 seek, endeavour 6/24; 6 consider, search out 21/11; **lokyd** *pp.* 26/404; **loke** *imp. pl.* 21/5, 25/103; 7 await the time *in* **loke** *pr. 1 sg.* 25/60; 8 look about *in* **loke** *pl.* 8/137; 9 observe *in* **loke** *imp. sg.* Pr 142, 32/70; 10 see to it (that) *in* **loke** *imp.* 2/27, 59, 130.

lokyn *pp.* 1 contained 1/17; 2 locked *2/233; **loke** *imp. pl.* 34/248.

lok(ke) *n.* lock 25/428, 34/248; **lokkys** *pl.* 42/50.

lokkys *n.* locks of hair 26/85.

lomb(e), lambe, lom *n.* lamb 3/68, 22/41, 45, 47, 27/349, 29/110; **lombys** *gen. sg.* 3/75.

lond(e) *n.* land Pr 445, 2/136, 322; the earth, this world 5/119, 18/3; region, country 12/22, 20/6, 23/175; *In dyverse* ~ 18/310; *Bedleem* ~ 20/4; **londys** *pl.* 20/123.

long(e) *adj.* long 10/62, 180, 25/393; ~-*pekyd* with long pointed toes 26/69; protracted 11/26; extensive, much 20/89; **lenger(e)** *comp.* longer 30/22, 34/151; *more* ~ 21/271; *adv.* for a long time Pr 428, 501, 1/46; ~ *bought* paid for at length 2/316; far 32/65, 74; **lenger(e)** *comp.* longer 9/281, 11/88, 21/72.

longe *v. impers.* be (one's) duty: *doth* ~ (*onto*) is one's duty 4/41; (with *to*) pertain to, be the concern of 21/125; **longyth, longyht, longygh** *pr. 3 sg.* belongs 6/176, 23/178; (with *to*) is appropriate (to), is used (in) 21/19, 27/

66; **longith** *impers. me* ~ *to* I long for 41/100; **longyth** *pl.* are appropriate to 21/20.

longyng *ppl. adj.* longing 9/135.

longynge *vbl. n.* distress 15/140.

lo(o) *interj.* behold 13/22, 22, 41/497; lo! 5/13, 9/65, 294.

loof see **loff.**

look see **lok(e).**

lordchep *n.* favour, *or* power 6/8; power, authority, status of a lord 18/3, 20/254.

lord(e) *n.* lord Pr 43, 44, 344; **lordys, lordeis** *gen. sg.* Pr 24, 402, 2/68, *9/127; **lordys** *pl.* 10/116, 16/111, 20/176.

lordyngys *n.* term of polite address 10/1.

lore *n.* doctrine, teaching 3/123, 11/111, 21/148; conduct 41/137; counsel, decision 24/221.

lose *v.* loosen, untie 26/128; **losyn** *imp. sg.* open 42/50; **losyth** *imp. pl.* loosen, untie 25/430.

losel *n.* scoundrel 3/144.

losse *n.* loss 25/364.

lost(e) *pp.* ruined, brought to ruin 2/303, 3/95, 11/140.

loth *n.* fault 36/59.

loth(e) *adj.* reluctant, unwilling 14/119, 25/149; *me be* ~ I do not wish to 3/49; *perto he were ful* ~ he would be most unwilling (to be angry) 13/143; (with *of*) displeased (with) 35/178; evil 38/19.

lothe *v.* loathe, be opposed to 8/178.

lothfolest *adj. sup. as noun* most loathsome one 8/151.

lott *n.* lot, destiny 24/158; what is allotted 39/90.

louris *pr. 3 sg.* (of a look) falls angrily 41/400.

love, loue *n.* love 3/119, 128, 4/44, 5/23, 27, 6/159; **lovys** *gen. sg.* 26/62.

love, loue, lovyn *v.* love 3/40, 145, 5/22, 38, 57, 9/187, 232, 10/313; **loue** *pr. 1 sg.* 38/195; **lovyst** *pr. 2 sg.* 8/155; **lovyth** *pr. 3 sg.* 11/91, 13/150, 14/87; **lovyn** *pl.* 27/56; **lovyd, louyd** *pa. t.* Pr 351, 9/176, 25/197, 360, 374; **lovyd, louyd** *pp.* 5/58, 9/79, 11/71; **loue, love** *imp. sg.* 9/178, 179, 180; **love, lovyth** *imp. pl.* 9/176, 178, 39/44; **loue** *pr. subj.* 27/497.

loveday *n.* reconciliation 11/185.

louely, lovely *adj.* excellent, lovely 5/181, 16/136, 18/157, 173, 23/57; **lovelyest** *sup.* 20/146; **louely(e)** *adv.* graciously, in a friendly manner Pr 7; splendidly 18/160.

louelyer *adj. comp.* more obedient and humble, *or* more lovable, lovelier 5/16.

louers *n.* lovers 24/202.

lovyngest *ppl. adj.* most loving 8/164.

lovyngely *adv.* lovingly 38/249.

lovnesse *n.* humility, *or* lovingness, love 41/95, 137, 166.

lowd(e) *adv.* loudly 13/57, 28/142.

lowe *adj.* humble 4/12, 10/1, 393; base, ignoble 18/176; low 26/15; *adv.* humbly 16/111, softly 28/142.

lowh see **lawh3**.

lowly(e) *adj.* humble, obedient 5/26, 237, 22/81; *as noun* 13/105.

lowlyness *n.* humility, meekness 39/85.

lowlyté *n.* humility 36/51.

lownes(se) *n.* humility 13/88, 41/243.

lowt(e), lowth *v.* bow, make obeisance 14/184, 18/158, 20/130, 279, 23/6, 33/40; obey 25/434; **lowte** *pr. subj.* (with *to*) 6/43.

lullay *interj.* soothing expression used in lullabies 14/197.

lullyd *pa. t.* slept peacefully 20/100.

lullynge *vbl. n.* soothing (a baby), singing (a lullaby) 20/89.

luminarye *n.* luminary PS 3; **luminaryes** *pl.* PS 17.

lunge *n.* lung 20/71.

lurdeyn, lordeyn *n.* rogue, rascal 4/183, 20/174, 179.

lust(e) *n.* desire, lust 14/271, 21/176; wish 15/109.

lust *pr. 1 sg.* wish 15/110.

lusty *adj.* healthy, full of vigour 8/136.

maculacion *n.* spot, mark 14/240, 349; defilement 14/334, 21/132; *to myn ~* that stained my honour 14/377.

magesté, majesté *n.* majesty, power 1/20, 47, 11/8, 23/85; (of God) *his ~* 8/72; i.e. God 21/71.

magnyficens *n.* munificence, magnificence 8/163.

magnefyeth *pr. 3 sg.* praises 41/169.

magré *prep.* in spite of: *~ þin heed* in spite of all that you do 14/360.

may *n.* virgin, young girl 6/143, 10/198, 12/44.

may *pr. 1, 3 sg.* may, can: (with ellips. of following vb.) 3/67, 4/88, 5/29;

mayst(e), mast *pr. 2 sg.* 2/202, 5/223, 10/264, 25/301; **may, mow, mon, mowne** *pl.* Pr 221, 1/39, 46, 11/64, 13/137, 29/189, 41/28, 42/20; (with ellips. of vb.) Pr 259, 280, 312; *with þat we ~* if we may 13/169; **myght, myth, myht** *pa. t.* Pr 37, 3/8, 4/146, 159, 227, 7/48, 8/234, 41/67, 143; **mytyst** *pa. 2 sg.* 28/164.

mayd(e), maide *n.* virgin Pr 114, 131, 160, 4/10; *~ childe* girl 8/71; male celibate 32/148, 41/197, 361.

maydenhed *n.* virginity 10/485.

maydon, maydyn, mayden *n.* virgin, girl Pr 143, 2/263, 6/114, 7/56, 66, 9/33, 246, 10/291, 296; maidservant 6/173; male celibate 10/179; **maydenys, maydonys, maydens, maidenys, maydynnys, maydyns** *gen. sg.* virgin's 7/120, 124, 10/132, 18/32, 64, 164, 236, 252, 21/101, *34/106; **maydenys, maydonys, maydenes** *pl.* Pr 155, 161, 9/194, 201, 214, 10/89; celibates 21/240.

mayn *n.* power, strength 2/113, 4/241, 5/240.

maynteyn *v.* maintain, support 10/468, 26/90.

maystyr, mayster *n.* master 2/197, 4/154, 166, 8/135, 137, 143; instructor 21/138, 147; **maysterys** *gen. sg.* master's 27/270; **maysterys** *pl.* learned authorities 31/137.

maystrye(e) *n.* pre-eminence: *bere þe ~* are pre-eminent 21/28; victory 21/139; **maystryes** *pl.* cunning tricks 23/200, 26/22; feats of arms 34/290.

make *n.* mate, spouse Pr 34, 2/19, 10/78.

make, makyn, maken *v.* **1** create, build Pr 15, 71, 2/134, 4/98; **mad(e)** *pa. t.* and *pp.* Pr 12, 31, 32; **2** express, experience (an emotion) Pr 343, 3/189, 4/250; **make** *pr. 1 sg.* 4/142, 199, 18/258; **makyst** *pr. 2 sg.* 15/138, 37/12; **makyth** *pr. 3 sg.* Pr 393; **make, makyn** *pl.* Pr 467, 19/62, 41/387; **make** *imp. pl.* 20/213, 35/118; **make** *pr. subj.* 32/237, 41/269; **3** make, do, cause 1/2, 29, 31/194; *~ pawsacyon* pause 9/304; *I xal 3ow ~* I shall force you to 14/155; **makyst** *pr. 2 sg.* 10/448; **makyth** *pr. 3 sg.* 8/132, 26/230, 27/304; *~ ... restynge* rests, pauses 11/260 s.d.; **make, makyn** *pl.* 8/66; *refl.* 26/449 s.d.; **mad(e)** *pa. t.* and *pp.*

make (*cont.*)

11/14, 35, 53; **make** *pr. subj.* (forming *imp.*) *teryenge* ... ~ tarry 34/151; **4** speak, utter 3/97, 4/179, 10/93; **make** *pr. 1 sg.* ~ ... *gratulacyon* thank 41/97; **makyn** *pl.* ~ *on hym a gret cry* cry out loudly against him 28/104 s.d.; **mad(e)** *pa. t.* and *pp.* 9/20, 35, 52; **makyght** *imp. pl.* ~ *no mone* don't lament 20/106; **5** perform 10/311; **make** *pl.* 1/64; **6** disseminate 15/308; **7** bring about, cause 25/106, 41/178; ~ *to myschefe* bring to ruin 41/64; **mad** *pa. t.* 41/95; **make** *imp. pl.* 5/159; **8** pretend *refl.* 32/176 s.d., 176 s.d.; **9** send *in* **make** *pr. 1 sg.* 4/245; **10** cause to be *in* **makyst** *pr. 2 sg.* 8/173; (with ellips. of 'thou') 30/200; **makyth, makyht** *pr. 3 sg.* 8/179, 10/434, 442; **mad(e)** *pa. t.* and *pp.* 2/197, 217, 3/161; **make** *imp. sg.* ~ ... *chere* cheer (sb.) 27/570; **11** celebrated *in* **made** *pa. t.* 29/11; **12** presented dramatically *in* **mad** *pp.* 8/9; **13** composed 13/151A.

Makere *n.* Creator 2/142, 5/1, 9/260; **Makers** *gen. sg.* 2/180.

maladyes *n.* maladies 26/414.

males *n.* malice, wickedness 11/45.

malycyous, malicious *adj.* malicious 26/50, 59, 41/19.

man, manne *n.* man Pr 12, 32, 65, 21/187; servant 8/65; **mannys, manis** *gen. sg.* Pr 33, 34, 2/211, 19/156; **mennys** *gen. pl.* 4/194, 34/50.

manas(e), manace *n.* threat of harm, menace 1/72, 4/33, 137, 27/208; *doth þis* ... ~ carries out this threat 27/241.

maner(e), manyr *n.* manner, way 10/73, 19/170; *in good* ~ in a proper way 2/55, 10/215, 368; *in all* ~ in every way 10/381, 19/142, 22/87; kind, variety 26/160, 161; *all* ~ every kind of Pr 499, 2/32, 4/208; *no* ~ not any kind (of) 8/29, 26/146, 28/168; *no* ~ *wyse* not at all 10/73; *in what* ~ *of wyse* how 11/246; *ony* ~ any kind of 14/327.

manhod, manhed *n.* human state or form 27/376, 32/150, 41/21, 498; manliness 26/113.

many *adj.* many a 8/132, 10/81, 156; ~ *on* many a man, many 6/137, 25/73, 29/37; ~ *way* (on) many a way 14/38; ~ *a folde* much 14/245.

mankend(e), mankynd(e) *n.* mankind 6/64, 7/24, 100, 12/158, 19/151, 31/134; human form 19/6, 32/186; *from* ~ *hyre* ... *excuse* exonerate herself of having known a man sexually 14/305; **mankyndys, mankende, mankendeis, mankynde his** *gen. sg.* 11/282, 19/118, 120, 154, 23/51, 25/453.

mankynne *n.* mankind 16/85.

manly *adv.* like a man 29/109, 41/421.

mansclawth *n.* manslaughter 31/107.

marchawnt *n.* merchant 27/245.

mary, maryn *v.* marry 10/173, 298; **maryed, maryde** *pp.* 8/12, 10/178, 181, 195.

maryage *n.* marriage Pr 123, 21/244.

marke, merke *n.* target 4/153, 158, 162, 165.

marre, marryn *v.* harm, destroy 18/73; confuse, lead astray 18/304; disturb 25/364.

massage, message *n.* messenger 4/245, 41/255; message 11/321, 25/250, 26/258, 41/132, 193; errand, service as messenger 21/209, 30/24, 41/116; *on* ~ ... *sent* dispatched with a message 27/39; **massagys** *pl.* errands 26/254, 38/158.

mas(s)anger(e), masager, messager *n.* messenger Pr 145, 164, 4/247, 26/256 s.d., 41/122.

masse *n.* the mass 42/110.

mast see **may**.

maystyr *pr. 1 sg.* rule, prevail over 18/6.

mateynes *n.* matins 42/110.

mater(e), matyr *n.* matter, subject Pr 201, 517, 7/118, 8/5, 15/240; reason, grounds 24/103; speech 26/117; business, affair 27/474; *in hire* ~ *clere* without bodily taint, sinlessly 41/5; **materys, materis** *pl.* matters, subjects, affairs 9/299, 26/119, 122, 124.

materyal, material *adj.* material, physical 23/96, 101.

matremony *n.* matrimony 10/331.

mawmentryes *n.* false gods, idols 41/469.

Mawndé, Maundé *n.* Last Supper Pr 314, 27/17, 42, 66, 366.

me *pron.*[1] *refl.* myself 2/175, 3/48, 50; (dat. of interest) for me 41/9, 403, 408; **my, mi** *poss.* my 1/1, 2, 3, 5/123; **myn(e), mene** 1/28, 82, 2/46, 11/327n.; *absol.* 12/108, 13/19, 14/81; those associated with me 3/54; **myself(f), mysylf(e)** myself 1/3, 16, 2/204, 319, 27/144; I myself 15/68, 24/14, 15.

me *pron.*² people, men 25/318, 39/25.

mech *n.* much 21/38.

mech(e), myche *adj.* great, abundant, much 8/163, 11/28, 68; many 29/158, 41/61; **mech(e). myche, moch** *adv.* much 14/57, 15/35, 26/149, 41/104; very 22/51; much of the time 41/23.

mede *n.* 1 reward Pr 524, 5/42, 192; **medys** pl. 20/122; 2 benefit 9/193; 3 bribe 14/158, 24/165, 35/255.

mede *v.* reward, bless 5/229.

medele see **mell(e)** *v.*¹

medycyn *n.* medicine, medical treatment 15/219; remedy 15/291, 41/431.

medyl-erth *n.* the earth 2/263.

medytacyon *n.* meditation 28/150; (as personif.) 9/198.

meef see **meve.**

meet see **mete** *adj.*

meke *adj.* humble, submissive 3/43, 7/4, 9/106; docile, gentle 26/380, 29/110; **mekest** *sup.* humblest 9/246, 263, 11/202; **meke** *as noun* the meek 8/141.

meke *v.* appease 11/8.

mekely *adv.* humbly 8/80, 172, 9/76; obediently 8/95, 29/10.

mek(e)nes(se) *n.* humility, obedience 3/67, 7/116, 8/63.

mekyl, mekel(l), mykyl *adj.* great 1/66, 2/187, 14/70, 18/246, 20/103, 35/101.

melyon *n.* million 28/128.

mell(e) *v.*¹ concern or occupy oneself, mix 1/71, 24/134, 35/8; have sexual intercourse 10/76, 14/78, 24/71; effect, bring about 16/131; (with *perwith*) deal (with) 35/247; **medele** *imp. sg. refl.* mix, join (oneself) 16/57; **medele** *pr. subj.* concern yourself, meddle 3/173.

mell *pr. subj.*² tell 21/199.

melody(e), melodé *n.* melody 1/34, 16/88, 39/46, 41/495.

membyr, membre *n.* bodily part 11/297, 26/95; **membrys** pl. 31/9.

memory(e), memorie *n.* memory 9/101, 27/482, 532, 33/26.

mend(e), mynde, meende *n.* mind Pr 512, 1/6, 2/329, 9/110, 24/290, 25/274, 28/174, 38/10; *haue ~, haue ~ on (of), haue ... in (pi) ~* remember Pr 223, 8/163, 199, 9/54, 152, 11/7, 32/188, 38/144; *fro oute of ~* from time immemorial 19/94; *has in ~* have concern for 32/139; remembrance 25/363; frame of mind,

disposition 2/329, 16/81; desire, inclination 5/56; **mendys** pl. memories, thoughts 26/25.

mendere *n.* one who corrects 41/280.

mene *n.* way, means 26/219; mediator, intercessor 41/280; **menys** pl. means, methods 26/298, 27/135, 274.

men(e), meen *v.*¹ 1 intend, have in mind 10/176, 22/175; **menyht** *pr. 3 sg.* 4/92; **menyth** *impers.* 10/41; **ment** *pp.* intended, planned Pr 59, 9/260, 28/57; *haue ~* are bent on, are planning 18/140, 20/79; 2 mean 14/346, 23/13, 27/10, 402; **mene** *pr. 1 sg.* 26/150; **menyth** *pr. 3 sg.* 6/17, 71, 12/34; 3 said *in* **ment** *pp.* 35/225; 4 told 41/259.

mene *v.*² mediate: *to ~* to mediate between, *or* as mediator 19/112.

mene ('my') see **me** *pron.*¹

menetyme *n.* meantime 26/208 s.d., 244 s.d., 280 s.d.

meny, mené *n.* company 27/339, 41/410; retinue 27/348 s.d., 32/168 s.d.

menstrell see **mynstrell.**

meracle, merakle *n.* miracle Pr 295, 406, 9/98, 41/287; **meraclis, meraclys, meracles** pl. 26/229, 295, 30/184, 196, 31/16.

mercyable, mercyabyl *adj.* merciful 11/84, 107, 24/33, 209, 260.

mercy(e) *n.* mercy Pr 289, 346, 3/74; (as personif.) 11/75, 89, 117.

mercyf(f)ul(l) *adj.* merciful 5/59, 8/121, 9/263.

mere *n.* country, i.e. route 18/322; boundary-marker 36/41.

mery *adj.* merry, happy 3/20, 8/211, 9/85; **meryer** *comp.* 8/77, 20/164.

merke see **marke** *n.*

merke *v.*¹ make dull or murky 23/59.

merke *v.*² mark 31/9.

merth(e) see **myrth(e).**

meruayll *adj.* marvelous 25/438.

mervayle *v.* marvel at 38/261; **merveyle** *pr. 1 sg.* marvel 38/138; **merveylyth** *impers. me ~* I am filled with wonder 11/89, 12/15; **merveyllys, merveylyth** pl. marvel 26/36, 32/177; **merveylyd** *pa. t.* wondered Pr 249; **merveyle** *imp. sg.* marvel 9/246.

merveyl(e) *n.* marvel, miracle 10/261, 15/227; **merveylis, mervaylys, merveles** pl. 27/80, 34/9, 38/290, 321.

mervelyous, merveylous, mervelous
adj. marvelous, miraculous, astonishing 8/188, 9/162, 11/229, 41/127, 193, 499; strange, exciting wonder 26/25, 31.

mesemyth *impers.* it seems to me 11/79, 121, 14/152.

messager see **mas(s)anger(e)**.

Messy(e) *n.* Messiah 7/44, 108.

mest(e) see **more**.

metall *n.* metal 18/239.

metaphesyk *n.* metaphysics 21/16.

mete *n.* 1 meal: *to ~, at ~* at table Pr 235, 20/155, 194; 2 food 2/164, 245, 9/248; **metys** *pl.* 20/147, 23/75.

mete, meet *adj.* appropriate 24/200, 32/95; of the right size 31/204, 32/50; properly spaced 32/60, 61.

mete *v.* meet 6/37, 8/199, 221; **metyth** *pr. 3 sg.* 26/256 s.d.; **mett, mete, metyth, metyn** *pl.* 26/288 s.d., 385 s.d., 453 s.d., 32/20 s.d.; **metyng** *pr. p.* 27/36 s.d.; **mete** *pr. subj.* 8/76.

meth *n.* gentleness: *mylde ~* mild manner 16/46.

methynkyth, methynkyht, methynke, methynkeht, methynkygh *impers.* it seems to me 3/116, 118, 122, 4/160, 10/236, 14/365, 18/23, 20/143, 24/225; **methought, methowut** *pa. t.* 16/70, 29/102, 113.

metyng(e) *vbl. n.* meeting 8/13, 81, 240.

meve *v.* tempt 22/153; **movyth** *impers.* arouses, disturbs 11/89; **mevyd** *pa. t.* incited 11/43, 38/357; **mevyd** *pp.* distressed 38/9; proposed, urged 31/188; **meef** *pr. subj.* move, set forward 26/119.

myche *n.* loaf of bread (suggesting sacramental wafer) 18/73.

myche see **mech(e)** *adj.*

mydday *as adv.* during the middle of the day 4/72, 20/95.

myddys *n.* midst 26/138; *in ~* in the midst 19/139.

mydnyth *n.* midnight 29/16; *as adv.* at midnight 20/95.

mydplace *n.* middle of the playing area 26/288 s.d.

mydwyff, mydwyfe *n.* midwife 15/136, 151, 215; **mydwyuys, mydwyuis** *pl.* Pr 189, 15/120, 129, 173, 198; **mydwyuis** *gen. pl.* 15/189.

myght, myth, myht *n.* might, power Pr 15, 27, 396, 4/9, 67, 101, 41/76, 150, 375;

natural ~ physical vitality 9/249; *sensual ~* power of the appetite 26/28; **myghtys, mythtis, myhtis, myhtys, mythis** *pl.* 9/60, 18/169, 20/129, 41/163, 351, 508; *wyth my ~* heartily 41/122; **wyth alle oure** *~* most willingly 41/175.

myghtf(f)ul(l) *adj.* mighty 15/226, 36/55, 38/96.

myghty(e), mythty, myhty *adj.* mighty, great 1/59, 5/1, 9/138, 11/9, 32/112, 41/149; **myghtyest** *sup.* 13/92.

myht see **may, myght**.

mykyl see **mekyl**.

mylde *adj.* gentle, humble Pr 127, 184, 5/17; kind, gracious 5/59.

myle *n.* mile Pr 255, 4/156, 8/212; **myles** *pl.* 13/9.

mylk(e) *n.* milk 15/236, 244, 18/236.

myllere *n.* miller 14/23.

mynde see **mend(e)**.

mynyster, mynystryn *v.* serve 8/73; provide religious services 9/208; **mynistere** *pl.* perform rites 8/28.

minster *n.* bishop's subordinate 9/277 s.d.; **ministerys** *pl.* priests 8/97 s.d.

mynystracyon, mynistracyon *n.* office or function of minister 8/31; serving, ministering 9/246; service as minister 13/26, 31.

mynstrell, mynstrall, menstrell *n. pl.* minstrels 18/19n., 20/153, 231.

myrable *adj.* wonderful 41/188.

myrke *adj.* dark, dense 18/304.

myrkenes *n.* darkness 25/228.

myr(r)e *n.* myrrh Pr 205, 18/61, 255.

myrroure *n.* example 38/383.

myrth(e), merth(e) *n.* mirth, joy Pr 201, 1/31, 71, 2/287, 19/70, 22/20, 33/8; melody, song, joyous behaviour 1/34, 38, 16/63; **merthis, myrthis** *pl.* 3/189, 16/131, 20/213, 244, 32/237, 35/31.

mys see **mys(se)** *n.* and *v.*

myschawns, myschauns, myschaunce *n.* misfortune, adversity, grief 14/266, 24/100, 213.

myschef(f), myschyf(f), myscheve, myschefe *n.* misfortune, affliction, trouble 1/72, 15/257, 264, 18/232, 27/224, 31/9, 41/64; *do . . . ~* harm, injure 27/127; evil 30/114; **myschevys** *pl.* 11/28.

myscheve *v.* do wrong 14/133; bring to

grief, ruin 27/84; **myschevyd** *pp.*
brought to harm 11/76.
mysdede *n.* misconduct, misdeeds 24/
39; *here* (*oure*) ~ 32/138, 42/36.
mysdemynge *vbl. n.* misjudgement 25/
67.
mysdoyng *vbl. n.* misconduct 2/279.
mysese *n.* suffering, distress 32/47.
myshappe *pr. subj.* go astray 24/21.
myslevyng *ppl. adj.* leading an evil life
4/92.
myslevyng(e) *vbl. n.* sinful living 24/155,
27/403.
mysrewle *n.* misconduct 3/8.
mys(se) *n.* sin, misdeed, wickedness
3/169, 4/95, 22/43; misfortune, harm
10/387; *withowtyn* ~ indeed, certainly
19/97.
mys(se) *v.* lack, lose 5/27, 42/56; (with
of) 1/39, 25/307, 26/12; **mys** *pr. 1 sg.* 32/
256, 38/143; 2 miss, fail 27/326; **mys** *pr.
subj.* 14/392.
myst(e) *n.* mist, fog 18/227, 304, 23/59.
mysthought *pp.* thought wrongly 12/169.
mystyr man *n. what* ~ what kind of man
14/288.
mystrost, mystruste *n.* lack of faith or
confidence 13/79, 25/70.
mysvse *v.* debauch 14/288.
myswrought *pp.* offended, done wrong
12/152, 167.
mytere *n.* mitre 26/164 s.d.
myth, mytyst see **may.**
myth, mythis, mythtis see **myght** *n.*
mythty see **myghty(e).**
mythtyly, myghtyly *adv.* mightily 27/
119, 38/62.
mo, moo *n.* more 27/494, 34/204; *withowtyn* ~ at once, certainly 13/160; **mo(o)**
pl. others 12/20, 30/62; *adj.* more 21/
195, 23/177, 31/52; *adv.* any more 3/189;
longer 8/106.
moch see **mech(e).**
mod see **mood(e).**
modyr, moder, moþyr *n.* mother Pr
253, 393, 429, 18/282, 41/2, 104, 115;
moderys, moderis *gen. sg.* 19/90, 21/
41, 41/107; **moderys** *pl.* 8/187, 13/
163A, 20/112; **moderys** *gen. pl.* Pr 226,
227.
modyrles *adj.* motherless 21/172.
mokador *n.* bib 21/42.
molde see **mo(o)lde.**

mon see **may.**
mone *n.*[1] moon 1/57, 2/10, 104; *vndyr* ~
on earth 2/197.
mon(e) *n.*[2] grief, complaint 10/263, 12/
41, 86.
mony(e), moné, monay *n.* money 14/
199, 26/83, 103, 27/197, 239.
monyth *n.* month 11/257; **monthis,
monethys, monethis, monthys** *pl.*
10/469, 13/73, 132, 160A, 30/183, 39/35.
mood(e), mod *n.* mind, heart, mood
3/124, 4/202, 6/79, 12/63.
mo(o)lde *n.* earth Pr 12, 68, 18/11.
moote *n.* conflict, struggle Pr 111.
moralysacyon *n.* spiritual commentary:
make ~ interpret spiritually 26/141.
more *n.* greater, more 8/74; 11/222, 21/
144; ~ *and lesse* people of all ranks,
everyone Pr 7, 39/81; ~ *and las* (*lesse*)
everything Pr 470, 14/376; *adj. comp. þe*
~ 25/376, 29/121; **most, mest(e)** *adj.
sup.* Pr 236, 239, 9/60, 18/169; *as noun*
3/93, 18/50; most important 26/405;
more *adv.* ~ *and lesse* altogether, completely 22/125; **most(e), moost** *adv.
sup.* 1/44, 47, 59, 29/27.
moreovyr *adv.* moreover 39/41.
morn, morwyn *n.* morning Pr 193, 407,
7/16; *evyn and* ~ at all times 5/212, 27/8.
morne see **murne.**
morny *adj.* sad, mournful 10/479.
mornyng(e) *vbl. n.* mourning, sorrow,
lamentation Pr 393, 467, 4/142; ~ *songe*
27/204.
mornyng *ppl. adj.* mournful 35/114.
mornynge *as adv.* in the morning 4/72.
mortal(l) *adj.* mortal 26/121; ~ *Dedys,
Dedys* ~ Deadly Sins 26/130, 411;
severe, extreme 26/479.
morwe *n.* morning 35/134.
most(e), moost see **more.**
mote *n. pyke out a* ~ dwell on trifles 10/
283.
mote, mut *pr. 1 sg.* 1 (usu. *subj.*) may 10/
178, 304, 29/202; **moty** may I 3/20, 13/7,
16/66; **mot(e), mut** *pr. 2, 3 sg.* 5/52, *6/
15, 8/4; þe deuyl* ~ may the devil 30/230;
mote, mut *pl.* 8/230, 248, 16/151; 2
must *in* **must(e)** *pr. 1 sg.* 5/47, 96, 170;
impers. ~ *me* I must 5/137, 171; (with
ellipsis of vb. of motion) 27/569;
must(e), mut, mot *pr. 3 sg.* 5/89, 99,
139, 13/67, 25/52, 41/262; **must(e)** *pl.*

mote *(cont.)*
Pr 186, 243, 2/333; (with ellipsis of vb. of motion) 10/183, 15/4, 19/100; *impers. vs.* *(us)* – we must 8/129, 13/156, 42/34.

mot-halle *n.* judgement hall, council chamber 30/5, 14, 21.

movyth see **meve.**

mow, mowne see **may.**

mowe *n.* (with *make*) make faces 32/200, 209.

mownteynes *n.* mountains 9/108, 32/17.

mowth(e), mouth(e) *n.* mouth Pr 63, 326, 5/25, 174, 12/187, 14/53; *hath . . . in his ~* is speaking 10/444; *be ~* i.e. through confession 26/411.

mullynge *n.* term of endearment: darling 16/144.

multyplye *v.* multiply, increase 5/216, 29/28; **multyply** *pl.* 8/136; **multyplyed** *pp.* 9/131.

mure *adj.* gentle, demure 41/119; humble 41/448.

murne, morne *v.* lament, mourn 25/136, 37/10; **murne** *pr. 1 sg.* grieve 10/481; **mornyng** *pr. p.* lamenting 32/92 s.d.; **murnyd** *pa. t.* 38/252.

mursel(e) *n.* morsel, small piece of food Pr 41, 2/129, 23/73; choice dish 14/92.

musyke *n.* music 21/11.

muste *n.* new wine 40/18.

must(e), mut see **mote.**

nacyon *n.* people, nation 41/440.

nay *n.* denial: *þis is no (n) ~, þis may not be seyd ~, withoutyn ony ~* it cannot be denied Pr 18, 263, 3/70, 26/20, 41/361; *adv.* not: *him thought ~* it seemed unbelievable to him 13/78.

nay *v.* to refuse (to act thus) 41/388.

nayl *n.* nail 31/204, 32/69, 72; **nayles, naylys, naylis** *pl.* 31/26, 200, 36/29, 38/323.

naylyn *v.* nail 32/48 s.d.; **nayle** *pl.* Pr 387; **naylid** *pa. t.* 38/70; **naylid, naylyd** *pp.* 32/265, 34/2, 20, 35/129, 36/91.

nakyd *adj.* naked Pr 387, 2/168, 176.

nale *n.* sett at þe ~ drinking in company, at the ale-house 6/91.

name *n.* reputation, renown 4/151, 6/153, 12/53; *of ryche ~* excellent, renowned 2/70; **namys, name, names** *pl.* 2/24, 9/197, 210, 10/332, 26/109.

namyth *pr. 3 sg.* names, calls Pr 169; **namyd** *pp.* 24/235, 32/180.

namely *adv.* especially 11/321, 13/16.

nat(t) see **not(t).**

naturaly *adv.* in natural terms, of natural processes 3/32.

natural(l), naterall *adj.* hereditary 7/26; physical 9/249; innate: *~ wytt* native intelligence 21/134; proper 26/66; following natural law, natural 26/111, PS 38.

nature *n. mannys ~* the human race 3/35; inherent nature, condition 21/98, 38/130; nature, natural law: *not ~ doth lothe* i.e. does not oppose procreation 8/178; *without ~* supernaturally, by miracle 8/196; *kynde ~* inherent nature 25/134; **natures** *gen. sg.* of natural affection, of parental love 41/101.

ne *adv.* not 4/51, 20/13, 96; **ne, nyn** *conj.* nor, or Pr 515, 2/42, 3/182, 8/15, 15, 9/149; *~ non* nor any 1/4.

necglygens *n.* negligence 26/400.

necke, nekke *n.* neck 5/113, 20/92, 31/212 s.d.; *~ bon* 2/307; **neckys** *pl.* 26/244 s.d.

ned(e) *n.* need 2/67, 5/47, 9/284; *it is grett ~* it is very necessary 8/145; *yt is no ~* it is unnecessary 10/167, 34/82; *what ~ was it here* why was it necessary for her 21/241; time of need 10/422, 15/48, 185; *adv.* necessarily 8/129. Cf. **nedys.**

nedful *adj.* necessary 10/95, 365, 29/129.

nedy *n.* the needy 11/49, 13/108.

nedys, nedis *adv.* necessarily 5/89, 96, 137, 178.

nedyth *pr. 3 sg.* needs 8/157, 11/163, 225; **nedyth, nedith** *impers. what ~ (sb.)* what need is there for (sb.) 25/377, 29/175, 41/125; *what ~ it to fere you* why do you fear 41/157; **nede** *pl.* 11/222; **nedyd** *pa. t. impers. it ~ not to bene* it wasn't necessary 19/113.

negremauncye see **nygramancye.**

neybore, nehebour *n.* neighbour, fellow man 6/178, 24/25, 29; dear or 'close' one 41/510; **neyborys** *gen. sg.* neighbour's 6/165, 168, 172; **neyborys** *pl.* 8/124, 10/184, 26/42.

neyth see **nyhyn.**

neyther *pron.* neither 8/102.

neyther, neythyr *conj.* neither 3/114, 115, 6/69, 10/271.

nempne, nemene *v.* name, mention 5/131; speak of (sb.) by his title 19/45.

ner(e), neyr *adv.*[1] nearly 3/95, 10/238, 22/172, 30/46; ~ *is* it is nearly 19/98; near 6/23, 37, 10/135.

nere *adv.*[2] not at all 19/157.

ner(e) *conj.* nor 4/148, 6/175, 176; *seyse ~ sessyon* at assizes or court sessions 26/114.

nerhonde *adv.* close at hand 31/96.

nesch *adi.* weak, soft 2/313.

nest *adv.* next 11/292 s.d.

nevyr, neuyr, never *adv.* never Pr 2, 381, 1/27, 46, 6/141; ~ *so* extremely, to whatever degree Pr 422, 6/120, 8/302; not at all Pr 351, 2/157, 3/190, 14/217; ~ *þe more* not at all 3/124, 11/108.

nevyrmo *adv.* nevermore 2/234.

nevyrmor(e), neuyrmor *adv.* never again Pr 98, 176, 1/69; never 5/259, 14/276, 15/203, 21/160.

nevyrþeles(se), neuyrtheles *adv.* nevertheless 10/183, 12/104, 25/229, 41/242, 262, 434.

new(e) *adj.* new 4/247, 8/35, 11/339; *adv.* recently 41/334.

ny(e), nyh, ny3 *adv.* near 4/157, 12/46, 18/152, 26/472; nearly 26/430, 435, 441, 35/76; ~ *almost* 10/228.

nyght, nyth, nyht *n.* night Pr 472, 506, 2/2, 3/72, 4/19, 73, 90, 5/51; **onyth** at night 26/80; **nyghtys, nygthtys, nyght, nyghtis, nythis** *pl.* Pr 268, 4/242, 22/125, 130, 23/66, 38/116, 41/174.

nygramancye, negremauncye, nygramansye *n.* necromancy, sorcery 21/117, 28/131, 30/47, 179.

nyhyn, neyth *v.* come near, approach 26/49, 41/159; **nyhith** *pr. 3 sg.* ~ . . . *ny* comes near 41/312; **nyghe** *pl.* ~ . . . *nye* 18/152; **neyhand** *pr. p.* ~ *nere* 19/4.

nyl *pr. 3 sg.* will not 41/145.

nyn see **ne**.

nynte *ord. num. as noun* ninth 9/134.

nynty *card. num. as adj.* ninety 8/181.

nyth, nythis see **nyght**.

no *conj.* nor 30/18.

nobyll *adj.* noble 7/121.

noyous *adj.* distressing 9/143.

noyse, noyis *n.* sound, noise 16/30, 28/148 s.d., 31/57 s.d.; *noyous is þe ~* distressing is the outcry 9/143.

noyther *adj.* neither 27/314.

nome *pp.* brought 10/205.

none *n.* nones, three o'clock p.m. 31/35; *as adv.* at nones 4/72.

non(e), noon *pron.* no one, not one Pr 162, 1/51, 3/35, 5/16, 29/23; neither 21/23.

non(e), noon *adj.* no, not any Pr 514, 1/4, 2/249, 4/91, 6/70, 85.

norch *v.* nourish 23/96; **norchyth** *pr. 3 sg.* 9/155.

nor(e) *conj.* nor, or Pr 130, 351, 3/114.

norsshere *n.* nourisher 26/5.

northe *n.* north 23/157.

nortur(e) *n.* moral discipline, *or* breeding 3/5; courtesy 41/123.

not *n.* nothing 8/161, 27/422, 426; *sett ~ be* have no regard for 26/93.

not *pr. 1 sg.* don't know 8/231, 41/375.

note *n.* song 16/62.

not3, noth, notht, notwh, notwth see **nowth** *adv.*

nother, nowther, nothyr *conj.* neither 6/159, 10/49, 162, 20/134, 214, 22/131, 42/18.

nothyng(e), noþing *pron.* nothing, nobody 9/186, 11/210, 259, 29/54; *fore ~* not for anything 26/439.

nothyng(e) *adv.* not at all 3/172, 10/252, 394; *ryght ~* 20/213.

notyd *pp.* reported 41/265.

not(t), nat(t) *adv.* not Pr 69, 116, 125, 2/204, 5/191, 6/167.

notwithstandyng, notwithstondynge *conj.* although 26/16, 39/9.

nought *pron.* none 24/275.

noumbryd *pp.* reckoned, considered (to be) 39/71.

novell *n.* tidings, news 38/298.

now(e) *adv.* now Pr 1, 7, 55.

nowth, nought, nouth *n.* nothing, nought 2/44, 3/63, 4/4, 5/257, 6/1, 13/62, 41/163, 411; *sett(e)* . . . *at ~* considered worthless 22/172; hold in contempt 26/76, 94.

nowth, not *adj.* pointless, futile 9/242, 27/77, 28/66.

nowth, nought, nowght, nouth, notwth, noth, nowht, nouht, notht, notwh, not3 *adv.* not, not at all Pr 341, 371, 2/38, 43, 194, 4/113, 185, 9/119, 10/72, 12/2, 150, 14/176, 21/72, 26/252, 28/144, 32/104, 284, 41/99, 268, 422.

nowthty *adj.* ineffectual; without worth 3/172.

numbre, novmbyr, noumbre *n.* number 7/81; company 27/543, 39/75.

nowther see **nother.**

o, a *prep.* of, concerning 21/19; out of: *bryng(e) ~ dawe* kill 29/38, 129.

o see **o(o).**

obecyon *n.* ground for reproach 30/81n.

obedyens, obedyence *n.* obedience 7/4, 9/114, 27/22, 30/156; *with ~* obediently 21/274.

obedyent *adj.* obedient 28/182.

obey(e) *v.* obey 9/235, 25/426, 439; *~ ... to, to ... ~* submit to, obey 5/111, 225; **ob(b)ey(e)** *pr. 1 sg.* 41/141; *refl.* am willing 5/148; am obedient 22/90; **obey, obeyth** *pl.* 20/160; *~ to* are obedient to 33/38.

obeschyauns, obeschaunce *n.* obeisance 41/97, 354.

oblé *n.* wafer, sacramental bread 27/372 s.d.

oblocucyon *n.* bad locution 8/5.

observaunce *n.* ceremony, rite 41/362, 368.

obstinacye *n.* obstinacy 11/44.

ocapve *v.* take (the place of): *~ þe lott of Judas plas* take Judas' place by lot 39/90; **occapyed, ocupyed** *pp.* engaged, occupied 9/296, 41/22.

oc(c)upacyon *n.* task, undertaking 9/214, 297; business 10/156; activity 11/326; (with *of*) solicitude for, occupation with 41/433.

odyr see **other(e)** *adj.*

of *adv.* off 5/168, 6/34, 35.

of(f) *prep.* **1** in Pr 1, 7/80, 26/66; **2** of Pr 8, 3/98, 11/292, 13/59; *foule ~ flyth* flying birds Pr 31; *sterrys ~ lyth* bright stars 1/30; *~ me* my 6/42, 95; *~ such informacyon* knowing so much 21/135; **3** about, concerning Pr 44, 55, 105; **4** by, through Pr 60, 63, 277; **5** made of 2/18, 18, 311; **6** from 3/120, 7/105; *~ ... come* descended from 10/207; **7** for 3/169, 4/216, 238; **8** because of, on account of 4/1, 27, 8/147; **9** out of: *~ wytt* insanely 4/144; **10** in respect of 4/147, 6/151; **11** ott of 6/30, 31/57 s.d.; **12** found in *or* on 6/68, 83, 115; **13** over 15/320, 30/124, 143; *~ all othere thyng* above all else 26/285; **14** at 26/36.

offende, affendyn *v.* offend, sin (against) 4/64, 15/259; *I to ~ hym day nor nyght that I may never* offend him 4/73; **offendyth** *pr. 3 sg.* 4/31; **offende** *pl.* 25/226; **offendyd** *pa. t.* and *pp.* 8/171, 9/78, 11/92; **offende** *pr. subj.* 15/313; *ageyn þe lawe ... ~* violate the law 24/26.

offens(e) *n.* transgression, sin 7/39, 8/158, 11/2; *~ to* sin against 4/232.

offyse, offyce, offis *n.* duty, task, function 11/36, 31/168, 41/359.

offre, offyr, offere *v.* offer, present 3/68, 5/127, 8/65, 10/140, 165, 204, 18/35, 28/64; **offre, offyr, offere** *pr. 1 sg.* 10/214, 243, 18/244; **offeryth** *pr. 3 sg.* 19/196 s.d.; **offre, offere** *pl.* 8/26, 9/60, 10/129; **offeryd** *pa. t.* Pr 148; **offeryd, offryd, offered, offred, offerde** *pp.* Pr 86, 3/77, 8/11, 193, 9/6, 10/65, 67, 11/80, 19/82; **offyr** *imp. sg.* 5/82; **offyr, offeryth** *imp. pl.* 3/42, 8/98, 107.

offryng(e), offerynge(e) *vbl. n.* offering Pr 140, 3/87, 141, 8/105, 19/183.

ofte *adv.* often 9/140, 11/327, 25/228.

ofte-tyme *adv.* often Pr 302, 14/96.

oftyn *adv.* often 3/37, 6/95, 108.

oftyntyme *adv.* often 6/96, 106, 107.

oftyntymes *adv.* often 10/284, 29/123.

ogyl *v.* quiver (with fear) 41/382.

oy *interj.* hear ye 10/142.

oyle *n.* oil 28/9.

oynement, onyment *n.* ointment 27/163, 190, 194, 34/140.

okys *n.* oak trees 20/186.

old(e), hoold, eld(e), holde *adj.* old Pr 248, 403, 4/127, 26/47, 164 s.d., 164 s.d., 27/370, 394; *as noun* 7/96, 8/96, 10/98.

olyve *n.* *~ bush* branch of an olive tree 4/251.

omage *n.* homage 16/152.

omnypotent(e) *adj.* omnipotent 2/140, 8/19, 14/252.

on, vn *prep.* on Pr 68, 71, 84, 27/553; over Pr 260, 31/131; in, into Pr 352, 4/11, 177; *~ lyve, ~ lyue* alive 3/182, 4/209, 217; about, concerning 14/253, 28/192, 38/200; for 25/376; against 27/473, 543, 28/104 s.d.; with respect to 38/125.

on *adj.* a certain 26/26, 178, 217.

on see **on(e)** *pron.*

onbete *pp.* unbeaten 20/34.

onbokyll *v.* unbuckle 22/32.

onclose see **vnclose.**

ondyr see **vndyr.**
ondothe see **vndo.**
on(e) *pron.* one 2/77, 3/93, 4/49; *a merveyl*
~ a miracle 10/261; *in* ~ in unity 7/134,
9/157; *in* ~ together PS 19, 41/285.
onest *adj.* proper 11/114.
onesté *n.* honour 26/111.
onethys *adv.* scarcely 15/72, 25/8.
onhangyd *ppl. adj.* not (yet) hanged 30/
221.
ony *n.* honey 10/446.
ony see **any.**
onyment see **oynement.**
onys *adv.* once 3/77, 7/78, 9/239; *for* ~,
evyr, and ay once and for all 12/61; ever,
at all 8/127, 27/31, 559.
onyth see **nyght.**
only(e) *adv.* only 6/81, 13/101, 14/319.
on lyve, on lyue see **lyf(f)(e).**
onlose *v.* unloose: ~ *hese lyppys* speak 29/
24; **vnlosne** *imp. pl.* untie 26/351.
onowryd see **honour(e).**
onpossyble *adj.* impossible 21/77.
onrekenyd *ppl. adj.* not spoken 18/178.
onsondyr *adj.* split into parts 4/174.
onsownd *adj.* wicked 14/372.
ontyl(l)(e) *prep.* to PS 4, 30/227, 38/70.
onto(o), vnto *prep.* to Pr 182, 223, 278,
429, 3/4, 8/27, 35/154; tor, to obtain
2/41, 29/36; on 2/307, 19/196 s.d.; as
10/323; into 10/364, 14/313.
o(o) *card. num. as adj.* one Pr 33, 1/12, 13;
each 27/322.
o(o)n *card. num. as adj.* one 5/251, 9/23, 59.
ope *v.* open Pr 508.
opyn *adj.* open, clear, unobstructed Pr
29, 21/102, 22/106; readily perceived
14/219; public 24/162; clear, audible
36/118, 37/82; *adv.* publicly, without
concealment 7/8, 29/134.
opyn *pr. 1 sg.* open 42/53; **opynd** *pp.*
made known 12/136; **oppyn** *imp. pl.* 32/
18.
opynly *adv.* publicly, without concealment Pr 494, 12/110, 14/352; distinctly,
manifestly 15/228, 23/168, 25/435.
oppynyon *n.* belief, doctrine 26/239.
oppressyon *n.* harm 26/234.
or, ore, er *conj.¹* or Pr 506, 1/41, 3/67, 13/
180A, 14/225, 31/87, 34/161.
or, er(e), her, eer *conj.²* before 4/117,
5/173, 199, 9/84, 10/45, 34/125, 37/98; ~
þat 10/390, 23/112, 32/263; ~ *þan* 27/
138, 367, 34/85.

oratory *n.* chapel 26/288 s.d.
ordeyn(e) *v.* 1 provide, supply 5/129, 10/
412, 11/175; prepare, provide 27/40;
ordeyn *pa. t. I* ~ . . . *for me* I planned to
use as my own 34/143; **ordeyn** *imp. sg.*
27/341; 2 ordain, decree 24/158;
ordeyned, ordeynyd *pp.* 4/203, 25/
203, 28/27; 3 prepare 27/47, 37/50, 56;
ordeyn *imp. sg.* 27/42, 347; 4 bring
about 27/100; 5 arrange or conduct
(matters) 27/326; 6 plot, plan *in*
ordeyne *pl.* 41/226; 7 appointed,
assigned *in* **ordeyned** *pa. t.* 13/24;
ordeyned, ordayned *pp.* 19/150, 21/
252, 26/363, 39/74.
**ordenawns, ordenauns, ordenaunce,
ordenawnce** *n.* plan, decree 4/216, 14/
236, 27/1, 16, 53, PS 24; scheme 26/57,
27/134; preparation 27/52 s.d., 61.
ordyr *n.* order 6/116.
ore *n.* grace, favour 8/247.
ore 'our', see **we.**
orygynal *adj.* original: ~ *synne* 19/47.
orryble, horible, horryble *adj.* horrible
27/241, 31/1st s.d., 38/32, 41/155, 159.
ortografye *n.* orthography 21/6.
ost *n.* army, host 35/211.
ostage *n.* dwelling place, inn 15/66.
oth(e) *n.* oath 6/89; *withowte* ~ truly 13/
140; *for an* ~ because of an oath 29/210;
othis, othys *pl.* 6/85, 87, 93, 26/89, 95.
other, othyr, othir *pron.* (the) other 21/
115, 24/33, 27/533, 32/84 s.d., 41/202;
non ~ *than trowth is* nothing but the
truth 6/160; *it may non* ~ *be* it cannot be
otherwise 15/46; *non* ~ nothing else 25/
153; **otherys** *gen. sg.* 26/282, 27/535;
other(e), othyr *pl.* 11/128, 278, 15/230,
38/97.
other(e), othyr, odyr *adj.* other Pr 29,
2/249, 6/70, 144, 14/174, 27/81, 28/80
s.d.; any other 10/78, 21/10; another 19/
183.
**ought, owth, outh, owgth, owught,
howth, aught** *adv.* at all, in any respect
10/143, 13/4, 14/42, 18/153, 21/50, 27/
462, 28/94, 36/49, 41/37, 374.
oure, howre, hour(e) *n.* hour, time 14/
47, 25/132, 26/23, 27/431, 435, 41/308,
432; *the* ~ *of incense, þe* ~ *of incensynge*
(at) the time appointed for burning

oure (*cont.*)
　　incense 13/31, 77; **howrys, owrys** *pl.*
　　25/221; *all* ~ at all hours 9/259.

our(e) see **we.**

out, outh, owt *interj.* (expressing dis-
　　tress, anger, indignation) 4/174, 174,
　　186, 41/389, 401, 475, 42/31, 32, 35; ~
　　upon (*on*) a curse on 31/38, 32/97, 35/
　　170.

outborn *adj.* born out of the region 30/
　　122n.

outcrye *pr. subj.* proclaim, denounce 24/
　　239.

out(e), owt(e), owth, outh, owughte
　　adv. out, forth Pr 76, 107, 175, 14/241,
　　264, 15/252, 19/145, 20/200, 26/364, 27/
　　491, 28/148 s.d.; *all* ~ *and* ~ completely
　　23/8; away, gone Pr 252, 10/466, 12/148;
　　openly 14/241, 281, 27/234; *prep.* out of
　　8/108.

outh see **ought** *adv.*, **out** *interj.*, **out(e)**
　　adv., **owght** *n.*

outrage *v.* act outrageously, sin 14/132.

outrage *adj.* wicked, outrageous
ouyr, ovyr, over *prep.* across, along,
　　upon Pr 445, 4/228, 5/107, 18/280, 19/
　　143; over, above 4/248, 16/19, 22/94;
　　above in authority 5/2, 242, 245; in con-
　　travention of 14/243; surpassing 16/
　　103.

ouyr *v.* hover: ~ *hym on* hover above him
　　Pr 260.

ovyrall *adv.* everywhere 4/150.

ovyrcome *v.* **1** surpass 5/219; **ovyr-
　　comyth** *pr. 3 sg.* 11/115; **2** overcomes Pr
　　409; **ouercam** *pa. t.* Pr 248; **ouyrcom**
　　pp. 23/201.

ovyrdon *adv.* exceedingly 2/80.

ouyrest *adv.* on top of the rest 31/1st s.d.

ouyrhie *adv.* too high 41/58.

ovyrlayd *pp.* lain upon, had sexual inter-
　　course with 14/216.

ouyrlede *v.* overcome, overmaster 27/96.

ovyrlonge *adv.* too long 24/113.

ovyrsen *v.* attend to, keep watch over 21/
　　264.

ouyrsprede *v.* spread or extend over 22/
　　94.

ouyrthrow(e) *v.* vanquish 16/113; cast
　　down, destroy 27/119; **overthrowyht**
　　pr. 3 sg. 8/141; **ovyrthrowyn** *pa. t.* fell
　　down 29/107; **ovyrthrowyth** *imp. pl.*
　　32/19.

ovyrtok *pa. t.* caught up with Pr 468;
　　ovyrtake *pp.* 38/41.

ovyrwood *adj.* exceedingly mad 6/78.

ovyth *quasi-impers.* behoves 5/110.

ow *interj.* oh! alas! 4/92, 12/34, 15/37.

owe, howe *pr. 1 sg.* **1** ought 21/276, 26/
　　401n., 41/104; **howyth, owyght** *pr. 3 sg.*
　　10/232, 309; **owe, howe** *pl.* 10/303, 41/
　　24; *what þat ʒe* ~ your duty, obligation
　　10/7n.; **2** possesses *in* **owth** *pr. 3 sg.* 10/
　　70; **3** owe *in* **owyn** *pl.* 41/354.

owght, owth, ought, outh *n.* aught, any-
　　thing 9/289, 12/4, 14/66, 15/107, 27/
　　413, 41/162.

owyn, owe, own *adj.* own Pr 15, 63, 420,
　　2/199, 5/172, 10/411, 25/67.

ownere *n.* owner 22/159.

owr(e) see **we.**

owrys see **oure** *n.*

owth see **ought** *adv.*, **out(e)** *adv.*, **owe** *pr.
　　1. sg.*, **owght** *n.*

owtrage *adj.* wicked, outrageous 4/18,
　　6/138.

owught(e) see **ought** *adv.*, **out(e)** *adv.*

ox(e) *n.* ox 6/175, 29/125, 36/19.

pace see **pas(se).**

pacyens *n.* patience 9/298, 305, 13/178A.

pad(de) *n.* toad 18/88, 20/211.

page *n.* boy 20/45, 30/23; (term of con-
　　tempt) knave 20/168, 171.

pagent *n.* play, scene, act Pr 14, 27, 53.

pay *n.* satisfaction, pleasure: *to þi* ~ so as
　　to please you 5/8; *plesyth to þi* ~, *is ples-
　　ynge to ʒoure* ~ pleases you 10/254, 25/
　　103.

payd *pa. t.* paid 29/124; **payd, payed** *pp.*
　　pleased 9/44, 12/197, 41/89, 296; *wers
　　. . . * ~ treated worse 14/86; **pay** *pr. subj.*
　　give (one's) just deserts 24/189.

payn see **peyn(e).**

pak *n.* bundle, package 14/193.

paleys *n.* palace 18/14, 16.

palme *n.* palm-tree branch or leaf 41/
　　113, 220, 357; palm tree 41/134; ~ *Sun-
　　day* Pr 308.

palsye *n.* palsy 13/141.

pap(pe) *n.* breast 21/43; *here moderys* ~ Pr
　　227; ~-*hawk* suckling child (hawk after
　　the pap) 18/88; ~-*hawkys* *pl.* 20/11;
　　pappys *pl.* 20/100.

Paraclyte *n.* Holy Ghost PS 7.

paradys(e), paradis(e) *n.* Eden Pr 35, 51, 2/31, 86; heaven Pr 426, 7/80, 16/97.

parayl *n.* appearance 27/322.

paramoure *n.* (of a child) darling 5/37.

pardé *interj.* by God, indeed 12/163.

parfyte *adj.* complete, perfect 11/294, 294, 298.

park *n.* grove 28/16 s.d.; **parkys** *pl.* enclosed tracts of land 18/182.

parlement *n.* parliament Pr 270, 9/307, 28/57.

parochonerys *n.* parishioners 8/56.

partabyl *adj.* able to share 27/483.

part(e) *n.* 1 part, portion 8/55, 56, 57; **partys** *pl.* 8/51, 21/83; 2 duty, office 26/231, 301, 34/206; 3 party 27/314.

parte *v.* 1 part company, depart 13/164, 24/114, 32/262; **parte** *pr. 1 sg.* 20/199; **partyth** *pr. 3 sg.* 23/220; **partyn, part** *pl.* 13/166 s.d.; 27/348 s.d.; ~ *atwynne* 23/112; **parte** *pr. subj.* 10/390; 2 divide *in* **parte** *pr. 1 sg.* 2/5.

partenere *n.* ~ *of* sharer in 34/117.

party *n. on his* ~ for his part 27/97, 341.

pas *n.* course, way 9/95, 25/316, 36/23; strange phenomenon, miracle 16/23n.; pace 30/40.

paschal(l) *adj.* paschal 27/43, 76 s.d., 369.

Pasche *n.* Passover 27/44; ~ *day* 31/96, 175.

passage *n. take* ~ go 3/190; pregnancy 11/257, 327.

pas(se), pace, passyn *v.* 1 penetrate Pr 401; 2 go, proceed 4/140, 10/372, 11/148, 14/385, 19/147, 26/235, 31/71; *out of* ... ~ escape from 26/244; **pas(se), pace** *pr. 1 sg.* 1/76, 5/199, 22/121; **passyth** *pr. 3 sg.* 26/453 s.d.; **pas(se), pace** *pl.* Pr 466, 6/109, 41/182; ~ *... lythly away* present in haste or incompletely 9/299; **passent** *pr. p. evyn* ~ steadily journeying 38/276; **passe** *pr. subj.* (forming *imp.*) 3/12; 3 go by 16/23; 4 surpass, exceed 21/105, 24/7; **passyth, passeth** *pr. 3 sg.* 10/17, 21/54, 34/32, 35/133; ~ *... of powsté* is more powerful than 20/169; **passyn, passe** *pl.* 10/7, 15/75, 26/82; 5 continue, proceed 26/327; 6 passes *in* **passyth** *pr. 3 sg.* 34/149; **passe** *pl.* 9/4; **past, passyd** *pp.* 26/204, 276, 30/33, 32/56; *(awey) is* ~ has come to an end 2/282, 13/172; 7 departed *in* **paste** *pp.* 41/227; **pace** *pr. subj.* 12/121.

Passyon *n.* the Passion Pr 296, 13/182A, 19/87.

patryarke *n.* patriarch 5/10; bishop PS 24; **patryarchys, patryarkys** 11/35, 15/50.

pat(t)h(e) *n.* path 26/144, 148, 157; **pathys, patthis** *pl.* 26/135, 164.

pawsacyon *n.* pause, intermission 9/304.

peerles, pereles *n.* peerless 16/91, 34/13.

pe(e)s *n.* peace 2/56, 7/124, 126; (as personif.) 11/120, 143; quiet 8/17; **Pesys** *gen. sg.* 11/166.

peyn *v.* inflict pain 36/30; **peyn** *pr. 1 sg.* suffer 28/36; **peynyth, peyneth** *pr. 3 sg.* grieves 31/15; *it* ~ 11/169, 29/42, 32/160; **peynyd** *pp.* subjected to suffering 13/18.

peynde *v.* press, torment 32/187.

peyn(e), payn *n.* suffering, torment, pain Pr 321, 323, 1/74, 3/180, 4/239, 34/194; *is grett* ~ is very distressing 23/209; punishment, penalty Pr 47; *in* ~ *of* on pain of losing 34/194; on pain of 41/62, 397; **peynes, peynys** *pl.* sufferings, torments, pains 11/3, 27, 72, 28/15, 41/444.

peynful *adj.* distressing 41/178.

peynfully *adv.* with pain and suffering 20/257, 38/364.

peynfulnes(se) *n.* pain, suffering 3/77, 22/8.

peyr(e) *n.* pair Pr 74, 4/114, 133.

peys *n.* weight 25/406.

peler(e) *n.* pillar 31/195, 210 s.d., 41/245.

pelle, pellys *n.* furred cloaks, furs 18/198, 26/208 s.d.

penauns, penawns, penawnce, penaunce *n.* penance 22/16, 24, 137, 139, 140, 143, 149, 151, 154, 26/131; pain, suffering 25/7.

penne *n.* pen 32/176 s.d.

pens *n.* pence Pr 366, 19/178, 27/198.

pepyl(l), pepil, peple *n.* people, company Pr 6, 8/106, 9/10, 14/337, 41/43, 61.

pepyr *n.* pepper 2/35.

perayl, peryl *n.* peril 26/195; *per is* ~ *in* it is dangerous 34/175; **perellys** *pl.* 8/2, 27/557.

peraventure, perauenture *adv.* perhaps 9/121, 15/187, 30/206.

perce, perysch, perchyn *v.* pierce 19/89, 21/97, 25/454.

perdure *v.* persist 26/411.
pere *n.*[1] peer Pr 24, 2/108, 121.
pere *n.*[2] pear 2/37.
pere *v.* appear 14/8, 41/337.
pereles see **peerles.**
perfyght *adv.* perfectly, completely 12/132.
perfyth *n.* perfection, fulfilment 26/467.
performe *v.* perform 10/308; **performyd** *pp.* 40/6.
perysch see **perce.**
perysch(e) *v.* perish 11/5, 127, 142; **peryschyd** *pp.* 11/139.
perjory *n.* perjury 26/114.
perle *n.* pearl 16/91.
perpetual(l) *adj.* perpetual 9/173, 41/196.
perplexité *n.* distress 41/112.
persecucyon *n.* persecution, oppression 26/49, 27/2, 41/241.
perseverawns *n.* in ~ steadfastly 26/408.
persevere *n.* preserver 11/281.
person(e) *n.* **1** person 8/6, 21/96, 27/264; *þi* ~, *ʒoure* (*youre*) ~ you 8/162, 28/151, 41/124; *þin owyn* ~ yourself 26/407; *his* ~ him 26/447; **personys** *pl.* people 8/3, 27/117, 28/80 s.d.; **2** person of the Trinity 11/266, 21/111; *þe secunde* ~ *attrybute* the attribute of the Son 21/129; **personys** *pl.* 1/12, 16, 9/23.
perteyneth *impers.* is (one's) duty or function 8/40.
pertly *adv.* publicly, *or* expertly Pr 5.
perverte, peruertyth *pr. 3 sg.* misleads, corrupts 26/218, 41/43.
pes *imp. pl.* stop (talking) 41/27.
pes see **pe(e)s.**
pet see **pitt.**
pete see **put(t).**
peté, pyté, pety *n.* pity, mercy Pr 289, 371, 5/264, 8/172, 9/293, 10/482, 11/6, 34, 12/25; cause for pity 5/100.
petéfful, petyful *adj.* pitiful 25/412; full of pity, merciful 28/183.
petycyons *n.* petitions, requests 9/230.
peusawns *n.* number, crowd 27/79.
Pharao *n.* Pharaoh 27/386.
Pharysew *n.* Pharisee 24/65; **Pharasy** the Pharisaic sect 26/223; **Pharaseus** *pl.* Pharisees 26/288 s.d.; **Pharysewys** *gen. pl.* Pr 284.
phesyk, fesyk *n.* medical science 21/20, 29/89.

phylosophye *n.* philosophy 21/14.
pyan *n.* peony 2/35.
pychyn, pyth *v.* thrust Pr 404; pierce 20/12; **pyght** *pa. t.* thrust 38/126; **pyght(e), pyht, pyth, pygth** *pp.* placed, set, established, situated Pr 21, 1/74, 80, 2/149, 15/264, 23/70, 32/268; implanted Pr 167; arranged 27/212; thrust 38/364.
pygth *n.* pith, essential quality 10/433.
pyke *v.* pick 10/283.
pylgrym *n.* pilgrim 38/49; **pylgrimys, pylgrymys, pylgrymes** *pl.* 8/53, 38/53, 54.
pylgrymagys *n.* pilgrimages 13/17.
pylis *n.* towers, strongholds 23/176.
pylle *imp. pl.* tear, pluck 29/190, 190.
pillid *adj.* tonsured, *or* bare, miserable 41/33.
pyn(e) *n.* pain, suffering 15/221, 25/43.
pynnacle *n.* pinnacle 23/109, 114, 26/30.
pynne *n.* marker at centre of a target 14/222; point, peak 23/110.
pynne *v.* fix, confine 2/190; imprison 27/256.
pynt *n.* pint 20/148.
pyté see **peté.**
pyth see **pychyn.**
pitt, pyt(t)(e), pet *n.* grave, pit Pr 307, 25/140, 149, 157, 161, 422; pit (of hell) 2/269, 6/90, 20/253, 41/482, 487; hole 38/325; **pyttys** *gen. sg.* of the grave 25/259.
place, plas(e) *n.* place, *or* playing-place Pr 399, 2/57, 219, 9/95, 10/374, 23/185; *to* ~ into the (playing-)place 14/151; dwelling place Pr 300, 8/251, 12/168; *In dyverce* ~ 26/35; situation, employment 27/211; position 39/90; **placys** *pl.* dwelling places 18/263; places 26/462, 41/16.
plage *n.* affliction 13/35.
play, pley(e), pleyn *v.* **1** perform dramatically Pr 14, 28, 314, 359, 23/115; **pleyth** *pr. 3 sg.* 31/1st s.d.; **pleand, pleyand** *pr. p.* 8/3, 41/25; **pleyd** *pp.* Pr 519, 31/1st s.d.; **2** be joyful, enjoy oneself 2/218; **3** (euphem.) have sexual intercourse 14/265, 271; **4** perform: *gan þer do* ~ caused to be performed there 26/22; **5** play 29/189; **pleyth** *pr. 3 sg.* 19/146 s.d.

playn, pleyn *n.* plain, meadow land 4/244, 25/223.

planetys *n.* heavenly bodies 9/115.

plas(e) see **place**.

plasmacyon *n.* forming, creation 21/60.

plate *n.* plate-armour 41/393; **platys** *pl.* pieces of silver money Pr 318, 27/305, 29/14.

pley(e), play *n.* 1 dramatic performance Pr 102, 309, 526; **pleys** *pl.* Pr 6; 2 pleasure, joy 2/300, 25/127, 35/32; **pleys** *pl.* 33/6; 3 sexual play, intercourse 6/142, 42/121; 4 **pleys** *pl.* games, amusements 20/235.

pleyn(e), playn *adj.*[1] open to view, unobstructed Pr 399, 38/188; ordinary 9/174; unconfined, open 18/182; clear, readily understood 34/163, 37/83, 39/6; bare 41/457; *as absol.* plain fact 24/205; *adv.* plainly, clearly, manifestly Pr 264, 4/180, 6/63, 27/554; directly 23/157, 26/351, 34/148; openly 34/168.

pleyn, playn *adj.*[2] perfect, complete 7/80, 26/40, 33/6; ~ *bench* full council 41/72; *adv.* fully 28/9.

pleyng *vbl. n.* performance (of a play) Pr 237.

pleynge *ppl. adj.* playing 11/315.

pleynyn *v.* complain 12/110.

pleynly *adv.* openly, plainly 7/3, 36, 54.

plenté, plenty *n.* abundance 2/300, 10/11, 16/97, 23/90; (*of*) *gret* ~ abundant 2/63, 85, 301.

plenté *adj.* plentiful, in abundance 5/125, 27/199; *anow* ~ in great abundance 3/19.

plentevous *adj.* plentiful 26/64.

plentevously *adv.* abundantly 4/3.

plesande see **plesyng(e)** *ppl. adj.*

plesaunt *adj.* agreeable, pleasing 14/398, 22/150, 26/110.

plesawns, plesauns, plesans *n.* pleasure, wish, will 1/9, 6/14, 26/270, 406, 29/134, 42/121; *after my* ~ as I please 1/9; *to* (*at*) (*one's*) ~ as pleases (sb.) 9/234, 22/181, 25/5; *take þat to* ~ take pleasure in that 26/449; *very* ~ true bliss 29/34; pleasure-giving: *prevy* ~ prostitution 26/104.

plese, plesyn *v.* please Pr 6, 2/40, 3/55, 4/13, 6/9; **plesyth** *pr. 3 sg.* 27/536, 38/171; *impers.* 3/130, 12/17, 13/146; *as* ~ *us tyll* as we please 2/79; *as* ~ *the* as you

please 6/92; *as* ~ *to þi pay* as pleases you 10/254; **plesyd** *pa. t.* and *pp.* 8/176, 11/69, 136; **plese, plesyth, plesyt** *pr. subj.* 37/99; *impers.* 8/169, 9/50, 66; ~ *it* may it please 11/33, 152; ~ *3ow* may it please you 26/225; **plesyd** *pa. subj. impers.* 15/35.

plesyng(e) *vbl. n.* liking, pleasure: *to* (*one's*) ~ as pleases (sb.) 3/2, 27/282; *to his* ~ pleasing to him 3/59; *be 3oure* ~ pleases you 8/94; *to 3oure* ~ as you please; *at oure* ~ as we wish 27/65.

plesyng(e), plesande *ppl. adj.* pleasing 9/34, 25/103, 26/139, 382.

pleson *n.* *to my* ~ pleases me (best) 11/117.

plete *v.* plead 20/198.

ply *v.* work at accomplishing 26/208.

plyght, plyth, plight *n.*[1] manner Pr 402; state, condition 4/71, 12/129, 14/304, 15/148.

plyght *n.*[2] danger 23/120.

plyght, plyth, plyte, plyht, plyghtys *pr. 1 sg.*[1] 1 assure, promise Pr 33, 395, 2/102, 150, 18/14, 22/110, 34/240, 38/148; *I* ~ I assure (you) 20/38; 2 pledge 14/52, 82; **plyth** *pr. 3 sg.* Pr 153; **plyght** *pp.* 6/146.

plyght *v.*[2] close, fold (one's hand) 15/261.

plucke, pluk *v.* pluck 15/37, 39; **pluk** *imp. pl.* ~ *up 3oure herte* cheer up, take heart 25/79.

poer see **pore** *adj.*, **power(e)** *n.*

poynt *n.* smallest part, jot 26/477; **poyntys** *pl.* feats 30/179; laces 26/72.

polycye *n.* political science 21/26.

polucyon *n.* uncleanliness, pollution 15/232.

polutyd *pp.* befouled 15/303.

pompe *n.* pomp Pr 21, 6/107, 18/133.

poosté see **powsté**.

popetys *n.* (used ironically of children) 'darlings' 20/11.

pore, poer, power *adj.* poor 2/171, 6/103, 109, 15/268, 27/71, 196, 200, 32/88 s.d.; *as noun* 13/108, 42/18; **porys** *gen. sg.* 11/50.

pore see **power(e)** *n.*

portys *n.* gates 5/226.

portature *n.* appearance 3/36.

possede *v.* possess 5/226.

possyble *adj.* possible 21/55, 26/214; able, sufficient (to do sth.) 26/211.

posté see **powsté.**
postelis see **apostel.**
potacyon *n.* drink, potion 14/237, 333, 347.
potage *n.* soup, meal 14/272.
pourge *v.* purge 14/141.
pousté see **powsté.**
poverté, povert *n.* poverty 8/56, 10/419, 19/203, 26/64.
power(e), poer, pore *n.* **1** power, ability 4/2, 7/32, 13/100, 15/75, 30/123, 31/82, 131; **powerys** *pl.* 26/211; **2** vigour 34/172.
power see **pore** *adj.*
pownde, pounde *n. pl.* pounds 20/148, 35/199.
powndys *n.* enclosures for cattle, *or* ponds 18/182.
powsté, pousté, po(o)sté *n.* power 1/10, 18, 2/107, 12/218, 16/141, 38/63, 41/412.
pray *n.* prey 24/115; preying, seizing 32/152.
pray, prey, preyn, preyen *v.* pray, beseech Pr 322, 8/144, 145, 146, 11/130, 32/84, 276, 41/247; **pray, prey** *pr. 1 sg.* 2/127, 3/69, 4/70; (with ellips. of 'I') 24/216; **prayth, prayt** *pr. 3 sg.* Pr 136, 378, 26/247, 28/24 s.d.; **pray, prey(e), prayth** *pl.* Pr 523, 527, 4/12; **praynge(e), preyand, preyng** *pr. p.* 7/131, 10/244, 13/68, 41/23, 26; **prayd, preyd, prayed** *pa. t.* 10/55, 25/92, 199, 30/14, 41/294; **pray, prey(e)** *imp.* 5/87, 21/43, 26/200; **pray, prey** *pr. subj.* 10/105; (forming *imp.*) 10/111, 15/80.
prayng *vbl. n.* praying 8/41.
prayour, prayer(e), preyere, preyour, prayჳer, prayr *n.* prayer 8/161, 176, 220, 9/190, 10/62, 106, 230, 19/42, 28/19, 41/107, 246; **prayers, prayorys, prayerys** *pl.* 8/162, 9/243, 11/36, 53, 80.
praty *adj.* pleasant, fine 10/459; ingenious, cunning 23/108; excellent, clever 30/15.
pratyly *adv.* skilfully, nicely 9/95.
precepte *pp.* laid down as a precept 27/385.
precept(t)ys *n.* precepts 6/59, 27/428, 436.
prech(e) *v.* preach 22/55, 102, 140; **prechyth** *pr. 3 sg.* Pr 99, 22/3, 23/18; **prechyn, preche** *pl.* 41/69, 268; **prechyng** *pr. p.* 41/190; **prechid** *pa. t.* 41/283;

prechyd, prechid *pp.* 23/95, 26/462, 29/134; **preche** *imp. sg.* 6/45; **preche** *pr. subj.* 6/41, 24/102.
precher *n.* preacher PS 11; **prechouris, prechours** *pl.* 41/33, 270, 398.
prechyng(e) *vbl. n.* preaching Pr 288, 23/103, 24/54.
precyous *adj.* precious 13/182A, 26/436, 27/438.
pref see **preve.**
pregnaunt *adj.* full of significance or consequence 40/34.
preyse *v.* praise 10/432; **prayse** *imp. pl.* 8/207.
preysyng(e), preysenge *vbl. n.* praising 10/301, 444, 13/67, 120.
prelat *n.* prelate 26/165.
prendyd *pp.* seized, taken 20/211.
prent(e) *imp. pl.* impress, fix Pr 512. 6/66.
prerogatyff *n.* divine privilege, distinction 11/304n.
pres *pr. pl.* assail, beset 7/127; **pressyd** *pp.* afflicted 32/228.
pres(e) *n.* crowd, throng Pr 5, 325, 2/29; *put... in* ~ put (oneself) forward, in the thick of things 29/98, 34/200.
presens(e), presence *n.* presence 3/11, 8/28, 11/328, 12/179, 19/106, 29/23; **his** ~ him Pr 207, 26/260, 265; *to ჳoure (oure)* ~ tò you (us) 8/161, 21/12, 24/197; *in* ~ present 21/138, 25/354; *ჳoure* ~ you 26/275, 27/64, 29/77; place 41/130.
present *n.* present time: *in* ~ immediately, *or* then Pr 149.
present *adj. in place* ~ in this very place 11/268; *adv.* here and now 26/188, 27/76, 30/162; *anon* ~ 2/146, 30/146; here 26/174; there 26/287.
present(e) *v.* **1** present, report 11/36, 24/84, 26/284; **2** represent *in* **present** *pr. 1 sg.* 26/209; **3** presents, offers *in* **presentyth** *pr. 3 sg.* 19/201; **presente** *pl.* 9/17 s.d.; **presentand** *pr. p.* 41/133; **4** claims, represents *in* **present** *pr. 3 sg.* 26/295; **present** *pl.* 14/123.
presentacyon *n.* presentation 9/295.
presentys, present *n. pl.* presents 9/277 s.d., 18/23, 139.
presydent *n.* head, chief PS 14.
preson, presyn *n.* prison, confinement 26/240, 27/104, 252, 38/315.

preson *v.* imprison 41/76; **presonde** *pp.* 31/107.

presoner *n.* prisoner 42/106.

prest *adj.* ready Pr 358, 10/29; inclined 42/113; keen 32/277; *adv.* quickly 18/14, 35/163, 41/505.

prest(e), prysste *n.* priest 7/38, 8/61, 9/65, 42/14; **prestys, prestes** *pl.* 8/26, 30, 94, 9/50, 278.

presthood *n.* priests 28/64.

presume *v.* presume to go 8/103; **presumyd** *pa. t.* acted presumptuously 11/109; **presume** *pr. subj.* presume to go forward 14/244.

presumpcyon *n.* arrogance 11/98; presumption (of salvation) 26/160.

pretende *v.* try, attempt (to act) 41/161n.; **pretendist** *pr. 2 sg.* intend 41/217; **pretendyth** *pr. 3 sg.* claims to be 26/41; **pretende** *imp. sg.* direct (one's course) 9/95; proffer 41/113.

preudent, prudent *adj.* prudent, wise 26/209, 257, 29/45.

preuayll, prevayll see **provayl(e)**.

preve, prove, preue, preuyn, prevyn, pref *v.* 1 approve of, *or* prove the worth of 5/195; 2 make trial of, put to the test 14/299, 18/88, 20/12, 38/85; **preve** *pr. subj.* 15/246; 3 prove to be 14/351, 15/180; **preve** *pr. 1 sg.* 14/131, 324, 41/45; **prevyd** *pa. t.* 14/401; 4 prove, demonstrate 21/79, 38/296, 39/5; **preve** *pr. 1 sg.* 38/115; **preue** *pl.* 34/12; **prevyd, previd** *pa. t.* 38/227, 279; 5 try out 31/57; 6 prove to be true 38/381, 387; 7 (with fut. sense) find out by testing *in* **preue** *pr. 1 sg.* 23/111.

prevely, preuyly, prevyly, preuely *adv.* secretly, stealthily 10/200, 24/175, 27/268 s.d., 347, 32/192, 34/251, 35/258, 36/162, 41/378.

prevv *adi.* intimate 26/104; secret 26/298, 27/269, 274.

prevyd *ppl. adj.* proven 26/191.

prevyde *imp. pl.* go beforehand 11/149n.

prevydens *n.* provision: *with good ~* properly and fully 9/300.

preuylage *n.* privilege 11/323.

pryde, pride *n.* pride Pr 22, 236, 239, 1/66, 2/259, 6/107.

pryk, prycke *n.* prick, puncture: *dethis ~* mortal wound 2/229; target 4/156, 157.

primat *n.* primate 26/209.

prime *n.* first hour of the day 30/17, 22.

prime *adj.* young, excellent 16/91.

prynce, prince *n.* prince, ruler 2/57, 7/48, 124, 126, 16/72, 19/133; *~ of prestys* (*prestes*) high priest 8/30, 94, 9/50; **princys, prynces, pryncys, prynsis, pryncis, prynsesse** *pl.* 20/169, 26/296, 27/277, 285, 29/89 s.d., 90, 30/19, 31/137, 41/29, 39, *40, 51, 390.

pryncepaly, pryncypaly *adv.* principally 5/19, 26/172.

prynces *n.* princess 41/117, 179.

pryncypal, pryncipal, prynspal *adj.* royal 11/332; principal, of highest importance 26/203, 39/4.

prys(se), prise, price *n.* value, worth: *of ~* worthy, excellent 2/33, 4/57, 16/91; *plenty of ~* abundance of precious things 16/97; pre-eminence: *bere þe ~* surpass all others 21/7; payment of money 31/99.

prysste see **prest(e)** *n.*

pryvyté, privité *n.* 1 private parts 2/174; **pryuytés** *pl.* 2/171; 2 privacy 12/134.

procede, prosede *v.* 1 proceed 9/28, 302, 10/166, 26/183; **procedyth** *pr. 3. sg.* 27/1st s.d.; **procede** *pr. subj.* 26/179, *187, 220; (forming *imp.*) 27/57; 2 issue 8/60, 11/181; **procedyng** *pr. p.* Pr 498; 3 proceed with 29/6, 17; **proced** *pl.* 9/6.

proces(se), prossesse *n.* course of proceeding or presentation 8/16; *be ~ in* due time 8/223; *be ~ in* time 26/224; story, performance 13/40.

processyon *n.* procession 14/238, 249, PS 10; *go þi ~* go in procession 14/331.

proferre *v.* promote, advance 29/57.

profyr *pr. subj.* proffer 27/282.

profyte, profite *v.* profit, be of benefit 8/6, 161, 13/64; **profyteth** *impers.* 23/145; **prophete** *pl.* 27/78.

progenitouris *n.* progenitors 7/75.

promese, promys *n.* 1 promise 27/561; **promessys** *pl.* 29/59; 2 fulfilment of a promise 39/50.

promysyd *pa. t.* promised *28/178.

promyssyon, promiscyon *n.* promise 7/28; fulfilment of a promise 39/21.

prongys *n.* pangs of distress 28/176.

pronunciacyon *n.* pronunciation 8/3.

properyd *pp.* empowered 26/165.

prophecy(e), prophesye, prophecie, prophesé, prophesey *n.* prophecy Pr

prophecy(e) *n*(*cont.*)
108, 7/3, 94, 12/173, 13/127, 16/38, 58, 74, 26/426, 28/4; **profecyes** *pl.* 8/70.

prophecy(e), prophesy(e) *v.* prophesy Pr 110, 114, 27/390, 29/182, 186; **prophesye** *pr. 1 sg.* 26/125; **prophesyed, prophecyed** *pa. t.* 13/170A, 26/395.

prophete *n.* prophet 7/1, 33, 53; **prophetys, prophetis** *gen. sg.* 18/30, 26/426, 41/385; **prophetys** *pl.* Pr 109, 471, 11/35.

prophetes *n.* prophetess 19/64.

prophytabyll, profytable *adj.* fruitful 5/224; beneficial, valuable 29/56.

propyr, propire *adj.* true, perfect 9/118; (my) own 41/316.

propyrly *adv.* correctly, *or* severally 24/235.

propyrté *n.* attribute, quality 21/121, 132.

proporcyon *n. of* ~ proportionately 26/78.

prose *n.* story 26/177.

prosodye *n.* prosody and phonology 21/8.

prossesse see **proces(se)**.

prosperité *n.* prosperity 8/154.

prostrat *adj.* prostrate 8/162, 9/243.

protestacyon *n.* solemn affirmation 7/77.

provayl(e), preuayll, prevayll *v.* 1 avail, be effectual 26/193, 251; **provaylys** *pl.* 26/37n.; 2 prevail, be victorious 25/440; 3 be accepted or used (as a custom) 27/528.

proverbe *n.* proverb 12/81.

provyde, provide *v.* arrange, prepare, provide 26/51, 122, 165, 182.

provynce, province *n.* district, territory 29/76, 34/75.

prow *n.* benefit 12/89, 13/173, 34/56.

prowde, proude *adj.* proud 13/104; *as noun* 8/141, 13/101.

prowdely *adv.* proudly 20/194.

prudens *n.* wisdom, prudence 26/60.

prune *v.* trim, preen, *or* cut down 18/88.

psalme *n.* psalm 10/454; sacred song 13/81, 127, 19/146 s.d.; **psalmys, psalmes, psalmus** *pl.* 9/101, 10/430, 437, 445, 449.

pshalmodyeth *pr. pl.* celebrate by singing psalms, 'hymn' 41/167.

puere see **pure**.

pullyn, pull(e) *v.* 1 6/34, 29/180 s.d., 31/210 s.d., 212 s.d., 32/48 s.d.; **pullyn, pulle** *pl.* 28/104 s.d., 30/236 s.d.; **pul(le)** *imp.* 32/53, 62, 65; 2 drink (with fut. sense) *in* **pulle** *pr. 1 sg.* 14/362.

punche *v.* pierce *or* torment 36/30.

punchement *n.* punishment 11/93.

punchyth *imp. pl.* punish 8/159.

purcatorye *n.* purgatory 33/48.

pure, puere *adj.* physically pure, clear 15/231, 239, 22/27.

purenesse *n.* spiritual purity 6/15.

purgacyon *n.* purgation Pr 186, 14/235, 284; exculpation 14/179, 400, 403.

purgyd *pp.* exculpated 14/292.

puryfyed, purefyed *pp.* made ceremonially clean 19/104, 107.

purpyl *adj.* purple 31/212 s.d.

purpos(e) *n.* assertion 14/223; purpose, objective 24/46, 26/46, 250.

purpose *pr. 1 sg. refl.* intend, plan 4/67, 26/39, 41/173; **purpos(e)** *pl.* Pr 53, 59, 309; *refl.* Pr 5, 297.

purpure *n.* purple robes 41/51.

purs(e) *n.* money-bag, purse 14/25, 199, 26/83.

pursewe *v.* persecute 28/167.

purveyd *pa. t.* provided 12/224.

puruyauns, purvyauns, purvyaunce *n.* preparation, provision 26/35, 101, 27/55.

put(t), puttyn, pete *v.* put, place Pr 415, 480, 15/250, 18/124n., 20/11; ~ *away* put aside, abolish Pr 324; *he gan vs* ~ he brought us 2/226; ~ *ryght freschly owte* press forward energetically, extend 14/264; ~ (*sb.*) *in ... blame* accuse, disgrace (sb.) 12/73, 24/58; ~ *on* (*sb.*), ~ *aȝens* (*sb.*) accuse (sb.) of 27/94, 31/73, 185; ~ (*sb.*) *to* subject (sb.) to 27/85, 31/115; **putt** *pr. 1 sg. refl.* 24/276; **puttyst** *pr. 2 sg.* 16/97; ~ .... *to his fenaunce* brings to his end 25/2; **puttyth** *pr. 3 sg.* ~ ... *away* drives away 10/436; **put, puttyn** *pl.* 31/212 s.d., 212 s.d.; **put(t)** *pa. t.* ~ *me in blame* rebuked me 7/107; (with *fro*) removed, deposed 13/104; **puttyst** *pa. 2 sg.* ~ *from* deprived of 42/117; **put** *pp.* ~ *out* expelled 2/93; ~ *awey* driven away 10/438; ~ *at* subjected to 14/341; ~ ... *from* deprived of 20/223; thrust 2/229; **put(t)** *imp.* 38/386; ~ *in* entrust to 11/123; ~ *out* expel 22/87; ~ *hem to* subject him (them) to 26/116, 29/53.

quan see **whan** *adv.*
quelle see **qwelle.**
qwelp see **whelpe.**
queme see **qweme.**
quene, qwene *n.* quean, whore 24/69, 119, 149, 41/392; **qwenys, quenys** *pl.* 20/58, 67, 107.
quen(e) see **qwen(e).**
quer see **qwere.**
quyk see **qwyk(e).**
quyte, quyth see **qwyt(t)e** *v.*
quod *pa. t.* said 11/25.
qwake, quake, qweke *v.* quake Pr 507, 2/272n., 14/157, 35/138, 37/23, 41/382; **qwake** *pr. 1 sg.* 8/78, 9/270, 12/180; **qwakyth** *pr. 3 sg.* 28/20, 43, 34/7; **qwakyng** *pr. p.* 27/571.
qwall *n.* whale 7/72; **whallys** *gen. sg.* 38/116.
qwan see **whan** *adv.*
qwarel *n.* accusation 24/57; quarrel 27/296.
qwart *n.* health 25/61. Cf. **qwert(e).**
qwat see **what** *pron.*
qweche see **which(e)** *pron.*
qwed *adj.* evil Pr 422.
qwedyr *pr. 1 sg.* quiver 12/180.
qweynt *adj.* strange, unusual 23/115.
qweke *n.* the living 29/172.
qweke see **qwyk(e).**
qwelle, quelle *v.* kill Pr 378, 12/97, 18/91; vanquish, overcome 16/132, 35/66; destroy 41/228; **qwelle** *pr. subj.* kill 24/177.
qwelp see **whelpe.**
qweme, queme *v.* gratify 11/122, 41/202.
qwen(e), quen(e) *n.* queen Pr 110, 9/29, 11/335, 18/272, 41/278.
qwene, qwenys see **quene.**
qwens *adv.* whence 9/109.
qwere, quer *n.* company PS 13; choir, court 41/317.
qwere see **wher(e).**
qwert(e) *adj.* whole and sound 22/111, 38/256. Cf. **qwart.**
qwest *n.* pursuit 35/261.
qwestyon, questyon *n.* question 3/158, 21/93, 233, 23/8.
qwhan see **whan** *adv.*
qwhat see **what** *pron..*
qwher see **wher(e).**
qwheth, qweth *pr. 1 sg.* bequeath, assign

24/136, 25/107; **qwethyng** *in phrase quyk and* ~ alive and able to speak 37/61.
qwhy see **why** *adv.*
qwhich see **which(e).**
qwhyl see **whyl(l).**
qwy see **why** *adv.*
qwyk(e), quyk, qweke, qwycke *adj.* alive, live 10/450, 25/356, 26/86, 35/180, 37/61, 37/89, 38/221, 304; ~ *with childe* pregnant 11/209.
qwyl see **whyl(l).**
qwyle see **whyle.**
qwyppys see **whippe.**
qwyte, qwyght *adj.* free 24/207, 31/101, 37/77.
qwyt(t)e, qwyght, quyte *v.* **1** requite, pay 4/133, 5/42, 18/196; **quyth** *imp. sg.* 42/129; **qwyte** *pr. subj.* Pr 524, 10/253; **2** *refl.* clear (oneself) 35/151; **3** deliver 38/151.
qwyte see **white.**

race *n.* hurry 14/156.
race *v.* tear, go (in pieces) 21/208.
radyant *adj.* radiant 41/118, 177.
raftys *n.* sticks 20/32n.
rage *v.* take sexual pleasure 10/297.
ray *n.* array: *with a reed* ~ covered in blood 20/33; *as adj.* striped 26/244 s.d., 244 s.d.
rayed *pp.* prepared, furnished 41/298.
rayn *n.* rain 4/242.
rake *v.* sweep away, destroy 20/136n.
rakyl *adj.* rash 2/80.
rakynge *ppl. adj.* fast-moving 20/32.
ransake *imp. pl.* examine thoroughly 15/252.
rape *n.*[1] blows, *or* haste 20/10.
rape *n.*[2] haste 25/256.
rape *imp. pl. refl.* hasten 42/5.
rapely *adv.* quickly 42/16.
rappe *v.*[1] smite, *or* seize 20/136n.
rappe *pr. 1 sg.*[2] rush about 41/416.
rather(e) *adv.* rather 12/110, 21/113, 22/69.
raunsom, rawnsom *n.* ransom 24/14, 32/150.
rave, raue *v.* be insane, talk wildly 4/144, 10/277, 15/194, 28/144, 38/79; **raue** *pr. subj.* 18/145.
ravaschyd *ppl. adj.* ravaged 38/353.
ravyn *n.* raven 35/208.
rebate *v.* lessen 8/200.

rebawdye *n.* ribaldry 42/115.

rebawdys *n.* rogues 20/136.

rebukys *n.* rebukes 26/56.

receyve, reseyve *v.* **1** admit to one's company, welcome 9/205, 10/147, 153; **resseyuynge** *pr. p.* 41/112; **2** eat 9/249, 27/408, 412, 440; **reseyvyd** *pp.* 27/456 s.d.; **3** receive 19/188; **resseyved** *pa. t.* 41/355; **receyvyd** *pp.* 19/138; **receyve** *imp. sg.* receive, accept 19/170; **receyve, receyvyth, reseyve** *imp. pl.* 19/198, 205, 29/92; **receyve** *pr. subj.* 27/148.

rech(e) *v.* spread 18/134; attain, come to 18/233, 21/145.

recistens, recystence see **resystens**.

recke *pr. 1 sg.* (with *of*) care about 20/96; **rowth, routh** (with present sense) *ne I ~ nere* nor am I at all reluctant 19/157; *ne ~ nowth* don't care 41/418; **rowth** *impers. me ~ nowth* (*of*) I am not troubled by 30/61.

reclyne *v.* tend to return to 14/313.

recomaunde *pr. 1 sg. refl.* commend (oneself) 41/164.

recomende *pr. 1 sg. refl.* commend (oneself) 26/253; *absol.* 11/388; **recomende** *pl.* 25/195; **recomendynge** *pr.p.* 9/277; **recomende** *imp. pl.* 9/282, 11/308, 25/93.

reconsyle *imp. pl. refl.* restore (oneself) to purity 22/150; **reconsylid** *pp.* readmitted 9/56.

reconsyliacyon *n.* reconciliation 11/52.

record(e) *n.* record, evidence 14/396; *ber it ~ record* *18/238; *a gret ~* a long record (of crimes) 30/113; *bere ... ~* bear witness 36/105; witness: *take ~ of* call to witness 29/211.

record(e) *v.* bear witness to 10/333; declare as one's verdict 14/284; bear witness 26/338, 30/119; **record** *imp. sg.* (with *of*) have mind of 38/306; **record** *imp. pl.* (with *of*) give heed to 4/152.

recure, recuryn *v.* cure 26/476; obtain 27/75; restore to life 30/75; **recure** *pl.* obtain 10/106; **recuryd** *pa. t.* regained 26/38.

reddure *n.* severity *26/416; *settyn ~ (to)* to deal severely with 41/49.

rede see **reed** *n.*

red(e), reed *adj.* red 2/23, 18/35, 26/208 s.d.; red with blood 20/10, 33, 35/82.

rede, redyn *v.*[1] read 9/209, 10/424, 452, 32/176 s.d.; **rede** *pr. 1 sg.* 6/99, 41/22; **rede, redyn** *pl.* Pr 52, 108, 10/346, 13/160A, 15/52; **rede** *pp.* read, *or* spoken 18/253; **rede** *imp. pl.* 9/281.

rede *v.*[2] advise 38/317; **red(e)** *pr. 1 sg.* 6/185, 8/250, 10/169; direct 41/396; **rede** *pr. subj.* guide, protect 10/402.

redem *v.* redeem 28/8; **redempt, redemyd** *pp.* 23/136, 28/58.

redempcyon *n.* redemption 11/14, 150, 19/92.

redy *adj.* ready, willing Pr 336, 2/41, 4/134; *~ bent* drawn and ready Pr 85; *~ sowth* sought out 2/48; *~ dyht* given, dedicated 3/64; *~ bent, ~ dyght* prepared and ready 10/146, 154, 213, 20/151; *~ is dyth þe to* is prepared and ready for you 26/379.

redyly *adv.* readily Pr 414; without delay 42/5.

redynge *vbl. n.* reading, expounding 21/6.

redolens *n.* the redolence 26/449.

redresse *v.* amend, redress 26/410.

reducyd *pp.* recalled 28/48.

reed, rede *n.* advice, plan Pr 136, 2/141, 155, 207, 4/58, 6/95.

reed see **red(e)** *adj.*

refeccyon *n.* spiritual refreshment PS 36.

reforme *pr. subj.* amend 26/129.

refreyn *v.* restrain 6/184; **refreyn** *imp. pl.* 25/336.

refresch *v.* refresh 25/367.

refreschynge *vbl. n.* spiritual refreshment 13/157.

refuse *v.* deny 14/286, 28/113; **refusynge** *pr. p.* refusing 10/420; **refusyd** *pa. t.* rejected 31/20.

regal(l) *adj.* royal 7/29, 32, 8/40.

regyon *n.* realm, kingdom 9/265, 11/157, 18/1.

regne, reyn *n.* **1** reign, royal power 11/244, 20/9; **2** kingdom 18/178, 27/123, 483; *ȝoure ~* 18/22.

rehers *v.* name individually 26/117; relate 26/288; **rehercyd** *pp.* spoken *27/381.

rehersall, rehersayl *n.* recitation 26/418, PS 12.

reyn(e) *v.* **1** reign 20/119, 41/511, 514; **regne, reyne** *pr. 1 sg.* 18/69, 31/1; **regnyst** *pr. 2 sg.* 41/502; **regnyth** *pr. 3* *sg.* 4/24; **reynyth** *pl.* 11/331; **reygn-yng, reyneng, reynyng** *pr. p.* 3/66, 9/265, 11/244; **2** prevail, hold sway 26/173; **reyn** *pr. subj.* 26/170, 41/74; **3** flourished *in* **reyned** *pa. t.* 35/34.

reynenge *vbl. n.* rule 1/3.

Reynes *n.*[1] linen cloth of Raines 26/74.

reynes *n.*[2] loins 27/358, 417.

reyse *v.* give rise to, set going 14/40, 72; *vp* ~ raise up, arouse 18/225; raise, lift 25/231, 404, 408; **reysn't** raise it up, restore it 27/120, 32/108; raise (to life) 33/19, 38/146, 41/492; **reysed, reysid** *pa. t.* raised Pr 307, 38/149; **reysed** *pp.* raised up 35/127; **reyse** *imp. sg.* raise 41/503.

rejoycyd *pp.* rejoiced 20/247; **rejoyse** *imp. sg.* enjoy by possessing (a woman) 6/168.

rejoyse *n.* joy: *haddyst* ~ rejoiced 42/114.

rek(e)nyd *pp.* ~ *be rowe* named or considered in order 5/220, 18/175, 33/47.

rekenyng *n. make* ~ enumerate 29/160.

relacyon *n.* statement of clarification, explanation 10/105, 41/237; statement 15/90; *make* ~, *gyf* ~ tell 26/258, 30/121.

relefe *v.* remain 41/63n.

releffe *n.* relief, help 15/126.

relese *v.* relieve 23/72; abate 25/28.

relesere *n.* (with *of*) deliverer (from) 41/515.

releve *v.* relieve 25/326; assist 26/362; **releve** *pr. subj.* relieve 2/329.

relevys *n.* remainder 9/290.

rem *n.* realm 16/19; **remys** *pl.* 18/2, 23/164.

rememberawns *n.* memory 26/25.

remembyr *v.* remember 9/19; **remembyr** *pl.* 32/48; **remembryng** *pr. p.* 3/7; **remembryd** *pp.* 26/47; **remembyr** *imp. sg. refl.* take thought, bethink 27/267; **remembre, remembyr** *imp. pl.* 26/121, 189, 285, 28/2.

remeve, remeffe *v.* go elsewhere 26/122, 28/23; **remevyd** *pp.* removed 36/152; **remeve** *imp. sg.* remove 28/38; withdraw 38/383.

remyssyon *n.* forgiveness, pardon 7/131, 26/40.

rend(e) *v.* tear, tear out 20/10, 28/176, 29/36; **rende** *pr. 1 sg.* 25/109.

ren(ne), rennyn *v.* run Pr 331, 10/188, 20/32, 24/140, 28/148 s.d.; **renne** *pr. 1 sg.* 36/123, 41/416; **renne, rennyn** *pl.* Pr 333, 445, 26/25; **rennyng** *pr. p.* 29/89 s.d., 31/57 s.d., 34/100 s.d.; **ronne** *pp.* traversed, run 11/157; **renne** *imp.pl.* make haste 42/16; **renne** *pr. subj.* (forming *imp.*) run 36/126.

renogat *n.* renegade 41/42.

renown(e) *n.* renown 32/116, 42/18.

repelle *imp. sg.* repel 11/45.

repent *v. refl.* repent, be sorry 14/366, 26/179; **repentyd** *pa. t.* 11/44; **repent** *pr. subj. refl.* 27/93.

repentaunce *n.* repentance 24/2, 212, 41/448.

repentaunt *adj.* repentant 22/146, 24/285.

replett *adj.* replete 7/2.

replyeth *imp. pl.* apply (yourselves), *or* reply 41/173n.; **replye** *pr. subj.* apply 27/396n.

report *n.* statement 15/53.

repref(f), repreve, reprefe *n.* **1** shame, disgrace 3/103, 8/177, 12/115, 14/136, 27/85; **2** reproof, rebuke 14/341, 26/84, 116, 41/62; *withowt* ~ undeniably 26/366; **reprevys** *pl.* 26/51.

reprevable *adj.* deserving of reproof; *a mene onto hym* ~ a way to cast him in blame 26/219.

reprove, repreff *v.* reprove 10/73, 13/149; **repreff** *pl.* 26/76; **reprevyd** *pp.* 10/50; **repreve** *pr. subj.* 26/91.

reputacyon *n.* honour, reputation 11/278.

requyryth *pr. 3 sg.* demands, requires 29/88; **requyrand** *pr. p.* asking, entreating 41/126.

rere *v.* raise up 38/139; **rere** *pr. subj.* utter 6/161.

resch *n.* rush (the plant) 18/289.

rescu *n.* rescue 11/276.

reseyve, reseyvyd see **receyve.**

resemblauns *n.* appearance, features 26/67n.

resydens *n.* place of residence 21/143.

resystens, recystence, resistens, recistens *n.* resistance, opposition 7/5, 26/422, 30/159, 41/160; *is no* ~ there can be no opposition 21/15, 25/357, 447.

reson, resoun *n.* reason (the power or faculty) 3/116, 18/36, 26/28; ~ *is, is* ~ *is*

reson (*cont.*)
agreeable to reason 5/176, 27/130, 268;
man of ~ reasonable man 8/15; *be* ~ as
reason dictates 11/103; reasoning 21/
85; *sey grett* ~ make very reasonable
arguments 11/116; reason (why), justification 24/99, 105; **resonys** *pl.* reasons
42/16.

resonable *adj.* reasonable 9/191, 27/309.

resorte *v.* go 8/88; come 11/75, 26/451;
resortyng *pr. p.* returning 27/348 s.d.

responcyon *n.* response 41/41.

resseyved, resseyuynge see **receyve**.

rest(e), ressté *n.* repose, rest Pr 356,
15/2, 61, 27/251.

rest *v.*[1] **1** *refl.* rest 13/44, 29/87, 41/298;
restyth *pr. 3 sg.* 27/204 s.d.; **restyng** *pr.
p.* 41/463; **rest(e)** *imp. pl.* 41/331; *refl.*
25/19; **reste** *pr. subj. refl.* (forming *imp.*)
41/457; **2** be at ease, have repose 29/
215; **3** (with *on*) hang from 31/200; **4**
(with *in*) is founded on, vested in *in*
restyth *pr. 3 sg.* 1/3; **5** (with *in*)
depends on 30/85.

rest *v.*[2] stop 18/296.

restynge *vbl. n.* pause for rest 11/260 s.d.

res(s)tor(e), restoryn *v.* restore 2/295,
11/63, 39/33; ~ *þe place* fill the place 11/
48; set right, repair, cure 11/106, 203,
15/293.

restreyn *v. refl.* restrain (oneself) 25/371;
restreyn *imp. sg. refl.* restrict (oneself)
6/186.

resurreccyon, resurrexion *n.* resurrection 7/83, 25/301, 39/82.

retoryke *n.* rhetoric 21/23.

returne *v.* return 7/83, 8/222, 27/186;
returnyth *pr. 3 sg.* reverses course: ~
his trace comes back 5/243; **returne,
returnyth** *imp. pl.* return 8/118, 39/48.

reve *v.*[1] lacerate, *or* rob 18/147.

reve *v.*[2] remove 32/193; **revid** *pp.* taken
away 35/142.

revere *n.* river 40/21.

reuerens, reverens *n.* reverence Pr 196,
415, 6/127, 8/72, 14/381, 21/140;
respect, deference 21/276.

reverens *v.* reverence, worship 1/41, 25/
442.

revyfe *v.* revive 26/465; **revyfe** *pr. 3 sg.*
26/197.

revyled *pa. t.* reviled 9/54; **revylyd** *pp.*
8/128, 10/51.

reward(e) *n.* reward 15/273, 27/76, 29/
121.

reward(e) *v.* give (as a reward) 27/539;
reward 13/183A.

rewe *n. on* ~ in order, in a line Pr 313.

rew(e) *v.* feel regret for, rue 3/167, 14/
137, 27/336; grieve, feel compassion 34/
124, 35/130; *doth me* ~ fills me with
regret 4/106; **rewyst** *pa. 2 sg.* (with *on*)
felt pity for 42/104.

rewful *adj.* rueful 32/5.

rewle *n.* rule Pr 42; *in what* ~ ... *be
brought* how should (one) be punished
24/228.

rewle *v.* guide 4/131; *refl.* govern (oneself) 23/203; **rewlyd** *pp.* governed 3/29,
9/169, 10/123.

rewly, ruly *adj.* rueful, pitiable Pr 229,
402, 25/410, 31/57 s.d.; *adv.* shamefully,
pitifully 7/68, 38/268.

rewthe see **ruthe.**

ryal(l) *adj.* royal 18/2, 16, 240.

ryalté *n.* regal state or dignity 18/1, 27/4.

ryb *n.* rib Pr 33; **rybbys** *pl.* 20/10, 33.

ryc(c)hes *n.* riches 6/76, 77, 10/420.

rych(e), riche *adj.* excellent 2/70, 20/145;
costly, elegant 6/102, 18/197, 198;
wealthy 6/107, 110, 23/162; ~ *of* wealthy
in 6/120, 10/413; powerful, exalted,
noble 10/418, 20/9, 120; *so* ~ as noble
(as lord as I) 18/1; *as noun* 6/105, 13/
109, 42/18; **rycheste** *sup.* most valuable
18/239; *adv.* richly, splendidly 18/69.

ryde, rydyn *v.* ride 18/90, 26/377, 427,
35/239; **ryde** *pr. 1 sg.* 18/2; *I* ~ *on my
rowel* I spur my horse 20/9; **rydyth** *pr. 3
sg.* 26/385 s.d.; **rydyng** *pr. p.* 18/22; **ryd**
imp. sg. 20/74; **rydyth** *imp. pl.* 35/280;
ryde *pr. subj.* 34/280.

ryf(f) *adv.* promptly, readily Pr 87, 155,
178.

ryght, ryth, ryte *n.* righteousness, justice, right Pr 42, 1/24, 16/34, 26/216, 42/
128; *of* ~ rightly, with reason 9/182; (as
personif.) 11/116, 141; *þe* ~ 32/6; justi-
fiable reason 12/198; one's rightful
claim 20/223; law 27/106; duty 41/181;
as ~ *is oure* as is our duty 15/63.

ryght, ryth *adj.* proper, fitting Pr 19, 19/
122, 31/100, 41/504; true, right 11/29,
22/141, 36/6; right (side or direction)
13/100, 18/314, 26/137; straight, direct
18/298, 26/135, 164; correct 21/85.

ryght, ryth, ryht, rygh, rith, rythis, rithis, rythtis *adv.* very Pr 78, 89, 177, 2/283, 3/88, 143, 4/33, 127, 210, 14/97, 23/25, 41/402; ~ *a* (with *adj.*) a very 7/128, 24/67, 30/40; just, exactly Pr 152, 4/206, 5/142, 25/19, 36/41; *now* ~ right now 41/162, 303, 497; properly, correctly 4/131, 25/173; truly, indeed 4/170, 10/215, 41/140; straight, directly 8/251, 16/19, 18/16; at all 10/305, 15/223, 31/91; ~ *nowth* (*nowght, nought, nouth*), ~ *nothynge* not at all 3/143, 5/95, 15/110, 20/213; ~ *nought* nothing 4/4, 41/411; rightly, *or* indeed 18/203; immediately 25/425, 34/239, 38/157; upright 32/89.

ryghtful, rythful*adj.* righteous Pr 383, 8/50, 11/91, 14/281, 30/26.

ryghtfful(l)nes *n.* righteousness 11/91, 22/72.

ryghtwysnes, rythwysnesse *n.* righteousness 11/100, 29/257; (as personif.) 11/90, 105, 131.

ryme *pr. subj.* rhyme, i.e. make rhyme or reason 26/79.

ryng(e) *n.* ring 10/318, 320; **rynggys** *pl.* 18/70.

rynge *pr. subj.* make a ringing sound: ~ *wele in ȝoure purs* pay me well 14/25.

rynggyng *ppl. adj.* resounding 31/1.

rys *n.* rice 2/37.

ryse, rysyn *v.* 1 rise Pr 428, 509, 7/70, 11/51, 28/92 s.d., 31/210 s.d.; **ryse** *pr. 1 sg.* 25/425; **rysyth, ryseth** *pr. 3 sg.* 27/268 s.d., 32/291; **rysyn, ryse** *pl.* 18/297, 307, 28/92 s.d.; **ro(o)s, rese** *pa. t.* 39/63, 41/20, 502; **resyn, rysyn, reson** *pp.* 7/78, 86, 34/169, 35/82, 111, 36/138; **ryse, rysyth** *imp. pl.* 13/167, 28/73, 39/29; **ryse** *pr. subj.* 34/232; **2** raise (to life) 33/5, 35/67; **3** rise in rebellion 41/81.

rysyng *vbl. n.* uprising 41/55.

ro *n.* roe 35/298.

roberych *n.* rubric 27/515 s.d.

robys *n.* robes 18/70.

rochand *n.* (?) lord, ruler 31/1.

rodde *n.* rod 10/197, 231, *5/158n.; **roddys** *pl.* 10/196.

rode, rood *n.* rood Pr 390, 2/293, 7/68, 19/85, 22/49, 36/150; ~ -*tre* Pr 387.

rokkys *n.* rocks 4/233.

rolle *pr. subj.* enrol 14/156n.

rollyd *pp.* wrapped, covered 18/70.

Romaynes *n.* Romans 27/84.

rop *n.* rope 32/65, 73; **ropys** *pl.* 31/212 s.d., 32/67.

rosch *n.* rush (the plant): *not wurth a* ~ valueless 2/309.

rote *n.* root, source 18/46.

rought see **rowte**.

routh see **recke**.

rowe *n.* row: *on* ~ together, *or* in order 4/11, 18/90; *be* ~ in succession 5/220, 18/175, 33/47.

rowel *n.* pointed wheel on a spur 20/9.

rowncys *n.* horses 20/32.

rownd(e) *adj.* round 6/29, 18/129, 23/181; *adv.* all over 11/157; ~ *aboute* (*abowte, abowtyn, abowth*) everywhere, all around Pr 254, 4/25, 14/279.

rowne *v.* tell, 42/16.

rowse *v.* (?) declare 10/18n.; **rowse** *pp.* raised up, spoken 10/472.

rowte, rought, rowthte, rowth *n.* company, assemblage 20/229, 277, 23/2, 29/95; *allþe* ~ everyone present 14/6; *on* ~ as a group 20/136n.; *in every* ~ everywhere 4/24.

rowth *n.* uproar, *or* blow, stroke 31/1.

rowth see **recke**.

rubbe *pr. pl.* run about 42/68n.

ruyne *n.* ruin, destruction 11/204.

rulere *n.* ruler 18/2; **rewelerys** *pl.* 26/317.

ruly see **rewly**.

rustynes *n.* corrosion, corruption 4/230.

ruthe, rewthe, rowthe *n.* pity 15/268; *for* (*gret*) ~ what a shame 4/214, 5/100, 38/31; matter of sorrow or regret 11/59, 14/132, 31/144.

sa see **so(o)**.

Sabath *n.* Sabbath 34/96.

sacerdotale *adj.* priestly 7/13.

sacrement *n.* sacrament 22/64; **sacramentys, sacrementys** *pl.* 16/5, 18/74.

sacryd *adj.* consecrated 27/371, 501.

sacryfice, sacrefyse, sacrifice, sacrefyce, sacryfyce, sacrafice, sacryfyse, sacrefice *n.* sacrifice (the act) 3/42, 53, 5/80, 115, 119, 8/37, 39, 45, 59, 84, 95; sacrificial offering 5/126, 131, 8/75, 19/116, 27/370, 372.

sad(de) *adj.* dignified, sober Pr 4, 10/394, 15/188; steadfast, trustworthy 3/23, 38; sorrowful 5/133, 8/79, 208; correct,

sad(de) (*cont.*)
strong 8/4; vigorous 20/201; heavy 25/406; *adv.* sorrowfully 4/198, 37/24; soberly, seriously 41/223.

sadelys *n.* saddles 35/278.

sadly *adv.* resolutely, vigorously 4/191, 15/3; profoundly, soberly 21/146; in earnest 35/251.

saff, save *adj.* safe, unharmed 14/210, 25/233, 34/144; secured, unable to harm 30/40.

saff, save *conj.* except, save (that) Pr 38, 4/124, 19/14; *prep.* except for 2/39, 3/34.

sage *n.* *in old* ~ in ancient sage writings 10/346; wise woman 13/38.

sayd, seyd *ppl. adj.* spoken 9/7; mentioned before 39/70.

sayll *v.* assail 4/171.

sayn see **se.**

sake *n.* *Godys* ~ for God's sake! 13/5.

saluse *v.* salute 41/194.

salutacyon *n.* salutation 8/12, 9/272, 309.

salve, salue *n.* 1 remedy 16/11, PS 6; 2 ointment 36/48; **salvys** *pl.* 36/3.

salvyn *v.* salve, heal 26/390.

salver *n.* healer 19/124.

sapyens *n.* sapience 11/175.

Sarazyn *n.* Saracen 26/164 s.d.

sarteyn see **serteyn(e)** *adv.*

satan *n.* satin 26/105.

satysfaccyon *n.* penitential acts 22/176.

savacyon, saluacyon, salvacyon *n.* salvation 11/176, 282, 19/154, 156, 26/42, 39/24, 41/95, 279.

saue, save, savyn, sauyn, sawe *v.* 1 save, spare, preserve Pr 116, 197, 290, 375, 380, 1/8, 2/294, 3/44, 4/115, 28/140; **savyth** *pr. 3 sg.* Pr 411; **saue** *pl.* Pr 384, 6/129; **sauyd** *pa. t.* Pr 91; **savyd** *pp.* Pr 73, 4/217, 9/111; **saue, save** *imp. sg.* 4/5, 5/72, 262; **saue, save** *pr. subj.* Pr 3, 522, 4/84; *~ us sekyr, ~ us sownd* keep us safe 4/90, 6/12; 2 make safe 34/179.

save see **saff** *adj.* and *conj.*

savyng *conj.* saving, except that 26/208 s.d., 449 s.d.

savynge *vbl. n.* saving 41/52.

Savyour, Sauyour, Savyure, Saveyour *n.* Saviour Pr 319, 363, 8/197, 18/24, 19/149, 25/442, 41/187, 434.

savowrys *n.* savours 9/256.

sawe *n.* words, speech 10/2, 30/95;

decree 10/8; tale 35/274; **sawys** *pl.* words 9/253.

Sawtere *n.* Book of Psalms 10/431, 453; *~-book* 10/424; *Oure Ladyes* ~ the rosary 13/156A.

scappys *n.* slips 23/121.

schadu *v.* overshadow 1/252.

schaffald(e), skaffald, skafhald, scafald, shaffald *n.* scaffold 26/208 s.d., 29/1st s.d., 30/10 s.d., 152 s.d., 31/57 s.d., 210 s.d., 32/168 s.d., 182 s.d.; **schaffaldys, skaffaldys** *pl.* 29/1st s.d., 34/269 s.d.

schaf(f)tys, shaftys *n.* spears, lances 18/89, 20/30, 34/292.

schamfast, shamfast *adj.* shamefast 13/15, 26/99.

schamyd *pp.* shamed 14/319.

schamly *adv.* shamefully 41/228.

schape, skape, shape *v.* escape 14/230, 316, 24/111, 25/12, 34/195; **skapyst** *pr. 2 sg.* (with future sense) 2/43, 4/185.

schapyn *v.* 1 cause, bring about 34/293; **shapyht** *imp. pl.* 20/31; 2 given shape, fashioned in **shapyn** *pp.* 16/17.

schapman *n.* merchant 27/304; **chapmen** *pl.* 27/309.

schap(p) *n.* shape, form 11/295, 14/95.

scharlys see **charle.**

scharpe see **sharp(e).**

schedyn, shedde *v.* shed 18/150, 19/84; **xad** *pp.* 27/485.

scheeld, shylde *pr. subj.* shield 8/89, 10/477.

schelchownys *n.* women, *or error for* **scheltrownys** formations of troops 20/31n.

schende, schent see **shende.**

schep *n.* abundance: *for* ~ *nor derth* on account of abundance nor scarcity 15/108.

schep see **shep(e).**

schet see **shete** *v.*

schewyn, schewyng see **shew(e).**

schon see **sho.**

schonde *n.* ruin 34/293.

schortyn *v.* cut short 41/57; **short** *pl.* 25/334.

schote *n.* arrow 4/173.

schoure, shoure *n.* shower 5/36, 16/78; **schouris** *pl.* attacks, blows 41/402.

schrewde, shrewyd, shrewde *adj.* bad 27/83, 31/37, 43.

schrewe see **shrewe** *pr. 1 sg.*

schryf(f)te, shryf(f)t *n.* shrift 22/151, 176; ~ *of mowth(e)* auricular confession 22/155, 167, 177.

schryve, shryve *v.* shrive 9/208; *refl.* make confession 37/82; **shrevyn** *pp. be* ~ be confessed 22/163; **shryve** *pr. subj. refl.* 22/147.

schrowde *n.* clothing 2/120.

scyens *n.* branch of learning 21/5, 10, 26; knowledge 21/21.

sclawndryd, sclaundryd *pp.* slandered Pr 185; accused, charged 24/173.

scle see **sle(e).**

sclep see **slep(e)** *n.*

sclepe, sclepyng, sclepp see **slepe** *v.*

sclepyr *adj.* deceitful, slippery 10/347.

sclyde *v.* pass away, disappear 25/188; **slyde** *pl.* slip, slide 8/56; **slyde** *imp. sg.* go, pass 1/70.

sclyly *adv.* stealthily 40/18.

scloo, sclow see **sle(e).**

scolde *n.* scold 24/149.

score, skore *n.* score, group of twenty 4/200, 19/158, 21/151, 154, 24/53, 41/380.

scorgys, skorgys *n.* scourges 30/231, 38/22.

scorn see **shorn.**

scorn(e) *v.* deride, scorn 35/206, 38/69; **scorne** *pl.* 40/28; **skornyng** *pr. p.* 31/212 s.d.

scowte *n.* term of contempt 14/182, 24/145, 24/177.

scrapyth *pr. 3 sg.* erases (with a knife) 4/34.

scrybe *n.* scribe 24/49, 65.

scripture, scrypture, scryptour *n.* Holy Scripture, sacred writing 9/109, 10/94, 101, 22/37, 23/184, 38/227, 248.

se *n.*[1] sea Pr 71, 2/105, 135.

se *n.*[2] seat, throne 1/56, 7/87, 11/243.

se, sen(e) *v.* **1** see Pr 47, 63, 82, 102, 518, 9/32; **se** *pr. 1 sg.* 1/16, 2/168, 194; **seyst** *pr. 2 sg.* 28/77, 32/98; (with fut. sense) 10/469; **seyth** *pr. 3 sg.* 8/177, 32/160; **se, se(e)n** *pl.* Pr 108, 162, 2/183, 26/449 s.d.; **seyng** *pr. p.* 34/121 s.d.; **saw, sey, sawghe, say** *pa. 1, 3 sg.* 7/62, 16/15, 16, 18/323, 29/197, 34/130, 36/86; **saw, sowe, seyn** *pa. pl.* 27/317, 36/152, 163, 39/53; **sen(e), seyn(e), sayn** *pp.* Pr 30, 232, 3/181, 6/108, 9/294, 10/202, 13/15,

27/12, 35/156; *þat is* ~ that is apparent 10/82; **se** *imp.* 9/156, 160, 206; **se** *pr. subj.* Pr 505, 3/21, 32/371; **sey** *pa. subj.* 32/239; **2** look 3/184; **3** ascertain, discern 18/142, 23/192, 26/109; **seest** *pr. 2 sg.* learn (by reading) 8/181; **seyn** *pl.* 30/97; **seinge, seyng** *pr. p.* perceiving *13/34, 41/360; **se** *imp. sg.* find 31/70; **4** see to it (that) *in* **se** *imp.* 8/142, 9/191, 34/65; **5** consider *in* **seyth** *imp. pl.* 26/22.

seal(e), sele *n.* seal 34/239, 242, 254.

seche see **sek(e)** *v.*, **such(e).**

secund(e) *ord. num. as adj.* second Pr 27, 2/3, 4/14; *as noun* 9/106, 232, 10/354.

sed(e), seed, seyd *n.* offspring 5/216, 218, 223, 228, 10/56, 63; seed 14/73, 18/85.

sede *v. dede* ~ was born 41/313.

se(e)l, seyl *n.* time 27/473, 28/105, 29/116, 161.

sees see **ses(e).**

sefne, seven, sevyn *card. num. as adj.* seven 8/151, 9/115, 207, 10/246, 26/130; *as noun* 7/81.

sefnt(e), sefte *ord. num. as adj.* seventh Pr 106; *as noun* 9/126, 238.

sey(e), say(e), seyn, sayn *v.* say, tell, speak Pr 144, 218, 224, 2/235, 4/109, 6/22, 65, 7/90, *10/115 s.d., 27/419; **sey(e), say(e)** *pr. 1 sg.* Pr 183, 257, 304; **seyst** *pr. 2 sg.* 8/156, 10/40, 11/83; (with ellips. of 'thou') 29/160, 30/57, 31/118; **seyth, seyt, sseyth** *pr. 3 sg.* Pr 137, 301, 8/97 s.d., 11/81, 26/453 s.d., 27/268 s.d.; **sey, seyn, say** *pl.* 4/154, 9/26, 11/116; **seyng(e), sayng(e), seyand, seyinge** *pr. p.* 9/17 s.d., 13/78, 26/164 s.d., 256 s.d., 27/1st s.d., 41/24, 110, 114, 131; **seyd(e), sayd(e)** *pa. 1, 3 sg.* Pr 178, 2/95, 156, 179, 15/237, 41/200; **seydest, seydyst** *pa. 2 sg.* 11/61, 21/75; **seyd, seyden, seydyn** *pa. pl.* 14/65, 77, 21/94, 180, 27/545; **seyd(e), sayd(e), seyn** *pp.* Pr 135, 7/58, 75; **sey, say** *imp. sg.* 2/215, 3/111, 4/109; **sey, seyth, seyn, say** *imp. pl.* 9/169, 10/99, 15/289, 16/121; **sey** *pr. subj.* (forming *imp.*) 18/269, 35/157, 40/13; ~ *wrech* pronounce punishment 24/91.

seyl see **se(e)l.**

seyn *n.* see **se, sygne.**

seyne *ppl. adj.* visible, seen 18/23.

seyse see **syse** n.[1]

seke adj. sick 25/11, 251, 38/36; as noun 8/86, 42/83.

sek(e), seche, sekyn v. 1 seek Pr 439, 4/244, 5/136, 18/32, 201, 208; **seke** pr. 1 sg. 18/45; **seke, sekyn, sech** pl. 18/24, 183, 28/84, 85, 93; **sowth, south, sought** pa. 3 sg., pl. Pr 210, 254, 29/104, 38/78; **sowtyst** pa. 2 sg. 2/251; **sowth, sought, sowght** pp. 14/174, 21/261, 28/102, 37/66; **seke** imp. pp. 21/2, 36/70; 2 search 20/172; **sowte** pp. 11/153; **seke** imp. pl. 11/151; 3 come in **seke** pr. 1 sg. 28/151; **sowth** pa. t. and pp. 26/464, 27/189; 4 visiting in **sekynge** pr. p. 13/38; 5 attempted in **sowte** pa. t. 25/219; 6 afflicted in **sought** pp. 25/69, 32/231; 7 sought out, found in **sowth, sought, sowght** pp. 2/48, 3/26, 4/186, 15/72, 20/126, 26/77, 27/159; 8 sought to obtain or receive 21/52, 22/69, 26/97.

sek(e)nesse, seknes see **syknes(se)**.

sekyr adj. secure, safe 4/90, 34/236; certain 24/77, 27/469, 34/240; adv. safely or truly 12/23; certainly 15/11, 35/265.

sekyrly(e) adv. certainly Pr 490, 7/96, 15/36.

sel see **se(e)l**.

sele n. see **seal(e)**.

sele v. place a seal on 34/231; **sele** pr. 1 sg. 34/243; **selyd, sealyd** pp. 34/235, 38/311; **sele** imp. pl. 34/247.

selkowth adj. wonderful, strange 16/16.

selle v. 1 sell 27/195, 309; ~ lechory prostitute oneself 26/106; 2 betray (for a price) 27/215, 217, 231; **sellyth** pr. 3 sg. 27/240; **seldyst** pa. 2 sg. 30/31; solde pa. 3 sg. and pp. Pr 363, 27/335, 464; **solde** pa. subj. 27/227; 3 deliver up 18/93.

seme v. 1 befit, beseem 41/204; **semyth** impers. 41/359; 2 seems, appears in **semyth** pr. 3 sg. 12/25; **seme** pl. 15/58; **semyd** pa. t. 14/76; **seme** impers. me xulde ~ it would seem to me 11/125; **semyth** impers. 21/156, 32/203; ~ me it seems to me 9/24, 159, 14/92; ~ you does it seem to you 41/500; vs ~ it seems to us 41/504; is seen, is manifested 34/6.

sem(e)ly adj. seemly 2/126, 30/11; seemly, or becomingly 3/23; **semelyeste** sup. 18/10.

semlant n. appearance, demeanour 18/55.

sen see **syn** conj.

send(e), sendyn v. 1 send 4/244, 247, 7/92; **sendyth** pr. 3 sg. Pr 220, 377, 418; **sende** pl. Pr 273; **sent(e)** pa. t. Pr 70, 76, 77; **sent, sende** pp. Pr 145, 5/215, 6/53, 11/189; **sende** imp. sg. Pr 139; **send(e)** pr. subj. 26/194, 31/53; 2 grant, ordain 5/56, 67, 10/113, 27/168; **sendyst** pr. 2 sg. 41/215; **sentyst** pa. 2 sg. 3/89; **send(e)** pr. subj. 8/23, 71, 147; 3 sent word in **sent** pp. 20/77, 41/255; 4 caused 20/102.

sengler see **syngulere**.

sendyng vbl. n. sending 30/194.

sensyble quasi-adv. before your eyes 26/209.

sensual adj. (of the appetite) physical 26/28.

sensualyté n. sensuality 26/153.

sentens, sentence n. meaning: acorde in all ~ completely agree 7/34; portion of discourse, speech 8/4, 9/7; decision 10/102; putt bothe zoure ~ in entrust your decision to 11/123; punishment 24/194, 219; statement, dictum 26/421, 27/430; significance 30/202.

senues n. sinews 32/70.

separacyon n. make ~ divide 26/44.

septer n. sceptre 31/212 s.d.

sepulcre n. sepulchre 34/157 s.d., 36/61.

sepulture n. burial 25/136, 41/334.

sequens n. liturgical composition 8/97 s.d.

ser adj. withered 41/425.

seraphyn n. one of the seraphim Pr 49.

ser(e), ssere n. 1 sir (as title) Pr 347, 366, 8/82; 2 (as respectful term of address) 2/127, 4/62, 5/75, 27/262; **serys, seris** pl. 4/10, 8/98, 9/216, 26/269, 41/79.

serge n. search 29/80.

seryattly adv. seriatim, one by one 27/440.

serteyn, sertayn, certeyn, sertan, certayn adj. certain Pr 487, 6/62, 89, 25/133, 26/251, 33/18, 35/191, 37/92.

serteyn(e), sertayn(e), certeyn, sarteyn, certan, serteayn adv. certainly, indeed Pr 179, 268, 320, 5/146, 7/73, 10/222, 14/238, 18/8, 23/163, 26/353, 34/245.

serteyn see **certayn** n.

serteynly, certeynly *adv.* (as emphatic) certainly 12/111, 20/97, 35/259; *ful* ~ indeed 3/81.

sertyfie *v.* declare, affirm 7/119; **serte-fyeth** *pr. 3 sg.* 41/171; **certyfyenge** *pr. p.* notifying 8/32; **certefye** *imp. pl.* report (on sb.) officially 26/169.

sertys *adv.* (as emphatic) surely, indeed 10/44, 207, 21/15.

servaunt, seruuaunte, serwaunt, seruuant, seruaunt *n.* servant 4/97, 5/66, 72, 238, 6/173, 9/21, 36; **servaun-tys, seruauntys, servaunt, seruaun-tis, servauntis** *pl.* Pr 412, 1/33, 4/5, 9/161, 285, 26/121, 38/224, 41/170, 478.

serve, servyn, serue *v.* 1 serve 3/2, 72, 5/40, 55, 8/120, 9/189; **serue** *pr. 1 sg.* 32/287; **servyng** *pr. p.* 8/52; **servyd** *pp.* 20/156; 2 treated *in* servyd *pa. t.* 42/85; **servid** *pp.* 35/144.

servys(e), servyce, service, servise *n.* public worship 8/97; service 9/52, 10/77, 83, 14/381, 19/36, 27/517, 520; food 9/279, 287, 20/146; treatment 12/52.

ses(e), sees, sesyn, sesse, ces *v.* 1 (intr.) cease Pr 98, 11/134, 22/114, 27/361, 29/100; ~ *of* desist from 4/29, 8/93, 11/93; *of my tonge* . . . ~ stop talking 13/42; **sees** *pl.* 2/53; **sesyd** *pa. t.* 14/85; **se(e)s** *imp. pl.* 30/245; *of* . . . ~, ~ *of* desist from 2/52, 25/139, 330; **ses** *pr. subj.* 2/27, 6/46; **sese** *pl.* cease (talking) Pr 3; **ses** *imp. pl.* 41/26; 2 put a stop to Pr 323, 11/138, 19/69.

sesyd *pp.* in legal possession 12/127.

sessyon *n.* court session 26/114.

sete *n.* seat, throne Pr 23, 348, 1/61; *oure* ~ 20/159; **setys** *pl.* 8/151, 13/104.

sethe, sethyn see **syth(e), sythyn.**

set(t), settyn *v.* 1 set, place 14/129, 23/110, 29/180 s.d., 32/92 s.d., 176 s.d., 34/118 s.d.; **settyn't** set it 29/152; *onto hem* ~ *awe* overawe them 41/44; ~ *reddure* (*to*) to deal severely with 41/49; **settyth** *pr. 3 sg. refl.* 28/24 s.d.; **settyn** *pl.* 31/212 s.d.; **sett** *pa. t.* Pr 17; **set(t)(e)** *pp.* placed, fixed, established Pr 22, 239, 349, 9/116; **set(t)** *imp.* 4/163, 6/188, 14/260; ~ *nevyr ʒoure hert amys vpon* never wrongfully place your hope in 6/73; ~ *to þe shuldyr* put your shoulder to it 24/122; ~ *to ʒoure handys* grab hold, lay your hands (on it) 25/391, 402; ~ *on*

ʒowre hand grab him 38/179; **set(t)** *pr. subj.* 6/75; ~ *on þe his syse* should judge you 14/318; 2 seat *refl.* 27/491 s.d.; **set-tyth** *pr. 3 sg. refl.* 27/527 s.d.; **settyng** *pr. p.* 32/92 s.d.; **set(t), ssett** *pp.* Pr 235, 348, 473, 35/278; 3 establish, ordain *in* sette *pl.* 18/74; 4 attached *in* sett *pa. t.* 29/101; 5 valued *in* sett *pp.*: ~ *wul nere at nought* considered very nearly worthless 22/172; **sett(e)** *imp. sg.* ~ . . . *at nowth* hold in contempt 26/76, 94; **sett** *pr. subj.* ~ *not be* have no regard for 26/93; 6 prepare (a table) *in* sett *imp. pl.* 20/144.

seuer(e) *pr. 1 sg.* affirm, assert 41/121; promise 41/439.

seustere see **systyr.**

severe *adv.* surely 41/336n.

seuere *v.* distinguish, sever 26/216.

sevyle see **cevyle.**

sewe *n.* (as term of abuse) sow 42/118.

sew(e) *v.* proceed Pr 429; follow 26/148; plead, appeal 11/336, 27/152; adopt, put into practice 40/12; **suenge** *pr. p.* following, imitating 3/5; **sewe** *imp. pl.* *do* ~ go 31/76; **sewyng** *pr. p.* following 27/424.

sewre see **sure.**

sewte, sute *n.* (legal) action 21/131; *fol-wyth* . . . ~ does the same as 22/160.

sex *card. num. as adj.* six Pr 29, 11/1, 13/73.

sexte *ord. num. as adj.* sixth Pr 92, 2/14, 6/139; *as noun* 9/122, 236.

shaffald see **schaffald(e).**

shaftys see **schaf(f)tys.**

shake, schake *v.* 1 shake 24/192, 28/15, 44, 35/215; **shake** *pp.* 35/139; 2 wield 34/292.

shame, schame *n.* shame, disgrace Pr 389, 2/93, 173, 176, 187, 4/81; shame-fastness, modesty 9/253, 280; matter for severe reproach 10/337, 24/174; *speke* . . . ~ (*of*) speak of so as to dishonour 14/106, 38/88; infliction of shame 14/372.

shamfast see **schamfast.**

shamfastnes *n.* shamefastness, modesty 11/236.

shamful(l), schameful, shameful *adj.* shameful Pr 324, 2/167, 22/47, 27/126, 32/96; **xamefullest** *sup.* 29/61; *adv.* shamefully 28/184.

shamfully *adv.* shamefully 27/212, 32/267, 38/24.

shanke *n.* knees, legs 20/93.

shape see **schape.**

shapyht, shapyn see **schapyn.**

sharp(e), scharp(e), sharppe *adj.* sharp Pr 404, 4/173, 233, 20/65; keen 4/181; heavy 5/36; intensely painful 19/88; fierce 41/402.

sharply *adv.* severely, harshly 20/17.

she, sche *pron. 3 sg.* she Pr 129, 156, 160, 377, 435, 460; **here, hyre, hir(e)** *acc. and dat.* Pr 115, 155, 161, 9/40, 10/361, 12/159, 14/108, 110, 285; **her(e), hire, hyre** *poss.* Pr 116, 132, 430; **hereself** *refl.* 25/348.

shede *n.* sheath 28/107.

sheff *n.* sheaf 3/101, 112.

shelde *n.* shield 21/104; **scheldys** *pl.* 18/89, 20/30.

shende, schende *v.* **1** ruin, destroy 1/8, 3/173, 20/17; **shent, schent** *pp.* 21/37, 26/315, 27/92, 28/184, 31/83, 41/76; **2** kill 5/99, 20/80, 222; *refl.* 25/348; **shent, schent** *pp.* 5/143, 204, 38/29; **3** disgraced 6/153, 12/33, 53; **4** punished 2/142, 9/25, 14/166.

shendynge *vbl. n.* disgrace 18/313.

shene *adj.* bright, shining 16/15.

shenshipp, shenschepe, shenschepp *n.* disgrace 5/51, 10/477, 40/17.

shep(e), schep *n.* sheep Pr 90, 3/83, 5/200, 201, 27/497.

sheppherdis *n. gen. sg.* shepherd's 24/43; **shepherdys** *pl.* Pr 193, 195, *8/130n.

shert *n.* shirt 26/73, 31/57 s.d.; **shyrtys, shertys** *pl.* 26/449 s.d., 31/170 s.d.

shete, chete *n.* winding-sheet 25/146, 36/127, 131, 135.

shete *v.* shoot 4/160, 163; **shete** *pr. 1 sg.* 4/171; **schet, shote, shett** *pa. t.* 4/148, 173, 14/166; **shet** *pp.* cast 25/63; **shete** *imp. sg.* ~ **oute** send forth PS 4.

shetyng *vbl. n.* shooting 4/181.

shew(e), shove, shewyn *v.* **1** show, reveal, display Pr 10, 28, 53, 26/147, 164 s.d.; ~ *wyttnes* bear witness 14/145, 21/165; ~ *it owth* reveal it 14/241; **shewe** *pr. 1 sg.* 5/84, 27/395; **shewyst** *pr. 2 sg.* 3/109, 116; **shewyth, shewyght** *pr. 3 sg.* 16/25, 26/208 s.d.; ~ *as* appears to be 27/382; (with ellips. of 'he') that he shows 30/48; *impers. it* ~ it is shown

8/166, 14/352; **shewyth, shewe, schewyn** *pl.* 9/253, 13/135, 26/244 s.d.; **shewyng, schewyng** *pr. p.* 26/428, 27/76 s.d., 348 s.d., 30/152 s.d.; **shewyd** *pa. t. and pp.* 9/1, 15/275, 25/449; ~ *experyence* demonstrated 26/463; **shewe** *imp. sg.* 3/107, 14/253, 23/219; ~ *owughte* reveal 14/281; **shewe, shewyth** *imp. pl.* 20/3on., 208, 23/27; **shewe** *pr. subj.* 14/327; **2** say 3/125; **3** grant 10/451; **shewyd** *pp.* 4/211; **4** perform openly 23/116, 34/9; **shewyth** *pr. 3 sg.* 26/295; **5** allow to be heard *in* **shewe** *pr. subj.* 41/264.

shewyng *vbl. n.* presenting 19/201.

shylde see **scheeld.**

shyne *n.* brightness, radiance 16/15.

shyne *v.* shine 16/27, 39; **shyneth** *pr. 3 sg.* 35/42; **shynand** *pr. p.* 19/153; **shyne** *pr. subj.* 14/311.

shynynge *vbl. n.* shining 16/25.

shynyng *ppl. adj.* shining 5/36.

shyp(p), schypp *n.* ship Pr 71, 4/98, 111, 207.

shyppbord(e) *n.* side of a ship: *within þe (my)* ~ on board the (my) ship 4/121, 209.

shyrle *adv.* shrilly 12/147. Cf. **shrylle.**

shyrlyng *ppl. adj.* shrill-sounding 20/31.

shytte *pr. pl.* shut, close up 25/163; **shytt, schet, shitt** *pp.* shut, locked 2/302; shut 27/185; confined, shut up 27/252, 38/312.

sho *n.* shoe 2/210; **schon, shon** *pl.* 6/29, 34, 35, 22/32, 26/128.

shodyr *v.* shudder 16/78.

shorn, scorn *pp.* shorn 20/91, 25/324.

short(e), schort *adj.* brief 2/316, 9/306, 14/68, 23/26.

short *v.* see **schortyn.**

short(e)ly *adv.* briefly 9/171; quickly, with little delay 32/76 s.d.

shoure see **schoure.**

shoue *v.* **1** expel, banish 10/71; **showe** *pr. subj.* 3/129; **2** thrusts, shoves *in* **showyth** *pr. 3 sg.* 34/100 s.d.; **show** *imp. sg.* 34/100, 100.

shove see **shew(e).**

shray *n.* outcry 20/31.

shrevyn see **schryve.**

shrewde, shrewyd see **schrewde.**

shrewe *n.* **1** rascal 14/82, 258, 270; **shrewys** *pl.* 24/138; **2** something troublesome 23/29; **3** shrew 42/120.

shrewe, schrewe *pr. 1 sg.* curse, beshrew 14/49, 26/85.

shrylle *adj.* keen, piercing 36/89.

shrynkyd *pa. subj.* contracted into oneself 23/148.

shuldyr *n.* shoulder 24/122; **shulderys, shulderyn** *pl.* 20/30, 93.

syb(b)(e) *adj.* related by blood 5/172; *as noun* kinswoman 14/113, 114, 355; kinsman 25/37; **sybbest** *adj. sup.* ~ *blood* closest relative 25/112.

syde *n.* 1 side (of one's body) Pr 240, 2/260, 11/13; oure ~ 35/196; **sydys** *pl.* 15/97, 36/58; 2 party, faction 1/68; 3 place, direction 9/206, 23/170; *on every (a)* ~ everywhere 3/100, 4/220, 20/172; *on þat other* ~ on the other hand 10/101; 4 region 26/336.

syde *adj.* long 26/85.

syenge *vbl. n.* sighing 3/193.

syght, syth, ssyht, syht, syte, sygth, ssyght, sythte, sithis, sythis, sith *n.* sight Pr 229, 232, 393, 3/134, 195, 4/146, 159, 6/17, 14/50, 25/410; *by opyn* ~ in plain view Pr 29; *in* ~ in (one's) sight, before (one's) eyes 4/69, 103; *within* ~ in open view 10/214; *to þi* ~ to you 11/31, 26/382; *in* ~ open, manifest 12/199; *to* ~ to see 14/91; *knowe with ful opyn* ~ see very clearly 34/1; *haue in* ~ have in mind 41/80; *in this virgyne* ~ in sight of this virgin 41/305; appearance 16/102, 41/164; *in the Trynité* ~ in the judgement of the Trinity 41/138; **syghtys** *pl.* (tempting) sights 9/139.

sygne, syne, seyn, synge *n.* sign, token 9/159, 10/229, 16/16, 25/234, 26/106; *in* ~ *of* in the shape of 41/250; *our* ~ *make* make the sign of the cross 41/455; **sygnes** *pl.* 9/253.

sygnyfye *v.* signify 40/32; **signefye** *pl.* 41/374.

signifure, sygnyfure *n.* signification, token 22/29, 38/92, 133.

syhyn *v.* sigh 41/258; **syenge** *pr. p.* 4/198.

syknes(se), seknes, sek(e)nesse *n.* malady, sickness 11/20, 14/369, 19/124, 25/7, 12, 18, 41/443, 467, 471.

sylens *n.* silence Pr 4.

sylk *n.* silk 31/212 s.d.

sylver, sylvyr, syluer *n.* silver 14/160, 23/167, 24/163, 26/72, 27/230, 237, 298.

sympyl, sympil *adj.* 1 humble, plain, of low rank 3/70, 6/104, 9/145, 41/169, 172; **sympelest, sympilest** *sup.* 9/261; *as noun* 9/38, 41/96; 2 of little value 22/172; *adv.* with simplicity or sincerity 8/144.

symulacyon *n.* trickery, simulation 30/48.

syn, sen *conj.* 1 since, seeing that *8/129, 19/75, 28/189, 29/214; ~ þat 30/137; 2 since the time that 30/116, 41/53; ~ whan since when 3/162; ~ þat 29/198; *prep.* after 13/73, 41/55.

synagog *n.* synagogue 29/135.

syndony *n.* linen shroud 34/138.

syne see **sygne.**

synful(l) *adj.* sinful Pr 45, 350, 2/143; *as noun* 8/86, 11/336, 41/311; **synfolest** *sup. as noun* 8/166.

synfully *adv.* sinfully 4/224.

syng(e) *v.* sing Pr 192, 4/253, 8/97 s.d.; **synge** *pr. 1 sg.* 16/7; **synge, synggyn** *pl.* 1/40, 13/185A, 26/453 s.d.; **syngyng(e)** *pr. p.* 8/172 s.d., 9/245 s.d.; **songe** *pa. t.* 16/65; **songyn, songe** *pp.* 13/129, 16/63, 19/146 s.d.

synge *n.* see **sygne.**

syngynge *vbl. n.* singing 16/152.

syngulere, sengler *adj.* singular, special 11/323, 41/177.

syngulerly, syngulyrly *adv.* particularly 3/39, 8/192.

synke *v.* penetrate 21/80; descend 27/223; **synke** *pr. 1 sg.* sink 4/189.

syn(ne) *n.* sin Pr 69, 2/167, 183; *oure (here)* ~ 7/131, 42/78; **synnys** *pl.* Pr 276, 22/26, 23/50; **synnys** *gen. pl.* 22/24.

synne *v.* sin 23/106; **synnyst** *pr. 2 sg.* (with ellips. of 'thou') 26/154; **syn** *pl.* 12/72; **synnyd** *pa. t.* 11/102, 34/19, 42/30; **synnyd** *pp.* 2/195, 11/61, 14/289; **synne** *pr. subj.* 23/44, 24/21.

synners *n.* sinners 26/10.

synnyng *vbl. n.* sinning 2/251.

syre *n.* lord 7/128, 18/10, 23/5; master, *or* father 20/221.

syse, seyse *n.*[1] assize Pr 354, 14/318, 26/114; *þe grett last* ~ Judgement Day 25/299; *sett in* ~ properly or legally established 18/309.

syse, syghys *n.*[2] sighs 2/287, 8/79.

systyr, sustyr, suster, systere, seustere *n.* sister 11/90, 105, 315, 15/211, 234, 25/270, 337, 41/83, 348, 352;

systyr (*cont.*)
   systerys *gen. sg.* 36/17; **systerys, systeryn** *pl.* 9/204, 227, 284, 25/25, 108, 194.
sith, syte, syth see **syght**.
syth(e), sethe *adv.* then, subsequently 8/11, 11/297, 13/79, 29/18; *conj.* since, seeing that 11/179, 25/177, 26/434; ~ *þat* 19/160; since (the time that *or* of) 19/99, 26/24; ~ *þat* 12/29, 20/165.
sythe *v.* sigh 37/23.
sythyn *adv.* then, subsequently 27/107, 452 s.d., *527 s.d.; **sythyn, sethyn** *conj.* since, seeing that 27/454, 38/189; ~ *þat* 26/369; since (the time that *or* of) 31/64; ~ *þat* 14/229.
sythys *n.* times 39/10.
sithis, sythis, sythte see **syght**.
syt(t), sitt, syttyn *v.* **1** sit 1/56, 6/88, 7/87, 13/44, 14/2, 35/207, 38/220, 42/62; **sytt** *pr. 1 sg.* 10/483; ~ *in ondyr* am subordinate (only) to 18/84; **sittiste** *pr. 2 sg.* 41/249; **syt(t), syttyth, syttyht, syttys** *pr. 3 sg.* 2/260, 3/127, 5/129, 8/160, 10/300, 12/174, 30/10 s.d., *31/170 s.d.; **syt(t)** *pl.* Pr 3, 226, 21/29; **syttyng(e)** *pr. p.* 1/61, 10/197, 27/76 s.d.; **syt(t)** *imp.* 20/157, 21/41, 27/514; **syttyn** *pr. subj.* 5/263; **2** sit (as a judge) 31/168; **3** be situated 34/242; **4** is fitting or proper *in* **syt, syttyth** *impers.* 11/113, 26/437.
syttynge, syttenge, sittyng *ppl. adj.* fitting, appropriate 11/125, 23/141, 41/246.
syxti *card. num. as adj.* sixty 38/275.
skape, skapyst see **schape**.
skarlet *adj.* scarlet 26/164 s.d.
skele see **skyl(l)(e)**.
sky(e) *n.* sky 2/239, 26/27, 63; *on* ~ in the sky 1/57; star 16/39n.; cloud 39/67; **skyes** *pl.* the heavens 9/117, 16/17.
skyl(l)(e), skele *n.* reasoning power 3/109; perception, understanding 5/189; what is reasonable or right: *is* (*good*) ~ is reasonable 10/307, 361, 19/206; *were more* ~ would be more reasonable 27/195; cause, reason 27/169, 41/195.
skyp(pe) *v.* skip, leap 30/238; (with *fro*) get away 31/23; **skyppe** *pr. 1 sg.* leap, hurry 18/17.
skore *v.* scour 13/133.
skore see **score**.

skorgyn *v.* scourge, flog 31/210 s.d.; **skorgyd** *pp.* 19/84, 31/212 s.d.; **skorge** *imp. pl.* 31/196.
skorn(e), scorn *n.* scorn 14/341, 21/61, 29/165, 30/222; matter for scorn 26/23.
skornfully *adv.* scornfully 32/168 s.d
slauth, slowth *n.* sloth 42/109, 113.
slawe *adj.* slow 26/330.
slawndyr *n.* disgrace, opprobrium 8/62; slander *14/40, 46.
sle(e), slo, slen, scle, scloo *v.* slay Pr 220, 228, 2/311, 3/146, 177, 5/91, 6/132, 16/48, 20/85, 25/156, 30/98, 41/77; **sle** *pr. 1 sg.* 5/180, 184, 200; **sleyth, sleth** *pr. 3 sg.* 8/139, 25/363; **slew(e), scle, slow** *pa. t.* 3/168, 4/184, 33/11, 39/62, 41/53; **slayn, slawe, sclayn(e)** *pp.* Pr 82, 292, 3/153, 179, 4/175, 182, 189, 16/37, 24/108; **scle, scloo** *imp. sg.* 5/88, 6/132, 134; **sle, sleyth, slo** *imp. pl.* 5/166, 20/48, 41/405; **sle(e)** *pr. subj.* 5/79, 41/82; **sclow, slewe** *pa. subj.* 2/319, 41/81.
sleytys *n.* tricks 23/206; ~ *sly3* wise devices 16/13.
slep(e), sclep, slepp *n.* sleep Pr 374, 4/75, 20/81, 28/70, 34/304; *haue a* ~ sleep 18/281.
slepe *v.* sleep Pr 358, 6/189, 11/86; **slepe** *pr. 1 sg.* 34/316; **slepyst** *pr. 2 sg.* 28/33; **slepyth** *pr. 3 sg.* 25/232; **slepe** *pl.* 9/84; **sclepyng, slepyng** *pr. p.* 28/32 s.d., 68 s.d., 31/63; **slept(e)** *pa. t.* 14/306, 41/360; **sclepe** *imp. sg.* 28/34; **slepe** *pr. subj.* 6/50, 9/245, 18/274; **sclepp** *v.* sleep, *or* slip 4/36n.
slepynge *vbl. n.* sleeping 25/236.
sleve *n.* sleeve 38/380.
slye, sly3 *adj.* sly Pr 285; wise 16/13, 18/153.
slynge *pr. subj.* cast, sling 14/27.
slytt *v.* slit, sever 25/141.
slought *adj.* slow 38/89.
sloveyn *n.* (term of opprobrium) wicked woman 24/150.
slowth see **slauth**.
slutte *n.* slut, loose woman 24/150.
smal(e) *adj.* small 6/93, 26/79, 87.
smellyng *vbl. n.* odour 2/7.
smert(e) *adj.* severe 1/76, 19/88, 32/249; sharp 38/91; *adv.* sharply, distinctly 22/109.
smertly *adv.* quickly 5/86, 20/144.
smyle *pr. 1 sg.* smile 15/181.

smyte, smyght *v.* **1** smite, strike 28/106, 29/141 s.d.; *of* ~ cut off 5/168; **smyte** *pr. 1 sg.* 20/190; **smytyht, smytyth, smyth** *pr. 3 sg.* 9/81, 28/108; ~ *of* cuts off 28/106 s.d.; **smet** *pa. t. of* ~ 29/204; **smet(e)** *pp.* 28/108, 31/28; **smyth** *imp. pl.* ~ *up* strike up (an agreement) 27/311; **smyte** *pr. subj.* ~ *of* 41/93; **2** driven *in* **smet** *pp.* 31/203.

snayle *n.* snail, *or* turtle 23/148.

snarle *v.* entrap, snarl 41/402.

snelle *adj.* wise, good 12/141.

sneveleris *n.* snivellers 41/402.

snow(e) *v.* snow 14/307.

snowte *n.* (in imprecation) nose, face 14/262.

sobbe *pr. pl.* sob 11/20.

sobyr *adj.* solemn, sober 10/354.

soch see **such(e)**.

socour(e), socowre *n.* succour 10/219, 27/168, 41/176; helper 11/336.

socowre *v.* succour 10/56, 42/124; **socour, socowre** *pr. subj.* Pr 3, 6/192.

socurraunce *n.* succour 24/215.

sodeyn(e) *adj.* sudden Pr 240, 41/195, 235.

sodeyn(e)ly *adv.* suddenly Pr 475, 20/265, 270.

soevyr *adv. what man* ~ whoever 27/233.

sofer(e), sof(e)ryd, soferyth, sofre, sofron see **suffyr**.

soferauns *n.* patient endurance 9/138; permission 29/5.

sofreynes see **souereyn**.

softe *adj.* gentle, mild 9/146.

softyd *pp.* softened with balm, balmed 36/54, 57.

sokelyng *n.* clover 27/354, 401.

sokyn see **sowkyn**.

sokyng *vbl. n. 3evyn* ~ suckle, nurse 32/14.

solace, solas *n.* pleasure, solace 5/20, 197, 9/222, 15/288, 25/317, 28/154.

solacyth *impers.* cheers, comforts 12/14.

solemply *adv.* solemnly, ceremoniously 8/193.

solempn(e) *adj.* sacred Pr 491, 10/333.

solennyté, solempnité *n.* observance 31/175; solemnity 41/335.

solennyzacyon *n.* ceremonial celebration 8/33.

somdel see **sumdel(e)** *adv.*

somewhath, somwhat *n.* somewhat 29/132, 31/22.

somnorys *n.* summoners 14/161.

somowne *v.* summon 14/3; **somown** *pr. 1 sg.* 14/6.

somtyme see **sumtyme**.

son see **sownde** *n.*[1]

sond(e) *n.*[1] **1** sending, dispensation 2/328, 12/24, 14/291; **2** envoy, messenger 5/116, 10/163; **sondys** *pl.* 20/14.

sond(e) *n.*[2] **1** shore, land: ~ *and se, se and* ~ everything 2/105, 135; *on* ~ *and se* everywhere 4/84; *se nor on* ~ (not) anywhere 5/260; **2** sand 5/221.

son(e), ssone *n.* son Pr 80, 84, 116, 23/118; **sonys** *gen. sg.* 11/324, 19/55, 99; **sonys** *pl.* 3/32, 38.

son(e), soon *adv.* soon, quickly Pr 89, 147, 315, 34/43; **soner(e), sunere** *comp.* 25/68, 342; *þe (the)* ~ 4/20, 41/93; **sonest** *sup.* 23/52, 27/9.

song(e) *n.* song Pr 18, 1/40, 4/253.

sonne see **sunne**.

so(o), sa *adv.* such Pr 22, 4/227, 234; thus, so Pr 126, 3/46, 144, 13/117; ~ *þat* provided that 24/164.

sool *n.* sole 26/68.

sopere *n.* supper 27/40.

sophestrye *n.* sophistry 21/14.

sor *n.* ailment, affliction 15/291.

sore *adj.* bitter Pr 362, 3/193, 32/276; painful, grievous 20/201, 25/361, 32/154; distressing 29/62; *adv.* sternly Pr 124, 6/148; greatly, deeply Pr 133, 134, 484; bitterly, severely Pr 177, 3/167, 4/94; violently 34/7; tightly, firmly 31/195, 41/424; with great effort 32/62n.

sory *adj.* sorry, grieved Pr 364, 15/133, 24/264; vile 2/184, 35/35; *as noun* 8/86.

sorynes *n.* sorrowfulness 25/264.

sorwatorie *n.* haughty pride 33/25n.

sorwe, ssorwe, sorow *n.* sorrow Pr 238, 343, 394, 11/18, 22/51; **sorwyn, sorwys** *pl.* 8/200, 18/85, 20/94, 25/324.

sorwe(f)ful *adj.* remorseful 27/170; sad, sorrowful 28/163, 32/20.

sorwyn *v.* sorrow 37/28; **sorwe** *pr. 1 sg.* 19/13; **sorwyth** *pr. 3 sg.* 8/160.

sorwynge *vbl. n.* mourning, sorrowing 20/102, 25/139, 335.

soserye *n.* sorcery 30/177.

sote *adj.* sweet Pr 109, 7/24, 8/26.

sotely, sotylly *adv.* subtly, craftily 27/333, 336 s.d.

soth *adj.* true 29/212; *adv.* truly 38/17.

soth(e) *n.* truth Pr 144, 218, 328; *in ~* truly 10/239, 411, 11/154.

sothfast *adj.* true 35/42.

sothly *adv.* truly 3/37, 12/14; **ssothly** 9/35.

sotyl(le) *adj.* cunning, crafty, skilful 23/42, 26/27, 27/134.

sotylté *n.* wily stratagem Pr 286, 26/59, 119; **sotyltés** *pl.* 27/98.

sottys *n.* fools 18/74, 85, 20/14.

soundry *adj.* sundry 39/11.

south see **sek(e)**.

souereyn, sovereyn *n.* sovereign, lord 26/205, 245, 29/78; **sovereynes, sofreynes, sovereynys, souereynes** *pl.* (as term of address) excellent pĕople 9/1, 294, 13/23, 105A, 29/1, 41/1.

sovereyn, souereyn *adj.* sovereign, supreme 3/23, 66, 9/175, *254, 23/5, 25/353.

sovereynly *adv.* supremely *9/174.

souereynté *n.* supremacy 21/30.

sowe *v.* sow 14/73, 18/85, 26/13.

sowyht *pr. 3 sg.* sews 8/138.

sowke *n.* suck (of milk from the breast) 21/46.

sowkyn *v.* suck Pr 227; **sokyn** *pp.* sucked the nourishment from 2/184; sucked 25/37.

sowle, soul(l)e *n.* 1 soul Pr 372, 408, 425, 427, 4/30, 6/80; *~-helth* spiritual well-being 10/475; *~-drynk* 33/16; **sowlys, soulys, sowles, soules** *pl.* Pr 242, 410, 6/58, 8/208, 10/434, 11/19, 86, 41/456; **sowlys** *gen. pl.* 16/48; 2 people Pr 73, 4/111.

sownde, sound, son *n.*[1] speech 11/212, 41/368; 2 sound 41/489.

sownde *n.*[2] swoon, torpor 4/5.

sownd(e), sounde *adj.* in good condition 3/94; (spiritually) sound 3/172; safe, secure 6/12, 10/388, 399; solid, substantial 20/144; healthy, free (from disease) 20/263, 25/30, 38/327.

sowre *adj.* bitter 18/93.

sowth see **sek(e)**.

space, spas *n.* period of time 9/306, 11/269, 12/162, 21/272, 30/38; opportunity 19/52, 20/191, 24/40.

sparyst *pr. 2 sg.* 1 refrain 5/191; **sparyd** *pa. t.* 2/204, 38/39; 2 preserves, i.e. keeps barren *in* **sparyth** *pr. 3 sg.* 8/179.

spech(e) *n.* 1 speaking, words, speech Pr 162, 432, 456; **speches** *pl.* 11/113; 2 faculty of speech 13/169A.

specyal *adj.* special 36/2; **specyal(l)** *adv.* especially 8/43; *in ~* 41/197.

specyal(l)y, specyalé, specialy *adv.* especially, particularly 8/32, 9/289, 10/449, 11/317; in a special way, with special force 9/83, 11/80, 13/147A.

specyfy(e) *v.* speak of, specify 11/311, 27/394, 41/12.

sped(e) *n.* one who promotes success or prosperity Pr 528, 5/45, 9/8; prosperity, good fortune 8/147, 23/26; speed 2/145; *in ~* speedily 9/105, 145.

spede *v.* 1 cause to succeed or prosper 3/44, 10/422, 13/20; **spede** *imp. sg.* 10/456; **sped(e)** *pr. subj.* 5/50, 10/269, 396; 2 hasten 10/157; **sped** *pr. 1 sg.* 2/58; **sped** *imp. sg.* *~ up* speed up 27/474; **spede** *pr. subj.* 10/474; 3 succeed, prosper, fare 10/376, 14/26, 24/36; 4 send with speed 15/317; 5 go with speed 20/61; **spede** *pl.* 18/195; **spede** *imp. pl.* 30/145. 6 accomplish, carry out 20/267, 23/64; **spad, sped** *pp.* 30/149; accomplished (one's task) 20/113; 7 succeed in getting 25/295; 8 fulfilled *in* **spad, sped** *pp.* 16/58, 74.

spedful *adj.* helpful 10/98.

spedly *adv.* speedily 16/74.

speke, spekyn *v.* 1 speak, say 3/32, 8/139, 13/144, 14/110, 27/380 s.d., 31/37 s.d.; **spekyst** *pr. 2 sg.* 27/202, 29/138, 32/136; (with ellips. of 'thou') 30/209, 31/127; **spekyth** *pr. 3 sg.* Pr 390, 12/7, 22/3; **speke, spekyth** *pl.* 12/2, 13/142, 14/106, 26/441 s.d.; **spekyng** *pr. p.* 15/45; **spak, spoke** *pa. t.* Pr 471, 13/116, 168A, 27/544; *hem ~* they spoke Pr 499; **spokyn, spoke** *pp.* 2/178, 12/173, 19/50, 32/135, 38/92, 281; **speke** *imp.* 5/122, 24/218, 29/164; **speke** *pr. subj.* 26/202; 2 speak of 14/61.

spekyng *vbl. n.* talk 3/17.

spelle *n.* speech, words 12/221, 27/265.

spelle *v.* tell, declare 16/53, 18/170, 26/4; **spelle** *pl.* say 41/224.

spent, spende *pp.* consumed 14/363; used 36/48.

spere *n.* spear Pr 401, 404, 20/12; *~-poynt* 38/364; **sperys** *gen. sg.* 20/220, 38/325.

spere *pr. 1 sg.* close off 2/290; **sperd** *pp.* shut, fastened 7/47, 31/48.

spetously *adv.* spitefully, cruelly 28/160.

spycery *n.* spices 23/171.

spye *pr. subj.* spy 41/378.

spyes *n.* spies 26/337.

spyl(l)(e), spyllyn *v.* **1** kill Pr 383, 4/172, 5/172; **spille** *pr. 1 sg.* *41/37; **spylt** *pp.* 30/84; **2** destroy, bring to ruin or misery 2/154, 204, 4/30, 24/61; **spylle** *pr. 1 sg.* 20/186; **spylte** *pp.* 42/25; **3** go to waste 27/194; **4** perish 28/30, 31/134, 32/98; **5** shed, spill (blood) 31/144; **spylle** *pr. 1 sg.* 5/184; **spylt** *pp.* 4/204; **6** spoils *in* **spyllyth** *pr. 3 sg.* 14/62.

spynne *v.* spin (wool, etc.) 2/326, 333.

spyryt(e), Sprytt, Spryte *n.* animating influence 7/3; Holy Ghost 7/92, 95, 22/94; *þe Holy ~* 12/135; spirit, soul 13/85, 32/216; **spyrytys, spyritys** *pl.* supernatural beings 11/270, 27/176.

spyteful *adj.* shameful 37/55.

spyth *n.* spite, defiance 41/387.

spyttyn *v.* spit 29/180 s.d.

splendure *n.* brightness 21/82.

sport(e) *n.* entertainment, amusement 10/271, 20/189, 24/66; **sportys** *pl.* *~ of oure gle* entertainments that amuse us 20/243.

spot(t)(e) *n.* spot, blemish Pr 130, 14/349, 15/232.

spoused *n.* wedlock 41/15, 306.

spowsage *n.* marriage 10/13.

spowse, spouse, spovse *n.* spouse 2/126, 185, 304, 10/14, 28/8.

spowsyng *vbl. n.* marriage 10/90.

sprawlyd *pa. t.* sprawled 20/220.

sprede *v.* **1** spread 4/26, 151, 15/319; **sprad** *pp.* 38/299, **sprede** *pr. subj.* 10/400; **2** cover 27/417; **sprad** *pp.* 2/78; **3** shed over an area 38/326.

sprynge *v.* **1** issue, arise Pr 107, 4/26, 7/19; **spreng** *pa. t.* 41/279; **spronge, sprongyn** *pp.* 7/90, 98, 41/383; **2** grow, blossom Pr 142.

Spryte, Sprytt see **spyryt(e)**.

ssalte *adj.* lecherous: *~ sewe* sow in heat 42/118.

staf(f) *n.* staff 10/187, 190, 26/164 s.d.; **stavys, stauys** *pl.* 27/359, 427.

stage *n.* raised platform, station 3/188n., 21/159, 26/164 s.d.; *in ~* on the scaffold 10/350n.

stalke *v.* walk stealthily 34/298.

stall(e) *n.* stable, manager Pr 213, 16/118,

20/51; place, (ironically) seat of dignity 2/268.

starkly *adv.* vigorously 13/22.

stat *n.* status, office 21/32; **statis** *pl.* lords 41/30.

staunche *v.* stanch, quench 11/13.

sted(e), steed *n.*[1] space of time, time 2/159, 14/357; place 4/240, 25/244, 39/74.

stede *n.*[2] steed 18/10, 17; **stedys** *pl.* 20/121.

stedfast *adj.* steadfast 38/331, 342; *adv.* steadfastly 26/471.

stedfastly *adv.* steadfastly 26/485, 30/74, 38/318.

stey, steyng see **stye** *v.*

steyn *pr. pl.* vilify, stain 41/71.

steke *v.* pierce, stab 18/78, 20/60.

stele *n.* steel 34/269; *adj.* 34/288.

stele *v.* **1** steal 34/252, 256, 281; **stolyn** *pp.* 36/161, 37/8, 15; **stele** *imp. sg.* 6/147; **stele** *pr. subj.* 34/167; **2** (with *awey*) depart stealthily *in* **stelyn** *pl.* 20/3.

stent *imp. pl.* bring to a halt 41/408n.

steppys *n.* footsteps 8/150, 27/424.

steracle *n.* spectacle, show 23/115.

steryd see **styrth**.

sterne *adj.* bold, stern 18/205.

ster(r)e *n.* star Pr 212, 18/26, 60; **sterrys** *pl.* stars, celestial bodies 1/30, 57, 2/10.

sterte see **styrte**.

stevene, stewyn, stevyn *n.* voice, speech 10/244, 19/41, 39/45; song 16/7.

sty *n.* sty, place of moral pollution 2/241.

stye *n.* path 18/280.

stye, stey *v.* ascend Pr 481, 7/86, 37/47, 39/68; **stey** *pr. 1 sg.* 39/47; **steyng** *pr. p.* 39/54; **styed** *pp.* Pr 461.

styff *adj.* stiff 15/261.

styk(ke) *n.* stick Pr 150, 15/261, 38/129.

stylle *adj.* quiet Pr 4, 16/120; still, motionless 26/380; **styll(e)** *adv.* ever, always Pr 5, 11/102, 25/448; motionless 4/167, 20/188, 29/111; quietly 5/121, 36/33; without change of place 10/415, 13/159A, 166A; secretly 20/3; now as formerly 24/101, 25/395, 28/68 s.d.

stynge *v.* pierce 20/72; **stunge** *pp.* 20/70.

stynk(e) *n.* stink 25/396, 27/477, 38/32.

stynkygh *pr. 3 sg.* stinks 25/393; **stynkyn** *pl.* 20/238; **stynkyd** *pa. t.* 38/148.

stynkyng(e) *ppl. adj.* stinking 2/268, 3/144, 4/183.

styrte, sterte *v.* **1** spring away 31/26; **2** go swiftly 41/421; **styrte** *pr. subj.* 26/199.

styrth *pr. 3 sg.* stirs 15/97; **steryd** *pp.* stirred up 2/212; troubled 9/125; moved, prompted 10/435, 12/19.

styward *n.* steward Pr 206, 18/95.

stody(e) *n.* study 9/106, 21/197; state of abstraction 24/225.

stodye *pr. pl.* study 21/194; **stody** *imp. sg.* think intently 28/15.

stok *n.* kindred, line of descent 7/102; stick 10/262.

stol *n.* chair, stool 29/180 s.d., 31/212 s.d.; **stolys** *pl.* 26/288 s.d.

stomak *n.* stomach 23/4.

stomachere *n.* waistcoat 26/74.

stomble, stomblyd, stomele see **stumbyll.**

stond(e), stondyn, stand(yn) *v.* **1** stand Pr 332, 6/32, 10/162, 15/176, 30/152 s.d., 32/52, 88 s.d.; ~ *at . . . syse* stand trial Pr 354; *to hy3e doth* ~ is too large 12/26; *a3ens . . .* ~ withstand, resist 33/37, 42; **stond** *pr. 1 sg.* 28/78, 95; **stondyst, standyst** *pr. 2 sg.* 29/126, 30/210, 37/9; **stondyth** *pr. 3 sg.* 5/14; **stande, stondyth, stondys** *pl.* 10/233, 20/275, 25/417, 31/179, 34/80 s.d.; **standyng(e), stondyng** *pr. p.* 15/25, 26/164 s.d., 164 s.d., 29/109, 31/170 s.d.; **sto(o)d** *pa. sg.* 25/365, 29/110; **stodyn** *pa. pl.* 27/357; **stonde** *pp.* 4/157; **stonde** *pr. subj.* 5/263; **2** be (in a specified condition): *how þat it doth now* ~ how matters stand now 10/371; **stonde** *pr. 2 sg.* 14/287; **stondyth** *pr. 3 sg.* ~ *in dowt* is in danger 27/236; **stande, stonnde** *pl.* ~ *in dowte* 20/275, 35/244; **stood** *pa. t.* 15/148; *in oo persone* ~ one person was 21/96; *impers.* 38/199; **3** be located 23/166; **stant, stondyth, standyth** *pr. 3 sg.* 15/84, 23/159, 160, 26/347, 30/136; **4** (with *as*) hold the position of, act as *in* **stonde** *pr. 1 sg.* PS 9; **standyst** *pr. 2 sg.* 11/281; **5** considering that, since *in* **stondynge** *pr. p.* 24/169, 25/150; ~ *þat* 21/49; **6** **stood** *pa. t. mannys lyff 3itt* ~ man remained alive 23/92.

ston(e) *n.* stone 23/127, 25/163, 259; *stalk and* ~ 2/305; *strete and* ~ 18/137; *at stake and at* ~ 35/75; **stonys** *pl.* Pr 292, 12/97, 23/82.

stonyd *pp.* stoned 24/220, 227.

stopage *n.* obstacle 21/247.

stoppe *v.* block 24/129; **stoppyth** *pr. 3 sg.* 25/259; **stoppyd** *pp.* stopped 25/105.

store *n. no 3onge* ~ no recent acquisition 21/149.

story *n.* historical works 15/52.

stott(e) *n.* (term of contempt) whore 24/145, 160; **stottys** *pl.* 24/166.

stow *imp. sg.* arrest 24/125; **stow** *pr. subj.* 24/127.

stownde, stounde *n.* time: *in þat* ~ at that time Pr 398; *this* ~, (*in*) *þis* ~, *in* ~ now 3/96, 6/26, 18/127, 266; moment, short time 20/265.

stowte *adj.* stout, valiant 31/29; haughty 42/93.

straunge, strawnge *adj.* strange 3/134, 10/182, 25/51, 29/102, 117.

straw *n. a* ~ *for þi tale* your words are worthless 25/377.

streyt(e), streyth *adv.*[1] directly, straight 2/242, 14/232, 15/157, 159, 25/241, 246; straightway 21/217, 25/174; at once, *or* tightly 24/203.

streyte *adv.*[2] tightly, securely 38/70, 312.

streytly *adv.* strictly 6/181.

strekyn *pp.* streaked 18/165.

strem *n.* outflow, stream 9/123.

strenght, strenth *n.* strength, power 9/122, 14/205, 38/178, 283; *with* ~ by force 14/205, 38/178, 283; **strenghthis, strenthis** *pl.* 9/184, 19/27.

strengthe *v.* strengthen 25/238.

strete *n.* street 3/188n., 15/69, 72.

strewe *v.* cover Pr 311; strew, spread 23/31.

stryff(e), sstryff *n.* strife Pr 111, 351, 10/322, PS 32; trouble 2/212.

stryke *pr. 1 sg.* go 18/60.

stryve, stryvyn *v.* quarrel, struggle 9/242, 10/272, 25/446, 32/92 s.d.

strong(e) *adj.* strong 1/44, 20/185, 28/71; guilty 18/78; severe 23/70, 76, 144; zealous 30/247; **strongere, strengere** *comp.* 26/127; *as noun* 8/185; **strong** *adv.* strongly 34/199.

stro(o)k *n.* stroke, blow 3/152, 20/191; ~ *and stryf(f)* 35/19, 36/68; **strokys** *pl.* 20/201.

stuffe *v.* stuff 26/78.

stumbyll, stomble *v.* stumble 18/289, 25/223; **stomble** *pr. 1 sg.* 2/305; **stomblyd** *pp.* 35/75; **stomele** *pr. subj.* 23/127.

suenge see **sew(e)**.

subjecte *adj.* submissive, obedient 2/275.

submyt *imp. pl.* submit: ~ *egal* be equally submissive 27/534.

substancyall *adj.* wealthy 8/46.

substauns, substawns *n.* essential nature, being 1/13, 21/92, 25/4; (spiritual) substance or stature 26/405, 27/443; *of gret* ~ very substantial 24/103.

subuertyd *pp.* subverted 29/127.

successyon *n.* succession 7/26, 74.

such(e), swych(e), swech(e), suych, suech, swiche, seche, soch *adj.* such, such a Pr 21, 248, 250, 431, 9/140, 12/52, 19/88, 26/396, 444, 27/121, 259, 32/109, 34/9; ~ *on* such a person 11/149; *pron.* 8/188, 10/86, 98.

sudary *n.* napkin (around Jesus' head) 36/132, 135.

suerd see **swerd(e)**.

suerly see **surely**.

suete see **swete** *adj.*

suffyce *v.* suffice 9/301; **sufficyth** *pr. 3 sg.* 9/304; *not* ~ does not satisfy 9/254; **ssuffysed** *pp.* 41/315.

sufficyent *adj.* qualified 11/161.

suffyr, suffre, sofer(e), sofre, suffer, sofron *v.* 1 undergo, submit to, endure 7/11, 11/159, 170, 14/280, 22/48, 50, 135, 23/209, 28/68, 166, 170, 181, 32/155; **suffyr, suffre** *pr. 1 sg.* 23/74, 76, 202; **sufferyth** *pr. 3 sg.* 32/250; **sufferyn** *pl.* 32/264; **suffryd, sufferyd** *pa. t.* 35/134, 37/54; **soferyd, sofryd, sufferyd** *pp.* 35/19, 74, 38/338; 2 patiently endure 8/129; 3 allow, tolerate: ~ *to haue* allow (you) to have 27/32; **soferyth** *pr. 3 sg.* 8/129, 34/16; **sufferyd** *pp.* 41/70; **suffyr** *imp. sg.* 11/86, 22/71; **sofre** *imp. pl.* 27/515; **suffre** *pr. subj.* 41/63; 4 waited patiently *in* **soferyd** *pp.* 4/210.

sum, som(e) *pron.* some 10/453, 13/80, 14/65, 26/57, 294, 398; *all and* ~ every bit 30/27; *all an* ~ one and all 42/6.

sumdele *n.* part, some 15/139; **sumdel(e), somdel** *adv.* to some extent 27/147, 29/179, 38/122.

sum(me), som(e), ssum *adj.* some Pr 156, 2/172, 328, 3/119, 21/228, 27/273, 32/289; an unspecified (person or thing) Pr 163, 4/162; ~ *way* somehow 4/21.

sumthyng *n.* something 41/377.

sumtyme, somtyme *adv.* formerly 2/240, 34/143.

sumwhat *adv.* in some degree 23/27.

sumwhere *adv.* somewhere 24/245.

sunere see **son(e)** *adv.*

sunne, sonne *n.* sun 1/57, 2/10, 104, 12/16, 29/167, 38/163.

sunnebe(e)m, sonnbem *n.* sunbeam 16/18, 18/317, PS 18.

suppe *v.* sup 27/368.

supplycacyon, supplicacyon *n.* supplication 11/35, 53.

supportacyon *n.* support 13/179A.

supporte *n.* support 26/454.

suppose, suppoce *pr. 1 sg.* suppose, imagine 2/225, 14/189, 306, 28/171; **supposyd** *pa. t.* 38/246.

sure, sewre *adj.* trustworthy, steadfast 3/23, 38; unfaltering 8/4; certain, sure 26/474, 27/73, 330; unable to harm: ~ *anow* i.e. dead 34/81; *adv.* for a certainty 11/161.

surely, suerly *adv.* surely 12/15, 26/197, 34/64.

susteyn *v.* uphold 26/172; endure 28/173.

sustenauns, sustenawns *n.* sustenance, food 2/332, 10/414, 27/441, 29/36.

sustentacyon *n.* nourishment 9/248.

suster, sustyr see **systyr**.

sute see **sewte**.

suterys *n.* adherents, followers 42/43.

swage *v.* 1 assuage 10/348; 2 (intr.) abate, cease *in* **swage** *pl.* 20/47; **swage** *pr. subj.* 4/20.

swap *n.* stroke: *at a* ~ with a blow Pr 228.

swappynge *ppl. adj.* smiting 20/91.

swech(e), swych(e) see **such(e)**.

swelle *v.*[1] swell Pr 172, 14/80, 115.

swelle *v.*[2] swallow 9/121.

swem(e) *n.* grief 8/78; *it wore* ~ it would be a pity 11/127.

sweme *v.* be overcome 41/198; **swemyth** *impers.* distresses, grieves 15/98.

swemful *adj.* distressing 8/66.

swemynge *vbl. n.* grieving 9/81.

swepe *v.* sweep 13/133.

swerd(e), suerd *n.* sword Pr 50, 82, 85, 2/280; **swerdys** *pl.* 20/65, 27/344, 28/80 s.d.

swere, sweryn *v.* swear Pr 341, 6/96, 20/111, 29/116; **swere** *imp. sg.* 6/85, 95.

swet *n.* sweat 32/42.

swete, suete *adj.* sweet 2/7, 35, 5/14, 19, 21, 24; unleavened 27/353, 399; **swetter(e)** *comp.* 7/20, 10/446, 16/47.

swete *v.* sweat, toil 3/115; *hym owt* ~ sweat out of him 20/200n.; **swete** *pr. 1 sg.* 28/52.

swetyng *n.* sweet one 16/149, 21/227.

swetly *adv.* pleasurably Pr 227; pleasingly to the senses 15/29.

swet(t)nes *n.* gentleness, sweetness 9/153, 40/7.

swiche, swych(e) see **such(e)**.

swyfte *adv.* swiftly 25/401.

swymmen *v.* float Pr 71; **swymme, swymmyn** *pl.* swim 2/12, 20.

swyn *n.* swine 20/237.

swynk(e) *n.* labour 2/245, 14/101.

swynke *v.* labour 3/115; take trouble 22/127.

swyth *adv.* at once, quickly 4/99, 167.

swollyn *ppl. adj.* swollen, enlarged 14/215.

swoot *n.* sweat 2/245.

swownde *pr. subj.* swoon 15/132.

swowne, swonge *v.* swoon Pr 394, 32/100 s.d.; **swuonyng** *pr. p.* 32/92 s.d.

tabbard *n.* tabard, upper garment 26/164 s.d., 208 s.d.; **tabardys** *pl.* 26/244 s.d.

tabernacle, tabernakyl *n.* tabernacle 13/138, 14/340, 41/511.

tabyl(l), table *n.* **1** tablet 6/63, 68, 83; **tabelys, tabellis, tablys** *pl.* Pr 93, 6/38, 60; **2** table 20/144, 151, 27/348 s.d.

tayle *n.* pudendum: *of hire* ~ . . . *be lyght* may be promiscuous 14/96; retinue: *I drowe in my* ~ I took along with me 26/17.

take, tan *v.* **1** undergo, suffer Pr 502, 5/154, 27/558; *of deth* . . . ~ die 27/545; *deth to* ~ died 32/233; **toke** *pa. t.* 29/19; **take** *pp.* 4/181; **2** take: *begynnyng nevyr dyd* ~ never began 1/27; *on hond to* ~ to undertake 4/98; ~ *lynage* be descended 7/38; ~ *ensawmple* (*by*) to follow the example of 22/76; ~ *exaunple* follow this example 22/80; ~ . . . *cowncelle* consider (an issue) 30/192; **take** *pr. 1 sg.* ~ *to borwe*, ~ *wyt(t)nes* (*of*), ~ *record* of call to witness 8/169, 14/170, 247, 29/211; **takyth** *pr. 3 sg.* 27/511 s.d., 515 s.d., 31/117 s.d.; ~ *wonynge* dwells 18/209; **take** *pl.* ~ *ȝe on with* go on with, behave

toward 29/193; **toke** *pa. t.* Pr 83, 302; *vp* ~ raised up 13/112n.; **take, tan** *pp.* Pr 437, 6/35, 25/235; ~ *hym* brought to him 32/176 s.d.; **tak(e), takyth, takyght** *imp. pl.* 2/128, 12/186, 14/384, 27/486, 499, 29/179; ~ *it into vsage* make it a practice 11/325; ~ *good kepe* (*of, to*) look after 20/82, 25/27, 27/499; ~ *ȝoure stodye* study 21/197; ~ . . . *ȝoure cowncel* 29/114; ~ *cure* take charge of, care for 41/332; **3** accept 3/102, 8/39, 24/165; **toke** *pa. t.* 15/273; **take** *imp. sg.* 11/46; **4** assume, take on (human form) 7/14, 19/6, 21/166; **takynge** *pr. p.* 11/297; **toke, took** *pa. t.* 21/94, 109. ~ *ȝoure incarnacyon* assumed your human form 21/284; *blood I* ~ 35/49; **take** *pp.* ~ *incarnacyon* 15/92, 21/67; **5** choose 10/352, 27/50; **take** *imp. sg.* 34/171; **6** go on, follow 18/333; ~ *passage* go 3/190; **take** *pr. 1 sg.* 1/79, 14/254, 27/58; *my chawmere I* ~ I retire 15/94; **toke** *pa. t.* 24/72; ~ *þe pas* went 25/316; **tak** *imp. pl.* 18/298; **take** *pr. subj.* (forming *imp.*) 36/144; **7** give 19/179, 24/190; ~ (*good*) *hede* pay attention, consider 10/102, 26/181, 30/181; ~ *hede* attend (to) 34/207; **take** *pr. 1 sg.* 6/38, 10/313, 32/199; **takyng** *pr. p.* 31/212 s.d.; **toke, took** *pa. sg.* Pr 40, 41, 93; ~ *tent* gave heed Pr 88; ~ *me tylle* gave to me 2/205; **tokyn** *pa.* 38/284; **take** *pp.* ~ *good hede* 28/124; **take** *imp. sg.* 2/21, 4/167; ~ (*good*) *hede* (*heyd, heed*) 5/44, 209, 10/31; ~ *tent* 10/124; ~ (*good*) *hed* (*eyd*) *to* attend to 32/58, 212; **tak(e), takyth, takyht** *imp. pl.* 14/294, 34/134; ~ (*good*) *hed*(*e*) (*heyd*) 6/51, 8/18, 10/2; ~ *good intent*, ~ . . . *tent* pay attention 6/52, 10/142, 12/49; **take** *pr. subj.* 14/158; ~ (*good*) *hede* 34/63, 207; **toke** *pa. subj.* ~ *hede* 24/243; **8** experience, feel 23/69; ~ *it to grame* be angered by it 15/184; ~ *to ȝow good chere* be cheerful 25/62; ~ *þat to plesawns* take pleasure in that 26/449; **take** *imp.* Pr 138, 2/157, 11/237; ~ *good comforte to ȝow* be comforted 5/151; ~ *it nat at no greve*, ~ *this at no greff* don't be disturbed 16/144, 26/364; ~ *ȝe no care* have no concern 20/149; **take** *pr. subj.* 25/262; **9** understand 27/407; **10** receive 22/23, 63, 27/519; **toke** *pa. t.* Pr 302, 35/210; **11** take responsibility for 30/32; ~ *on me*

11/182; ~ *this vpon yow* 41/236; **take** *pr. 1 sg. I ~ this vpon me* 41/248; **tak** *imp. pl.* 41/363; **12** commit or devote oneself *in* **take** *pr. 1 sg. refl.* 10/74, 38/365; **13** (with *for*) consider, suppose to be *in* **takyst** *pr. 2 sg.* 6/77; **take** *pl.* 1/63; **14** take (one's leave) *in* **takyn, take** *pl.* 14/389, 27/348 s.d., 34/121 s.d.; **toke** *pa. t.* 13/175A; **15** captured, seized *in* **toke** *pa. t.* 29/16, 205; **take, takyn** *pp.* 29/89 s.d., 89 s.d., 93, 41/19; ~ *in hondys* made captive 27/102; **take** *pp.* caught Pr 283, 24/247; **16** assigned to *in* **toke** *pp.* Pr 155; **17** entered upon, occupied *in* **takyn** *pp.* 29/1st s.d.; **18** taken (as spouse) 10/323.

takyll *n.* weapon 4/169.

takyng *vbl. n.* capture 28/148 s.d.

takke *v.* fasten, tack 31/26; **takkyd** *pp.* 32/77.

tale, tall *n.* **1** account, information, tale Pr 441, 6/194, 7/111; *tell þu þat* ~ speak such words 2/317; **talys** *pl.* 14/134, 18/217, 35/286; *withoute mo* ~ I say no more 23/177; **2** statement 7/70.

talkyn *v.* say 38/175; **talkyn** *pl.* 29/84; **talkyd** *pp.* 8/14.

talkyng(e) *vbl. n.* speech Pr 4, *8/18, 29/21; *what xal be his* ~ what he will say 3/15.

tall *adj.* handsome, bold 24/71.

tan see **take.**

tary *v.* tarry 26/126, 30/151, 41/8; **tery** *pr. 1 sg.* 30/18; **taryst** *pr. 2 sg.* 10/222; **taryeth** *pr. 3 sg.* 14/259;. **tary** *pl.* 24/113; **taryed** *pa. t.* Pr 501, 12/124; **tary(e)** *imp. sg.* 5/85, 11/23; **tary, taryeth** *imp. pl.* 10/151, 32/280, 35/239; **tary, tery** *pr. subj.* 14/176, 30/8.

taske *v.* ~ *a wynke* have a nap 34/324n.

tast *n.* taste 32/204.

tast, tastyn *v.* taste 2/85, 164, 286; **tast** *imp. pl.* test, examine 15/225.

tech(e) *v.* **1** teach 4/42, 6/55, 9/208; **teche, techyn** 3/46, 38/102, 41/266; **tawth, tauht** *pa. t.* 34/34, 41/3; **tawth, taught, tawght** *pp.* 6/59, 194, 19/2, 22/74, 180; **teche** *imp. sg.* 6/14; **2** show (the way) 18/130, 231, 36/6; **taught** *pa. t.* 18/321; **3** tell 18/271.

techer *n.* teacher PS 9.

techyng(e) *vbl. n.* teaching, instruction 6/52, 27/498.

tedyous *adj.* tedious 8/14.

tee *v.* proceed 3/14.

teer *n.* tear 24/12; **terys** *pl.* 8/66, 177, 37/2.

teyl *imp. sg.* work for 2/245.

teynt *ppl. adj.* tainted, infected, corrupt 41/400.

tekele *pr. pl.* tickle 26/86.

tekyl *adj.* easily moved: ~ *vndyr þe too* easily swept off her feet 14/97.

tell(e), tellyn *v.* **1** tell Pr 56, 168, 193, 488, 14/190, 231; **tel(l)(e)** *pr. 1 sg.* Pr 100, 159, 170; **tellyth** *pr. 3 sg.* Pr 440, 29/89; **telle, tellyth** *pl.* Pr 443, 25/40, 29/63, 36/145; **telland** *pr. p.* 41/127; **told(e)** *pa. t.* and *pp.* Pr 66, 209, 441; **tel(l)(e)** *imp. sg.* 2/317, 4/178, 5/124; **tell(e), tellyth** *imp. pl.* 5/76, 135, 9/32; **telle** *pr. subj.* (forming *imp.*)) 38/235; **2** discern 23/194, 25/121; **3** count 27/273, 291; **telle** *pr. 1 sg.* reckon 11/1; **4** proclaimed *in* **tolde** *pp.* 10/15; **5** direct *in* **telle** *imp. sg.* 18/173.

teme *n.* theme: *sayd vs this* ~ s oke these words to us 41/200.

temperal *adj.* secular 26/195.

temperawnce *n.* temperance 26/213.

temple, tempyl(l) *n.* temple Pr 245, 397, 7/42, 9/237, 10/19, 21; **templys** *pl.* 27/15.

temptacyon *n.* templtation 9/138, 11/174, 21/130.

tempt(e) *v.* tempt, put to the test Pr 274, 15/262, 23/41; **temptyth** *pr. 3 sg.* Pr 376; **temptynge** *pr. p.* 15/275; **temptyd, tempte** *pa. t.* 21/118, 120, 123, 26/27; **temptyd** *pp.* Pr 276; **tempte** *pr. subj.* 23/213.

tende *ord. num. as adj.* Pr 119; *as noun* 9/138.

tend(e) *v.* **1** attend (to), look after 9/212, 18/264, 41/432; **tender** *pr. subj.* 9/215; **2** intends *in* **tendyth** *pr. 3 sg.* 27/235n.; **tende** *pl.* 4/252.

tendyr *adj.* young 9/5; soft, fresh 23/82.

tendyrly *adv.* with tender feeling 9/215; with kind attention 10/2.

tene *n.* malice Pr 185; trouble, harm Pr 236, 522, 10/480.

tene *v.* be distressed 41/400; **tene** *imp. sg.* harass, distress 10/84.

tent *n.* heed, attention Pr 88, 10/124, 142.

tent *imp. pl.* attend to 41/297.

terestyall *adj.* terrestrial 41/203, 492.

tery see **tary.**

teryeng(e) *vbl. n.* delay 9/25, 19/38, 27/ 345.

terys see **teer.**

term(e) *n.* length of time Pr 267, 22/124; ~, *tyme, and tyde* always 10/330; saying 26/58; **termys** *pl.* ways of speaking: *old ~ the* old expression 27/303.

termynable, termynabyle *adj. in me (you) is* ~ I (you) make the final decision 26/216, 29/51.

testyficacyon *n.* testimony 7/123.

testyfie, testefy *v.* attest, declare (to be true) 7/130, 26/52.

testymonyall *n.* witness 26/420.

testymonye *n.* testimony 31/148.

testymonye *v.* bear witness 26/338.

tetys *n.* breasts 32/14.

þan, than *conj.* than Pr 416, 1/54, 4/161, 193, 237, 5/58.

thank *v.* (with *of* 'for') 13/170; **thank(e)** *pr. 1 sg.* (with *of*) 4/238, 5/17; *I ~ it God* I thank God for it 15/42; **thank** *pl.* (with *of*) 13/178A; **thankyng(e)** *pr. p.* 13/161A, 27/378, 41/132; **thankyd** *pp.* 4/216; **thank** *imp. pl.* (with *of*) 13/148, 21/36; **thank(e)** *pr. subj.* 9/74, 41/184.

thank(e) *n.* thanks 29/120, 30/194, 32/28.

thankyng *vbl. n.* thanks 27/374.

than(ne), þan(ne), then *adv.* then Pr 18, 21, 25, 43, 46, 61; *conj.* therefore, that being the case Pr 291, 8/206, 10/186.

þar *pr. pl.* need 27/436.

þat, that *pron.* that 5/129, 7/93, 12/25, 37, 34/109, 41/83; ~ *þer* Pr 509; *pron. rel.* who, whom, that, which Pr 3, 78, 93; that which, those who, he who Pr 197, 411, 471; one whom *29/97; *adj.* that Pr 20, 45, 46; so great 11/158; those 21/113.

þat, that *conj.* that Pr 23, 125, 163, 210, 528, 2/239; so that Pr 190, 2/29, 4/77; (introd. exclam. clause) Pr 363, 2/178, 188; in consequence of which 4/139; since, seeing that 5/195, 41/168; because 13/85; in that 26/235.

the, then, þe *v.* thrive, prosper 3/20, 10/ 178, 13/7, 29/102, 30/234, 34/223; *evyl mot(e) þu (he)* ~ may you (he) have misfortune 30/234, 32/53.

thedyr *adv.* to that place, thither 8/88, 15/157, 24/73; ~ *ward* going there 9/47; towards that place 27/52 s.d.

thedom *n.* prosperity: *evil ~ bad luck* 14/ 262.

thef(f)(e), þeff *n.* **1** thief Pr 353, 31/97, 32/139, 224; **thevys** *gen. sg.* 28/136; **thevys, þewys, þevys** *pl.* Pr 350, 388, 31/170 s.d., 181, 32/88 s.d.; **thevys** *gen. pl.* 32/96; **2** scoundrel Pr 384, 4/187, 31/ 106, 173; **thevys** *pl.* 18/78.

thefte *n.* theft 6/147.

þei, they, thei, þey *pron.* they Pr 37, 38, 42, 114, 147, 163, 4/112, 114, 5/228, 18/ 224; **them, þem** *acc.* and *dat.* Pr 44, 367, 441, 468, 470, 522; **þem** *refl.* 27/491 s.d.; **þer, ther(e)** *poss.* Pr 44, 242, 293, 11/80, 25/228, 41/31.

theys see **þis** *adj.*

then see **the** *v.*

þenge see **thyng(e).**

thenke, þenke, thenkyth *see* **thynk(e).**

thens *adv.* thence Pr 211, 10/237, 11/104.

þeras, ther(e)as *conj.* where 15/153, 22/ 20, 25/242, 244, 260, 31/179.

þerat(t)e *adv.* at it 14/69; to it 29/20.

þerbesyde *adv.* near there 28/16 s.d.

þerby, þerbe *adv.* by means of that 10/ 438; in consequence of that 11/140, 27/ 361, 38/287; near there 20/238, 23/160, 34/250.

þer(e), ther(e), thore, þare, þore *adv.* there Pr 30, 36, 37, 63, 132, 2/32, 9/92, 11/173, 201; ~ *may no man* no man can 4/23, 5/57, 119; ~ *myht nevyr man* no one could 4/146; ~ *is no more* there is nothing more to say 8/74; ~ *is not may* nothing can 8/161; ~ *can (kan) no tounge telle (expres)* nobody can tell (express) 8/232, 37/78; ~ *was nevyr joy* no joy ever before 8/243; ~ *may no myrth* no joy can 25/326; where Pr 430, 14/39, 15/280; in that respect 8/104; then 11/61; whereas 25/128, 160.

þerf(f)or(e), ther(e)f(f)or(e) *adv.* therefore Pr 180, 2/99, 160, 4/44, 225, 6/138; for it, for that 5/136, 13/145, 24/52; *cawse ~ reason why* 25/230.

þerin(ne), therin *adv.* in it Pr 17, 266, 410, 23/139; in that (undertaking) 9/193; in them 26/134.

therkeness, thyrknes *n.* darkness 10/ 436, PS 27.

therlys *n.* piercings (i.e. wounds) 20/58n.

þerof, therof *adv.* of it, of that 2/110, 129,

138, 41/113; concerning that 2/112, 3/22, 23/4; from that 14/71, 309, 31/84.

þeron *adv.* on it, on that 7/64, 15/27, 29/157; on which 15/73.

þerowte *adv.* out of doors, abroad 4/23.

þerqwyl *adv.* meanwhile 19/146 s.d.

þerto, therto *adv.* to it, to that 2/206, 3/48, 10/308, 41/354; for that purpose 3/73, 27/140, 31/204; also 6/126; concerning that 9/62, 19/187, 34/119; i.e. to be angry 13/143; for that 10/305; on that place 29/141; added to that 34/202; to that place 41/421.

þerupon *adv.* upon them, upon it 26/449 s.d., 27/454.

þerwhylys *adv.* meanwhile 32/92 s.d.

þerwith, therwith, therwyth *adv.* thereupon 8/13; in addition to that 9/150; with that, with it 9/251, 258, 10/432, 21/126, 41/442; against that 9/242; by means of that 14/72.

þewys see **thef(f)(e)**.

thyk *adj.* thick, numerous 2/228; abundant 38/131.

thyng(e), þing(e), þenge, thing *n.* 1 thing Pr 30, 2/6, 32, 255, 3/173, 12/34, 41/59; **thyngys, thyng(e), þing** *pl.* 9/296, 10/413, 448, 13/92, 26/285, 28/144, 29/158; 2 anything 5/68, 12/102, 28/169; 3 person 16/148, 18/157, 316.

thynk(e), thynkyn *v.*[1] 1 consider to be 11/212, 41/507; **thynkyst** *pr. 2 sg.* (with ellips. of 'thou') 30/246; **thynkyth, thynke** *pl.* 24/200; ~ *longe* yearn 11/260; 2 conceive 13/66; 3 think 13/113, 29/224; **thynke** *pr. 1 sg.* 11/137, 231, 25/359; **thynk(e), þinkyth, thynkyth** *pl.* 29/177, 30/77, 78, 34/83, 210; **thowth** *pa. t.* 28/169; **thynk** *imp. sg.* (with *on*) think about, have in mind 9/80, 28/192; **thynkys, thynke** *imp. pl.* 25/65; ~ *no greff* don't be distressed 13/147; 4 believe 21/78; 5 think of 25/104; 6 intend 27/221; **thynke** *pr. 1 sg.* 27/152; **thenkyth, thynk** *pr. 3 sg.* Pr 176, 9/100; **thynk(e), thenke, þenke** *pl.* Pr 14, 28, 215, 359, 517, 25/148; **thowth, thought** *pa. t.* Pr 293, 10/68; **thenke** *pr. subj.* Pr 104; 7 have in mind *in* **thynk** *pl.* 15/107; 8 remember 41/199; 9 supposed, expected *in* **thouth** *pa. t.* Pr 86.

thynkyth *pr. 3 sg. impers.*[2] ~ *me* it seems to me 40/23; **thought** *pa. impers.* *hym* ~

nay it seemed unbelievable to him 13/78.

thynkynge *vbl. n. as to my* ~ it seems to me 21/269.

thyrlyng *pr. p.* piercing Pr 497; **thyrlyd** *pp.* 28/174. Cf. **thrylle**.

þis, this, thys, þese, thes *pron.* this Pr 18, 50, 64, 6/68, 71, 7/90, 8/129, 11/168, 307, 12/206, 26/188; *he* ~ this man 23/188; this place 41/480; **þese, these** *pl.* 4/40, 6/187, 15/51, 21/255, 30/201.

þis, this, thes(e), þese *adj.* this Pr 5, 9, 11, 519, 3/68, 4/92, 25/315, 26/188, 27/486; **þese, thes(e), þis(e), this(e), theys** *pl.* Pr 96, 443, 2/97, 4/194, 201, 230, 6/66, 181, 10/469, 13/132, 14/134, 41/9, 33; **this, þis** *adv.* thus 32/190, 38/261.

tholyn *v.* suffer, endure 18/63; **tholyd** *pa. t.* 34/272, 35/81, 36/4; **tholyd** *pp.* 20/118.

thondyrblast *n.* clap of thunder 31/66.

thonge *n.* strap, lace 26/128.

þo(o), tho *pron.* those Pr 3, 103, 391, 8/38, 14/4, 38/350; those who 31/49, 41/267, 42/43; *ad.* those Pr 161, 226, 336.

tho(o) *adv.* then 23/218, 41/211, 291.

thore, þore see **þer(e)**.

thorn *n.* thorn-bearing plant 15/304; *crowne of* ~ 25/454; **þornys** *pl.* thorns 31/212 s.d.

thorw(e), þorwe, þurowe, thurwe, throw, throwh, thourgh, þurwe, þour, thorow *prep.* by means of Pr 15, 281, 400, 406, 1/28, 2/265, 3/47, 74, 7/4, 14/291, 16/4, 25/7, 27/379, 41/71, 466, 521; (of direction) through 18/59, 19/90, 20/4; *adv.* through 32/76.

thorweouth *prep.* throughout 14/47.

þough see **þow** *conj.*

thought, thowth, thouth, þowth, thouht *n.* 1 thought, thinking Pr 337, 3/24, 65, 4/6, 5/92, 240, 6/174, 41/413; *with a* ~ instantly 11/214; *haue in* ~ keep in mind 22/176; **thoughtys** *pl.* 11/137; 2 intention, idea 14/171, 32/279, 34/22; *al my* ~ my sole intention 9/228, 12/6; 3 distress, anxiety 25/47, 27/191, 30/28, 32/99.

þow, thow, þowh, þough *conj.* although 2/231, 3/21, 49, 103, 6/166, 9/245, 25/440, 36/93; ~ *þat* 6/119, 12/109, 198; though 28/136.

thowsand *card. num. as adj.* thousand 11/1, 157A, 14/48; *as noun* 30/118, 34/204; *many a* ~ 31/3; **thowsandys** *pl.* 30/180.

thrall(e) *n.*[1] thrall 5/247, 23/186; **thrall(e)** *pl.* 6/13, 20/204, 23/125.

thrall *n.*[2] while 35/234.

thrawe see **throwe.**

thre *card. num. as adj.* three Pr 252, 276, 350; *as noun* 6/61, 10/355, 11/37.

thred *n.* thread 42/125.

thred(de) see **thryd(de).**

threte, thrett *n.* threat 2/147, 18/94.

threte *v.* threaten 2/97.

threttene *as ord. num., as noun* thirteenth 9/150.

thretty(e) *card. num. as adj.* thirty Pr 492, 11/11, 27/305.

thryd(de), thredde *ord. num. as adj.* third Pr 53, 8/57, 27/120, 41/293; **thrydde, thyrde, thred** *as noun* 9/110, 233, 10/355, 21/114, 31/203.

thryes *adv.* thrice Pr 341, 8/79, 16/21.

thryff, thryfe *v.* thrive 10/278, 304; ~ *schul ye late* you won't prosper soon 41/394.

thryfte *n.* prosperity: (in oath) *be my* ~ 29/116.

thrylle *v.* pierce Pr 240. Cf. **thyrlyng.**

thrysté *n.* thirsty (ones) 11/13n.

thrysty, thrusty *adj.* thirsty 42/97; *as noun* 42/79.

throte *n.* throat 25/143.

throwe *v.* cast, throw: *such thrett wolde me* ~ (who) would threaten me in this way 18/94; **throwe** *pr. 1 sg.* 33/45; **throwe, thrawe** *pp.* 2/189, 201, 24/248, 26/240.

throw, throwh see **thorw(e).**

throwys *n.* throes, labour-pangs 15/131.

thrust, thurste *n.* thirst 32/194, 196, 198, 38/29.

thrusty see **thrysty.**

þurowe, thurwe, þurwe see **thorw(e).**

þu, thou, thu, thow *pron. 2 sg.* you Pr 3, 138, 139, 1/66, 2/227, 259, 3/170, 5/37, 10/258, 18/245, 248, 26/457; **þe, the** *dat.* and *acc.* 1/45, 50, 63, 64, 67, 3/68; **þe, the** *refl.* 2/60, 6/79, 101; **þin(e), thyn, þinne** *pron. poss.* yours 10/221, 14/81, 31/136; *adj.* 2/41, 109, 111, 163, 5/114, 124, 139; **þi, thy, thi, þy** your Pr 2, 179, 1/65, 75, 2/249, 3/132, 6/124, 126, 172, 18/257; **þiself(e), thys(s)elf,**

þiselph, þisylf, þiselff *pron.* yourself 2/24, 5/232, 6/186, 12/33, 23/117, 120; you 10/344, 14/116, 286, 21/155, 25/398, 27/265.

thurste see **thrust.**

þus, thus *adv.* thus, so Pr 42, 165, 293, 301, 344, 7/133.

tyde *n.* time, while 10/330, 35/238; *þis* ~ now Pr 9, 3/104, 14/274; *withinne (in) a* ~ soon 5/48, 23/56, 27/203; *in no* ~ never 23/143; *at every* ~ constantly 25/189.

tide *v.* happen, betide 41/80.

tydyng(e) *n.* news Pr 78, 8/218, 18/101; **tydyngys, tydandys, tydyngis** *pl.* Pr 443, 4/245, 8/206, 31/78, 35/178, 36/97, 41/213, 259, 458.

tyed *pp.* tied 26/350.

tyght, tyth *adv.* quickly Pr 508, 25/383; *as* ~ immediately 3/160.

tyl(l), til *conj.* until Pr 461, 2/263, 292, 41/46, 76; ~ *þat* 19/23, 25/28, 188.

tyll(e), tyl *prep.* to 18/321, 27/30, 32/124, 38/250, 273; *hym (me, us)* ~ to him (me, us) Pr 89, 2/79, 156; ~ *fortene ʒere* up to the age of fourteen 9/15; *doth charge us* ~ commands us 24/183.

tymbre-wryth *n.* carpenter 15/6.

tyme *n.* time 8/41, 97 s.d., 9/4; *þat* ~, *in þe* ~ *þat*, *what* ~ *(þat)*, *swyche* ~ *as* when 4/155, 223, 5/180, 9/195, 10/129, 21/212, 19/1st s.d.; *þis* ~ now 8/59, 14/257, 24/216; ~ *of mete* period set aside for eating 9/281; ~ *of ʒere* the proper season 15/27; **tymes, tyme** *pl.* 14/279, 297, 26/123, 32/36.

'tys *phrase* 'tis 28/106 s.d.

tyth see **tyght.**

tythe *v.* offer as tithe 3/94, 97, 126; **tythe** *pr. 1 sg.* 3/85, 88, 101; **tythe** *imp. sg.* 3/108.

tythyng *n.* tithe Pr 57, 3/91, 132.

tythyng *vbl. n.* act of tithing Pr 64, 3/148; **tythyngys** *pl.* Pr 55.

tythis *n.* tithes 3/137.

tyxt *n.* text 26/47.

to see **to(o)** *adj.*

to *adv.* too Pr 388, 1/46, 11/68.

to *prep.* with respect to Pr 510, 6/13, 8/47; against 4/232, 27/235; in accordance with 9/12; in 9/177; as 10/302, 310, 11/95; on, against 14/88; for 16/11, 18/39, 28/190; (with ellips. of vb. of motion)

22/137; of 26/353, 27/499; **to(o)** to Pr 4, 65, 71; expressing contact, *or* too 34/248.

to-breke *imp. sg.* break open 16/56.

to-drawe *v.* tear to pieces 41/476.

tofore *prep.* to the front of 41/404.

togedyr *adv.* together 5/104, 10/25, 111.

tokenyng(e) *vbl. n.* token, portent 16/24; *in ~* as a token 41/133.

tokyn *n.* **1** token, sign 4/252, 8/104, 155; *in ~* as a sign 8/198, 11/208, 16/51; **tokenys** *pl.* 34/3, 12, 38/92; **2** proof, evidence 12/102.

tolle *n.* tools (of war), weapons 20/44.

tombe *n.* tomb 34/147.

tomorwe *n.* tomorrow 11/23; *as adv.* 8/168, 27/434, 29/74.

tomorwyn *n.* tomorrow 34/51.

tonge, tounge, tung *n.* tongue Pr 199, 8/232, 19/34, 20/240, 30/239, 37/78; *is sclēpyr of ~* speaks deceitfully 10/347; *of my ~ . . . ses* stop talking 13/42.

tonyght *adv.* tonight 34/318.

too *n.* toe 14/97, 32/244; **ton** *pl.* 14/260.

to(o), two *card. num. as adj.* two 4/194, 13/9, 19/31, 158, 26/72, 79; *as noun* 12/72, 14/46, 21/2; *hem ~* both of them Pr 469; *both ~* both 3/51, 53, 11/84.

toost *n.* toasted bread 20/133.

to-pende *v.* press severely, torment 20/12n.

to-pynde *pp.* reduced 2/325n.

torchys, torchis *n.* torches 27/342, 28/80 s.d.

to-rent *pp.* utterly torn apart 20/33, 32/244.

tormentry *n.* infliction of torment 21/188.

torne *n.* turn of affairs 31/43.

tose *v.* elicit, search out 42/12.

toth *n.* tooth: *withdrawe my gret rough ~* 'pull back my fangs', cease to trouble you 14/159; **teth** *pl.* 24/191.

tother *pron.* other one 34/121 s.d.; **tother** *pl. þat ~* the others 21/113; **tother(e)** *adj.* other 6/64, 9/206, 29/194 s.d.

to-torn(e) *pp.* torn to pieces 2/265, 20/93, 258.

toure, towre *n.* tower, stronghold 5/39, 8/24, 10/223, 23/158, 37/49, 41/182; **towrys, touris** *pl.* 27/15, 41/404.

towaly *n.* towel 27/511 s.d., 515 s.d.

towche *n.* stroke, blow 29/99.

towch(e) *v.* **1** touch Pr 39, 2/67, 139; **towchyd** *pa. t.* and *pp.* 2/181, 297; **towch(e)** *imp.* 2/38, 15/251, 280; **2** pertain, pertain to *in* **towch** *pl.* 6/62, 64; **towchyd** *pa. t.* and *pp.* 12/103; *was only ~ be temptacyon* the temptation concerned only 21/130.

towchynge *vbl. n.* touching 15/247.

town(e) *n.* town 10/183, 14/47, 15/66; *in felde and* (*nor*) *~* 3/188, 5/260, 6/154.

trace *n.* course, path 5/243; way of life 27/186.

tray *v.* betray 35/46.

trayn *n.* deceit 35/189.

traytour, tretour(e), tretowre, tretore *n.* traitor Pr 317, 325, 361, 26/55, 309, 28/86, 121, 31/97; **traytorys, tretowrys, tretorys, tretour, tretouris** *pl.* 29/32, 42, 48, 55, 31/12, 41/400.

transgressyon *n.* transgression 11/77.

tras *v.* travel Pr 405; devise 27/209.

trast *v.* trust 10/45.

travayl(e), traveyl, trauayle *n.* labour, effort 23/146, 208; *~ hye* holy labour 11/319; hardship, suffering 15/1, labour and pain of childbirth 15/205, 206.

trauayle, travayl *pr. pl.* are in labour 15/152; *~ of childe* suffer the pains of childbirth 15/121; **trauelyng** *pr. p. ~ of chylde* 15/141.

travalynge *vbl. n. gon in ~* are in labour 15/135.

traveyll, travayl *v.* travel 13/156; *me to ~* for me to travel, *or* to weary me 10/167; **trauaylid** *pp.* 18/43.

travelynge *ppl. adj.* suffering the pains of childbirth 15/130.

tre *n.* tree Pr 370, 2/38, 67; *~ and frute* 2/22; *~ . . . erbe and floure* 2/6—7; **tres** *pl.* 20/185, 35/139.

trede *v.* (with *down*) trample 7/52.

trey, tray *n.* abuse Pr 185; trouble, grief Pr 522, 10/480.

trekyl *v.* trickle 8/66.

Trenyté see **Trinyté.**

trepett *n.* tripping up 20/188.

treson, tresson *n.* treason 26/58, 27/116, 132; betrayal 27/209, 214, 220, 221.

tresorere *n.* treasurer PS 22.

tresour, tresowre, tresure, tresoour *n.* treasure Pr 318, 365, 10/403, 18/197, 26/112, 27/237.

trespacyd *pa. t.* and *pp.* transgressed 14/290, 27/109, 447; **trespas** *imp. sg.* 6/143.

trespas(e), tres(s)pace, tresspas *n.*
transgression Pr 364, 381, 4/29, 63, 138,
213, 12/165; fault 31/73.

tretable *adj.* able to be entreated 24/35.

tretore, tretour(e), tretowre see **tray-tour.**

trew(e), trowe *adj.* honest, sincere, vir-tuous Pr 64, 2/116, 4/110, 35/33; faithful
Pr 412, 10/329, 14/226; true, genuine
1/14, 4/154, 5/23; *adv.* with confidence,
truly 38/195, 280.

trew(e)ly(e), truly, treuly(e) *adv.* truly,
indeed Pr 287, 2/198, 3/31, 36/115, 41/
127, 268, 277, 359; faithfully 5/150, 22/
113.

trewth(e), truth(e), threwth *n.* 1 truth
Pr 56, 271, 352, 18/271, 24/84, 38/79; (as
personif.) 11/57, 81, 116; (as asseveration) *be my* ~ 14/44, 50, 90; *of* ~ truly
26/233; **trewthis** *pl.* 26/171, 466; **2**
solemn promise 10/313.

trybulacyon, tribulacyon *n.* tribulation
5/208, 8/156, 11/74, 26/431; **tribulacyouns** *pl.* 41/339.

tribus *n.* tribes 8/32, 62.

trybute *n.* tax 15/4, 63.

try(e) *v.* ascertain 26/171, 303, 29/73;
tryed(e) *pp.* 26/43, 466; ~ *owth* found
out 14/181; **trye** *imp. pl.* ~ ... *owth* 15/
252.

tryne *adj.* threefold 9/277.

**Trinyté, Trynyté, Trynité, Trinité,
Trenyté** *n.* Trinity 1/14, 4/65, 8/120,
10/301, 11/171, 240, 312, 333, 12/68, 13/
48, 138, 15/44, 18/248, 19/21; **Trynité**
gen. sg. 41/138.

tryst *n.* trust 41/231.

tryste *pr. 3 sg.* (with *to*) trusts in 18/303;
tryst *pr. subj.* may believe 30/220.

trobelyth *pr. 3 sg.* troubles 10/92, 23/4;
trobyl *pl.* 10/81; **trobelyd** *pp.* 11/230,
29/127.

trobyl *n.* trouble, distress 9/104, 27/14.

trone(e) *n.* throne Pr 262, 498, 1/21.

trost(e), truste *n.* trust, faith 26/58, 38/
73, 145; *in* ~ *þat* trusting that 26/152.

troste, trust *v.* 1 trust, believe 38/309; ~
to 36/112; **trost, trust, trostyn** *pr. 1 sg.*
10/219, 14/322, 25/84; **trostyth** *pr. 3 sg.*
Pr 371; **trustyd** *pa. t.* 38/229, 369, 379;
trust(e) *imp. sg.* 38/318, 344, 375;
trust(e), trostyth, trost *imp. pl.* 36/
115, 37/91, 38/104, 195, 280; **2** believe
sth. will happen 26/156.

trow(e) *v.* 1 believe, think, suppose
5/223, 12/81, 15/246; **trow(e)** *pr. 1 sg.*
3/134, 9/284, 13/9; **trowyste** *pr. 2 sg.*
41/67; **trowe** *imp. pl.* 41/146; **2** trust *in*
trowe *pr. 1 sg.* 13/142.

trowe see **trew(e).**

trowth(e) *n.* 1 troth 6/146, 14/52, 82; (as
asseveration) *be my(n)* ~ 14/64, 155,
222; *be* ~ 14/70; **2** truth 6/157, 160, 14/
253; *for* ~ as being true 7/119, 130; *in* ~
truly 10/236, 11/129; (as personif.) 11/
153.

trus *pr. 1 sg.* pack, truss 20/84.

tundyr *n.* (?) tinder 4/176n.

tung see **tonge.**

turmentouris, tormentours *n.* tor-turers 41/91, 394.

turne *v.* 1 change 14/312, 24/60, 26/56;
turnyd *pp.* 2/287, 8/125, 25/127; *is* ~
has become 11/219; **turne** *imp.* 2/310,
23/81, 38/103; **2** convert, pervert 24/50;
turnyd *pp.* 30/118; **3** alter (one's course
in life) 27/481, 32/12; **turne** *imp. pl.*
22/6; ~ *зoure faye* be converted 34/35; **4**
turns *in* **turnyth** *pr. 3 sg.* 32/8 s.d., 20
s.d.; **turnyng** *pr. p. refl.* 34/121 s.d.;
turne *imp.* Pr 180, 5/167, 15/28; ~ *aзen*
change (one's) course, return 24/22;
refl. 23/170; **5** moved *in* **turnyd** *pa. t.*
13/55.

turtyl *n.* turtle-dove 11/313; **turtelys** *pl.*
8/75, 19/116.

twey, tway *adj.* two 11/64; *on* ~ in two
38/285.

tweyn(e), twayn *adj.* two Pr 93, 486,
4/177, 6/60; *on* ~ in two 4/177, 25/324,
28/172; *as noun* 4/41, 5/251, 6/129;
tweyners *gen. pl.* 13/39.

twelfte *ord. num. as noun* twelfth 9/146.

twyes *adv.* twice 25/407, 27/562.

twynne *v.* split in two 32/229.

vmbyl *adj.* humble 27/534.

vn see **on** *prep.*

vnbegete *ppl. adj.* unbegotten 27/460.

vnbynde *v.* 1 undo, dissolve 16/77; **2**
untie *in* **vnbynde** *pl.* 25/433; **3** set free,
delivered *in* **vnbownde** *pp.* 16/4, 92,
36/8; **vnbynde** *pr. subj.* 24/295.

vnborn *ppl. adj.* unborn 4/236, 27/260,
460.

vnclose, onclose *v.* open 26/62, 27/76
s.d., 348 s.d., 30/152 s.d.; **onclose** *imp.
pl.* 28/74.

vndefyled, vndefylde, vndefylyd *ppl.*
adj. undefiled 14/324, 15/241, 21/184,
22/95.

vndefowlyd *pp. adj.* undefiled 19/110.

vndyr, ondyr, vnder, vndre *prep.* subject to Pr 293, 26/45, 29/83; *in* ~ subordinate to 18/84; under Pr 448, 2/197,
4/166, 18/278; among 25/408.

vndyrlyng *n.* underling 2/253.

vndyrstonde, vndyrstand(e) *v.* **1**
understand 2/132, 10/175, 191, 26/142,
27/406; **vndyrstand(e)** *pr. 1 sg.* 11/322,
19/127, 30/139; **vndyrstond(e)** *imp. sg.*
6/40, 133, 10/124; **vndyrstonde,
vndyrstondyth, vndyrstande** *imp. pl.*
6/71, 13/23, 31/94; **vndyrstande** *pr.
subj.* 27/415; **vndyrstod** *pa. subj.* 19/81;
2 attend to, give heed to 12/209.

vndyrtake *v.* **1** take upon oneself 4/128;
vndyrtake *pr. 1 sg.* 10/136; **2** venture to
assert 24/67, 29/208.

vndo *imp. sg.* unfasten and open 42/50;
vndo, ondo, ondothe *imp. pl.* 12/1, 1,
5, 8, 33/25.

vndowteful *adj.* certain 9/126.

vndryd see **hundryd.**

vnete *pp.* uneaten 27/413.

vngry *adj.* hungry 2/247.

vnhede, vnhyde *v.* reveal 2/167, 21/200;
vnhyd *pp.* 24/251.

vnhende *adj.* discourteous 20/224.

vnherborwed, vnherborwyd *ppl. adj.*
having no shelter or refuge 42/85; *as
noun* 42/116.

vnyté *n.* the unity of the Godhead, God
11/135, 184, 207; unity 41/494.

vnkende, vnkynde *adj.* unnatural,
wicked, unkind Pr 219, 513, 2/170, 283,
11/59, 15/45.

vnkendely *adv.* cruelly, improperly 28/
134.

vnkendenesse *n.* unkindness 28/14.

vnknowe *ppl. adj.* unknown 18/177.

vnknowlage *n.* lack of knowledge 12/130.

vnlokyn *pp.* opened, unlocked 2/182, 35/
39.

vnlosne see **onlose.**

vnnumerabyll *adj.* innumerable: *many* ~
5/222.

vnpynne *v.* unbolt 33/30.

**vnprophitable, unprofytabyl, vnpro-
fytable** *adj.* without value or use 3/171,
187, 11/162.

vnqwyt *ppl. adj.* unrequited 31/21.

vnrecurabyl *adj.* unrecoverable 31/140.

vnresonable *adj.* unreasonable, senseless 24/263.

vnryth, vnryght *n.* wrong, iniquity 28/
133, 38/365.

vnstable, vnstabyl *adj.* morally
unstable, apt to fall 24/27, 261; inconsistent 24/92.

vntey *imp. pl.* unbind 25/429.

vnthende *adj.* poor in quality 3/101.

vntrewe *adj.* dishonest, false 3/166.

vntrost *n.* disbelief 15/257.

vnwys(e) *adj.* foolish, unwise 2/215, 283,
38/302.

vnworthy, vnwurthy *adj.* unworthy 11/
235, 41/239, 247.

vnwurthynes *n.* unworthiness 13/34.

up, vp *adv.* up Pr 481, 1/21, 3/68, 10/196,
13/112, 18/225; *bothe* ~ *and down* 14/49;
upwards 18/132; open 24/121; *prep.* up
9/165.

upholdyn *v.* guarantee 31/150; **upholde**
pr. subj. succeed in, achieve 24/46.

vpon, upon, vppon *prep.* on, upon Pr 16,
72, 87, 370, 387, 390; over, about, concerning 25/70, 27/1st s.d., 35/174; ~ *me
crye* cry out against me 24/172; on condition of, *or* for (this) 35/255; toward
24/25.

vpryght *adj.* vertical 9/165.

vprysyng *vbl. n.* resurrection 38/244.

vpryth *adv.* face upward 29/108.

upteyd *pp.* tied, fastened 24/139.

vpward *adv.* upward 27/372 s.d.

vsage *n.* use, employment 11/259; practice, habit 11/325.

vse *n.* custom 41/350.

vse *v.* use 39/6; **vsyth** *pr. 3 sg.* recites 10/
441; **vsyd** *pp.* used 27/370, 372;
observed, followed 30/60; **vse** *imp. sg.*
engage in 26/432; **vse** *pr. subj.* are wont
6/96.

vterest *adj. sup.* farthest *19/144.

uttyrly *adv.* utterly 31/20, 39/42.

vaylyth *pr. 3 sg.* avails 20/198.

vayn(e) see **veyn** *adj.*

valure, valour *n.* worth, importance 22/
31; value 38/132; *for 3oure* ~ (as payment) appropriate to your value 38/93.

vanyté *n.* futile conduct, vain pursuits
3/16, 4/46, 6/74.

varyable *adj.* inconstant 24/93, 26/217.

varyauns, varyaunce, varyawns *n.* debate, discord Pr 188, 41/350; variance, inconsistency 24/98, 26/212; variety 26/65n.

vath *interj.* (expressing contempt) 32/105, 105.

veyn *n.* vein: *flesch and* ~ 20/117, 32/68.

veyn, vayn(e) *adj.* without worth 3/172, 187, 9/296, 35/190; *in* ~ in vain 6/84, 9/133.

veynglory(e) *n.* vainglory 9/130, 23/144, 26/32.

velany, velony(e) *n.* villainy, wrongdoing, evil 2/236, 12/103, 114, 14/110, 42/116.

vemynyd *pp.* envenomed 8/150.

venge *v.* avenge 4/195, 26/59; **vengyd** *pp.* (usu. with *on, of*) 4/21, 95, 191.

veng(e)abyl, vengeable *adj.* vengeful, cruel 11/105, *12/99, 24/25, 90.

vengeauns, vengeaunce, venjauns, vengeawns, vengeance *n.* vengeance, punishment 3/169, 4/117, 137, 203, 214, 13/172, 14/233, 24/210, 27/12.

venym *adj.* venomous 22/147.

verament *adv.* truly Pr 455, 11/266, 18/62.

verdyth *n.* conclusion 38/80.

veryfye *v.* prove true 12/171.

ver(r)y, ver(r)ay *adj.* true Pr 50, 7/84, 11/132, 25/436, 26/419, 465; *in* ~ *feyth* truly 21/85; *adv.* truly 15/181, 21/128, 172.

ver(r)yly(e) *adv.* truly 7/45, 8/134, 139.

vers *n.* verse 19/146 s.d.

versyfyeng *vbl. n.* versification 21/10.

vertu, uertu *n.* miracle Pr 427; virtue 3/5, 4/47, 11/270; power 11/252, 14/236, 405, 25/380; power, virtue 4/3; **vertuys, vertues** *pl.* virtues 4/125, 9/234, 18/50, 39/3, 4; moral influences or powers 10/433; members of one of the classes of angels 11/114.

vertuysful *adj.* full of virtue 10/439.

vertuous, vertuis *adj.* virtuous 4/82, 12/201, 27/422.

veruent see **fervent**.

veruently *adv.* as fire Pr 496.

vesage *n.* face 3/184, 5/181, 21/156.

vesytacyon *n.* visitation 5/206, *13/144.

vesyte, vicyte, vycyte *v.* visit 11/327, 26/415, 443, 27/45, 42/82; **vesyte** *imp. sg.* 11/15.

vesselys *n.* table vessels or utensils 9/283.

vetaylys *n.* victuals 27/50.

vexacyon *n.* vexation, affliction 9/140.

victoryously *adv.* victoriously 41/20.

vyl see **wyll(e)**.

vyolens *n.* violence 41/158.

virgyn(e), virgine *n.* virgin 10/298, 11/202, 13/60, 14/79; **virgynes, virgyne** *gen. sg.* 21/100, 41/305.

virginyté, virginité, virgynyté *n.* virginity 11/248, 14/335, 15/233, 305, 41/115.

vysion *n.* prophetic vision 7/45.

voydnes *n.* emptiness, futility 13/109.

voys *n.* voice, sound Pr 261, 2/194, 9/145.

vowchsaffe *v.* **1** agree, deign, vouchsafe 34/320; **vowchesaff** *imp. sg.* 39/31; **vowchesave** *pr. 1 sg.* (with sep. adj.) 34/144; **vowchesaf(f), vowchsaue, vowchesave** *pr. subj.* 3/54, 15/208, 37/40, 38/4, 39/87.

wachyn, wachith see **weche**.

wagour *n.* wager 4/164.

way, wey *adv.* away: *do* ~ Pr 459, 12/74, 32/121.

way(e), wey(e), weyys, weyis *n.* **1** course of travel Pr 212, 476, 2/58, 6/194, 8/212, 10/168, 18/229n., 231; **weys, waye** *pl.* 5/50, 10/398, 14/390, 15/54; **2** road, path Pr 311, 1/79, 2/48; **3** way, manner Pr 521, 4/21, 26/395; **weys** *pl.* 23/130, 31/19; **4** direction 8/215; **5** distance 32/36, 38/243; **6** ways (of living) *in* **weys** *pl.* 9/137, 22/99, 26/133.

wayle *v.* wail 27/9.

wayten *v.* keep watch 34/229; **wayted** *pp.* observed, spied 20/2.

wake, wakyn *v.* pass the night in prayer 8/41; watch, guard 1/31, 34/228, 287; **wakyng(e)** *pr. p.* being awake 4/75, 41/307.

wakyn *ppl. adj.* wakened, awake 18/299.

walk(e), walkyn *v.* walk, move about 2/62, 322, 5/47, 107; **walk(e)** *pr. 1 sg.* 2/122, 209, 5/97; **walkyn** *pl.* 5/15, 41/86; **walkyng(e)** *pr. p.* 1/15, 27/554, 36/66; **walkyd** *pa. t.* and *pp.* Pr 469, 20/1, 38/245; **walke** *imp. sg.* 18/96, 23/46; **walkyth, walke** *imp. pl.* 27/49, 38/188; **walk(e)** *pr. subj.* 5/263, 6/50, 25/225; (forming *imp.*) 15/159, 25/213.

walkyn *n.* firmament 2/4.

walkyng(e) *vbl. n.* walking 10/189, 38/
205.

walterid *pp.* soaked, weltered 34/297.

wand(e), wond, whande *n.* rod, stick
10/165, 177, 185, 193.

wante *pr. 1 sg.* lack 19/11.

wantowne *adj.* reckless 38/302.

wantruste *n.* lack of trust 25/76.

wardeyn *n.* guardian 10/290.

ware *n.* sheep, *perhaps* possessions 21/
263.

ware *adj.* aware 18/30, 20/268, 25/334;
careful, wary 29/115, 34/160; *be ~* take
note Pr 120.

ware see **was(e)**.

wark see **werk(e)**.

warly *adj.* warily 34/100 s.d.

warnyn *v.* warn 31/31; **warn(e)** *pr. 1 sg.*
2/264, 4/49, 14/5.

warnyng *vbl. n.* warning 27/456.

warse see **wers(e)**.

wasch(e), wassche, wesche *v.* 1 wash
13/133, 27/518, 38/363, 41/349, 353;
wasch(e) *pr. 1 sg.* 31/157, 37/2;
wasshyth *pr. 3 sg.* 27/527 s.d.; **wasch,
wasschyd** *pp.* 27/531, 38/348, 363;
wasch(e) *imp.* 20/152, 27/155, 526; **2**
wash away 22/43.

waschynge, wasshyng *vbl. n.* washing
15/230, 27/528.

was(e) *pa. 1, 3 sg.* was Pr 30, 31, 32, 37/4;
were, wore, wace *pa. 2 sg.* 25/218, 28/
59, 104, 35/14, 102, 41/427, 42/103;
**were, wore, weryn, ware, wern,
worn, was** *pa. pl.* Pr 36, 94, 185, 4/222,
8/102, 10/50, 54, 13/173A, 15/51, 21/
151, 153, 26/14, 35/181, 41/105, 284n.;
**were, wore, worn, where, weryn,
ware** *pa. subj.* were 4/153, 158, 161, 15/
30, 26/439, 32/281, 35/278; *to ~* were
completed 10/190n.; would be Pr 291,
2/72, 80.

wast *n. but ~* to no purpose, in vain 32/
203, 33/41.

wast *pp.* (with *awey*) lost, destroyed
2/288.

watyr, water *n.* water Pr 72, 258, 2/3, 5;
watyrys *pl.* 4/248.

watt *n.* fellow 29/117.

wawys *n.* waves 4/230.

wax(e) *v.* grow 18/219, 32/261; **waxit** *pr. 3
sg.* 38/162; **waxe** *pl.* 34/11; **wax** *pp. am
~ wood* have gone mad 30/28; **waxyn**
pr. subj. ~ wood 18/146.

we, whe *pron.* we Pr 5, 10, 10, 26/288; **us,
vs** *dat.* and *acc.* Pr 7, 112, 116, 1/45,
2/168, 176; *us (vs) must* we must 13/156,
42/34; *refl.* ourselves Pr 5, 297, 8/211;
our(e), owr(e), houre, ore *poss.* our Pr
4, 43, 44, 18/230, 267, 269, 26/98, 27/78,
32/100 s.d., 41/45; *absol.* ours 10/221,
20/233, 233; **oureself(e), ouresylf** *pron.
pl. refl.* 2/152, 183, 15/64.

weche, wachyn *v.* watch 28/18, 34/172;
keep watch 41/181, 305; **wachith** *imp.
pl.* watch over 41/174, 299.

wech(e) see **which(e)**.

wechecrafte see **wichcraft**.

wedde *v.* wed Pr 143, 10/19, 265; **wedde**
pr. 1 sg. 10/320; **weddyd** *pa. t.* 21/256; *~
... onto his wyff* married 21/238; **weddyd, wedde** *pp.* 10/86, 11/192, 12/222,
14/99; **wedde** *imp. sg.* 10/318; **weddyth**
imp. pl. 12/50.

weddyng *vbl. n.* wedding Pr 121, 10/6, 42.

wede *n.* garment, clothing 2/209, 11/178,
18/12.

wedyr *n.* weather: *grett ~* severe weather,
storms 34/8.

wedyr see **whedyr**.

wedlock *n.* wedlock Pr 151, 21/247.

wedow(e) *n.* widow 6/144, 15/270.

weel see **wel(l)**.

wey(e), weyis, weyys, weys see **way(e)**.

weyl(l) see **wel(l)**.

weyth *n.* weight 25/406.

wekys see **woke**.

wel-belouyd, wel-belovyd *ppl. adj.* well-
beloved 5/81, 22/93, 178.

welcomyng *vbl. n.* welcoming 27/48.

welde *pr. 1 sg.* rule, reign over 18/11, 20/
182; **weldyth, weldygh** *pr. 3 sg.* possesses, has at (one's) command 1/21,
10/248.

wele *n.* well-being, prosperity, good fortune 2/65, 5/219, 6/149.

wel(e), weyl *adj.* happy 9/210, 35/123;
well 26/255, 31/77, 36/94.

wele see **wel(l)** *adv.*, **wyl(l)** *v.*

welyn see **wyl(l)** *v.*

**weleaway(e), wel(l)away, weelaway,
weleway** *interj.* alas! 2/296, 3/178, 12/
57, 78, 15/254, 20/245, 25/113, 29/213,
213; *n.* lamentation 3/193.

wel(l), wel(l)e, weyl(l), wul, weel, wyl
adv. well Pr 64, 474, 512, 519, 4/45, 59,
5/38, 42, 74, 6/71, 32/254, 39/76;

wel(l) (*cont.*)
certainly, indeed Pr 64; much 4/236, 14/87; very 5/17, 22/172, 24/213, 36/89; safely 8/91; readily, fully 11/82, 21/73; (to introd. a statement) well 30/137.

wel(l)com(e), wolcom(e), welcum, welkom *adj.* welcome 27/69, 38/192, 41/253, 281, 42/62, 65; *interj.* 8/135, 10/31, 12/9, 41/121, 122, 42/63.

wellys *n.* springs of water 11/25.

welsom *adj.* desolate, wild 2/298.

welth(e) *n.* prosperity, well-being Pr 112, 1/21, 2/62; **welthis** *pl.* costly possessions 10/420.

wem *n.* moral stain Pr 130, 21/184.

wench(e) *n.* woman 12/51, 14/99, 103.

wend(e), wendyn *v.*[1] go, travel 1/2, 3/192, 5/104, 18/325; **wende** *pr. 1 sg.* 2/298, 5/97; **wende** *pl.* 14/178, 19/27, 21/281; **wentyst** *pa. 2 sg.* went 2/219; **went** *pa. 3 sg.* went to 41/17; **went, wenten** *pa. pl.* went 13/36, 38/274, 276; **went** *pp.* gone 21/202, 25/159; **wend(e)** *imp. sg.* 2/250, 266, 10/138; **wendyth, wende** *imp. pl.* 18/262, 308, 36/63; **wende** *pr. subj.* 3/171; (forming *imp.*) 25/346, 32/259, 38/234.

wende *pr. pl.*[2] think, suppose 9/285.

wen(e) *n.* doubt Pr 112, 234.

wen(e) *v.* **1** believe, think 10/181, 40/29; **wene** *pr. 1 sg.* Pr 32; **wenyth** *pr. 3 sg.* Pr 454, 20/169, 23/16; ~ *to be* thinks himself to be 20/170, 171; **wend** *pa. t.* 11/309, 31/44; **2** expects *in* **wenyth** 20/195.

wepe, wepyn *v.* **1** weep 8/90, 9/82, 11/26, 29/212 s.d.; **wepe** *pr. 1 st.* 8/162, 240, 10/481; **wepyst** *pr. 2 sg.* 12/147; **wepyth** *pr. 3 sg.* Pr 177, 37/1st s.d.; **wepyng(e)** *pr. p.* Pr 254, 4/196, 27/1st s.d. *with þe leste teer* ~ by weeping the smallest tear 24/12; **wepte** *pa. t.* 10/53; **wepyth, wepe** *imp. pl.* 32/9, 10, 35/96; **2** pray for with weeping *in* **wepe** *pr. 1 sg.* 9/243.

wepyng(e) *vbl. n.* weeping Pr 362, 2/315, 5/133; *ppl. adj.* 10/55, 36/69, 37/2; ~ *dale* pit of tears 2/321; ~ *wylle* tearful desire 27/167.

wepoun, weponys *n. pl.* weapons 28/80 s.d., 148 s.d.

werd see **word(e).**

werd(e), world(e), werld(e), word(e), werdl *n.* world Pr 11, 2/250, 4/102, 123, 16/96, 19/39, 20/108, 134, 21/136, 150,

30/70, 41/154; **werdlys, worldys, wordlys, werdys** *gen. sg.* 5/182, 6/74, 80, 21/56, 22/43, 25/315, 27/388, 39/42.

werdly, wurdly, worldly *adj.* earthly, mundane Pr 318, 6/76, 78, 10/413, 41/112.

were *v.* wear 11/178.

weryng *vbl. n. to* ~ for wearing 18/240.

were, werfor see **wher(e).**

wery, weré *adj.* weary 13/10, 43, 15/60, 18/171.

weryd *pa. t.* (with *awey*) drove away 36/11.

weryn see **was(e).**

werk(e), wark *n.* work 1/2, 29, 2/14; action, deed 4/6, 55, 11/265; things done or made 34/6, 28, 29; **werkys** *pl.* actions, deeds 3/44, 4/43, 60; creatures 11/107.

werke, werkyn *v.* **1** do, act 2/68, 141, 3/96; **wrought** *pa. t.* 38/37; **wrought, wrouth, wrowth** *pp.* done Pr 339, 2/192, 4/183, 219, 32/125; acted 2/203, 20/125, 27/106; **werk** *imp. pl.* 18/292; **2** perform, carry out 4/137, 5/96, 150; **werke** *pr. 1 sg.* 1/75, 32/279; **werkyst** *pr. 2 sg.* 41/189; **werkyth, werke** *pr. 3 sg.* 22/161, 26/229; ~ *with* practices 26/325; **wrought, wrouth** *pa. t.* Pr 296, 2/331, 35/20; **wrought, wrowth, wrougth** *pp.* 4/117, 5/90, 6/47, 27/80, 30/47, 54, 201, 204; **werk, werkyth** *imp. pl.* 5/160, 165, 26/370; **3** bring about, cause 11/206, 23/30, 24/45; **werkyht, werkyth, werke** *pr. 3 sg.* 6/135, 22/5, 26/322; **wrought, wrowth** *pp.* 14/208, 15/1, 257; **4** created, made *in* **wrought, wrowth, wrougth, wrouth** *pp.* Pr 30, 34, 1/11, 41/417; *to here is* ~ is made to suit her 24/88; **5** worked 4/206; **6** written, recorded 16/68; **7** strive *in* **werch** *pr. subj.* 6/130.

werker(e) *n.* maker 16/105; worker 16/115.

werkyng(e) *vbl. n.* performance of work 2/8, 49, 52; deeds, works 20/180, 26/403, 28/132.

werld(e) see **werd(e).**

werm(e), worm *n.* serpent 2/209, 220, 227, 259, 262; sea monsters, sea creatures: ~ *and fysch* 2/12; **wurmys, wormys, wyrmys** *pl.* worms 20/273, 281, 42/44; **wormys** *gen. pl.* worms' 20/256.

wers(e) *adj. comp.* worse 8/152, 13/62, 31/44; *absol.* 3/113; **wers, wurs, warse** *adv. comp.* 14/86; *þe* ~ 14/26, 201, 18/275.

werst *n.* 3/81, 95, 97.

wese see **wys(e)** *adj.*

wete *adj.* wet 4/248, *34/296; *as noun* rainy weather 5/35.

wete, wetyn *v.* **1** know, find out 3/31, 6/36, 8/134, 28/152, 29/186; **wot(e), woot, wott** *pr. 1 sg.* 2/244, 3/190, 8/215, 10/373, 12/119, 21/203, 25/299, 32/254; **wotys(s)t, wost** *pr. 2 sg.* 9/180, 27/268, 28/50, 34/162; **wete, wote, woot** *pl.* 8/69, 19/98, 180, 21/262, 32/104; **wyst** *pa. t.* and *pp.* 12/163, 14/71, 28/104; **wete** *imp. pl.* 13/160; **wete** *pr. subj.* 10/294; **wyst** *pa. subj.* 12/100, 9/64, 25/83; **2** understand 11/160; **3** recognize, discover 18/123n.

wethyr see **whethyr.**

whallys see **qwall.**

whan *adj.* dark, gloomy 34/11; wan 35/184.

whan, quan, when, qwhan, qwan *adv.* when Pr 42, 75, 148, 12/16, 19/146 s.d., 26/449 s.d., 28/92 s.d., 30/244 s.d., 41/200, 227, 306; ~ *þat*, ~ *that* Pr 441, 518, 5/168; *conj.* while by contrast 22/174, 23/137.

whande see **wand(e).**

whanhope *n.* hopelessness, despair Pr 369.

whantynge *vbl. n.* lack, wanting 4/145.

whantownnesse *n.* wantonness, lasciviousness 24/116.

whar *imp. sg.* be on your guard! 29/185, 185.

what, qwhat, qwat, whath *pron.* what Pr 168, 272, 339, 2/192, 8/173, 31/173, 38/45; ~ *þat* what, that which 10/7, 122, 23/111; whatever, that which 2/255, 8/142, 26/397; ~ *þat* 5/76, 34/68.

what, whath, whatt *adj.* what Pr 30, 3/131, 8/232, 26/193, 27/215; ~ *man* who 4/179; ~ *tyme* (*þat*) when 4/223, 25/131, 41/154; whatever, whichever 4/153, 158, 27/24; ~ *day* on the day that 2/96; ~ *þing* (*thynge*) whatever 3/173, 25/294; ~ *man* whoever, he who 3/179, 4/36, 14/237; *in* ~ *place þat* wherever 5/32, 10/377; which 12/119, 30/132; *adv.* how 3/111.

what(h) *interj.* (exclamation of surprise, astonishment) 3/117, 144, 10/233; ~ *devyl* 41/410.

whatso *pron.* whoever 10/10; whatever 25/296, 27/43, 34/48.

whatsoevyr *pron.* whatever 8/214.

whatsumeuyr *pron.* whoever, whatever 41/376.

whedyr, wedyr *adv.* whither, where 3/183, 190, 8/100; ~ *þat* 21/203; to whatever place 26/377; ~ *as* 12/145.

wheyle see **whyle** *n.*

whele *imp. pl.* turn, wheel 29/190, 190.

whelpe, qwelp *n.* young dog, offspring of a noxious creature 24/112; *helle* ~ 5/72; *Mahownd* ~ 34/311.

wher(e), qwere, were, qwher *adv. interrog. and rel.* where 2/192, 3/159, 165, 11/149, 21/207, 29/215, 37/35; ~ *þat* 3/163, 194, 21/228; wherever, in what place 20/190, 26/39, 77; ~ *þat* 6/50, 32/273; **wher(e)as** where 2/240, 10/336, 27/336 s.d.; wherever 29/41; **wher(e)for(e), whereffore, werfor** and therefore Pr 527, 3/38, 4/196, 8/105, 27/496; for which reason 2/235; on account of which 27/212; why 28/170, 37/12; **wher(e)so** wherever 3/171, 4/80, 5/63; **wheresoevyr, wheresoever** wherever 22/133, 35/302, 36/129; **wherevyr** wherever Pr 124, 10/386.

where ('were') see **was(e).**

whethyr, wethyr, whether, whedyr *conj.* whether 5/263, 15/253, 23/193, 27/434, 30/257, 36/160, 38/79; ~ *þat* 6/189, 18/299; if 27/465 s.d.; (introd. a disjunctive question) 31/109.

why *n.* reason 4/184.

why, whi, qwy, qwhy *adv.* why 2/195, 212, 215, 12/100, 20/90, 25/171, 29/162, 31/127, 32/97; ~ *þat* 2/215–16, 10/193, 26/147–8.

which(e), wech(e), whech(e), wich(e), qwych(e), wych(e), qwhich, qweche *pron. rel.* which, who, whom Pr 289, 1/45, 3/75, 26/4, 26, 175, 204, 430, 473, 27/54, 72, 318, 501, 41/167, 221; *þe* (*the*) ~ Pr 94, 107, 111, 26/412; ~ *þat* who, which 5/35, 7/43, 9/137, 25/197; ~ *þat* he who 19/83; *adj.* whichever Pr 259; which Pr 492, 10/431, 27/546; of what kind: ~ *peusawns* what a crowd 27/79.

whight, whyght, whyht see **wyght** *n.*

whyght see **white** *adj.*

whylde see **wyld(e).**

whyle, wyle, qwyle, wheyle, wel *n.*
time, short time 8/100, 14/68, 15/179,
18/287, 26/173, 31/116; *in þis* ~ at such
a young age Pr 251; *ony* ~ at or for any
time *40/20.

whyle, whylys see **wyle.**

whylys, whilys *conj.* while 19/186, 22/
111; ~ *þat* 28/116.

whyl(l), whil(e), qwhyl, qwyl *conj.*
while, as long as 3/25, 4/146, 6/149,
8/170, 9/36, 25/283, 41/304; ~ *þat*
4/159, 14/307, 21/138, 31/1st s.d.

whylsum *adj.* wild and lonely 22/123.

whylt see **wyl(l).**

whipyng *vbl. n.* wiping 32/45.

whippe *n.* whip 30/240; **whyppys,
qwyppys** *pl.* 30/236 s.d.; 241, 31/196.

whysest see **wys(e).**

whysshe *v.* wish 27/260.

whyt *adj.* swift 30/10.

whit see **with.**

whyt see **wyght** *n.*

white, whyte, qwyte, whyght *adj.* white
Pr 141, 2/23, 6/166, 10/128, 141, 149,
212, 218; *noun* white clothing, fur 9/17
s.d., 26/164 s.d., 208 s.d.

whith, whithtys see **wyght** *n.*

whith see **with.**

who see **wo(o).**

whonde *imp. pl.* refrain, hesitate: *nothynge*
~ exclude nothing, *or* don't hesitate at
all 12/211.

who(o), ho(o) *pron.* **1** whoever, he that Pr
505, 11/225, 13/156A; ~ *þat* 10/441, 12/
18, 42/23; **2** who 3/161, 8/234, 9/86, 10/
87, 11/25, 104; ~ *þat* 27/253; *as* ~ like
one who 29/222; **3** if anyone: ~ *vndyrstod* if the truth were known 19/81.

whoo see **wo(o).**

whos(e), whoys, whoos *pron. rel.* whose
Pr 300, 4/2, 4, 8/179, 26/121; *interrog.*
1/40, 12/47.

whov, whow see **how** *adv.*

wichcraft, wechecrafte, wychecrafte *n.*
witchcraft 26/228, 325, 28/131.

wich(e), wych(e) see **which(e).**

wyckyd, wykkyd *adj.* wicked Pr 416,
2/238, 259, 4/60, 190, 6/135; *as noun* 10/
50.

wyckydnes, wykkydnes *n.* wickedness
3/76, 11/137.

wyd(e) *adj.* wide, large Pr 117, 4/123, 215;
(of time) long Pr 267, 22/124; *adv.* over
a large area, extensively 8/135, 14/38,
18/253.

wyde *v.* go, move 18/131n.

wyf(f)(e), wyve *n.* **1** wife Pr 153, 179, 182,
10/274; **wyfys** *pl.* 34/196; **2** woman
2/87, 36/69.

**wyght, whyght, whith, whight, wythe,
wyhgt, whyt, whyht, wyht** *n.* person
6/132, 134, 140, 144, 12/201, 13/62, 14/
397, 15/81, 268, 20/251, 22/112, 25/119,
179, 277, 37/70; *sum erthely* ~ somebody
24/125; **wyghtys, wytys, whithtys** *pl.*
18/11, 34/22, 35/287.

wyght, wyth, wight *adv.* without delay,
quickly 4/162, 34/91; quickly, *or* strong
36/11.

wyghtly *adv.* swiftly, nimbly 18/17.

wyk *adj.* wicked 2/227.

wyl see **wel(l).**

wyld(e), wyllde, whylde *adj.* undomes-
ticated 2/13, 19/193, 20/183; tumultu-
ous, unconfined 4/139; sinful 4/202,
10/394, 22/99; imprudent, unreasonable 15/19, 37; wild, fierce 27/111, 29/
32, 31/66; extremely disturbed 35/123;
as noun cruel ones 10/50.

wyldirnese, wyldernes, wyldyrnes *n.*
wilderness 22/2, 121, 137.

wyle, whyle *n.* wile 14/356, 31/43, 46, 34/
88; **wylys, whylys** *pl.* 2/227, 23/42.

wyle see **whyle** *n.*

wylfully *adv.* willingly 32/233.

wyl(l), wol(e), wele, woll, wul, will *pr. 1,
3 sg. and pl.* **1** *auxil.* (expressing futurity) Pr 13, 58, 103, 1/29, 2/49, 4/95,
6/110, 8/146, 10/170, 173, 179, 462, 15/
93, 18/231, 27/172, 36/146, 41/70; **wylt,
whylt** *pr. 2 sg.* 2/148, 151, 10/42, 29/213,
30/235, 32/141; **welyn** *pl.* 31/150;
wold(e), wulde *pa. 1, 3 sg. and pl.* Pr
129, 2/92, 169, 25/143; **woldyst** *pa. 2 sg.*
5/211, 213, 11/9; **2** wish, desire *in* **wyl**
pr. 1 sg. 10/294; **wolt** *pr. 2 sg.* 28/185;
wol(e), wyl *pr. 3 sg.* 8/74, 10/273, 288;
wyl(l)(e), wele, wole, wolne *pl.* 5/253,
12/4, 13/46, 25/102, 102, 31/153; **wyl**
imp. sg. 24/280; **wolne** *pr. subj.* 27/465
s.d.; **3** want *to in* **wole** *pr. 1 sg.* 34/49, 59;
wolte *pr. 2 sg.* 27/17; **wyl** *pr. 3 sg.* 20/85,
22/163; **wolde** *pa. t.* 11/97, 38/85; **wole,
wolyn** *pl.* 9/195, 27/384, 31/114;

wyl(l)(e), wole *pr. subj.* 6/42, 21/11, 26/
385 s.d.; **4** requires, demands *in* **wole**
pr. 3 sg. 30/83; **5** *auxil.* (with futurity obscured) will prove to (be) 41/377; **6**
wold(e) *1, 3 sg.* and *pl.* (with infin.)
want to 5/181, 8/134, 9/93; (with *fayn*)
very much want to 2/172, 114, 3/1;
(without infin.) 10/225; **7 wold(e)** wish,
desire 8/87, *10/190, 24/245; **woldyst** *2
sg.* 24/30; (with ellips. of 'thou') 28/181;
8 wold *subj.* (used optatively as expression of desire, longing) ~ (*to*) *God* 10/
201, 11/9, 14/43; **9 wolde** should 13/17.

wyll(e), wyl, vyl, wyle *n.* will, intention,
desire Pr 88, 384, 468, 1/75, 2/81, 3/88,
28/32, 30/225; **wyllys** *pl.* 29/7.

wyndand *ppl. adj.* (see note) 41/417n.

wynde *n.* wind Pr 217, 34/262; breathing
25/105.

wynde *v.* wrap up, enclose 34/139; *in cloth
to* ~ to clothe 2/327; **wynde** *pr. 1 sg.* 35/
51; **wounde, woundyn** *pp.* 3/174, 185,
25/59, 145, 35/6, 59; **wynde** *pr. subj.*
5/54, 38/340.

wyne *n.* wine 20/215; **wynes** *pl.* 20/147.

wynke *n.* short sleep 34/325.

wyn(ne), wynnyn, wyne *v.* **1** obtain,
gain, get Pr 112, 18/44, 22/11, 17, 23/
207; ~ *to be* (*in*) arrive at 22/18; **wynnyst** *pr. 2 sg.* 23/210; **wan** *pa. t.* 26/24;
wonnyn, wonne *pp.* 16/6, 24/289;
wynnyth *imp. pl.* 15/189; **2** get by
labour 2/332; **3** save, redeem 4/121, 16/
10, 115; **wynnyst** *pr. 2 sg.* 16/96;
wunne, wonnyn *pp.* 35/41, 36/5; **4**
entice, prevail upon 14/224; **5** make
your way *in* **wynne** *imp. sg.* 19/43.

wynnere *n.* one who gains sth. by effort
or merit 16/106.

wynnynge *vbl. n.* money-making 27/248.

wyntyr *n. pl.* winters: *þis thretty* ~ for
thirty years 34/103.

wype *v.* wipe 34/100 s.d.; **whypyth** *pr. 3
sg.* 27/527 s.d., 32/44 s.d.

wyrmys see **werm(e)**.

wysdam, wysdome, wisdam *n.* wisdom, knowledge 2/132, 161, 9/180, 21/
38, 41/31; i.e. Christ 11/134, 41/94; wise
action 41/57.

wyse *n.* way, manner Pr 352, 2/82, 4/54; *in
no* ~, *in no maner* ~, *in no kynnys* ~ not
at all Pr 39, 1/50, 10/73, 12/50; *in many*
~ in many ways 10/81; *in what* (*manere*

of) ~ how 11/246, 12/32; *on þis* ~ in this
way 14/182; *in all* ~ in every way 26/
139.

wys(e), wysse, wese *adj.* learned Pr 246,
21/4, 49; wise 2/113, 120, 6/56, 8/40, 18/
238; ~ *of connyng* (*kunnyng*) having
knowledge and understanding 2/102,
150; skilful, clever 20/41; *as noun* 10/98;
wysest, whysest *adj. sup.* 10/116, 21/
142, 23/2; *as noun* 26/222.

wys(e)ly *adv.* skilfully, wisely 3/96, 8/205,
15/54; attentively, carefully 6/24.

wysse *v.* guide, conduct 22/99, 25/181,
41/168; **wysse** *pr. subj.* instruct 10/385;
guide 14/390, 15/310.

wyst see **wete** *v.*

wyte *v.* (with *them*) blame (for) 12/200.

with, wyth, whith, whit *prep.* with Pr 4,
6, 18, 9/44, 16/105, 26/438, 41/7, 38; ~
þat if 13/169; by means of Pr 18, 51, 57;
through, because of 2/288; towards,
against 24/63, 41/401.

wyth see **wyght** *adv.*

wythal(l)(e) *adv.* as well 1/26; *prep.* with
8/217, 14/148, 26/78.

withdrawe *v.* remove 9/233, 14/159.

wythe see **wyght** *n.*

within(ne) *adv.* inside: ~ *and withowte,
withowt and* ~ 9/147, 11/153; *prep.*
inside of Pr 473, 4/121, 209; within (a
period of time) 2/159, 5/48, 14/47.

**withowtyn, withowt(e), without(e),
withoutyn, withowth, withouth** *adv.*
outside 9/147, 11/153, 15/69; abroad
41/379; *prep.* without Pr 94, 111, 119,
146, 234, 247, 2/16, 54, 3/4, 4/16, 9/119,
10/263, 11/55, 12/106, 26/260, 304, 30/
22; outside of, contrary to 8/196; *conj.*
unless 15/205.

withsett *pr. subj.* withstand, resist 23/212.

withsytt *v.* withstand, resist 23/216.

withstande, withstonde *v.* withstand,
resist 20/266, 34/203; **withstonde** *pr.
subj.* 23/210.

wytys see **wyght** *n.*

wyt(t)(e), witt(e) *n.* judgement, understanding 2/80, 309, 313, 36/159, 38/103,
329; reason, sanity 2/306, 18/275, 38/
353; *of* ~ insanely 4/144; skill 4/126;
mind, memory 16/68; knowledge,
learning 21/34, 38, 54; wise plan 23/40,
49, 53; **wyttys, wittys** *pl.* wits 2/59, 18/
123n., 148, 35/250; bodily senses 9/241,
10/317.

wytte *pr. 2 sg.* go 8/100.

wytty *adj.* learned, sagacious 21/49.

wyt(t)nes(s)(e) *n.* **1** testimony, evidence 6/156, 158, 161; ~ *I take* I take as evidence 42/76; **2** witness 22/119; *take* ~ (*of*) call to witness 14/170, 247; *God to* ~ God is my witness 14/211; **wyttnes** *pl.* 39/43.

wyt(t)nes(se) *v.* **1** bear witness to, attest to 4/152, 22/112, 29/143; **wytnessyth** *pr. 3 sg.* PS 39; **wyttnessynge** *pr. p.* 7/123; **2** witness *in* **wytnesse** *pl.* Pr 449.

Wyttsunday *n.* Pentecost Pr 491.

wo see **wo(o)**.

wod(e) see **wood**.

woful *adj.* woeful 26/54, 27/1, 3.

woke *n.* week Pr 99; **wekys** *gen. pl.* 20/101.

wolcom(e) see **wel(l)com(e)**.

wolde see **wo(o)lde** *n.*

wol(e), woll see **wyl(l)**.

wolle *n.* wool 26/77.

wombe *n.* **1** womb Pr 172, 8/179, 11/239; **wombys** *pl.* 32/13; **2** belly, abdomen 2/266, 12/26, 30.

wom(m)an *n.* woman Pr 34, 282, 287, 2/174.

won *v.* hesitate, refrain 41/48n.

wond see **wand(e)**.

wondyr, woundyr, wundyr, wonder *n.* object of wonder, marvel 3/133, 25/432, 35/148, 38/140, 41/290; *no* ~ *is* it is no wonder 27/205; sense of wonder: *haue grett* ~ marvel greatly 36/155, 38/257, 289; **wondrys, woundrys, wonderis** *pl.* astonishing acts, miracles, wonders 29/65, 68, 41/189.

wondyr, woundyr *adj.* wondrous 15/101, 16/62, 26/291, 30/197, 38/321.

won(e) *n.* place 1/15; *every* ~ in every place 15/68.

wonyn, wone, wonne *v.* dwell 16/105, 19/136, 27/476, 31/36, 32/242; **wonyght** *pr. 3 sg.* 16/9; **wone** *pl.* 31/8.

wonyng(e) *vbl. n.* dwelling-place 10/336, 18/209; place 18/116.

wonte *pp.* wont, accustomed 11/186.

wo(o), who(o) *n.* woe 2/16, 232, 277, 321, 3/174, 24/192; *adj.* woeful Pr 467, 13/162, 21/201; *interj. me is ful* ~ I grieve sorely 8/213; *so* ~ *is me* so disturbed am I 41/416.

wood, wod(e) *adj.* raging Pr 72, 4/201; insane, senseless Pr 388, 3/122, 18/146, 28/104 s.d., 35/70, 36/93; ~ *man* madman 41/241; ~ *men* 28/143.

wo(o)lde *n.* plain, hill, forest land Pr 445; ground, earth 4/190, 5/15, 18/96.

woot see **wete** *v.*

worchep(e), wurchep(p), worschepe, wurchipe, worchipe, wurchipp *n.* worship, veneration, honour 1/40, 2/30, 10/242, 248, 249, 18/188, 26/445, 27/128, 40/1, 45/450, 500; renown, good name 8/85, 14/151, 344.

worchep(e), worchepyn, worchip, worschepe see **wurchep(e)** *v.*

worchepful, wurchepful *adj.* honourable 8/82, 15/57, 41/1.

worchepyng *vbl. n.* worshipping Pr 196.

word(e), wurd(e), werd, wourd(e) *n.* **1** word, statement Pr 337, 5/231, 6/134, 135, 8/109, 11/288, 13/64, 15/289; *at a* ~ as soon as the word is given 27/300; *at o* ~ succinctly 30/108; **wurdys, wordys, wourdys** *pl.* Pr 96, 109, 315, 390, 442, 2/97, 8/78, 39/19, 60; **2** command, bidding 2/169, 10/134, 26/357; **3** information, report 5/215, 21/228.

word(e), wordlys, worldys see **werd(e)** ('world').

wore, worn see **was(e)**.

worm, wormys see **werm(e)**.

wost, wot(e), wotys(s)t, wott see **wete** *v.*

wounde, wownde *n.* wound Pr 405, 11/159, 24/128, PS 36; injury 16/6, 96, 20/27; *gostly* ~ spiritual injury 14/212; **woundys** *pl.* Pr 117, 480.

wounde *v.* wound 8/153, 25/160.

woundere *v.* **1** marvel Pr 484; **wundyr** *pr. 1 sg.* 25/71; **wonderyth** *pr. 3 sg.* Pr 134; **woundyr** *pl.* 21/146; **2** wonder *in* **woundyr** *pr. 1 sg.* 23/188, 27/253.

woundyr, wundyr *adv.* exceedingly, wondrously 2/77, 24/48, 25/56, 34/8.

woundyr see **wondyr** *n., adj.*

woundyrf(f)ul(l) see **wundyrful(l)**.

woundyrly *adv.* to an astonishing degree 25/11, 358, 374.

wourd(e), wourdys see **word(e)**.

wourthy see **wurthy(e)**.

wrake *n.* enmity; *withowtyn* ~ willingly 10/134; harm 14/208, 31/30; distress, suffering, injury 22/51, 23/30; punishment 42/75.

wrappyd *pp.* clothed 18/12; wrapped, covered, enveloped 25/412, 27/142, 35/6.

wrastele *pr. 1 sg.* wrestle 20/187.

wrecch(e), wretche *n.* outcast, wretch 2/250, 298, 3/185, 11/67; **wrecchis** *pl.* 2/283, 13/62, 136; ~ *of* ~ *be* wretches (who) have come from wretches 11/17.

wrech(e) *n.* misery, affliction 23/30, 36/5; punishment 24/91.

wrechid *adj.* wretched 41/256.

wreke *v.* 1 deliver, rescue 33/32; **wrokyn** *pp.* 2/232; **wreke** *imp. sg.* 16/55; 2 avenged *in* **wreke, wrokyn** *pp.* 14/329, 18/80, 20/64.

wretchydnes, wrecchydnes, wrecchid- nesse *n.* wretchedness 11/49, 25/315; wickedness 22/4.

wreth, wrat(t)h *n.* wrath 2/238, 24/31, 290, 26/113, 39/44, 42/101.

wry *v.* swerve, deviate 26/144.

wryngyn *v.* make twisting movements (or error for **wryngyng**) 31/212 s.d.

wryte *v.* write 7/94, 24/236, 242; **wryte** *pl.* ~ *hym to be* write that he is 32/178; **wrot** *pa. t.* 41/3; **wretyn, wrete** *pp.* Pr 94, 6/39, 60, 63.

wrythe *imp. sg.* (with *onto*) twist, wring 2/307.

wrytynge *vbl. n.* written literature, Scrip- tures 8/185, 18/238; penmanship, *or* literary composition 21/6.

wronge *n.* wrong, wrongdoing 12/199, 26/129, 39/44; *do me* ~, *dedyst me* ~ 1/42, 12/123.

wrong(e) *adj.* wrongful 4/43, 23/75; *adv.* wrongfully, wrong 27/202, 498, 29/82.

wroth(e) *adj.* grieved, vexed Pr 43, 68; violent, stormy Pr 217, 34/262n.; very angry 9/77, 13/142, 21/224; sad, appre- hensive 36/60.

wrouth see **werke** *v.*

wul see **wel(l), wyl(l).**

wulf *n.* wolf 7/104.

wundyrful(l), woundyrı(f)ul(l) *adj.* wonderful, inspiring astonishment 10/ 260, 15/167, 21/64, 34/3, 37/91, 38/77.

wurchepful see **worchepful.**

wurchep(e), worchep(e), wur- chepp(yn), wurchip(e), worchip,

wurchyp, worchepyn, wurchipp, worschepe *v.* worship, honour Pr 19, 216, 1/34, 38, 41, 46, 64, 3/72, 4/240, 5/196, 233, 13/137, 19/30, 78, 41/353; **wurchyp(p), wurchep, worchep** *pr. 1 sg.* 5/60, 22/115, 27/188; **wurchyp, wur- chipe, wurchepp** *pl.* 1/44, 49, 2/55; **wurchep(p)yd** *pa. t.* and *pp.* 5/249, 258, 7/106; **wurchep** *imp. sg.* 15/279; **wur- chyp** *imp. pl.* 1/59; **wurchipe, wur- chep** *pr. subj.* 1/42, 6/121.

wurd(e), wurdys see **word(e).**

wurdly see **werdly.**

wurmys see **werm(e).**

wurs see **wers(e).**

wurth(e) *adj.* worth 2/309, 20/133, 21/27; valuable 18/198.

wurthely, worthely, wurthylye *adv.* worthily, nobly 15/49, 18/12, 20/156; with due devotion 16/87.

wurthy(e), worthy, wourthy *adj.* 1 worthy, excellent 1/47, 55, 63, 6/110, 32/78, 91; **wurthyer, worthyer** *comp.* 1/53, 54; **wurthyest** *sup.* 1/43, 13/60, 20/147; *as noun* 20/170; 2 deserving, worthy (to do or be) 3/79, 5/90, 8/99, 149, 207; 3 fitting, appropriate 11/304, 14/389, 21/266.

wurthynes *n.* worthiness 40/5.

xad see **schedyn.**

xal, xall(e), schal(l), shal(l)(e), xul *pr. 1, 3 sg. auxil.* shall, will Pr 30, 67, 106, 7/5, 8/109, 238, 10/186, 359, 18/227, 19/5, 24/124, 26/145, 28/15, 30/168; **xalt(e), xalle, shalt, schalt** *pr. 2 sg.* 1/72, 2/32, 116, 5/226, 10/122, 27/40, 41/109; (with ellips. of 'thou') 19/44; **xal, xul, xall(e), schul(l), schal, shul(l), shal(l), xull, xaln, xule, xuln** *pl.* Pr 10, 19, 47, 110, 192, 231, 280, 336, 483, 3/25, 7/63, 8/119, 16/127, 18/90, 23/63, 24/78, 207, 32/76 s.d., 84 s.d., 38/ 352, 41/31, 34, 46, 175, 181; *sg. and pl.* (with ellips. of vb. of motion) 8/203, 238, 27/15; **xuld(e), schuld(e), shuld(e)** *pa. t.* Pr 38, 73, 81, 5/154, 9/121, 10/276, 18/100, 21/62, 27/401; (with ellips. of following vb.) 9/89, 32/ 247; **xuldyst** *pa. 2 sg.* 25/398, 28/55, 30/ 164.

xamefullest see **shamful(l).**

yate see **gate** *n.*[1]

yis, ȝys, ȝis *adv.* yes 10/169, 29/178, 178, 178, 38/308, 41/126, 146.

yit see **ȝit(t)**.

yong see **ȝonge** *adj.*

PROPER NAMES

Aaron 27/351, 38/97, 129.

Abacuch, Abbacuc Habakkuk 7/85, 41/147.

Abdias Obadiah 7/77.

Abel, Abell(e) Pr 54, 57, 3/131, 159, 4/193.

Abyacar a bishop Pr 118.

Abias King Abijah 7/57.

Abysakar, Abizachar a bishop 10/1st s.d., 14/105 s.d.

Abraham Pr 79, 83, 90, 5/9 etc., 11/277, 13/115, 117, 35/1st s.d., 33.

Achas King Ahaz 7/105.

Adam Pr 41, 2/15 etc., 4/16, 9/264, 11/61, 139, 277, 19/96, 21/117, 126, 26/24, 35/1st s.d., 1, 35; **Adamys, Adamis** *gen.* 11/29, 32/150, 35/18.

Affraunt Pilate's knight 34/184.

Aggee Haggai 7/101.

Almonye Germany 23/172.

Amon King Amon 7/129.

Amorawnt, Amaraunt Pilate's knight 34/182, 214.

Amos 16/46.

Andrewe St Andrew the apostle PS 15.

Annas the high priest 26/164 s.d. etc., 27/76 s.d., 29/1st s.d. etc., 30/152 s.d., 31/170 s.d., 32/168 s.d., 34/237 s.d., 259, 269 s.d., 35/260 s.d.

Anne, Anna, An St Anne Pr 127, 8/10 etc., 9/2, 17 s.d., 19, 10/14, 32, 21/185, **Annys** *gen.* 36/27.

Anne Anna the prophetess 19/64, 164.

Aragon 23/172.

Aramathy see **Joseph of Baramathie**.

Archage (?) Arcadia 18/53, 23/164.

Archas a place seen from the mount 23/172.

Arfexe Annas' messenger 26/199.

Arphaxat Pilate's knight 34/183.

Artyse Pilate's man 31/155.

Asa King Asa 7/65.

Babylony(e), Babolony Babylon 9/99, 41/147; *Towre of* ~ 23/158.

Bakbytere 14/41, 62.

Balaam 16/26, 38, 18/159.

Baltazare one of the Magi 18/29.

Baramathie see **Joseph of Baramathie**.

Bar(r)abas Pr 385, 31/106 etc.

Baruk Baruch 7/125.

Bedle(e)m Bethlehem 15/12, 16/20, 29, 79, 18/315, 20/4, 172, 23/15, 30/134, 35/15; ~ *Judé* 30/134.

Belyal(l) Belial 35/225, 41/477.

Belyard Belial 23/1.

Belzabub, Belsabub Beelzebub 23/1, 41/477.

Bertylmew St Bartholomew the apostle PS 28.

Betany Bethany 27/567; ~-*ward* 28/1st s.d.

Boosras, Boosdras one of the shepherds 16/22, 74.

Caym(e) Cain Pr 54, 62; 3/3, etc., 4/180, 182, 192; **Caymys** *gen.* 4/224.

Cayphas Caiaphas, the high priest Pr 335, 366, 26/186 etc., 28/122, 146, 29/1st s.d. etc., 30/13, 152 s.d., 31/170 s.d., 32/168 s.d., 176 s.d., 34/157 s.d. etc., 35/260 s.d.; **Cayfas** *gen.* 41/427.

Caluerye, Caluarye, Kalvarye, Calvary Calvary 25/455, 31/210, 32/27, 34/70, 36/134.

Caton 21/22 (see the note).

Cavdas Queen Candace PS 22.

Cephas St Peter PS 24.

Cham Ham 4/66.

Cleophas Pr 464, 38/8 etc.

Coleyn Cologne Pr 208.

Cosdram Pilate's knight 34/184.

Cryst(e), Crist(e), Chryst Pr 191 etc., 8/1, 8, 70, 15/92, 16/59, 104, 18/284, 20/173, 22/134, 136, 23/14, 145, 25/82, 311, 26/26 etc., 27/1st s.d. etc., 28/36 s.d. etc., PS 16, 20, 29/37, 110, 31/212 s.d., 32/43, 120, 168 s.d., 33/9, 34/121 s.d., 137 s.d., 36/4 etc., 37/84, 88, 93, 38/10 etc., 39/62, 41/5 etc.; **Crystys, Cristis, Chrystys, Crystis** *gen.* Pr 202 etc., 13/182A, PS 36, 32/176 s.d., 35/222, 36/128, 147, 38/86, 99, 39/82, 41/192, 360.

Danyel Daniel 7/61, 16/54, 41/148.

Davyd, Dauyd, Dauid, David, Davyth, Dauyth King David Pr 139, 7/25, 35, 9/152, 10/126 etc., 11/194, 243, 277, 13/

Davyd (*cont.*)
23, 15/7, 26/454, 470, 39/60; **Dauyd, Dauydis, Dauythis, Dauidis** *gen.* Pr 146, 10/139 etc.

Dysmas thief crucified with Jesus 31/179, 207.

Doctrynal 21/22 (see the note).

Egypt(e), Egypth, Egythp Egypt Pr 223, 8/184, 20/78, 86, 21/249, 27/352.

Elyzabeth, Elizabeth(h) St Elizabeth 8/13, 11/208, 255, 310, 13/2 etc.

Emanuel(le) Emmanuel 7/10, 112.

Emawus, Emaws Emmaus 38/3, 273, 308.

Erlonde Ireland 23/175.

Eve, Eue, Eva, Eua Eve Pr 40, 41, 7/55, 11/219, 19/96, 26/24, 35/1st s.d., 1, 18.

Ezechyas King Hezekiah 7/113.

Ezechiel Ezekiel 7/46.

Flom Jordon, Flum Jordon the River Jordan Pr 258, 22/28, 65, 35/27, 41/18.

Fraunce France 23/169.

Gabryel(l), Gabriele Gabriel Pr 157, 11/189, 307, 317, 12/214, 13/32, 37, 69, 14/342, 41/1st s.d.

Galylé, Galelye Galilee 8/42, 11/190, 20/6, 23/160, 27/555, 29/80, 85, 208, 30/45 etc., 36/64.

Galys Galicia 23/173.

Gyldyn (Goldyn) Gate the Golden Gate 8/198, 221.

Gylle in *Jakke and* ~: lad and lass; everyone 34/219.

Gryscysme 21/22 (see the note).

Heyn Herod's knight 20/15.

Hely Elijah 32/190.

Heloy Eli 32/183.

Herowde, Herownde, Herowdys, Herode King Herod the Great Pr 209 etc., 18/115 etc., 20/75, 85, 246, 21/250; **Herowdys, Herodys** *gen.* Pr 206, 18/292.

(þe) Herowd(e), Herowdys, Herownd(e), Herowndys Herod Antipas 29/1st s.d., 20 s.d., 25, 30/128 etc., 31/79, 90; **þe Herowdys** *gen.* 30/152, 152 s.d.

Hoberd Herod's knight 20/15; *Sere* ~ (used contemptuously of Jesus) 32/198, 206.

Ypotan A realm of Jasper 18/153 (see the note to 18/25–68).

Ysaac, Isaac Isaac Pr 80, 84, 5/13 etc., 8/182.

Ysaie, Isaye, Ysaye Isaiah 7/1 etc., 11/7, 21/181.

Ysakar(e), Isaker(e) a high priest 8/30, 97 s.d., 9/278, 286.

Israel(l) 9/141, 13/112, 20/19, 27/352, 32/173, 39/33; ~ *-countré* 38/74.

Itayl Italy 23/164.

Jacob 11/244, 16/39, 41/120; **Jacobys** *gen.* 18/162.

Jakke see **Gylle.**

James þe Lesser PS 23.

James James the Greater PS 17.

Januense (?) Genoa 23/165.

Japhet Japheth 4/79.

Jasper one of the Magi 18/57.

Jeremye Jeremiah 7/33, 11/25.

Jerusalem, Jherusalem, Hierusalem, Jheruselem Pr 255, 494, 8/36, 44, 198, 9/99, 125, 19/1, 43, 21/217, 23/159, 27/1, PS 20, 29/10, 32/9, 38/51 etc., 39/20, 40, 49.

Jesmas a thief crucified with Jesus 31/179, 209.

Jesse 7/98, 105, 15/49; **Jesses** *gen.* 9/266.

Jesu, Jesus, Jhesus, Jhesu Jesus Pr 169 etc., 8/16, 196, 224, 11/241, 334, 12/64, 13/155A, 164A, 20/23, 21/179 etc., 22/136, 24/42, 83, 120, 25/82 etc., 26/178 etc., 27/37 etc., 28/1st s.d. etc., 29/15 etc., 30/40 s.d. etc., 31/1st s.d. etc., 32/1 etc., 33/9, 34/37 etc., 36/28, 62, 37/93, 38/65 etc., 39/51, 72, 40/10, 41/87 etc.; **Jesus, Jesuis** *gen.* 30/236 s.d., 31/1st s.d., 47, 34/49 etc.

Joachym, Joachim Pr 127, 8/10 etc., 9/2 etc., 10/31, 172, 21/185.

Joathan King Jotham 7/97.

Joel, Johel 7/93, 40/34.

Johan, John, Jhon St John the Baptist Pr 256, 13/164A, 167A, 177A, 22/54, 71, 119, 26/125, 395, 27/390, PS 37, 29/37, 35/1st s.d., 25, 39/24.

Johan, Jhon, Jon St John the apostle Pr 395, 444, 26/385 s.d., 27/36 s.d., PS 17, 32/92 s.d., 146, 274, 36/124, 38/85, 314, 41/3 etc.

Jonas Jonah 7/69, 38/115, 118, 123.

Joras King Joram 7/81.

Joseph St Joseph Pr 148 etc., 8/12, 10/159
etc., 11/193, 12/138, 147, 13/143, 165A,
14/82 etc., 15/104, 157, 19/97, 181, 20/
73, 21/237, 252, 256, 26/26.

Joseph the patriarch 8/184.

**Joseph (Josepht) of Baramathie (ab
Aramathy)** Joseph of Arimathea Pr
412, 34/57 etc.

Joseph Justum Joseph Justus 39/82 s.d.

Josophat, Josephat King Jehoshaphat
7/73; *Vallé of* ~ 41/333.

Juda Judah *cety of* ~ 13/8.

Judas Judas Pr 317, 325, 360, 27/268 s.d.
etc., 28/71 etc., 29/13, 30/24 s.d., 25, 32
s.d., 31/10, 36/104, 38/19, 39/61, 70;
Judas *gen.* 39/90.

Judas Jude the apostle PS 30.

Juré, Jury(e) Judea 23/165, 25/214, 30/12,
103, 39/40, 41/14, 32, 147.

Lameth Lamech 4/150.

Lazare, Lazarus Lazarus Pr 299, 304,
25/17 etc., 26/38, 38/147.

Legenda Sanctorum the *Legenda Aurea*
41/13.

Libano Lebanon 41/326.

Lyon, Leyon, Leon 26/194 etc.

Longeys, Longeus Longinus Pr 403, 34/
88 s.d. etc.

Lucas, Luke St Luke Pr 465, 38/1, 9, 307.

Lucyfer(e), Locyfere, Lucifer Lucifer
Pr 20, 1/66, 11/48, 23/57, 26/1.

Lumbardye Lombardy 23/170.

Mahound, Mahownd(e) 18/92 (see the
note), 20/36, 209, 23/63, 29/26, 43, 58,
30/165, 34/311, 317, 41/391; *Seynt* ~ 34/
305.

Malcus 29/98; **Malchus, Malcus** *gen.*
28/106 s.d., 29/101.

Manasses King Manasseh 7/122.

Maria Jacobi 36/1st s.d.

Maria (Mary) Salomé 36/1st s.d., 25.

Mary(e), Maria, Mari(e) the Virgin
Mary Pr 128, 184, 8/190, 224, 9/22 etc.,
10/29 etc., 11/196 etc., 12/36 etc., 13/11
etc., 14/75 etc., 15/10 etc., 16/28, 18/
161, 282, 19/123 etc., 21/185, 34/122,
134, 41/2 etc.; **Maryes** *gen.* 26/26, 41/
334.

**Mary(e) (Maria) Mawdelyn, Magda-
lyn(e), Magdalen(e), Mavdelyn**
Mary Magdalene Pr 451, 455, 462, 25/9

etc., 27/149, 204 s.d., 28/148 s.d., 155,
37/1st s.d., 42, 38/306, 313, 385.

Maryes (thre) the Three Marys Pr 438,
32/92 s.d., 34/157 s.d.

Martha St Martha 25/9 etc.

Mathew St Matthew PS 25.

Mathiam St Matthias 39/82 s.d.

Maunfras one of the Shepherds 16/14.

Melchizar one of the Magi 18/37.

Michaele the archangel Michael 42/1st
s.d.

Mycheas Micah 7/53.

Moyse one of the Shepherds 16/31.

Moyses Moses Pr 92, 98, 6/5 etc., 16/33,
24/106 etc., 26/168, 215, 27/351, 38/97;
Moyses *gen.* Pr 291, 19/114, 24/201.

Montana 13/7 (see the note).

Naverne Navarre 23/161.

Nazareth 7/21, 8/43, 10/462, 11/191, 21/
179, 23/161, 26/178, 28/88, 92, 97, 29/63
etc., 30/158, 31/183, 38/65.

Neptalym Naphtali 13/162.

Nychodemus, Nycodemus Nicodemus
Pr 412, 34/113 s.d., 118, 121 s.d.

Noe Noah Pr 67, 70, 76, 4/10 etc.; **Noes**
gen. 35/34.

Normandye Normandy 23/169.

Octauyan Octavian 15/3.

Olyvet(e) Olivet 28/16 s.d., 24 s.d., 36
s.d., 39/30.

Osyas Hosea 7/110.

Ozyas King Uzziah 7/89.

Parys Paris 23/172.

Petyr, Peter, Petir St Peter Pr 338, 343,
444, 26/385 s.d., 27/36 s.d. etc., 28/16
s.d. etc., PS 14, 29/194 s.d., 212 s.d., 36/
73 etc., 38/85, 301, 377, 41/238 etc., 42/
49.

Phelypp Philip the evangelist PS 21 (see
the note).

Pheso Ephesus 41/190.

Pycardye Picardy 23/174.

Pylat(e), Pilat(t), Pylatt Pilate Pr 347
etc., 29/1st s.d., 18, 30/3 etc., 31/1st s.d.
etc., 32/168 s.d., 176 s.d., 177, 34/41 etc.,
35/152 etc., 38/108; **Pylatys, Pylatus**
gen. Pr 373, 31/50, 57 s.d.

Poperynge Poperinghe 23/174.

Portyngale Portugal 23/173.

Poul(e), Powle St Paul PS 33, 41/236 etc.

Pownteys 23/174 (see the note).

Rachel 8/183.
Rebecca Mary's maiden 10/354.
Reysesclaundyr 14/66.
Rewfyn 26/194 etc.
Roboas King Rehoboam 7/50.
Rome 23/166, 35/280.

Saba Saba in Arabia 18/25.
Salamon King Solomon 7/41, 23/167.
Salmana 23/163 (see the note).
Salomé see **Maria Salomé**.
Salomee, Salomé a midwife 15/150, 175, 234.
Samary Samaria 39/41.
Samaryan the Samarian PS 21.
Sampson Samson 8/185.
Samuel 8/186.
Sara Sarah 8/181.
Sathan, Sathanas, Satan, Ssathan Satan Pr 273, 277, 2/225, 7/52, 20/221, 23/5, 183, 26/3, 97, 469, 31/1st s.d., 5, 41/477, 489.
Scottlonde Scotland 23/175.
Sephore Mary's maiden 10/355.
Sesar(e), Sezar Caesar 18/84, 26/184, 308, 310, 27/116, 30/50.
Shem 4/57.
Sybile Sclutte 42/118.

Sym Somnore 14/138.
Symeon Simeon 19/20 s.d. etc.
Symeon Zelotes Simon the apostle PS 29.
Symon (leprows), Seymon Simon the leper 27/36 s.d. etc.
Symonem, Symon Simon of Cyrene 32/20 s.d., 40 s.d.
Syon Mount Zion 9/124, 27/25, 41/14.
Sophonye Zephania 7/117.
Spayn Spain 23/161.
Susanne Mary's maiden 10/353.

Tarys Tarshish 18/41.
Thomas the apostle Pr 478, 479, PS 35, 38/297 etc.

Veronyca St Veronica 32/45.

Walys Wales 23/175.

Zabulon 7/6 (see the note).
Zabulon Zebulun 23/162.
Zakary(e), Zakarie, Zacharye Zachariah 13/6 etc.
Zebee 23/163 (see the note).
Zelomye a midwife 15/154, 175.

NAMES IN THE SUMMONER'S PROLOGUE (PLAY 14)

Bertylmew þe bochere 16.
Betrys Belle 13.
Bette þe bakere 24.
Boutyng þe browstere 30.

Cok Crane 21.
Colle Crakecrust 23.
Colett Crane 17.

Davy Drydust 21.

Geffrey Gyle 9.
Gylle Fetyse 18.

Jak-at-þe-Stylle 11.
(fayr) Jane 18.
Johan Jurdon 9.

Kate Kelle 15.
Kytt Cakelere 17.

Letyce Lytyltrust 22.
Luce Lyere 22.

(fayr) Mabyle 10.
Malkyn Mylkedoke 10.
Megge Merywedyr 31.
Miles þe myllere 23.

Peyrs Pottere 14.
Pernel Prane 19.
Phelypp þe good flecchere 20.
Powle Pewterere 19.

Robyn Rede 24.

Sabyn Sprynge 31.

Sawdyr Sadelere 12.

Sybyly Slynge 30.

Symme Smalfeyth 15.

Stevyn Sturdy 11.

Thom Tynkere 13.

Tyffany Twynkelere 32.

Whatt-at-þe-Welle 14.